Employment Law

ASPEN PUBLISHERS

Employment Law: A Guide to Hiring, Managing, and Firing for Employers and Employees

LORI B. RASSAS

Wolters Kluwer
Law & Business

AUSTIN   BOSTON   CHICAGO   NEW YORK   THE NETHERLANDS

http://paralegal.aspenpublishers.com

To contact Customer Care, e-mail customer.care@aspenpublishers.com, call 1-800-234-1660, fax 1-800-901-9075, or mail correspondence to:

Aspen Publishers
Attn: Order Department
PO Box 990
Frederick, MD 21705

Printed in the United States of America.
1 2 3 4 5 6 7 8 9 0
ISBN 978-0-7355-8421-1

Library of Congress Cataloging-in-Publication Data

Rassas, Lori B., 1972-
   Employment law : a guide to hiring, managing, and firing for employers and employees / Lori B. Rassas.
      p. cm.
   Includes bibliographical references and index.
   ISBN 978-0-7355-8421-1 (alk. paper)
   1. Labor laws and legislation — United States. I. Title.

   KF3319.85.R37 2011
   344.7301 — dc22

                                                                              2010024509

About Wolters Kluwer Law & Business

Wolters Kluwer Law & Business is a leading provider of research information and workflow solutions in key specialty areas. The strengths of the individual brands of Aspen Publishers, CCH, Kluwer Law International and Loislaw are aligned within Wolters Kluwer Law & Business to provide comprehensive, in-depth solutions and expert-authored content for the legal, professional and education markets.

CCH was founded in 1913 and has served more than four generations of business professionals and their clients. The CCH products in the Wolters Kluwer Law & Business group are highly regarded electronic and print resources for legal, securities, antitrust and trade regulation, government contracting, banking, pension, payroll, employment and labor, and healthcare reimbursement and compliance professionals.

Aspen Publishers is a leading information provider for attorneys, business professionals and law students. Written by preeminent authorities, Aspen products offer analytical and practical information in a range of specialty practice areas from securities law and intellectual property to mergers and acquisitions and pension/benefits. Aspen's trusted legal education resources provide professors and students with high-quality, up-to-date and effective resources for successful instruction and study in all areas of the law.

Kluwer Law International supplies the global business community with comprehensive English-language international legal information. Legal practitioners, corporate counsel and business executives around the world rely on the Kluwer Law International journals, loose-leafs, books and electronic products for authoritative information in many areas of international legal practice.

Loislaw is a premier provider of digitized legal content to small law firm practitioners of various specializations. Loislaw provides attorneys with the ability to quickly and efficiently find the necessary legal information they need, when and where they need it, by facilitating access to primary law as well as state-specific law, records, forms and treatises.

Wolters Kluwer Law & Business, a unit of Wolters Kluwer, is headquartered in New York and Riverwoods, Illinois. Wolters Kluwer is a leading multinational publisher and information services company.

In Memory of My Grandparents

Debora and Isak Diamond

Molly and Ben Rassas

And to My Parents

Marge and Aaron Rassas

Who All Said I Could

Summary of Contents

Contents

 **INTRODUCTION TO EMPLOYMENT LAW AND THE EMPLOYMENT RELATIONSHIP**

PART I WORKPLACE DISCRIMINATION 13

2 TITLE VII—THE FOUNDATION OF WORKPLACE DISCRIMINATION LAW

X. REMEDIES UNDER TITLE VII   41

3 RACE, COLOR, AND NATIONAL ORIGIN DISCRIMINATION

I. RACE AND COLOR DISCRIMINATION   52

II. NATIONAL ORIGIN   55

---

4   RELIGIOUS DISCRIMINATION

5 SEX, PREGNANCY, AND GENETIC DISCRIMINATION

6 AGE DISCRIMINATION

Chapter Objectives   99

7   DISABILITY DISCRIMINATION

 **HIRING** **137**

 EMPLOYEES VERSUS INDEPENDENT CONTRACTORS

⑨ RECRUITING AND ASSEMBLING A DIVERSE APPLICANT POOL

10 COLLECTION OF INFORMATION: THE APPLICATION AND INTERVIEW

11   PRE-EMPLOYMENT TESTING

PART III **MANAGING**   **245**

12 **COMPENSATION AND BENEFITS**

13 PAID AND UNPAID LEAVE

Chapter Objectives 263

14   PERFORMANCE MANAGEMENT

Chapter Objectives   307

15   WORKPLACE HARASSMENT

16   WORKPLACE PRIVACY AND PERSONAL EXPRESSION

17   REGULATION OF OFF-DUTY CONDUCT

PART IV   FIRING   391

18   EMPLOYMENT AT WILL

---

19 ENDING THE EMPLOYMENT RELATIONSHIP

20 SEVERANCE AND POST-EMPLOYMENT OBLIGATIONS

About the Author

Lori B. Rassas, Esq., has more than a decade of experience working on employment and labor issues. She received an LL.M. in Labor and Employment Law from New York University Law School, a J.D. from the George Washington University Law School, and a B.A. from Tufts University. Throughout her career she has provided extensive guidance and counsel on all phases of the employment process to both employers and employees. She has developed a pragmatic approach to the navigation of employment relationships that is derived from her experience working to resolve complex legal issues that have arisen on both sides of the bargaining table.

Preface

At the end of a job interview, a potential employer asks an applicant, "And what starting salary are you looking for?"

The applicant responds, "In the neighborhood of $150,000 a year, depending on the benefits package."

The interviewer sits back in her chair a moment, considers the statement, and responds, "What would you say to a package of six weeks' vacation, 14 paid holidays, fully paid medical benefits, a defined benefit retirement plan equal to 50% of your salary, a corner office, and a company car?"

The applicant stands up from his chair and responds, "Wow! Are you kidding?"

And, to that, the potential employer replies, "Yes, but you started it."

* * * * * * * *

People need to work to live, and yet it is never as simple as performing services in exchange for compensation. The employer-employee relationship is actually incredibly complex, and despite this, employers and employees often enter into working relationships absent a clear understanding of their mutual expectations. Quite often the parties also enter into working relationships without a basic understanding about the laws that govern the creating, maintaining, and ending of those employment relationships. This lack of awareness has the potential to place both parties at a significant disadvantage when discussing employment issues because they will not have an appreciation of their rights and obligations under the law.

Employment Law: A Guide to Hiring, Managing, and Firing for Employers and Employees is designed to address this situation by providing an overview of employment law and identifying the most significant rights and obligations employers and employees have during the key phases of the employment relationship. The textbook begins with a discussion about the prohibition against workplace discrimination, and then tracks the employment process—from job creation, to recruitment, to compensation and benefits, to leave entitlements, and to performance management, all the way to the conclusion of the employment relationship.

I. TEXTBOOK STRUCTURE

This book is divided into four parts, covering workplace discrimination and the hiring, managing, and firing of employees. The information is further divided into 20 chapters, which explain basic legal principles in clear and concise language.

A. Part I, Workplace Discrimination

Part I, Workplace Discrimination, focuses on Title VII, which makes it illegal for employers to discriminate against individuals on the basis of their race, color, religion, sex, and national origin; the Age Discrimination in Employment Act (ADEA), which makes it illegal for employers to discriminate against individuals who are 40 years of age or older on the basis of their age; and the Americans with Disabilities Act (ADA), which makes it illegal for employers to discriminate against qualified individuals with disabilities and requires employers to provide a disabled job applicant or employee with a reasonable accommodation unless doing so would cause an undue burden. This purpose of this part of the textbook is not to educate litigators or to provide detailed guidance about the mechanics of presenting a case in a judicial forum. Instead, the goal is to alert employers to the types of workplace behavior that may subject them to liability for discriminatory conduct, and to alert applicants and employees to the types of workplace behavior that may infringe upon their rights.

The chapters covering workplace discrimination should be thought of as the umbrella you remember to bring with you to school or work on the days when it never rains. Armed with this basic knowledge about the litigation process, the hope is that you will never be placed in a situation where you have to use it — either by having a need to file a claim alleging discriminatory conduct, or having a need to present a defense to an allegation that an employment decision was based upon improper motivations. If, however, you become a party to a legal claim, you will be a well-informed participant in the process.

B. Part II, Hiring

Part II, Hiring, lays out the components of a nondiscriminatory recruitment and hiring process and provides employers with guidance about soliciting candidates for an open position from a diverse applicant pool, and collecting information (through the use of employment applications and interviews) in a manner to minimize potential claims for workplace discrimination. Both employers and applicants will learn how to distinguish appropriate employer conduct from conduct that suggests an employer used improper motivations as the basis for an adverse employment decision, which could be the basis for the filing of a discrimination claim.

C. Part III, Managing

Part III, Managing, covers issues relating to terms and conditions of employment, focusing on compensation and benefits, leave entitlements, performance management, harassment, and privacy rights. This part includes an extensive discussion about the appropriate use of performance management tools, including probationary periods, progressive discipline policies, and performance evaluations, geared toward minimizing the potential for their use to constitute discriminatory employer conduct. The balance that must be achieved between the rights of employers to manage their businesses and the rights of employees to be free from employer intrusions, both while at work and also when engaging in conduct outside their regularly scheduled work hours (often within the context of privacy rights), is also discussed in detail.

D. Part IV, Firing

Part IV, Firing, the final part in this textbook, focuses on the ending of employment relationships. It examines the concept of employment at will, which is the legal doctrine that governs most working relationships and provides the parties with the right to terminate their employment relationship for any reason at any time, but that is subject to a number of limitations. There is also a significant discussion about layoffs and the just-cause standard for terminations as well as how employers can minimize the potential for liability once a relationship ends. The significance of separation packages (including the use of knowing and voluntary waivers of employees' rights) and restrictive covenants is also explored.

II. TEXTBOOK RESOURCES

As you move through this book you will find that each of the 20 chapters includes illustrative examples, key terms and definitions, and a number of discussion questions to test students' knowledge of the most significant concepts presented. A comprehensive index and glossary of the key terms can also be found at the end of this book. In addition, there are a number of other available resources.

- The companion website for this textbook at www.aspenparalegaled.com/rassas_employment includes additional resources for students and instructors, including
  - □ Study aids to help students master the key concepts for this course. Visit the site to access interactive StudyMate exercises such as flash cards, matching, fill-in-the-blank, and crosswords. These activities are also available for download to an iPod or other hand-held device.
  - □ Instructor resources to accompany the text.
  - □ Links to helpful websites and updates.
- The textbook comes packaged with four months of prepaid access to Loislaw's online legal research database, at http://www.loislawschool.com.
- Blackboard and eCollege course materials are available to supplement this text. This online courseware is designed to streamline the teaching of the course, providing valuable resources from the book in an accessible electronic format.
- Instructor resources to accompany this text include a comprehensive Instructor's Manual, Test Bank, and PowerPoint slides. All of these materials are available on a CD-ROM or for download from our companion website.

* * * * * * * *

Employment law is a challenging area of law, but it is also an exciting field that has widespread relevance to all individuals who receive compensation in exchange for the providing of a service. There are certainly times when employers and employees have similar interests and truly benefit from each other's success. However, it would be naïve to ignore the reality that there are times when their interests will diverge. Both parties have a vested interest in possessing a basic understanding of their entitlements and obligations in order to anticipate the types of employment issues that might materialize, expend efforts to resolve them at the earliest stage possible, and be prepared to defend their interests in the absence of a mutually agreeable resolution. This book is designed to be a resource for both parties to an employment relationship who want to obtain a solid foundation of knowledge to further each of these goals.

Acknowledgments

I have always wanted to write a book. The subject changed, the point of view changed, and the format changed. However, what never changed was the unwavering support of my family and friends. First, I want to thank my family: my parents Marge and Aaron Rassas; Stacey, Jeff, and Logan Klinge; Jessica, Eric, Danica, and Jamie Rosenbloom; and Melissa Rassas. Each of you has always been incredibly supportive of everything I set out to do and encouraged me to continue to pursue my goals even when others suggested I pursue a different path. I know how lucky I am to have each of you, and I hope I make you proud. (Melissa, now that you are a lawyer, I cannot wait to see you take the world by storm!)

I am also very fortunate to be unable to express my gratitude to my mentors and friends separately because each of the following people has been more than willing to take on both roles. A very special thank you to Scott, Beth, and Aidan Atkins; Liz Bishop; Jayne Bower; Dominique Bravo and Eric Sloan; Irene Dorzback; Wendy Freedman; Greg Hessinger; Marci, Jason, Harper, and Sloane Kroft; Sharon and Fred Kroft; Ryan Kroft and Adam Zeller; Richard Larkin; Mike McPherson; Becky Nelson; Debra Osofsky; John Russum; Parisa Salehi; Judy Sanders; Wendy Siegel and Randy Frisch; Jayne Wallace; Ronnee Yashon; and Ana Venegas—all of whom barely have time to recover from providing me guidance and support relating to one project before I reach out to them to discuss something new. I am also grateful to Alexis Belladonna, Jen Biderman ("B"), Donna Fenn, and Beth Wang, who, along with my family, not only accepted the fact that writing was my priority but also made it theirs any time I asked them to review some of my earlier drafts.

Stephen Pollan, thank you for your wise and seasoned advice, which kept me moving not only forward but also in the right direction. Also, I have you to thank for the introduction to Deborah Harkins, whose copyediting expertise helped me to create an instructor's manual that I am confident will be a valuable teaching resource. Dr. Ellen Cohn, and Marsha and Morey Rosenbloom, thank you not only for your support but also for your practical advice about how to navigate the publishing industry for the first time. (Yes, I realize I no longer have an excuse for a weekend getaway that does not last at least 24 hours.)

Ken Husserl, I am grateful to you for providing me with my first opportunity to teach a class of my own and for your continued friendship, guidance, and support. Marisol Abuin, thank you for your friendship and well-grounded advice, as well as for consistently encouraging me to pursue my writing goals. I also have you to thank for the introduction to David Herzig, who became the Executive

Editor for this book. Thank you to the entire team of people at Aspen Publishers who put so much time and energy into the publication of this book. I am especially grateful to Kaesmene Harrison Banks, Christie Rears, and Susan Junkin for truly embracing this project. Thanks also to the *Amarillo Globe-News* for granting me the permission to reprint one of their articles in this book and particularly to Susie Self for her responsiveness. I (along with all of the students who will likely initially breeze through my writing to locate the cartoons sprinkled throughout the text) also want to thank Cartoonist Randy Glasbergen, whose illustrations are found throughout the text. Randy, I have always admired your talent and am thrilled to have this opportunity to have my work published alongside yours.

I would also like to thank the following reviewers, whose suggestions and insightful commentary helped to shape the content of the book:

Laura Barnard, Lakeland Community College
Lisa Burke, University of Tennessee — Chattanooga
Paul Guymon, Harper College
Bruce Hamm, Onondaga Community College
Jason Harris, Augustana College
Kathleen Reed, University of Toledo
Thomas Tudor, University of Arkansas — Little Rock

And, finally, I want to pay a special tribute to my friend Jen Giegerich, who lost her courageous battle with cystic fibrosis this past year. Jen was not only a treasured daughter, sister, and friend, but also a passionate teacher who inspired each of the students who were lucky enough to be assigned to her class. Her unwavering dedication and passion for teaching was known to everyone who came in contact with her and particularly to her colleagues and students at Accompsett Elementary School located in Smithtown, New York, which recently renamed a fifth-grade hallway the "Miss G Wing" in her memory. Jen, I will always remember how incredibly supportive you were of my writing of this book, and I am just sorry you never had the chance to finish your own.

Introduction to Employment Law and the Employment Relationship

Welcome to employment law! Tackling this field of study is a challenging under-taking. However, it is also an exciting and dynamic topic that will likely be relevant to students regardless of the career path they decide to pursue.

Chapter Objectives

This chapter introduces employment law and explains its relevance to all individuals who intend to work in exchange for compensation. It also places the presented information in context and clarifies its intended use.

Upon completion of this chapter students should have a basic understanding of what the course will cover. Specifically, upon mastering the main objectives of this chapter, students should be able to

■ explain the potential relevance of employment law to their careers;
■ explain the difference between employment law and labor law;
■ explain why this textbook is not a substitute for legal advice;
■ identify a number of sources of law; and
■ list some characteristics of the employer-employee relationship that make it unique.

After reading this basic introduction students will be prepared to learn about workplace discrimination and the rights and obligations of the parties in an employment relationship during each phase of the employment process.

RELEVANCE OF EMPLOYMENT LAW AND RELATED ISSUES

Every individual who studies employment law will find himself or herself in a number of situations during professional life that will be relevant to the issues presented in this text. First, there are an infinite number of job opportunities directly related to this field. For example, many attorneys and paralegals specialize in employment law and handle disputes that materialize within the context of employment relationships. In addition, these professionals often hire staff to support them in their work. There are also a number of job opportunities in the human resources departments of small and large companies that require the management of day-to-day employment issues relating to the recruiting, hiring, managing, and training of employees. Furthermore, there are individuals in every industry who are responsible for supervising other employees, and these professionals will benefit from possessing knowledge about how to effectively hire, manage, and fire employees in a manner consistent with the law.

For those individuals who have no intention of pursuing opportunities in the field of employment law or working in positions that include supervisory responsibilities, the issues presented here will still be relevant to their personal career paths. For example, even a basic job search involves employment matters, such as the information potential employers are legally permitted to solicit and to consider when making employment decisions, the obligations of job applicants to provide accurate information, and other rights and obligations of both parties who are considering entering into an employment relationship.

Once an individual accepts a position and starts to work, other employment issues could surface, such as whether employer conduct that has a negative impact on a working condition (i.e., the assignment of an undesirable work task to an employee, a demotion, or the giving of a negative performance appraisal) is motivated by discriminatory conduct, whether an employer has a legal obligation to provide an employee with a certain benefit, whether an employer has the legal right to end an employment relationship, and whether both parties continue to fulfill their post-termination obligations to one another.

Regardless of whether the knowledge individuals obtain from this book turns out to be relevant to the substance of a career choice, or whether they draw upon it as they pursue their employment goals, they will likely find that it is an interesting course of study. Before tackling the substantive components of the law, however, it is important to have a firm understanding of what the textbook does and does not cover, as well as how to use the information appropriately and to recognize its limitations.

EMPLOYMENT LAW VERSUS LABOR LAW

This textbook focuses on employment law, which is a broad term that covers all areas of the employer-employee relationship. Despite the extensive scope of this field of study, employment law generally does not include coverage of the collective bargaining process, the process by which employers and the labor unions that represent their employees reach an agreement about the employees' terms and conditions of employment. Issues related to collective bargaining would be covered in the study of labor law, which focuses on the National Labor Relations Act (NLRA) and other state laws that regulate the rights of employees who are, or want to become, members of a labor union.

Many employment law textbooks dedicate a number of chapters to labor law and provide information relating to the laws governing the relationship between employers and their unionized employees. For a number of reasons, the study of labor law is not covered extensively in this textbook.

A. SUBSTANTIVE DIFFERENCES

Although many people refer to employment law and labor law interchangeably, these fields of law are substantively different. A labor law course would analyze the NLRA and the obligations that employers and labor unions have toward one another. Such a course would also explain the types of conduct that are appropriate for employers and labor unions to exert to further their respective goals.

There is no question that individuals employed in a unionized environment must have a working knowledge of labor law and the obligations of employers and labor unions with respect to dealing with one another. These obligations are extensive, and a failure to abide by these laws has the potential to have a significant impact on the operations of a business. Based on these stakes, a significant number of chapters would be needed to provide the level of coverage necessary to guide employers and employees through the process.

Because the relevance of information about labor law would be limited to individuals who are working in a unionized environment, and because the majority of workplaces in the United States are not unionized, this textbook does not devote a significant amount of attention to labor law. This choice was not intended to minimize the importance of this field of study but rather to steer those working in a heavily unionized environment to seek out more expansive resources that are specific to that area of the law.

B. CHANGING LANDSCAPE

Another reason extensive coverage on labor law is not presented is that now, more than ever, this area of law is in a state of flux. Although laws are always changing, the Obama Administration has expressed what many have recognized as an unprecedented level of interest and support for a number of pieces of legislation that have the potential to dramatically impact how labor unions organize and how collective bargaining agreements (the contracts negotiated between labor unions and employers) are negotiated. The complexity of labor law, coupled with the fact that sweeping changes to the current laws are likely on the horizon, is another reason these topics are not presented in detail.

Even though this textbook does not provide extensive coverage of labor law, this does not detract from the value of this textbook for both unionized and nonunionized employees. This is because most major employment laws apply to employees regardless of whether or not they work in a unionized environment. In addition, the text does highlight those areas in which the most significant differences in the treatment of union and nonunion employees might materialize.

C. SIGNIFICANT UNION ISSUES ARE IDENTIFIED

Although individuals working in heavily unionized environments should seek out additional sources of information, this textbook does not ignore the reality that labor unions play a significant role in employment relationships. Based on this, the text identifies and explains a number of the significant differences that may exist between the treatment of unionized and nonunionized employees. For example, Chapter 19, Ending the Employment Relationship, includes an extensive discussion about the just cause standard for terminations. When this standard applies, its elements are analyzed to determine whether a termination is appropriate. The just cause standard may apply to nonunionized employees, but it is most often negotiated as part of a collective bargaining agreement to apply to unionized employees. The purpose of these types of references is to highlight potentially significant issues so that those individuals working in a unionized environment will recognize the need to seek out more extensive and specialized knowledge about that particular area of the law.

TEXTBOOK IS NOT A SUBSTITUTE FOR LEGAL ADVICE

This textbook focuses on the general legal parameters that govern each phase of an employment relationship — from the initial decision to solicit applicants and fill a position to the ultimate decision to end a working relationship. This includes information about how employers can minimize their potential liability for workplace discrimination claims, as well as how employees can assert their rights and receive the employment benefits available under the law. Although this information represents general trends that govern employment relationships in the United States, for a number of reasons, it is neither intended to be legal advice nor intended to be a substitute for it.

A. NUMBER OF SOURCES OF LAW

As a starting point, one reason for the need to solicit legal advice to address an employment issue is the fact that the laws that govern employment relationships come from a number of sources. Some of the most significant sources include statutory law, common law, administrative law, and federal and state constitutions. Each has the potential to alter the rights and obligations of the parties who enter into an employment relationship.

1. STATUTORY LAW

Statutory law refers to legislative acts passed by a controlling authority such as Congress or a state legislature.[1] Statutory law is a critical component of employment law and is covered extensively in this textbook. Examples of important federal statutory laws relevant to employment law are Title VII, which is the foundation of workplace discrimination law; the Family and Medical Leave Act (FMLA), which provides unpaid job-protected leave for employees to tend to family and medical (and under the recent amendments, some expanded military-related) issues; and the Americans with Disabilities Act (ADA), which prohibits discrimination against qualified individuals with disabilities.

> **statutory law**
> laws passed by Congress and state legislatures

Federal statutory laws such as these are emphasized in this textbook and apply to employees working in any state. However, because states have the right to offer individuals greater benefits and protections than those offered by federal laws, some examples of state statutes will be referenced for illustrative purposes and to highlight significant differences that exist.

a. Variations in Types of Issues Regulated

Because variations exist between federal and state laws, both must be considered when making decisions about an appropriate course of conduct. For example, as discussed in Chapter 12, Compensation and Benefits, the Fair Labor Standards Act (FLSA) is the federal law that governs minimum compensation and the payment of overtime. The FLSA does not regulate the number of hours an employee can be required to work in one day, nor does it define what constitutes a part-time or full-time employee. A seasoned employment attorney would know, however, that a number of state laws do regulate these terms and conditions of employment. Thus legal research must be performed before making a determination about whether certain conduct is permissible or whether it could subject an employer to liability.

b. Variations on Available Causes of Action and Defenses

This textbook provides information on a broad range of claims an applicant or employee may file to address an employment issue, as well as a number of arguments an employer might assert to defend its conduct. However, laws relating to what claims and defenses are recognized in a particular jurisdiction vary from state to state. For example, as discussed in Chapter 18, Employment at Will, some states recognize that an employee may assert a **promissory estoppel** claim to enforce a promise made by an employer, such as a promise of continued employment for a certain length of time. The assertion of such a claim has the potential to result in the imposition of significant liability on an employer.

> **promissory estoppel**
> legal theory that a promise should be enforced if an individual reasonably relied on the promise and injustice can only be avoided by enforcement of that promise

However, the availability of relief under a promissory estoppel claim would depend on whether the claim was filed in a jurisdiction that recognizes that particular cause of action. This claim would not be an available option for an individual who filed the claim in a state such as New York, for example, because the state does not recognize a promissory estoppel cause of action.

2. COMMON LAW

Not only is it essential to research the laws passed by federal and state legislatures, but it is also important to gain a comprehensive understanding of the legal cases that have been decided on a particular issue to determine how the provisions of those laws have been applied. In some instances, there may not be a state or federal law that regulates a particular employment matter, but judicial decisions might impose obligations on the parties. **Common law**, also referred to as case law, refers to the principles that are established by courts through the issuance of judicial decisions.[2]

For example, within the context of a discussion about discrimination based on an individual's disability, a statement relating to how the Supreme Court defines the term *reasonable accommodation*, or a list of factors the courts will consider to make a determination as to whether a particular workplace accommodation is reasonable or whether it would represent an undue burden an employer would not be obligated to undertake, would be examples of principles established by common law. See Chapter 7, Disability Discrimination.

Common law refers to the general body of cases that interpret and apply certain legal principles, and the number of cases involving a particular matter may be extensive. However, particular attention is often paid to a court that is hearing an issue that has not been subject to prior judicial review. This is because the first time a court renders a ruling on a particular issue, the resulting decision establishes a **precedent**, which sets the framework for how the matter will likely be interpreted or applied in the future.[3]

3. ADMINISTRATIVE REGULATIONS

In other instances, guidance about a particular issue might be provided by a federal or state government agency through the issuance of an **administration regulation**, which is another source of law that has the potential to have a significant impact on the determination of whether particular employer or employee conduct is legally permissible. These rules passed by federal and state agencies, the administrative regulations, have the same effect as law.[4] Congress delegates this rulemaking authority to federal agencies, and state legislatures delegate this authority to state agencies.

For example, the regulations put forth by the Department of Labor (DOL), a federal agency, relating to how a provision of a federal law such as the FLSA should be interpreted, are administrative regulations. The Equal Employment Opportunity Commission (EEOC) is another federal agency that issues administrative regulations relating to the federal employment laws it is responsible for enforcing (such as Title VII, which is the foundation for workplace discrimination law and is discussed in detail throughout this textbook). The regulations put forth by a state agency such the New York State Division of Human Rights (which is the New York equivalent of the EEOC on the state level) are another example of administrative law.

common law
also referred to as case law; the principles established by the courts through the issuance of judicial decisions

precedent
the decision by a court the first time the court hears an issue and makes a ruling, which establishes how that issue should be interpreted or applied in future cases

administrative regulations
rules promulgated by federal and state agencies that have the powers delegated to them by Congress or a state legislature

4. FEDERAL AND STATE CONSTITUTIONS

Federal and state constitutions represent another source of law. A **constitution** is a group of principles that govern the relationship between the government and the people it represents.[5]

The United States **Constitution** establishes the structure of the federal government as well as its relationship to state governments and their citizens. The federal Constitution is applied only to the federal government; therefore, it applies only to employment relationships in the public sector because, under those circumstances, the government is the employer. The federal Constitution does not govern the relationships between individuals and private employers.

In limited instances, however, a federal (or state) constitutional provision may be referenced and used by arbitrators (neutral third parties who are retained to resolve employment disputes) as the basis for imposing obligations upon private-sector employers. For example, the U.S. Constitution includes a **due process clause,** which provides individuals with the right to a fair legal proceeding, including the opportunity to be heard.[6] Based on this provision, within the context of employment law, it has been suggested that an employer might be required to provide an employee with due process before imposing discipline on that employee, a topic covered extensively in Chapter 14, Performance Management.[7]

However, because the U.S. Constitution governs public-sector employment relationships, an individual who wants to apply a principle rooted in the federal constitution to an employment relationship between a private employer and employee must find an alternative source for any due process obligation or some legal support for the application of a due process requirement. This is a task that would be performed by an attorney or an individual with legal training and is another reason why individuals should seek legal advice for employment issues rather than relying on the broad principles presented in this textbook.

constitution
group of principles that govern the relationship between a government and the people it represents

due process clause
constitutional provision that, among other things, provides individuals with the right to a fair legal proceeding, including the opportunity to be heard

B. LAWS APPLY TO DIFFERENT EMPLOYERS

Even if an individual is able to determine which sources of law would be substantively relevant to a particular situation, this knowledge will not necessarily determine the appropriate course of conduct. This is because not all laws apply to all parties, and this is another example of an issue that would likely need to be researched by an attorney or an individual with extensive legal training. For example, a law might cover only employers who employ a minimum number of employees. Title VII, which prohibits workplace discrimination based on race, color, religion, sex, and national origin, applies to private employers who have 15 or more employees who worked for the employer for at least 20 calendar weeks. In contrast, an employer will be covered by the Age Discrimination in Employment Act (ADEA) if it has 20 or more employees who worked for the company for at least 20 calendar weeks.[8] A law might also apply only to an employer with a certain amount of business. For example, the FLSA (which, as noted above, is the federal law that governs the payment of a minimum wage rate and overtime) generally does not cover enterprises that do not have at least $500,000 in annual dollar volume of business.[9] Furthermore, some laws apply to employers in certain industries or in certain geographic locations.

An attorney working to resolve an issue or to determine the appropriateness of pursuing a particular claim would research these variations in coverage and discuss her conclusions with her client. This level of detail falls outside the scope of the information provided in this textbook, the purpose of which is to provide a broad overview of the law. Nevertheless, such detailed analysis would be a necessary part of the decision-making process to determine how to proceed in an employment-related matter. If it is determined that an employer is covered by a particular law, seeking legal advice is also essential to understand and interpret the language of the law.

C. LAWS ARE COMPLEX

Individuals who want to provide legal advice and counsel must undergo extensive training prior to receiving a license to practice law in the United States. The language of each law is often complicated, and the proper application of the terms of a particular law may be subject to interpretation and, in many cases, extensive litigation. This reality is another reason it is important to solicit advice from an attorney to handle an employment issue.

1. DETERMINATIONS ARE FACT SPECIFIC

One of the reasons for the complexity of laws governing employment relationships is the fact that the appropriateness of an employment decision is usually based on the specific details surrounding it. Thus, while overriding principles provide a foundation for making well-informed decisions, the presence or absence of what may seem like an insignificant detail might have an impact on whether a particular action is legally permissible. Thus, while the examples used in this text provide basic fact patterns to illustrate how a law would be applied, a legal determination as to the appropriateness of a response would require a more extensive fact-gathering process.

2. DETERMINATIONS ARE SUBJECTIVE

Even if extensive details about a situation are available, specialized legal advice is likely still necessary to assess the appropriateness of certain conduct. This is because employment law, like all other areas of law, is often open to varying interpretations, which are based on a number of subjective considerations.

For example, the law imposes obligations on employers with respect to the rights of employees to engage in religious conduct during work time. Specifically, as discussed in Chapter 4, Religious Discrimination, employers have an obligation to provide a reasonable accommodation to employees who request work relief to engage in such conduct, provided the granting of this relief does not impose an undue burden on the employer or the business operation.

The extensive litigation on these issues offers significant common law guidance relating to what is reasonable and what constitutes an undue burden, and this is a source of law emphasized throughout this text. However, the final determination relating to what conduct would fall within these parameters is an inquiry that would require an examination of subjective considerations. This is because what is reasonable to one person may be considered unreasonable to another, just as different people may have different opinions as to what constitutes an undue burden. In many cases, two parties may present logical but opposing views relating to the appropriateness of particular conduct, in which case a third party (a judge or arbitrator) might be asked to decide which interpretation should be sustained. This reality is another reason it is advisable to consult an attorney who has specialized knowledge about the common law interpretation of terms such as *reasonable* and *undue burden* (which, within the context of a legal dispute related to religious discrimination or disability discrimination, is often critical) for advice and counsel before deciding how to proceed.

D. LAWS CHANGE

Another factor that necessitates the solicitation of legal advice on employment issues is the fact that the law is always in a state of flux, with courts continually shaping the interpretation of existing laws by issuing decisions, and Congress and state legislatures passing, amending, and in some cases repealing laws on the same rigorous schedule. Therefore, even if the legal information that is presented in the textbook is updated on the day an individual reads this text, it is always possible that a different version will be in effect at the time a legal issue arises, or that other judicial interpretations will have been rendered by the time a particular case is heard in a particular judicial forum.

E. LAWS PLAY VARIOUS ROLES

All of the factors outlined above should be considered while moving through this text. Further, because there are a number of different sources of law, in many cases the rights and obligations of the parties to an employment relationship will be derived from a number of sources and may overlap. For example, Title VII and other sources of statutory law are central to the discussion relating to discrimination, but common law and administrative law each play a role in how those statutes are interpreted. Further, the principles presented represent the general trends across the country and are derived from a number of different sources that may or may not apply to a particular situation. Thus, the information provided should be viewed as a starting point for making legally sound employment decisions since the laws that apply to a particular issue that an individual seeks to resolve may be different than those discussed in this text.

In addition, when learning about these general employment law trends, it is important to realize that the information leading to their creation often materializes based on a number of factors that make the employment relationship unique.

IV   EMPLOYMENT RELATIONSHIP

The employer-employee relationship has many unique characteristics, and each must be considered when trying to resolve employment issues.

A. CONSISTENT AND INCONSISTENT GOALS

First, unlike other relationships, when two individuals enter into an employment relationship, their interests may be consistent and inconsistent at the same time. On the one hand, in a traditional employer-employee relationship, success for an employer could translate into success for an employee because higher profits could lead to the offering of higher salaries and enhanced benefits. On the other hand, however, these improvements may not materialize because if an employer increases the salaries of its employees, it will decrease its own profits.

In addition, even if an employer decides that earned profits will be reinvested into a business, the employer might decide to use the funds for something other than the salaries of its employees. This might include, for example, using the profits for workplace renovations, technological upgrades, or additional advertising aimed at earning even greater profits. Decisions such as these could actually have a negative impact on employees if, for example, a technological enhancement leads to increased efficiency, or some functions previously performed by an employee are automated; either of these changes could result in the elimination of an employee's position.

B. UNSTABLE RELATIONSHIP

Another source of tension in the traditional employer-employee relationship is its inherent instability. First, the needs of employers may change over time, which could result in the reduction of the number of individuals employed or in significant changes in job responsibilities and expectations for job performance. The needs of employees are just as dynamic. Individuals may decide to pursue new employment opportunities to enhance their skills or to earn more money, to move to a different part of the country, or to reprioritize their life goals.

C. SYMBOLISM OF A JOB

The emotions that are inextricably linked to employment relationships represent an additional challenge. On the most fundamental level, the majority of individuals work because they need to survive; people need money for food, shelter, and other necessities to live. Thus, when employees sense that their source of income is in jeopardy, emotions enter into the mix.

In addition, career choices are often based on both objective and subjective factors, and compensation represents only one component. For example, an individual may place a high value on the prestige associated with a position (such as a specific job title or a geographically desirable office), opportunities for advancement, a flexible work schedule, or other perks. In other cases, people view their jobs as a measurement of self-worth or their ability to make a valuable contribution to society.

Each of these factors has the potential to impact an individual's job performance and commitment to a particular position. This could influence how both parties view the employment relationship and the importance they place on issues that arise with respect to it. Thus, the significance of these concerns should not be discounted as students move through this book, which as they will see, first provides an overview of workplace discrimination, followed by a chronological overview of the employment process.

TEXTBOOK STRUCTURE

The first part of this textbook focuses on workplace discrimination and the pursuit of such a claim in a judicial forum. Because employees seek to pursue career opportunities without being hindered by workplace discrimination, and because employers seek to recruit, hire, manage, and terminate their employees without being hindered by discrimination litigation, it makes sense to start with an overview of Title VII and a number of other significant federal anti-discrimination laws that set the groundwork for the entire process.

Further, since litigation may be unavoidable, in the event it does occur employers who work within the parameters outlined in this book will be in the best position to defend their conduct, and employees who have gained a working knowledge of their rights and obligations will be in the best position to assert their rights. After the initial overview, the textbook moves on to the significant stages of the employment process, which include the hiring, managing, and firing of employees.

With a firm understanding of the appropriate use of this textbook and the information presented within it, you are now prepared to jump into this exciting, interesting, and relevant area of the law. Good luck!

KEY TERMS

✓administrative regulations
✓common law
✓constitution
✓due process clause
✓precedent
✓promissory estoppel
✓statutory law

DISCUSSION QUESTIONS

1. Provide some examples of different sources of employment law.
2. Explain some reasons why a law may apply to some employers and not to others.
3. Explain why an attorney should be consulted for legal advice related to employment law issues.
4. Explain some of the factors that make the relationship between employers and employees unique.
5. Stacey is a college student whose career goal is to become the CEO of a large company that designs and sells educational toys. She tells you she will not enroll in an employment law class because she wants to limit her course selections to those that are relevant to her goals. What do you think about her statement?
6. Jessica, the CEO of a large New York company, tells Stacey (from the question above) she should have a basic understanding of employment law. She also tells Stacey she can obtain the necessary knowledge by consulting the volumes of books Jessica has owned for years, which include the text of all New York laws. What do you think about this advice?

ENDNOTES

1. *See* Black's Law Dictionary 1180 (8th ed. abridged 2005).
2. Black's Law Dictionary 231 (8th ed. abridged 2005).
3. Black's Law Dictionary 986 (8th ed. abridged 2005).
4. *See* Black's Law Dictionary 40 (8th ed. abridged 2005).
5. The federal government consists of three branches. The legislative branch (Congress) makes the law, the executive branch (the President) enforces the laws, and the judicial branch (the courts) interprets the laws.
6. Black's Law Dictionary 424 (8th ed. abridged 2005).
7. *See, e.g., Cameron Iron Works*, 25 Lab. Arb. (BNA) (1955) (Boles, Arb.).
8. *See* U.S. Equal Employment Opportunity Commn., Coverage of Business/Private Employers (available at *http://www.eeoc.gov/employers/coverage_private.cfm*).
9. Fair Labor Standards Act of 1938 (FLSA) (available at *http://www.dol.gov/whd/regs/statutes/ FairLaborStandAct.pdf*), *as amended*, 29 U.S.C. §§ 201 *et seq.* (available at *http://www4.law .cornell.edu/uscode/29/201.html*); 29 C.F.R. pts. 510-794 (available at *http://www.dol.gov/ dol/allcfr/ESA/Title_29/Chapter_V.htm*); U.S. Dept. of Labor, Employment Law Guide, Wages and Hours Worked: Minimum Wage and Overtime Pay (available at *http://www .dol.gov/compliance/guide/minwage.htm#who*).

Workplace Discrimination

"They say we're not placing enough emphasis on diversity."

2

Title VII—The Foundation of Workplace Discrimination Law

Chapter Objectives

This chapter provides an introduction to employment discrimination through a detailed examination of Title VII of the Civil Rights Act of 1964, which prohibits workplace discrimination based on race, color, religion, sex, and national origin. The chapter explains who is entitled to the benefits and protections provided by the Act and identifies the type of employer conduct Title VII prohibits.

A significant portion of the chapter focuses on the framework for presenting proof for a disparate treatment claim, which relates to intentional discrimination, and for a disparate impact claim, which relates to facially neutral conduct that produces a discriminatory result. The well-established structure and shifting of the burden of proof between the employer and employee (or applicant) are discussed in detail. Having this knowledge will help employees (and applicants) assess whether they have sufficient evidence to support a discrimination claim and will help employers determine how to present the most appropriate defense in the event a claim materializes.

Upon completion of this chapter, students should have a fundamental understanding of Title VII. Specifically, upon mastering the main objectives of this chapter students should be able to

- explain the purpose of Title VII, what it prohibits, and who it is designed to protect;
- explain the different types of evidence that might support an employment discrimination claim;
- define *disparate treatment* and *disparate impact*, and provide examples of employer conduct that might result in the filing of each type of claim;
- present the framework for the presentation of proof for both a disparate treatment claim and a disparate impact claim;
- define the terms *prima facie case* and *pretext*
- explain some defenses to discriminatory conduct that might be available to an employer;
- provide an example of a bona fide occupational qualification (BFOQ) that might absolve an employer of liability under Title VII;
- explain what types of employer conduct would support a retaliation claim; and
- identify the types of remedies that are available under Title VII.

INTRODUCTION

Employment discrimination is a complex area of law, and because it has the potential to expose employers to significant liability, the extensive litigation arising under it is not surprising. Specifically, the Equal Employment Opportunity Commission (EEOC), which is the federal agency responsible for enforcing Title VII, reports that in 2009, 93,277 charges were filed under the statute, which represents a significant increase over the 77,444 charges filed in 1999.[1] In addition, between 1990 and 2006, employment discrimination cases accounted for about half of all of the civil rights complaints filed in federal court, which translates into 8,413 cases filed in 1990 and 14,353 filed in 2006, and this does not account for the thousands of claims that were settled before the reaching of a judicial resolution.[2] Further, of those employment discrimination claims that resulted in a finding of discriminatory conduct, 81% resulted in some type of monetary award, and the average award between 2000 and 2006 was $158,460.[3] See Exhibit 2-1.

Based on the expansive and complex nature of workplace discrimination, there are a number of books that focus on one specific statute or type of discrimination. Further, it is not uncommon for attorneys (or paralegals) to specialize in one particular area of employment discrimination or one stage of the employment process. For example, an attorney might decide to handle claims of racial discrimination or sexual harassment exclusively, or limit her practice to wrongful terminations or to compensation discrimination claims. It is critical, however, for anyone who handles workplace issues to possess at least a basic understanding of the entire landscape of discrimination, because the issues often occur in conjunction with one another.

Employers must provide individuals with equal employment opportunities, and there are a number of laws that are designed to ensure this result. See Exhibit 2-2. The most significant federal employment discrimination statutes are covered in this textbook and include

- ✓ **Title VII of the Civil Rights Act of 1964**, which prohibits discrimination based on race, color, religion, sex, and national origin;
- ✓ the **Equal Pay Act of 1963 (EPA)**, which prohibits unequal compensation for men and women who perform substantially equal work in the same establishment;
- ✓ the **Age Discrimination in Employment Act of 1967 (ADEA)**, which prohibits discrimination against individuals who are 40 years old or older;
- ✓ the **Americans with Disabilities Act of 1990 (ADA)**, which prohibits discrimination against qualified individuals with disabilities; and
- ✓ the **Genetic Information Nondiscrimination Act of 2008 (GINA)**, which prohibits discrimination based on genetic information.[4]

Employees asserting a discrimination claim under one of these federal statutes are not permitted to file a claim directly with a court but instead must pursue the matter through the EEOC, which is the government agency responsible for enforcing the federal discrimination laws.[5]

Title VII of the Civil Rights Act of 1964
federal law that prohibits workplace discrimination based on race, color, religion, sex, and national origin

Equal Pay Act of 1963 (EPA)
federal law that requires equal pay for equal work

Age Discrimination in Employment Act of 1967 (ADEA)
federal law that prohibits discrimination against individuals who are 40 years old or older

Americans with Disabilities Act of 1990 (ADA)
federal law that prohibits workplace discrimination against qualified individuals with disabilities

Genetic Information Nondiscrimination Act of 2008 (GINA)
federal law that prohibits employers from discriminating based on genetic information

Exhibit 2-1
Number of Charges Filed with the U.S. Equal Employment Opportunity Commission 1997- 2009[1]

	FY 1997	FY 1998	FY 1999	FY 2000	FY 2001	FY 2002	FY 2003	FY 2004	FY 2005	FY 2006	FY 2007	FY 2008	FY 2009
Total Charges	80,680	79,591	77,444	79,896	80,840	84,442	81,293	79,432	75,428	75,768	82,792	95,402	93,277
Race	29,199	28,820	28,819	28,945	28,912	29,910	28,526	27,696	26,740	27,238	30,510	33,937	33,579
	36.2%	36.2%	37.3%	36.2%	35.8%	35.4%	35.1%	34.9%	35.5%	35.9%	37.0%	35.6%	36.0%
Sex	24,728	24,454	23,907	25,194	25,140	25,536	24,362	24,249	23,094	23,247	24,826	28,372	28,028
	30.7%	30.7%	30.9%	31.5%	31.1%	30.2%	30.0%	30.5%	30.6%	30.7%	30.1%	29.7%	30.0%
National Origin	6,712	6,778	7,108	7,792	8,025	9,046	8,450	8,361	8,035	8,327	9,396	10,601	11,134
	8.3%	8.5%	9.2%	9.8%	9.9%	10.7%	10.4%	10.5%	10.7%	11.0%	11.4%	11.1%	11.9%
Religion	1,709	1,786	1,811	1,939	2,127	2,572	2,532	2,466	2,340	2,541	2,880	3,273	3,386
	2.1%	2.2%	2.3%	2.4%	2.6%	3.0%	3.1%	3.1%	3.1%	3.4%	3.5%	3.4%	3.6%
Retaliation— All Statutes	18,198	19,114	19,694	21,613	22,257	22,768	22,690	22,740	22,278	22,555	26,663	32,690	33,613
	22.6%	24.0%	25.4%	27.1%	27.5%	27.0%	27.9%	28.6%	29.5%	29.8%	32.3%	34.3%	36.0%
Retaliation— Title VII only	16,394	17,246	17,883	19,753	20,407	20,814	20,615	20,240	19,429	19,560	23,371	28,698	28,948
	20.3%	21.7%	23.1%	24.7%	25.2%	24.6%	25.4%	25.5%	25.8%	25.8%	28.3%	30.1%	31.0%
Age	15,785	15,191	14,141	16,008	17,405	19,921	19,124	17,837	16,585	16,548	19,103	24,582	22,778
	19.6%	19.1%	18.3%	20.0%	21.5%	23.6%	23.5%	22.5%	22.0%	21.8%	23.2%	25.8%	24.4%
Disability	18,108	17,806	17,007	15,864	16,470	15,964	15,377	15,376	14,893	15,575	17,734	19,453	21,451
	22.4%	22.4%	22.0%	19.9%	20.4%	18.9%	18.9%	19.4%	19.7%	20.6%	21.4%	20.4%	23.0%
Equal Pay Act	1,134	1,071	1,044	1,270	1,251	1,256	1,167	1,011	970	861	818	954	942
	1.4%	1.3%	1.3%	1.6%	1.5%	1.5%	1.4%	1.3%	1.3%	1.1%	1.0%	1.0%	1.0%

[1] The U.S. Equal Employment Opportunity Commission (available at *http://www.eeoc.gov/eeoc/statistics/enforcement/charges.cfm*). The number of charges corresponds to each fiscal year and reflects the number of individual charge filings. Because individuals often file charges claiming multiple types of discrimination, the number of total charges for any given fiscal year will be less than the total of the eight types of discrimination listed.

Exhibit 2-2

Equal Employment Opportunity is

THE LAW

Private Employers, State and Local Governments, Educational Institutions, Employment Agencies and Labor Organizations

Applicants to and employees of most private employers, state and local governments, educational institutions, employment agencies and labor organizations are protected under Federal law from discrimination on the following bases:

RACE, COLOR, RELIGION, SEX, NATIONAL ORIGIN

Title VII of the Civil Rights Act of 1964, as amended, protects applicants and employees from discrimination in hiring, promotion, discharge, pay, fringe benefits, job training, classification, referral, and other aspects of employment, on the basis of race, color, religion, sex (including pregnancy), or national origin. Religious discrimination includes failing to reasonably accommodate an employee's religious practices where the accommodation does not impose undue hardship.

DISABILITY

Title I and Title V of the Americans with Disabilities Act of 1990, as amended, protect qualified individuals from discrimination on the basis of disability in hiring, promotion, discharge, pay, fringe benefits, job training, classification, referral, and other aspects of employment. Disability discrimination includes not making reasonable accommodation to the known physical or mental limitations of an otherwise qualified individual with a disability who is an applicant or employee, barring undue hardship.

AGE

The Age Discrimination in Employment Act of 1967, as amended, protects applicants and employees 40 years of age or older from discrimination based on age in hiring, promotion, discharge, pay, fringe benefits, job training, classification, referral, and other aspects of employment.

SEX (WAGES)

In addition to sex discrimination prohibited by Title VII of the Civil Rights Act, as amended, the Equal Pay Act of 1963, as amended, prohibits sex discrimination in the payment of wages to women and men performing substantially equal work, in jobs that require equal skill, effort, and responsibility, under similar working conditions, in the same establishment.

GENETICS

Title II of the Genetic Information Nondiscrimination Act of 2008 protects applicants and employees from discrimination based on genetic information in hiring, promotion, discharge, pay, fringe benefits, job training, classification, referral, and other aspects of employment. GINA also restricts employers' acquisition of genetic information and strictly limits disclosure of genetic information. Genetic information includes information about genetic tests of applicants, employees, or their family members; the manifestation of diseases or disorders in family members (family medical history); and requests for or receipt of genetic services by applicants, employees, or their family members.

RETALIATION

All of these Federal laws prohibit covered entities from retaliating against a person who files a charge of discrimination, participates in a discrimination proceeding, or otherwise opposes an unlawful employment practice.

WHAT TO DO IF YOU BELIEVE DISCRIMINATION HAS OCCURRED

There are strict time limits for filing charges of employment discrimination. To preserve the ability of EEOC to act on your behalf and to protect your right to file a private lawsuit, should you ultimately need to, you should contact EEOC promptly when discrimination is suspected:

The U.S. Equal Employment Opportunity Commission (EEOC), 1-800-669-4000 (toll-free) or 1-800-669-6820 (toll-free TTY number for individuals with hearing impairments). EEOC field office information is available at www.eeoc.gov or in most telephone directories in the U.S. Government or Federal Government section. Additional information about EEOC, including information about charge filing, is available at www.eeoc.gov.

Exhibit 2-2 *(continued)*

Employers Holding Federal Contracts or Subcontracts

Applicants to and employees of companies with a Federal government contract or subcontract are protected under Federal law from discrimination on the following bases:

RACE, COLOR, RELIGION, SEX, NATIONAL ORIGIN

Executive Order 11246, as amended, prohibits job discrimination on the basis of race, color, religion, sex or national origin, and requires affirmative action to ensure equality of opportunity in all aspects of employment.

INDIVIDUALS WITH DISABILITIES

Section 503 of the Rehabilitation Act of 1973, as amended, protects qualified individuals from discrimination on the basis of disability in hiring, promotion, discharge, pay, fringe benefits, job training, classification, referral, and other aspects of employment. Disability discrimination includes not making reasonable accommodation to the known physical or mental limitations of an otherwise qualified individual with a disability who is an applicant or employee, barring undue hardship. Section 503 also requires that Federal contractors take affirmative action to employ and advance in employment qualified individuals with disabilities at all levels of employment, including the executive level.

DISABLED, RECENTLY SEPARATED, OTHER PROTECTED, AND ARMED FORCES SERVICE MEDAL VETERANS

The Vietnam Era Veterans' Readjustment Assistance Act of 1974, as amended, 38 U.S.C. 4212, prohibits job discrimination and requires affirmative action to employ and advance in employment disabled veterans, recently separated veterans (within

three years of discharge or release from active duty), other protected veterans (veterans who served during a war or in a campaign or expedition for which a campaign badge has been authorized), and Armed Forces service medal veterans (veterans who, while on active duty, participated in a U.S. military operation for which an Armed Forces service medal was awarded).

RETALIATION

Retaliation is prohibited against a person who files a complaint of discrimination, participates in an OFCCP proceeding, or otherwise opposes discrimination under these Federal laws.

Any person who believes a contractor has violated its nondiscrimination or affirmative action obligations under the authorities above should contact immediately:

The Office of Federal Contract Compliance Programs (OFCCP), U.S. Department of Labor, 200 Constitution Avenue. N.W., Washington, D.C. 20210, 1-800-397-6251 (toll-free) or (202) 693-1337 (TTY). OFCCP may also be contacted by e-mail at OFCCP-Public@dol.gov, or by calling an OFCCP regional or district office, listed in most telephone directories under U.S. Government, Department of Labor.

Programs or Activities Receiving Federal Financial Assistance

RACE, COLOR, NATIONAL ORIGIN, SEX

In addition to the protections of Title VII of the Civil Rights Act of 1964, as amended, Title VI of the Civil Rights Act of 1964, as amended, prohibits discrimination on the basis of race, color or national origin in programs or activities receiving Federal financial assistance. Employment discrimination is covered by Title VI if the primary objective of the financial assistance is provision of employment, or where employment discrimination causes or may cause discrimination in providing services under such programs. Title IX of the Education Amendments of 1972 prohibits employment discrimination on the basis of sex in educational programs or activities which receive Federal financial assistance.

INDIVIDUALS WITH DISABILITIES

Section 504 of the Rehabilitation Act of 1973, as amended, prohibits employment discrimination on the basis of disability in any program or activity which receives Federal financial assistance. Discrimination is prohibited in all aspects of employment against persons with disabilities who, with or without reasonable accommodation, can perform the essential functions of the job.

If you believe you have been discriminated against in a program of any institution which receives Federal financial assistance, you should immediately contact the Federal agency providing such assistance.

EEOC 9/02 and OFCCP 8/08 Versions Useable With 11/09 Supplement

EEOC-P/E-1 (Revised 11/09)

APPLICABILITY OF TITLE VII OF THE CIVIL RIGHTS ACT OF 1964

The most comprehensive federal law that governs employment discrimination is Title VII of the Civil Rights Act of 1964, which prohibits discrimination in employment based on race, color, religion, sex, and national origin.[6] The law became effective on July 2, 1965, and has been amended a number of times.

On the most basic level, Title VII makes it illegal for employers to discriminate in all aspects of employment. This prohibition attaches at the early stages of the hiring process, imposing obligations on employers as they advertise for a position and start to recruit and to interview applicants.

A. COVERED EMPLOYERS

When Title VII was first contemplated, its broad application compelled small business owners to strenuously lobby Congress to exclude them from the Act's coverage. Specifically, these business owners argued that the financial burden of defending a discrimination lawsuit would have a significant impact on their ability to remain in business, even if it was eventually determined that there was no unlawful conduct. Their efforts succeeded in convincing Congress to limit the statute's applicability to public- and private-sector employers who employ at least 15 employees.[7] Today, however, most states have passed laws that prohibit workplace discrimination and that apply to employers of all sizes.

B. DISCRIMINATION DEFINED

The language of Title VII does not include a precise definition of the term *discrimination*. The term is broadly interpreted and, even though discrimination is commonly discussed within the context of wrongful terminations, this is just one small part of the employment process. Specifically, the prohibition against discrimination under Title VII and other workplace anti-discrimination laws requires that employers not impose adverse actions upon individuals based upon the individuals' membership in a protected class.

1. ADVERSE ACTION

adverse action
a decision that has a negative impact on the working conditions of an individual and cannot be imposed based on an individual's membership in a protected class

An **adverse action** is an employment decision that has a negative impact on an individual's working conditions that may be the basis of a workplace discrimination claim. A failure to hire or train an individual, a discharge or layoff, and a decision to offer an individual reduced compensation or level of benefits are examples of adverse actions. Adverse actions can relate to any term and condition of employment, and Title VII prohibits workplace discrimination as it relates to each of them, including decisions relating to

- ✓ hiring;
- ✓ firing;
- ✓ compensation;
- ✓ work assignments;
- ✓ classification of employees;
- ✓ transfers, promotions, layoffs, or recalls;
- ✓ job postings;
- ✓ recruiting;
- ✓ testing;
- ✓ use of company facilities;
- ✓ training and apprenticeship programs;
- ✓ allocation of fringe benefits;
- ✓ retirement benefits;
- ✓ disability leave; and
- ✓ all other terms and conditions of employment.[8]

2. MEMBERSHIP IN A PROTECTED CLASS

Individuals can assert a claim under Title VII only if they are subjected to discriminatory treatment (in the form of an adverse action) based on their membership in a **protected class**, which refers to a group of people who have one or more characteristics in common and are protected from discriminatory and harassing conduct.

protected class
group of people who share a common characteristic that entitles them to protection from discriminatory and harassing conduct under Title VII or other anti-discrimination laws

a. Nature of Protected Class

The protected classes under Title VII are race, color, religion, sex, and national origin. Individuals are protected from the imposition of adverse employment decisions based on their membership in each of these protected classes, on a stereotype associated with each of these protected classes, or on an individual's marriage to or association with someone who is a member of one of these protected classes.[9] In addition, Title VII prohibits employers from retaliating against an employee for filing a discrimination claim under Title VII by imposing an adverse employment decision upon that employee.

b. Membership in a Protected Class Is Nonexclusive

An individual might be subjected to discriminatory conduct based on membership in more than one protected class. For example, an employer who imposes an adverse action on an individual based on his anti-Semitic beliefs might be subject to a claim for religious discrimination, national origin discrimination, or both. Likewise, a female employee subjected to discriminatory treatment based on the fact that she is a woman and a member of a particular minority group might assert a claim under Title VII for discrimination based on sex and race.[10]

c. Limitations on Protections

Individuals who are discriminated against based on a characteristic *not* linked to a protected class cannot assert a discrimination claim under Title VII. For example, an individual could not file a claim under Title VII asserting that she was discriminated against because she had young children, because neither parents nor caregivers are a protected class under Title VII. Instead, to file a claim under Title VII for workplace discrimination based on either of these classifications, the individual would be required to link the discriminatory conduct to her membership in a protected class, such as gender or race.

Based on this, the same woman might have a viable claim under Title VII if she could show that women were assigned to less desirable work shifts, based on the assumption that women would be less committed to their jobs because usually they had the primary responsibility to care for a family's young children.[11] Under these circumstances, the employee would assert her rights as a woman, a member of the protected class that relates to sex, as opposed to asserting her rights as a caregiver, which is not a protected class under Title VII.

d. Expansion of Protections

Although protection from workplace discrimination under Title VII is limited to membership in the delineated list that includes race, color, religion, sex, and national origin, this is not the full scope of potential protections because individuals may be entitled to protections under other federal laws, state laws, or other sources. Some states have anti-discrimination laws extending the prohibition against workplace discrimination to a greater number of protected classes than those protected under Title VII. For example, New York law prohibits workplace discrimination based on age, race, creed, color, national origin, sexual orientation, military status, sex, disabilities, predisposing genetic characteristics, and marital status.[12] Therefore, for the purposes of an employment discrimination claim, whether or not an individual is a member of a protected class will depend on the law under which the individual asserts the claim.

TYPES OF EVIDENCE

Regardless of the legal source of a workplace discrimination claim, there are a number of types of evidence that might be used to support a showing that discriminatory conduct occurred. This information is important for employers because it will shed light on the nature of employer conduct that may be the basis for the imposition of liability. It is equally important for applicants and employees to be aware of the type of proof necessary to sustain a discrimination claim.

A. DIRECT EVIDENCE

In 1964 when Title VII was passed and signed into law, employment discrimination was highly visible in the workplace. As a result, there was a significant amount of evidence indicating that employment decisions had been made based on discriminatory factors prohibited by the new legislation. These circumstances resulted in the presentation of **direct evidence** that proved discrimination had occurred, meaning that an individual could show that his membership in a protected class was used as the basis for the making of an adverse employment decision in violation of Title VII.

direct evidence
information that is clear proof that particular conduct occurred

Testimony that an employer made a staff meeting announcement that members of a certain race would not be eligible for promotional opportunities is an example of direct evidence of intentional discrimination. A letter from an employer saying that a female applicant would not be considered for a training program because it was designed to provide strength training that would be more beneficial to men and the types of careers they seek is another example of direct evidence of discrimination. Along these same lines, the presentation of a company policy limiting hiring for loading dock positions to male applicants would be another example of direct evidence of discriminatory conduct.

Courts have also held that individuals can support discrimination claims by showing that a stereotype was the basis for an adverse employment decision. For example, one court found that an employer's instructions to its female employees to wear jewelry, work in a more feminine manner, and attend charm school to enhance their chances of being promoted, was sufficient evidence to show an employer's actions violated Title VII's prohibition against sex discrimination.[13]

If an individual presents direct evidence of intentional discrimination, it is likely that her employer will be held liable for unlawful conduct, unless the employer presents a viable defense for the discriminatory decision as discussed below.

B. CIRCUMSTANTIAL EVIDENCE

After Title VII was passed, employers started to understand the prohibition against workplace discrimination, and direct evidence of its occurrence became more difficult to obtain. This decline might have been the result of a change in employer conduct in response to the legislation, or it might have been the result of an adjustment of discriminatory conduct to decrease the likelihood that it would be detected. Regardless of the reason for the decline, because direct evidence of discrimination became less readily available, aggrieved individuals started to look for alternate ways to prove their discrimination claims, and the courts started to consider **circumstantial evidence** in support of such claims. Unlike direct evidence, circumstantial evidence does not prove that workplace discrimination occurred. Instead it merely suggests that this prohibited behavior took place.

circumstantial evidence
information that suggests particular conduct occurred but that does not prove it definitively

Individuals might present circumstantial evidence to show that groups of employees belonging to a protected class were routinely treated less favorably than those who were not members of it. This evidence could be presented through the use of statistics related to different groups of employees within a workplace, or through the introduction of testimony supporting the claim of differential treatment. Although the presentation of statistics has been sufficient to satisfy the initial burden of proof in a discrimination claim, the Supreme Court has held that such a presentation alone is not sufficient to prove intentional discrimination.[14]

In determining how much weight statistics should receive, courts look to a number of factors, such as the relevant labor pool and the level of skill that is needed for a particular job. Courts have reasoned that this evidence is circumstantial because if statistics show that members of a specific protected class rarely held certain skilled positions, for example, it might be evidence of discrimination, or it might represent the fact that fewer people possessed the required skills or had an interest in applying for those positions.[15] This is not direct evidence because it does not conclusively prove that an individual's protected class membership was considered when decisions were made.

Along the same lines, an employee might assert a sex discrimination claim by presenting circumstantial evidence that women were regularly assigned to less desirable overnight shifts while men were routinely assigned to more desirable day shifts. This is not direct evidence because it only suggests, but does not prove, discriminatory conduct occurred. Despite the inference of sex discrimination that can be drawn from the presentation of this circumstantial evidence, the employer would likely avoid liability for discrimination if the evidence also illustrated that all of the women working the night shift actually requested those hours so they could tend to other responsibilities during the day. Circumstantial evidence remains significant today because there is rarely a "smoking gun" that can be used as direct evidence to prove that discrimination occurred.

As Title VII evolved and individuals started to assert their rights under the statute, the Supreme Court faced questions about how employees could best position themselves to sustain a discrimination claim, and how employers could place themselves in the best position to defend themselves in the event a situation resulted in litigation. The eventual result was the development of a framework for the presentation of evidence, and the shifting of the burden of proof within the context of workplace discrimination claims.

FILING A CLAIM UNDER TITLE VII

An individual alleging workplace discrimination under Title VII is not permitted to file a claim directly with a court. Instead, the charge must be filed with the EEOC.

A. EQUAL EMPLOYMENT OPPORTUNITY COMMISSION (EEOC)

Equal Employment Opportunity Commission (EEOC)
federal agency responsible for the enforcement of Title VII and a number of other federal anti-discrimination laws

The **Equal Employment Opportunity Commission (EEOC)** is the federal agency that is responsible for enforcing Title VII and a number of other federal employment discrimination laws, including the EPA, the ADEA, and the ADA.[16] The Agency is made up of five commissioners, each appointed for staggered five-year terms, and is responsible for making policy and approving most employment discrimination litigation. The EEOC's general counsel is appointed by the President for a four-year term and oversees the enforcement of the litigation.[17]

B. STATUTE OF LIMITATIONS

A **statute of limitations** refers to the time limit for filing a claim asserting a violation of a particular law.[18] For example, if the statute of limitations under a particular law is one year, an individual who intends to file a claim asserting a violation of that law is required to take that legal action within the one-year period following the alleged unlawful conduct. If a claim is filed after the one-year period, the claim will generally be considered untimely and be dismissed from further consideration.[19]

statute of limitations
time period during which an individual can file a claim asserting that a legal violation occurred under a particular statute

1. ONE HUNDRED AND EIGHTY (180) DAYS

Generally speaking, an individual must file a charge for employment discrimination under any federal discrimination statute enforced by the EEOC within 180 days of the alleged violation.[20] This is significant because all laws that are enforced by the EEOC (with the exception of the EPA) require individuals to file a charge with the Agency before filing a private claim in court.[21] Thus, individuals must file the charge within this 180-day statute of limitations to protect their rights.

Although the application of the statute of limitations to a particular law may seem straightforward, the issue is actually frequently the subject of litigation. This is because some laws use the alleged unlawful conduct as the triggering point for the calculation of the time limit for the filing of the claim, while other laws use different triggering points, such as the time the individual knew or should have known about the alleged misconduct. In addition, some laws leave the issue subject to interpretation. The complexity of the issue relating to the 180-day statute of limitations for compensation discrimination has specifically materialized with respect to identifying the event that should be considered the starting point for calculating the statute of limitations when the alleged prohibited conduct continues over an extended period of time. As discussed below, the Supreme Court issued a decision on this matter within the context of compensation discrimination, but Congress subsequently overturned the judicial interpretation of the law.

2. TRIGGERING EVENT FOR COMPENSATION CLAIMS UNDER THE LEDBETTER FAIR PAY ACT OF 2009

The Supreme Court recently tackled the issue of the appropriate application of the statute of limitations for compensation claims under Title VII, and Congress then issued a legislative response to the Court's ruling. Specifically, in a particular compensation discrimination case, the employer argued that the 180-day statute of limitations for filing a claim under Title VII should run from the date of the initial discriminatory decision, regardless of the period of time during which an individual was compensated at the discriminatory rate. In contrast, the employee argued that *any* paycheck that included the discriminatory compensation rate could be used as the starting point for the calculation of the 180-day time limit.

In its decision the Supreme Court agreed with the employer, holding that the statute of limitations for filing a compensation discrimination claim under Title VII starts from the time of the *initial* compensation decision rather than providing employees the opportunity to initiate a claim within 180 days from each offending paycheck.[22]

Ledbetter Fair Pay Act of 2009
federal law that states the statute of limitations for filing a compensation discrimination claim starts to run each time the discriminatory wages are paid, as opposed to from the initial discriminatory decision

Soon after the issuance of that decision Congress revisited this issue and reversed the Court's ruling with the passage of the **Ledbetter Fair Pay Act of 2009**, which states that the discriminatory conduct occurs "each time wages, benefits, or other compensation is paid, resulting in whole or in part from [a pay] decision or other practice," as opposed to at the time of the initial compensation decision.[23] Therefore, pursuant to this Act, an individual may now file a discriminatory compensation claim under a law enforced by the EEOC within 180 days after the receipt of any paycheck that reflects the alleged improper rate of pay.

C. EEOC RESPONSE TO THE FILING OF A CLAIM

Once an individual files a charge with the EEOC within 180 days of the appropriate triggering event, the EEOC will initiate and conduct an investigation, attempt to settle the charge, submit the charge to mediation, or dismiss it, depending on the facts of the specific case.[24]

right to sue letter
document from the EEOC that provides an individual with the right to file a workplace discrimination claim in federal court

In the event the EEOC finds evidence of discrimination, it will attempt to work with the employer to determine the appropriate remedy and, if an agreement cannot be reached, the Agency will decide whether it will file a lawsuit in federal court on behalf of the charging party. If the EEOC decides not to bring a suit (or if the EEOC initially finds no evidence of discrimination), then the Agency will issue a **right to sue letter** that provides the individual with 90 days to file a lawsuit on his own.[25] This right to sue letter is what provides an individual with the right to file a workplace discrimination claim in federal court.

 FILING A DISCRIMINATION CLAIM IN FEDERAL COURT

When Congress passed Title VII, there was a notable absence of a road map for individuals to use to assert a discrimination claim or for employers to use to defend their employment decisions. Based on the significance of these omissions, it was not surprising that after the passage of Title VII, the Supreme Court agreed to hear these issues to provide clarification and review.

As Title VII cases began to be filed in federal court, two distinct trends developed relating to the type of discrimination alleged. Some discriminatory conduct appeared to be intentional, and some conduct appeared to unintentionally produce discriminatory results. Today, discrimination claims are filed based on these divisions, with the filing of disparate treatment claims to address intentional discriminatory conduct and the filing of disparate impact claims to address conduct that appears neutral but produces a discriminatory result.

VII. DISPARATE TREATMENT CLAIMS

The first category of discrimination claims that arise under Title VII are **disparate treatment claims**, which relate to intentional discrimination. *McDonnell Douglas Corporation v. Green* is the 1973 Supreme Court case that established the framework for proving employment discrimination claims that allege an employer engaged in intentional discrimination.[26] This decision sets out the framework for presenting evidence for disparate treatment discrimination claims, and for shifting the burden of proof between the employee (or applicant) alleging discriminatory conduct occurred and the employer defending its employment decisions.

disparate treatment claim
an employment discrimination claim alleging an employer engaged in intentional discrimination

McDonnell Douglas Corporation v. Green
the Supreme Court case that established the framework for the presentation of proof for a claim of intentional discrimination

A. *PRIMA FACIE* CASE

The first step for an individual asserting an employment discrimination claim is the presentation of a *prima facie* case of discriminatory conduct. This is the most fundamental explanation of the nature of alleged discrimination used by the court to determine whether the facts, if true, would support the imposition of liability under the statute. The initial presentation is a simple one as the Supreme Court stated that the "burden of establishing a *prima facie* case of disparate treatment is not onerous."[27] The lax standards for the presentation of a *prima facie* case are consistent with its limited purpose, which is to show the existence of facts that illustrate a *possibility* that discrimination occurred, as opposed to showing that it actually did.

prima facie **case**
an individual's initial burden of proof when asserting an employment discrimination claim

To establish a *prima facie* case of discrimination in hiring, for example, the individual filing the discrimination claim must show that

1. the individual belongs to a protected class; and
2. the individual applied for and was qualified for a position for which the employer was seeking applicants; and
3. despite the individual's qualifications, she was rejected for the position; and
4. even after the rejection the position remained open, and the employer continued to seek applicants with similar qualifications.[28]

1. MEMBERSHIP IN A PROTECTED CLASS

Within the context of a *prima facie* case, a court would dismiss a claim filed under Title VII if it is not filed by an individual who is a member of a protected class (or a representative of such a member) that the statute seeks to protect. For example, if an individual files a claim under Title VII asserting that he was discriminated against because the employer said he was overweight, this would not satisfy the initial element of a *prima facie* case, because the claim does not allege that the employer engaged in discriminatory conduct based on race, color, religion, sex, or national origin, which are the protected classes under the statute.

2. QUALIFIED FOR THE POSITION

The second element of a *prima facie* case relates to whether the applicant is qualified for the position. When initially presenting evidence relating to qualifications, all that is required is a showing of the possession of the minimum qualifications required for the position. Individuals do not need to prove they were the ideal candidate, only that they had the qualifications the employer could reasonably expect its job candidates to possess.

In evaluating the *prima facie* case for discrimination, courts will usually focus on objective qualifications, which are generally measurable skills. The significance of subjective criteria, which relate to the personal opinions of the person evaluating the candidate, become relevant only when the employer defends its behavior and presents evidence to show that the adverse decision was not based on discriminatory motives.

3. ADVERSE ACTION

The next element of the *prima facie* case relates to the presentation of evidence that an adverse employment decision was actually imposed. For a claim based on discriminatory hiring, an adverse employment decision could be a showing that the individual was not hired. Depending on the nature of the alleged discrimination, the adverse decision could be a showing that an individual did not receive a promotion, was denied access to a training program, was terminated, or was subjected to any other employment decisions that would have a negative impact on an individual's terms and conditions of employment.

This is critical, because the basis for the filing of a Title VII claim is the imposition of an adverse decision that was motivated by consideration of an individual's membership in a protected class. Therefore, if the individual asserting the claim was not subjected to an adverse action, the individual will be unable to establish a *prima facie* case of discrimination and the claim will be dismissed.

4. CANDIDATES WITH COMPARABLE QUALIFICATIONS CONTINUE TO BE CONSIDERED

The final element of a *prima facie* case of discrimination in hiring requires demonstrating that after rejecting the applicant, the employer continued to interview and consider candidates with comparable qualifications. For example, a female applicant for a position as a plumber, with three years of relevant experience and all of the other qualifications required for the position, could satisfy this element by showing that after the employer rejected her application, other male candidates with significantly less experience were interviewed for the position.

The requirements for the *prima facie* case are flexible, depending on the specific nature of the asserted claim. Thus, an individual asserting a hiring discrimination claim would present a slightly different *prima facie* case than an employee asserting a claim of discrimination related to the denial of a promotion. Specifically, an individual could satisfy the burden relating to the fourth element of a *prima facie* case for a discriminatory promotion by showing an employee with comparable qualifications (but not a member of a protected class) was promoted; for a discriminatory denial of access to a training program, by showing an employee with comparable qualifications (but not a member of a protected class) was granted access; and for a discriminatory termination, by showing an employee who engaged in the same misconduct (but not a member of a protected class) continued to be employed.

B. EMPLOYER'S BURDEN: ARTICULATE A LEGITIMATE, NONDISCRIMINATORY REASON FOR ITS ADVERSE DECISION

Once an individual presents a *prima facie* case of discrimination, the burden of proof shifts to the employer to articulate a legitimate, nondiscriminatory reason for the adverse employment decision.

1. APPROPRIATE JUSTIFICATIONS FOR MAKING ADVERSE DECISIONS

Employers are provided with a great deal of latitude with respect to the reasons they may have for making a decision that has an adverse impact on an applicant (or an employee) and the reasons vary depending on the nature of the decision. Within the context of a claim for a discriminatory termination, some examples of legitimate reasons for terminating an employee include

- ✓ inability to perform the work the job requires;
- ✓ inability to work the schedule needed by the employer;
- ✓ injuring a co-worker;
- ✓ falsifying time sheets or other documents;
- ✓ failing to meet production requirements;
- ✓ reduction in workforce (provided the reduction is not based on discriminatory considerations);
- ✓ refusal to follow the managerial directives; and
- ✓ insubordination (failing to follow the instructions of a supervisor).

2. EXTENT OF BURDEN

The burden on the employer to present its reason for making an adverse decision is not particularly high, and the Supreme Court went so far as to say that the employer "need not persuade the court that it was actually motivated by the proffered reasons, but it is sufficient if the . . . evidence raises a genuine issue of fact as to whether it discriminated against the plaintiff."[29]

a. Appropriateness of Objective and Subjective Considerations

An employer may offer objective or subjective reasons for its determination that the adverse decision was warranted. An objective consideration would be based on a measurable fact, such as a showing that most employees working as data processing clerks for the employer process 150 invoices in a day and the employee who was terminated consistently processed 25. A subjective consideration would be based on the personal opinion or observation made by the employer and, when offered as the basis for the imposition of an adverse decision, should have some basis in fact. For example, an employer's statement that an employee "did not fit in" will likely be considered less credible than a similarly subjective statement that a candidate's personality seemed to be "laid back and flexible," which was incompatible with the rigid corporate culture in which the job existed.

b. Deference to Employer

Even though the courts will review an employer's justifications for making an adverse decision, they will not second-guess any business decisions and generally will defer to the employer's expertise. It is only when an employer asserts a reason that appears to be untrue or inconsistent with other presented evidence that the court will challenge the employer's stated rationale for making the decision.

C. EMPLOYEE TO SHOW EMPLOYER'S JUSTIFICATION FOR DECISION IS A PRETEXT

Once an employer presents its reason for the adverse decision, the burden of proof shifts back to the individual asserting that claim to show that the provided reason is actually a **pretext** (a cover-up) for the employer's true discriminatory motives.[30]

This inquiry often focuses on the credibility of the employer's explanation of the reason for the adverse employment decision. For example, if an employer defends its decision to terminate an individual of a particular race based on the employer's need to reduce payroll costs, the employee claiming that the decision was discriminatory would be provided with the opportunity to show that this justification was not the employer's true motivating factor for making the decision. The employee might show that the employer was recruiting new employees to work in the exact role he performed before being terminated as evidence that the employer's stated reason for the termination was a pretext for its discriminatory intent.

pretext
employer's explanation for making an adverse decision that is actually a cover-up for the true discriminatory motivating factor

1. PRETEXT-PLUS

In 1993 the Supreme Court issued a significant decision that continues to have an impact on the litigation of employment discrimination claims. Specifically, the Court introduced a "pretext-plus" component of a discrimination claim. Under the **pretext-plus** theory, once an employee establishes that the employer's asserted nondiscriminatory reason for its adverse decision is a pretext, the employee has an additional obligation (the "plus") to show that consideration of an individual's membership in a protected class was the motivating factor behind the adverse decision.[31]

Under the above facts, in response to the employer's statement that the basis for making an adverse decision was to reduce payroll costs, the employee asserting the racial discrimination claim could show the employer's stated reason was a pretext by introducing evidence that the employer was recruiting new employees to work in the exact role he performed before the termination. This evidence would support the employee's claim that the need to reduce payroll costs was not the true reason for the adverse decision. Under the pretext-plus theory, the employee would be required to go one step further ("the plus") and prove that the true motive for the adverse decision was discriminatory. Therefore, once the employee illustrated that the employer did not terminate the individual because of a need to reduce payroll costs, the employee would have the additional burden of proving that the employee's race was actually the motivating factor behind the termination.

a. *Prima Facie* Case May Be Sufficient to Satisfy Pretext-Plus Burden

The Supreme Court has continued to grapple with the question of the appropriate burden to be imposed on an applicant (or employee) once the employer's reason for the adverse decision is shown to be a pretext. Seven years after it first established the pretext-plus theory, the Court revisited the issue and presented somewhat of a middle ground. The Court explained that the employee may or may not have the additional burden to prove the employer's motives were discriminatory based on the type of evidence that was previously presented. The Court clarified that once the plaintiff shows that the employer's asserted reason is false (a pretext), there might *not* be a need for additional proof of discrimination provided the appropriate level of evidence was presented within the *prima facie* case or at some other point in the litigation.

However, despite what seemed to be a judicial determination that the "plus" of the pretext-plus theory might not be required, the Court seemed to reaffirm its initial commitment to placing the burden of proof on the individual asserting the claim by stating that the key question to be answered is whether the employer engaged in intentional discrimination, *not* whether the reason it provided was false. Specifically, the Court stated that a plaintiff's *prima facie* case, combined with sufficient evidence to find that the employer's asserted justification is false, may permit the trier of fact to conclude that the employer unlawfully discriminated, but there was no guarantee that this would be the result.[32]

b. Plaintiff Continues to Have Ultimate Burden of Proof

This shifting of the burden of proof ensures the continued recognition of the initial judicial decision to require the individual asserting the claim to prove discriminatory conduct occurred — in other words, it ensures that "[t]he ultimate burden of persuading the trier of fact that the defendant intentionally discriminated

pretext-plus
requirement for an applicant (or employee) to show both that the employer's explanation for making an adverse employment decision was untrue *and* that the true motivating factor was discriminatory

against the plaintiff remains at all times with the plaintiff."[33] Therefore, the employee will always have this burden, but there may be more than one way to satisfy it.

2. MIXED-MOTIVE CLAIMS

mixed-motive
an action that is motivated by both legitimate and discriminatory considerations

Another significant factor in employment discrimination litigation is whether an employer can illustrate that a **mixed motive** was the basis for the adverse employment decision, which refers to a decision based on both legitimate and discriminatory factors. The key issue under these circumstances is whether an employer would have reached the same conclusion absent consideration of the discriminatory factor.

Civil Rights Act of 1991
federal law that, among other things, subjects employers to liability for adverse employment decisions that are motivated by both legitimate and discriminatory considerations

The Supreme Court initially determined an employer who presented evidence of a mixed-motive decision could escape liability under Title VII.[34] Congress disagreed, however, and through the passage of the **Civil Rights Act of 1991** clarified that employers are prohibited from considering discriminatory factors in making employment decisions—even if other factors contributed to the decision.[35]

Therefore, despite some earlier judicial decisions that reached different conclusions, today an employer who shows that a decision was based on both discriminatory and legitimate considerations will not be able to escape liability for discriminatory conduct under Title VII. However, mixed motives can be a significant element of an employer's defense because their presence significantly limits the types of damages that may be awarded, as explained in the section on remedies found at the end of this chapter.

VII   DISPARATE IMPACT CLAIMS

In addition to facing liability for decisions based on a combination of discriminatory and nondiscriminatory motives, employers may also be subject to liability for the unintentional discriminatory result of their conduct which has an adverse impact on members of a protected class. Under this theory of liability, the alleged discrimination is not the result of employer conduct that is intentionally discriminatory but is instead the consequence of the implementation of a policy or practice that is neutral on its face but that produces a discriminatory result. An employee facing this type of discrimination is able to file what is classified as a **disparate impact claim**.

disparate impact claim
employment discrimination claim alleging that an employer implemented a practice or policy that was neutral on its face but that resulted in an adverse impact on members of a protected class

A. SIGNIFICANCE OF UNINTENTIONAL DISCRIMINATION

As Title VII evolved, the Supreme Court recognized that workplace discrimination was not always the result of intentional discriminatory conduct and made it clear that Title VII was never intended to be limited to intentional discriminatory behavior. The Court provided for the filing of a disparate impact claim if an individual was discriminated against as a result of the implementation of a facially neutral policy or practice that produced a discriminatory result.[36]

B. EMPLOYER'S INTENT IS IRRELEVANT

Under the disparate impact theory, the intent of the employer is irrelevant, so an employer's assertion that it implemented a neutral policy and did not intend to discriminate would not absolve the employer from liability for the discriminatory consequences of the conduct. The Supreme Court held that "practices, procedures, or tests neutral on their face, and even neutral in terms of intent, cannot be maintained if they operate to 'freeze' the status quo of prior discriminatory practices."[37] The Court went on to say that "good intent or absence of discriminatory intent" would not legitimize conduct that produces a discriminatory result.[38] In short, any employment decision or practice that has an impact on a protected class that is less favorable than the impact it has on those who are not in a protected class could subject an employer to liability under the disparate impact theory.

C. BASIS FOR DISPARATE IMPACT CLAIMS

Because employers are responsible for the impact of their policies, they must carefully craft any guidelines used to recruit applicants and to determine the terms and conditions of employment for their employees. For example, the use of pre-employment testing, education and language requirements, and height and weight restrictions for its job applicants could subject an employer to liability for discrimination based on a disparate impact claim. This is because these tests and standards have the potential to disproportionately impact members of a protected class. See Chapter 11, Pre-Employment Testing.

More specifically, suppose an employer is seeking applicants for a job unloading delivery trucks and posts a notification that it is looking for male applicants for the position. This conduct could be the basis for filing a *disparate treatment claim* based on intentional discrimination, because the job posting is intentionally discriminating against female applicants in violation of the prohibition against sex discrimination under Title VII.

Now, suppose the employer decides she wants to hire strong people to unload delivery trucks and posts a new notification indicating her interest in interviewing applicants who can comfortably lift 75-pound boxes. This posting may appear to be nondiscriminatory because it does not mention, reference, or exclude members of a protected class. However, by posting a notification that applicants must be able to lift 75 pounds, the employer might be discouraging qualified female applicants from applying for the position if they are less likely to be able to lift this amount of weight, especially if the job only requires individuals to comfortably lift 50-pound boxes. Under these circumstances, the employer might be subject to liability for *disparate impact* sex discrimination for using a facially neutral job posting that has an adverse impact on members of a protected class.

D. PRESENTATION OF PROOF FOR A DISPARATE IMPACT CLAIM

The presentation of proof for a disparate impact claim, just like the presentation of proof for a disparate treatment claim, involves the shifting of the burden of proof between the individual filing the claim and the employer defending its actions. Specifically, the framework for asserting a disparate impact claim is as follows:

1. The plaintiff (applicant or employee) must establish a *prima facie* case of discrimination by presenting an employment practice or decision that

   a. is neutral on its face; and
   b. has a disproportionate impact on members of a protected class.

2. Once the *prima facie* case is established, the burden shifts to the defendant (employer) to show that the challenged policy or practice is job related *and* that there is a business necessity for it.

3. After the employer satisfies this burden, the applicant or employee can still sustain his claim by presenting a less discriminatory alternative that would have a lesser impact on members of a protected class.

1. *PRIMA FACIE* CASE

The presentation of a *prima facie* case for a disparate impact claim requires the individual alleging the discriminatory conduct to produce evidence of an employment policy or practice that is neutral on its face but that, when implemented, has an adverse impact on members of a protected class.[39] Evidence of a disparate impact on members of a protected class is usually presented through the use of statistical evidence that compares members of a protected class with those who fall outside it. For example, an individual might show that a pre-employment test used to disqualify applicants has a disparate impact on minorities by presenting evidence that only 15% of the minority applicants pass the test, as compared to 95% of the non-minority applicants. These results indicate that the test violates the **four-fifths (or 80%) rule**, which states that if the selection rate of the group with the lowest selection rate is less than 80% of the selection rate of the group with the highest selection rate, then there is a presumption that a disparate impact exists.[40] See Chapter 11, Pre-Employment Testing, for a detailed example of how this test is applied.

four-fifths (or 80%) rule
standard established by the EEOC that quantifies an adverse impact on a protected class as a selection rate that is less than 4/5 (or 80%) of the selection rate for the group with the highest selection rate

2. SHOWING OF BUSINESS NECESSITY

Once the employee satisfies the burden of presenting a *prima facie* case, the burden of proof shifts to the employer to show that its employment policy or practice is "job related for the position in question and consistent with **business necessity**."[41] A business necessity is a showing by an employer that a practice or policy is essential to its operations, despite its disparate impact on members of a protected class.

business necessity
a showing by an employer that a practice or policy is essential to its operations, despite its disparate impact on members of a protected class

A number of factors are used to determine whether there is a business necessity to justify the discriminatory result of a facially neutral policy. Specifically, the employer may justify a qualification as necessary for a position by showing (1) a strong statistical correlation exists between the requirement and successful job performance; (2) the job requirement relates to a skill that is necessary for performance of the job; (3) the requirement enables the employer to select candidates who possess the necessary skills for successful job performance; or (4) the possession of the particular skill is statistically correlated to strong performance.[42]

For example, an employer will likely be able to show that granting interviews for a counselor position only to those applicants with a college degree in psychology is a job-related requirement and constitutes a business necessity, even though the policy may exclude a disproportionate number of applicants from certain protected classes who may be less likely to have an advanced degree.[43] Employers will be less likely, however, to be able to justify the imposition of a similar educational requirement for applicants for blue-collar jobs or clerical positions, because it is less likely an advanced degree will be relevant to the tasks associated with those positions.[44]

3. LESS DISCRIMINATORY ALTERNATIVES

Even if an employer is able to illustrate that the policy that creates the disproportionate impact is a business necessity, the applicant or employee could still sustain a disparate impact claim by presenting a less discriminatory method the employer could have used to achieve the same result.[45] For example, under the facts relating to the job unloading delivery trucks noted above, the employer might assert that it has a business necessity to hire strong applicants because the boxes to be unloaded are heavy. Even if the court accepted this business need to hire strong candidates, an applicant might present evidence that the heaviest boxes employees are required to unload weigh only 60 pounds.

Under these circumstances, the employer's liability would stem from the fact that it could have advertised for applicants who could comfortably lift 60 pounds instead of 75 pounds. This adjustment would have addressed the employer's business need and might have also resulted in the hiring of a larger number of female applicants. This is because as it is more likely that more women possess the strength to lift 60 pounds than 75 pounds, the reduction of this weight requirement could have increased the number of qualified female applicants, which in turn could have reduced the discriminatory impact the policy would have on members of the protected class.

VIII ALLOWANCE FOR CONDUCT THAT WOULD OTHERWISE BE DISCRIMINATORY

Although Title VII prohibits workplace discrimination, it actually recognizes a limited number of instances when an employer might be permitted to consider membership in a protected class when making an employment decision.

A. WORK PRODUCTION

As a starting point, employers are generally permitted to base an employee's compensation on the quantity or quality of that employee's work, even if this practice results in paying some employees who are members of a protected class less than nonmembers. However, it would be impermissible to utilize this practice if the shifts or tasks most likely to lead to greater production (and therefore greater compensation) are assigned in a discriminatory manner.

B. SENIORITY SYSTEMS AND PROFESSIONALLY DEVELOPED TESTS

bona fide seniority system
policy that provides enhanced benefits to employees based on their length of employment and is permissible under Title VII despite the disparate impact it might have on members of a protected class, provided the system was not designed to produce discriminatory results

Section 703(b) of Title VII permits the use of **bona fide seniority systems**, which use an employee's length of service as a factor to determine certain terms and conditions of employment.

Despite the legal challenges to these systems based on the disparate impact they may have on members of certain protected classes, the Supreme Court has supported their use and reasoned that absent a discriminatory purpose, the operation of a seniority system is not an unlawful employment practice even if the system results in the perpetuation of discrimination that predated the passage of Title VII.[46] Along these same lines, employers are permitted to make decisions based on the results of a "professionally developed test" provided it was not "designed, intended or used to discriminate."[47]

C. BONA FIDE OCCUPATIONAL QUALIFICATIONS (BFOQs) AS A DEFENSE TO DISCRIMINATORY CONDUCT BASED ON RELIGION, SEX, AND NATIONAL ORIGIN

bona fide occupational qualification (BFOQ)
employer's defense to an employment discrimination claim that illustrates the business necessity of considering an individual's protected class status (other than race and color), which is conduct that would be otherwise prohibited

Employers who consider protected class membership when making employment decisions might be able to avoid liability by showing that membership in the protected class is a **bona fide occupational qualification (BFOQ)** for a position. Section 703(e) of Title VII sets forth the BFOQ defense stating that an employer is permitted to base an adverse employment decision on an individual's religion, sex, or national origin (but not race or color) if the consideration is "reasonably necessary to the normal operation of the particular business or enterprise."[48] An employer who successfully asserts the BFOQ defense will not be subject to liability under Title VII.

The appropriateness of the BFOQ defense is determined by a fact-specific inquiry that looks to the nature of the job, the requirements to perform it, and the purpose for which the employer's business exists. Courts carefully scrutinize the assertion of the BFOQ defense because it allows an employer to consider membership in a protected class when making an employment decision, which is the precise behavior Title VII is designed to prohibit. Although employers always have the option to assert this defense to justify discriminatory behavior under Title

VII based on religion, sex, or national origin, courts have been most willing to accept it within the context of issues relating to safety, privacy, and religious beliefs. (Note that, as referenced above, the BFOQ defense cannot be used to justify discriminatory behavior based on race or color.[49])

1. SAFETY

In a number of instances, courts have permitted the BFOQ defense when it is linked to a safety issue. For example, the Supreme Court refused to impose liability on an employer who refused to consider women applicants for prison jobs requiring physical contact with prisoners in male maximum security prisons. The Court justified the acceptance of the employer's BFOQ defense based on extensive evidence highlighting the dangerous conditions in the prisons and the fact that many of the inmates were sex offenders who would be more likely to harm women than they would be to harm their male counterparts. The Court reasoned that this discriminatory conduct was not prohibited because placing female guards in those positions had the potential to endanger the female guards as well as the prisoners and other employees.[50]

2. PRIVACY

Employers have also successfully asserted the BFOQ defense within the context of claims that involve privacy concerns. For example, employers will likely be able to use the BFOQ defense to justify hiring at least one staff member of the same gender for a patient care position, which requires providing assistance with personal hygiene such as showering and getting dressed.[51]

3. RELIGION

Courts have also permitted employers to recruit applicants of a certain religion in limited instances by accepting a BFOQ defense.[52] For example, one court held that an employer could defend its decision to require a pilot to be a Muslim using a BFOQ defense because the employer presented evidence that non-Muslim employees caught flying in Mecca would be beheaded pursuant to Saudi Arabian law.[53] In another instance, an employer was allowed to use the BFOQ defense to limit its recruitment of applicants for a faculty position in a university philosophy department to Jesuits where all of the undergraduates were required to take philosophy, the university was founded by Jesuits, and the university was centered around Jesuit traditions.[54]

4. NARROW APPLICATION OF DEFENSE

The BFOQ defense is narrowly applied to instances where there is business necessity for considering protected class membership. For example, an employer would not be able to successfully assert that being a non-Jewish doctor was a BFOQ for a position with a university that provided physicians to a Saudi Arabian hospital because there was no evidence that the hospital would refuse to grant a visa to a

Jewish faculty member, nor was there any evidence to suggest that a Jewish doctor could not satisfactorily complete the job tasks.[55]

5. CUSTOMER PREFERENCE

Because employers are prohibited from discriminating against members of a protected class, they are not permitted to use the bias of their customers as the basis for the assertion of the BFOQ defense. Thus, courts generally reject the BFOQ defense when an employer asserts that the preference of its managers or a potential customer base is what creates the business need to consider protected class membership. For example, to capitalize on the principle that "sex sells," one airline made the decision to appeal to its wealthy male business travelers by limiting its hiring to female flight attendants and requiring them to wear provocative uniforms. When a number of male job applicants claimed the practice was discriminatory, the employer asserted the BFOQ defense and claimed the policy was intended to create an image that was essential to its business clients, the majority of whom were men.

In rejecting the company's claim that the consideration of sex was a business necessity that supported the assertion of the BFOQ defense, the court found that the fundamental purpose of the airline was to transport passengers. The court reasoned that because the employer's image was not central to this purpose, the BFOQ defense could not be used by the employer to justify the resulting sex discrimination.[56]

 IX

RETALIATION

retaliation
an employer's imposition of an adverse action in response to an individual's assertion of a legal right

In addition to being prohibited from engaging in discriminatory conduct, employers are also prohibited from retaliating against an individual for attempting to assert a legal right under Title VII. A **retaliation** claim under Title VII relates to the imposition of an adverse action upon an individual in response to his asserting (or intending to assert) his rights by filing a discrimination claim, or by participating in the process to assert the rights of someone else.

The EEOC reports that in 2009 it received 33,613 charges of retaliation discrimination based on all statutes it is charged with enforcing, with 28,948 charges arising under Title VII.[57] In 2008, it resolved 25,999 retaliation charges and recovered more than $111 million for aggrieved parties, which does not include monetary benefits obtained through litigation.[58]

A. SCOPE OF PROTECTION

The Supreme Court has supported the broadest possible interpretation of Title VII's prohibition against retaliation, finding it significant that the statute prohibits discrimination in "terms and conditions of employment" but excludes this qualifier when referencing the prohibition against retaliation and just states that retaliation is prohibited.[59]

An individual subjected to adverse consequences for challenging employer behavior believed to be discriminatory, for providing assistance in a proceeding to determine whether workplace discrimination occurred, or for requesting a reasonable accommodation for a religious belief or practice can file a retaliation claim under Title VII.[60] The protection from retaliation also extends to individuals who are subjected to adverse consequences for associating with someone who engaged in this behavior, such as an employee who is demoted because his spouse filed a discrimination claim.[61] The critical issue in a retaliation claim is whether an individual was subjected to an adverse action in response to his assertion of a right provided for under Title VII.

B. IMPOSITION OF AN ADVERSE ACTION IN RESPONSE TO ASSERTION OF A LEGAL RIGHT

Under some circumstances employers have a right to engage in conduct that may have a negative impact on the working conditions of its employees to manage their performance and enforce workplace rules. However, just as employers are prohibited from imposing adverse actions such as declining to promote or terminating an employee based on discriminatory considerations, they are also prohibited from imposing these actions in response to an employee's assertion of a legal right.

Employers are prohibited from imposing an adverse action (such as assigning an individual to an undesirable shift) if the purpose is to discourage an individual from opposing a discriminatory practice or from filing or supporting the filing of a discrimination claim. This prohibition also extends to the coercion, intimidation, threats, and harassment if the purpose is to achieve this same result.

Adverse actions that could be the basis for a retaliation claim could take a number of forms, such as a termination, demotion, issuing of a negative job performance evaluation, or even increasing the monitoring of an individual in response to the filing of a workplace discrimination claim.[62] The issue in a retaliation claim is whether an any employment decision that has a negative impact on an individual's working conditions is imposed to discourage an individual from asserting their legal rights under the statute.

C. TYPES OF RETALIATION CLAIMS

The type of retaliation claim an individual pursues will depend on the behavior the employer is allegedly attempting to hinder or prevent.

1. PROTECTED ACTIVITY

Protected activity refers to the exercising of a right that an individual is legally entitled to assert, and retaliation occurs when an individual is subjected to an adverse action for engaging in such conduct. Depending on the nature of the asserted right, the retaliation claim will be in the form of either an opposition or participation claim.

protected activity
conduct that generally cannot be the basis for the imposition of an adverse employment action because the right to engage in the conduct is provided under a law

2. OPPOSITION CLAIMS

opposition claim
retaliation claim based on an employer's imposition of an adverse action on an individual in response to the individual's conduct that challenges employer behavior believed to be discriminatory

Opposition claims arise when an individual is the target of an adverse decision for challenging employer conduct on the basis that it is discriminatory. Put simply, an individual has a right to challenge behavior she believes is illegal (in violation of Title VII) and cannot be subjected to an adverse decision for doing so.

Although raising an issue about an employer's conduct is protected behavior, the challenge must be based on a reasonable, good-faith belief that the conduct is discriminatory, and the conduct must be opposed in a reasonable manner. For example, upon discovering that an employer is engaging in discriminatory behavior, an employee might bring the situation to the attention of a supervisor, threaten to file a discrimination claim if the behavior does not stop, or participate in a picket line to oppose the conduct.[63] However, an employee who decides to express such opposition through actions that interfere with job performance, or activities that involve threats or acts of violence, is not protected, even if the purpose of this conduct is to alert others to the discriminatory conduct.[64]

3. PARTICIPATION CLAIMS

participation claim
retaliation claim based on an employer's imposition of an adverse action on an individual in response to the individual's decision to participate in a proceeding relating to an employment claim or to assist another individual in filing a claim

Participation claims arise when an individual is the target of an adverse decision as a result of his participation in a proceeding relating to an employment discrimination claim or assisting another individual to assert a right. Individuals also have the right to participate in an investigation relating to an employment discrimination claim, and this right is protected even if the ultimate decision is that the claim is without merit. A participation claim is asserted in response to the imposition of an adverse decision based on an individual's decision to file an employment discrimination claim, cooperate with anyone conducting an investigation, or appear as a witness at a proceeding. Individuals are also protected from retaliation under Title VII after requesting a reasonable accommodation to engage in religious conduct.[65] See Chapter 4, Religious Discrimination.

D. EMPLOYER LIABILITY FOR UNSUBSTANTIATED DISCRIMINATION CLAIMS

Employers should know that retaliation claims filed under Title VII may be separate from claims of discriminatory conduct. Therefore, a court could determine that the underlying discrimination claim filed by the employee was unsubstantiated but still impose liability on the employer for retaliatory conduct. Thus, employers are prohibited from engaging in retaliatory conduct, regardless of whether there is merit to the underlying claim.

For example, suppose an employee files a claim against an employer for religious discrimination and retaliation under Title VII. If an employer presents evidence that a court determines satisfied the employer's legal obligation to provide a reasonable accommodation to enable an employee to engage in a religious practice, the employer will not be subject to liability for religious discrimination under Title VII for that component of the claim. However, the employer could still face liability for retaliation under Title VII if, for example, after the reasonable accommodation was initially requested, the employer gave the employee an unjustified negative performance evaluation.[66] See Chapter 4, Religious Discrimination.

 ## REMEDIES UNDER TITLE VII

Once it is determined that an employer engaged in conduct that violated Title VII by engaging in either discriminatory or retaliatory conduct, the next issue relates to assessing the appropriate measure of damages for the behavior. The nature of the damages imposed under Title VII will vary depending on the specific facts of the case as well as the type of relief requested.

A. TYPES OF DAMAGES

In the most basic sense, the types of damages that might be demanded by a plaintiff in a Title VII claim include

- ✓ **back pay** (wages lost as a result of the unlawful conduct);
- ✓ **front pay** (future wages from the time of a judgment until reinstatement, or until a certain date if the reinstatement is not possible);[67]
- ✓ hiring of an individual;
- ✓ reinstatement of an individual;
- ✓ promotion of an individual;
- ✓ the providing of a reasonable accommodation; or
- ✓ other actions that would make the individual whole, meaning that the individual would be placed in the same position she would have been in had the discriminatory conduct not occurred.[68]

In addition to the damages outlined above, fees for attorneys, witnesses, and court costs might also be requested and awarded, depending on the nature of the claim. Further, a court could determine that requiring an employer to post a notice addressing the discrimination claims and/or educating employees about their rights to work free from discrimination is the appropriate remedy.[69] There are also a number of other types of damages available for claims of intentional discrimination.

back pay
damage award that represents wages lost as a result of the unlawful conduct

front pay
damage award that represents future wages from the time a judgment is made until reinstatement or until a certain date if the reinstatement is not possible

B. CIVIL RIGHTS ACT OF 1991 ESTABLISHES AUTHORITY FOR EXPANDED DAMAGES FOR INTENTIONAL DISCRIMINATION

Civil Rights Act of 1991
the federal law that, among other things, allows for the awarding of compensatory and punitive damages for intentional discrimination claims

In response to a number of Supreme Court decisions limiting the types of damages that could be imposed under Title VII, Congress passed the **Civil Rights Act of 1991**, which is the federal law that, among other things, allows for the awarding of compensatory and punitive damages for intentional discrimination claims.[70]

1. COMPENSATORY DAMAGES

compensatory damages
damages awarded to an individual in recompense for actual losses suffered based on a finding of intentional discrimination

If there is a determination that an employer engaged in intentional discrimination, **compensatory damages** may be awarded to an individual as compensation for actual losses suffered as a result of the discriminatory conduct.[71] These damages might include monetary losses, future monetary losses, costs associated with a job search or medical expenses as well as costs associated with any resulting emotional harm such as mental anguish, inconvenience and loss of enjoyment of life.[72]

2. PUNITIVE DAMAGES

punitive damages
damages awarded to an individual that are designed to punish an employer for inappropriate conduct

A judicial finding that an employer engaged in intentional discrimination could also result in the imposition of **punitive damages**, which are designed to punish the employer for engaging in prohibited reckless, malicious, or deceitful behavior.[73]

3. STATUTORY CAPS ON DAMAGES

Although the Civil Rights Act of 1991 legislated the availability of compensatory and punitive damage awards, the amount of such awards is not unlimited. Instead, the Act places a statutory cap on the amount of damages, which represents the maximum amount of money that may be awarded. These limitations are based on the size of the employer in accordance with the following schedule:

- $50,000 for employers with 15 to 100 employees;
- $100,000 for employers with 101 to 200 employees;
- $200,000 for employers with 201 to 500 employees; and
- $300,000 for employers with more than 500 employees.[74]

C. MITIGATION OF DAMAGES

mitigation of damages
affirmative obligation imposed on an individual asserting a claim to make a reasonable effort to limit the damages he incurs as a result of the employer's discriminatory conduct

An individual who asserts a claim under Title VII has a general obligation to limit the potential damages that are incurred as a result of an employer's discriminatory conduct. The **mitigation of damages** refers to this affirmative obligation, which requires the aggrieved individual to make a reasonable effort to reduce the damages incurred. Within the context of a discriminatory termination, the complainant must be "ready, willing, and able" to work during the relevant time period, and will not be entitled to back pay for the time period during which the individual declines to be available for work.[75]

An employer can attempt to minimize a potential damage award by asserting that an individual has failed to fulfill this obligation. In addition, there are a number of types of employer conduct that may have an impact on the amount of the damages awarded.

D. CONSIDERATIONS THAT MAY AFFECT THE AMOUNT OF DAMAGES AWARDED

A number of factors will be considered significant when determining the amount of the damages to be imposed on an employer for discriminatory conduct. For example, an employer might present evidence of a legitimate, nondiscriminatory reason for the adverse decision in the form of a mixed motive, the discovery of information that would support the adverse decision after it was imposed. In addition, an employer might assert that, despite the discriminatory conduct, it made reasonable efforts to comply with the law.

1. LEGITIMATE, NONDISCRIMINATORY REASON FOR THE ADVERSE DECISION

a. Mixed Motive

As discussed above, in an attempt to justify an adverse employment decision, an employer might present evidence of a **mixed motive**, which is the presence of both discriminatory and legitimate reasons for the imposition of the adverse decision, and which is a factor to be evaluated by a court that is assessing the appropriate level of damages. Although a mixed motive will not completely absolve an employer from liability under Title VII, such a showing will limit the court's power to impose certain remedies. On a showing of a mixed motive, the charging party may be entitled to injunctive relief and attorney's fees but would not be entitled to reinstatement, back pay, or compensatory or punitive damages.[76]

mixed motive
the presence of both discriminatory and legitimate reasons for the imposition of the adverse decision, and which is a factor to be evaluated by a court that is assessing the appropriate level of damages

b. After-Acquired Evidence Rule

An employer may also suggest that the **after-acquired evidence rule** be applied when the appropriate level of damages is being assessed. The after-acquired evidence rule is the judicial consideration of a legitimate reason that would justify an adverse employment decision, which is discovered *after* the imposition of the adverse decision for a discriminatory reason, that may be considered by a court charged with assessing the appropriate damage award.

    The Supreme Court has held that an employer could still be subject to liability for a discriminatory termination even if the employer uncovered behavior after the termination that would have provided a legitimate basis for ending the employment relationship. The Court also ruled, however, that because it could not completely ignore a legitimate reason an employer might have for terminating an employee, this type of information could be considered when determining the appropriate remedy for the discriminatory conduct.[77]

after-acquired evidence rule
judicial consideration of a legitimate reason that would justify an adverse employment decision, which is discovered *after* the imposition of the adverse decision for a discriminatory reason, that may be considered by a court charged with assessing the appropriate damage award

2. EMPLOYER EXERTED REASONABLE EFFORTS TO COMPLY WITH THE LAW

An employer might also assert that a reduced award is appropriate by showing that, despite the resulting discriminatory conduct, it made reasonable efforts to comply with the law. An employer might show that it implemented anti-discrimination policies, provided training for its supervisors, or established a clear process for raising and addressing complaints, which it communicated to its workforce. Although these practices would not relieve an employer of liability for its discriminatory conduct, their presence could support the imposition of a reduced damage award.[78]

KEY TERMS

- ✓ adverse action
- ✓ after-acquired evidence rule
- ✓ Age Discrimination in Employment Act of 1967 (ADEA)
- ✓ Americans with Disabilities Act of 1990 (ADA)
- ✓ back pay
- ✓ bona fide occupational qualification (BFOQ)
- ✓ bona fide seniority system
- ✓ business necessity
- ✓ circumstantial evidence
- ✓ Civil Rights Act of 1991

- ✓ compensatory damages
- ✓ direct evidence
- ✓ disparate impact claim
- ✓ disparate treatment
- ✓ Equal Employment Opportunity Commission (EEOC)
- ✓ Equal Pay Act of 1963 (EPA)
- ✓ four-fifths (or 80%) rule
- ✓ front pay
- ✓ Genetic Information Nondiscrimination Act of 2008 (GINA)
- ✓ Ledbetter Fair Pay Act of 2009

- ✓ *McDonnell Douglas Corporation v. Green*
- ✓ mitigation of damages
- ✓ mixed motive
- ✓ opposition claim
- ✓ participation claim
- ✓ pretext
- ✓ pretext-plus
- ✓ *prima facie* case
- ✓ protected activity
- ✓ protected class
- ✓ punitive damages
- ✓ retaliation
- ✓ right to sue letter
- ✓ statute of limitations
- ✓ Title VII of the Civil Rights Act of 1964

DISCUSSION QUESTIONS

Explain your response to each of the following questions with the understanding that in some cases there is no right or wrong answer. If you cannot make an informed decision with the facts provided, indicate the nature and significance of the additional information you would need. For the purposes of these questions, you can assume that the employers and employees mentioned below are covered by Title VII.

1. Randy tells you he just read a newspaper article about a $2 million judgment against a company for discriminatory hiring in violation of Title VII. He tells you he is thankful that he does not have to worry about a Title VII claim because he has employed the same 88 employees for years and has no intention of hiring additional staff. What do you think?

2. Explain the difference between a disparate treatment claim and a disparate impact claim and provide an example of a set of facts that would support a claim under each theory.

3. If Daphne was presenting a claim against her employer asserting she was denied a promotion because she was a woman, what would be her initial burden in court?

4. Explain the difference between a pretext and a mixed motive as each relates to the reason for the imposition of an adverse employment decision.

5. Norma interviews applicants for a number of new sales positions at a local car dealership. She eliminates all but three candidates, and then decides to hire Annie because she knows her clients like red curly hair like Annie's. Herb, who has brown hair, immediately sends Norma a letter saying he is suing the company for workplace discrimination under Title VII unless she offers him a job. What do you think about his claim?

6. Logan says her boss, Diego, told her (and five other women) that they were his top employees but none of them would be offered promotional opportunities with the company. When they asked for an explanation, Diego told them that some of his traditional clients told him they would refuse to work with women, and if any of those clients decided to take their work to another vendor, he would suffer a significant economic loss. In a private conversation, Diego also told Logan she should be patient because she was still in the early stages of her career, so there was still a significant amount of time for her to receive a promotion during her time with the company. Do you see any problems with Diego's conduct?

7. Ruth has been rejected for promotional opportunities four times in the past six months. After each rejection, her boss told her she needed to tone down her rhetoric because her demeanor was too aggressive for the positions for which she was applying. Do you think she has a valid claim of discrimination under Title VII?

8. Wendy served as the President of a large fashion empire for ten years, and she attributed much of her success to the education she received at Lincoln Towers University. When her company decides to open a new office, she writes a letter to the Dean of the University saying that, as a token of her appreciation to the school, she will recruit solely from Lincoln Towers to staff the new satellite office. The Dean is thrilled with this development and assures Wendy he will screen the potential applicants and forward her the resumes of upcoming graduates who will mostly likely be interested in a career in fashion. Do you see any problems with this recruitment plan?

9. Two employers engage in the exact same discriminatory conduct, but one is required to pay $100,000 in damages while the other employer is required to pay $50,000. What might account for this difference?

ENDNOTES

1. U.S. Equal Employment Opportunity Commn., Charge Statistics FY 1997 Through FY 2009 (available at *http://www.eeoc.gov/eeoc/statistics/enforcement/charges.cfm*).
2. *See* U.S. Dept. of Justice, Special Report, Civil Rights Complaints in U.S. District Courts, 1990-2006 (Aug. 2008) (available at *http://bjs.ojp.usdoj.gov/content/pub/pdf/crcusdc06.pdf*).
3. *Id.*
4. Other significant federal laws include Sections 501 and 505 of the Rehabilitation Act of 1973 (which prohibits discrimination based on disabilities against individuals working in the federal government); and the Civil Rights Act of 1991 (which provides for, among other things, monetary damages as a sanction against those employers who have engaged in intentional employment discrimination). U.S. Equal Employment Opportunity Commn., The Rehabilitation Act of 1973 Sections 501 and 505 (available at *http://www.eeoc.gov/laws/statutes/rehab.cfm*); U.S. Equal Employment Opportunity Commn., The Civil Rights Act of 1991 (available at *http://www.eeoc.gov/eeoc/history/35th/1990s/civilrights.html*).
5. U.S. Equal Employment Opportunity Commn., Filing a Lawsuit in Federal Court (available at *http://www.eeoc.gov/federal/fed_employees/lawsuit.cfm*).
6. Some countries offer greater federal protection than what is provided for under Title VII, some offer less protection, and some countries provide different types of protection. For example, some countries do not prohibit discrimination against women based on sex (less protection), and some countries specifically prohibit discrimination based on a person's last name (more protection, although it is possible that this type of discrimination could be linked to a protected class under Title VII).
7. 29 U.S.C. §§ 2000e *et seq.* Title VII also covers private and public employment agencies, labor organizations, and joint labor-management committees that oversee apprenticeship and training.
8. *See generally* U.S. Equal Employment Opportunity Commn. website (available at *http://www.eeoc.gov*).
9. A number of states also have laws prohibiting harassment based on sexual orientation, parental status, marital status, and political affiliations.
10. *See, e.g., Tolani v. Upper Southampton Twp.*, 158 F. Supp. 2d 593 (E.D. Pa. 2001) (alleging discrimination based on race, religion, and national origin by an Asian employee who was from India, based on employer comments relating to the way Indian people worshipped); *see generally* U.S. Equal Employment Opportunity Commn., Discrimination by Type (available at *http://eeoc.gov/laws/types/index.cfm*).
11. U.S. Equal Employment Opportunity Commn., Questions and Answers About EEOC's Enforcement Guidance on Unlawful Treatment of Workers with Caregiving Responsibilities (available at *http://www.eeoc.gov/policy/docs/qanda_caregiving.html*). The guidelines also state that in the absence of the finding of a federal protection, a caregiver might be entitled to some type of relief under a state or local law.
12. N.Y. Exec. Law § 296(1)(d) (Unlawful Discriminatory Practices).
13. *Equal Empl. Opportunity Commn. v. Joe's Stone Crab*, 220 F.3d 1263 (11th Cir. 2000).
14. *Hazelwood Sch. Dist. v. United States*, 433 U.S. 299 (1977).

15. *See Teamsters v. United States*, 431 U.S. 324 (1977).

16. U.S. Equal Employment Opportunity Commn., The Commission (available at *http://www.eeoc.gov/eeoc/commission.cfm*).

17. *Id.*

18. *See* Black's Law Dictionary 1179 (8th ed. abridged 2005).

19. Many laws use the alleged unlawful conduct as the triggering point for the calculation of the time limitation for the filing of the claim. However, some laws use other triggering points, such as the time the individual knew or should have known about the misconduct.

20. U.S. Equal Employment Opportunity Commn., How to File a Charge of Employment Discrimination (available at *http://www.eeoc.gov/employees/howtofile.cfm*); *see also* U.S. Equal Employment Opportunity Commn., Filing a Charge of Discrimination (available at *http://www.eeoc.gov/employees/charge.cfm*). The 180-day statute of limitations extends to 300 days if the charge is covered by state or local anti-discrimination laws in addition to a federal law enforced by the EEOC. U.S. Equal Employment Opportunity Commn., Filing a Charge of Discrimination (available at *http://www.eeoc.gov/employees/charge.cfm*); U.S. Equal Employment Opportunity Commn., Filing a Charge of Employment Discrimination (available at *http://eeoc.gov/charge/overview_charge_filing.html*). For claims arising under the ADEA, only state laws extend the filing limit to 300 days.

21. U.S. Equal Employment Opportunity Commn., Filing a Charge of Employment Discrimination (available at *http://eeoc.gov/charge/overview_charge_filing.html*). Since an individual can file a claim under the EPA directly with a court as opposed to being required to first file a charge with the EEOC, a claim arising under the EPA can be filed within two years of the violation and within three years if the violation is willful. *Id.* See Chapter 12, Compensation and Benefits.

22. *Ledbetter v. Goodyear Tire & Rubber Co.*, 550 U.S. 618 (2007). The same rules apply to claims that arise under the ADA and the ADEA, which track much of Title VII's enforcement language. *See* U.S. Equal Employment Opportunity Commn., Notice Concerning the Lilly Ledbetter Fair Pay Act of 2009 (available at *http://www.eeoc.gov/laws/statutes/epa_ledbetter.cfm*).

23. 42 U.S.C. § 2000e-5(e)(4), (5); *see generally* Press Release, Acting EEOC Chairman Ishimaru Lauds Final Passage and Signing of Lilly Ledbetter Fair Pay Act (Jan. 29, 2009) (available at *http://www.eeoc.gov/eeoc/newsroom/release/archive/1-29-09.html*).

24. Since many states have anti-discrimination statutes that overlap with federal statutes enforced by the EEOC, the EEOC coordinates with local agencies to prevent the duplication of efforts and to ensure the rights of employees are protected. U.S. Equal Employment Opportunity Commn., How to File a Charge of Employment Discrimination (available at *http://www.eeoc.gov/employees/howtofile.cfm*).

25. *Id.*

26. *McDonnell Douglas Corp. v. Green*, 411 U.S. 792 (1973).

27. *Texas Dept. of Cmty. Affairs v. Burdine*, 450 U.S. 248, 253 (1981).

28. *McDonnell Douglas Corp. v. Green*, 411 U.S. 792, 802 (1973).

29. *Texas Dept. of Cmty. Affairs v. Burdine*, 450 U.S. 248 (1981).

30. *McDonnell Douglas Corp. v. Green*, 411 U.S. 792, 805 (1973).

31. *St. Mary's Honor Ctr. v. Hicks*, 509 U.S. 502 (1993).

32. *Reeves v. Sanderson Plumbing Prods.*, 530 U.S. 133 (2000).

33. *Texas Dept. of Cmty. Affairs v. Burdine*, 450 U.S. 248, 253 (1981).

34. *Price Waterhouse v. Hopkins*, 490 U.S. 228 (1989).

35. Pub. L. No. 102-166, § 107(a), 105 Stat. 1071 (codified at 42 U.S.C. § 2000e-2(m) (2000)).

36. *See e.g., Griggs v. Duke Power Co.*, 401 U.S. 424, 430-431 (1971); *see also* 42 U.S.C. § 2000e-2(a)(1) (disparate treatment); 42 U.S.C. § 2000e–2(k)(1)(A)(i) (disparate impact); U.S. Equal Employment Opportunity Commn., Employment Tests and Selection Procedures (available at *http://www.eeoc.gov/policy/docs/factemployment_procedures.html*).

37. *Griggs v. Duke Power Co.*, 401 U.S. 424, 430-431 (1971).

38. *Id.*

39. 42 U.S.C. § 2000e-2(k)(1)(A)(i).

40. *See* 29 C.F.R. pt. 1607 (Uniform Guidelines on Employee Selection Procedures). Questions and answers to clarify and interpret the Uniform Guidelines were adopted by five federal agencies. *See* 44 Fed. Reg. No. 43 (Mar. 2, 1979) (available at *http://www.eeoc.gov/policy/docs/qanda_clarify_procedures.html.*).

41. 42 U.S.C. § 2000e-2(k)(1)(A)(i).

42. *See* 29 C.F.R. pt. 1607 (Uniform Guidelines on Employee Selection Procedures). Questions and answers to clarify and interpret the Uniform Guidelines were adopted by five federal agencies. *See* 44 Fed. Reg. No. 43 (Mar. 2, 1979) (available at *http://www.eeoc.gov/policy/docs/qanda_clarify_procedures.html*); *see generally* Lawrence Ashe, Recent Developments in Scored Test Case Law, Equal Employment Opportunity Commn., Meeting of May 16, 2007—Employment Testing and Screening (available at *http://www.eeoc.gov/eeoc/meetings/archive/5-16-07/testcase_ashe.html*).

43. *Briggs v. Anderson*, 796 F.2d 1009, 1023 (8th Cir. 1996); *see Griggs v. Duke Power Co.*, 401 U.S. 424 (1971).

44. *See Griggs v. Duke Power Co.*, 401 U.S. 424 (1971).

45. 42 U.S.C. § 2000e-2(k)(1)(A)(ii).

46. *Pullman-Standard v. Swint*, 456 U.S. 273 (1982).

47. Section 703(h) of Title VII, 42 U.S.C. § 2000e-2(h) (1976).

48. 42 U.S.C. § 2000e-2(e). An employer is not permitted to assert this defense in response to Title VII claims based on race and color. The BFOQ defense is, however, available for age discrimination claims filed under the ADEA. See Chapter 6, Age Discrimination.

49. 42 U.S.C. § 2000e-2(e)(1).

50. *Dothard v. Rawlinson*, 433 U.S. 347 (1977). In a footnote, one of the Justices further stated he would have reached a different conclusion if the prison had additional safeguards in place such as better management of dangerous conditions or the separation of sex offenders from the general prison population.

51. *See, e.g., Automobile Workers v. Johnson Controls Inc.*, 499 U.S. 187 (1991); *City of Philadelphia v. Pennsylvania Human Relations Commn.*, 300 A.2d 97 (Pa. 1973).

52. 42 U.S.C. § 2000e-2(e)(1); EEOC Compl. Man. § 12 (Religious Discrimination) (July 22, 2008) (available at *http://www.eeoc.gov/policy/docs/religion.html*).

53. *Kern v. Dynalectron Corp.*, 577 F. Supp. 1196 (N.D. Tex. 1983), *aff'd*, 46 F.2d 810 (5th Cir. 1984).

54. *Pime v. Loyola Univ. of Chi.*, 803 F.2d 351 (7th Cir. 1986).

55. *Abrams v. Baylor Coll. of Med.*, 805 F.2d 528 (5th Cir. 1986).

56. *Wilson v. Southwest Airlines*, 517 F. Supp. 292, 304 (N.D. Tex. 1981).

57. U.S. Equal Employment Opportunity Commn., Sex-Based Charges FY 1997–FY 2008 (available at *http://archive.eeoc.gov/stats/charges.html*).

58. U.S. Equal Employment Opportunity Commn., Charge Statistics FY 1997 Through FY 2009 (available at *http://www.eeoc.gov/eeoc/statistics/enforcement/charges.cfm*).

59. *Burlington N. & Santa Fe (BNSF) Ry. Co. v. White*, 548 U.S. 53 (2006).

60. Retaliation claims based on age discrimination can be filed under the ADEA, and retaliation claims based on disability discrimination can be filed under the ADA. See Chapter 6, Age Discrimination and Chapter 7, Disability Discrimination.

61. U.S. Equal Employment Opportunity Commn., Retaliation (available at *http://www.eeoc.gov/laws/types/retaliation.cfm*).

62. *Id.*

63. *Id.*

64. *Id.*

65. This same protection relating to the right to request a reasonable accommodation for a disability is available under the ADA. See Chapter 7, Disability Discrimination.

66. EEOC Compl. Man. § 8 (Retaliation) (May 20, 1998) (available at *http://www.eeoc.gov/federal/digest/xi-5-3.cfm*). The same rationale would apply in a situation in which an individual requests and is granted a reasonable accommodation for a disability but then is the subject of an adverse employment decision such as a demotion. U.S. Equal

Employment Opportunity Commn., Disability Discrimination (available at *http://www.eeoc.gov/types/ada.html*); see Chapter 7, Disability Discrimination.

67. U.S. Equal Employment Opportunity Commn., Front Pay (available at *http://www.eeoc.gov/federal/digest/xi-7-4.cfm*).

68. U.S. Equal Employment Opportunity Commn., Federal Laws Prohibiting Job Discrimination Questions and Answers (available at *http://www.eeoc.gov/eeoc/publications/qanda.cfm*).

69. *Id.*

70. U.S. Equal Employment Opportunity Commn., Enforcement Guidance: Compensatory and Punitive Damages Available under § 102 of the Civil Rights Act of 1991 (available at *http://www.eeoc.gov/policy/docs/damages.html*).

71. U.S. Equal Employment Opportunity Commn., Federal Laws Prohibiting Job Discrimination Questions and Answers (available at *http://www.eeoc.gov/eeoc/publications/qanda.cfm*); *see* Special Report, U.S. Dept. of Justice, Civil Rights Complaints in U.S. District Courts, 1990-2006 (Aug. 2008) (available at *http://www.ojp.usdoj.gov/bjs/pub/pdf/crcusdc06.pdf*).

72. U.S. Equal Employment Opportunity Commn., Enforcement Guidance: Compensatory and Punitive Damages Available under § 102 of the Civil Rights Act of 1991 (available at *http://www.eeoc.gov/policy/docs/damages.html*). The Civil Rights Act of 1991 amended Title VII, the ADEA, and the ADA. The 1991 Act also provided individuals with the right to jury trials for Title VII claims involving intentional discrimination, a right that was previously not available. *See* U.S. Equal Employment Opportunity Commn., The Civil Rights Act of 1991 (available at *http://www.eeoc.gov/eeoc/history/35th/1990s/civilrights.html*). *See* U.S. Dept. of Justice, Special Report, Civil Rights Complaints in U.S. District Courts, 1990–2006 (Aug. 2008) (available at *http://bjs.ojp.usdoj.gov/content/pub/pdf/crcusdc06.pdf*); *see also* U.S. Equal Employment Opportunity Commn., Remedies for Employment Discrimination (available at *http://www.eeoc.gov/employees/remedies.cfm*).

73. *See* U.S. Dept. of Justice, Special Report, Civil Rights Complaints in U.S. District Courts, 1990–2006 (Aug. 2008) (available at *http://bjs.ojp.usdoj.gov/content/pub/pdf/crcusdc06.pdf*); *see also* U.S. Equal Employment Opportunity Commn., Remedies for Employment Discrimination (available at *http://www.eeoc.gov/employees/remedies.cfm*).

74. U.S. Equal Employment Opportunity Commn., Enforcement Guidance: Compensatory and Punitive Damages Available Under § 102 of the Civil Rights Act of 1991 (available at *http://www.eeoc.gov/policy/docs/damages.html*); U.S. Equal Employment Opportunity Commn., The Civil Rights Act of 1991 (available at *http://www.eeoc.gov/eeoc/history/35th/1990s/civilrights.html*).

75. 5 C.F.R. § 550.805(c)(1), (2); *See Ford Motor Co. v. EEOC*, 458 U.S. 219 (1982); *see generally* U.S. Equal Employment Opportunity Commn., Remedies: Back Pay — A Primer, 13 Digest Equal Empl. Opportunity, L. No. 3 (Summer Quarter 2002) (available at *http://www.eeoc.gov/federal/digest/xiii-3.cfm*).

76. EEOC Compl. Man. § 13 (National Origin Discrimination) (Oct. 6, 2008) (available at *http://www.eeoc.gov/policy/docs/national-origin.html*).

77. *McKennon v. Nashville Banner Publg. Co.*, 513 U.S. 352 (1995).

78. U.S. Equal Employment Opportunity Commn. website (available at *http://www.eeoc.gov*). For damage awards imposed under the ADA, if the employer can illustrate it engaged in a "good faith" effort to provide a reasonable accommodation, this could also reduce damage awards because it would prohibit the awarding of compensatory or punitive damages. U.S. Equal Employment Opportunity Commn., Federal Laws Prohibiting Job Discrimination Questions and Answers (available at *http://www.eeoc.gov/eeoc/publications/qanda.cfm*).

Race, Color, and National Origin Discrimination

3

Chapter Objectives

This chapter explores the prohibition against race, color, and national origin discrimination under Title VII, as well as the associated characteristics employers are prohibited from using as the basis for making adverse employment decisions.

After completing this chapter, students should have a basic understanding of the type of employer conduct that has the potential to materialize into a claim of discrimination based on race, color, and national origin. Students will learn about disparate impact, disparate treatment, and hostile work environment claims, as well as how fluency requirements, consideration of an individual's accent, and workplace rules requiring employees to communicate in English can subject an employer to liability under Title VII.

Upon mastering the main objectives of this chapter, students should be able to

- explain the characteristics linked to an individual's race and national origin that are protected under Title VII;
- explain the type of employer conduct that could result in a disparate treatment claim and a disparate impact claim based on race, color, and national origin discrimination;
- explain the protections available to individuals subjected to an adverse employment decision based on their citizenship;
- explain the obligations of employers under the Immigration Reform and Control Act (IRCA) and the Act's relevance to national origin discrimination;
- explain the significance of the Immigration and Nationality Act (INA) and the obligations the Act imposes on employers;
- explain why it may be problematic for an employer to consider an applicant's accent when making a hiring decision, and when an accent might be an appropriate reason for disqualifying an applicant;
- define English-only rules and explain when their imposition might be appropriate; and
- explain the types of conduct that could create a hostile work environment.

The population of the United States is approximately 300 million people, and about a third of these individuals are members of different racial minority groups, including 42.7 million Hispanics, 39.7 million African-Americans, 14.4 million Asian-Americans, and 5.5 million people of Native ancestry.[1] The problem of racial discrimination continues to be a significant concern, as evidenced by one poll which indicated that 84% of Blacks/African-Americans surveyed and 66% of non-Hispanic Whites/Caucasians surveyed believed that racial discrimination is a "very serious" or "somewhat serious" problem in the United States.[2] This is supported by the fact that the Equal Employment Opportunity Commission (EEOC) reports that it received 36 claims relating to hangman's nooses in 2007. Further, in one case the Agency recovered $290,000 from an Oklahoma company that subjected its Black/African-American employees to a hostile work environment that included derogatory name-calling and the display of nooses at a worksite.[3]

RACE AND COLOR DISCRIMINATION

Race and color are protected classes under Title VII, so employers with 15 or more employees are prohibited from discriminating in any aspect of employment based on race, color, ethnicity, or any characteristics associated with these classifications. This prohibition applies to discrimination based on an individual's actual or perceived racial classification, a feature associated with a particular racial group (such as hair texture), and an individual's marriage to or association with someone who belongs to a particular group.[4] In addition, Title VII prohibits employers from retaliating against individuals for filing a racial discrimination claim or for assisting another individual in pursuing a racial discrimination claim under the statute.[5]

A. EXTENT OF DISCRIMINATORY CONDUCT

The EEOC reports that discrimination, harassment, and retaliation claims based on race continue to be the most common employment discrimination claims under Title VII. In 2009 the EEOC received 33,579 charges of racial discrimination under Title VII, and in the same year it resolved 31,129 charges and recovered $82.4 million for aggrieved parties, which does not include monetary benefits obtained through litigation.[6] In addition, according to the EEOC, new forms of racial discrimination continue to emerge. See Exhibit 3-1.

Exhibit 3-1
Emergence of New Forms of Racial Discrimination[1]

✓ With a growing number of interracial marriages and families and increased immigration, the racial demographics of the workforce have changed bringing new issues of race and color discrimination to the workplace;

✓ Advances in technology, such as the use of video resumes, may influence recruitment and hiring decisions based on race, color, gender or national origin, or disproportionately exclude applicants who lack access to computers and video cams;

✓ Selection or screening criteria — such as credit scores, certain employment tests and the use of computer software that flags addresses or zip codes — may screen out individuals based on race and ethnicity.

Current Forms of Discrimination Based on Race and Color

✓ Racial slurs, nooses, KKK propaganda, and other racist insignia still exist in the workplace;

✓ Racial and cultural stereotypes continue to influence employment decisions;

✓ Intolerance, disrespect, and exclusion along racial and color lines remain in the work environment.

---

[1]The U.S. Equal Employment Opportunity Commission, E-RACE (Eradicating Racism and Colorism from Employment) *Why Do We Need E-RACE?* (available at *http://eeoc.gov/initiatives/e-race/e-race-facts.html*). The E-RACE Initiative is a five-year national outreach, education, and enforcement campaign implemented to advance the legal right to a workplace free of race and color discrimination.

B. BROAD APPLICATION

The prohibition against racial and color discrimination relates to all phases of the employment process, from recruiting and interviewing applicants, to compensating, promoting, disciplining, and terminating employees. Employers should recognize potential vulnerabilities that exist at each stage of the process. See Exhibit 3-2. This is critical because an employer who engages in racially discriminatory conduct could be faced with significant liability. For example, one employer agreed to settle a racial discrimination claim alleging it refused to promote a group of Blacks/African-Americans by paying a $425,000 penalty, establishing a written promotion policy, and implementing a training program.[7] In addition, because a racial discrimination claim could be filed under Title VII, an employer may be subject to liability based on the filing of a disparate treatment claim (for intentional discrimination) or a disparate impact claim (for unintentional discrimination).

Exhibit 3-2
How to Prevent Race and Color Discrimination[1]

Recruitment, Hiring, and Promotion

- Recruit, hire, and promote by implementing practices designed to widen and diversify the pool of candidates considered for employment openings, including openings in upper level management.
- Monitor for EEO compliance by conducting self-analyses to determine whether current employment practices disadvantage people of color, treat them differently, or leave uncorrected the effects of historical discrimination in the company.
- Analyze the duties, functions, and competencies relevant to jobs. Then create objective, job-related qualification standards related to those duties, functions, and competencies. Make sure they are consistently applied when choosing among candidates.
- Ensure selection criteria do not disproportionately exclude certain racial groups unless the criteria are valid predictors of successful job performance and meet the employer's business needs.
- Make sure promotion criteria are made known, and that job openings are communicated to all eligible employees.
- When using an outside agency for recruitment, make sure the agency does not search for candidates of a particular race or color. Both the employer that made the request and the employment agency that honored it would be liable.

Terms, Conditions, and Privileges of Employment

- Monitor compensation practices and performance appraisal systems for patterns of potential discrimination. Make sure performance appraisals are based on employees' actual job performance.
- Develop the potential of employees, supervisors, and managers with EEO in mind, by providing training and mentoring that provides workers of all backgrounds the opportunity, skill, experience, and information necessary to perform well, and to ascend to upper-level jobs. In addition, employees of all backgrounds should have equal access to workplace networks.
- Protect against retaliation. Provide clear and credible assurances that if employees make complaints or provide information related to complaints, the employer will protect employees from retaliation, and consistently follow through on this guarantee.

---

[1]Best Practices for Employers and Human Resources/EEO Professionals, The U.S. Equal Employment Opportunity Commission, E-RACE (Eradicating Racism and Colorism from Employment) (available at *http://eeoc.gov/initiatives/e-race/bestpractices-employers.html*). The E-RACE (Eradicating Racism and Colorism from Employment) Initiative is a five-year national outreach, education, and enforcement campaign implemented to advance the legal right to a workplace free of race and color discrimination.

C. DISPARATE TREATMENT DISCRIMINATION

Disparate treatment discrimination based on race relates to employer conduct motivated by discriminatory intent or motive. An employer could be liable for a disparate treatment claim for racial discrimination by refusing to hire individuals belonging to a certain race, segregating certain classifications of people at their workplace, or physically isolating members of this protected class from particular clients or customers. Along these same lines, it is impermissible to exclude members of certain races from specific positions based on the fact that historically they have not held or been interested in those positions.[8]

disparate treatment discrimination
employment discrimination claims alleging that an employer engaged in intentional discrimination based on an individual's membership in a protected class

D. DISPARATE IMPACT DISCRIMINATION

Disparate impact discrimination based on race materializes when an employer engages in what appears to be neutral conduct, but the conduct results in a disproportionate impact on individuals belonging to a particular race.

Specifically, employers could be subject to liability for limiting their recruitment efforts to non-diverse applicant pools such as certain schools or universities, or the social networks of their current employees. This is because this type of conduct, while on its face appearing neutral and nondiscriminatory, could deny certain minority groups access to an employer's recruitment process. Requiring applicants to have a particular educational background that is not necessary to perform a job is another example of a policy that may appear to be neutral but could result in liability if its implementation produces a discriminatory result.[9]

disparate impact discrimination
employment discrimination claims alleging that the implementation of a policy that is neutral on its face results in a disproportionate impact on members of a protected class

 NATIONAL ORIGIN

In addition to the protections that are offered to individuals based on their race and color, Title VII protects employees from discrimination based on their national origin within the same framework as another protected class set out in the statute. Employers who employ 15 or more individuals are prohibited from making adverse employment decisions based on an individual's country of origin or ancestry. This would include, for example, declining to promote an employee because her ancestry is Mexican, Ukrainian, Filipino, Arab, Native American, or any other nationality. This protection is available regardless of whether the individual was born in the United States or abroad, and regardless of whether the individual is a U.S. citizen. The EEOC reports that in 2009 it received 11,134 charges for national origin discrimination under Title VII, and in the same year it resolved 9,644 charges and recovered $25.7 million for aggrieved parties, which does not include monetary benefits obtained through litigation.[10]

A. BROAD APPLICATION

Consistent with other protected classes under Title VII, the prohibition against national origin discrimination relates to all phases of the employment process. Just as with all of the other protected classes under the statute, claims can be filed under a disparate treatment or disparate impact theory, depending upon whether the alleged misconduct was intentional or unintentional. Such claims often arise within a number of contexts.

1. BIRTHPLACE

On the most basic level, an employer cannot use an individual's birthplace as the basis for an adverse employment decision. The location may be a particular country or an area, such as Kurdistan, which is home to people who share a common language, culture, and ancestry.[11]

2. NATIONAL ORIGIN OR ETHNIC GROUP

national origin group or ethnic group
group of people who share one or more social characteristics

The prohibition against national origin discrimination also extends to **national origin or ethnic groups**, which refers to individuals who share one or more social characteristics. This consideration relates to ethnicity; physical, linguistic, or cultural traits; or perception. For example, if an employer uses the fact that an individual is Hispanic as the basis for an adverse employment decision, it could constitute the basis for a national origin claim based on ethnicity. If an employer makes a hiring decision based on an individual's traditional African wardrobe, it could constitute national origin discrimination based on a cultural trait. Discrimination based on a perception is present when an individual is subjected to an adverse employment decision based on the assumption that he is from a particular birthplace or has a certain ancestry, regardless of whether this is an accurate characterization.[12]

3. CITIZENSHIP

Even though Title VII does not explicitly prohibit discrimination based on citizenship, for a number of reasons, a brief discussion of it is warranted here. First, using citizenship as the basis for an adverse employment decision would fit within the scope of the statute if use of the information has the "purpose or effect" of engaging in discriminatory conduct based on an individual's national origin, which is specifically protected.[13] Further, there are a number of other laws that restrict the consideration of citizenship status when making employment decisions (and in other contexts), and these laws provide overlapping, and in some cases more extensive, protections.

a. Immigration Reform and Control Act of 1986 (IRCA)

Immigration Reform and Control Act of 1986 (IRCA)
federal law that prohibits employment discrimination based on an individual's citizenship status

The Immigration Reform and Control Act of 1986 (IRCA) is the federal law that prohibits discrimination based on citizenship status when making decisions about hiring, referrals, and terminations.[14] IRCA also provides overlapping protections with Title VII because it, too, prohibits national origin discrimination. The Act also provides more expansive coverage because it applies to all employers, including those who employ between 4 and 14 individuals, who would not be covered by Title VII because it, in contrast, applies only to employers who employ 15 or more individuals.[15]

Because employers have independent obligations to verify the working status of their employees, collecting citizenship information has the potential to raise concerns about national origin discrimination in that employers will then have information that could be used as the basis for discriminatory conduct if considered in making a hiring decision, or in making any other decisions relating to the individual's terms and conditions of employment.

b. Immigration and Nationality Act (INA)

Federal law limits the rights of some individuals to work in the United States, and the **Immigration and Nationality Act (INA)** is the federal law that amends the IRCA and provides, in part, that employers can only hire individuals who have the legal right to work in the United States or who are aliens authorized to work here.[16] The INA imposes an obligation on employers to verify an individual's eligibility to work, which requires the completion of the **employment eligibility verification form**, commonly referred to as an **I-9** form.[17] This form requires individuals to provide documentation such as a passport, or a combination of documents such as a driver's license and Social Security card to establish both their identity and their employment eligibility.[18] See Exhibit 3-3.

> **Immigration and Nationality Act (INA)**
> federal law that prohibits employers from hiring individuals who are not legally authorized to work in the United States

> **employment eligibility verification (I-9) form**
> federal document used by employers to verify an individual's eligibility to work in the United States

Therefore, to comply with this law, employers will collect information that is likely to reveal information about an individual's protected class status — in particular, information relating to an individual's national origin. If the information is considered when making a hiring decision (or in any subsequent decisions relating to the individual's terms and conditions of employment), it could subject an employer to liability under Title VII.

Employers also could be subject to liability for collecting the information in a discriminatory manner. For example, an employer who limits the verification process to people of a certain national origin or to foreigners may be subject to liability for national origin discrimination for treating individuals differently based on their protected class status. To minimize the potential for this type of liability, employers should verify whether each employee is authorized to work in the United States rather than limiting this inquiry to a specific group.[19] Employers should also ensure that the information that must be collected to comply with the INA is only used for the limited purpose contemplated by the statute.

B. LANGUAGE ISSUES

Even after an employer makes a nondiscriminatory decision to hire an individual and verifies the individual's eligibility to work, national origin discrimination claims may still surface in other contexts, such as those that relate to language issues. Accent discrimination, fluency requirements, and English-only rules often materialize into national origin discrimination claims.

1. ACCENT DISCRIMINATION

Title VII's prohibition against national origin discrimination forbids employers to make an adverse employment decision based on an individual's accent.[20] Even if an

Exhibit 3-3

OMB No. 1615-0047; Expires 06/30/09

Department of Homeland Security
U.S. Citizenship and Immigration Services

Form I-9, Employment
Eligibility Verification

Instructions
Please read all instructions carefully before completing this form.

Anti-Discrimination Notice. It is illegal to discriminate against any individual (other than an alien not authorized to work in the U.S.) in hiring, discharging, or recruiting or referring for a fee because of that individual's national origin or citizenship status. It is illegal to discriminate against work eligible individuals. Employers **CANNOT** specify which document(s) they will accept from an employee. The refusal to hire an individual because the documents presented have a future expiration date may also constitute illegal discrimination.

What Is the Purpose of This Form?

The purpose of this form is to document that each new employee (both citizen and non-citizen) hired after November 6, 1986 is authorized to work in the United States.

When Should the Form I-9 Be Used?

All employees, citizens and noncitizens, hired after November 6, 1986 and working in the United States must complete a Form I-9.

Filling Out the Form I-9

Section 1, Employee: This part of the form must be completed at the time of hire, which is the actual beginning of employment. Providing the Social Security number is voluntary, except for employees hired by employers participating in the USCIS Electronic Employment Eligibility Verification Program (E-Verify). **The employer is responsible for ensuring that Section 1 is timely and properly completed.**

Preparer/Translator Certification. The Preparer/Translator Certification must be completed if **Section 1** is prepared by a person other than the employee. A preparer/translator may be used only when the employee is unable to complete **Section 1** on his/her own. However, the employee must still sign **Section 1** personally.

Section 2, Employer: For the purpose of completing this form, the term "employer" means all employers including those recruiters and referrers for a fee who are agricultural associations, agricultural employers or farm labor contractors.

Employers must complete **Section 2** by examining evidence of identity and employment eligibility within three (3) business days of the date employment begins. If employees are authorized to work, but are unable to present the required

document(s) within three business days, they must present a receipt for the application of the document(s) within three business days and the actual document(s) within ninety (90) days. However, if employers hire individuals for a duration of less than three business days, **Section 2** must be completed at the time employment begins. **Employers must record:**

1. Document title;
2. Issuing authority;
3. Document number;
4. Expiration date, if any; and
5. The date employment begins.

Employers must sign and date the certification. Employees must present original documents. Employers may, but are not required to, photocopy the document(s) presented. These photocopies may only be used for the verification process and must be retained with the Form I-9. **However, employers are still responsible for completing and retaining the Form I-9.**

Section 3, Updating and Reverification: Employers must complete **Section 3** when updating and/or reverifying the Form I-9. Employers must reverify employment eligibility of their employees on or before the expiration date recorded in **Section 1**. Employers **CANNOT** specify which document(s) they will accept from an employee.

A. If an employee's name has changed at the time this form is being updated/reverified, complete Block A.

B. If an employee is rehired within three (3) years of the date this form was originally completed and the employee is still eligible to be employed on the same basis as previously indicated on this form (updating), complete Block B and the signature block.

C. If an employee is rehired within three (3) years of the date this form was originally completed and the employee's work authorization has expired **or** if a current employee's work authorization is about to expire (reverification), complete Block B and:

1. Examine any document that reflects that the employee is authorized to work in the U.S. (see List A **or** C);
2. Record the document title, document number and expiration date (if any) in Block C, and
3. Complete the signature block.

Exhibit 3-3 *(continued)*

What Is the Filing Fee?

There is no associated filing fee for completing the Form I-9. This form is not filed with USCIS or any government agency. The Form I-9 must be retained by the employer and made available for inspection by U.S. Government officials as specified in the Privacy Act Notice below.

USCIS Forms and Information

To order USCIS forms, call our toll-free number at **1-800-870-3676**. Individuals can also get USCIS forms and information on immigration laws, regulations and procedures by telephoning our National Customer Service Center at **1-800-375-5283** or visiting our internet website at **www.uscis.gov**.

Photocopying and Retaining the Form I-9

A blank Form I-9 may be reproduced, provided both sides are copied. The Instructions must be available to all employees completing this form. Employers must retain completed Forms I-9 for three (3) years after the date of hire or one (1) year after the date employment ends, whichever is later.

The Form I-9 may be signed and retained electronically, as authorized in Department of Homeland Security regulations at 8 CFR § 274a.2.

Privacy Act Notice

The authority for collecting this information is the Immigration Reform and Control Act of 1986, Pub. L. 99-603 (8 USC 1324a).

This information is for employers to verify the eligibility of individuals for employment to preclude the unlawful hiring, or recruiting or referring for a fee, of aliens who are not authorized to work in the United States.

This information will be used by employers as a record of their basis for determining eligibility of an employee to work in the United States. The form will be kept by the employer and made available for inspection by officials of U.S. Immigration and Customs Enforcement, Department of Labor and Office of Special Counsel for Immigration Related Unfair Employment Practices.

Submission of the information required in this form is voluntary. However, an individual may not begin employment unless this form is completed, since employers are subject to civil or criminal penalties if they do not comply with the Immigration Reform and Control Act of 1986.

Paperwork Reduction Act

We try to create forms and instructions that are accurate, can be easily understood and which impose the least possible burden on you to provide us with information. Often this is difficult because some immigration laws are very complex. Accordingly, the reporting burden for this collection of information is computed as follows: **1)** learning about this form, and completing the form, 9 minutes; **2)** assembling and filing (recordkeeping) the form, 3 minutes, for an average of 12 minutes per response. If you have comments regarding the accuracy of this burden estimate, or suggestions for making this form simpler, you can write to: U.S. Citizenship and Immigration Services, Regulatory Management Division, 111 Massachusetts Avenue, N.W., 3rd Floor, Suite 3008, Washington, DC 20529. OMB No. 1615-0047.

Exhibit 3-3 *(continued)*

OMB No. 1615-0047; Expires 06/30/09

Department of Homeland Security U.S. Citizenship and Immigration Services	**Form I-9, Employment** **Eligibility Verification**

Please read instructions carefully before completing this form. The instructions must be available during completion of this form.

ANTI-DISCRIMINATION NOTICE: It is illegal to discriminate against work eligible individuals. Employers CANNOT specify which document(s) they will accept from an employee. The refusal to hire an individual because the documents have a future expiration date may also constitute illegal discrimination.

Section 1. Employee Information and Verification. To be completed and signed by employee at the time employment begins.

Print Name: Last	First	Middle Initial	Maiden Name
Address *(Street Name and Number)*		Apt. #	Date of Birth *(month/day/year)*
City	State	Zip Code	Social Security #

I am aware that federal law provides for imprisonment and/or fines for false statements or use of false documents in connection with the completion of this form.	I attest, under penalty of perjury, that I am (check one of the following): ☐ A citizen or national of the United States ☐ A lawful permanent resident (Alien #) A _____ ☐ An alien authorized to work until _____ (Alien # or Admission #) _____

Employee's Signature	Date *(month/day/year)*

Preparer and/or Translator Certification. *(To be completed and signed if Section 1 is prepared by a person other than the employee.)* I attest, under *penalty of perjury, that I have assisted in the completion of this form and that to the best of my knowledge the information is true and correct.*

Preparer's/Translator's Signature	Print Name
Address *(Street Name and Number, City, State, Zip Code)*	Date *(month/day/year)*

Section 2. Employer Review and Verification. To be completed and signed by employer. Examine one document from List A OR examine one document from List B and one from List C, as listed on the reverse of this form, and record the title, number and expiration date, if any, of the document(s).

List A	OR	List B	AND	List C
Document title:				
Issuing authority:				
Document #:				
Expiration Date *(if any)*:				
Document #:				
Expiration Date *(if any)*:				

CERTIFICATION - I attest, under penalty of perjury, that I have examined the document(s) presented by the above-named employee, that the above-listed document(s) appear to be genuine and to relate to the employee named, that the employee began employment on *(month/day/year)* _____ **and that to the best of my knowledge the employee is eligible to work in the United States. (State employment agencies may omit the date the employee began employment.)**

Signature of Employer or Authorized Representative	Print Name	Title
Business or Organization Name and Address *(Street Name and Number, City, State, Zip Code)*		Date *(month/day/year)*

Section 3. Updating and Reverification. To be completed and signed by employer.

A. New Name *(if applicable)*	B. Date of Rehire *(month/day/year) (if applicable)*

C. If employee's previous grant of work authorization has expired, provide the information below for the document that establishes current employment eligibility.

Document Title:	Document #:	Expiration Date (if any):

I attest, under penalty of perjury, that to the best of my knowledge, this employee is eligible to work in the United States, and if the employee presented document(s), the document(s) I have examined appear to be genuine and to relate to the individual.

Signature of Employer or Authorized Representative	Date *(month/day/year)*

Exhibit 3-3 *(continued)*

LISTS OF ACCEPTABLE DOCUMENTS

LIST A	LIST B	LIST C
Documents that Establish Both Identity and Employment Eligibility	Documents that Establish Identity	Documents that Establish Employment Eligibility
OR		**AND**
1. U.S. Passport (unexpired or expired)	1. Driver's license or ID card issued by a state or outlying possession of the United States provided it contains a photograph or information such as name, date of birth, gender, height, eye color and address	1. U.S. Social Security card issued by the Social Security Administration *(other than a card stating it is not valid for employment)*
2. Permanent Resident Card or Alien Registration Receipt Card (Form I-551)	2. ID card issued by federal, state or local government agencies or entities, provided it contains a photograph or information such as name, date of birth, gender, height, eye color and address	2. Certification of Birth Abroad issued by the Department of State *(Form FS-545 or Form DS-1350)*
3. An unexpired foreign passport with a temporary I-551 stamp	3. School ID card with a photograph	3. Original or certified copy of a birth certificate issued by a state, county, municipal authority or outlying possession of the United States bearing an official seal
4. An unexpired Employment Authorization Document that contains a photograph (Form I-766, I-688, I-688A, I-688B)	4. Voter's registration card	4. Native American tribal document
	5. U.S. Military card or draft record	5. U.S. Citizen ID Card *(Form I-197)*
5. An unexpired foreign passport with an unexpired Arrival-Departure Record, Form I-94, bearing the same name as the passport and containing an endorsement of the alien's nonimmigrant status, if that status authorizes the alien to work for the employer	6. Military dependent's ID card	6. ID Card for use of Resident Citizen in the United States *(Form I-179)*
	7. U.S. Coast Guard Merchant Mariner Card	
	8. Native American tribal document	7. Unexpired employment authorization document issued by DHS *(other than those listed under List A)*
	9. Driver's license issued by a Canadian government authority	
	For persons under age 18 who are unable to present a document listed above:	
	10. School record or report card	
	11. Clinic, doctor or hospital record	
	12. Day-care or nursery school record	

Illustrations of many of these documents appear in Part 8 of the Handbook for Employers (M-274)

individual never affirmatively reveals his national origin, or even if the employer does not have knowledge of the precise national origin of an applicant, liability could still arise if an inference suggests that national origin was considered. For example, if an employer indicates an unwillingness to extend an offer of employment to a "foreign-sounding" individual, this would suggest the decision was motivated by the individual's national origin and is, therefore, in violation of Title VII.[21] As one court reasoned, an individual's accent and national origin are so "obviously inextricably intertwined," that such a consideration necessitates a "very searching look" at a decision based on either.[22]

If an employer makes an adverse employment decision based on an individual's accent but claims the decision was not discriminatory, the significant issue becomes whether the accent would materially interfere with the individual's ability to perform the job requirements. Courts will not permit the use of a foreign accent as the basis for an adverse employment decision if the accent interferes only with a peripheral job function.[23] When assessing whether disqualifying an applicant based upon an accent is permissible, courts tend to provide employers with greatest flexibility within the context of teaching, customer service, and telemarketing positions, because oral communication is a central component of these positions. Even in these instances, however, the employer will have to sustain the high burden of showing that the individual's accent will interfere with the completion of the primary job responsibilities of the position.[24]

2. FLUENCY REQUIREMENTS

Employers may also be subject to liability for making an adverse employment decision based on an individual's lack of fluency in English, unless fluency is required to perform the primary job responsibilities associated with the position. For example, it might be necessary for individuals applying for managerial positions in a restaurant to be fluent in English, but the same degree of fluency might not be necessary for each of the cashiers the manager would supervise.[25]

The same limitations on an employer's right to require fluency in English are applicable to other fluency requirements. For example, an employer who has Spanish-speaking–only customers might have a legitimate business reason for hiring some Spanish-speaking employees, but this might not be sufficient reason to require Spanish fluency for all positions. Therefore, an employer might be prohibited from using Spanish fluency as the basis for disqualifying applicants because this could have a disparate impact on individuals based on their national origin. Based on these variations, employers should be certain that any fluency requirements are closely linked to a specific business need.

3. ENGLISH-ONLY RULES

English-only rules
workplace rules that prohibit employees from speaking any language other than English while at work

English-only rules require employees to communicate solely in English while at work. English-only rules are generally disfavored, and Title VII permits their use only in very limited instances where the rule serves a business necessity and is imposed in a nondiscriminatory manner.[26] Such rules cannot be imposed to discriminate based on an individual's national origin and cannot prohibit the speaking of certain foreign languages and allow the speaking of others.[27] Because the EEOC disfavors English-only rules, they are closely scrutinized. For example, one company agreed to pay $90,000 to settle a discrimination claim filed by a group of Haitian and Jamaican employees based, in part, on the employer's outright prohibition against their speaking Creole while at work.[28]

a. Must Support a Business Necessity

Because employers are permitted to impose English-only rules only based on a showing of a business necessity, the EEOC has provided some guidance on this issue. Specifically, the need for (1) employees to communicate with customers, co-workers, and supervisors who only speak English; (2) employers to promote safety and enable the rapid dissemination of emergency information; (3) employers to facilitate the completion of group projects; and (4) supervisors to appropriately evaluate work performance related to customer interaction, have been used to support a showing that the rules serve a business necessity.[29]

b. Must Be Narrowly Tailored

Even in instances in which an English-only rule is permissible, it must be narrowly tailored to remedy the problem it is designed to address.[30] For example, if an employer cites safety concerns as the business necessity in support of an English-only rule in a factory, the employer should limit the prohibition against other languages to the time when employees are actually performing job duties or on the factory floor, and allow the speaking of other languages in break areas and restrooms.[31] In addition, even if a rule is permissible, employers should place employees on notice about the scope of the rule as well as the consequences for violating it.[32]

C. CUSTOMER PREFERENCE

Employers must also recognize that because Title VII prohibits discrimination based on an individual's national origin, an employer cannot use the prejudices of others as a defense to discriminatory conduct. Title VII makes no distinction between an employer's decision not to hire someone based on his own prejudices, and an employer's decision not to hire someone based on the prejudices of co-workers or customers. Thus, an employer could not justify the consideration of an applicant's national origin when making a decision to hire based on an assertion that its customers refuse to work (or even prefer to work) with individuals from particular countries. Because this prohibition applies to all terms and conditions of employment, the same rationale will apply to all employment decisions, such as an employer's decision to decline to promote certain individuals based upon the discriminatory preferences of its customers.

D. MEMBERSHIP IN MORE THAN ONE PROTECTED CLASS

When making employment decisions, employers should also be aware that an individual who files a claim under Title VII may be a member of more than one protected class and may simultaneously file a claim of discrimination based on each. This may occur within the context of a national origin discrimination claim when there is a significant link between an individual's ethnic identity and religious beliefs. For example, if a dark-skinned Muslim individual who was born in Saudi Arabia is subjected to an adverse employment decision, he could presumably file a discrimination claim under Title VII based on religion, national origin, race, and/or color.[33] This is significant because, although an employer does not have an obligation to provide a reasonable accommodation to an individual based on the individual's national origin, in the event that a national origin claim is linked to a religious practice, the employer may have an obligation to accommodate the religious practice to the extent it does not impose an undue burden. See Chapter 4, Religious Discrimination.

HOSTILE WORK ENVIRONMENT CLAIMS BASED ON RACE, COLOR, AND NATIONAL ORIGIN

hostile work environment claims
discrimination claims that arise when individuals are subject to unwelcome, offensive, and pervasive behavior and ridicule at the workplace based on their protected class membership

In addition to avoiding making decisions about the terms and conditions of an individual's employment based on considerations of race, color, and national origin, employers also have an obligation to ensure that their employees are not subjected to hostile work environments based on their protected class membership. This is important because the broad prohibition against race, color, and national origin discrimination extends to **hostile work environment claims**, which may be asserted under Title VII. Employers have an obligation to prevent the harassment of individuals based on their race, color, and national origin, which could materialize in the form of racial or ethnic slurs, or in derogatory comments directed toward particular individuals based on their membership or perceived membership in any of these protected classes.

Employers are obligated to address this type of behavior and should train their supervisors about the inappropriateness of the conduct, and punish those who engage in it. By providing this training and making supervisors accountable for their behavior, employers will minimize the likelihood that a hostile work environment claim would materialize under Title VII. In addition, in the event an employer is found liable for such a claim, the employer can present evidence of this training as a factor to be considered when the amount of the damage award is being assessed, asserting that it made reasonable efforts to comply with the law.[34] See Chapter 15, Workplace Harassment.

KEY TERMS

- ✓ disparate impact claims
- ✓ disparate treatment claims
- ✓ employment eligibility verification (I-9) form
- ✓ English-only rules
- ✓ hostile work environment claims
- ✓ Immigration and Nationality Act (INA)
- ✓ Immigration Reform and Control Act of 1986 (IRCA)
- ✓ national origin group or ethnic group

DISCUSSION QUESTIONS

Explain your response to each of the following questions with the understanding that in some cases there is no right or wrong answer. If you cannot make an informed decision with the facts provided, indicate the nature and significance of the additional information you would need. For the purposes of these questions, you can assume that the employers and employees mentioned below are covered by Title VII.

1. Explain the type of characteristics that are protected within the context of racial discrimination.
2. Provide a set of facts that would support a claim under a disparate treatment and disparate impact theory for national origin discrimination.
3. Does an employer have the right to require its employees to speak only English while at work?
4. Can the owner/administrator of a foreign language school require all employees to be fluent in two languages? Why or why not?
5. Harvey graduated from Superstar University, where he had the best four years of his life and obtained a top-notch college education. When he started his own law firm he decided that, as a way to support his school, he would only interview and hire applicants who graduated from the school. Could this decision materialize into a discrimination claim under Title VII?
6. Erin is the manager of a restaurant, and her customers often complain they have a difficult time understanding Devon because of his thick accent. She really likes Devon, but when her customers tell her they will refuse to return to her restaurant unless he is terminated, she agrees to terminate his employment and hire a waitress who has grown up in the neighborhood. Do you see any problems with Erin's decision? Assuming you determine the law would prohibit Erin from terminating Devon under these circumstances, do you think it should?
7. Beth is a wonderful boss who prides herself on her close-knit workforce. After hiring two bilingual employees, she posts a sign in the lunchroom saying that all employees are expected to speak English during work hours to ensure that

all of the employees will be able to understand one another and become friends. Are there any problems with Beth's imposing this rule? Do you think she should have the right to impose rules if she thinks it will benefit her employees?

ENDNOTES

1. *See* U.S. Equal Employment Opportunity Commn., Transcr. Commission Meeting (Feb. 28, 2007) (available at *http://www.eeoc.gov/eeoc/meetings/archive/2-28-07/*).

2. U.S. Equal Employment Opportunity Commn., Why Do We Need E-RACE? (available at *http://www.eeoc.gov/eeoc/initiatives/e-race/why_e-race.cfm*) (citing Poll: Most Americans See Lingering Racism — in Others (Dec. 12, 2006) (available at *http://cnn.com/2006/US/12/12/racism.poll/index.html*)).

3. *EEOC v. Helmerich Payne Intl. Drilling Co.*, No. 3:05-CV-691-DPJ-JCS (S.D. Miss. filed Oct. 9, 2007) (consent decree) (available at *http://www.websupp.org/data/SDMS/3:05-cv-00691-68-SDMS.pdf*).

4. U.S. Equal Employment Opportunity Commn., Race/Color Discrimination (available at *http://www.eeoc.gov/laws/types/race_color.cfm*); *Chacon v. Ochs*, 780 F. Supp. 680 (C.D. Cal. 1991) (prohibiting discrimination against a non-Hispanic woman because she was married to a Hispanic man).

5. U.S. Equal Employment Opportunity Commn., Race/Color Discrimination (available at *http://www.eeoc.gov/eeoc/statistics/enforcement/race.cfm*).

6. U.S. Equal Employment Opportunity Commission, Race-Based Charges FY 1997-FY 2009 (available at *http://www.eeoc.gov/eeoc/statistics/enforcement/race.cfm*).

7. *See* EEOC Press Release, Tobacco Superstores, Inc. to Pay $425,000 for Race Discrimination Against Blacks (Aug. 5, 2008) (available at *http://www.eeoc.gov/eeoc/newsroom/release/archive/8-5-08.html*).

8. U.S. Equal Employment Opportunity Commn., Race/Color Discrimination (available at *http://www.eeoc.gov/laws/types/race_color.cfm*).

9. *Id.*

10. U.S. Equal Employment Opportunity Commn., National Origin-Based Charges FY 1997–FY 2009 (available at *http://www.eeoc.gov/eeoc/statistics/enforcement/origin.cfm*).

11. EEOC Compl. Man. § 13 (National Origin Discrimination) (Oct. 6, 2008) (available at *http://www.eeoc.gov/policy/docs/national-origin.html*).

12. *Id.*

13. *Espinoza v. Farah Mfg. Co.*, 414 U.S. 86, 92 (1973); 29 C.F.R. § 1060.5(a).

14. 8 U.S.C. § 1324b(a)(1)(B). The prohibition against discrimination also protects some foreign nationals authorized to work in the United States, and employers who do hire such employees working under special visa programs may also have obligations relating to wages and other working conditions. *See generally* U.S. Dept. of Labor, Wage & Hour Div. (available at *http://www.dol.gov/esa/whd*).

15. 8 U.S.C. § 1324b(a)(1)(B).

16. This component of the INA is enforced by the Department of Homeland Security. U.S. Dept. of Labor, Employment Law Guide, Authorized Workers (available at *http://www.dol.gov/compliance/guide/aw.htm*).

17. 8 U.S.C. § 1101. *See generally* U.S. Dept. of Labor, Employment Law Guide, Authorized Workers (available at *http://www.dol.gov/compliance/guide/aw.htm*).

18. The list of acceptable documents is part of the I-9 form (available at *http://www.uscis.gov/files/form/I-9.pdf*). Once this information is collected, employers must retain the documents for three years, or for one year after the employment ends, whichever is longer.

8 U.S.C. § 1101; *see generally* U.S. Dept. of Labor, Employment Law Guide, Authorized Workers (available at *http://www.dol.gov/compliance/guide/aw.htm*).

19. U.S. Equal Employment Opportunity Commn. website (available at *http://www.eeoc.gov*).

20. 29 C.F.R. § 1606.1.

21. *See* EEOC Compl. Man. § 13 (National Origin Discrimination) (dated Oct. 6, 2008) (available at *http://www.eeoc.gov/policy/docs/national-origin.html*) (citing 45 Fed. Reg. 85,632, 85,633 (Dec. 29, 1980) (preamble to "Guidelines on Discrimination Because of National Origin")).

22. *Fragante v. City & County of Honolulu*, 888 F.2d 591, 596 (9th Cir. 1989).

23. *See, e.g., Carino v. University of Okla. Bd. of Regents*, 750 F.2d 815 (10th Cir. 1984) (finding a noticeable Filipino accent could not be used as the basis for a demotion or for declining to consider an applicant for a supervisory position).

24. EEOC Compl. Man. § 13 (National Origin Discrimination) (Oct. 6, 2008) (available at *http://www.eeoc.gov/policy/docs/national-origin.html*).

25. *Id.*

26. 29 C.F.R. § 1606.7.

27. EEOC Compl. Man. § 13 (National Origin Discrimination) (Oct. 6, 2008) (available at *http://www.eeoc.gov/policy/docs/national-origin.html*).

28. *EEOC v. Flushing Geriatric Ctr., Inc.*, No. 05-4061 (E.D.N.Y. Apr. 23, 2007).

29. EEOC Compl. Man. § 13 (National Origin Discrimination) (Oct. 6, 2008) (available at *http://www.eeoc.gov/policy/docs/national-origin.html*). Courts have different views as to the appropriateness of English-only rules. *See, e.g., EEOC v. Synchro-Start Prods., Inc.*, 29 F. Supp. 2d 911 (N.D. Ill. 1999) (holding English-only rules may create discriminatory working environments based on national origin); *Garcia v. Gloor*, 618 F.2d 264 (5th Cir. 1980) (upholding an English-only rule).

30. EEOC Compl. Man. § 13 (National Origin Discrimination) (dated Oct. 6, 2008) (available at *http://www.eeoc.gov/policy/docs/national-origin.html*).

31. *Id.*

32. U.S. Equal Employment Opportunity Commn. website (available at *http://www.eeoc.gov*).

33. *See, e.g., Tolani v. Upper Southampton Twp.*, 158 F. Supp. 2d 593 (E.D. Pa. 2001) (alleging discrimination based on race, religion, and national origin by an Asian employee who was from India, based on employer comments relating to the way Indian people worshiped).

34. *See, e.g. Faragher v. City of Boca Raton*, 524 U.S. 775 (1998); *see Burlington Indus., Inc. v. Ellerth*, 524 U.S. 742 (1998).

Religious Discrimination

4

Chapter Objectives

This chapter explores the prohibition against religious discrimination under Title VII. The text explains how religion is defined under the statute and discusses the wide range of religious practices and conduct that are within the scope of protected activity. In addition, the text explores the extent of an employer's obligations to provide a reasonable accommodation and the factors used to determine whether an accommodation would be required of the employer or whether it would constitute an undue burden the employer would not be required to undertake.

After completing this chapter, students should have a fundamental understanding of the analysis used to assess whether a practice or conduct is religious in nature and falls within the scope of behavior Title VII intends to protect. In addition, students should be able to discuss the concept of a reasonable accommodation and undue burden, and explain the number of ways an employer might elect to alter the working condition of an employee to satisfy its obligations under Title VII.

Upon mastering the main objectives of this chapter students should be able to

- explain how religion is defined under Title VII, as well as identify the types of conduct and practices that the statute protects;
- explain the four elements that establish the basis for a religious discrimination claim;
- discuss the extent to which an employer will be required to provide a reasonable accommodation and provide examples of accommodations that might be appropriate;
- list some factors that might be used to determine whether providing an accommodation would constitute an undue burden; and
- define *religious expression* and explain how a limitation on it might materialize into a religious discrimination claim.

INTRODUCTION

Religion is a protected class under Title VII, so employers are prohibited from discriminating on the basis of religion when making decisions about hiring, promoting, compensating, and firing employees, as well as all other terms and conditions of employment. Consistent with other types of discrimination claims, employers also have an obligation to ensure that employees are not subject to religious harassment at their workplace, and employers are prohibited from retaliating against individuals for filing a religious discrimination claim or participating in the investigation of a religious discrimination claim. This prohibition covers employers with 15 or more employees, and prohibits discrimination against both employees and applicants.[1]

A. SCOPE OF PROTECTION

According to the Equal Employment Opportunity Commission (EEOC), the federal agency responsible for enforcing Title VII, the prohibition against religious discrimination extends to employer conduct such as the refusal to hire individuals of a certain religion, the imposition of more stringent promotional requirements for individuals who practice certain religions, and the imposition of additional or different work requirements on certain employees because of their religious beliefs or practices. Further, an individual's employment cannot be conditioned on his participation in, or refusal to participate in, a religious activity.[2]

The prohibition against religious discrimination imposes an obligation on a covered employer to accommodate an individual's religious beliefs and practices unless doing so would impose an undue burden on an exployer. This obligation distinguishes religion from the other protected classes, because it is the only protected class under Title VII for which an accommodation might be required.[3]

B. EXTENT OF DISCRIMINATION

The EEOC reports that in 2009 it received 3,386 charges of religious discrimination, and in the same year it resolved 2,958 charges and recovered $7.6 million in monetary benefits for aggrieved parties, which does not include monetary benefits obtained through litigation.[4] In addition, the Agency reports that the number of claims of religious discrimination filed in 2009 was more than two times more than the number filed in 1992.[5]

religious corporation
employer for which there is a limited exception to the prohibition against religious discrimination under Title VII that permits it to consider an individual's religion when making employment decisions

C. EXCEPTION FOR RELIGIOUS CORPORATIONS

Despite the prohibition against religious discrimination, Title VII provides a limited exception for **religious corporations** and permits such employers to consider religion as a factor in making some employment decisions.[6] For example, a church that meets the definition of a religious corporation may decline to consider non-Baptist applicants when seeking to hire a Baptist preacher to lead its congregation. In contrast, a construction company seeking to hire two employees would not be permitted to consider an individual's religion in making its hiring decisions and could be subject to liability for engaging in discriminatory conduct if it did so.

This exception for religious corporations is very limited, and secular employers who seek to impose their own religious beliefs on their employees fall outside its scope.[7] Additionally, while religious corporations may consider religion as a factor in making employment decisions, they are still prohibited from discriminating based on race, color, sex, and national origin on the same terms as other secular employers.[8]

D. BONA FIDE OCCUPATIONAL QUALIFICATIONS (BFOQs) AS A DEFENSE TO DISCRIMINATORY CONDUCT

An employer might defend its consideration of an individual's religion when making an employment decision if religion constitutes a **bona fide occupational qualification (BFOQ)** for a position. As discussed in Chapter 2, Title VII — The Foundation of Workplace Discrimination Law, an employer who can show that an individual's religion (or another protected class status other than race or color) is a BFOQ for a position will not be subject to liability for discriminatory conduct for considering an individual's protected class membership in making an employment decision. Pursuant to this statutory exception, an employer is permitted to base an adverse employment decision on an individual's religion (or another protected class status other than race or color) if the consideration is "reasonably necessary to the normal operation of the particular business or enterprise."[9]

For example, one court held that an employer could defend its decision to require a pilot to be a Muslim using a BFOQ defense, because the employer presented evidence that non-Muslim employees caught flying in Mecca would be beheaded pursuant to Saudi Arabian law.[10] See Chapter 2, Title VII — The Foundation of Workplace Discrimination Law, for a more detailed discussion of the BFOQ defense.

> **bona fide occupational qualification (BFOQ)** employer's defense to a discrimination claim that illustrates the business necessity of considering an individual's protected class status, which would be otherwise prohibited

---

   **BASIS FOR A CLAIM**

An employee filing a religious discrimination claim must show that

1. the practice at issue is religious in nature;
2. the practice is based on sincerely held religious beliefs;
3. the employer was aware of the conflict between the employee's ability to perform her job responsibilities and the religious practice; and
4. the employee was subjected to discriminatory treatment for engaging in the religious practice.

Once an employee sets forth the elements of a claim, the employer has the burden to show that it is "unable to reasonably accommodate [the] employee's religious observance or practice without undue hardship on the employer's business."[11]

A. RELIGION AND RELIGIOUS PRACTICES

Copyright 2006 by Randy Glasbergen.
www.glasbergen.com

"My company does not discriminate on the basis
of religion. Worshiping me is totally voluntary."

1. DEFINITION OF RELIGION

religion
broad term that covers all aspects of religious observances, practices, and beliefs

Title VII leaves much leeway for determining what constitutes a **religion** by merely stating that it "includes all aspects of religious observance and practice, as well as belief."[12] The EEOC and a number of judicial decisions have provided significant guidance on the scope of Title VII's coverage of religion, indicating that it covers organized religions (such as Catholicism, Judaism, or Islam) as well as moral or ethical beliefs that may not be part of an organized faith. The Supreme Court has issued a number of opinions that reinforce this expansive interpretation, stating that "[r]epeatedly and in many different contexts, we have warned that courts must not presume to determine the place of a particular belief in a religion or the plausibility of a religious claim."[13]

Because the relevant judicial inquiry as to whether the practice for which an employee is seeking an accommodation is religious is based on that "person's own scheme of things," an employee's belief may be considered religious under Title VII even if the individual is the sole person who adheres to it.[14] In addition, this broad and personal interpretation may require employers to accommodate religious beliefs and practices they find unreasonable and distasteful.[15] This broad interpretation includes **atheism**, which is the

atheism
the absence of religious belief,

absence of religious belief. However, some beliefs, such as those associated with politics or personal preferences, are excluded and not provided with any protection.[16]

2. DEFINITION OF RELIGIOUS CONDUCT OR PRACTICE

Once it is determined that a situation has religious implications, the next question is whether the specific behavior for which an employee seeks protection constitutes **religious conduct or a religious practice.**

a. Broadly Defined

Attending religious services, praying, wearing religious symbols or clothing, and declining to participate in certain activities are all examples of actions that may constitute religious conduct.[17] Other activities, such as attending weekly bible study classes and church conventions, might also fall under Title VII's coverage.

b. Reason for Participating in Practice

The issue relating to whether conduct constitutes religious behavior does not focus on the nature of the activity but instead on the individual's reason for engaging in it. Based on this, it is possible that an activity might be protected when engaged in by one person but not protected when engaged in by another.[18] For example, one person might refrain from eating a particular type of food for religious reasons (protected religious conduct), but another person might follow the same rule based on health considerations (not protected religious conduct).

B. SINCERITY OF BELIEF

Despite the wide latitude employees have to establish that a particular practice is religious in nature, they must also show that the belief is sincerely held.[19] Courts will consider varying types of informal evidence in assessing this sincerity, because requiring formal proof, such as a letter from a church official, would be too restrictive based on the extension of religious protections well beyond organized religions.[20]

1. EMPLOYER'S RIGHT TO CHALLENGE SINCERITY

Because employers have an obligation to accommodate only the sincerely held religious beliefs of their employees, they have the right to challenge the asserted sincerity. Employers that show a belief is not sincerely held will not have an obligation to accommodate it. For example, an employer might show that an employee who seeks a religious accommodation to relieve him of a Sunday work schedule has actually worked a number of Sundays in the past. The employer might also question the sincerity of a belief if the resulting benefit is one that is popular among

---

which is protected under Title VII's prohibition against religious discrimination

religious conduct or a religious practice behavior for which an employer might be required to provide a reasonable accommodation to avoid liability for discriminatory conduct under Title VII, provided the accommodation will not impose an undue burden on the employer

other employees, or if in the past, the employee had asked for and was denied the benefit for secular reasons.[21]

2. LEVEL OF SINCERITY MAY CHANGE

When asserting these challenges, the employer's burden is very high because of the judicial recognition that an individual's religious beliefs may change over time based on life events or the passage of time. In these types of cases, courts consider a number of factors, such as when the individual started to engage in a particular practice and what might have motivated the change in behavior.[22]

C. AWARENESS OF THE CONFLICT

Individuals seeking religious accommodations are responsible for informing their employers about the conflict between their religious practice and work obligations.[23] Thus, an employer could likely discipline an employee for reporting to work late because he was attending a religious service if the employee did not inform his employer of the reason for the tardiness until after the imposition of discipline.[24] Based on this, employees should learn about the types of conduct that constitute religious beliefs or practices for which an employer might be required to provide a reasonable accommodation, so they can make the appropriate request in a timely fashion.

D. PRESENCE OF DISCRIMINATORY CONDUCT

Once an individual illustrates the presence of a sincerely held religious belief, the next step is demonstrating that the employer engaged in discriminatory conduct based on it. For example, an applicant might show that she was not considered for a position based on her religious beliefs, or an employee might show that he was not considered for a promotional opportunity because of his participation in a particular religious practice.

DUTY TO PROVIDE A REASONABLE ACCOMMODATION

reasonable accommodation
employer's obligation to alter an individual's working conditions, to allow participation in religious conduct, provided it would not impose an undue burden on the employer's business

Once an employer is on notice about an individual's desire to engage in conduct that constitutes a sincerely held religious belief or practice that will conflict with a work responsibility, the employer must offer a **reasonable accommodation** unless it can show that any accommodation would impose an undue burden on the employer's business.[25]

A. DEFINING A REASONABLE ACCOMMODATION

In the most basic sense, a reasonable accommodation relates to relieving or altering a work obligation so an employee can engage in religious conduct.

1. FACT-SPECIFIC INQUIRY

The determination as to what constitutes a reasonable accommodation is a fact-specific inquiry and therefore must be evaluated on a case-by-case basis. A request might be narrow, such as a request not to deduct money from an employee's paycheck for the payment of union dues if the money will be used for a purpose inconsistent with that individual's religious beliefs.[26] The request might also be much broader, such as the assignment to a flexible schedule that permits an employee to attend religious services throughout the year.

A reasonable accommodation for a religious belief or practice may take a number of forms. It might include providing an employee with additional unpaid leave, allowing employees to change shifts, or offering a job reassignment or lateral transfer. An employee might also ask an employer for permission to use its facilities, such as a quiet conference room, to pray.[27]

2. EXTENT OF OBLIGATION

An employer's obligation to provide a religious accommodation is "plainly intended to relieve individuals of the burden of choosing between their jobs and their religious convictions, where such relief will not unduly burden others."[28]

a. Full Accommodation Is Desirable

Employers have an obligation to completely eliminate the conflict between their employees' desire to engage in a religious practice and their work responsibilities, provided it is not an undue burden. Therefore, an employer may not offer a partial accommodation unless it can show a full accommodation would rise to this level.[29] For example, if an employee requests Friday evenings and Saturdays off to celebrate a religious holiday, the employer will not fulfill its obligation under Title VII by providing only Friday evenings off, unless he can illustrate that providing Saturdays off as well (the full accommodation) would constitute an undue burden.[30]

b. Partial Accommodation Might Be Sufficient

In some cases, an accommodation that provides only partial relief might be sufficient. Suppose an employee asks to be relieved from her two Saturday shifts to attend a Saturday religious convention, and her employer, who needs 24-hour coverage for his business, attempts to secure a volunteer to cover the employee's weekend shifts. If the employer is able to find a volunteer willing to accept only one weekend shift and declines to force another employee to work the second weekend shift or to offer additional compensation as an incentive for another volunteer to accept the shift, the court would likely determine that this partial accommodation was sufficient. Although Title VII requires employers to reasonably accommodate the religious practices of their employees, it does not guarantee that employees will be provided with the full opportunity to fulfill their religious obligations; in this instance, a partial accommodation would likely be sufficient based on a showing that providing a full accommodation would impose an undue hardship on the employer.[31]

c. No Obligation to Offer the Accommodation Proposed by an Employee

The Supreme Court has specifically held an employer is not required to offer any particular accommodation, including a reasonable accommodation proposed by the employee making the request. Instead the Court reasoned, "[W]here the employer has reasonably accommodated the employee's religious needs, the statutory inquiry is at an end. The employer need not further show that each of the employee's alternative accommodations would result in an undue hardship."[32]

For example, under the facts stated above, if the employer offered the employee Saturday off in exchange for working two shifts on Sunday, and the employee said she would prefer to work on Monday rather than the weekend, it is unlikely the employer would have to grant her request, because the initial accommodation would be deemed reasonable.[33]

B. UNDUE BURDEN

undue burden
burden that is beyond what an employer is obligated to undertake to accommodate an individual's religious beliefs or practices

de minimis
Latin term for minimal importance, referring to a burden an employer would likely be obligated to undertake in an effort to reasonably accommodate an individual's religious belief or practice

An employer's obligation to provide a reasonable accommodation is not absolute. Instead, the employer is required to provide an accommodation only to the extent it will not impose an **undue burden,** which is a cost or hardship that is "more than a *de minimis* cost."[34] *De minimis* is the Latin term for minimal importance, and it refers to an insignificant or minimal burden, which an employer would likely be required to withstand in an effort to reasonably accommodate an individual's religious belief or practice.

For example, an employer might have an obligation to allow an employee to leave work at sundown on Friday to attend a religious service if the employee would not be paid for the missed time and if a number of other employees would be available to cover his shift. Even though this change might require the employer to undertake a minimal administrative burden to process the shift change request, or it might result in a financial cost if the covering employee earned a higher hourly rate than the employee who was relieved from work, it is doubtful that either of these costs would rise above the *de minimis* standard, which would be necessary to give the employer the right to refuse to accommodate the religious practice of the employee.[35] In contrast, a small employer probably would likely not have to relieve its single employee from a worksite on its busiest day of the year, even if this refusal would prevent the individual from being able to engage in a religious practice, since the employer could likely show that providing this relief would constitute an undue burden.[36]

1. RELEVANT CONSIDERATIONS

In determining whether an accommodation would constitute an undue burden, courts consider a number of financial and nonfinancial factors, such as the type of workplace, the nature of the employee's duties, and the cost of the accommodation as compared to the budget of the employer.[37] To illustrate that an accommodation would impose an undue burden, the employer must submit tangible proof of the cost of providing the accommodation or the level of disruption it would cause. An employer will likely not be able to sustain this burden either by suggesting the accommodation might elicit an adverse reaction from other employees or by projecting a financial cost that might be incurred by providing it.[38]

For example, an employer would generally not be permitted to refuse to grant permission to an employee for the use of the conference room to recite a daily prayer based on the potential it would encourage others to request the same. Instead, the employer must grant the permission, assuming it is otherwise reasonable and would not be an undue burden, and wait until the issue materializes to determine whether an adjustment to the accommodation is necessary.[39]

2. FINANCIAL CONSIDERATIONS

Because courts recognize that employers may be subject to financial constraints, they will consider the size and budget of an employer, along with the number of employees requesting an accommodation, when determining what constitutes a reasonable accommodation and what would represent an undue burden. As a general rule and as described above, an employer will not have an obligation to incur any more than a *de minimis* additional cost to provide a reasonable accommodation to an employee.

a. Cost-Neutral Arrangements

Employers seeking to use a financial situation as a justification for the refusal to provide a reasonable accommodation must show that providing the accommodation would result in a cost that they would not incur in the absence of the particular arrangement. An accommodation that would result in a cost to the employer that the employer would be obligated to pay, even in the absence of granting the accommodation request, will not be sufficient. For example, a court would be unlikely to allow an employer to refuse to provide an accommodation based on a claim that the proposed accommodation would require the payment of overtime to a particular employee if, in the absence of an accommodation, the overtime would still have to be paid, but to a different person.[40]

b. Obligation to Absorb *de Minimis* Costs

The Supreme Court has explained that even though an employer is usually not required to provide an accommodation that would cause the employer to incur a financial cost, an employer might be required to accept a *de minimis* expense. This is because it is unlikely a nominal cost would constitute an undue hardship such that an employer would have the right to refuse to offer the accommodation.[41]

The obligation to absorb *de minimis* costs might include the absorption of minimal administrative costs or the temporary payment of overtime while alternative arrangements are investigated. In addition, an employer might be required to accept the burden of the administrative costs associated with rearranging the schedules of other employees if those costs are necessary to implement the accommodation.[42]

3. NONFINANCIAL CONSIDERATIONS

Courts have also recognized a number of nonfinancial factors that would support a finding that an employer would not be obligated to offer an accommodation based on the undue burden it would represent.

a. Impact of the Accommodation on Others

Courts recognize that providing an accommodation may significantly affect the productivity of a workforce, or result in the imposition of burdensome responsibilities on co-workers.[43] There is also judicial guidance indicating that the infringement on the rights and benefits of other employees, safety concerns, and the potential for the accommodation to cause the employer to violate another law would represent an undue burden, which Title VII would not require the employer to undertake.[44]

b. Some Disruption May Result

Although Title VII attempts to address the needs of employers to manage their business operations, this does not mean that an employer will not be required to tolerate some interruptions. As one court stated, a showing of "[u]ndue hardship requires more than proof of some fellow-workers' grumbling or unhappiness with a particular accommodation to a religious belief."[45] Instead, an employer would have to present evidence relating to the extent of the disruption that would result, and this would be used to assess whether it would constitute an undue burden or whether the disruption would represent a *de minimis* burden the employer would be required to accept.

4. EXTENT OF HARDSHIP MUST BE CONSIDERED

Courts have insisted that the extent of the hardship an accommodation would have on an employer continues to be a relevant consideration. For example, the Supreme Court invalidated a Connecticut statute that prohibited an employer from requiring an employee to work on a day the employee designated as his Sabbath in recognition of the fact that an employee might be required to work if such an accommodation would result in an undue burden on the employer.[46]

Along these same lines, an employer probably would not be permitted to mandate that all new employees be available to work seven days a week, because this would constitute a refusal to consider an applicant who was unavailable to work on Saturdays for a religious reason absent an inquiry as to whether the employer might be able to offer an accommodation that would not constitute an undue burden.[47]

C. CATEGORIES OF ACCOMMODATIONS

The wide range of accommodations that might address the conflict between an individual's religious belief and practice and a work responsibility does provide employers with significant flexibility to provide a reasonable accommodation absent an undue hardship. There is no definitive list of the types of accommodations that might be deemed reasonable; instead, the determination is made on a case-by-case basis.

1. FLEXIBLE SCHEDULES AND SWAPPING OF SHIFTS

As a starting point, an employee may request an accommodation in the form of a flexible schedule or a shift change.

a. Presence of Policy Not Determinative

It is unlikely that an employer could escape liability for refusing to approve the swapping of shifts based solely on the existence of a policy that would prevent it. In fact, a number of courts specifically acknowledge that an employer might have to make an exception to its governing policy to provide an accommodation.[48] The Supreme Court does, however, impose limits on the extent to which an employer must deviate from its policies. Specifically, the Court stated that the intent of Title VII was not to mandate that "an employer must deny the shift and job preference of some employees, as well as deprive them of their contractual rights, in order to accommodate or prefer the religious needs of others. . . ."[49]

The extent to which an employer might be required to deviate from an established policy, or whether it would constitute an undue hardship, would be determined based on a review of the types of factors outlined above, as well as the specific nature of the policy, which would include a consideration of the amount of effort it would take for the employer to deviate from it.

b. Employer Effort to Alleviate Burden

If the employer can show that requiring employees to exchange shifts represents an undue hardship, the employer might still have an obligation to permit exchanges on a volunteer basis. This might satisfy the obligation of the employer even if the result was only a partial accommodation due to the number of employees who elected to participate.[50] The employer would likely not be required to permit these swaps, however, if the voluntary nature of the shift changes did not alleviate the issue that would result in an undue burden on the employer, which was the reason the employer was relieved of its obligation to accommodate the employee's request for work relief in the first place.

Even if permitting a voluntary shift change would require minimal employer effort, there might be other factors that would prevent the accommodation from being reasonable. For example, one court determined that an employer was not required to exclude an employee from a rotating schedule (even though failure to do so would interfere with that employee's ability to engage in a religious practice) because the employer illustrated that working alongside a number of different supervisors, which could only be accomplished by the rotation of shifts, was a significant component of the training program.[51]

2. WORK RESPONSIBILITIES

In some cases an employer might be obligated to modify the job tasks assigned to an employee in order to provide a reasonable accommodation.

a. Reassignment of Peripheral Job Tasks

Most jobs require the performance of critical tasks as well as other responsibilities that are not directly tied to the particular position. In instances where a peripheral job task conflicts with an employee's religious beliefs, the employer might have an obligation to relieve the individual of that responsibility. The determination will be based on a fact-specific inquiry looking to such factors as whether the task is a central component of the job, whether there are other employees available to perform the work, and whether the individual seeking the accommodation can perform other job responsibilities in place of the tasks that cause the conflict.[52]

For example, one court found an employer had to permit a pharmacist to assign requests for contraceptives to one of his co-workers when he indicated that his religious beliefs prevented him from providing contraceptives to customers.[53] However, it is unlikely a court would require an employer to accommodate a pharmacist who indicates that his religious beliefs prevent him from providing any prescription medication to customers, because filling prescriptions is likely the primary purpose for his employment. Depending on the specific nature of the accommodation that might be necessary, however, and whether it would represent an undue hardship, an employer might have an obligation to place such an employee in a different position in order to provide a reasonable accommodation.

b. Lateral Transfers

An employer who cannot accommodate an employee in her current position might have an obligation to consider a lateral transfer, particularly if a position with the same salary and benefits is available and if the change would not impose an undue hardship on the employer's business. If a comparable position is not available, a transfer to a lower-level position might be deemed reasonable.[54]

3. DRESS CODES AND GROOMING REQUIREMENTS

In a number of instances, employees have used the imposition of dress codes and grooming requirements as the basis for religious discrimination claims because practices such as wearing certain religious garb and shaving facial hair could have religious implications. Just as with all other employment policies, employers will be required to provide a reasonable accommodation to any employees who indicate that such a dress code or grooming policy conflicts with a sincerely held religious belief or practice, unless providing the accommodation would impose an undue burden on the employer.

For example, an employer who refuses to hire a job applicant because the applicant's religion would prevent him from getting a "short and neat" haircut might be held liable for religious discrimination, particularly if the applicant could have pulled his hair back to address the employer's concerns.[55] In contrast, an employer would likely be permitted to refuse to allow employees to wear pants, even if this conflicted with an employee's sincerely held religious belief, if wearing the pants would pose a danger to the employee or to others. See Chapter 16, Privacy and Personal Expression, for a more detailed discussion about dress codes and grooming policies.

 RELIGIOUS EXPRESSION

Although religious discrimination claims often arise within the context of religious conduct and practices, Title VII also protects religious expression. Therefore, an employer must provide employees with a reasonable accommodation to allow them to engage in religious expression unless doing so would impose an undue burden on the employer's business.

A. DEFINITION OF RELIGIOUS EXPRESSION

There is no precise definition of **religious expression** and it can include such behavior as displaying religious icons or messages in a work area, speaking with people about religious beliefs, passing out literature, or greeting others with religious messages.

religious expression
term used to describe the displaying of or speaking about religious content, which is protected under Title VII's prohibition against religious discrimination

B. REGULATION OF RELIGIOUS EXPRESSION

As a general rule, the prohibition against discrimination based on religious expression would prevent an employer from regulating religious speech differently than it regulates other expression that is not work-related. In addition, even if religious expression is treated in the same manner as other types of expression, the employer may be required to provide an accommodation for the religious expression unless it would impose an undue burden on the employer's business.

An issue might arise if, for example, an employer tells an employee who displays a copy of the Quran that it must be kept out of the view of customers because it might not be well-received. A court assessing an employer's right to restrict this type of religious expression in this manner would consider a number of factors, such as whether the individual is a receptionist whose work space is in clear view of all employees and customers, or whether the individual sits in isolation in a private cubicle. In addition, a court could consider whether the employer permits other employees to retain other religious items such as Bibles on their desks, or whether all religious material is prohibited.[56]

C. FACT-SPECIFIC INQUIRY

The issue of what is reasonable and what constitutes an undue burden, again, is a fact-specific inquiry. For example, in one instance a court rejected an employer's assertion that allowing an individual to say "have a blessed day" to customers was an undue burden because this was a brief interaction and there was no evidence that it affected whether a customer continued to do business with the employer.[57] In contrast, another court found that an employer did not have to accommodate an employee's desire to include "in the name of Jesus Christ of Nazareth" in her regular statements to customers, because it offended some customers and resulted in the loss of business.[58]

D. ACCOMMODATION OF EMPLOYEES WHO DO NOT SHARE BELIEFS OF EMPLOYER

Although private-sector employers are generally permitted to incorporate their own religious practices into the workplace, they will likely be required to accommodate an individual who does not share the same religious beliefs and practices. For example, an employer would probably be required to provide employees with the opportunity to leave a meeting at the time a religious prayer is chanted. It is unlikely this would be an undue hardship because it does not impose a cost on the employer and would not disrupt the operation of the business.[59] In contrast, an employer's instructions to an individual to "close her ears" during the portion of the meeting that conflicts with her religious beliefs would likely not satisfy that employer's obligation to provide a reasonable accommodation.[60]

KEY TERMS

✓ atheism
✓ bona fide occupational qualification (BFOQ)
✓ *de minimis*
✓ reasonable accommodation
✓ religion
✓ religious conduct or religious practice
✓ religious corporation
✓ religious expression
✓ undue burden

DISCUSSION QUESTIONS

Explain your response to each of the following questions with the understanding that in some cases there is no right or wrong answer. If you cannot make an informed decision with the facts provided, indicate the nature and significance of the additional information you would need. For the purposes of these questions, you can assume that the employers and employees mentioned below are covered by Title VII.

1. Provide a set of facts that would support a claim of disparate treatment religious discrimination and another to support a claim of disparate impact religious discrimination.
2. Do you agree with the statement that an employer who considers an individual's religion in the hiring process will always be subject to liability for religious discrimination? Why or why not?
3. Explain how religion is defined under Title VII and the types of conduct that will and will not be protected.
4. Provide two examples of reasonable accommodations that are related to the work schedule of an individual.
5. Provide two examples of accommodations that might constitute an undue burden and two examples of accommodations that would not constitute an undue burden. Explain the factors you considered to reach each conclusion.
6. Explain why an employer might be subject to liability for asking an individual not to wear a bracelet that has a number of religious charms attached to it.
7. Ilyse runs a small business with 20 employees and decides she will only hire employees who guarantee they will work on a set schedule throughout the year. She says this will significantly ease the administrative burden of scheduling employees for different shifts and will minimize the amount of overtime that she might incur if employees ask to switch their shifts. Do you think this is a sound business plan? Why or why not?
8. Hailey says that because she wants to protect herself from claims of religious discrimination, she plans to implement a company policy that will offer all employees three weeks of paid vacation each year, along with an additional week of paid vacation to be used for religious purposes. Will this satisfy her obligations under Title VII to reasonably accommodate the religious beliefs and practices of her employees? Why or why not?
9. Greg is an employee who wants to take time off to attend a church convention. Greg approaches his employer, who tells Greg he has already taken too much time off, he cannot attend the convention, and he should not make any requests for additional time off during the next six months. Do you see any problems with his employer's response?
10. Liz is the head of a company that is on the verge of bankruptcy, and she tells her employees they will all be required to work seven days for the next three months to assist her in increasing revenues to save the business. Assuming Liz

said this policy will be implemented uniformly for all employees, do you think this could result in a potential claim of religious discrimination under Title VII?

11. Every few weeks, Rich reports to work late and submits a letter to his employer saying his lateness should be excused because he felt overwhelmed and decided he needed to go to church. His employer believes that because Rich brings a letter from his pastor explaining his lateness, this constitutes a religious practice, so the employer must permit the practice to continue. Do you agree?

ENDNOTES

1. 42 U.S.C. § 2000e(j).
2. EEOC Compl. Man. § 12 (Religious Discrimination) (July 22, 2008) (available at *http://www.eeoc.gov/policy/docs/religion.html*).
3. The Americans with Disabilities Act (ADA) also requires a covered employer to provide a reasonable accommodation to an employee or job applicant with a disability, unless doing so would cause an undue burden. See Chapter 7, Disability Discrimination.
4. U.S. Equal Employment Opportunity Commn., Religion-Based Charges FY 1997–FY 2009 (available at *http://www.eeoc.gov/eeoc/statistics/enforcement/religion.cfm*).
5. EEOC Compl. Man. § 12 fn. 8 (Religious Discrimination) (July 22, 2008) (available at *http://www.eeoc.gov/policy/docs/religion.html*) (stating 1,388 claims were filed in 1992); U.S. Equal Employment Opportunity Commn., Religion-Based Charges FY 1997–FY 2009 (available at *http://www.eeoc.gov/eeoc/statistics/enforcement/religion.cfm*) (stating 3,386 claims were filed in 2009).
6. 42 U.S.C. § 2000e-1(a). The term *religious corporation* has been defined as an employer that has a "purpose and character that are primarily religious." *EEOC v. Townley Engg. & Mfg. Co.*, 859 F.2d 610, 618 (9th Cir. 1988).
7. *Corporation of Presiding Bishop of Church of Jesus Christ of Latter-Day Saints v. Amos*, 483 U.S. 327 (1987).
8. *See, e.g., EEOC v. Fremont Christian Sch.*, 781 F.2d 1362 (9th Cir. 1986) (prohibiting religious corporations from providing "head of household" healthcare benefits to unmarried employees and married men); *DeMarco v. Holy Cross High Sch.*, 4 F.3d 166 (2d Cir. 1993) (prohibiting age discrimination by religious institutions).
9. 42 U.S.C. § 2000e-2(e).
10. *Kern v. Dynalectron Corp.*, 577 F. Supp. 1196 (N.D. Tex. 1983), *aff'd*, 46 F.2d 810 (5th Cir. 1984).
11. 42 U.S.C. § 2000e(j). The establishment of a claim of religious discrimination relating to a hiring decision is slightly different and requires the individual filing the claim to show (1) the individual belongs to a protected class; (2) the individual applied for and was qualified for a position for which the employer was seeking applicants; (3) despite the individual's qualification, the individual was rejected; and (4) even after the rejection, the position remained open and the employer continued to seek applicants from candidates with similar qualifications. *See McDonnell Douglas Corp. v. Green*, 411 U.S. 792, 802 (1973). *See* Chapter 2, Title VII — The Foundation of Workplace Discrimination Law.
12. 42 U.S.C. § 2000e(j).
13. *Employment Div. of Dept. of Human Res. of Or. v. Smith*, 494 U.S. 872, 878 (1990).
14. *See United States v. Seeger*, 380 U.S. 163 (1969).

15. *See Dettmer v. Landon*, 799 F.2d 929, 932 (4th Cir. 1986) (holding religious beliefs do not need to be "acceptable, logical, consistent, or comprehensible to others" to be protected).

16. U.S. Equal Employment Opportunity Commn., Questions and Answers: Religious Discrimination in the Workplace (July 22, 2008) (available at *http://eeoc.gov/policy/docs/qanda_religion.html*).

17. EEOC Compl. Man. § 12 (Religious Discrimination) (July 22, 2008) (available at *http://www.eeoc.gov/policy/docs/religion.html*).

18. *Id.*

19. *United States v. Seeger*, 380 U.S. 163, 185 (1969).

20. *See, e.g., EEOC v. Tyson Foods, Inc.*, Civil Action No. 99-5126 (W.D. Ark. consent decree entered Aug. 14, 2000) (settlement based on employer's agreement to revoke its policy requiring all accommodation requests to include a letter from a church).

21. *See generally* U.S. Equal Employment Opportunity Commn., Questions and Answers: Religious Discrimination in the Workplace (July 22, 2008) (available at *http://www.eeoc.gov/policy/docs/qanda_religion.html*).

22. *See, e.g., EEOC v. Ilona of Hung., Inc.* 108 F.3d 1569 (7th Cir. 1997) (rejecting the challenge to the sincerity of an employee's request for an accommodation to celebrate a religious holiday based, in part, on the showing that the birth of her son and death of her father caused her to become more religious).

23. *See, e.g., Redmond v. GAF Corp.*, 574 F.2d 897, 902 (7th Cir. 1978) (holding "an employee who is disinterested in informing his employer of his religious needs may forego the right to have his beliefs accommodated by his employer"). *But see Heller v. EBB Auto Co.*, 8 F.3d 1433, 1439 (9th Cir. 1993) (requesting time off to attend a religious ceremony was sufficient notice to an employer of a need for an accommodation).

24. *Elmenayer v. ABF Freight Sys.*, 318 F.3d 130 (2d Cir. 2003).

25. 42 U.S.C. § 2000e(j).

26. *See, e.g., EEOC v. University of Detroit*, 904 F.2d 331 (6th Cir. 1990).

27. *See* EEOC Compl. Man. § 12 n.188 (Religious Discrimination) (July 22, 2008) (available at *http://www.eeoc.gov/policy/docs/religion.html*) (citing Federal Workplace Guidelines § 1(c) n.1: "[W]orkplaces that allow employees to use facilities for non-work related secular activities generally are required to allow the privilege on equal terms for religious activities").

28. *Protos v. Volkswagen of Am., Inc.*, 797 F.2d 129, 136 (3d Cir. 1986).

29. *See, e.g., EEOC v. Universal Mfg. Corp.*, 914 F.2d 71 (5th Cir. 1990) (finding that accommodating an employee for five days of a seven-day religious conference was insufficient absent a showing that the full accommodation would result in an undue burden).

30. *Baker v. Home Depot*, 445 F.3d 541 (2d Cir. 2006).

31. *See Morrissette-Brown v. Mobile Infirmary Med. Ctr.*, 2006 WL 1999133 (S.D. Ala. July 14, 2006) (accommodating an employee by providing her with the opportunity to trade shifts with co-workers based on a mutual agreement was sufficient to satisfy an employer's obligation to provide a reasonable accommodation).

32. *Ansonia Bd. of Educ. v. Philbrook*, 479 U.S. 60, 69 (1986).

33. *See Wilshin v. Allstate Ins. Co.*, 212 F. Supp. 2d 1350 (M.D. Ga. 2002).

34. 29 C.F.R. § 1605.2(e)(1). The *de minimis* burden is a very low threshold, and there have been a number of legislative attempts to require employers to bear a more significant cost. For example, the Workplace Religious Freedom Act (WRFA) would require employers to offer an accommodation for a religious belief or practice unless it would be a "significant or difficult expense." To date, this legislation has not passed. *See* H.R. 1431, 110th Cong. (2007).

35. *Brown v. General Motors*, 601 F.2d 956, 959 (8th Cir. 1979).

36. *See, e.g., Tooley v. Martin Marietta Corp.*, 648 F.2d 1239, 1243 (9th Cir. 1981).

37. U.S. Equal Employment Opportunity Commn., Guidelines on Discrimination Because of Religion, 29 C.F.R. § 1605.2(e).

38. *EEOC v. Alamo Rent-A-Car, LLC*, 432 F. Supp. 2d 1006 (D. Ariz. 2006) (rejecting the employer's position that allowing the wearing of a religious headscarf would be an undue

burden because of the disruption that would be associated with the opening of "the floodgates to others violating the uniform policy").

39. U.S. Equal Employment Opportunity Commn., Questions and Answers About the Workplace Rights of Muslims, Arabs, South Asians and Sikhs Under the Equal Employment Opportunity Laws (available at *http://www.eeoc.gov/facts/backlash-employee.html*).

40. *Redmond v. GAF Corp.*, 574 F.2d 897, 904 (7th Cir. 1978) (rejecting the argument that the payment of overtime is an undue hardship because the overtime would have been paid to an employee regardless of whether the accommodation was offered).

41. *See Trans World Airlines, Inc. v. Hardison*, 432 U.S. 63 (1977).

42. U.S. Equal Employment Opportunity Commn., Guidelines on Discrimination Because of Religion, 29 C.F.R. § 1605.2(e)(1).

43. *Trans World Airlines, Inc. v. Hardison*, 432 U.S. 63, 84 (1977).

44. *See* EEOC Compl. Man. § 12 (Religious Discrimination) (July 22, 2008) (available at *http://www.eeoc.gov/policy/docs/religion.html*).

45. *Burns v. Southern Pac. Transp. Co.*, 589 F.2d 403, 407 (9th Cir. 1978).

46. *Estate of Thornton v. Caldor, Inc.*, 472 U.S. 703 (1985).

47. EEOC Compl. Man. § 12 (Religious Discrimination) (July 22, 2008) (available at *http://www.eeoc.gov/policy/docs/religion.html*).

48. *See, e.g., Minkus v. Metropolitan Sanitary Dist.*, 600 F.2d 80 (7th Cir. 1979).

49. *Trans World Airlines, Inc. v. Hardison*, 432 U.S. 63 (1977). In *Trans World Airlines*, the Supreme Court also rejects the notion that "an agreed-upon seniority system must give way when necessary to accommodate religious observances." 432 U.S. at 79.

50. *See, e.g., Morrissette-Brown v. Mobile Infirmary Med. Ctr.*, 2006 WL 1999133 (S.D. Ala. July 14, 2006).

51. *Beadle v. Tampa*, 42 F.3d 633, 636 (11th Cir. 1994).

52. EEOC Compl. Man. § 12 (Religious Discrimination) (July 22, 2008) (available at *http://www.eeoc.gov/policy/docs/religion.html*).

53. *Noesen v. Medical Staffing Network, Inc.*, 2007 WL 1302118 (7th Cir. 2007).

54. *Cook v. Lindsay Olive Growers*, 911 F.2d 233, 241 (9th Cir. 1990).

55. EEOC Compl. Man. § 12 (Religious Discrimination) (July 22, 2008) (available at *http://www.eeoc.gov/policy/docs/religion.html*).

56. *See id.*

57. *Anderson v. U.S.F. Logistics (IMC), Inc.*, 274 F.3d 470, 476 (7th Cir. 2001).

58. *Johnson v. Galls Merch.*, 1989 WL 23201 (W.D. Mo. Jan. 17, 1989).

59. *EEOC v. Townley*, 859 F.2d 610, 620-621 (9th Cir. 1988).

60. *Young v. Southwestern Sav. & Loan Assn.*, 509 F.2d 140 (5th Cir. 1975).

Sex, Pregnancy, and Genetic Discrimination

Chapter Objectives

This chapter explores workplace discrimination based on sex, pregnancy, and genetics. Title VII prohibits employers from considering sex or sexual stereotypes when making employment decisions, and the Pregnancy Discrimination Act (PDA), which is an amendment to Title VII, prohibits discrimination based on pregnancy. Workplace discrimination based on genetics is also prohibited by Title VII, pursuant to the Genetic Information Nondiscrimination Act of 2008 (GINA), which recently amended the statute.

After completing this chapter, students should have a working knowledge of what constitutes sex discrimination under Title VII, which includes the obligations an employer has to employees who are on pregnancy leave. In addition, students should be able to explain what constitutes genetic information and the limitations GINA places on employer conduct.

Upon mastering the main objectives of this chapter students should be able to

■ define sex discrimination and provide examples of the types of information that, if considered, could subject an employer to liability for sex discrimination under Title VII;

■ define sex-plus discrimination;

■ explain the purpose of the PDA and the obligations an employer has to an employee on pregnancy leave;

■ explain the difference in coverage of a claim of sex discrimination under Title VII and a claim under the Equal Pay Act (EPA); and

■ define *genetic testing* and *genetic information* and explain their significance to GINA.

DISCRIMINATION BASED ON SEX

sex discrimination
discrimination based on sex or
gender stereotypes that is
prohibited by Title VII

The prohibition against sex discrimination under Title VII applies to employers with 15 or more employees and prohibits the imposition of adverse employment decisions on individuals based on sex or on gender stereotypes.[1] In addition, the Supreme Court has held that this prohibition against sex discrimination includes the prohibition against sexual harassment, which is discussed in detail in Chapter 15, Workplace Harassment.[2]

Consistent with all other protected classes under Title VII, this prohibition extends to all phases of the employment process, and individuals can file disparate treatment or disparate impact claims. In addition, employers are not permitted to retaliate against individuals for filing a sex discrimination claim, or for participating in the investigation or prosecution of an employer for sex-based discrimination under Title VII.[3] See Chapter 2, Title VII — The Foundation of Workplace Discrimination Law.

The significance of educating employers about the prohibition against sex-based discrimination is best illustrated by some settlements reached and penalties imposed. For example, two large financial services companies paid out a sizeable amount of money in response to sex discrimination claims alleging unequal treatment in compensation and opportunities for promotional advancements. One company was ordered to pay $2.2 million to a female broker, and another agreed to pay $54 million to settle a claim filed on behalf of 340 women who worked in investment banking.[4] The EEOC reports that in 2009 it received 28,028 charges for sex-based discrimination under Title VII. In the same year it resolved 26,618 charges and recovered $121.5 million for aggrieved parties, and this figure does not include monetary benefits obtained through litigation.[5]

A. PROHIBITION APPLIES TO MEN AND WOMEN

The prohibition against sex discrimination applies to men on the same terms as it does to women. For example, if an employer grants its female employees three weeks of childcare leave in addition to the time provided for the actual birth, but does not offer this comparable three-week leave to men, the policy would violate Title VII's prohibition against sex discrimination because it treats employees differently based on their gender.[6]

B. BASIS FOR THE CLAIM

**"The local business journal wants to do an article on
the 10 most powerful women in our company.
Quick, go hire 7 more women!"**

As a starting point, an employer is not permitted to exclude applicants on the basis of sex, such as imposing a rule that only men or only women can apply for certain positions. The prohibition against sex discrimination, however, extends beyond these basic considerations.

1. STEREOTYPES

The prohibition against sex discrimination extends beyond the making of decisions based on the fact that an individual is a male or a female, and also prohibits employers from refusing to "hire an individual based on stereotyped characterizations of the sexes."[7] For example, an employer cannot advertise a position seeking a "male construction worker," or a "female nurse," based on preconceived determinations that these are the individuals who would be the most likely to apply for such positions. Recruiting and hiring only men for certain mechanical positions because of the stereotype that men are more mechanically inclined than women, or recruiting and hiring only women for caregiving positions based on the stereotype that women are more nurturing than men, are equally impermissible.[8] Employers are also prohibited from making decisions based on employment statistics about men and women, such as a finding that in some instances the turnover or absenteeism rates are higher for women than for men because of childcare obligations.[9]

2. CUSTOMER PREFERENCE

Employers are also prohibited from discriminating based on sex in response to the preference of its customers. For example, an employer would be subject to liability under Title VII for deciding not to hire a female CEO because some of its customers objected to working with women in powerful positions.[10]

C. EMPLOYEE BENEFITS

The protection against sex discrimination is not limited to hiring and firing but rather applies to all other terms and conditions of employment, which includes the providing of employee benefits. Therefore, because medical benefits must be provided to men and women on the same terms, a health plan that excludes certain prescriptions that are only appropriate for women (such as birth control pills) would likely be considered discriminatory. This obligation extends to providing medical benefits for spouses. Therefore, an employer's policy that provides different levels of coverage to the spouses of male employees than it provides to the spouses of female employees would violate Title VII's prohibition against sex-based discrimination.[11]

D. SEX-PLUS DISCRIMINATION

sex-plus discrimination
discrimination based on an individual's gender as well as on an additional characteristic not unique to the gender

Employers must also avoid **sex-plus discrimination,** which relates to less favorable treatment of individuals based on both their gender and an additional characteristic shared by both genders.[12]

For example, under the sex-plus theory, it would be unlawful for an employer to refuse to hire women with young children while hiring men with young children based on the assumption that women are more likely to take on the primary caretaker role and therefore less likely to prioritize work responsibilities.[13] This decision would be unlawful because it treats women less favorably, both because they are females and because they have children. The "plus" in the sex-plus theory relates to having young children because it is a characteristic that is common to both men and the women.

E. BONA FIDE OCCUPATIONAL QUALIFICATION (BFOQ)

bona fide occupational qualification (BFOQ)
employer's defense to an employment discrimination claim that illustrates the business necessity of considering an individual's protected class status, a consideration that otherwise would be prohibited

Consistent with the treatment of other protected classes under Title VII (other than race and color), there are limited instances in which an employer can appropriately defend the selection of a candidate based on sex. Specifically, an employer might avoid liability for sex discrimination under the statute by showing that sex is a **bona fide occupational qualification (BFOQ),** meaning the consideration of an individual's sex is necessary because being a particular gender is central to the performance of the position. For example, a casting director might limit the recruitment for a movie role to male or female applicants when a particular gender is necessary for "authenticity or genuineness."[14] See Chapter 2, Title VII — The Foundation of Workplace Discrimination Law, for a more detailed discussion of BFOQs.

⫼ DISCRIMINATION BASED ON PREGNANCY

© 1999 Randy Glasbergen.
www.glasbergen.com

"If you plan to stop working to have your baby, please do it during a coffee break and try not to disturb your coworkers."

In addition to Title VII's prohibition against discrimination based on sex, the statute also offers protection based on pregnancy. The **Pregnancy Discrimination Act of 1978 (PDA)** amended Title VII to prohibit discrimination in all aspects of employment based on pregnancy, childbirth, and related medical conditions.

The PDA, which covers employers with 15 or more employees, requires that employers treat pregnant women in the same manner as others who may be unable to perform their usual job functions based on a disability. Some state laws provide more expansive protections and specify that their prohibition extends to questions about whether an individual intends to become pregnant, plans to have children, or uses birth control.[15]

Under Title VII, this prohibition against discrimination based on pregnancy relates to all aspects of employment, meaning employers cannot discriminate against pregnant employees with respect to decisions relating to the hiring, firing, disciplining, and promoting of its employees. The EEOC reports that in 2009 it received 6,196 charges for pregnancy discrimination under Title VII, and in the same year it resolved 5,594 charges and recovered $16.8 million for aggrieved parties, which does not include monetary benefits obtained through litigation.[16]

Pregnancy Discrimination Act of 1978 (PDA)
federal law that prohibits discrimination in employment based on pregnancy, childbirth, and related medical conditions

A. PREGNANCY AND MATERNITY LEAVE

With respect to pregnancy and maternity leaves, employers must treat women in the same manner as other temporarily disabled employees. Specifically, women on pregnancy leaves should not be treated differently than employees on other types of leave, nor can they be offered less than what they would be entitled to had the leave been requested and granted for a different medical condition. For example, employers who request medical documentation supporting an employee's request for medical leave can request the same information from pregnant employees. However, employers cannot impose this requirement on pregnant employees or women on maternity leave unless it is also requested from other employees with temporary disabilities.[17]

Similarly, if employers offer short-term disability leave to their employees, this leave must be extended to pregnancy-related conditions. Employers must also hold the jobs of women out on pregnancy or maternity leave open for the same length of time as for those employees who are on other types of leave.[18] In the same way, employers are prohibited from implementing a policy that would prevent pregnant employees from returning to work after suffering from a medical condition relating to pregnancy unless comparable restrictions are imposed upon employees with other medical conditions.[19]

B. MEDICAL AND FRINGE BENEFITS

With respect to providing medical and fringe benefits to women on pregnancy and maternity leave, the same guidelines apply, meaning pregnant employees must be offered benefits on the same terms as those offered to employees with other medical conditions. For example, pregnant employees must be reimbursed for pregnancy-related medical conditions at the same rate as that which applies to other medical conditions unrelated to pregnancy. In addition, women on pregnancy-related leaves must accrue vacation pay, seniority rights, salary increases, and so forth on the same basis as employees on medical leaves that are not pregnancy related.[20]

SEX DISCRIMINATION AND THE EQUAL PAY ACT (EPA)

Equal Pay Act (EPA)
an amendment to the FLSA that requires equal pay for equal work

Although the prohibition against sex discrimination is specifically referenced in Title VII, the **Equal Pay Act (EPA)** — an amendment to the Fair Labor Standards Act (FLSA) — provides another source of protection against sex-based discrimination because it is the federal law requiring employers to offer equal pay for substantially equal work. Title VII, however, has a broader scope than the EPA because it prohibits employers from compensating one employee more than another based on sex, regardless of whether the work they perform is equal.

For example, an employer who compensates its male waiters more than its female hostesses based on the assumption that men are more likely to be the primary bread winners in a family may be subject to liability under Title VII for sex discrimination — for considering a gender stereotype when making decisions about compensation. This set of facts would not, however, support a claim under the EPA because presumably a waiter and hostess do not perform equal work, which is the foundation for a claim under the statute.

If, however, the same employer pays male waiters more than female waitresses, and justifies the pay differential by stating that men tend to be the bread winners for their families, the employer could be subject to liability both for sex discrimination under Title VII (for treating women less favorably than men based on a gender stereotype) and for compensation discrimination under the EPA (for failing to offer women and men equal pay for equal work). See Chapter 12, Compensation and Benefits, for a detailed discussion of the EPA.

 ## DISCRIMINATION BASED ON GENETICS

Title VII was recently amended to prohibit the use of genetic information as the basis for making adverse employment decisions, providing individuals with an additional source of protection from workplace discrimination. Legislation related to genetics has particular significance because technological advancements have increased the availability and accuracy of information relating to the potential for individuals to develop certain diseases.

A. GENETIC TESTING

Genetic testing refers to tests performed to assess the likelihood that an individual will develop certain diseases that are hereditary in nature. Despite the increased availability and accuracy of these tests, some individuals have been reluctant to undergo them due to the concern that the results might be used as the basis for an adverse employment decision. For example, there is the fear that employers might discriminate against individuals with certain genetic predispositions to avoid the potential need of these individuals for extensive sick or medical leave, their resignations for medical reasons (which could result in increased recruitment costs), or increased healthcare costs for the employers. These apprehensions contributed to the passage of the Genetic Information Nondiscrimination Act of 2008 (GINA), which prohibits workplace discrimination based on genetics and genetic information.[21]

genetic testing
tests used to assess the potential for an individual to develop certain diseases that are hereditary in nature

B. GENETIC INFORMATION NONDISCRIMINATION ACT OF 2008 (GINA)

The **Genetic Information Nondiscrimination Act of 2008 (GINA)** amended Title VII to include a prohibition against workplace discrimination based on genetics. GINA subjects covered employers to an absolute prohibition against

Genetic Information Nondiscrimination Act of 2008 (GINA)
federal law that prohibits workplace discrimination based on genetics and genetic information

the use of genetic information in making employment decisions under any circumstances.[22]

The Act was designed to address on a national level some of the concerns about genetic discrimination by prohibiting workplace discrimination against applicants and employees based on genetic information in hiring, promotion, discharge, compensation, fringe benefits, job training, and all other terms and conditions of employment.[23]

1. GENETIC INFORMATION

genetic information
broad term for information revealed through an individual's genetic test or the test of a family member, as well as a family medical history

GINA broadly defines **genetic information** to include information revealed through an individual's genetic test or the tests of an individual's family members, as well as information revealed in an individual's family medical history. Information about an illness an individual has already developed, and tests for alcohol or drugs, are outside the scope of GINA's coverage and the type of information the Act is designed to protect.[24]

GINA recognizes limited instances when an employer might gain access to such information, such as by overhearing a discussion among co-workers, or receiving genetic information in support of a request for a reasonable accommodation pursuant to the Americans with Disabilities Acts (ADA). In these limited instances, GINA recognizes that employees may possess this genetic information but subjects such employers to stringent confidentiality requirements relating to the storage and dissemination of this information.[25] See Chapter 7, Disability Discrimination.

2. RIGHTS AND REMEDIES UNDER GINA PARALLEL TITLE VII

The rights of individuals under GINA parallel the rights of individuals under Title VII. Specifically, GINA makes it unlawful for employers to refuse to hire an individual, to decide to terminate an employee, or to discriminate against an employee with respect to any terms and conditions of employment, based on genetic information.[26] Further, employers are not permitted to use genetic information to segregate or classify employees in a way that would deny them employment opportunities or adversely impact their employment.[27] For example, an individual who was not hired due to the results of a genetic test that indicated a genetic predisposition to cancer would likely have a viable claim under GINA, even if the individual never actually developed the disease.

The remedies available under GINA also track those available under Title VII. Specifically, an aggrieved individual may seek reinstatement, hiring, promotion, back pay, injunctive relief, pecuniary and non-pecuniary damages (including compensatory and punitive damages), attorneys' fees, and costs. Consistent with Title VII, the statutory caps on the amount of damages that may be awarded for future losses, pain and suffering, and punitive damages (ranging from $50,000 for employers with 15 to 100 employees, to $300,000 for employers with more than 500 employees) are also applicable.[28] See Chapter 2, Title VII — The Foundation of Workplace Discrimination Law, for a detailed discussion of available remedies.

KEY TERMS

- ✓ bona fide occupational qualification (BFOQ)
- ✓ Equal Pay Act (EPA)
- ✓ genetic information
- ✓ Genetic Information Nondiscrimination Act of 2008 (GINA)
- ✓ genetic testing
- ✓ Pregnancy Discrimination Act (PDA)
- ✓ sex discrimination
- ✓ sex-plus discrimination

DISCUSSION QUESTIONS

Explain your response to each of the following questions with the understanding that in some cases there is no right or wrong answer. If you cannot make an informed decision with the facts provided, indicate the nature and significance of the additional information you would need. For the purposes of these questions, you can assume that the employers and employees mentioned below are covered by Title VII.

1. Provide a set of facts that would suggest a job applicant has a viable disparate treatment claim for sex discrimination under Title VII.
2. Provide a set of facts that would suggest a terminated employee has a viable disparate impact claim for sex discrimination under Title VII.
3. Explain the type of information that the Genetic Information Nondiscrimination Act of 2008 (GINA) would prohibit an employer from using when making a decision relating to whether to hire a particular job applicant.
4. Jill is opening a new business. She creates a list of job responsibilities for a new receptionist and tells her recruiter to focus on male candidates, because they would be more likely to possess those traits than female candidates. Do you think this is a wise business strategy?
5. John owns a high-end lingerie store and conducts a survey to determine whether his customers would prefer to shop with a male or female salesperson. Because more than 90% of his customers said they would prefer a female salesperson, he decides to terminate all of his male employees and hire women to fill each of these positions. Do you think this is a sound business decision?
6. J.J. owns a toy store. He decides he is over-staffed, and plans to terminate the employment of one of his cashiers. He decides to terminate a pregnant employee instead of her male counterpart, because he knows his pregnant employee will request maternity leave and he wants to ensure that the store has appropriate sales coverage. Do you think J.J. can be held liability for sex discrimination for this decision? Why or why not?
7. In question 5 above, what if John has a male employee and a female employee and decides to terminate the female employee because she earns more money

than her male counterpart. Do you think this decision might subject him to liability for discriminatory conduct? Why or why not?

ENDNOTES

1. 42 U.S.C. § 2000e-2.
2. *Meritor Sav. Bank, FSB v. Vinson*, 477 U.S. 57, 65 (1986).
3. U.S. Equal Employment Opportunity Commn., Sex-Based Discrimination (available at *http://www.eeoc.gov/laws/types/sex.cfm*).
4. Patrick McGeehan, *What Merrill's Women Want, N.Y. Times*, Aug. 22, 2004, at 31 (available at *http://www.nytimes.com/2004/08/22/business/what-merrill-s-women-want.html?pagewanted=1*).
5. U.S. Equal Employment Opportunity Commn., Sex-Based Charges FY 1997–FY 2009 (available at *http://www.eeoc.gov/eeoc/statistics/enforcement/sex.cfm*).
6. U.S. Equal Employment Opportunity Commn., The Family and Medical Leave Act, the Americans with Disabilities Act, and Title VII of the Civil Rights Act of 1964 Fact Sheet (available at *http://www.eeoc.gov/policy/docs/fmlaada.html*).
7. U.S. Equal Employment Opportunity Commn., Guidelines on Discrimination Because of Sex, 29 C.F.R. § 1604.1(a)(1)(ii).
8. *See* 29 C.F.R. § 1604.1.
9. *Id.*
10. *See id.*
11. *Id.*
12. *See, e.g., Phillips v. Martin Marietta Corp.*, 400 U.S. 542, 544 (1971); *see also Fischer v. Vassar Coll.*, 70 F.3d 1420, 1448 (2d Cir. 1995), *on reh'g en banc*, 114 F.3d 1332 (2d Cir. 1997), *cert. denied*, 522 U.S. 1075 (1998).
13. *See Phillips v. Martin Marietta Corp.*, 400 U.S. 542 (1971).
14. 29 C.F.R. § 1604.1.
15. N.Y. Exec. Law § 296.1(g).
16. U.S. Equal Employment Opportunity Commn., Pregnancy Discrimination Charges EEOC & FEPAs Combined: FY 2008–FY 2009 (available at *http://www.eeoc.gov/eeoc/statistics/enforcement/pregnancy.cfm*).
17. U.S. Equal Employment Opportunity Commn., Pregnancy Discrimination (available at *http://www.eeoc.gov/laws/types/pregnancy.cfm*).
18. *Id.*
19. *Id.*
20. *Id.*
21. *See* U.S. Equal Employment Opportunity Commn., Background Information for EEOC Notice of Proposed Rulemaking on Title II of the Genetic Information Nondiscrimination Act of 2008 (available at *http://www.eeoc.gov/policy/docs/qanda_geneticinfo.html*). Individuals might also have a concern that the discovery of a predisposition to a particular disease might result in a denial of medical coverage or increased out-of-pocket costs. *Id.* Doctors have also stated that this fear of genetic discrimination is problematic because it prevents thousands of at-risk individuals from using these tests to manage their long-term healthcare needs. *See* Amy Harmon, *Congress Passes Bill to Bar Bias Based on Genes*, N.Y. Times, May 2, 2008 (available at *http://www.nytimes.com/2008/05/02/health/policy/02gene.html*).
22. U.S. Equal Employment Opportunity Commn., Background Information for EEOC Notice of Proposed Rulemaking on Title II of the Genetic Information Nondiscrimination Act of 2008 (available at *http://www.eeoc.gov/policy/docs/qanda_geneticinfo.html*). Prior to

the passage of GINA about 35 states had passed genetic anti-discrimination laws that prohibit the consideration of information received from genetic testing when making decisions about hiring, firing, and other terms and conditions of employment. *See, e.g.,* Connecticut (Conn. Gen. Stat. § 46a-60), Louisiana (La. Stat. Ann. § 23:302-:303), Rhode Island (R.I. Gen. Laws § 28-6.7-1); *see generally* Genetic Employment Laws, National Conference of State Legislatures (updated Jan. 2008) (available at *http://www.ncsl.org/default.aspx?tabid=14280*). Other states have passed laws that offer more limited protections for specific diseases, such as a Florida statute that prohibits mandatory testing for sickle cell anemia, a hereditary blood disorder, for employment purposes. Fla. Stat. §§ 228.201, 63.043, 448.076. The statute also prohibits this mandatory testing for admission into a state education institution or for adoption.

23. Genetic Information Nondiscrimination Act of 2008, tit. II, § 202(a) ("EEO is the Law" Poster Supplement) (available at *http://www.eeoc.gov/employers/upload/eeoc_gina_supplement.pdf*). The Act also prohibits insurance companies from requesting or demanding a genetic test, or using any test results to reduce coverage or adjust the cost of coverage. *See* Office for Human Research Prots. (OHRP), U.S. Dept. of Health & Human Servs. (HHS), Guidance on the Genetic Information Nondiscrimination Act: Implications for Investigators and Institutional Review Boards (available at *http://www.hhs.gov/ohrp/humansubjects/guidance/gina.html*). In 2000 then President Clinton did sign an executive order (a declaration from a President or Government that has the same impact as a law) that prohibited genetic discrimination. That order, however, only applied to federal employers and had a limited application because it did not prohibit the consideration of results from all types of genetic tests or the consideration of family medical histories. Exec. Order 13145: To Prohibit Discrimination in Federal Employment Based on Genetic Information, President Clinton, The White House, Feb. 8, 2000 (available at *http://www.eeoc.gov/abouteeoc/history/35th/thelaw/13145.html*); *see* Questions and Answers: EEOC Policy Guidance on Executive Order 13145 Prohibiting Discrimination in Federal Employment Based on Genetic Information (available at *http://www.eeoc.gov/policy/docs/qanda-genetic.html*).

24. *See* U.S. Equal Employment Opportunity Commn., Background Information for EEOC Notice of Proposed Rulemaking on Title II of the Genetic Information Nondiscrimination Act of 2008 (available at *http://www.eeoc.gov/policy/docs/qanda_geneticinfo.html*).

25. *Id.*

26. Genetic Information Nondiscrimination Act of 2008, Pub. L. No. 110-233, § 202(a)(1), 122 Stat. 881.

27. Genetic Information Nondiscrimination Act of 2008, Pub. L. No. 110-233, § 202(a)(2), 122 Stat. 881.

28. *See* U.S. Equal Employment Opportunity Commn., Background Information for EEOC Notice of Proposed Rulemaking on Title II of the Genetic Information Nondiscrimination Act of 2008 (available at *http://www.eeoc.gov/policy/docs/qanda_geneticinfo.html*). Punitive damages are not available in an action against federal, state, or local government employers.

Age Discrimination

6

Chapter Objectives

This chapter provides a basic introduction to age discrimination, focusing on the Age Discrimination in Employment Act (ADEA), which is the federal law that prohibits age discrimination in the workplace against individuals who are 40 years of age and older. The mechanics of filing an age discrimination claim based on intentional and unintentional discrimination are discussed, along with employer defenses that can block the imposition of liability under the statute. In addition, this chapter discusses the administration of employment benefits and retirement plans because age discrimination issues often arise in these contexts.

After completing this chapter, students will have a fundamental understanding of age discrimination. Specifically, upon mastering the main objectives of this chapter students should be able to

- explain the most significant provisions of the ADEA and the scope of its coverage;
- identify the terms and conditions of employment that are often the subject of a claim under the ADEA;
- describe a situation that would lend itself to the filing of an age discrimination claim under the disparate treatment theory (for intentional discrimination), and explain the shifting of the burden of proof that would occur in any resulting litigation;
- describe a situation that would lend itself to the filing of an age discrimination claim under the disparate impact theory (for unintentional discrimination), and explain the shifting of the burden of proof that would occur in any resulting litigation;
- define *reasonable factor other than age (RFOA)* and *bona fide occupational qualification (BFOQ)*, and explain the significance of each; and
- explain the obligations an employer has to provide benefits to employees on the same basis, and the rights employers have to provide different levels of benefits to its older employees.

Title VII of the Civil Rights Act of 1964 prohibits workplace discrimination based on race, color, national origin, religion, and sex, but it does not prohibit discrimination based on age. Although age was discussed during the Congressional debates to determine the categories of individuals that would be covered by Title VII, it was found to be inappropriate for inclusion in the statute. After the passage of Title VII, however, Congress suggested that the Department of Labor (DOL) propose legislation to remedy age discrimination. The suggestion eventually materialized in the passage of the ADEA, which tracks much of the language of Title VII but has some components that are unique to it.

SCOPE OF COVERAGE OF THE AGE DISCRIMINATION IN EMPLOYMENT ACT (ADEA)

Copyright 2002 by Randy Glasbergen.
www.glasbergen.com

"We do not have a bias toward younger applicants and it wasn't necessary to write your résumé in crayon."

Age Discrimination in Employment Act (ADEA) federal law prohibiting workplace discrimination against individuals 40 years of age and older

The **Age Discrimination in Employment Act of 1967 (ADEA)** is the federal law that prohibits public- and private-sector employers with 20 or more employees from discriminating against individuals who are 40 years of age and older. Consistent with other workplace anti-discrimination laws, the ADEA is enforced by the EEOC.[1]

Employers are generally prohibited from considering an individual's age when making employment decisions. For example, the ADEA would prohibit an employer from deciding it will interview only young applicants for a position, or that it will not consider applicants over 50 years of age. The EEOC reports that in 2009 it received 22,778 charges of age discrimination, and in the same year it resolved 20,529 claims and recovered $72.1 million in monetary benefits for aggrieved parties, which does not include monetary benefits obtained through litigation.[2]

A. INDIVIDUALS COVERED

Individuals who work for employers with fewer than 20 employees, or who are discriminated against because they are less than 40 years of age may have a viable age discrimination claim under a state anti-discrimination law but will fall outside the scope of the individuals entitled to the federal benefits and protections provided by the ADEA. Those individuals who are covered by the ADEA, however, will be protected from age discrimination during each phase of the employment process.

B. RECRUITMENT

The ADEA protects individuals from the early stages of the employment process. The prohibition against age discrimination applies to job postings and classified advertisements, making it generally unlawful to include age preferences (such as indicating a desire to hire a candidate between 20 and 30 years of age or a candidate who has graduated from college within the past three years), age limitations (such as indicating candidates over 50 years of age will not be considered), or other age-related specifications within them. Although the Act does not specifically prohibit an employer from asking prospective employees to provide their date of birth on employment applications, the inquiry is closely scrutinized, because it suggests an employer is considering an applicant's age in the hiring process.

C. TERMS AND CONDITIONS OF EMPLOYMENT

In addition to placing limitations on the age-related factors that employers can consider in the hiring process, the ADEA prohibits employers from discriminating based on age when making decisions about promotions, terminations, compensation, and all other terms and conditions of employment. Therefore, employers would not be permitted to limit access to apprentice or training programs based on age or characteristics linked to age. In addition, consistent with other federal anti-discrimination laws, the ADEA makes it unlawful for employers to retaliate against employees for challenging practices that discriminate based on age by filing a claim under the statute, or by participating in an investigation, hearing, or litigation for a claim arising under it.

DISPARATE TREATMENT DISCRIMINATION

An individual claiming that an employer used age or an age-related factor as the basis for an adverse employment decision can file a **disparate treatment claim** for intentional discrimination.

> **disparate treatment claim**
> employment discrimination claim alleging an employer engaged in intentional discrimination

Because the ADEA tracks much of the language of Title VII, the framework for asserting a disparate treatment claim under the ADEA tracks the framework established by the Supreme Court in *McDonnell Douglas* and its progeny.[3] Although the presentation of a disparate treatment claim is covered extensively in Chapter 2, Title VII — The Foundation of Workplace Discrimination Law, it is worth revisiting here.

A. *PRIMA FACIE* CASE

> ***prima facie* case**
> individual's initial burden of proof when asserting an employment discrimination claim

Consistent with filing a disparate treatment claim under Title VII, an individual filing a disparate treatment claim under the ADEA must first present a ***prima facie* case** of age discrimination. Under the ADEA, this would require showing that an individual who was 40 years of age or older was subjected to an adverse employment decision. This initial burden is a minimal one, but it must be established to proceed with a claim.

B. PROOF

Once the minimal burden of proof is established, the individual must provide direct or circumstantial evidence suggesting that the adverse employment decision was based on the individual's age or an age-related factor.[4]

1. DIRECT EVIDENCE

direct evidence
clear proof that discriminatory conduct occurred

The most straightforward way to prove age discrimination is by presenting **direct evidence** that it occurred. A supervisor's testimony that his company prefers not to hire older individuals because they tend to resist using computers and other new forms of technology is an example of direct evidence of age discrimination. In this case, the supervisor is making it clear that the company is using age as a motivating factor in making employment decisions, which violates the ADEA.

Although direct evidence is desirable, it is often difficult to obtain. Most employers have a basic knowledge of workplace anti-discrimination laws and do not engage in intentional discrimination. Further, even if an employer knowingly engages in discriminatory behavior, it is not likely to openly share its discriminatory motives. Even in the absence of direct evidence, however, there are other ways an individual can establish that an employer unlawfully considered her age when making an employment decision.

2. CIRCUMSTANTIAL EVIDENCE

circumstantial evidence
proof that suggests, but does not conclude, that discriminatory conduct occurred

In the absence of direct evidence, an individual can present **circumstantial evidence** to support an age discrimination claim. While this evidence is not conclusive proof that age was the motivating factor in making an adverse decision, it suggests that age was considered.

For example, an employee might present evidence showing that employees in their early 30s were compensated at a higher rate than similarly situated employees who were in their early 50s. This evidence does not necessarily prove that the employer engaged in discriminatory conduct, but it does suggest the possibility that such conduct did occur. This evidence probably would be sufficient to shift the burden of proof to the employer to defend the employee's claim of age discrimination by showing that the employer's decision to pay the different rates of compensation was not based on age or on an age-related factor.

C. EMPLOYER DEFENSES TO EVIDENCE OF DISCRIMINATORY CONDUCT

In response to the presentation of direct or circumstantial evidence of age discrimination, the burden of proof shifts to the employer to defend its employment decision.

1. LEGITIMATE, NONDISCRIMINATORY REASON

Employers have significant latitude to explain the basis for making an adverse employment decision and to illustrate that age or an age-related factor was not the motivating consideration. For example, employers can defend an allegation of discriminatory conduct based on age by providing evidence to support a **legitimate, nondiscriminatory reason** for the imposition of the adverse decision on the older employee. Specifically, the statutory language of the ADEA provides that an employer would not be subject to liability for the imposition of an adverse action on an individual 40 years old or older if the basis for its decision was a **reasonable factor other than age (RFOA)**.[5]

An RFOQ will be "reasonable" only if it has a bearing on whether the individual can perform the key job tasks, and is unrelated to age (which, if permitted, would undermine the purpose of the ADEA). A factor will not be reasonable if it is inherently linked to the passage of time, because that would disadvantage older individuals. For example, an employer could not promote an employee under the age of 40 years instead of an employee who was 50 years of age, claiming "more time left on the job" was an RFOQ.[6] Similarly, an individual could not be rejected for a position because he had too much work experience, because this would also disadvantage older individuals (as they would be more likely than younger individuals to have more experience) and being overqualified is not necessarily linked to whether the individual can perform the job.[7]

Considerations that fall under this exception might relate to education, prior experience, and other measures of the quality or quantity of an individual's work performance. For example, employers who can illustrate that they uniformly apply performance standards and terminate employees who do not meet those standards would not be subject to liability under the ADEA, even if the policy results in termination of some employees who are 40 years of age or older.[8] In addition, as discussed immediately below, an employer may be permitted to consider the amount of time an employee has worked for the employer as the basis for administration of an employer benefit even if this conduct has an adverse impact on older employees.

legitimate, nondiscriminatory reason
employer's burden of proof to present evidence illustrating a valid business justification for the imposition of an adverse employment decision that an individual alleges was based on a discriminatory motivation such as age

reasonable factor other than age (RFOA)
employer's basis for the imposition of an adverse decision on individuals 40 years of age and older that is unrelated to age and therefore not a violation of the ADEA

2. BONA FIDE SENIORITY SYSTEM

The statutory language of the ADEA recognizes that age might be an appropriate basis for an employment decision if consideration of age is necessary to observe the terms of a bona fide seniority system.[9] **Seniority** is a measure of an employee's years of service with an employer, and a **bona fide seniority system** uses this length of service to determine the appropriate benefit level for the employee.

The Supreme Court reinforced the permissibility of considering age for purposes of a bona fide seniority system. Specifically, the Court allows such systems to operate even if the result has a disparate impact on older employees or perpetuates discrimination that occurred before the passage of the ADEA provided the seniority system is not *designed* to produce the discriminatory result.[10]

seniority
measure of an employee's length of service with an employer

bona fide seniority system
arrangement that provides benefits based on an individual's number of years of service, which is not considered discriminatory provided there is no discriminatory intent

bona fide occupational qualification (BFOQ)
employer's defense to an employment discrimination claim that illustrates the business necessity of considering an individual's membership in a protected class, a characteristic that would be otherwise prohibited

3. BONA FIDE OCCUPATIONAL QUALIFICATION (BFOQ)

Outside the framework of a bona fide seniority system, an employer may have the right to consider an individual's age when making employment decisions by showing that there is a business necessity that warrants this consideration. The statute provides an exception to the prohibition against age discrimination if the employer can show that age is a BFOQ, meaning the consideration of age is "reasonably necessary to the normal operation of the particular business."[11]

For example, the BFOQ defense is available if an employer can show that because individuals over a certain age cannot perform certain job tasks, it is appropriate to categorically decline to consider such applicants for a position. This exception is interpreted narrowly, which is appropriate based on the statutory language, the ADEA's legislative history, and the limited circumstances under which the EEOC accepts this defense when enforcing the statute.[12]

When asserting the BFOQ defense to justify the disqualification of older employees, the burden is on the employer to illustrate that applicants in that age group are unable to perform the key job responsibilities of the position. This determination must be based on objective considerations that relate to the actual performance of a task or to safety concerns rather than stereotypes or generalizations about the abilities of older employees.[13]

For example, an employer would likely be prohibited from asserting the BFOQ defense to justify an upper age limit for individuals applying for a position requiring physical labor because "[t]he basic research in the field of aging has established that there is a wide range of physical ability regardless of age."[14] Instead, the employer would have a legal obligation to evaluate the physical ability of each individual applicant to determine whether he or she has the strength necessary to perform the job tasks.[15] An employer would not be required to engage in this individualized analysis and the BFOQ would likely be accepted, however, if it could show that the discriminatory policy is necessary because of "conditions that pertain to that age group," and the situation makes it "highly impractical to deal with the older employees on an individual basis."[16]

The Supreme Court applied this standard when ruling on the appropriateness of an employer's assertion of the BFOQ defense to justify its policy, which imposed a firm cutoff of 60 years of age for flight engineers. In rejecting the employer's position that the defense was appropriate based on safety concerns, the Court reasoned that there were likely a number of older individuals who would be perfectly capable of continuing to perform the work beyond age 60.[17] The Court also found it particularly significant that the employer relied on individualized testing to address other safety concerns, that other industry employers only required mandatory retirement at age 70, and that the Agency responsible for airline safety previously determined that individualized testing would not be an undue burden.[18]

Despite decisions such as this, the BFOQ defense for age discrimination is most successful when asserted within the context of safety concerns linked to positions that require driving or flying. However, the well-established narrow application of the BFOQ defense requires an employer to show that the individuals who would be eliminated from consideration based on the restriction would be unable to safely perform the job tasks (if at all), and that individualized testing would not be an option.[19] See Chapter 2, Title VII — The Foundation of Workplace Discrimination Law.

D. PRETEXT

pretext
employer's justification for making an adverse employment decision, which is a cover-up for the true discriminatory motivation

Because the ultimate burden of proof in a discrimination claim rests with the individual filing the claim, after an employer presents a legitimate, nondiscriminatory reason for its decision, the burden of proof shifts back to the individual making the allegation to show that the justification presented by the employer is actually a pretext, or a cover-up, for the true discriminatory motive.

For example, if an employer states that a 45-year-old employee was not promoted because of the employer's new policy that requires all high-level employees to possess a graduate degree, the employee can attempt to establish that this is a pretext by showing that two recently promoted high-level employees, both younger than 40 years old, did not have that level of education. If the individual asserting the claim is successful in proving that the employer's stated reason for making the decision was a pretext, the employer will likely be subject to liability for discrimination and damages will be awarded.

It is possible, however, that even after an individual shows that an employer's motivation was a pretext, pursuant to the pretext-plus theory, the individual will have an additional burden (the "plus") to show that consideration of an individual's age was the motivating factor behind the employer's adverse decision. Further, there are a number of ways an employer might assert that a reduced damage award for the discriminatory conduct is appropriate, particularly if the employer made the adverse decision based on a mixed-motive, meaning the decision was based on both legitimate and discriminatory considerations. See Chapter 2, Title VII — The Foundation of Workplace Discrimination Law, for a detailed discussion about the pretext-plus theory and mixed-motive claims.

DISPARATE IMPACT DISCRIMINATION

disparate impact claim
employment discrimination claim based on a policy or practice that is neutral on its face but results in a disproportionate impact on members of a protected class.

Under Title VII, an individual has the right to file both disparate treatment claims, based on intentional discrimination, and **disparate impact claims**, based on the implementation of a policy or practice that is neutral on its face but that produces a discriminatory result.

Assuming that an individual was alleging that the employer engaged in intentional age discrimination, the shifting of the burden of proof as set out above would govern the presentation of proof. Because the statutory language of the ADEA tracks much of Title VII, and the framework for the presentation of proof for a disparate treatment claim under the ADEA tracks the presentation of a comparable claim under Title VII, this suggests that the same parallels would apply to disparate impact claims. However, whether the disparate impact theory established for unintentional discrimination under Title VII would be transferable to claims of unintentional discrimination under the ADEA was historically a legal question that was answered differently by different courts.[20] This uncertainty remained until the Supreme Court determined that a disparate impact claim was available within the context of age discrimination but that its application was narrower than its application under Title VII, which makes it easier for an employer to present a defense to it.

A. APPLICABILITY OF ANALYSIS

In a number of instances in which this issue of whether an individual could file a disparate impact claim under the ADEA was initially raised, the Supreme Court declined to rule on it.[21] When the issue continued to surface, the Court issued a 1999 concurring opinion suggesting that this framework would not necessarily apply to claims of age discrimination because stereotypes relating to age might be used for different purposes than those linked to race, color, religion, sex, and national origin, which are the protected classes under Title VII.[22] Due to this lack of definitiveness, however, even after this decision, the issue remained an open legal question.

It was not until 2005 that the Supreme Court determined that disparate impact claims would be available for ADEA claims, based on the statutory language stating that an employer could not impose an employment action that resulted in an adverse impact "because of such individual's age."[23] However, the Court also decided that employers would have much more flexibility to defend a disparate impact claim for age discrimination than for a similar claim that arose under Title VII, because the older individuals availing themselves of this theory would have to identify the specific practice that had the adverse impact and the employer would have the opportunity to defend its conduct by illustrating that the reason for the adverse decision was any "reasonable factor other than age."[24] Because an individual can file a disparate impact claim under the ADEA, it is important to understand how the disparate impact analysis applies, including the initial burden of proof for the individual asserting the claim, and the manner in which an employer could defend its unintentional discriminatory conduct.

B. FRAMEWORK

Because Title VII is the statute for which the framework was initially established, a detailed explanation of the presentation of a disparate impact claim is provided in Chapter 2, Title VII — The Foundation of Workplace Discrimination Law. However, due to its applicability to ADEA claims, a brief review is warranted here.

The presentation of a disparate impact claim, like the presentation of a disparate treatment claim, involves shifting the burden of proof between the individual filing the claim and the employer defending its actions. The individual asserting the claim must present a *prima facie* case of age discrimination, which is the imposition of a facially neutral policy that has a disproportionate impact on individuals 40 years of age and older. After the *prima facie* case is established, the burden shifts to the employer to show that the challenged policy or practice is both job related and a business necessity. Once the employer satisfies this burden, the employee can still sustain his claim by presenting a less discriminatory alternative that would have had a lesser impact on the protected class.

 ## BENEFITS

Disparate treatment and disparate impact age discrimination claims may stem from any terms and conditions of employment. Nevertheless, there are a few areas that are particularly susceptible to allegations of age discrimination claims, and many relate to the availability of employee benefits.

A. EMPLOYEES MUST GENERALLY RECEIVE SAME BENEFITS

Because the ADEA prohibits discrimination against individuals who are 40 years of age or older, employers are generally required to provide the same level of benefits to employees regardless of their age. For example, employers should not offer job training only to laid-off employees under the age of 50, or provide life insurance only to employees of a certain age. Further, benefits will not be considered the same if there is a specific age after which the benefits are no longer provided. Thus, it would be impermissible for an employer to provide disability benefits to employees only until they reach age 62, because this policy results in the denial of a benefit to older employees, such as those who are 63 years old, based solely on their age.[25]

Despite the importance of providing and administering benefits in a nondiscriminatory manner, the goal is balanced against the reality that, because providing certain benefits to older employees might cost significantly more than providing comparable benefits to younger employees, employers might be reluctant to hire older employees. Based on this, there are some circumstances under which an employer might present a valid defense for the unequal treatment of older employees or a statutory exception might apply.[26]

B. EQUAL-COST DEFENSE TO JUSTIFY OFFERING OF REDUCED BENEFITS

In some cases, an employer may be permitted to provide older employees with reduced benefits by asserting the **equal-cost defense**, which is an employer's explanation for providing older employees with lesser benefits based on a showing that it spent an equal amount of money to provide the reduced benefits as it spent to provide younger employees with the same type of benefits.[27] For example, an

equal-cost defense
employer's explanation for providing older employees with lesser benefits based upon showing that it spent an equal amount of money to provide the benefits as it spent to provide younger employees with the same type of benefits

employer might assert this defense to justify its decision to provide $50,000 life insurance policies to its younger employees and $40,000 policies to its older employees if the cost incurred to provide these two levels of coverage is equal.[28]

The equal-cost defense is available only for life insurance, health insurance, and disabilities benefits, because these costs increase with age.[29] Employers cannot use this defense to explain providing fewer sick days or vacation days to older employees, because there is no inherent increased cost associated with providing these benefits to aging employees.

C. ALTERNATIVE SOURCE OF FUNDING

Employers might also be able to reduce certain benefits if, as employees age, they become entitled to enhanced benefits and other sources of income pursuant to federal and state laws. Thus, for example, an employer might be permitted to reduce the benefits it offers to older employees if the affected employees will be able to make up for the difference from other sources such as Medicare and Social Security.[30]

D. BONA FIDE EMPLOYEE RETIREMENT PLANS

In addition to the identification of circumstances that might permit an employer to offer different levels of benefits to older employees based on financial considerations, the ADEA also allows for the consideration of age "to observe the terms of a . . . bona fide employee benefit plan such as a retirement, pension, or insurance plan, which is not a subterfuge to evade the purposes of this Act."[31]

Retirement plans are a particularly important component of employee compensation packages and are discussed in further detail in Chapter 12, Compensation and Benefits. An additional discussion about these plans is also warranted here because such benefits have the potential to raise a number of issues under the ADEA due to the unavoidable link between retirement and an individual's age.

1. MANDATORY RETIREMENT PLANS

As a general rule the ADEA prohibits mandatory retirement plans because they force employees to leave employment upon reaching a certain age. There are a few exceptions, however, for employees working in law enforcement, as firefighters, and for some highly compensated executives and other policy makers.[32]

2. VOLUNTARY EARLY RETIREMENT INCENTIVES

In some circumstances the ADEA allows employers to provide early retirement incentives to encourage older employees to leave their employment to offset the salary and benefits costs that would otherwise be paid by the employer.[33] In creating early retirement incentives employers are permitted to (1) determine eligibility based on a minimum age or number of years of service; (2) require employees to decide whether they want to accept this incentive by a certain deadline; and (3) offer the incentive to a select group of employees, such as those holding a position of a certain level or working in a particular facility.[34]

Even though voluntary early retirement plans and incentives are permissible and not necessarily evidence of discriminatory conduct, such plans are regulated and closely scrutinized because of the inherent link between retirement and the age of an employee. For example, employers that offer early retirement incentives are not permitted to discriminate against different segments of the aging population by offering those employees who decide to retire in their 60s greater incentives than those who decide to retire in their 70s.[35] In reviewing these plans, significant attention is paid to these plans to ensure that voluntary retirement plans are nondiscriminatory and truly voluntary, and this is a recurring theme in both judicial decisions and Congressional legislation designed to guarantee these results.

a. Judicial Decisions to Ensure Voluntariness

In determining whether a retirement plan is voluntary, courts look to a number of factors to ensure that continued employment remains a viable option for aging employees. Courts will consider whether (1) employees are given sufficient time to consider their options; (2) employees are provided with sufficient information to make informed decisions; (3) employees were coerced into making their decisions; (4) employees would be subject to adverse employment consequences for declining the offer; and (5) employees had the opportunity to receive independent advice as to the appropriate decision.[36]

b. Congressional Action to Ensure Voluntariness

In response to the increasingly common employer defense to age discrimination claims that older employees were retiring voluntarily, Congress passed the **Older Workers Benefit Protection Act (OWBPA)**, which amended the ADEA and requires employers to ensure that any agreement designed to prevent an employee from filing a claim under the ADEA must provide older employees with sufficient information to ensure that the agreement represents a knowing and voluntary waiver of their rights.[37]

Older Workers Benefit Protection Act (OWBPA) federal law requiring that agreements intended to prevent employees from asserting their rights under the ADEA be knowing and voluntary waivers

For a waiver to apply to claims that would be filed under the ADEA it must (1) be in writing and be understandable; (2) specifically reference the ADEA; (3) waive only past claims and have no impact on claims that might arise in the future; (4) be in exchange for valuable consideration; (5) include a written provision suggesting that the affected employee consult an attorney prior to signing the waiver; and (6) provide the employee with at least 21 days to review and consider the agreement (45 days in a group layoff) and a 7-day period after its execution during which the individual retains the right to revoke the agreement.[38] Absent a valid waiver, an individual who retires would retain the right to pursue a claim under the ADEA alleging that her decision to retire was not voluntary but instead was the result of discriminatory conduct that would subject an employer to liability. See Chapter 20, Severance and Post-Employment Obligations for a detailed discussion about release agreements and the significance of the OWBPA.

KEY TERMS

- ✓ Age Discrimination in Employment Act (ADEA)
- ✓ bona fide occupational qualification (BFOQ)
- ✓ bona fide seniority system
- ✓ circumstantial evidence
- ✓ direct evidence
- ✓ disparate impact claim
- ✓ disparate treatment claim
- ✓ equal-cost defense
- ✓ legitimate, nondiscriminatory reason
- ✓ Older Workers Benefit Protection Act (OWBPA)
- ✓ pretext
- ✓ *prima facie* case
- ✓ reasonable factor other than age (RFOA)
- ✓ seniority

DISCUSSION QUESTIONS

Explain your response to each of the following questions with the understanding that in some cases there is no right or wrong answer. If you cannot make an informed decision with the facts provided, indicate the nature and significance of the additional information you would need. For the purposes of these questions, you can assume that the employers and employees mentioned below are covered by the ADEA and other relevant federal workplace anti-discrimination laws.

1. Provide a set of facts that would support a claim of age discrimination under the disparate treatment theory and one that would support a claim of age discrimination under the disparate impact theory.
2. Provide an example of a statement by an employer that would be considered direct evidence of age discrimination.
3. Do you agree with an employer's statement that he will never be permitted to terminate a 72-year-old employee without being subject to liability for age discrimination? Why or why not?
4. Provide a set of facts that would support an employer's defense that age is a BFOQ.
5. Provide a set of facts that would likely not be sufficient to support an employer's BFOQ defense in response to a claim of age discrimination.
6. Buddy is an engineer who owns a farmer's market and wants to hire 25 additional employees to assist him in planting a garden that will feed the entire town. Because Buddy believes young people are stronger than those who have aged, he decides to ask his children, Richard, Glen, and Ellen, whether they have any friends in their 20s who might be interested in the position. Buddy knows about the prohibition against age discrimination, but he says his need for strong employees is a "reasonable factor other than age," so he is not concerned about any potential liability. What do you think?

7. Beverly applies for a position as a salesperson at a local car dealership despite the fact that she has no prior sales experience. The employer says she has great potential but asks whether she intends to retire in the near future because he is concerned about investing a significant amount of money to train her if she does not intend to work for at least four more years. Beverly responds that she is only 50 years old and intends to work for at least 20 years. After further consideration, the employer decides to hire a 34-year-old candidate with ten years of prior sales experience. Do you think Beverly might have a claim of age discrimination?

8. It is a known fact that Ellen's catering business is in financial trouble. In response to the concern that the business will go bankrupt and all of the employees will lose their jobs, a group of older employees approach Ellen and tell her if she offers them early retirement incentives, they might consider retiring, which would significantly reduce the company's payroll costs. Ellen explains this is not an option, because any consideration of age with respect to employment matters will subject her to liability under Title VII for age discrimination, which would only add to her dire financial situation. What do you think?

9. Rosemarie owns a company that sells roller blades. She decides she will not hire salespeople over the age of 50 because it is unlikely they will know how to use the equipment. When a group of 55-year-old men file a claim of age discrimination, she asserts that age is a BFOQ for the position. Do you think this is a valid defense?

ENDNOTES

1. 29 U.S.C. § 630(b). Some state laws protect employees who are younger than 40 years of age. *See, e.g.*, Minn. Stat. § 363A.03 (prohibiting age discrimination in employment practice against persons over the age of majority).

2. U.S. Equal Employment Opportunity Commn., Age Discrimination in Employment Act (includes concurrent charges with Title VII, ADA, and EPA) FY 1997–FY 2009 (available at *http://www.eeoc.gov/eeoc/statistics/enforcement/adea.cfm*).

3. *McDonnell Douglas Corp. v. Green*, 411 U.S. 792 (1973).

4. The Supreme Court has held that a person who is age 40 or over and discriminated against based on age in favor of another person age 40 or over (and therefore also in the protected class) might still have a viable claim of age discrimination if there is a significant age difference between the two. *O'Connor v. Consolidated Coin Caterers Corp.*, 517 U.S. 308 (1996). The Supreme Court clarified this position in subsequent cases, holding that even if age was a motivating factor in selecting one member of a protected class over another, the protection would only be available if one individual was relatively older than the other. *General Dynamics Land Sys. v. Cline*, 540 U.S. 581 (2004).

5. *Geller v. Markham*, 635 F.2d 1027, 1035 (2d Cir. 1980).

6. *Taggart v. Time, Inc.*, 924 F.2d 43 (2d Cir. 1991).

7. 29 U.S.C. § 623(f)(1).

8. 29 U.S.C. § 623(f)(3).

9.   29 U.S.C. § 623(f)(2).

10. *Pullman-Standard v. Swint*, 456 U.S. 273, 276 (1982).

11. 29 U.S.C. § 623(f)(1); *see* 29 U.S.C. §§ 621-634; 42 U.S.C. § 2000-2(e).

12. *Western Airlines v. Criswell*, 472 U.S. 400, 409-412 (1985); *Dothard v. Rawlinson*, 433 U.S. 321, 334 (1977) (stating the BFOQ exception was meant to be an extremely narrow exception to the general prohibition against age discrimination contained in the ADEA); *see also* 29 C.F.R. § 1604.2(a) (2008) (stating the BFOQ exception for sex should be construed narrowly).

13. *Western Airlines v. Criswell*, 472 U.S. 400 (1985).

14. *Western Airlines v. Criswell*, 472 U.S. at 409 (citing Report of the Secretary of Labor, The Older American Worker: Age Discrimination in Employment 9 (1965); EEOC, Legislative History of the Age Discrimination in Employment Act 26 (1981); S. Rep. No. 95-493, at 2 (1977); and Legislative History 435).

15. *See* New York State Div. of Human Rights, Recommendations on Employment Inquiries (rev. Dec. 2004) (available at *http://www.dhr.state.ny.us/pdf/employment.pdf*).

16. *Western Airlines v. Criswell*, 472 U.S. 400, 418 (1985).

17. *Id.*

18. 472 U.S. at 423.

19. 472 U.S. at 401.

20. *See, e.g., Smith v. City of Des Moines*, 99 F.3d 1466 (8th Cir. 1996); *Mangold v. California Pub. Utilities Commn.*, 67 F.3d 1470 (9th Cir. 1995) (permitting disparate impact claims for age discrimination). *But see Ellis v. United Airlines, Inc.*, 73 F.3d 999 (1995); *EEOC v. Francis W. Parker School.*, 41 F.3d 1073 (7th Cir. 1994) (refusing to permit disparate impact claims for age discrimination).

21. *See, e.g., Markham v. Geller*, 451 U.S. 945 (1981) (Rehnquist, J., dissenting) (disagreeing with the Court's refusal to hear the question of whether the disparate impact model should apply to claims filed under the ADEA).

22. *Hazen Paper Co. v. Biggins*, 507 U.S. 604, 618 (1993) (Kennedy, J. concurring).

23. *Smith v. City of Jackson*, 544 U.S. 228 (2005) (citing 29 U.S.C. § 623 (a)(2)).

24. *Id; see also* U.S. Equal Employment Opportunity Commn., Background Information for EEOC Notice of Proposed Rulemaking on the Definition of "Reasonable Factors Other Than Age" Under the Age Discrimination in Employment Act of 1967 (available at *http://www.eeoc.gov/laws/regulations/qanda_reasonable_factors.cfm*).

25. *See generally* EEOC Compl. Man. ch. 3 (Employee Benefits) (available at *http://www.eeoc.gov/policy/docs/benefits.html*).

26. An employer's assertion that its medical plan complies with the Employee Retirement Income Security Act of 1974 (ERISA), the federal law that governs employee benefit plans, will not constitute a valid defense to an age discrimination claim. EEOC Compl. Man. chs. 3 (Employee Benefits), 1 (Introduction) (available at *http://www.eeoc.gov/policy/docs/benefits.html*).

27. *See* 29 C.F.R. § 1625.10; *see* EEOC Compl. Man. chs. 3 (Employee Benefits), 1 (Introduction) (available at *http://www.eeoc.gov/policy/docs/benefits.html*). To prevent the imposition of liability based on this defense, an employer must show the following elements: (1) the benefit must become more expensive with age; (2) the benefit must be part of a bona fide employee benefit plan; (3) the actual amount of the payments made or the cost incurred on behalf of an older worker is not less than the payment made on behalf of a younger worker; and (4) the benefits provided to the older employee is reduced only to the extent necessary to equalize these costs. 29 U.S.C. § 623(f)(2)(B)(i). To the extent an employer is permitted to impose this reduction due to the increased out-of-pocket cost to cover older employees, those employees may be provided with the option to contribute to the benefit costs to maintain the prior level of coverage. This employee contribution, however, can reflect only the increased cost tied to the aging of the employee, and while employees may agree to pay the difference, an employer cannot require that they do so. 29 C.F.R. § 1625.10(d)(4).

28. *Id.*

29. *See generally* U.S. Equal Employment Opportunity Commn., Informal Discussion Letter, ADEA: Benefits (available at *http://www.eeoc.gov/eeoc/foia/letters/2001/adea_benefits.html*); *Erie County Retirees Assn. v. County of Erie, Pennsylvania*, 220 F.3d 193 (3d Cir. 2000) (allowing equal cost defense for retiree medical benefits).

30. EEOC Compl. Man. ch. 3 (Employee Benefits) (available at *http://www.eeoc.gov/policy/docs/benefits.html*).

31. 29 C.F.R. § 1625.10 (benefit plans); 29 U.S.C. § 623(f)(2)(B) (retirement), (f)(2)(A) (seniority system).

32. 29 U.S.C.A. §§ 623(j) (law enforcement officers and firefighters), 631(c) (bona fide executives or high-level policy makers), 630(f) (government policy makers).

33. EEOC Compl. Man. chs. 3 (Employee Benefits), 1 (Introduction) (available at *http://www.eeoc.gov/policy/docs/benefits.html*).

34. EEOC Compl. Man. ch. 3 (Employee Benefits) § 6 (Early Retirement Incentives) (available at *http://www.eeoc.gov/policy/docs/benefits.html*).

35. *See, e.g., Jankovitz v. Des Moines Indep. Cmty. Sch. Dist.*, 421 F.3d 649 (8th Cir. 2005).

36. *See, e.g., Auerbach v. Board of Education*, 136 F.3d 104, 113 (2d Cir. 1998) (holding plan was voluntary since employees received complete and accurate information, received four months to make a decision, and did not present evidence suggesting decisions were coerced); *Anderson v. Montgomery Ward & Co., Inc.*, 650 F. Supp. 1480 (N.D. Ill. 1987) (holding the voluntariness of a retirement plan was a factual issue to be decided by a court when some employees were encouraged to reject the offer and others were threatened with termination if they decided to reject it); *see generally* EEOC Compl. Man. ch. 3 (Employee Benefits) (available at *http://www.eeoc.gov/policy/docs/benefits.html*).

37. The OWBPA also requires employers to present a cost-based justification for treating older employees differently than other plan participants. *See, e.g., Auerbach v. Board of Educ.*, 136 F.3d 104, 113 (2d Cir. 1998) (citing 123 Cong. Rec. 34,295 (1977)).

38. 29 U.S.C. § 626(f); *see* EEOC Regulations, Waiver of Rights and Claims Under the Age Discrimination in Employment Act (ADEA); 29 C.F.R. pt. 1625.

Disability Discrimination

7

Chapter Objectives

This chapter explores the prohibition of workplace discrimination against qualified individuals with physical and mental disabilities as provided for under the Americans with Disabilities Act (ADA) and the ADA Amendments Act of 2008 (ADAAA). The text begins with a description of conditions that would constitute a disability by substantially limiting a major life activity. This is followed by a discussion about the obligations employers have to reasonably accommodate disabled individuals provided it does not impose an undue burden on the employer, as well as the types of alterations to working conditions that might be appropriate.

After completing this chapter, students should have a fundamental understanding of how to determine whether an individual is entitled to benefits and protections under the ADA and the amendments to the Act. In addition, students should understand the extent of an employer's obligation to provide a reasonable accommodation to a qualified individual with a disability, and be able to identify the factors that are used to determine whether an accommodation would impose an undue burden on an employer.

Specifically, upon mastering the main objectives of this chapter students should be able to

- define *disability* under the ADA and its amendments, and identify the types of medical conditions that fit within and fall outside the Act's coverage;
- provide examples of major life activities and explain their relevance to determining whether an individual is entitled to the benefits and protections of the ADA;
- explain the extent to which an employer is obligated to provide a reasonable accommodation and what might impose an undue burden;
- provide examples of reasonable accommodations that an employer might provide to a qualified individual with a disability;
- describe the framework for presenting an ADA claim in a judicial forum; and
- explain the circumstances that might obligate an employer to approve an individual's request for a disability leave, as well as the employer's obligations to an employee returning from such a leave.

INTRODUCTION TO THE AMERICANS WITH DISABILITIES ACT (ADA) AND THE ADA AMENDMENTS ACT OF 2008 (ADAAA)

Americans with Disabilities Act of 1990 (ADA)
federal law that prohibits discrimination against qualified individuals with physical and mental disabilities

ADA Amendments Act of 2008 (ADAAA)
amendments to the ADA that reinforce the broad scope of the term *disability* and provide guidance relating to types of conditions protected by the Act and the extent of limitations to the protections

The **Americans with Disabilities Act of 1990 (ADA)** prohibits discrimination against qualified individuals based on their physical and mental disabilities. The **ADA Amendments Act of 2008 (ADAAA)** amended the ADA and reinforces the broad scope of the term *disability* and provides guidance relating to the types of conditions of conditions that are protected by the Act and the extent of limitations to those protections.[1]

Consistent with other workplace anti-discrimination laws, the ADA is enforced by the Equal Employment Opportunity Commission (EEOC), and it applies to public- and private-sector employers with 15 or more employees, although many states have laws that apply to employers with fewer employees.[2] Both the ADA and the amendments to it apply to all terms and conditions of employment, from creating job applications and arranging interviews, to recruiting, hiring, training, promoting, compensating, and terminating employees.

A. POTENTIAL LIABILITY

According to the EEOC, in 2009 it received 21,451 charges of disability discrimination. In the same year it resolved 18,776 charges, recovering $67.8 million for aggrieved parties, which does not include monetary benefits obtained through litigation.[3] Employers must know their obligations under the ADA because they can be subjected to significant penalties for refusing to offer accommodations to disabled employees and for terminating such employees because of their inability to perform the essential job functions. For example, one employer agreed to pay $250,000 to settle a disability discrimination lawsuit for its failure to accommodate a disabled employee and subsequently terminating his employment.[4]

B. EMPLOYMENT NOT GUARANTEED

Although the ADA imposes some obligations on an employer, the obligations do not include offering positions to unqualified applicants or guaranteeing continued employment. Instead, employers are required to assess whether a disabled individual is qualified for a position and if so, the employer may have an obligation to provide the individual with a reasonable accommodation. Because these obligations are applicable only to individuals who have a disability, the first question to tackle is whether the individual's condition constitutes a disability. An individual might have a serious medical condition but not be entitled to any benefits or protections under the ADA if the condition does not fit within the definition of *disability*.

 **DEFINITION OF *DISABILITY***

The ADA prohibits workplace discrimination against qualified individuals with disabilities, and the prohibition applies to all terms and conditions of employment. The ADA applies to a wide range of medical conditions and the ADAAA, which reinforces the Congressional intent to interpret the term broadly. Specifically, the ADAAA defines an individual with a disability as someone who

1. has a physical or mental impairment that substantially limits one or more major life activities; or
2. has a record of such an impairment; or
3. is regarded as having such an impairment.[5]

A. IMPAIRMENTS

There is no exhaustive list of the conditions that constitute *disabilities*. The statutory language of the ADA makes it clear that the term *impairment* should be interpreted broadly and include both physical and mental conditions.

1. TYPES OF IMPAIRMENTS

a. Physical Impairments

An individual may be entitled to the benefits and protections of the ADA based on a physical impairment. **Physical impairments** include any "physiological disorder, or condition, cosmetic disfigurement, or anatomical loss that affects one or more of the following body systems: neurological, musculoskeletal, special sense organs, respiratory (including speech organs), cardiovascular, reproductive, digestive, genito-urinary, hemic and lymphatic, skin, and endocrine conditions."[6] In addition, courts have held that individuals infected with contagious diseases such as tuberculosis and HIV are entitled to protection under the ADA.[7]

physical impairment
physiological disorder or condition, cosmetic disfigurement, or anatomical loss that may constitute a disability under the ADA

In some instances physical conditions are easy to identify, but in other instances they may not be so obvious. For example, an individual who is in a wheelchair would have an obvious physical impairment. But, an individual's respiratory condition, which also constitutes a physical impairment, would not be detectable by an employer or potential employer.

b. Mental Impairments

The ADA also applies to **mental impairments,** which are mental or psychological disorders, such as an emotional or mental illness.[8] These impairments are often difficult to assess because they are rarely readily identifiable.

mental impairment
a mental or psychological disorder that may constitute a disability under the ADA

Courts have provided some guidance relating to mental impairments, determining, for example, that dyslexia, retardation, emotional illnesses, and learning disabilities are considered mental impairments under the ADA.[9] The ADA also makes it clear that compulsive gambling, kleptomania, and pyromania are conditions that are outside the coverage of the Act.[10]

2. IMPAIRMENT MUST SUBSTANTIALLY LIMIT A MAJOR LIFE ACTIVITY

After it is determined that an individual has a physical or mental impairment, the next relevant inquiry is whether the condition substantially limits a major life activity.

a. Major Life Activity

major life activities
functions that are significant to an individual's daily life (e.g., walking, speaking, breathing) that must be substantially limited by a condition for the condition to constitute a disability for the purposes of the ADA

Major life activities are those functions that an average person can engage in with little or no difficulty, such as walking, breathing, seeing, hearing, and speaking.[11] The ADAAA provides significant guidance about what constitutes a major life activity. Most notably, the amendments include an extensive but nonexclusive list of major life activities, which include caring for oneself, performing manual tasks, seeing, hearing, eating, sleeping, walking, standing, lifting, bending, speaking, learning, reading, thinking, and communicating.[12] Further, the ADAAA makes it clear that major bodily functions, such as those associated with the immune system, normal cell growth, and digestive, bowel, bladder, neurological, brain, circulatory, respiratory, endocrine, and reproductive functions, all constitute major life activities.[13]

The purpose of the more expansive list included in the ADAAA was to make it more likely that individuals with certain impairments would fall within the class of individuals the ADA was designed to protect. For example, an individual with cancer who can demonstrate that the disease has resulted in a substantial limitation to normal cell growth would be entitled to protection under the ADA because cell growth constitutes a major life activity under the ADAAA.[14] Further, an individual who is undergoing chemotherapy treatments and is too exhausted to care for herself would likely be considered disabled under the ADA because caring for oneself is a major life activity.[15]

b. Substantial Limitation

substantial limitation
extent to which a major life activity must be restricted by an impairment for it to be considered a disability for the purpose of ADA coverage

For the condition that causes the impairment of a major life activity to constitute a disability, the impairment must result in a **substantial limitation** of the activity, as opposed to being a condition that merely makes it a challenge to perform the particular function. For example, a person with varicose veins would not be entitled to protection under the ADA unless the condition substantially limited the individual's ability to walk or stand (or engage in another major life activity), despite the fact that the condition might be incredibly painful.[16]

Courts have historically determined that an impairment had to prevent or severely restrict the ability of an individual to perform a major life activity before the resulting limitation would constitute a substantial limitation. Congress concluded these standards were too restrictive, and through the passage of the ADAAA, it decided that the determination of the presence of a substantial limitation should be based on a commonsense assessment that compares an individual's ability to perform a major life activity with the ability of those who do not have the condition.[17] Therefore, under the current law, the ability of the individual with an impairment to walk (a major life activity) would have to be compared to the ability of those in the general population who engage in the same practice (walking) to determine whether a substantial limitation exists.[18]

i. Limitation Might Stem from a Related Condition

In some circumstances, an individual might have a disability based on a condition that developed as a result of an underlying medical condition that would not independently be protected under the ADA. For example, someone might have an illness such as diabetes that does not substantially limit a major life activity. However, the resulting depression (possibly caused by such a diagnosis) might be severe enough to entitle the individual to protection under the ADA if the depression lasts for a significant period of time and limits the individual's ability to sleep or to eat, as compared to those in the general population.[19]

ii. Mitigating Measures

Mitigating measures refer to devices or other types of assistance that eliminate or reduce the symptoms or impact of an impairment. The ADAAA provides a number of examples of mitigating measures, such as medication, medical equipment, medical devices, and prosthetic limbs. It is important to identify these measures because the ADAAA prohibits consideration of most mitigating measures when determining whether an individual is disabled under the ADA but permits their consideration when determining the nature of a reasonable accommodation that might be appropriate.

mitigating measure
assistance that may eliminate or reduce the extent to which an impairment limits a major life activity

(a) Relevance of Mitigating Measure to Determine Whether an Individual Is Disabled
In determining whether an individual's impairment substantially limits a major life activity, the relevant inquiry is whether, *without* the use of any mitigating measures, an individual would be substantially limited in the performance of a major life activity. For example, an individual who is unable to walk would have an impairment that substantially limits a major life activity, even if, through the use of a prosthetic limb, the individual could walk alongside those in the general population. In this case, the mitigating measure — the prosthetic limb — is not considered when determining whether the individual's ability to walk is substantially limited.[20]

(b) Determining Whether a Reasonable Accommodation Is Required
Despite being prohibited from considering mitigating measures when determining whether an individual is disabled under the ADA, an employer *can* consider the impact of any mitigating measures when determining whether it has an obligation to provide a reasonable accommodation to a disabled individual. Thus, if an individual who walks with a prosthetic limb asks for a reasonable accommodation, the employer can base its decision about what accommodation (if any) would be appropriate on the individual's ability to walk *with* the use of the mitigating device (the prosthetic limb) rather than having to make the determination based on the individual's ability to walk *without* it.[21]

(c) Exception for Ordinary Eyeglasses and Contact Lenses
Although the ADAAA does not permit the consideration of mitigating measures when determining whether a major life activity is substantially limited, there is an

exception related to the use of eyeglasses and contact lenses. Specifically, lenses that are designed to correct vision *can* be considered when assessing whether the performance of a major life activity (seeing) is substantially limited by an impairment.[22] Therefore an individual who is able to achieve 20/20 vision with corrective lenses would not have a medical condition that substantially limits a major life activity (sight), regardless of the extent to which his vision is limited without the lenses. Put simply, the fact that the individual is not able to enjoy this level of eyesight absent that mitigating measure (the corrective lenses) would not entitle him to the benefits and protections under the ADA.[23]

iii. Conditions That Generally Do Not Constitute a Substantial Limitation

Although impairments must be considered on a case-by-case basis to determine whether they would be considered a disability under the ADA, the EEOC provides some guidance about conditions that would generally not substantially limit a major life activity. Specifically, the Agency suggests that a common cold, seasonal or common influenza, a sprained joint, or a broken bone that is expected to heal completely, would not rise to the level of a medical condition warranting protections under the ADA.[24]

Nevertheless, individuals who do not have an impairment that substantially limits a major life activity might still be entitled to the benefits and protections of the ADA if they are subjected to an adverse employment decision based on a record of an impairment.

B. RECORD OF AN IMPAIRMENT

record of an impairment
history of a past medical condition that might entitle an individual to benefits and protections under the ADA

An individual who recovers from a disability may still be entitled to protections under the ADA if the **record of an impairment** is the basis for the imposition of an adverse employment decision. This might occur if an individual is not offered a position because an employer learns of a past psychiatric illness from which the individual has recovered, and uses this past record as the basis for an adverse employment decision.

1. EMPLOYER PREJUDICE AND IGNORANCE

An individual who is discriminated against because of ignorance about the contagious nature of a disease or a stigma associated with a past disability would be protected from an adverse employer action that is based on a record of an impairment. For example, in one case the Supreme Court found that a woman who was terminated because her employer learned she had tuberculosis and feared she would contract the disease again and infect others was entitled to protection under the ADA. Even though this individual was not inflicted with a condition that substantially limited a major life activity at the time of the adverse action (the termination), she would still be entitled to protections under the ADA because the record of her past disability was the basis for the adverse decision.[25]

2. VOLUNTEERED INFORMATION ESTABLISHES RECORD

An individual does not have an obligation to provide a prospective employer with information about a disability. However, once this information is disclosed it will establish a record of an impairment and entitle the individual to benefits and protections under the ADA, meaning an employer can be subject to liability under the Act for using this information as the basis for an adverse decision.[26]

For example, if an individual applies for an opportunity for promotional advancement and demonstrates his ability to overcome challenges by revealing he was in an accident that caused permanent hearing loss, that revelation would establish a record of impairment. Even if the applicant also reveals he currently hears better than he did before the accident with the assistance of two hearing aids, he would still be protected under the ADA, because his comments established a record of an impairment.[27] Thus, once the information is revealed, the individual would have a disability based on a record of impairment, as defined by the ADA, and be entitled to the benefits and protections provided under it.

3. EMPLOYER KNOWLEDGE OF PAST IMPAIRMENT

The ADAAA did not amend the language of the disability definition relating to the record of an impairment, but it did clarify that an individual will not have to illustrate that an employer relied on a written document, such as a medical record, to determine that the individual had a record of an impairment. Instead, the relevant inquiry is whether the employer had knowledge of an individual's past impairment, an impairment that substantially limited a major life activity, and whether this knowledge was considered when making an adverse employment decision.[28]

C. REGARDED AS HAVING SUCH AN IMPAIRMENT

An individual might be entitled to the benefits and protections of the ADA if she is **regarded as having an impairment**, meaning an employer makes an adverse employment decision based on an impairment the employer believes the individual has.[29] Thus, an individual might have a viable claim under the ADA even if she never had a physical or mental impairment that substantially limited a major life activity.

This interpretation, which is found in the ADAAA, is broader than the Act's original language, which required the aggrieved individual to show that the employer made an adverse decision based on an impairment or perceived impairment that substantially limited the performance of a major life activity. Under the current law as amended, the aggrieved individual must show only that the motivation for the employer's adverse conduct (such as the allegation of a discriminatory termination) was the employer's belief that the individual's impairment or perceived impairment was not minor or transitory as opposed to proving the employer believed the impairment would substantially limit a major life activity.[30]

regarded as having an impairment
basis for adverse employer action rooted in the employer's belief that an individual has a disability, which could entitle an individual to benefits and protections under the ADA

For example, if an employer declines to extend an offer of employment to an applicant based on the belief that the applicant has cancer, the applicant might file a claim under the ADA. The basis for the claim would be that the employer engaged in discriminatory conduct based on the applicant being regarded as having this impairment, even if the applicant was not afflicted with the disease. Under this set of facts, the applicant would have to illustrate that the employer made the adverse employment decision based on the belief that the applicant had an impairment that was not minor or transitory. This is in contrast to how the law was interpreted before the passage of the ADAAA, which, as explained above, would have required the applicant to show that the employer made the adverse decision based on the employer's belief that the applicant had an impairment (cancer) *and* that it substantially limited a major life activity.[31]

1. INACCURATE CHARACTERIZATION

Employers might also be subject to liability under the ADA for acting upon information that mischaracterizes the impact of an individual's disability, or that stems from fear, gossip, or misinformation. For example, the EEOC issued a report about hearing impairments in the workplace. The report noted that many employers incorrectly assume that individuals with hearing impairments will cause safety issues, increase employment costs, or find it challenging to work in fast-paced environments. Therefore, an employer who decides not to hire an applicant based on such misperceptions could be subject to liability under the ADA.[32]

2. POTENTIAL RISK OF BECOMING DISABLED

An employer is prohibited from making employment decisions based on the possibility that an individual might become disabled. For example, if an employer declines to hire someone because of a family history of cancer (based on the potential for increased medical costs or job attendance issues), the rejected applicant could file a claim under the ADA based on the employer's treating her as if she were disabled even though, in fact, she was not.[33]

D. ILLEGAL DRUG USE AND ALCOHOLISM

Employees who are currently using illegal drugs fall outside the scope of the ADA's coverage and therefore would not be entitled to its protections.[34] However, recovering drug addicts *do* fall within the class of individuals the ADA is intended to protect, and would be entitled to its benefits and protections.[35] Specifically, individuals no longer using illegal drugs could meet the definition of a disability if they (1) have successfully completed a supervised drug rehabilitation program or have otherwise been rehabilitated successfully, or (2) are participating in a supervised rehabilitation program such as Narcotics Anonymous.[36]

Furthermore, an individual with alcoholism is considered disabled and falls within the scope and protections of the ADA if the alcoholism currently substantially limits a major life activity, if the individual has a record of such an impairment, or if the individual is regarded as having such an impairment and either is used as the basis for an adverse employment decision.

The first inquiry, then, is whether the individual falls within the scope of the class of people the ADA is designed to protect. Once it is determined that the individual has a disability in accordance with the definition, the next issue is what obligation, if any, is imposed on an employer or potential employer of that individual.

OBLIGATIONS IMPOSED ON THE EMPLOYER

The ADA does not require an employer to extend an employment offer to a disabled individual, nor does a finding that an individual is disabled guarantee continued employment. Instead, an employer has an obligation to provide a **reasonable accommodation** to qualified individuals with disabilities provided the accommodation will not impose an undue burden on the employer.[37]

reasonable accommodation
alteration made to the working conditions of a qualified individual with a disability that must be provided unless it imposes an undue burden on the employer

A. QUALIFIED INDIVIDUAL WITH A DISABILITY

As a starting point the relevant question is whether an individual is a **qualified individual with a disability**, defined as someone who possesses the skills, experience, and ability to perform the essential functions of the job, with or without a reasonable accommodation.[38] If the disabled individual is qualified for the position, the next issue is what obligation an employer has, if any, to provide a reasonable accommodation to the individual if it is necessary to enable the individual to perform the essential functions of the job.

qualified individual with a disability
individual possessing skills and experience to perform the essential functions of a job with or without a reasonable accommodation

B. EXTENT OF OBLIGATION TO PROVIDE A REASONABLE ACCOMMODATION

Employers have an obligation to provide reasonable accommodations to qualified individuals with a physical or mental impairment that substantially limits at least one major life activity, or to those individuals who have a record of such impairments.

Pursuant to the ADAAA, employers do *not* have an obligation to provide reasonable accommodations to those individuals who fit within the definition of a disabled individual based on being *regarded* as having such impairments.[39] For example, the employer of an individual who is in a car accident and becomes confined to a wheelchair would have to assess whether the employee must be offered a reasonable accommodation, because confinement to a wheelchair is a physical impairment that substantially limits the ability of the employee to walk. In contrast, if an individual is considered disabled because an employer regarded him as having an impairment (such as by drawing the inaccurate conclusion that a diabetic employee would not be able to work long shifts), then the ADA would *not* obligate the employer to provide a reasonable accommodation. Under this set of facts, the diabetic comes within the scope of the definition of *disability* because of being *regarded as having an impairment,* and employers have no obligation to provide reasonable accommodations to such individuals who are entitled to the benefits and protections of the ADA pursuant to this prong of the definition.[40]

1. OBLIGATION APPLIES TO ALL TERMS AND CONDITIONS OF EMPLOYMENT

If an individual is disabled for a reason other than being regarded as having an impairment, the employer's obligation to provide an accommodation is extensive because it applies to all terms and conditions of employment. This includes applying for a position, performing the essential job tasks, and taking advantage of all of the benefits and privileges associated with employment.[41] Therefore, the employer's obligation extends to applicants who are interested in pursuing an employment opportunity, an employee who requests relief from working a particular shift, and an employee who expresses an interest in a particular opportunity for promotional advancement.

Even when the obligation to provide an accommodation exists, however, it is not absolute. The employer is required to provide a reasonable accommodation only to the extent it does not cause an undue burden on the employer. Despite this obligation there is neither a precise definition of reasonableness nor a precise definition of undue burden; both determinations are made based on a fact-specific inquiry.[42]

2. REASONABLENESS OF THE ACCOMMODATION

Whether a particular accommodation is reasonable will depend upon a number of factors, such as whether an employer has limited or extensive flexibility to alter the working conditions of a disabled individual who requests an accommodation. For example, it might be unreasonable to require a small employer who runs a 24-hour operation to relieve a disabled individual from work three times a week to report to medical appointments, but it might be reasonable to impose this obligation upon a larger employer, who presumably has more flexibility to alter its employees' shifts.

3. UNDUE BURDEN

undue burden
burden that an employer will not be required to undertake in an effort to offer a qualified individual with a disability a reasonable accommodation

Even if an accommodation is possible, an employer will not be required to implement it if doing so would impose an **undue burden** on the employer. For example, a nightclub waitress might ask her employer to maintain bright lighting in the club because her permanent vision problem makes it difficult for her to see under dim lights. In this case the employer might be able to show that this accommodation, while necessary for the waitress to continue to perform her work, would constitute an undue burden because it would significantly impact the club's atmosphere and interfere with the ability of its patrons to view the entertainment that is the core of its business.[43]

a. No Obligation to Alter Essential Job Functions

One important consideration used to assess whether an accommodation will impose an undue burden on the employer is whether the individual's disability will prevent the performance of **essential job functions**, which are critical responsibilities associated with the position. If an employer is unable to provide a reasonable accommodation that would enable a qualified individual with a disability to perform an essential job function, it might be an appropriate basis for disqualification of the applicant from consideration, or the termination of a current employee, because requiring an employer to reassign a significant job task would likely constitute an undue burden the employer would not be required to undertake.

> **essential job function**
> a critical responsibility associated with a position; an employer will not be required to significantly alter or reassign it to accommodate a qualified individual with a disability

If, however, a qualified individual with a disability is unable to perform a **tangential task,** which is a noncritical responsibility associated with a position, an employer might be required to modify or reassign that responsibility to accommodate him because it is not a key duty associated with the position, and it is therefore unlikely the change would constitute an undue burden.

> **tangential task**
> noncritical responsibility associated with a position; an employer might be required to alter or reassign it to accommodate a qualified individual with a disability

b. Identifying Essential Job Functions

There is no precise definition of what constitutes an essential versus a tangential task — the determination depends upon the nature of the position — but there are some general guiding principles. For example, a task is considered essential if it is the reason the job exists, such as the need for a proofreader to be able to see the text to be reviewed. In one case the Supreme Court held that an employer did not have an obligation to provide an accommodation to a deaf applicant for a position as a nurse trainee because her disability would prevent her from performing significant job responsibilities associated with the position.[44]

Similarly, if the primary reason an employer seeks to hire a building inspector is to ensure that new buildings are built to code, it is unlikely that the employer would be required to accommodate an employee who was unable to climb into buildings by eliminating the work that needs to be performed on-site.[45] Additionally, tasks that can be completed by only a select number of people would likely be considered essential job functions.[46] It is also generally well established that an employer's obligation to provide a reasonable accommodation would not require the employer to alter production standards or provide assistive devices, such as reading glasses or hearing aids.[47]

4. PRESENCE OF A DIRECT THREAT

The ADA also gives employers the right to refuse to hire an applicant or the right to terminate an employee if her disability would pose a direct threat to the health or safety of the individual or to others. The rationale is that an individual who poses a threat would not be qualified, nor would any accommodation be deemed reasonable, based on the potential risk of harm.[48]

a. Absence of Alternatives

To have the right to reject a disabled individual's request for an accommodation based on safety concerns, an employer must show that the threat poses a significant risk that could result in substantial harm and that providing a reasonable accommodation would not eliminate the danger.

b. Relevant Considerations

To determine whether a potential danger would eliminate the obligation to provide an accommodation, the employer should consider (1) the duration of the risk involved, (2) the nature and severity of the potential harm, (3) the likelihood the harm will occur, (4) the imminence of the potential harm, and (5) the availability of a reasonable accommodation that might reduce or eliminate the threat.[49] For example, if a pizza delivery person has a medical condition that constitutes a disability and causes him to fall asleep without warning, the employer would likely be unable to offer a reasonable accommodation if driving a car is the sole purpose for which he was hired. In this case, the employer would probably be permitted to terminate the employee based on his disability without being subjected to any liability for disability discrimination under the ADA.[50]

C. EMPLOYERS RETAIN THE RIGHT TO DETERMINE THE NATURE OF THE ACCOMMODATION WITHIN THE STATUTORY PARAMETERS

Employers are generally encouraged to work with qualified individuals with disabilities to determine the most appropriate accommodation, particularly when an employer is considering a number of options.[51] Despite the EEOC's desire for the parties to work collaboratively to make these decisions, however, employers are not required to accept an accommodation proposed by the disabled individual. Instead, employers have the right to select the reasonable accommodation that will minimize the impact on its business operations.[52]

Consistent with this, the EEOC has specifically supported the employer's right to make the ultimate decision about which accommodation is to be provided, as long as it is reasonable, eliminates the workplace barrier, and enables the disabled individual to enjoy the same benefits and protections afforded to co-workers. Such benefits and privileges would include such things as ensuring that all employees have the same access to the same opportunities for promotional advancements as well as the same chance to attend educational programs and social events.

D. TYPES OF ACCOMMODATIONS

In considering the types of accommodations that might be appropriate, employers generally have a number of options available to them. There is no exhaustive list of the types of accommodations that might be considered reasonable or that might cause an undue burden, because the determination in each case will be based on the totality of the circumstances relating to the type of disability and job function for which the accommodation is being offered.

1. COMMON ACCOMMODATIONS

Common accommodations include granting leave to an employee to report to scheduled doctor appointments or to heal from surgical procedures, or granting work relief to administer medication. Further, disabled employees might request a change in work schedule, permission to work from home or from a different location, modification of the temperature of the office, or permission to make personal telephone calls (such as those to a doctor) during work time.[53] Other examples are reassigning job duties, offering additional unpaid leave, or modifying the equipment necessary to perform a job function.[54]

2. ACCOMMODATIONS TIED TO A SPECIFIC DISABILITY

Some accommodations are associated with specific disabilities. For example, an employer might provide a sign language interpreter or an appropriate emergency notification system (such as strobe lighting of fire alarms) to an individual with a hearing disability.[55] A person with diabetes that rises to the level of a disability under the ADA might request a number of breaks throughout the day and a private area to test his blood sugar.[56]

3. DISABILITY LEAVE

Under some circumstances, an accommodation might take the form of a disability leave. This might arise if an accommodation involving a reduced schedule or temporary reassignment is not a viable option. In the event an employer grants a leave of absence, it will have a number of obligations to the employee during the leave as well as on the employee's return.

a. Continuation of Health Insurance

Because employers are prohibited from discriminating against individuals with disabilities, they are prohibited from treating disability leaves differently than other types of leaves. For example, employers are required to continue health insurance coverage for employees on disability leave on the same terms and conditions as for individuals who are on other types of leave. Thus, if an employer pays the healthcare premiums for its employees who are on other nonmedical leaves, the employer must pay the healthcare premiums for its employees who are on disability leaves. If an employer requires employees on other types of leave to pay their medical premiums while they are away from work, then the employer can require employees on disability leave to make these same payments.

b. Rights of Returning Employees

Employers also have obligations to disabled employees upon their return to work. Generally speaking, at the end of the leave period an employee is entitled to return to the same job he held before the leave, provided the employer is unable to demonstrate that holding it open would constitute an undue burden. In the event the exact job is unavailable, the employer is usually required to place the returning employee in a vacant equivalent position provided doing so does not constitute an undue burden. If an equivalent position is unavailable, the employer would need to determine whether a vacancy exists at a lower level.[57]

IV. REQUESTING MEDICAL INFORMATION AND MEDICAL EXAMINATIONS

When an employee returns from a disability leave, or if there is a question as to whether an employee will be able to perform the essential tasks associated with a job, an employer might want to request an employee to provide certain medical information. Such requests are only permissible in limited circumstances and are closely scrutinized. The ADA also places significant restrictions on the rights of employers to ask job applicants and employees medical questions and to require that they undergo medical testing.[58]

A. PRE-EMPLOYMENT MEDICAL INQUIRIES AND TESTING

As a general rule, an employer may not ask an applicant about a disability, request answers to medical questions, or require a medical examination until after an offer is made. Even at that time, such requests are permissible only if they are job-related and only if all new employees in the same job are asked those medical questions and are required to take the same medical examination.[59] See Chapter 11, Pre-Employment Testing.

B. MEDICAL INQUIRIES ABOUT CURRENT EMPLOYEES

Requests for medical information from current employees are usually permissible so that employers may (1) determine the type of reasonable accommodation the employer might have an obligation to provide, (2) support an employee's request for sick leave (as long as it is asked of all of employees who request this type of leave), (3) determine the date an employee will likely return from a medical leave, and (4) demonstrate why an employee might be entitled to the extension of a current leave.[60] These types of inquiries would be appropriate if an employee requests an accommodation for a disability and the disability or the need for the accommodation is not obvious.[61] Employers are also permitted to request that an employee on a disability leave provide documentation about her ability to return to work if there is a reasonable belief that the employee may be unable to perform the essential functions of the job or would pose a direct threat to herself or to others.[62]

C. MEDICAL INFORMATION THAT IMPACTS WORK PERFORMANCE

Other than in the instances outlined above, the ADA generally prohibits employers from asking employees about a medical condition absent objective evidence and a reasonable belief that the condition is affecting work performance or that an employee is posing a threat to himself or others. If one of these circumstances exists, the employer may inquire about the *possibility* of a condition or request that the employee undergo a medical examination. An employer cannot, however, inquire about an employee's medical condition merely because there are job performance issues.[63]

For example, if an employer notices that a receptionist is away from her desk for extensive periods of time, the employer can discipline the employee for leaving her work station — but cannot inquire about a medical condition. If, however, the supervisor overhears the employee saying she is always tired, is always thirsty, and has a constant need to use the restroom, this could constitute objective evidence of a reasonable belief that the employee is suffering from a medical condition. Under these circumstances the employer might be permitted to inquire about the employee's medical condition, because the condition could prevent the employee from being able to sit at her desk for extended periods of time, which is likely an essential function of the job of a receptionist.[64]

V　PRESENTING A DISCRIMINATION CLAIM UNDER THE AMERICANS WITH DISABILITIES ACT (ADA)

An individual who claims she was subjected to an adverse employment decision based on a disability can assert a disparate treatment claim (for intentional discrimination) or a disparate impact claim (for unintentional discrimination) under the ADA.

A. DISPARATE TREATMENT DISCRIMINATION

The presentation of proof for a **disparate treatment claim** under the ADA follows the same framework as those claims brought under Title VII.

1. PRESENTATION OF PROOF

The specific nature of the presentation of an ADA claim will vary, depending upon which terms and conditions of employment are the subject of the discrimination. Specifically, an individual asserting a claim for disability discrimination in hiring must first establish a *prima facie* case of discrimination by showing that

1. he had a defined disability; and
2. he was qualified for the position and could perform the essential job functions with or without a reasonable accommodation; and

disparate treatment claim
discrimination claim alleging that the basis for an employer's adverse conduct is the intent to discriminate based on an individual's membership in a protected class such as having a physical or mental disability

***prima facie* case**
individual's initial burden of proof when asserting a claim for employment discrimination

3. he applied for an available position and was rejected; and
4. the employer offered the position to an applicant without a disability or continued to seek applicants with similar qualifications.

2. SHIFTING OF BURDEN OF PROOF

After the prospective employee provides evidence of a *prima facie* case of discrimination, the burden of proof shifts to the employer to present evidence of a legitimate, nondiscriminatory reason for not hiring the prospective employee. If the employer sustains this burden, then the burden shifts back to the prospective employee to prove that the reason asserted by the employer was a pretext and that the applicant's disability was the motivating factor for the adverse decision.

disparate impact claim
a discrimination claim alleging that an employer implemented a practice or policy that was neutral on its face but that had an adverse impact on members of a protected class

B. DISPARATE IMPACT DISCRIMINATION

The presentation of proof for a **disparate impact claim** under the ADA will follow the same framework used for claims brought under Title VII, meaning an individual could sustain a claim for discrimination if the employer implements a policy that is neutral on its face but results in a disproportionate impact on qualified individuals with disabilities.

For example, if the employer requires prospective employees to pass a written test and an individual is unable to successfully complete the test due to dyslexia, the employer will likely be subject to liability under the ADA unless it can show that the test was a "business necessity" and that there was no reasonable alternative (such as a similar test in a non-written form) that could be administered to the disabled individual that would not constitute an undue burden.[65] Under this set of facts, although it is not clear that the employer intended to discriminate against qualified disabled applicants by using this test, the test may have had an adverse impact on disabled applicants, which could constitute unintentional discriminatory conduct under the ADA. See Chapter 2, Title VII — The Foundation of Workplace Discrimination Law, for a more detailed discussion of these types of claims.

KEY TERMS

- ✓ ADA Amendments Act of 2008 (ADAAA)
- ✓ Americans with Disabilities Act of 1990 (ADA)
- ✓ disparate impact claim
- ✓ disparate treatment claim
- ✓ essential job function
- ✓ major life activity
- ✓ mental impairment
- ✓ mitigating measure
- ✓ physical impairment
- ✓ *prima facie* case
- ✓ qualified individual with a disability
- ✓ reasonable accommodation
- ✓ record of an impairment
- ✓ regarded as having an impairment
- ✓ substantial limitation
- ✓ tangential task
- ✓ undue burden

DISCUSSION QUESTIONS

Explain your response to each of the following questions with the understanding that in some cases there is no right or wrong answer. If you cannot make an informed decision with the facts provided, indicate the nature and significance of the additional information you would need. For the purposes of these questions, you can assume that the employers and employees mentioned below are covered by the ADA.

1. Provide examples of situations that would support a disparate treatment claim and a disparate impact claim under the ADA.
2. Robert is diagnosed with diabetes, and you overhear him telling his wife the condition is actually a blessing in disguise, because once he tells his boss he is disabled, he will have the right to take off as much time as he wants under the ADA, and there is nothing anyone can do about it. What do you think?
3. David was in a serious skiing accident while on vacation. When he returned to work, his employer said he was terminated because he could no longer perform his work. Do you think he might have a claim under the ADA? Why or why not?
4. Randy is a successful music attorney who wants to expand his practice and hire two additional attorneys to join his firm. He has available office space on the third floor of the building he owns, but because there is no elevator, he declines to interview a candidate who is in a wheelchair. Do you think this candidate would have a valid claim under the ADA? Why or why not?
5. Ruth is the CEO of a company that is hosting a conference celebrating its 100th anniversary. At a staff meeting she announces that employees will not be permitted to take any time off during the six weeks before the conference. Because she does not want to be accused of discriminatory behavior, she also issues a memo confirming that everyone has advance notice of the rule and no exceptions will be considered. Do you see any potential problems with this policy under the ADA?

ENDNOTES

1. *See generally* U.S. Equal Employment Opportunity Commn., Questions and Answers on the Notice of Proposed Rulemaking for the ADA Amendments Act of 2008 (available at *http://www.eeoc.gov/policy/docs/qanda_adaaa_nprm.html*).
2. 42 U.S.C. §§ 12,101-12,118 (2006). The ADA also covers private and public employment agencies, labor organizations, and joint labor-management committees that oversee apprenticeship and training. Title I of the Act prohibits discrimination in employment, Title II prohibits discrimination in public services, and Title III prohibits discrimination in public accommodations and services operated by private entities. Note also that the Rehabilitation Act of 1973 overlaps with the ADA significantly and applies to federal

employers, federal contractors, and recipients of federal grants. 29 U.S.C. §§ 701-796 (2005). The Rehabilitation Act is substantively similar to the ADA but provides claimants with some administrative remedies that are not available under the ADA.

3. U.S. Equal Employment Opportunity Commn., Americans with Disabilities Act of 1990 (ADA), Charges (includes concurrent charges with Title VII, ADEA, and EPA) FY 1997–FY 2009 (available at *http://www.eeoc.gov/eeoc/statistics/enforcement/ada-charges .cfm*).

4. Press Release, U.S. Equal Employment Opportunity Commn., Wal-Mart to Pay $250,000 for Disability Bias (June 9, 2008) (available at *http://www.eeoc.gov/press/6-9-08.html*).

5. ADA Amendments Act of 2008, Pub. L. No. 110-325, § 4(a), 122 Stat. 3553 (available at *http://www.eeoc.gov/policy/adaaa.html*) (amending section 3 of the ADA (42 U.S.C. § 12,102); *see* U.S. Equal Employment Opportunity Commn., Questions and Answers on the Notice of Proposed Rulemaking for the ADA Amendments Act of 2008 (available at *http://www.eeoc.gov/policy/docs/qanda_adaaa_nprm.html*). Note that the term *disability* is defined differently under statutes such as the Family and Medical Leave Act and some workers' compensation laws. This variation may result in a determination that an individual is disabled for the purpose of one statute but not for the purpose of another. In addition, some states have disability discrimination laws that include a definition of the term *disability* that is much more expansive than the definition under the ADA. *See, e.g.,* A.B. 2222, Cal. Assem. (requiring a condition to limit a major life activity (as opposed to "substantially limit" as required by the ADA) to constitute a disability for the purpose of coverage under California's Fair Employment and Housing Act).

6. 29 C.F.R. § 1630.2(h) (2009).

7. *School Bd. of Nassau County v. Airline*, 480 U.S. 273 (1987).

8. *Id.*

9. *Wynne v. Tufts Univ. Sch. of Med.*, 932 F.2d 19 (1st Cir. 1991).

10. 42 U.S.C. § 12,211(b)(2); 29 C.F.R. § 1630.3(d).

11. U.S. Equal Employment Opportunity Commn., Questions and Answers on the Notice of Proposed Rulemaking for the ADA Amendments Act of 2008 (available at *http://www.eeoc .gov/policy/docs/qanda_adaaa_nprm.html*).

12. ADA Amendments Act of 2008, Pub. L. No. 110-325, § 4(a), 122 Stat. 3553 (available at *http://www.eeoc.gov/policy/adaaa.html*) (amending section 3 of the ADA (42 U.S.C. § 12,102); *see* U.S. Equal Employment Opportunity Commn., Questions and Answers on the Notice of Proposed Rulemaking for the ADA Amendments Act of 2008 (available at *http://www.eeoc.gov/policy/docs/qanda_adaaa_nprm.html*).

13. U.S. Equal Employment Opportunity Commn., Summary of Key Provisions: EEOC's Notice of Proposed Rulemaking (NPRM) to Implement the ADA Amendments Act of 2008 (ADAAA) (available at *http://www.eeoc.gov/laws/regulations/adaaa-summary.cfm*). The courts have provided some guidance as to what it means for an impairment to substantially limit one or more major life activities. For example, before the passage of the ADAAA, the Supreme Court held that because reproduction is a major life activity, a person who is undergoing chemotherapy and becomes sterile is considered to be disabled and would be entitled to protections under the ADA. *See also Bragdon v. Abbott*, 524 U.S. 624 (1998) (holding reproduction is a major life activity); U.S. Equal Employment Opportunity Commn., Questions and Answers About Cancer in the Workplace and the Americans with Disabilities Act (ADA) (available at *http://www.eeoc.gov/facts.cancer .html*).

14. U.S. Equal Employment Opportunity Commn., Questions and Answers on the Notice of Proposed Rulemaking for the ADA Amendments Act of 2008 (available at *http://www.eeoc .gov/policy/docs/qanda_adaaa_nprm.html*).

15. U.S. Equal Employment Opportunity Commn., Questions and Answers About Cancer in the Workplace and the Americans with Disabilities Act (ADA) (available at *http://www .eeoc.gov/facts/cancer.html*).

16. *Oesterling v. Walters*, 760 F.2d 859 (8th Cir. 1985).

17. ADA Amendments Act of 2008, Pub. L. No. 110-325, § 2(b)(6), 122 Stat. 3553; U.S. Equal Employment Opportunity Commn., Questions and Answers on the Notice of Proposed Rulemaking for the ADA Amendments Act of 2008 (available at *http://www.eeoc.gov/ policy/docs/qanda_adaaa_nprm.html*).

18. *See* U.S. Equal Employment Opportunity Commn., Questions and Answers on the Notice of Proposed Rulemaking for the ADA Amendments Act of 2008 (available at *http://www .eeoc.gov/policy/docs/qanda_adaaa_nprm.html*).

19. *See id.*

20. U.S. Equal Employment Opportunity Commn., Questions on the Notice of Proposed Rulemaking for the ADA Amendments Act of 2008 (available at *http://www.eeoc.gov/ policy/docs/qanda_adaaa_nprm.html*).

21. *Id.*

22. *Id.*

23. *See Sutton v. United Air Lines, Inc.*, 527 U.S. 471 (1999).

24. U.S. Equal Employment Opportunity Commn., Questions and Answers on the Notice of Proposed Rulemaking for the ADA Amendments Act of 2008 (available at *http://www.eeoc .gov/policy/docs/qanda_adaaa_nprm.html*).

25. *School Bd. of Nassau County v. Airline*, 480 U.S. 273 (1987).

26. U.S. Equal Employment Opportunity Commn., Questions and Answers About Deafness and Hearing Impairments in the Workplace and the Americans with Disabilities Act (July 26, 2006) (available at *http://www.eeoc.gov/facts/deafness.html*).

27. *Id.*

28. U.S. Equal Employment Opportunity Commn., Questions and Answers on the Notice of Proposed Rulemaking for the ADA Amendments Act of 2008 (available at *http://www.eeoc .gov/policy/docs/qanda_adaaa_nprm.html*).

29. ADA Amendments Act of 2008, Pub. L. No. 110-325, § 3, 122 Stat. 3553 (Definition of Disability) (amending section 3 of the ADA (42 U.S.C. § 12,102)) (available at *http://www .eeoc.gov/policy/adaaa/html*).

30. U.S. Equal Employment Opportunity Commn., Notice Concerning the Americans With Disabilities Act (ADA) Amendments Act of 2008 (available at *http://www.eeoc.gov/laws/ statutes/adaaa_notice.cfm*); U.S. Equal Employment Opportunity Commn., Questions and Answers on the Notice of Proposed Rulemaking for the ADA Amendments Act of 2008 (available at *http://www.eeoc.gov/policy/docs/qanda_adaaa_nprm.html*).

31. U.S. Equal Employment Opportunity Commn., Notice Concerning the Americans With Disabilities Act (ADA) Amendments Act of 2008 (available at *http://www.eeoc.gov/laws/ statutes/adaaa_notice.cfm*).

32. U.S. Equal Employment Opportunity Commn., Questions and Answers About Deafness and Hearing Impairments in the Workplace and the Americans with Disabilities Act (July 26, 2006) (available at *http://www.eeoc.gov/facts/deafness.html*).

33. U.S. Equal Employment Opportunity Commn., Questions and Answers About Cancer in the Workplace and the Americans with Disabilities Act (ADA) (available at *http://www .eeoc.gov/facts.cancer.html*). This employer could also be subject to liability under the Genetic Information Nondiscrimination Act (GINA), which prohibits discrimination based on genetics. See Chapter 5, Sex, Pregnancy, and Genetic Discrimination.

34. U.S. Equal Employment Opportunity Commn., Questions and Answers About Health Care Workers and the Americans with Disabilities Act (available at *http://www.eeoc.gov/ facts/health_care_workers.html*).

35. *Fuller v. Frank*, 916 F.2d 558 (9th Cir. 1990).

36. 29 C.F.R. § 1630.3(b).

37. 42 U.S.C. §§ 12,101 *et seq.*

38. 29 C.F.R. § 1630.2(m) (2005).

39. U.S. Equal Employment Opportunity Commn., Notice Concerning the Americans With Disabilities Act (ADA) Amendments Act of 2008 (available at *http://www.eeoc.gov/laws/ statutes/adaaa_notice.cfm*).

40. 29 C.F.R. § 1630.2(*l*), (o)(4); Notice Concerning the Americans With Disabilities Act (ADA) Amendments Act of 2008 (available at *http://www.eeoc.gov/laws/statutes/adaaa_ notice.cfm*).

41. U.S. Equal Employment Opportunity Commn., Disability Discrimination (available at *http://www.eeoc.gov/types/ada.html*).

42. *Id.*

43. U.S. Equal Employment Opportunity Commn., How to Comply with the Americans with Disabilities Act: A Guide for Restaurants and Other Food Service Employers (available at *http://www.eeoc.gov/facts/restaurant_guide.html*).

44. *See Southeastern Cmty. Coll. v. Davis,* 442 U.S. 397 (1979). Note that this case was filed under the Rehabilitation Act, which mirrors much of the language of the ADA.

45. *Chiari v. City of League City,* 920 F.2d 311 (5th Cir. 1991).

46. U.S. Equal Employment Opportunity Commn., Disability Discrimination (available at *http://www.eeoc.gov.types/ada.html*).

47. *Id.*

48. *Chevron U.S.A. Inc. v. Echazabal,* 536 U.S. 73 (2002).

49. U.S. Equal Employment Opportunity Commn., Questions and Answers About Deafness and Hearing Impairments in the Workplace and the Americans with Disabilities Act (July 26, 2006) (available at *http://www.eeoc.gov/facts/deafness.html*).

50. U.S. Equal Employment Opportunity Commn., How to Comply with the Americans with Disabilities Act: A Guide for Restaurants and Other Food Service Employers (available at *http://www.eeoc.gov/facts/restaurant_guide.html*).

51. U.S. Equal Employment Opportunity Commn., Questions and Answers About Deafness and Hearing Impairments in the Workplace and the Americans with Disabilities Act (July 26, 2006) (available at *http://www.eeoc.gov/facts/deafness.html*). The request for an accommodation as well as input into which accommodation might be the most desirable result may come from a family member, a friend of the disabled individual, a healthcare professional, or any other person acting on behalf of the disabled individual. Questions and Answers About Diabetes in the Workplace and the Americans with Disabilities Act (ADA) (available at *http://www.eeoc.gov/facts/diabetes.html*).

52. U.S. Equal Employment Opportunity Commn., Questions and Answers About Deafness and Hearing Impairments in the Workplace and the Americans with Disabilities Act (July 26, 2006) (available at *http://www.eeoc.gov/facts/deafness.html*).

53. U.S. Equal Employment Opportunity Commn., Questions and Answers About Cancer in the Workplace and the Americans with Disabilities Act (ADA) (available at *http://www .eeoc.gov/facts.cancer.html*).

54. U.S. Equal Employment Opportunity Commn., Disability Discrimination (available at *http://www.eeoc.gov/types/ada.html*).

55. U.S. Equal Employment Opportunity Commn., Questions and Answers About Deafness and Hearing Impairments in the Workplace and the Americans with Disabilities Act (July 26, 2006) (available at *http://www.eeoc.gov/facts/deafness.html*).

56. U.S. Equal Employment Opportunity Commn., Questions and Answers About Diabetes in the Workplace and the Americans with Disabilities Act (ADA) (available at *http://www .eeoc.gov/facts/diabetes.html*).

57. U.S. Equal Employment Opportunity Commn., Fact Sheet, The Family and Medical Leave Act, the Americans with Disabilities Act, and Title VII of the Civil Rights Act of 1964 (available at *http://www.eeoc.gov/policy/docs/fmlaada.html*).

58. *See id.* Employers should recognize that other federal laws also impose restrictions on the rights of employers to gather such information. For example, employers should refrain from requesting information or conducting medical tests that would solicit genetic information since this could subject an employer to liability under the Genetic Information Nondiscrimination Act of 2008 (GINA). *See* U.S. Equal Employment Opportunity Commn., Genetic Information Discrimination (available at *http://www.eeoc.gov/laws/ types/genetic.cfm*); U.S. Equal Employment Opportunity Commn., Background Information for EEOC Notice of Proposed Rulemaking on Title II of the Genetic Information

Nondiscrimination Act of 2008 (available at *http://www.eeoc.gov/policy/docs/qanda_geneticinfo.html*). See Chapter 5, Sex, Pregnancy, and Genetic Discrimination, for a more detailed discussion about GINA and the limitations it places on the collection of genetic information.

59. U.S. Equal Employment Opportunity Commn., Pre-employment Medical Information and Examinations (available at *http://www.eeoc.gov/laws/practices/inquiries_medical.cfm*).

60. U.S. Equal Employment Opportunity Commn., Questions and Answers About Cancer in the Workplace and the Americans with Disabilities Act (ADA) (available at *http://www.eeoc.gov/facts.cancer.html*). See Chapter 17, Regulation of Off-Duty Conduct, for a discussion about requesting medical information as part of a voluntary employer-sponsored wellness program.

61. 42 U.S.C. § 12,112(d)(4).

62. U.S. Equal Employment Opportunity Commn., Questions and Answers About Cancer in the Workplace and the Americans with Disabilities Act (ADA) (available at *http://www.eeoc.gov/facts.cancer.html*); U.S. Equal Employment Opportunity Commn., Questions and Answers About Diabetes in the Workplace and the Americans with Disabilities Act (ADA) (available at *http://www.eeoc.gov/facts/diabetes.html*).

63. U.S. Equal Employment Opportunity Commn., Questions and Answers About Diabetes in the Workplace and the Americans with Disabilities Act (ADA) (available at *http://www.eeoc.gov/facts/diabetes.html*).

64. *See* 42 U.S.C. § 12,112(d)(4); U.S. Equal Employment Opportunity Commn., Questions and Answers About Diabetes in the Workplace and the Americans with Disabilities Act (ADA) (available at *http://www.eeoc.gov/facts/diabetes.html*).

65. *Stutts v. Freeman*, 694 F.2d 666 (11th Cir. 1983).

Part III

Hiring

"Right now we have openings for a beach lifeguard, greenhouse gardener, and sauna manager."

Employees versus Independent Contractors

8

Chapter Objectives

This chapter explores how two parties can structure their working relationship when the goal is to exchange the performance of services for compensation. The primary focus is the difference between employer-employee and employer-independent contractor relationships, and the working conditions that distinguish the individuals working in those capacities. There is a significant discussion about the benefits and protections available to each as well as the differing legal obligations that will be imposed on the employer depending on the classification of the worker.

After completing this chapter, students should be able to distinguish between employees and independent contractors and explain the reasons people decide to enter into each relationship. Specifically, upon mastering the main objectives of this chapter students should be able to

- identify the working conditions that suggest an individual is working as an employee and those that suggest the individual is working as an independent contractor;
- explain the benefits and drawbacks of an individual's decision to work as an employee or as an independent contractor;
- explain the benefits and drawbacks of an employer's decision to hire an employee or an independent contractor;
- list the different tests that are used to determine whether an individual is an employee or an independent contractor, when such tests would be used, and how each is applied; and
- explain why the Internal Revenue Service (IRS) has an interest in how working individuals are classified and describe the type of assistance the IRS provides.

IMPORTANCE OF THE CLASSIFICATION

employment at will
doctrine that provides that
either the employer or the
employee can terminate the
employment relationship at
any time with or without cause,
and with or without notice

The majority of working individuals are **employees at will**, which is the classification of employees who can be terminated or can themselves end the employment relationship with or without cause, and with or without notice. In many instances the parties decide that the at-will doctrine will apply to an employment relationship without a thorough assessment of their needs. However, because there are a number of other types of employment relationships, for a number of reasons, the parties should carefully consider other options before making this commitment. See Chapter 18, Employment at Will.

Because some statutes require employers to provide particular benefits to their employees, the establishment of an employer-employee relationship will obligate an employer to provide those benefits and will entitle an employee to receive them. In contrast, establishing an employer-independent contractor relationship will relieve employers of the obligation to provide certain benefits and will prevent independent contractors from being entitled to them. Thus, the proper job categorization is significant for employers, so they know their legal obligations to provide certain benefits, and for working individuals, so they know the extent of their entitlements.

A. ASSESSING THE NEED TO HIRE

An employer's decision to hire an individual to perform services on its behalf is based in large part on the reason the employer needs the additional support, and this will likely steer the parties toward a particular employment relationship. For example, the owner of a toy store might need additional sales assistance only during the holiday season. The owner of a recently expanded restaurant might need additional wait staff to cover the new dining space. An employer such as a university may decide it needs significant mailroom assistance for photocopying materials during the fall and spring semesters, but significantly less assistance during the summer sessions when fewer students are enrolled.

Based on these differing needs, some employers might benefit from the use of temporary employees hired for a short period of time to fill a short-term and specific need. Other workers may be hired through temporary staffing agencies who "lease" the services of an individual to a number of different employers. Some employers have also created "perma-lance" positions (a cross between a permanent and freelance arrangement), "perma-temp" positions (a cross between a permanent and temporary arrangement), or other hybrid relationships.

B. OTHER ISSUES TO CONSIDER IN STRUCTURING THE RELATIONSHIP

In addition to evaluating the reason an employer needs additional support, there are a number of other factors that may impact which type of employment relationship will be most appropriate. For example, some employers may want to have significant control over how an individual completes the assigned work, while others may have little interest in how the work is performed provided it is completed by a set deadline. Some employers might be willing to provide workspace for the individuals performing work on their behalf, while others might not have the space, the financial resources, or the desire to offer a physical workspace.

Depending on the nature of the position that is being filled, copyright issues might also influence an employer's decision whether to hire an employee or an independent contractor. This is significant because of the judicial finding that an employer would be the owner of the copyright for work completed by an employee, but the copyright for work completed by an independent contractor would be owned by the individual who performed the work.[1]

C. VARIATIONS ON TRADITIONAL EMPLOYMENT RELATIONSHIPS

Due to the wide range of employment needs that may materialize, variations on traditional employment relationships continue to develop. Despite this, however, the employer-employee and employer–independent contractor relationships continue to be the most common classifications used. Because of this overwhelming presence, these two types of relationships are the focus of this text. Nevertheless, in the event an employer has a unique hiring need, other relationship permutations should be explored, and parties contemplating entering into an employment relationship that deviates from these common classifications should thoroughly understand the structure that will govern, as the obligations and entitlements may vary.

 **DISTINGUISHING BETWEEN EMPLOYEES AND INDEPENDENT CONTRACTORS**

Understanding the distinctions between these two types of common worker classifications is critical. This is because an employer may be exposed to significant liability for failing to structure its relationships with its independent contractors in a way that clearly distinguishes them from its traditional employees, who are entitled to certain benefits and protections under the law.

Employee is the broad term for an individual who is subject to the control of an employer and provides services on the employer's behalf in exchange for compensation, and **independent contractor** is the broad term for an individual who is generally not subject to the control of an employer and provides services on the employer's behalf in exchange for compensation.

employee
broad term for an individual who is subject to the control of an employer and provides services on the employer's behalf in exchange for compensation

independent contractor
broad term for an individual who is generally not subject to the control of an employer and provides services on the employer's behalf in exchange for compensation

A. COMPLEXITY OF CLASSIFICATION

If you ask someone what it means to be an employee, you will likely receive a wide range of responses. Some will say you are an employee if you have a job. But what does this mean? If you deliver newspapers for a national employer, are you its employee? What if your parents tell you it is your job to earn passing grades or to clean your room? What if a company offers to pay you $100 to paint a mural for its new office — are you the company's employee? If you baby-sit for your neighbors on a Saturday evening, are you their employee for the evening? What if you agree to baby-sit for free in exchange for your neighbor's agreement to water your lawn when you go on vacation?

If you pose this same question to someone with legal training, she is likely to respond with questions of her own. She may ask why you are posing the question, because there are a number of tests used to make this determination, and the purpose for which you are seeking the answer will determine which test should be applied. Those with legal training probably will ask a number of additional questions because they know determining whether an individual is an employee will require a fact-specific and detailed analysis of the conditions under which the individual is performing the job. Those legally trained will also know that because the nature of the relationship will determine the rights and obligations the parties have to one another, it is important to devote the appropriate amount of care to making such a determination.

B. ABSENCE OF DEFINITIVE CLASSIFICATION

The importance of properly classifying an individual as an employee or an independent contractor makes the current landscape, which includes the potential application of a number of different tests, challenging to navigate. However, it is likely that the establishment of different standards for classifying workers was intentional — making it unlikely that a universal standard will ever be imposed.

A number of statutes provide their own definition of the term *employee*, which is relevant to determining whether an individual would be entitled to the benefits and protections the particular law offers. In addition, the Supreme Court specifically noted the appropriateness of using different classification standards in different contexts.[2] To further complicate the issue, some lower courts and other entities charged with making classification decisions have established their own processes, based on a hybrid of existing tests. Thus, the consequences of the absence of one clear test to make this determination, coupled with the fact-specific nature of most tests, make it possible that someone may be appropriately classified as an employee for one purpose but as an independent contractor for another.

Despite this current landscape, there are a few tests that are well established and usually considered, in whole or in part, by whichever entity is determining whether an individual is an employee or an independent contractor.

C. COMMON LAW RIGHT TO CONTROL

If you have ever participated in a discussion relating to the determination of an individual's employment status, it is likely you have heard of the common law **right to control test**. This is the layperson's term for the most well-known test used to determine whether someone is entitled to the benefits and protections of an employee or is appropriately classified as an independent contractor.

right to control test
compilation of factors used to determine whether the extent of control an employer exerts over an individual supports the classification of that individual as an employee or an independent contractor

Put simply, employers generally have control over their employees but do not necessarily have control over their independent contractors. The issue of control is critical because in addition to having legal obligations to provide benefits to employees, an employer will generally be responsible for the conduct of the individuals over whom it has control.

1. *RESPONDEAT SUPERIOR*

The right to control test is rooted in the legal theory of ***respondeat superior***, which is the Latin term for "let the master answer." Under this theory, because an employer has the right to control its employees, it is responsible for harm caused by the actions of its employees that occur during the scope of their employment. Conduct generally falls within the scope of an individual's employment if it (1) relates to work the employee was hired to perform, (2) takes place at the workplace and during work hours, and (3) benefits the employer. Employers may also be responsible for employee conduct that falls outside these parameters if the conduct causes harm and the employer (1) intended the harm to occur, (2) was negligent or reckless in allowing the harm to occur, or (3) provided the employee with the actual or apparent authority to engage in the conduct.[3]

respondeat superior
Latin for "let the master answer"; legal theory that imposes liability on an employer for the actions of its employees that occur during the scope of their employment

The Restatement (Third) of Agency provides more general guidance, stating that an employee is acting within the scope of employment when performing work assigned by his employer or engaging in conduct subject to his employer's control. It also states that an employee's conduct is not within the scope of employment when it is an independent course of conduct that the employee does not intend to serve any purpose for the employer.[4]

Suppose, for example, that Eric, an employer and owner of a lawn service company, hires Brett, an employee, to mow the lawn of one of Eric's clients. As a general rule, under *respondeat superior*, if Brett accidentally damages a client's prized flower garden while raking the leaves, Eric, as the employer, would be responsible for the damages. Brett caused the damages while performing services for the benefit of his employer (his master), Eric, so Eric is responsible for (meaning he must answer for) the harm caused by the actions of his employee, Brett.[5]

The important point here is that employers may be subject to significant liability for the actions of their employees. Therefore, employers should consider this potential risk when making a determination as to whether they want to hire employees who are subject to their control, or whether they would prefer to limit (but not necessarily eliminate) this potential liability.

In determining whether this relationship exists (meaning that the situation warrants holding the employer responsible for the actions of the employee), the right to control test considers the extent to which one party controls the actions of another. Different sources list different factors to be considered when trying to determine whether the degree of control is present, and rarely is one factor controlling. It is the presence or absence of a *number* of factors that is used to assess the presence or absence of the right to control.

2. FACTORS USED TO DETERMINE EXISTENCE OF THE RIGHT TO CONTROL

Both the Restatement of Agency and the Supreme Court have provided guidance relating to the types of factors that should be evaluated to determine whether an employer has control over an individual to the extent necessary to classify the worker as an employee.

a. Restatement (Second) of Agency

One common source of considerations used to determine whether an individual is an employee or an independent contractor under the right to control test is Section 220 of the Restatement (Second) of Agency, which considers such factors as whether the worker is engaged in a distinct occupation, whether the work is usually done under supervision or independently by a specialist, whether the individual is compensated based on the amount of time worked or for the completion of the job, whether the worker is a part of the regular business of the employer, and the length of time for which the person is employed.[6] The more control the employer exerts over the worker, the more likely the worker will be classified as an employee under the common law right to control test.

b. Judicial Application of the Right to Control Test

To determine whether the right to control exists in an employment relationship, the Supreme Court has held that the factors listed in the Restatement, along with a few others — for example, whether the individual has the right to assign additional work, whether benefits are provided, and how the individual is treated for tax purposes — are relevant considerations.[7] The Court has also considered the extent to which services provided are central to the employer's business, the permanency of the relationship between the individual and the employer, and the service provider's opportunity for profit or loss to be significant factors in making the determination.[8]

3. APPLICATION OF FACTORS

Although the list of factors used in applying the right to control test may seem overwhelming, it becomes much more manageable when looked at in context. For example, let us assume Danica, the owner of a car dealership, hires Jamie to build ten chairs for the dealership's showroom. Danica then tells Jamie she can select the days and hours she wants to dedicate to building the chairs, as long as the chairs are delivered by the end of the month. Jamie has the option to work eight hours a day until the work is completed, or she may decide to work 14 hours a day to get the project done. Suppose Jamie also will retain the flexibility to determine what the chairs will look like, will build the chairs in a location of her own choosing, and will use her own materials and tools for the project. In this case, because Jamie retains significant control over how she completes her work, an application of the right to control test and the factors listed in the Restatement will likely result in a finding that Jamie is an independent contractor, not an employee.

Now, let us assume that in the example above, Danica hires Jamie to come to her dealership on Monday morning to pick up the materials and tools to build ten wooden chairs based on the specifications she lists on a piece of paper. Further, let us assume Danica directs Jamie to work in the back office from 9:00 a.m. to 5:00 p.m., with one hour for lunch, until the work is completed. Under these circumstances, Jamie would likely be considered an employee because Danica is exerting significant control over Jamie's work. Specifically, Danica is providing detailed instructions as to where to perform the services (at the dealership), how to build the chairs (based on the specifications she provides), what tools and materials to use (those provided by the employer), and when to perform the work (from 9:00 a.m. to 5:00 p.m., with an hour for lunch).

Many factors are used to assess whether an individual should be appropriately classified as an employee or an independent contractor. Factors that are indicative of the right of an employer to control the work of an individual are used to support an *employee* classification, while those that show the individual has the right to control her own work are used to support an *independent contractor* classification. See Exhibit 8-1. A few of the factors listed in Exhibit 8-1 do warrant some further explanation.

Exhibit 8-1
Factors Considered When Applying the Right to Control Test[1]

Consideration	Suggests Employer–Employee Relationship	Suggests Employer–Independent Contractor Relationship
Right to Control	Employer controls the work of the individual.	Employer exerts little or no control over the work of the individual.
Type of Business	Individual does not have an independent business.	Individual has a business that is distinct from the employer.
Supervision	Individual is supervised by the employer.	Individual is not supervised by the employer.
Workspace, Tools, and Materials	Individual is provided with tools, materials, and a workspace.	Individual has own tools and workspace, and provides materials.
Length of Employment	Individual has a long-term relationship with the employer and anticipates employment for an indefinite duration.	Individual is retained for a specific project or length of time.

Exhibit 8-1 *(continued)*

Consideration	Suggests Employer–Employee Relationship	Suggests Employer–Independent Contractor Relationship
Compensation	Individual is paid an annual salary or an hourly rate and works a fairly consistent number of hours.	Individual is paid per project.
Integration	The services provided are tied to the core of the employer's business.	The services provided are tangential to the core of the employer's business.
Customer Base	Individual does not provide the service for anyone other than the customers (clients) of the employer for whom the services are provided.	Individual provides the service for customers (clients) other than those of the employer for whom services are provided.

[1] Charles Muhl, *What is an employee? The answer depends on the Federal law*, Mthly. Lab. Rev. (Jan. 2002) (available at *http://www.bls.gov/opub/mlr/2002/01/art1full.pdf*).

a. Central versus Peripheral Job Task

The question of whether the work performed is central to the business being conducted or whether it plays a tangential role is a significant one. For example, if Marge is the owner of a furniture store and hires Aaron to build 50 chairs, this would suggest the existence of an employer-employee relationship because selling chairs is central to the retail furniture business. In contrast, if Marge is the CEO of a clothing store and hires Aaron to build her an office chair, this would suggest that he is an independent contractor, because here the primary purpose of Marge's business is selling clothing, not chairs.

b. Workspace and Number of Clients

Courts have noted that employees tend to provide a service for one employer, while independent contractors tend to provide services for a number of different employers. This framework for appropriately classifying the workers is supported by the independent contractor's maintenance of a separate business operation that is distinct from the employer and the right to advertise for other customers. With respect to work location, employees usually work on-site, while independent contractors usually complete their work off the premises and maintain office space that is distinct from that of the employer.[9]

c. Wages and Length of Employment

When determining whether an individual is an independent contractor or an employee, great significance is attached to how compensation is paid for the services rendered. Independent contractors are much more likely than employees to be paid a flat fee for the completion of a project. Employees are more likely to be paid an hourly rate or an annual salary. Further, independent contractors are typically hired for a specific length of time or for a project, while employees are usually hired for an indefinite period of time to complete a variety of tasks.

D. ECONOMIC REALITIES TEST

Another test used by some courts and federal agencies to classify working individuals is the **economic realities test**, which favors the finding that an individual is an employee.

economic realities test
a test that focuses on the extent to which an individual is economically dependent on an employer to determine whether she should be treated as an employee or an independent contractor

1. ECONOMIC DEPENDENCE IS DETERMINATIVE

The economic realities test looks to whether the individual performing the services is economically dependent upon the employer offering the compensation. Those who receive a significant portion of their income from a particular employer would likely be classified as an employee under this test. For example, under this test, if Logan is hired to build five chairs over a six-month period for $250, she will likely be considered an independent contractor, because the presumption is that she will earn the majority of her income from other sources. In contrast, if Logan is hired to build 20 chairs a week for a total weekly compensation of $1,000 for an indefinite period of time, she would likely be classified as an employee under the economic realities test, because this could represent her primary source of income.

2. RIGHT TO CONTROL IS NOT DETERMINATIVE

Under the economic realities test, the question of whether an employer controls the work of another is a relevant consideration, but only to the extent it impacts whether an individual is economically dependent on the employer.[10] Therefore, an individual who derives 100% of her annual income from a particular employer will likely be classified as an employee—even if the employer does not exert a significant amount of control over her work. An individual who completes one small project under an employer's direct and consistent supervision might still be classified as an independent contractor, despite the exertion of this control, since the key issue is whether the individual is economically dependent on the employer.[11]

The factors used to determine whether economic dependence exists are similar to those applied under the right to control test. However, the relevant factors are connected to the central theme of this test, which is whether the individual's terms and conditions of employment are conducive to his performance of services for other employers, or whether the individual is economically dependent upon a single employer. See Exhibit 8-2.

**Exhibit 8-2
Factors Considered When Applying the Economic
Realities Test[1]**

Consideration	Suggests Employer–Employee Relationship	Suggests Employer–Independent Contractor Relationship
Integration	Individual provides a service that is part of the employer's core business.	Individual has a number of clients as opposed to providing services for a single employer.
Workspace, Tools, and Materials	Individual is provided with tools, materials, and a workspace on the employer's premises.	Individual has own tools, provides materials, and works from a remote location.
Right to Control	Employer retains control over the individual's work.	Employer has little or no control over the work of the individual.
Potential for Profit and Loss	Individual is compensated a set fee without consideration of profit or loss.	Compensation may vary based on profits or losses of the employer.
Skills	Work does not require any specialized or unique skill.	Work requires specialized skill.
Nature of Relationship	Individual has a long-term relationship with the employer and anticipates employment for an indefinite duration.	Individual is retained for a specific project or length of time.

[1] Charles Muhl, *What is an employee? The answer depends on the Federal law*, Mthly. Lab. Rev. (Jan. 2002) (available at *http://www.bls.gov/opub/mlr/2002/01/art1full.pdf*).

3. USE OF ECONOMIC REALITIES TEST

In some instances, courts have specifically rejected the application of the factors outlined in the Restatement in favor of the economic realities test. This is the situation with respect to coverage under the Fair Labor Standards Act (FLSA), the Family and Medical Leave Act (FMLA), and the Worker Adjustment and Retraining (WARN) Act.[12] See Chapter 12, Compensation and Benefits; Chapter 13, Paid and Unpaid Leave; and Chapter 19, Ending the Employment Relationship, respectively. Thus, an individual who is not dependent on an employer for all or for a significant portion of her income would likely not be entitled to the benefits and protections of the FLSA, regardless of the extent to which an employer exerts control over the completion of the work. Similarly, an individual who earns 95% percent of his annual income from one employer would likely be entitled to assert his rights under the FLSA, even if the employer provides the individual with flexibility with respect to the completion of his work.[13]

The importance of understanding the application of the wide range of factors that might be relevant to this determination is widely recognized. This is evidenced, for example, by a statement by the Department of Labor (DOL) (which is the federal agency responsible for enforcing a number of federal employment laws including the FLSA), indicating that on a number of occasions the Supreme Court has made it clear that there is not one clear rule for determining the appropriate classification of an individual under the statute.[14]

E. FACTORS CONSIDERED BY THE INTERNAL REVENUE SERVICE (IRS)

Other federal agencies, such as the IRS, have a vested interest in ensuring that individuals are properly classified, because the classification of a worker has significant tax implications. The IRS estimates that the misclassification of employees as independent contractors results in the loss of billions of dollars in tax revenue each year. Based on this situation, it is not surprising that the IRS offers assistance to ensure that working individuals are properly classified.

1. SIGNIFICANCE OF CLASSIFICATION FOR TAX PURPOSES

The appropriate classification of an individual as an independent contractor or an employee has significant tax implications because employers are usually responsible for withholding and paying taxes on the salaries of their employees. Employers do not have the same obligation with respect to their independent contractors. Specifically, employers are not required to withhold federal income taxes for independent contractors, nor do they have to make contributions into the United States Social Security System (FICA) or pay federal unemployment insurance (FUTA) taxes on behalf of independent contractors.[15]

There are also different reporting obligations for the different classifications. Employers are required to provide their employees with a W-2 form, which details the withholding of the employee's income and social security taxes, while a business payment to a nonemployee must be reported to the IRS on a 1099 form. Thus, determining whether an individual is an independent contractor or an employee is critical, because employers may be subject to significant tax liability for misclassifying individuals and failing to pay the appropriate taxes on their behalf.

2. RELEVANT CONSIDERATIONS

Historically the IRS utilized a 20-factor test that included many of the same factors established by the right to control test and outlined in the Restatement. Today, however, the IRS has shifted its focus to an examination of factors that fit into three broad categories.

The first category consists of behavioral factors, which relate to whether the employer has the right to control the details of the final product as well as how the work is completed. Financial considerations comprise the second set of factors, and relate to whether the business components of the job (such as how compensation is paid, whether expenses are reimbursable, and who provides the materials) are controlled by the employer. The final category looks at the relationship between the two parties and examines such factors as whether there are written contracts governing the terms and conditions of the work, whether vacation and sick days are provided, and whether the relationship is likely to continue for the indefinite future.[16]

3. FORM SS-8

The significant financial impact that the misclassification of individuals can have on the revenue stream of the IRS, along with (perhaps) the recognition of the complexity of making this determination, has resulted in the availability of IRS classification assistance through the filing of **Form SS-8**.

Although Form SS-8 focuses on the three broad categories of factors explained above, it also requires that the employer or individual produce information relevant to many of the factors outlined in the Restatement to assist the IRS in determining the appropriate classification of the worker. See Exhibit 8-3.

Form SS-8
federal tax form that can be filed by an employer or individual to seek IRS assistance to determine the appropriate classification of an individual as an employee or independent contractor in conjunction with the performance of certain work

F. FACTORS CONSIDERED FOR DETERMINING ELIGIBILITY FOR WORKERS' COMPENSATION

workers' compensation
compensation provided to employees for injuries sustained during the course of their employment

Workers' compensation is compensation provided to employees for injuries sustained during the course of their employment. The question of an individual's status is an important consideration with respect to workers' compensation, because a prerequisite for coverage is the establishment of an employer-employee relationship. Specific factors are considered to determine whether an individual is an employee and therefore entitled to workers' compensation benefits, or whether the individual is an independent contractor (or some other classification) who would be excluded from coverage. Although the factors used in making the determination are similar to those found in the Restatement, the analysis examines factors that fall into four broad areas.[17]

1. RIGHT TO CONTROL

The first area relates to the *right to control* and examines the factors discussed above, such as whether (1) the person performing the service(s) is provided with clear instructions about the nature of the task and how it will be completed, (2) the individual is integrated into the business, (3) the individual must perform the task or whether it can be delegated, (4) the sequence of the task is dictated by the employer, (5) the employer requires status reports, and (6) the employer reimburses the individual for business and travel expenses.[18]

Exhibit 8-3

Form **SS-8** (Rev. November 2006) Department of the Treasury Internal Revenue Service	**Determination of Worker Status for Purposes of Federal Employment Taxes and Income Tax Withholding**	OMB No. 1545-0004

Name of firm (or person) for whom the worker performed services	Worker's name

Firm's address (include street address, apt. or suite no., city, state, and ZIP code)	Worker's address (include street address, apt. or suite no., city, state, and ZIP code)

Trade name	Daytime telephone number ( )	Worker's social security number

Telephone number (include area code) ( )	Firm's employer identification number	Worker's employer identification number (if any)

Note. If the worker is paid by a firm other than the one listed on this form for these services, enter the name, address, and employer identification number of the payer. ▶

Disclosure of Information

The information provided on Form SS-8 may be disclosed to the firm, worker, or payer named above to assist the IRS in the determination process. For example, if you are a worker, we may disclose the information you provide on Form SS-8 to the firm or payer named above. The information can only be disclosed to assist with the determination process. If you provide incomplete information, we may not be able to process your request. See *Privacy Act and Paperwork Reduction Act Notice* on page 5 for more information. **If you do not want this information disclosed to other parties, do not file Form SS-8.**

Parts I–V. All filers of Form SS-8 must complete all questions in Parts I–IV. Part V must be completed if the worker provides a service directly to customers or is a salesperson. If you cannot answer a question, enter "Unknown" or "Does not apply." If you need more space for a question, attach another sheet with the part and question number clearly identified.

Part I   General Information

1 This form is being completed by: ☐ Firm ☐ Worker; for services performed _____ to _____ .
   (beginning date)   (ending date)

2 Explain your reason(s) for filing this form (for example, you received a bill from the IRS, you believe you erroneously received a Form 1099 or Form W-2, you are unable to get worker's compensation benefits, or you were audited or are being audited by the IRS). ---------------
   ----
   ----

3 Total number of workers who performed or are performing the same or similar services _____ .

4 How did the worker obtain the job? ☐ Application   ☐ Bid   ☐ Employment Agency   ☐ Other (specify) _____

5 Attach copies of all supporting documentation (contracts, invoices, memos, Forms W-2 or Forms 1099-MISC issued or received, IRS closing agreements, IRS rulings, etc.). In addition, please inform us of any current or past litigation concerning the worker's status. If no income reporting forms (Form 1099-MISC or W-2) were furnished to the worker, enter the amount of income earned for the year(s) at issue $ _____ .
   If both Form W-2 and Form 1099-MISC were issued or received, explain why. ------------------------
   ----

6 Describe the firm's business. ---

   ----

7 Describe the work done by the worker and provide the worker's job title. ---------------------------
   ----
   ----

8 Explain why you believe the worker is an employee or an independent contractor. -------------------
   ----

   ----

9 Did the worker perform services for the firm in any capacity before providing the services that are the subject of this determination request?
   ☐ Yes   ☐ No   ☐ N/A
   If "Yes," what were the dates of the prior service? ---
   If "Yes," explain the differences, if any, between the current and prior service. ----------------------
   ----
   ----

10 If the work is done under a written agreement between the firm and the worker, attach a copy (preferably signed by both parties). Describe the terms and conditions of the work arrangement. --
   ----

For Privacy Act and Paperwork Reduction Act Notice, see page 5.   Cat. No. 16106T   Form **SS-8** (Rev. 11-2006)

Exhibit 8-3 *(continued)*

Form SS-8 (Rev. 11-2006)   Page 2

Part II   Behavioral Control

1 What specific training and/or instruction is the worker given by the firm? ....

2 How does the worker receive work assignments? ....

3 Who determines the methods by which the assignments are performed? ....
4 Who is the worker required to contact if problems or complaints arise and who is responsible for their resolution? ....

5 What types of reports are required from the worker? Attach examples. ....

6 Describe the worker's daily routine such as, schedule, hours, etc. ....

7 At what location(s) does the worker perform services (e.g., firm's premises, own shop or office, home, customer's location, etc.)? Indicate the appropriate percentage of time the worker spends in each location, if more than one. ....

8 Describe any meetings the worker is required to attend and any penalties for not attending (e.g., sales meetings, monthly meetings, staff meetings, etc.). ....
9 Is the worker required to provide the services personally? . . . . ☐ Yes ☐ No
10 If substitutes or helpers are needed, who hires them? ....
11 If the worker hires the substitutes or helpers, is approval required? . . . . ☐ Yes ☐ No
    If "Yes," by whom? ....
12 Who pays the substitutes or helpers? ....
13 Is the worker reimbursed if the worker pays the substitutes or helpers? . . . . ☐ Yes ☐ No
    If "Yes," by whom?

Part III   Financial Control

1 List the supplies, equipment, materials, and property provided by each party:
   The firm ....
   The worker ....
   Other party ....
2 Does the worker lease equipment? . . . . ☐ Yes ☐ No
   If "Yes," what are the terms of the lease? (Attach a copy or explanatory statement.) ....

3 What expenses are incurred by the worker in the performance of services for the firm? ....

4 Specify which, if any, expenses are reimbursed by:
   The firm ....
   Other party ....
5 Type of pay the worker receives: ☐ Salary   ☐ Commission   ☐ Hourly Wage   ☐ Piece Work
   ☐ Lump Sum   ☐ Other (specify) ....
   If type of pay is commission, and the firm guarantees a minimum amount of pay, specify amount $ _____ .
6 Is the worker allowed a drawing account for advances? . . . . ☐ Yes ☐ No
   If "Yes," how often? ....
   Specify any restrictions. ....

7 Whom does the customer pay? . . . . ☐ Firm   ☐ Worker
   If worker, does the worker pay the total amount to the firm? ☐ Yes   ☐ No   If "No," explain. ....

8 Does the firm carry worker's compensation insurance on the worker? . . . . ☐ Yes ☐ No
9 What economic loss or financial risk, if any, can the worker incur beyond the normal loss of salary (e.g., loss or damage of equipment, material, etc.)? ....

Form **SS-8** (Rev. 11-2006)

Exhibit 8-3 *(continued)*

Form SS-8 (Rev. 11-2006) Page **3**

Part IV Relationship of the Worker and Firm

1 List the benefits available to the worker (e.g., paid vacations, sick pay, pensions, bonuses, paid holidays, personal days, insurance benefits). ....

2 Can the relationship be terminated by either party without incurring liability or penalty? . . . . ☐ Yes ☐ No
   If "No," explain your answer. ....

3 Did the worker perform similar services for others during the same time period? . . . . ☐ Yes ☐ No
   If "Yes," is the worker required to get approval from the firm? . . . . ☐ Yes ☐ No

4 Describe any agreements prohibiting competition between the worker and the firm while the worker is performing services or during any later period. Attach any available documentation. ....

5 Is the worker a member of a union? . . . . ☐ Yes ☐ No

6 What type of advertising, if any, does the worker do (e.g., a business listing in a directory, business cards, etc.)? Provide copies, if applicable. ....

7 If the worker assembles or processes a product at home, who provides the materials and instructions or pattern? ....

8 What does the worker do with the finished product (e.g., return it to the firm, provide it to another party, or sell it)? ....

9 How does the firm represent the worker to its customers (e.g., employee, partner, representative, or contractor)? ....

10 If the worker no longer performs services for the firm, how did the relationship end (e.g., worker quit or was fired, job completed, contract ended, firm or worker went out of business)? ....

Part V For Service Providers or Salespersons. Complete this part if the worker provided a service directly to customers or is a salesperson.

1 What are the worker's responsibilities in soliciting new customers? ....

2 Who provides the worker with leads to prospective customers? ....

3 Describe any reporting requirements pertaining to the leads. ....

4 What terms and conditions of sale, if any, are required by the firm? ....

5 Are orders submitted to and subject to approval by the firm? . . . . ☐ Yes ☐ No

6 Who determines the worker's territory? ....

7 Did the worker pay for the privilege of serving customers on the route or in the territory? . . . . ☐ Yes ☐ No
   If "Yes," whom did the worker pay? ....
   If "Yes," how much did the worker pay? .... $ _____

8 Where does the worker sell the product (e.g., in a home, retail establishment, etc.)? ....

9 List the product and/or services distributed by the worker (e.g., meat, vegetables, fruit, bakery products, beverages, or laundry or dry cleaning services). If more than one type of product and/or service is distributed, specify the principal one. ....

10 Does the worker sell life insurance full time? . . . . ☐ Yes ☐ No

11 Does the worker sell other types of insurance for the firm? . . . . ☐ Yes ☐ No
    If "Yes," enter the percentage of the worker's total working time spent in selling other types of insurance . . . . _____%

12 If the worker solicits orders from wholesalers, retailers, contractors, or operators of hotels, restaurants, or other similar establishments, enter the percentage of the worker's time spent in the solicitation . . . . _____%

13 Is the merchandise purchased by the customers for resale or use in their business operations? . . . . ☐ Yes ☐ No
    Describe the merchandise and state whether it is equipment installed on the customers' premises. ....

Sign Here ▶

Under penalties of perjury, I declare that I have examined this request, including accompanying documents, and to the best of my knowledge and belief, the facts presented are true, correct, and complete.

_____   Title ▶ _____   Date ▶ _____
Type or print name below signature.

Form **SS-8** (Rev. 11-2006)

2. METHOD OF PAYMENT

The second area of consideration relates to *how compensation is paid for the performance of services*. The payment of a salary on a regular basis in a consistent amount suggests an employer-employee relationship, while a more dynamic payment method that might vary in the amount of compensation, as well as in the timing of the payments, suggests the services are being performed by an independent contractor.[19]

3. LOCATION OF WORK PERFORMANCE AND PROVISION OF MATERIALS

The third set of circumstances relates to *where the work is completed* and *who provides the materials*. The analysis here parallels a number of factors listed in the Restatement, focusing on the fact that employees generally work on an employer's premises and are provided with tools and materials. Independent contractors, in contrast, are more likely to be responsible for securing a workspace as well as the tools and materials necessary to complete a task.[20]

4. RIGHT TO TERMINATE

The final consideration focuses on which party has the *power to terminate the relationship* and which party would be *liable for any resulting damages*. If both parties have the right to end the relationship, this suggests an employer-employee relationship. In contrast, two parties who enter into an employer-independent contractor relationship would not have the same option.[18]

For example, an employer who hires an employee to build chairs would likely retain the right to terminate the relationship (subject to the progressive discipline process or whatever terms and conditions govern their employment relationship) if the chairs are not built to his satisfaction. However, this remedy would not be available if an independent contractor is building the chairs. Instead, because the work of an independent contractor is usually governed by contract, the employer's remedy would be established by the contract. Specifically, the employer might have to provide the independent contractor with the chance to correct the problem, or the employer might be permitted to adjust the negotiated price to account for any substandard work.[21]

G. STRUCTURING THE RELATIONSHIP TO BE CONSISTENT WITH THE DESIRED CLASSIFICATION

The variations among the tests discussed above illustrate the importance of understanding when a particular test is used and how to structure an employment relationship to ensure that the working conditions create the intended relationship. In most cases, an employer will assess its hiring needs and expectations, determine the type of relationship it seeks to establish, and seek out an individual willing to work under those conditions. Once the parties come to an agreement relating to the type of relationship they intend to create, they can further tailor the individual's terms and conditions of employment to increase the likelihood that the classification will withstand any judicial (or IRS) scrutiny.

A number of factors will have an impact on whether the needs of the employer and the individual being hired will be best served by the worker's classification as an employee or an independent contractor.

1. ASSESSING THE NEEDS OF AN EMPLOYER

As discussed above, employers should consider a number of issues when determining whether to hire an employee or an independent contractor. Employers should consider how long they anticipate they will need the services of this new hire, and how much money they have to retain those services. An employer with limited resources might consider hiring an independent contractor for a short period of time. In addition to the savings that can be achieved by limiting the period for which a salary will be paid, employers generally do not provide benefits to independent contractors, do not add independent contractors to their insurance policies, and do not pay taxes on the independent contractors' earnings.

Keep in mind, however, that because independent contractors usually do not receive many of the benefits provided to employees, they often expect a higher rate of pay than what might be offered to an employee. Therefore, if an employer has a need for services for an extended period of time, hiring an employee might be a more financially sound decision. An employer must also consider nonfinancial considerations, such as how much control it wants to exert over the work performed and whether it wants to be responsible for the individual's conduct during the scope of employment, as well as whether it wants an individual who is dedicated solely to it or whether it is comfortable with the individual performing work for other clients.

a. Hiring Employees

Employers whose needs can be *partially* addressed by hiring an independent contractor and *partially* addressed by hiring an employee should hire an employee. Because employers have greater obligations to employees than to independent contractors, the liability for misclassifying an employee as an independent contractor is much more significant than misclassifying an independent contractor as an employee. For example, in one highly publicized case that moved through the judicial system in the 1990s, Microsoft settled a claim for $97 million after it was determined they misclassified a number of individuals as independent contractors.[22] In addition, an employer may be subject to significant tax penalties for a misclassification because the IRS has the right to recover retroactive taxes and contributions that should have been made on behalf of a misclassified individual. The misclassified individual can also file an independent claim for employee benefits she would have been entitled to, had she been classified properly.[23] Based on this reality, employers who are unsure about how to classify an individual, or whose needs can be adequately addressed by either, should classify and treat such individuals as employees to minimize potential future liability.[24]

b. Hiring Independent Contractors

Employers who decide to hire an independent contractor should enter into a written agreement with the individual that establishes the terms and conditions of the employment relationship. Although the *actual relationship* between the two parties will be evaluated to determine whether an individual is properly categorized, the written agreement can be one piece of evidence that weighs in favor of independent contractor status, provided it indicates a mutual intent for this arrangement.

The agreement should confirm the expectations of the two parties and expressly state that the independent contractor, by virtue of his status, will only be entitled to the negotiated benefits. Employers who want to take an added precaution may want to make it clear in the written document that the independent contractor will not be entitled to any benefits offered to employees, including, but not limited to, those found in the company handbook.

2. ASSESSING THE NEEDS OF AN INDIVIDUAL

Individuals seeking employment should perform a similar analysis to determine whether they want to be classified as an employee or an independent contractor. Those seeking a flexible schedule might prefer to negotiate conditions of employment more like those of an independent contractor so they can retain significant control over their own work schedule. In contrast, individuals seeking the potential for greater job security, or entitlements to additional benefits and protections, might decide they are more interested in working as an employee.

3. ENSURING CONDUCT IS CONSISTENT WITH AGREED-ON CLASSIFICATION

After the parties determine which relationship meets their needs and negotiate the terms and conditions of employment, they should behave in a manner that is consistent with those terms. For example, assuming the right to control test governs the relationship, employers who hire independent contractors should provide those individuals with significant discretion to determine how the work is completed. In contrast, employers who decide to hire employees should exert significant control over those individuals and the performance of their work. This is significant — in the event the classification of an individual is challenged — because the actual conduct engaged in by the parties will be scrutinized to determine whether the level of control the employer exerted over the individual supports the selected classification.

KEY TERMS

✓ economic realities test   ✓ Form SS-8   ✓ *respondeat superior*
✓ employee   ✓ independent   ✓ right to control test
✓ employment at will   contractor   ✓ workers' compensation

DISCUSSION QUESTIONS

Explain your response to each of the following questions with the understanding that in some cases there is no right or wrong answer. If you cannot make an informed decision with the facts provided, indicate the nature and significance of the additional information you would need.

1. Why is it important for employers to ensure that individuals who perform services on their behalf are properly classified?
2. List a number of reasons why an employer might want to hire an employee and why an employer might want to hire an independent contractor.
3. Provide some examples of working conditions that would suggest an individual is an employee under the common law right to control test.
4. Provide some examples of working conditions that would suggest an individual is an independent contractor under the common law right to control test.
5. What is the economic realities test, and when might it be used? Provide a set of circumstances that would suggest an individual is an independent contractor if this test was applied.
6. Explain why the IRS has an interest in ensuring that individuals are properly classified as employees or as independent contractors.
7. Jeff does not want to withhold federal income taxes for two individuals he plans to hire, so he is going to ask them to sign a document confirming they are independent contractors. What do you think about this idea?
8. Julie is a high-powered executive who hires a new assistant, Mike. Because Mike has a stellar reputation in the industry, Julie tells him that he will be subject to minimal supervision and can make up his own hours as long as he gets his work completed on time. Do you see any problems with this arrangement?
9. Melissa owns a wine bar and wants to hire an independent contractor to help her advertise her new business. Because Melissa comes from a family of high-powered attorneys, she knows the importance of written agreements and drafts the following document:

INDEPENDENT CONTRACTOR AGREEMENT

_____ [hereinafter Independent Contractor] agrees to provide services to "Passing the Bar" [hereinafter Employer] as an independent contractor. These services will include creating advertisements, determining how to disseminate the advertisements, and working on any and all other tasks that might be assigned. Independent Contractor agrees to respond to requests for his/her services in a timely fashion but no later than one business day after the request is made. Independent Contractor realizes that s/he is free to work for other companies but must receive prior written consent from Employer. Independent Contractor agrees that s/he will be paid at the rate of $20/hr. for all time spent performing services under this Agreement.

Do you see any problems with this agreement? Will this agreement guarantee that the hired individual will be an independent contractor?

ENDNOTES

1. *Community for Creative Non-Violence v. Reid*, 490 U.S. 30 (1989).

2. *Bartels v. Birmingham*, 332 U.S. 126, 130 (1947). The Court has also said that when a federal law does not include a clear definition of what constitutes an employee for the purpose of applicability of the statute, the right to control should be determinative. *Nationwide Mut. Ins. Co. v. Darden*, 503 U.S. 318 (1992).

3. Restatement (Second) of Agency § 228. Another critical issue is whether seemingly separate companies should be treated as a single employer for the purpose of determining liability. This is particularly significant because a finding that a number of organizations constitute a single employer would mean the combination of their employees would determine whether the employees are entitled to certain benefits. For example, an employer with eight employees will not have the obligation to provide benefits under the Family and Medical Leave Act (FMLA) because the statute only applies to employers with 50 or more employees. However, if there is a judicial determination that the employer includes a number of enterprises in addition to this single company or worksite, for example, this could mean the employer meets or exceeds the minimum threshold for coverage. *See, e.g., Smith v. K & F Indus., Inc.*, 190 F. Supp. 2d 643 (S.D.N.Y. 2002).

4. Restatement (Third) of Agency § 7.07 (2006).

5. If Eric pays the damages, he might have a legal right to require Brett to reimburse him for this loss, depending on the nature of their employment relationship and applicable state laws. The significant point here, however, is that the client can recover, from Eric, the damages caused by Brett, because Eric is responsible for Brett's action that occurred during the scope of his employment.

6. Restatement (Second) of Agency § 220.

7. *Nationwide Mut. Ins. Co. v. Darden*, 503 U.S. 318, 323-324 (1992). The Supreme Court has also determined that although a central component of an employment relationship is the payment of compensation for services, the compensation does not have to take a certain form. Specifically, it has said that providing a benefit such as shelter or clothing would constitute compensation. *Tony & Susan Alamo Found. v. Secretary of Labor*, 471 U.S. 290 (1985).

8. *Nationwide Mut. Ins. Co. v. Darden*, 503 U.S. 318, 323-324 (1992). The Court has also held that, in the absence of a statutory definition of the term employee, the right to control test is generally applicable to determine whether an individual is an employee under a federal law. *Id.; see Bartels v. Birmingham*, 332 U.S. 126, 130 (1947). The Court, however, has also noted an exception to this, stating that if the law relates to social legislation, then the determination should be based upon whether the individual depends upon the employer for his economic livelihood. *See Bartels v. Birmingham*, 332 U.S. 126, 130 (1947).

9. *See, e.g., United States v. Silk*, 331 U.S. 704 (1947).

10. *See generally* Susan N. Houseman, Flexible Staffing Arrangements, A Report on Temporary Help, On-Call, Direct-Hire Temporary, Leased, Contract Company, and Independent Contractor Employment in the United States (Aug. 1999) (available at *http://www.dol.gov/oasam/programs/history/herman/reports/futurework/conference/staffing/9.1_contractors.htm#19*).

11. *See generally* Charles Muhl, *What Is an Employee? The Answer Depends on the Federal Law,* Mthly. Lab. Rev. (Jan. 2002) (available at *http://www.bls.gov/opub/mlr/2002/01/art1full.pdf*).

12. U.S. Dept. of Labor, Fact Sheet #13: Employment Relationship Under the Fair Labor Standards Act (available at *http://www.dol.gov/esa/whd/regs/compliance/whdfs13.pdf*).

13. *Id.*

14. *Id.*

15. 26 U.S.C. §§ 3401 *et seq.* (income tax), 3101 *et seq.* (Social Security), 3301 *et seq.* (unemployment).

16. *See* Independent Contractor (Self-Employed) or Employee?, Internal Revenue Service website (available at *http://www.irs.gov/businesses/small/article/0,,id=99921,00.html*).

17. The factors used to determine eligibility for workers' compensation benefits greatly vary, and research should be conducted to determine which factors are considered in the state in which an individual intends to apply for these benefits. *See, e.g.,* New York State Workers' Compen. Bd., Frequently Asked Questions, Who Is an Employee Under the Workers' Compensation Law? (available at *http://www.wcb.state.ny.us/content/main/Workers/ Coverage_wc/worker_empDefinition.jsp*); *see generally* Office of Workers' Compen. Programs (OWCP), U.S. Dept. of Labor, for additional state-specific information (available at *http://www.dol.gov/esa/owcp/owcpmiss.htm*).

18. *See, e.g.,* New York State Workers' Compen. Bd., Frequently Asked Questions, Who Is an Employee Under the Workers' Compensation Law? (available at *http://www.wcb.state.ny. us/content/main/Workers/Coverage_wc/worker_empDefinition.jsp*).

19. *See* New York State Workers' Compen. Bd., Frequently Asked Questions, Who Is an Employee Under the Workers' Compensation Law? (available at *http://www.wcb.state .ny.us/content/main/Workers/Coverage_wc/worker_empDefinition.jsp*); *see generally* Office of Workers' Compen. Programs (OWCP), U.S. Dept. of Labor, for additional state-specific information (available at *http://www.dol.gov/esa/owcp/owcpmiss.htm*).

20. *See* New York State Workers' Compen. Bd., Frequently Asked Questions, Who Is an Employee Under the Workers' Compensation Law? (available at *http://www.wcb.state .ny.us/content/main/Workers/Coverage_wc/worker_empDefinition.jsp*).

21. *Id.*

22. *Vizcaino v. Microsoft,* 120 F.3d 1006 (9th Cir. 1997).

23. *See generally* Charles Muhl, *What Is an Employee? The Answer Depends on the Federal Law,* Mthly. Lab. Rev. (Jan. 2002) (available at *http://www.bls.gov/opub/mlr/2002/01/art1full.pdf*).

24. Once it is determined that an individual is an employee entitled to certain benefits and protections, the focus shifts to determine which party is the employer and, therefore, responsible for providing them. The analysis required to identify the appropriate employer is beyond the scope of this book but worth mentioning, because properly classified employees are entitled only to receive benefits and protections from their employer, whose identity may be disputed.

Recruiting and Assembling a Diverse Applicant Pool

Chapter Objectives

This chapter explores the importance of clearly defining a hiring need and selecting a candidate from a diverse pool of qualified applicants. The text focuses on the creation of concise job descriptions that require only the minimum qualifications necessary to perform the essential job tasks, and the importance of using a number of techniques to ensure that a diverse group of qualified candidates have access to an employment opportunity.

After completing this chapter, students should have a fundamental understanding of the hiring process, from the initial identification of a hiring need through the time an employer determines who will be interviewed and subject to further consideration.

Specifically, upon mastering the main objectives of this chapter students should be able to

■ explain the benefits of a comprehensive hiring process;
■ explain the importance of listing only the minimum job qualifications in a job description and advertisement;
■ explain what is meant by an applicant pool;
■ discuss the benefits of advertising a position and how to reach the most diverse pool of qualified applicants; and
■ list a number of recruitment techniques and explain the benefits and drawbacks of using each.

NEED FOR A HIRING PROCESS

The recruitment of qualified candidates for employment opportunities is the foundation of the hiring process and can provide an employer with significant benefits.

A. IDENTIFY THE IDEAL CANDIDATE

A comprehensive recruiting process will assist an employer in identifying the ideal candidate to fill a position. Although there may be a number of individuals who possess the skills necessary to complete the job tasks, a comprehensive recruitment process increases the likelihood the employer will find the candidate best suited to meet its needs.

B. MINIMIZE COSTS ASSOCIATED WITH HIGH TURNOVER

A recruitment process has the potential to reduce a number of costs associated with a high turnover rate. If an employer uses an informal or truncated process and hires a candidate who remains in the position only for a short period of time, an additional investment of time and money will be required to move through the process a second, third, or even fourth time.

Even if an employer selects a second candidate from those already interviewed, the start-up costs associated with hiring a new employee must be repeated and will include such things as readying office space, setting up technological equipment, and ordering business cards and office supplies. These costs are in addition to those associated with training new employees as well as the loss in productivity for the other employees who might be required to divert their attention from their day-to-day responsibilities to provide this training, or whose responsibilities it might be to arrange for preliminary employment matters such as readying office space and setting up equipment, as referenced above.

C. ENHANCE EMPLOYEE MORALE

A comprehensive hiring process can also have a positive impact on current employees, because they might be more likely to exert their efforts to train and welcome new employees if they are confident the candidate is committed to the position for the long term and if they have the expectation they will receive the benefit of an additional person to share the workload.

A workplace that is viewed as having a revolving door (meaning that new employees continue to be hired to replace exiting and usually dissatisfied employees) might be plagued with bad morale, decreased productivity, and a workforce that is not fully dedicated, either to the new employee or to their employer. In addition, employers who make hiring decisions outside the framework of a structured plan may face additional problems because the absence of a plan may make them vulnerable to claims of workplace discrimination.

D. MINIMIZE WORKPLACE DISCRIMINATION CLAIMS

Employers who do not dedicate the appropriate level of resources to the hiring process increase the likelihood that their hiring decisions will be viewed as biased, unfair, or the result of discriminatory behavior. Those who do not apply the same standards to all applicants will have difficulty demonstrating that their decisions were consistent with Title VII and other anti-discrimination laws.

In contrast, employers who allocate resources to the recruitment process will minimize their potential liability. They will be prepared to identify and explain the factors used to make employment decisions—information that can be used to refute a claim that employment decisions were based on improper motives. This potential for liability has a significant impact on the structuring of a legally sound recruitment and hiring plan.

 **RELEVANCE OF THE PROHIBITION AGAINST DISCRIMINATION TO THE RECRUITMENT PROCESS**

Employers should structure their recruitment process to avoid discriminatory decisions, recognizing that even the inference that discriminatory motives were part of the decision-making process will be problematic. Further, employers must recognize that courts do not impose a particularly high initial burden on an individual asserting a claim, and the process is filled with numerous sources of potential liability. For example, in one case a court allowed an individual to pursue an employment discrimination claim based on the fact that testimony was presented to illustrate that the names of the applicants, their voices, and the names of organizations to which the applicants belonged were sufficient to suggest that the employer knew the race of the applicants when it made its adverse employment decision.[1]

A. EXTENT OF THE PROHIBITION UNDER FEDERAL LAW

The prohibition against workplace discrimination under federal anti-discrimination laws applies to all phases of the employment process, including advertising positions, soliciting resumes, interviewing candidates, and extending employment offers. For example, employers who solicit applications only from select national-origin groups or who implement a recruitment program that intentionally excludes applicants of a particular national origin could be subject to liability. Employers should also recognize that seemingly neutral practices such as the solicitation of referrals through informal networking processes and the use of any other practices that result in "limiting, segregating, or classifying employees or applicants in a way which would deprive or tend to deprive employment opportunities or otherwise adversely affect his status as an employee, because of such individual's race, color, religion, sex, or national origin" could result in liability.[2]

B. EXTENT OF THE PROHIBITION UNDER STATE LAW

Although the statutory language of Title VII is broad, many states offer additional protections. Some states expand the prohibition of printing or circulating job advertisements that discriminate based on protected-class membership under federal anti-discrimination laws such as Title VII (race, color, religion, sex, and national origin), the Americans with Disabilities Act (ADA) (disabilities), and the Age Discrimination in Employment Act (ADEA) (age), to prohibit job advertisements that discriminate on the basis of other characteristics such as military status and marital status.[3]

C. ALLOCATION OF RESOURCES

When determining how much effort to expend on the creation and implementation of a recruiting and hiring plan, employers should ensure there is significant oversight at each stage of the process. Individuals who have recruiting and hiring roles should have extensive knowledge of the minimum job requirements for each open position, and should be trained about workplace anti-discrimination laws to ensure that illegal factors are not considered when making decisions. Demographic information about applications received and individuals selected for interviews should also be reviewed to ensure that the process captures a diverse pool of candidates.

In the event a rejected candidate claims that the hiring process is discriminatory, the employer's explanation of each component of this process along with a showing that it is uniformly applied to all applicants, regardless of whether or not they are members of a protected class, will become the basis for its defense. This is important because a failure to comply with Title VII and other anti-discrimination laws could result in significant liability. For example, one well-known clothing retailer agreed to pay $50 million to settle a discrimination suit alleging, among other things, that it used recruitment and hiring practices that excluded minorities and women.[4]

Although there is no specific recruitment plan that will protect an employer from liability, employers can minimize the potential for a workplace discrimination claim and position themselves to defend a suit in the event one arises by creating and implementing an objective, neutral, and structured hiring process. For this reason, although employers may want to retain flexibility during the hiring process, to the extent possible they should incorporate measurable objective factors into the process, starting with the creation of a clear and concise explanation of the minimum qualifications necessary for the position.[5]

 **JOB DESCRIPTIONS**

Once an employer identifies a hiring need, it should draft a clear and concise job description that is narrowly tailored to target qualified candidates.

A. JOB TASKS AND RESPONSIBILITIES

A job description should be narrowly tailored and describe each task that will be performed by the person who fills the position. This will assist employers in finding the candidate who is the best match for the position. In addition, allocating the resources needed to craft an accurate job description will help to ensure that the job description serves as an effective tool for long-term planning, because it can be used to assist supervisors in determining the appropriate level of discipline if a candidate who is hired does not satisfactorily perform the job tasks. See Chapter 14, Performance Management.

1. ESSENTIAL VERSUS TANGENTIAL TASKS

When crafting a job description, employers should separate the **essential job tasks** from the **tangential tasks**, which may be desirable but are not essential. Making the distinction between the two is important because the essential job functions will dictate the minimum qualifications for the position, encourage those with the skills to perform the necessary job functions to submit an application, and increase the likelihood that the ideal candidate will be identified. Most significant, however, is that by accurately identifying the essential functions, employers will not discourage members of a protected class who will be able to perform the essential job tasks from applying for the position based on their inability to perform the tangential (non-essential) tasks.

For example, suppose an employer is seeking to hire a mechanic to perform basic oil changes and who may occasionally be asked to assist a senior mechanic to rebuild an engine. If the employer lists both tasks as essential, this could be problematic. This is because if members of a protected class would be less likely than nonmembers to have the skills necessary to rebuild an engine, identifying the rebuilding of engines as an essential task will discourage those members of a protected class who do not have the skills from applying for the position, and those skills were not necessary to successfully perform the essential job responsibilities. Therefore, by listing a tangential task as essential, the employer could be subject to liability for discriminatory conduct for discouraging (and in some cases eliminating) qualified candidates from consideration for the position. See Chapter 2, Title VII — The Foundation of Workplace Discrimination Law, for a further explanation of this type of situation, which would materialize as a disparate impact claim under Title VII if the discriminatory result was unintentional.

essential job tasks
responsibilities that represent the necessary components of a position and that will be performed by the individual filling the position

tangential job tasks
responsibilities that may be assigned to an individual working in a position but that are not a necessary component of the position

2. OTHER RELATED DUTIES

In the event an employer wants to retain some flexibility with respect to assigning job tasks, it is preferable for the employer to indicate that "other related duties" might be assigned to the job candidate as opposed to retaining the right to assign additional duties "at the employer's discretion."

This limitation on the right to assign work may be valuable in the event an employee challenges the assignment of a particular job task not delineated in the description, claiming it is an undesirable job function and assigned in a discriminatory manner. An employer will be in a better position to defend an assignment by showing that it is related to the essential tasks of the job than it would be by asserting the assignment is appropriate because the employer retained the sole discretion to determine appropriate work assignments. Even employers who retain broad rights to assign work have an obligation to ensure that such assignments are made in a uniform and nondiscriminatory manner.

B. MINIMUM QUALIFICATIONS

© Randy Glasbergen.
www.glasbergen.com

"I'm looking for someone I can mold and shape into management material. Aside from being a big lump of clay, do you have any other qualifications?"

For the same reasons employers should distinguish essential jobs tasks from those that are tangential, they should distinguish the minimum qualifications for a position from those that are desirable but not necessary. Employers should be able to justify each qualification by explaining why it is essential for a candidate to possess the qualification to be considered for the position. For example, if an employer determines that a position on the loading dock would require lifting 50-pound crates, it should not post a job description requiring candidates to have the ability to lift 60-pound crates. This is because the use of the enhanced requirement might discourage qualified applicants who are members of certain protected classes from applying for the position even though they might be able to lift 50 pounds and are therefore qualified for the position. If an employer indicates that the suitable candidate must have a college degree, the employer should be prepared to illustrate why a person without a college degree would be unable to perform the essential tasks. This is because imposing this requirement probably would discourage qualified applicants, who are members of certain protected classes and less likely to have college degrees, from applying for the position.

Further, because employers list only the qualifications required for the position, they should be prepared to disqualify all candidates who do not possess the minimum requirements. An employer who makes an offer to a candidate who lacks one of the qualifications listed as necessary for the position will leave itself open to a discrimination claim, particularly if there are other rejected applicants who do possess the minimum qualifications and are members of a protected class.

1. YEARS OF EXPERIENCE

Employers should also be careful about requiring applicants to have a minimum number of years of high-level experience. Although an employer might desire a candidate with 10 to 15 years of particular experience, it should be prepared to illustrate why fewer years of experience would prevent a candidate from performing the desired work. This is important, because by requiring a significant number of years of high-level experience, employers might eliminate some members of protected classes who have historically been denied advancement opportunities, through no fault of their own.

Employers should also avoid listing a maximum number of years of experience because it could be viewed as age discrimination, potentially discouraging a disproportionate number of older individuals from applying for a position because they would be more likely than younger candidates to have exceeded the upper limit on years of experience.

2. SUBJECTIVE VERSUS OBJECTIVE RESPONSIBILITIES

Job tasks should reference as many objective factors as possible rather than focusing on subjective considerations. This is because in the event a workplace discrimination claim materializes, it will be easier for an employer to illustrate a decision was nondiscriminatory if it can show a measurable explanation for the result.

For example, an employer who identifies the need to hire an individual who can type 70 words per minute should include this quantifiable measurement in a job description rather than just referencing a need for a fast typist. Under these circumstances, if an applicant asserts that the employer rejected his application based on an improper consideration such as his race, the employer can point to the applicant's ability to type 40 words a minute as the basis for the disqualification, as opposed to referencing a general dissatisfaction with the speed of the applicant's typing. Employers who do list an objective requirement in a job description, however, as discussed above, should be prepared to explain why an applicant who possesses a lower skill set, such as the ability to type 50 words per minute, would not be qualified for the position.

3. UNIFORM APPLICATION

Employers that have determined the minimum qualifications for a position must also ensure that the same standards are applied to all applicants. For example, an employer could require applicants for a support staff position to type 60 words per minute, but the employer could not list this qualification solely for its female applicants. Similarly, an employer may require that all applicants be able to lift 60 pounds, but it cannot set this standard for male applicants while establishing a different standard for female applicants. See Chapter 5, Sex, Pregnancy, and Genetic Discrimination.

After the employer has evaluated and determined its precise hiring needs, the next step is devising a plan to ensure that the most diverse group of qualified candidates are given the opportunity to apply for the position.

APPLICANT POOL

applicant pool
group of candidates who will be considered for an open position

Employers seeking to hire a diverse workplace must solicit candidates from a diverse **applicant pool**, which represents the group of qualified individuals who will be considered for the position.

A. OBLIGATION TO CONSIDER ALL QUALIFIED APPLICANTS

Once the minimum qualifications are established, employers should consider all applicants who meet those standards. Employers are not permitted to disqualify applicants based on their membership in a protected class. For example, in one instance the owner of a fast-food store refused to give an employment application to a biracial girl even though there was a "help wanted" sign in the window. Soon after, the girl sent her Caucasian friend into the store with the same request, and the friend was immediately provided with an application. Based on this, the biracial girl filed a claim for racial discrimination, which resulted in a $5,000 settlement on her behalf.[6]

1. CUSTOMER PREFERENCE

The prohibition against discrimination in hiring decisions applies to decisions based on the prejudices of both employers and their customers. Employers are prohibited from making discriminatory hiring decisions, and they cannot follow the discriminatory instructions of third parties. The EEOC, which is the federal agency that enforces Title VII, makes no distinction between decisions based on an employer's prejudices and those based on the prejudices of others but carried out by the employer. For example, an employer would not be permitted to decline to hire a Muslim who is the most qualified candidate for the counter person position at its coffee shop based on a concern that the individual's religion will make some customers uncomfortable.[7]

Similarly, the EEOC rejected the assertion that an employer had the right to decline to consider the application of a minority applicant for a job as a delivery person, due to concern that its customers would not be comfortable with a minority employee coming to their home.[8] An employer would also not have the right to reject the most qualified applicant (who happened to be a black female) based on a concern relating to how some customers might react to a Black/African-American customer service representative.[9] In one instance, a company agreed to settle a discrimination claim for more than $700,000 for, among other things, separating the applications for positions in an assisted-living facility based on minority groups, because certain residents indicated they preferred the assistance of non-minority caregivers.[10]

2. CO-WORKER PREFERENCE

Employers are also prohibited from making decisions based on the real or perceived prejudices of their existing workforce. An employer could not refuse to hire an applicant who did not ascribe to a particular religion based on a specific concern that the individual would feel uncomfortable with other employees who have strong ties to their religious beliefs.[11]

3. EMPLOYMENT AGENCIES

Not only are employers prohibited from engaging in discriminatory practices, but they are also prohibited from instructing or suggesting that recruitment firms engage in this same behavior. Furthermore, by following the discriminatory instructions or suggestions of an employer, recruitment firms could also be held liable for any resulting discriminatory conduct.

For example, an employer could be subject to liability for discriminatory conduct for instructing an employment agency to limit potential candidates to individuals who belong to a particular religion (or to screen out candidates belonging to a particular religion), and the employment agency would be subject to liability for complying with such a request. An employment agency would also be subject to liability under Title VII for complying with an employer's instructions to screen out applicants based on their national origin as evidenced by their last names, or on the fact that an applicant might need a reasonable accommodation for a disability or for a religious practice, and the employer would be subject to liability for making such a request.[12]

B. COST-EFFECTIVE RECRUITMENT TOOLS

Once an employer makes a commitment to soliciting and reviewing all candidates that possess the minimum qualifications for the position, there are a number of ways to reach the appropriate candidates. The ideal plan will utilize a number of different tools to provide a diverse group of qualified candidates with access to the opportunity. Although it may seem that the task of developing and implementing a nondiscriminatory recruitment plan will be an expensive process, it does not have to be cost prohibitive. Instead, there a number of inexpensive recruitment tools that can provide access to a diverse applicant pool and achieve the level of diversity contemplated by Title VII and other anti-discrimination laws.

1. EMPLOYEE REFERRALS/WORD-OF-MOUTH RECRUITING

Employers may be attracted to a recruitment process that focuses on asking current employees for referrals, based on the presumption that they would be in the best position to know which candidates would be best suited for an open position.

a. Intentional Discriminatory Result

Word-of-mouth recruitment techniques are prohibited if the intention is to deliberately recruit a homogenous workforce and exclude people based on membership in a protected class.[13] For example, because religion is a protected class under Title VII, an employer would be prohibited from engaging in word-of-mouth recruitment intended to limit the recruitment efforts to candidates that practice a certain religion. See Chapter 4, Religious Discrimination.

b. Unintentional Discriminatory Result

Even if an employer's use of employee referrals is not intended to be discriminatory, reliance on it as a sole recruitment tool is problematic. Because people tend to socialize and network with those similar to themselves, relying on this type of informal recruitment technique might deny access to an opportunity to a large number of qualified individuals who are members of a protected class not represented in the employer's workplace. This is particularly true in industries where minorities and women continue to be underrepresented.[14] Thus, it is critical that employers go beyond this traditional method of recruiting to minimize potential discrimination claims by soliciting qualified applicants from a diverse population.

2. NEPOTISM

nepotism
providing favorable treatment to family members of current employees when making employment decisions

Nepotism relates to favoring the relatives of employees when making employment decisions. Many employers have anti-nepotism policies to prevent the consideration of familial ties in making employment decisions.

Nepotism is generally not a favored recruitment tool for the same reasons that word-of-mouth recruiting and employee referrals are problematic. Specifically, if an employer's workforce is made up of primarily one ethnic group and the employer favors the relatives of current employees when making hiring decisions, that favoritism could violate Title VII's prohibition against discriminatory conduct. Employers who decide to use nepotism as a recruitment technique should maintain a firm commitment to using both objective and neutral hiring criteria when dealing with family members of current employees to minimize (but not eliminate) potential liability for discriminatory conduct.[15]

3. JOB FAIRS, INTERNSHIPS, AND PROFESSIONAL ORGANIZATIONS

Employee referrals, word-of-mouth recruiting, and nepotism are recruitment techniques that appeal to employers because they have the potential to minimize the time and money allocated to the hiring process. However, the EEOC actually provides guidance relating to a number of other recruitment tools that involve minimal cost, can alleviate some of the potential problems associated with informal recruitment techniques likely to target a homogenous applicant pool, and can assist an employer in reaching a diverse pool of qualified applicants.

For example, the Agency encourages employers to attend job fairs, offer internships, and seek assistance from professional groups and associations to enhance the diversity of their applicant pools.[16] These types of tools should be part of an employer's overall recruitment program, particularly if the employer has a homogeneous workforce. When making decisions about which job fairs to attend, employers should attempt to recruit at colleges that have a high population of minority students and members of other protected classes, particularly if their current workforce is not diverse.[17]

C. JOB POSTINGS AND ADVERTISEMENTS

Another way to solicit candidates from a diverse pool of qualified applicants is to advertise the position to a diverse group of potential candidates. Although there is likely a cost associated with advertising, it will be significantly less than a damage award that might be imposed should there be a finding that an employer engaged in discriminatory conduct by failing to provide members of a protected class the opportunity to apply for the position. In addition, technological advances allow for more targeted and less costly forms of advertising than what was previously available. Employers who decide to use advertising as part of their recruiting process must remember, however, that they can be subject to liability under Title VII for both the discriminatory content of a job posting as well as the discriminatory dissemination of it.

1. DRAFTING THE ADVERTISEMENT

The federal prohibition against workplace discrimination applies to job advertisements, and some state laws specifically reference the prohibition against printing or circulating job advertisements that discriminate based on protected class membership.[18] Because of this, it is critical to draft a nondiscriminatory job posting so that the use of the tool, designed to prevent discriminatory conduct by reaching out to a diverse audience, is not found to be discriminatory itself.

a. Using Neutral Terms

Employers should avoid terms that are linked to characteristics associated with protected-class membership because using such terms can be a powerful indicator of a discriminatory motive. Although terms that relate to any protected class should be avoided, issues commonly arise with respect to advertisements that reference age and gender.

i. Age

The ADEA is the federal law that prohibits most employers with 20 or more employees from discriminating against individuals who are 40 years of age and older, and some states prohibit discrimination against younger individuals.[19] Based on this, employers should not consider an applicant's age when making hiring decisions, and words suggesting an employer is seeking applicants of a particular age should be avoided.

For example, advertising for applicants in a particular age range, for young applicants, for college students, or for recent college graduates should not be used, because it implies that older candidates will not be considered. These terms have the potential to discourage older employees, who are protected by age discrimination laws, from applying for these positions. Advertisements seeking candidates over 65 years of age, retirees, or candidates interested in supplementing their pensions would also be considered discriminatory.[20] The use of these terms is problematic because it suggests that the employer intends to consider an applicant's age when making its hiring decisions. In addition, this type of advertising would undermine the employer's goal of encouraging a diverse group of qualified applicants to apply for the position. See Chapter 6, Age Discrimination.

ii. Gender

Because Title VII prohibits discrimination based on sex, terms relating to gender, such as those listed below, should be avoided in favor of gender-neutral alternatives. Employers who use gender-specific terms in job postings suggest that they are most interested in applicants of a particular sex, and basing a hiring decision on an individual's membership in a protected class constitutes discriminatory conduct under Title VII and could subject an employer to liability.[21] See Chapter 5, Sex, Pregnancy, and Genetic Discrimination.

Terms to Avoid	Comparable Substitutes[22]
Bellboy	Bell Person, Bellhop
Male, Female, Lady, Gentleman	Applicant, Candidate, Trainee
Steward/Stewardess	Flight attendant
Foreman	Supervisor
Draftsman	Drafter
Fireman	Firefighter
Policeman	Police Officer

b. Encouraging Diverse Applicants

In addition to engaging in conduct designed to recruit candidates from a diverse applicant pool, such as avoiding terms that suggest an employer may be considering discriminatory factors when making its hiring decisions, employers should make an affirmative commitment to a nondiscriminatory process. Employers should make it clear in their advertisements that they welcome and encourage applicants from a diverse applicant pool to apply for a position. The most direct way to convey this message is to include language in the advertisement stating that the employer is an "equal opportunity employer" committed to refraining from making hiring decisions based on membership in a protected class.[23]

2. POSTING THE ADVERTISEMENT

After the job posting is drafted, the employer should ensure that it is disseminated in a nondiscriminatory manner to reach a diverse applicant pool. One of the purposes of advertising a position is to solicit applications from individuals other than those who have a personal connection to current employees, so the distribution should not be limited to internal communications. An employer would likely be engaging in discriminatory conduct by limiting the posting of the advertisement to a Hindu temple, and distributing the advertisement only to members of the temple and asking them to refer their friends who are also members of the temple. In this instance, even if the advertisement included neutral and nondiscriminatory language, the dissemination of the information to a limited audience would undermine the benefits of the neutral language and commitment to diversity.[24]

a. Newspapers

In an effort to reach a diverse audience for a job posting, an employer could post the advertisement in a number of newspapers that have a diverse readership. Because the use of newspaper advertising is a way to enhance the diversity of the applicant pool, the benefit of this recruiting tool will be minimized (or even diminished) if the target audience of the newspaper mirrors the employer's workforce. Thus, employers that do not have a particularly diverse workforce should target minority or ethnic newspapers whose readers might not otherwise be aware of the open position.[25]

b. Internet

Employers may also decide to post an advertisement on the Internet based on the growing number of job sites that have become popular and that are cost-effective methods of targeting a diverse pool of potential candidates. Although the use of the Internet has the potential to enhance the diversity of the applicant pool, an employer should not rely on it exclusively. Because some segments of the working population do not own personal computers, or do not have Internet access, by limiting recruitment to online websites, an employer could be denying potentially qualified candidates access to the opportunity. In addition, because older applicants would be less likely to have computer skills than younger applicants, relying on online and electronic submissions could result in fewer submissions from older applicants, and this discriminatory result, even if unintentional, could constitute discriminatory behavior.[26]

D. MONITORING RESPONSES TO AN ADVERTISEMENT

After an employer sets an initial recruitment plan in motion, it should monitor the incoming applications to ensure that its efforts were sufficient to achieve the desired result of a diverse pool of qualified applicants. In the event the employer notices that members of a particular protected class seem to be underrepresented, the employer may wish to reexamine the qualifications and responsibilities to ensure each is necessary for the candidate who fills the position to possess.

When employers are satisfied that they have a diverse applicant pool with a number of qualified candidates, they should prepare to move on to the next step in the hiring process. Specifically, employers will use the employment application and interview process to gather additional information to assess each applicant's suitability for the position.

KEY TERMS

✓ applicant pool   ✓ tangential job tasks
✓ essential job tasks   ✓ nepotism

DISCUSSION QUESTIONS

Explain your response to each of the following questions with the understanding that in some cases there is no right or wrong answer. If you cannot make an informed decision with the facts provided, indicate the nature and significance of the additional information you would need. For the purposes of these questions, you can assume that the employers and employees mentioned below are covered by Title VII and other relevant federal workplace anti-discrimination laws.

1. Explain the benefits of a structured hiring process.
2. What information should be included in a job description?
3. Define *applicant pool* and explain its relevance to the hiring process and workplace anti-discrimination laws.

4. Provide some examples of cost-effective recruitment tools.
5. Your boss tells you he plans to exaggerate the qualifications he lists on a job description because he wants to hire an exceptional candidate. Do you think this is a good idea?
6. Scott works in the financial services industry and is hosting an informal reception to speak with anyone interested in applying for a position as his new executive assistant. He asks his co-workers to invite any of their friends who might be interested in applying for the position. What do you think about this recruiting technique?
7. Ariel is staffing her new Spanish restaurant, which she hopes will capture the essence of the country. To accomplish this goal, she plans to post "help wanted" signs written in Spanish to attract candidates who are fluent in the language. What do you think about this idea?
8. Francesca wants to hire two new housekeepers to work in her hotel and is working on a job description. She plans to require all candidates to be able to engage in heavy lifting because from time to time, housekeepers may be asked to move and set up tables for large conferences. She also plans to target younger employees because she has money in her budget to pay only minimum wage. Explain any issues that might materialize based on the writing of this job description and how you would address them.
9. Richard is the owner of a pharmacy and is looking to hire a new pharmacist. One of his employees, Hailey, says that her cousin Jake is relocating from another city, is looking for a new position as a pharmacist, and has an excellent reputation. Hailey's boss thanks her for the referral but says that it would be inappropriate for him to consider the relatives of current employees. What do you think?

ENDNOTES

1. *See EEOC v. Target Corp.*, 460 F.3d 946 (7th Cir. 2006).
2. 42 U.S.C. § 2000e-2(a)(2).
3. *See, e.g.*, N.Y. Exec. Law § 296(1)(d) ("It is unlawful for an employer or employment agency to print or circulate or cause to be printed or circulated any statement, advertisement or publication, or to use any form or application for employment, or to make any inquiry in connection with prospective employment, which expresses, directly or indirectly, any limitation, specification or discrimination as to age, race, creed, color, national origin, sexual orientation, military status, sex, disability, predisposing genetic characteristic, or marital status, or any intent to make any such limitation, specification, or discrimination . . .").
4. Press Release, EEOC Agrees to Landmark Resolution of Discrimination Case Against Abercrombie & Fitch (Nov. 16, 2004) (available at *http://www.eeoc.gov/press/11-18-04 .html*).
5. EEOC Compl. Man. § 13-III (National Origin Discrimination) (available at *http://www .eeoc.gov/policy/docs/national-origin.html*).
6. *EEOC v. Quiznos*, No. 2:06-cv-00215-DSFJC (C.D. Cal. settled Sept. 22, 2006).

7. EEOC Compl. Man. § 12 (Religious Discrimination) (July 22, 2008) (available at *http:// www.eeoc.gov/policy/docs/religion.html*).

8. *EEOC v. Schwan's Sales*, No. 4:0 CV 00221 AGF (E.D. Mo. Jan. 29, 2007).

9. *EEOC v. Con-Way Freight, Inc.*, No. 407 CV 01638 (E.D. Mo. Sept. 20, 2007).

10. *See EEOC v. Merrill Gardens, LLC*, No. 1:05-CV-004 (N.D. Ind. Oct. 6, 2005).

11. EEOC Compl. Man. § 12 (Religious Discrimination) (July 22, 2008) (available at *http:// www.eeoc.gov/policy/docs/religion.html*).

12. *See* U.S. Equal Employment Opportunity Commn., Guidelines on Discrimination Because of Religion, 29 C.F.R. § 1605.3; *see generally* EEOC Compl. Man. § 12 (Religious Discrimination) (July 22, 2008) (available at *http://www.eeoc.gov/policy/docs/religion .html*). Note that temporary agencies are subject to the same restrictions as other employers and these limitations apply beyond the making of hiring decisions. For example, if a temporary agency learns that one of its employees is assigned to a back-end position in response to his wearing of religious garb, the agency should insist that the employee be returned to the more desirable position. EEOC Compl. Man. § 13-III (National Origin Discrimination) (available at *http://www.eeoc.gov/policy/docs/national-origin.html*); *see also* Enforcement Guidance on Application of EEOC Laws to Contingent Workers Placed by Temporary Employment Agencies and Other Staffing Firms, Questions 8-9, 11 (BNA 1997) (available at *http://www.eeoc.gov/policy/docs/guidance-contingent.html*).

13. *See, e.g.*, EEOC Compl. Man. § 13-III (National Origin Discrimination) (available at *http://www.eeoc.gov/policy/docs/national-origin.html*).

14. Rania V. Sedhom, *The EEOC's eRace Initiative: Combating Systemic Racism*, Human Resources 2008 (Summer ed.) (available at *http://www.buckconsultants.com/buckconsultants/portals/0/ documents/publications/published_articles/2008/Articles_Sedhom_Human_Resources_summer_ 08.pdf*).

15. *See* U.S. Equal Employment Opportunity Commn., Informal Discussion Letter, All Statutes: Pre-employment Inquiries (Dec. 23, 2004) (available at *http://www.eeoc.gov/eeoc/ foia/letters/2004/all_statutes_inquiries.html*). In addition to concerns under Title VII, nepotism could result in liability under other laws such as those that relate to privacy.

16. *See* EEOC Comp. Man. § 13 (National Origin Discrimination) (Oct. 6, 2008) (available at *http://www.eeoc/gov/policy/docs/national-origin.html*).

17. *See* U.S. Equal Employment Opportunity Commn., Transcr. Commission Meeting (Feb. 28, 2007) (available at *http://www.eeoc.gov/eeoc/meetings/archive/2-28-07/*).

18. *See, e.g.*, N.Y. Exec. Law § 296(1)(d) ("It is unlawful for an employer or employment agency to print or circulate or cause to be printed or circulated any statement, advertisement or publication, or to use any form or application for employment, or to make any inquiry in connection with prospective employment, which expresses, directly or indirectly, any limitation, specification or discrimination as to age, race, creed, color, national origin, sexual orientation, military status, sex, disability, predisposing genetic characteristic, or marital status, or any intent to make any such limitation, specification, or discrimination. . . ."); *see generally* New York State Div. of Human Rights, Recommendations on Employment Inquiries (rev. Dec. 2004) (available at *http://www.dhr.state.ny.us/ pdf/employment.pdf*).

19. 29 U.S.C. § 630(b). Some state laws protect employees who are younger than 40 years of age. *See, e.g.*, Minn. Stat. § 363A.03 (prohibiting discrimination in employment practice against employees over the age of majority).

20. 29 C.F.R. § 1625.4(a).

21. New York State Div. of Human Rights, Recommendations on Employment Inquiries (rev. Dec. 2004) (available at *http://www.dhr.state.ny.us/pdf/employment.pdf*).

22. *Id.*

23. EEOC Comp. Man. § 13-III (National Origin Discrimination) (Oct. 6, 2008) (available at *http://www.eeoc.gov/policy/docs/national-origin.html*).

24. EEOC Compl. Man. § 12 (Religious Discrimination) (July 22, 2008) (available at *http:// www.eeoc.gov/policy/docs/religion.html*).

25. *See* U.S. Equal Employment Opportunity Commn., Transcr. Commission Meeting (Feb. 28, 2007) (available at *http://www.eeoc.gov/eeoc/meetings/archive/2-28-07/*).

26. *See* U.S. Equal Employment Opportunity Commn., Internet Hiring, EEOC Informal Discussion Letter (Oct. 2, 2005) (available at *http://www.eeoc.gov/eeoc/foia/letters/2005/ internet_hiring.html*).

Collection of Information: The Application and Interview

10

Chapter Objectives

This chapter explores how employers can appropriately gather information about job applicants to assess their qualifications for a position. The text focuses on the need to ask job-related and narrowly tailored questions to minimize the potential for discrimination claims.

After completing this chapter, students should have a fundamental understanding about the use of employment applications and the interview process. Students should be able to differentiate between questions that solicit information that can be appropriately considered as part of the hiring process, and questions that should be avoided.

Specifically, upon mastering the main objectives of this chapter students should be able to

■ explain the overriding themes governing the collection of information during the hiring process;

■ explain the types of exchanges between a prospective employer and applicant that would be considered part of an employment application and interview;

■ explain how facially neutral requests for information such as those relating to the applicant's contact information, marital status, credit history, and native language might subject an employer to liability under Title VII and other federal anti-discrimination laws;

■ explain why an employer should not discuss an applicant's medical condition during a job interview; and

■ explain the types of questions relating to an applicant's education and work history that employers should avoid asking during the hiring process.

COLLECTING INFORMATION FROM APPLICANTS

Once an employer has a diverse pool of candidates to consider, the next step is collecting additional information about each individual to assess his ability to perform the responsibilities associated with the open position. A significant amount of information is obtained through the applicant's completion of an employment application and participation in an interview. The law does not distinguish between information that is collected in written form and information that is acquired verbally, so the same laws govern the collection of information from both of these sources.

Employers usually require applicants to fill out an application, which is reviewed to determine whether the individual will move forward in the process and be granted an interview. Employers must be careful to screen the candidates without considering any information related to an applicant's membership in a protected class. After the employer selects the individuals it has determined are the most qualified for the position, interviews should be arranged to further assess their qualifications.

A. LIABILITY MAY ARISE FROM ANY INFORMATION EMPLOYER POSSESSES

As employers initiate the information collection process, they should understand that any information they possess, regardless of how it is acquired, may subject them to liability for a discrimination claim: *the presumption is that employers use all information they possess to make their employment decisions.*[1] Because this presumption applies to each stage of the recruitment process, employers should carefully consider each of their information requests to ensure that it is necessary for purposes of making a decision on whom to hire. If the requested information is not necessary or will not be considered as part of the decision-making process, then it should not be solicited.

For example, although there is no outright prohibition against asking for a candidate's date of birth or age, such requests are closely scrutinized because of the potential for such information to be used to screen out older applicants in violation of laws that prohibit age discrimination. Therefore, employers who ask for the information should be prepared to explain why a hiring decision cannot be made without it.[2]

B. NARROWLY TAILOR QUESTIONS TO SOLICIT JOB-RELATED INFORMATION

The purpose of the application and interview process is to assess a candidate's ability to perform the job functions. Employers should solicit only job-related information and ensure that the questions are narrowly tailored to avoid requesting information that is directly or indirectly related to characteristics of a protected-class membership. Questions that stem from stereotypes or generalizations linked to membership in a protected class should also be avoided. For example, female applicants should not be asked whether they have young children, based on the stereotype that if they do, they would likely have care-giving responsibilities that could prevent them from reporting to work on a consistent basis. Instead, the ideal questions are those that are fact specific and tied to the relevant job functions.

Employers should pay close attention to the information each question is intended to gather, as well as to inferences that can be drawn from any information produced in response to it. For example, national origin is a protected class under Title VII. If an employer seeks to hire a candidate who is fluent in Spanish, the interviewer should pose this question directly, as opposed to asking an applicant whether Spanish is her native language or whether the applicant was born in Spain. An employer will obtain similar information by asking an applicant whether he is fluent in Spanish or whether Spanish is an applicant's native language. However, if an employer declines to extend an offer to an applicant, and had previously requested information about his national origin when it could have obtained the information needed (level of fluency) without soliciting national origin information, this could suggest that the employer improperly considered the applicant's protected class membership in violation of Title VII.

C. UNIFORM PROCESS

Employers should also implement a uniform process and avoid the appearance of discriminatory motives by using the same application for all candidates and asking the same interview questions. In the event a discrimination claim does materialize, an employer could present evidence of this standardized treatment to refute a claim that individuals were subjected to different standards based on their membership in a protected class.[3]

 **EMPLOYMENT APPLICATION**

The guidelines for asking questions on employment applications and during interviews are similar, but there are some parameters that are unique to each method of information collection. The term **employment application** is broadly interpreted and relates to any written questions about and submissions by an applicant, including resumes and any other submitted information about a candidate's background.[4]

employment application
broad term for any written information provided by an applicant during the hiring process

The federal prohibition against workplace discrimination under Title VII applies to job applications. Some state laws specifically prohibit the use of applications that expressly, directly, or indirectly discriminate, based on an extensive list of protected classes beyond those protected by federal anti-discrimination laws.[5] An employer may be subject to liability for decisions relating to how the applications are submitted for consideration, as well as the type of information that is solicited.

A. ELECTRONIC APPLICATIONS

The increased reliance on computers and technology has led some employers to supplement, and in some cases to replace, its use of paper employment applications with electronic submissions via their websites, the websites of recruiting firms, or other job search engines. Using these submission formats may enhance the diversity of an applicant pool by enabling employers to reach out to a geographically diverse audience. The Equal Employment Opportunity Commission (EEOC), which is the federal agency that enforces Title VII, has, however, challenged the exclusive use of online applications, and courts have not ruled on whether the sole reliance on electronic applications would violate any federal anti-discrimination laws based on its potential to exclude members of certain protected classes. Thus, even though the use of electronic applications is not prohibited (and in fact is a widespread practice), employers should still be aware of the potential issues associated with their use.

1. DISPARATE TREATMENT DISCRIMINATION

An employer would be subject to liability under a disparate treatment claim for intentional discrimination under Title VII and other anti-discrimination laws for using electronic submissions to intentionally screen out applicants based on membership in a protected class. For example, if an employer required the submission of electronic applications so it could easily eliminate candidates over a certain age or that live in certain ethnic neighborhoods, this would constitute discriminatory behavior.[6]

2. DISPARATE IMPACT DISCRIMINATION

More challenging issues arise when analyzing conduct that might support a disparate impact claim, which is conduct that appears facially neutral but results in a disproportionate impact on members of a protected class. On the most basic level, by requiring applicants to log onto a website to apply for a position, employers are assuming that all qualified individuals have access to a computer to complete the process. On average, because minorities earn less money than nonminorities, they may be less likely to have access to computers and therefore be disproportionately impacted by a recruitment process that relies solely on electronic submissions.[7]

Even if all qualified applicants can gain access to a computer, another issue relates to whether all qualified applicants have the technical skills necessary to complete the electronic application process. This issue will be particularly problematic if the computer skills are not related to the minimum qualifications of the position for which the application is being used.

For example, if an employer requires all individuals interested in applying for a position to submit an application via the employer's website, and this includes jobs for individuals who will assist in building new office space, it potentially raises an issue because it is unlikely that computer skills would be necessary to complete the essential tasks for those positions. This might not be as problematic, however, if the positions that require online application submissions also require that applicants have those computer skills to complete the essential jobs tasks associated with the position.

Even if an employer can overcome this hurdle, online applications have the potential to surface within the context of other anti-discrimination laws. For example, because older applicants would be less likely than younger applicants to have computer skills, an employer's reliance on electronic applications could result in the exclusion of a significant number of qualified older applicants from the applicant pool in violation of the Age Discrimination in Employment Act (ADEA).[8] Using electronic applications also poses a potential risk of employer liability under the Americans with Disabilities Act (ADA), as evidenced by the filing of a claim against a number of employers by a group of blind individuals who relied on screen-reader software, because the employer's job websites were not compatible with these types of programs.[9] See Chapter 6, Age Discrimination, and Chapter 7, Disability Discrimination.

B. VIDEO RESUMES AND PHOTOGRAPHS

Generally speaking, employers should not ask applicants to provide video resumes or photographs before making a decision about whether a candidate will be invited for an interview. This is because an applicant's physical characteristics can provide a significant amount of information related to protected class membership. Specifically, both video resumes and photographs may reveal information about an individual's age, race, and national origin, or whether an individual has a visible physical disability. For example, an individual who wears a religious headdress and is asked to provide a photograph might file a claim for religious discrimination if subjected to an adverse employment decision.

Put simply, these types of requests have the potential to undermine the protections employers intend to achieve through implementing a nondiscriminatory hiring process. This is because by complying with the request of an employer for a video resume or photograph, an applicant will be revealing a significant amount of information about her protected-class status — which is the type of information the employer should be trying to avoid collecting.[10]

C. CONTENT OF APPLICATION

Once the employer decides which format will be used for the application, the next step is deciding what information the application will be designed to solicit from each applicant. The key to drafting a legally sound application is to clarify the purpose of the application, ensure all of the requested information is relevant, and avoid questions that intentionally or unintentionally solicit information that could be used for a discriminatory purpose. In addition, there are some provisions that are commonly included on an application to protect the interests of employers.

1. CLARIFYING THE IMPACT OF SUBMITTING AN APPLICATION

Employers should include language on their employment application clarifying that nothing contained in it, nor any subsequent request for an interview, should be construed as an offer of employment. For example, an employer can include language stating that the applicant "understands that the use of this application should not be construed as an offer of employment," or that the applicant "understands that the use of this application is not intended to obligate the employer in any way." This simple language can be one piece of evidence used to refute an applicant's claim that his submission of the application (or something that was said during the recruitment process) constituted an offer of employment or a guarantee of future work.

2. EXPLANATION OF REQUESTS FOR ADDITIONAL INFORMATION

To the extent the employer intends to request additional information from its applicants beyond what is requested on the form, this should be disclosed on the application to ensure the terms are agreeable to the applicant.

a. Verification of Information

An applicant should be notified on the application form if any of the provided information will be verified. To achieve this result, an application might include language stating that by completing this application the candidate authorizes the employer to "verify employment history, confirm academic credentials, and check references in its sole discretion to determine the applicant's suitability for this position."

b. Pre-Employment Testing

Applicants also should be told whether they will be required to take any tests as part of the application process, which might include a skills assessment test to determine whether an individual is qualified for the position. Employers who intend to conduct background checks (including a criminal history or credit check) should include language in the application outlining what will be performed; if an employer intends to retain a consumer reporting agency to provide this service, applicants should sign a separate document providing written authorization for the third-party agency to do this work. Because blanket policies that disqualify applicants based on arrest or conviction would likely violate Title VII, employers also often include language on the application stating that a past conviction or arrest will not necessarily disqualify an applicant from consideration.

Employers intending to condition an employment offer on the results of a drug test or medical examination should also include language to that effect. The application could state that the applicant "understands that the completion of this application does not guarantee an offer of employment, but in the event one is extended, the offer may be subject to the results of a medical and/or drug test." See Chapter 11, Pre-Employment Testing, for a detailed discussion of pre-employment tests and the limitations on the rights of employees to use them.

c. Verification of Eligibility to Work in the United States

Because federal law requires employers to verify an individual's eligibility to work in the United Sates, employers should also include language on their application that places applicants on notice of this obligation. An employer might indicate that "in compliance with federal law, all persons hired will be required to verify identity and eligibility to work in the United States and to complete the required employment eligibility verification document form upon hire."[11]

3. CONFIRMING EMPLOYER COMMITMENT TO AVOIDING DISCRIMINATORY CONDUCT

Employers should make it clear on their application forms that they are an equal opportunity employer and do not discriminate based on membership in a protected class.[12] This could be as simple as stating "this employer is an equal opportunity employer" or providing additional detail by listing the classes that are protected under Title VII (race, color, religion, sex, and national origin) as well as those protected under other federal and state anti-discrimination laws.

4. REQUESTING SIGNATURE OF APPLICANT

Employers usually ask applicants to sign the application to indicate that the information is accurate. The application might include language stating that the applicant represents that "the information provided is accurate and complete, and in the event the employer determines that information is false or misleading, my employment may be terminated at the time of the discovery."

After an applicant completes the employment application, the employer should review the information and determine whether the individual will be invited to interview for the position.

 **INTERVIEW**

The interview is an important component of the hiring process, but it also lends itself to a number of situations that might subject an employer to liability.

A. DEFINITION OF *INTERVIEW*

The law does not limit the definition of *interview* to a one-time face-to-face conversation between a prospective employer and a job applicant. Instead the **interview** extends to all formal or informal face-to-face, telephone, or e-mail exchanges between an employer and a candidate, which would include a conversation inviting the individual to apply for a position and a discussion to schedule the interview. The prohibition of asking certain questions and gathering certain information applies to each of these exchanges.

interview
broad term for exchanges between a potential employer and job applicant that occur during the recruitment and hiring process

B. PRELIMINARY CONVERSATIONS ARE RELEVANT

Because the presumption is that employers will consider any information that is revealed during the interview process when making a hiring decision, employers should provide training about workplace discrimination issues to anyone who might have contact with the job candidates. For example, suppose an applicant calls a recruitment office to inquire about the status of an application and the counselor comments on the individual's accent and asks where she was born. If the applicant is ultimately not granted an interview for the position, the rejected applicant could assert that her national origin was wrongfully considered by the employer in making the decision and that the employer had the information identifying the applicant's national origin based on the conversation that took place between the recruitment office counselor and the applicant.[13]

C. NO SPECIFIC REFERENCE TO MEMBERSHIP IN A PROTECTED CLASS IS NECESSARY

Employers should be aware that statements that suggest a discriminatory motive may be considered, even if there is no specific reference to the protected class status of the individual. For example, an employer who makes a comment that "those damned humanists are ruining the world," and then refuses to hire an individual of a particular religion, could be subject to liability because the statement suggests religion was a factor that influenced the adverse employment decision, even though there was no specific reference to the particular religion of the applicant.[14]

D. MANAGE DISCUSSION

Employers can use job descriptions as a source for interview questions because the content should have been reviewed previously to ensure that it was accurate and the minimum qualifications were job related. By creating a list of interview questions that track information previously vetted, employers will be better equipped to focus the conversation on the gathering of information necessary to make a final decision and avoiding discussions that could suggest discriminatory conduct.

Interviewers who have a list of appropriate questions will also be able to manage the interview process. Interviewers will be able to quickly identify conversations that are not directly tied to job responsibilities and redirect the exchange. This will prevent an inadvertent peripheral conversation, which is unrelated to whether the applicant is qualified to perform the job responsibilities and reveals information about an individual's membership in a protected class.

 IV FRAMING THE APPROPRIATE QUESTIONS

Although the specific information necessary to assess a candidate's ability to perform a job will vary depending upon the nature of the position, there are some general guidelines that frame the process. Some questions should be avoided because they seek out information that is directly related to an individual's membership in a protected class. These questions have the potential to subject an employer to liability for workplace discrimination even if there was never an intention to use the information in a manner that was inconsistent with the law.

Questions that are not job related should not be asked. If, however, particular information is necessary for an employer to make an informed decision, it should be asked in a targeted manner consistent with the following parameters. In the tables that follow are the types of questions and inquiries that should be avoided, as well as how an employer might consider rephrasing the question to solicit the minimum amount of information necessary to address its needs, while not soliciting extraneous information that could potentially result in liability under an anti-discrimination law.[15]

A. CONTACT INFORMATION

1. NAME AND ADDRESS

Subject	Recommended	Not Recommended[16]
Name	Have you ever worked for this company under a different name? Is additional information related to a name change, use of an assumed name, or nickname necessary to enable a check of your records? If yes, explain.	Inquiries about original names of an applicant whose name has been changed by court order or otherwise; inquiries about the birth name of a married woman.
Address or Duration of Residence	Identify your place of residence.	How long have you lived in this country? In what country did you live before?

Employers usually request basic information relating to an applicant's name, home address, telephone number, position applying for, and availability date. Although an employer will be able to justify a business need for requesting contact information for future communications, there is still potential for it to be used for discriminatory purposes. For example, information about an applicant's first or last name could be used to illegally eliminate a candidate based on the perception that she is a member of a certain protected class.[17] In addition, it has been suggested that some companies have unlawfully attempted to exclude certain minorities from the hiring pool by eliminating applicants based on their zip codes.[18]

Although employers are not prohibited from collecting contact information, the potential for an employer to misuse information about an candidate's name or home address as described above illustrates how the collection of facially neutral information can reveal an individual's membership in a protected class and subject an employer to liability for the improper use of the information. In response to these concerns, some particularly cautious employers remove the name, address, and contact information of its applicants during the application review process to minimize the potential for this information to impact hiring decisions and to avoid the suggestion that the information was improperly considered.[19]

2. EMERGENCY CONTACT INFORMATION

Subject	Recommended	Not Recommended[20]
Emergency Contact	None.	An employer should ask an individual to provide an emergency contact name and number at the start of their employment.

By asking a candidate for emergency contact information, an employer might receive information about an individual's marital status, which should not be considered as part of the hiring process. Depending on the inference drawn, it could result in a disparate impact on men or women. Although an employer may have a legitimate business need to have emergency contact information for employees in the event of an emergency, it is unlikely that an employer would have a business need to collect this information from an applicant who is at the employer's workplace only for an interview to discuss an employment opportunity.

B. FAMILY ISSUES

1. RELATIVES

Subject	Recommended	Not Recommended[21]
Relatives	Inquiries as to the names of an applicant's relatives already employed by the company.	Inquiries as to the names, addresses, and ages of an applicant's spouse, children, or relatives not employed by the company.

Questions about whether or not an applicant is related to a current employee may be relevant to ensure that the company complies with its nepotism policy, which establishes guidelines for hiring family members of current employees. However, whether or not an applicant has children or wants to have children should not be considered when making a hiring decision. Depending upon the inference made, using this type of information could have an adverse impact on women and constitute sex discrimination under Title VII. See Chapter 9, Recruiting and Assembling a Diverse Applicant Pool, and Chapter 5, Sex, Pregnancy, and Genetic Discrimination, respectively.

2. MARITAL STATUS

Subject	Recommended	Not Recommended[22]
Marital Status	None.	Do you wish to be addressed as Miss, Mrs., or Ms.? Are you married? Does your husband support your decision to apply for this position? Are you single? Are you divorced? Are you separated? Give the name of your spouse. Provide information about your spouse. Requirements for the production of any documents that would reveal marital status.

Employers should avoid asking applicants about their marital status unless there is a job-related reason for doing so. Although an employer might need the information to provide an individual with appropriate family health insurance forms or determine appropriate tax deductions, this information can be collected after an individual accepts an offer of employment. In addition, if an employer learns an applicant has children and inquires about the applicant's marital status, it could be problematic. This is because women are more likely than men to have primary physical custody of their children; therefore, basing a decision on this information could result in a disparate impact on women and constitute sex discrimination under Title VII. See Chapter 5, Sex, Pregnancy, and Genetic Discrimination.

3. SEXUAL ORIENTATION

Subject	Recommended	Not Recommended[23]
Sexual Orientation	None.	Inquiries about sexual orientation. Do you have girlfriend/ boyfriend?

Employers should not ask applicants questions about their sexual orientation. Title VII prohibits discrimination based on sex, but it does not prohibit employment discrimination based on sexual orientation.[24] However, there are a number of states and cities that do prohibit workplace discrimination based on sexual orientation in the private sector,[25] and some states provide protections to employees working in the public sector.[26] Based on these variations, in addition to the constant state of flux in the law in this regard, employers should avoid asking questions related to the sexual orientation of applicants. This is particularly true because it probably would be difficult for an employer to illustrate why it would need to know an applicant's sexual orientation to properly evaluate the applicant's ability to perform the essential job tasks.

C. HEIGHT AND WEIGHT

Subject	Recommended	Not Recommended
Height and Weight	None.	What is your height? What is your weight?

Employers should refrain from asking applicants questions about height and weight because these questions might have a disparate impact on members of particular protected classes. Certain ethnic groups tend to be taller or shorter than others, so excluding applicants based on height may have a disparate impact on those groups. Employers who do have a business need for this information should be prepared to explain why a particular characteristic is necessary. For example, an employer looking to hire individuals to lose a certain amount of weight for its new weight loss program designed for obese individuals may be able to request height and weight information, as would an employer seeking to hire models for its line of plus-sized women's clothing.

Employers may face liability for considering the physical appearance of candidates in the absence of a true business necessity, or for applying the standards in a discriminatory manner. For example, in one instance a company was required to pay $225,000 in lost wages and $95,000 for damages for imposing personal appearance requirements upon its female applicants, and not imposing comparable requirements upon the male candidates.[27] Therefore, employers requesting information about the height and weight of its applicant (or any other physical characteristics) should be prepared to show both the business need for the requirements and that they are imposed in a uniform and nondiscriminatory manner.

D. AGE

Subject	Recommended	Not Recommended[28]
Age	Are you 18 years of age or older? If not, state your age.	How old are you? What is your date of birth? What are the ages of your children, if any?
Birthday	None.	Requirement that the applicant produce proof of age in the form of a birth certificate or other record.

Because the ADEA prohibits discrimination based on age against individuals who are 40 years old and older, employers must ask age-related questions with significant care. Although employers are permitted to ask applicants to provide their age, since the mere request for this information might deter older applicants from submitting an application, these requests are reviewed carefully to determine whether the employer has a business need for the information.[29] Thus, because the age of an applicant is rarely necessary to assess whether the individual can perform the essential tasks associated with the job, this question should generally be avoided. See Chapter 6, Age Discrimination.

E. RACE AND COLOR

Subject	Recommended	Not Recommended[30]
Race and Color	None.	Questions about complexion or color of applicant's skin, eyes, hair, or other physical characteristics.

Because Title VII prohibits workplace discrimination based on race or color. employers should not ask any questions to solicit information about an individual's race or characteristics associated with an individual's race because it is unlikely the information would be necessary to assess whether an individual is qualified for a position. While employers may have a legal obligation to gather such information for affirmative action reporting requirements, it should be requested and maintained separately from information collected as part of the recruitment process.

F. RELIGION

Subject	Recommended	Not Recommended
Religion	None.	Questions about religious denomination, religious affiliation, house of worship, or the observance of religious holidays.

Because Title VII prohibits workplace discrimination based on religion, employers should not ask applicants to reveal information about their religion or religious practices unless it is job related or falls into one of the limited exceptions when such considerations may be appropriate. Specifically, employers who are defined as *religious corporations* under Title VII may consider an individual's religious affiliation when making a hiring decision, and it is also appropriate to consider this information when religion is a bona fide occupational qualification (BFOQ), which means that belonging to a particular religion is a necessary component of the position. Other than under these limited circumstances, however, questions of a religious nature should be avoided unless the employer can illustrate a business need for the information. See Chapter 4, Religious Discrimination.

G. SEX AND PREGNANCY

Subject	Recommended	Not Recommended
Sex	None.	Inquiry as to gender. Inquiries about capacity to reproduce, use of any form of birth control, or family planning issues.

Because Title VII prohibits workplace discrimination based on sex and pregnancy, employers should not ask applicants about any characteristics associated with their sex, sexual stereotypes, or family planning issues unless there is a job-related reason for doing so. These questions would likely be based on generalizations and could result in a sex discrimination claim under Title VII. Questions related to sex and pregnancy will be closely scrutinized because it is unlikely that questions of this nature would gather information relevant to whether or not an applicant is qualified for a position. See Chapter 5, Sex, Pregnancy, and Genetic Discrimination.

H. NATIONAL ORIGIN, BIRTHPLACE, AND CITIZENSHIP

Subject	Recommended	Not Recommended[31]
National Origin	None.	Inquiries about an applicant's lineage, ancestry, national origin, descent, parentage, or nationality. Inquiries about the nationality of an applicant's parents or spouse.
Birthplace	None.	Inquiries about an applicant's birthplace, or the birthplace of parents, spouse, or other relatives.
Citizenship	Are you a citizen of the United States, or do you have the legal right to remain permanently in the United States?	Of what country are you a citizen? Questions about whether an applicant, an applicant's parents, or an applicant's spouse are naturalized or native-born citizens. Requiring applicants to produce naturalization papers.

Because Title VII prohibits discrimination based on national origin, employers should refrain from asking questions related to it unless the questions are job related. Employers should also refrain from asking for information about an applicant's birthplace, since this information could be used to discriminate based on both national origin, which is prohibited conduct under Title VII, and citizenship.

The Immigration Reform and Control Act of 1986 (IRCA) is a federal law that specifically prohibits discrimination based on citizenship status when making hiring decisions. Further, although citizenship is not a protected class under Title VII, discrimination based on citizenship would fit within the scope of the statute if use of the information has the "purpose or effect" of engaging in discriminatory conduct based on an individual's national origin, which is specifically protected by Title VII.[32]

Immigration Reform and Control Act of 1986 (IRCA)

Employers will have an obligation to solicit information related to national origin and citizenship to comply with the Immigration and Nationality Act (INA), which is the amendment to IRCA that provides that employers can only hire individuals who have the legal right to work in the United States or who are aliens authorized to work here.[33] The INA requires employers to verify the identity and employment eligibility of all employees hired, which can be done by completing the Employment Eligibility Verification (I-9) form (see Exhibit 3-3). However, employers should require employees to complete the form after an offer of employment is made to avoid another potential source of liability for discriminatory conduct.[34] See Chapter 3, Race, Color, and National Origin Discrimination.

Immigration and Nationality Act (INA)

Employment Eligibility Verification (I-9) form

I. FOREIGN LANGUAGE SKILLS

Subject	Recommended	Not Recommended[35]
Foreign Language Skills	Inquiry into related work experience. If the position requires fluency in a particular language, inquiry may be made as to whether the applicant speaks that language fluently.	What is your native language? How did you learn to read, write, or speak the foreign language?

Employers should also not ask applicants about their native language, unless the information is necessary for the employer to make a decision as to whether the individual is qualified for the position. Even if a position requires familiarity with a particular language, the relevant questions should be geared toward fluency. This is because if an applicant is fluent in a particular language, it would be unlikely that the employer would need to know whether the language is the applicant's native language to determine whether the individual is qualified for the position.

J. MEDICAL ISSUES

1. DISABILITIES

Subject	Recommended	Not Recommended[36]
Disabilities	None.	Do you have a disability? Have you ever been treated for any of the following diseases? Do you have a drug or alcohol problem? Have you ever had a drug or alcohol problem?

The ADA prohibits workplace discrimination based on disabilities and places strict limitations on the types of medical information that can be solicited. Employers should not ask applicants questions about a disability or engage in a discussion that might elicit information related to it. For example, while an employer can ask applicants whether they can perform the essential job tasks required for a position with or without a reasonable accommodation, an employer cannot ask whether an accommodation would be needed.[37] Additionally, because alcoholism and past drug addictions are protected under the ADA, employers should avoid questions that would encourage applicants to reveal information related to those conditions.[38]

Employers should remember that an applicant has no obligation to inform an employer about a disability or about an intention to request an accommodation. Instead, applicants are required only to answer whether they can perform the essential job tasks with or without a reasonable accommodation. Therefore, both direct and indirect questions about an individual's disability must be avoided. This prohibition would include asking whether an applicant has ever been hospitalized, has seen a psychiatrist, or is taking medication. In addition, applicants should not be asked how many sick days they used in the previous year, as this could be a direct result of a disability.

The ADA also prohibits employers from asking an applicant about a medical condition until after a conditional job offer is made.[39] Once the offer is made, but prior to the start of employment, medical questions can be asked (and medical examinations may be administered) provided that all applicants for the positions are subjected to the same requirements.[40] See Chapter 7, Disability Discrimination, and Chapter 11, Pre-Employment Testing.

2. FAMILY MEDICAL HISTORY/GENETICS

Subject	Recommended	Not Recommended
Family History and Genetics	None.	Do any diseases run in your family? Do you plan to undergo any genetic testing? Do you have any ill family members?

Because the Genetic Information Nondiscrimination Act of 2008 (GINA) is a federal law prohibiting discrimination against applicants based on genetic information, employers must avoid asking applicants to provide any genetic information, which includes information about genetic tests, testing of family members, family member medical histories, or predisposition to certain diseases. GINA significantly restricts the rights of employers to collect genetic information, and even in the limited circumstances when it is permissible, the information must be collected and maintained pursuant to rigid guidelines.[41] See Chapter 5, Sex, Pregnancy, and Genetic Discrimination.

3. INJURIES

Subject	Recommended	Not Recommended[42]
Injuries	None.	How did you break your leg? It is difficult to use those crutches? How long will you be on crutches?

Even though all injuries will not rise to the level of a disability under the ADA, employers should refrain from asking applicants questions about any injuries. An employer might ask an applicant about a broken leg and learn it is an isolated injury incurred during a ski accident. However, depending on the nature of the injury, the question might also lead to further questions about how long the applicant expects it will take for the leg to heal, or whether the individual has broken other bones. The answers to these types of questions could result in the revelation of information related to a more serious medical condition that might constitute a disability and be protected under the ADA. Based on this potential risk, questions or discussions about injuries should be avoided.[43]

4. WORKERS' COMPENSATION

Subject	Recommended	Not Recommended
Workers' Compensation	None.	Do you have a pending workers' compensation claim? Have you ever filed a workers' compensation claim?

Employers should not ask applicants whether they have previously filed a claim for workers' compensation, which is a benefit provided to employees who experience a job-related illness or injury. Such questions would be soliciting medical information from an applicant, which could materialize into a claim under the ADA. In addition, because employees have the right to file a workers' compensation claim to address workplace injuries, an employer might be subject to liability for retaliation if the employer imposes an adverse employment decision upon an applicant based on the applicant's past assertion of this legal right.[44] See Chapter 8, Employees versus Independent Contractors, for a discussion about workers' compensation.

K. QUALIFICATIONS

1. EDUCATION

Subject	Recommended	Not Recommended[45]
Education	Inquiries about the applicant's academic, vocational, or professional education and the public and private schools attended.	Year(s) of attendance. Date(s) of graduation.

Employers can ask applicants whether they have a high school or college degree, as well as the highest level of education they have obtained, if this information is necessary to properly assess whether the candidate is qualified for a position. Applicants can also be asked to indicate the number of years of schooling they completed, but they should not be asked to provide their dates of graduation. This question would provide information about an applicant's age, which could suggest an employer was unlawfully considering age when making hiring decisions. See Chapter 6, Age Discrimination.

2. WORK EXPERIENCE

Subject	Recommended	Not Recommended
Work Experience	Inquiries about the prior work experience that is relevant to the applicant's ability to perform the responsibilities of the position.	Do you think you are overqualified for this position?

It is appropriate to inquire about the work experience of an applicant because there is a direct link between an individual's past experience and suitability for a position. The most common requests include the name and location of a number of past employers, the job titles held, the salaries paid, the name of supervisors, and the reason each employment relationship ended. However, because employers are not permitted to discriminate based on age, they should be prepared to defend each question if it is alleged that the information is being gathered to screen out older applicants. For example, an employer could be subject to liability for asking for information about job experience to determine how many more years an individual would likely continue to work, and then eliminating those applicants who would be likely to retire in the near future.[46]

A number of courts have also determined that an employer's decision not to hire an applicant due to concern that the individual is overqualified is impermissible under the ADEA because of the disparate impact this consideration might have on older applicants. One court reasoned that the fact an applicant is overqualified is not sufficiently linked to job performance to make it a permissible justification for eliminating older applicants. This is because it is unlikely that being overqualified would prevent an older individual from being able to perform the essential job tasks.[47] See Chapter 6, Age Discrimination.

3. PROFESSIONAL ORGANIZATIONS

Subject	Recommended	Not Recommended[48]
Organizations	Inquiry into an applicant's membership in organizations that are relevant to the ability to perform the job.	Requirement that applicants list all clubs, societies, and associations to which they belong.

Employers may ask applicants about their professional memberships to the extent the inquiry is narrowly tailored to elicit job-related information. A general question asking applicants to list all of their organizational affiliations could be problematic, because individuals may belong to associations based on their protected class membership such as religion or national origin, and the possession of such information by the employer, if not job related, could suggest that the information was being used as the basis for the making of a discriminatory decision.

An employer may, however, inquire about an applicant's membership in a professional organization that has a clear connection to the position. For instance, asking applicants for a patent attorney position whether they belonged to a particular professional association, in order to determine whether they have access to educational conferences that focus on the latest developments in that area of law, would be an appropriate inquiry.

L. TERMS AND CONDITIONS OF EMPLOYMENT

1. SCHEDULING

Subject	Recommended	Not Recommended[49]
Work Schedule	Determination regarding eligibility for weekend, evening, and overtime work if this is a business necessity and is asked of all applicants.	Does your religion prevent you from completing weekend work? Do you have a medical condition that will prevent you from working a double shift? Based on your age, do you think you can handle long work hours? Will your childcare arrangements prevent you from completing weekend work?

Although employers generally have the right to determine the work schedule of their employees, they must do so in a uniform and nondiscriminatory manner. Therefore, employers should be cautious about asking an applicant about her ability to work in a way that will elicit information about an individual's membership in a protected class. For example, this may be an issue for a disabled applicant who has a medical condition that might prevent the working of lengthy shifts, or for those who will require a reasonable accommodation to engage in a religious practice. In addition, employers would be subject to liability for sex discrimination if they make hiring decisions based on sexual stereotypes, such as the idea that women will be less willing to work flexible schedules or evening shifts because of child-rearing responsibilities.

2. ATTENDANCE

Subject	Recommended	Not Recommended[50]
Attendance	Are you able to comply with our attendance policy?	How many sick days did you use with your past employer? Will your childcare responsibilities prevent you from reporting to work on a regular basis?

An employer is permitted to inform applicants about its attendance policy and ask whether they can work in accordance with it. The ADA does not consider this to be soliciting information about a disability because there can be a number of explanations as to why an individual might not be able to report to work. Employers should not, however, ask about the number of sick days an applicant used in a prior position or anything related to the use of medical leave. This is because such information would be very likely to elicit information about an applicant's disability which, if considered, could subject an employer to liability under the ADA.[51]

An employer with a legitimate business need to control tardiness and excessive absenteeism is not violating the law by refusing to extend a job offer to an applicant who has a poor attendance record. However, because a policy such as this could have a disparate impact on applicants in certain protected classes, such as those with disabilities, employers who want to make such decisions should ensure that the policy is applied uniformly and there is a business need for it.

3. COMPENSATION

Subject	Recommended	Not Recommended
Compensation	What are your salary expectations?	What is the lowest salary you are willing to accept?

Compensation discrimination issues are particularly complex. Aside from the fact that employers cannot base compensation on whether or not an individual is a member of a protected class, even appropriate considerations such as work experience or level of education achieved can produce discriminatory results. These issues are discussed in detail in Chapter 12, Compensation and Benefits, which is dedicated to compensation. However, within the context of hiring, employers should establish a salary range for a position and should not deviate from it. Further, for the purpose of interview questions, employers should avoid asking questions about minimum salary requirements because, given the fact that women are generally paid less than men, women would be more likely than men to work for lower compensation. Thus, asking this question could result in compensation discrimination based on the disproportionate impact the consideration of this response would have on women.[52]

M. PERSONAL FINANCES

1. CREDIT

Subject	Recommended	Not Recommended
Credit	None.	What is your credit rating?

Employers should avoid asking questions relating to an applicant's credit history because making a decision based on this information could have a disparate impact on applicants belonging to certain protected classes. Studies have shown that certain minorities have lower credit scores than nonminorities, and older women may be less likely than younger women to have established a significant independent credit history. These findings make the consideration of credit history particularly problematic for these groups of applicants. Despite this potential disparate impact, however, questions relating to an applicant's credit history may be appropriate if there is a business need that justifies consideration of this information.[53] See Chapter 11, Pre-Employment Testing.

2. HOME OWNERSHIP

Subject	Recommended	Not Recommended
Home Ownership	None.	Do you own your home? Do you rent your home?

Employers should avoid asking questions about an applicant's home ownership unless the information is necessary to make a hiring decision. This is because home ownership is rarely relevant to the ability of an applicant to perform the essential tasks associated with a position, and minorities are generally less likely than nonminorities to own their homes.[54] Based on this, asking for this informa-tion (and therefore presumably using it to make a hiring decision) could subject an employer to a claim for discriminatory conduct due to the potential for its con-sideration to have a disparate impact on members of a protected class.

N. PERSONAL HABITS

Employers who are considering asking questions about the personal habits of their applicants should be aware that some states have privacy laws that prevent ask-ing questions about legal conduct. In addition, some states have passed lifestyle anti-discrimination laws, which protect applicants and employees from adverse employment decisions based on lawful conduct (such as drinking alcohol, smok-ing, or having an extramarital affair) that takes place outside their regularly sched-uled work hours.[55] See Chapter 17, Regulation of Off-Duty Conduct for an extensive discussion relating to the rights of employers to regulate lifestyle choices (such as diet and exercise) directly and through the implementation of voluntary wellness programs designed to provide employees with assistance in making informed decisions about personal habits.

1. SMOKING

Subject	Recommended	Not Recommended
Smoking	None.	Do you smoke?

There is no federal anti-discrimination law that prohibits employers from asking applicants whether or not they smoke; however, a number of states have passed legislation protecting the rights of individuals to smoke, particularly outside their regularly scheduled work hours. In addition, because certain addic-tions are covered by the ADA, asking a question about an applicant's smoking habits may provide an employer with information suggesting an applicant has a disability.[56]

This issue received media attention when a Texas employer implemented a policy to screen out applicants who smoked or used tobacco products. The employer justified its policy by saying that "hiring employees that are not tobacco users will take us one more step toward creating a healthy work environ-ment."[57] The announcement of this policy received significant media attention, and there were robust opinions on both sides. Some argue that because there is no Texas law that directly addresses the issue, employers should have the right to consider whether an applicant is a smoker when selecting their workforce. Critics of the policy have said that employers are violating the rights of applicants to make decisions about personal habits that do not affect job performance.[58] See Exhibit 10-1.

Exhibit 10-1

BSA to snuff out smoking

Hospital adopts no-hire policy for smokers

BY DAVID PITTMAN
david.pittman@amarillo.com

Baptist St. Anthony's Health System will not hire applicants who smoke or use other to-bacco products, according to a new policy implemented Friday.

"We feel that hiring employees that are not tobacco users will take us one more step toward creating a healthy work environment," said BSA spokeswoman Mary Barlow.

New hires will be subject to a blood test that now includes screening for recent tobacco use. Screenings test for coti-nine, a byproduct of nicotine produced when the drug is metabolized.

The new policy will not affect current workers who smoke on their own time, she said. Tobacco use was banned on all BSA property last year.

Barlow estimated that BSA, which employs roughly 3,300 people, hires from 60 to 90 people a month.

Neither Barlow nor the Amarillo Chamber of Commerce knew of another busi-

PLEASE SEE **BSA** ON PAGE 4A

BSA: Policy based on Cleveland Clinic's

FROM PAGE 1A

ness that prohibited the hiring of smokers.

Vicki Wilmarth, an Amarillo attorney who specializes in employment law, said BSA is well within its right to not hire smokers.

"There is no state or federal law that says an employer cannot discriminate on the basis of smoking," Wilmarth said.

Barlow said BSA based its policy on that of the Cleveland Clinic, one of the busiest hospital systems in the country with more than 37,000 employees. Many credit the clinic for enacting the first nonsmoker hiring policy in September 2007.

The clinic hires roughly 500 a month, and 2 percent of new hires tested had cotinine levels considered too high, said Dr. Michael Roizen, the clinic's chief wellness officer.

The policy hasn't impacted the number of employee applications.

"We did not notice a shortage because of the policy," Roizen said. "In other words, as many people were choosing us because of our policy as were avoiding us."

Roizen said a person who smokes on average 10 cigarettes a day can be smoke-free for five days and pass the clinic's screening.

Barlow said BSA would screen for roughly the same level as the Cleveland Clinic. BSA is using a blood test, and Cleveland uses a urine test.

"The cotinine test in urine is pretty accurate," Roizen said.

Cleveland Clinic conducts a second test to confirm positive results. It offers smoking cessation classes to applicants who test positive.

"Our commitment isn't to not hire people," Roizen said. "Our commitment is to hire people who don't smoke."

Roizen said secondhand smoke shouldn't produce a level high enough to detect.

BSA teamed with rival Northwest Texas Healthcare System to start tobacco-free campuses starting Jan. 1 last year. The change forced employees, patients, visitors and doctors to not smoke or use tobacco on its property.

Barlow said BSA fired two people who continued to violate the policy.

Northwest spokeswoman Caytie Martin said the hospital informs potential employees that they are a tobacco-free campus, then the employees decide if they want to work there or not.

"We don't have a policy in effect that screens them," Martin said.

Health care costs for Cleveland Clinic employees have dropped in a time when it has skyrocketed nationally.

"This year, the clinic's cost went down 8 percent as opposed to the national average, which went up 5 percent," Roizen said, who couldn't say how much of that was associated with the smoking policy or any aspect of the clinic's wellness program.

Smokers applying for work at BSA would have a difficult time avoiding a positive test because of the uncertainty of when they would interview and be called in for a test, Barlow said. A person is only tested after being offered a job.

"It'd be very hard to try to manipulate it," Barlow said of testing.

Scott Camarata, head of Speak Out Amarillo, which spoke against a May vote on banning public smoking in Amarillo, said his organization only voiced opposition to less government control, and BSA is a private business.

"Personally I think it's discriminatory," Camarata said. "But it's their house. It's their rules."

2. ALCOHOL USE

Subject	Recommended	Not Recommended[59]
Alcohol Use	Do you drink alcohol (if job related)? Have you ever been convicted of driving while under the influence (if job related)?	Have you even been addicted to alcohol? Have you ever been treated for alcohol addiction? Have you ever been treated for abuse of alcohol? Are you an alcoholic? Are any of your family members alcoholics?

Employers may ask applicants questions about their drinking habits. However, because there is always a risk that asking questions about drinking habits will elicit information about alcoholism, a protected condition under the ADA, employers should carefully consider whether knowing whether an applicant drinks alcohol, even on a casual basis, is necessary to make a hiring decision.[60]

3. DRUG USE

Subject	Recommended	Not Recommended[61]
Drug Use	None.	How often did you use illegal drugs in the past? Have you ever been addicted to illegal drugs? Have you ever been treated for drug addiction? Have you ever been treated for drug abuse?

Employers should not ask applicants about their drug use. Although the use of illegal drugs is not protected behavior, a past drug addiction constitutes a disability under the ADA. Therefore, by revealing a past drug addiction, an applicant would be placing the employer on notice of a record of an impairment, which is protected under the statute. If questions about past drug use are job related, however, then such questions would be permissible and should be asked.[62] See Chapter 7, Disability Discrimination, and Chapter 11, Pre-Employment Testing, for a discussion of medical testing and drug testing.

O. MISCELLANEOUS

1. ARREST AND CONVICTION RECORDS

Subject	Recommended	Not Recommended
Arrest Record	Have you ever been convicted of a criminal offense? Provide details.	Have you ever been arrested? Provide details.

Generally speaking, an employer should not ask applicants about their arrest record because an arrest is not conclusive proof that a crime was committed. Convictions may be considered if the conviction would affect an applicant's ability to perform the essential tasks associated with the position. See Chapter 11, Pre-Employment Testing for an extensive discussion about the appropriate use of arrest and criminal records within the context of background checks.

2. MILITARY EXPERIENCE AND DISCHARGE

Subject	Recommended	Not Recommended[63]
Military Experience	Inquiry into whether the applicant has any job-related military experience or training.	Inquiry into the applicant's military status, type of discharge, or future military commitments.

By making hiring decisions based on an applicant's military status, an employer is engaging in unlawful discriminatory conduct. Specifically, the Uniformed Services Employment and Reemployment Rights Act (USERRA) prohibits discrimination on the basis of military service against veterans and reservists in all aspects of employment.[64] See Chapter 13, Paid and Unpaid Leave, for a detailed discussion of USERRA and what it provides.

In addition, because men tend to participate in the armed forces in greater numbers than women do, a policy that excludes applicants based on military status would likely have a disparate impact on male candidates in violation of the prohibition against sex discrimination under Title VII. Based on this, applicants should generally not be asked about their past military service or whether their military duty would require them to be absent from work. If, however, there is a specific type of military training that has a direct link to the available position, a question related to it might be appropriate.[65] Questions about military discharge are generally not appropriate because at least historically minorities may have been more likely to be dishonorably discharged than nonminorities, so a policy of considering military discharge in making hiring decisions could have a disparate impact on members of a protected class.[66]

3. OPEN-ENDED QUESTIONS

Subject	Recommended	Not Recommended[67]
Request for Other Information	Provide any additional information relevant to the applicant's ability to perform the essential job tasks.	Provide additional information. Attach any other information you would like the employer to know.

Employers should avoid asking applicants open-ended questions as this would increase the likelihood that information might be provided that, if considered, could result in discriminatory behavior. For example, asking applicants to list the qualities that distinguish them from other applicants might result in the description of the challenges of growing up in a foreign country, or overcoming a disability. This is problematic because this information, if considered in the hiring process, could subject an employer to liability for national origin or disability discrimination. To minimize these types of issues, employers should avoid broad inquiries and focus on asking narrowly tailored questions that solicit information closely tied to job qualifications and that are necessary to make an informed decision as to whether the candidate will be able to perform the essential job tasks.

V. CONVERSATIONS THAT MAY BIND AN EMPLOYER

The guidance provided to employers about the interview process usually focuses on the avoidance of discrimination claims, but there are other sources of potential liability. For example, employer statements made during an interview have the potential to bind an employer in a way the employer might not have intended. Employers must be cautious about conversations they have with a job applicant throughout the recruitment process because their words might create an implied contract, obligating them to provide certain benefits.

implied contract
obligation that may arise based on employer statements or conduct

Implied contracts may be created by employer statements or conduct and could obligate the employer to provide certain benefits and protections. These contracts may be created within a number of contexts that relate to job security and other terms and conditions of an individual's employment.

A. LENGTH OF EMPLOYMENT

Employers should be careful about making any statements to applicants that might result in the imposition of a contractual obligation on them. For example, employers who intend to hire at-will employees, who can be terminated with or without cause and with or without notice, should avoid making statements suggesting the new hire will be entitled to any degree of job security.

Employers should be particularly careful about making promises that inadvertently guarantee a particular length of employment. For example, employers who want to retain the broad termination rights under the at-will doctrine should not tell applicants that they will have a job for as long as they perform their job responsibilities, that they will be terminated only for certain reasons, or that they will enjoy a lengthy and secure employment relationship with the company. Within the context of wrongful termination claims, at-will employees have used such employer statements to suggest that they were promised continued employment unless they engaged in misconduct that would warrant the ending of the employment relationship. See Chapter 18, Employment at Will, for a detailed discussion about implied contracts.

B. TERMS AND CONDITIONS OF EMPLOYMENT

During the interview process, employers should avoid speaking about terms and conditions of employment that may not materialize, because a failure to provide promised benefits could give rise to a claim for misrepresentation. This will be particularly problematic if the availability of the promised benefits enticed the individual to accept the employment offer. For example, an employer that tells an individual about the availability of flexible work schedules and childcare assistance could be subject to liability if, after the employee starts to work, she is informed that these benefits will not be offered. An employer that tells applicants that the future of the company looks bright and then decides to close the business shortly after the conversation might also be sued for fraud and misrepresentation.[68]

 ## VI MEMORIALIZING THE AGREEMENT

In an attempt to avoid a misunderstanding related to a newly established employment relationship, once the terms and conditions of employment are agreed upon, most employers will draft some type of document to highlight the agreed-on terms. There are a number of ways for the parties to document their mutual understandings.

A. EMPLOYMENT CONTRACT

In some instances, the parties entering into an employment relationship negotiate an employment contract to establish their respective obligations to one another. Discussion of the bargaining and drafting of such agreements is beyond the scope of this textbook, but employment contracts generally include a specific term of employment, a job title, the salary and available benefits, and the rights of the employer to terminate the employment relationship prior to the end of the specified term. In addition, many agreements include information about the employee's job responsibilities. The majority of working individuals, however, do not work pursuant to a written agreement but instead are considered at-will employees who can be terminated with or without cause and with or without notice. See Chapter 18, Employment at Will.

B. OFFER LETTER

Even if the parties do not negotiate an employment contract, they should still have a written document outlining the key elements of the contemplated employment relationship. Employers often provide new employees with an **offer letter**, which highlights the key terms of employment, such as the new employee's title and compensation. An offer letter might also include other pertinent information, such

offer letter
document provided to a new employee to confirm key terms and conditions of employment, such as compensation and job title

as benefit entitlements, job duties, supervisor name, start date and time, and the name of the person to contact with questions.

Employers who intend to maintain the right to terminate an employee for any reason at any time usually reiterate that condition in the offer letter to make it clear that the document is not intended to constitute an employment contract, or alter the individual's status as an at-will employee. An employer might include such language as "[t]his letter confirms our mutual understanding that your employment will be at-will, meaning that either party can end the relationship at any time." An employer might also state: "[c]onsistent with our discussions relating to the terms and conditions of your employment, [company name] retains the right to terminate your employment with or without cause and with or without notice pursuant to the at-will doctrine." See Chapter 18, Employment at Will.

 VIII POST–JOB-OFFER ISSUES

A. MAINTENANCE OF RECORDS

After the employer completes the hiring process for a particular position, the employer should ensure that the process that resulted in the creation of the employment relationship is properly documented for future reference. Because an individual may challenge a hiring decision well after the initial decision is made, employers should maintain accurate and detailed records of the factors used to reach the decision to select or reject a candidate.

Aside from the fact that an employer may not recall all of the details about a hiring decision long after the decision is made, it is also possible that the individuals who participated in the process will no longer be working for the company by the time a claim materializes. Based on this possibility, the individuals involved in the hiring process should be instructed to document as much objective detail as possible when noting the reasons for the decisions.

1. CHARACTERIZATION OF DECISION

Employers should train individuals who participate in the hiring process to recognize that a legitimate reason for an adverse employment decision might be construed as inappropriate based upon how it is characterized on paper. For example, a supervisor who notes that an applicant was not a match for the workplace culture might be accused of discriminatory conduct if the workforce consists of predominantly white men and the rejected applicant was an Asian female. However, if the individual had a written document to support the employer's determination that the applicant was not a match because the position required significant face time with clients and the applicant indicated her desire to work extensively from home, it would be a significant piece of evidence that an employer could use to defend a claim alleging that the rejection was discriminatory.

2. LIMIT RECORD TO RELEVANT CHARACTERISTICS

Employers should also ensure that any notes summarizing the interview process reflect the specific information used to make the hiring decision. This is important to prevent any post-hiring documentation from undermining the careful planning and execution of the hiring process. For example, the notes of an employer referencing an applicant's identifying characteristics (such as his race, or the fact that he is an older man) could be used as evidence that a characteristic was used in the ultimate hiring decision, even if the reason for making the notation was merely to distinguish one candidate from another.

B. POST-HIRING COLLECTION OF INFORMATION

In some instances, employers are required to maintain information about the diversity of its workforce. Specifically, all employers who employ 100 or more individuals are required to complete an **EEO-1 survey**, which is a government form requiring a count of the employees by job category and then by ethnicity, race, and gender.[69]

EEO-1 survey
government form employers must submit on an annual basis that counts workforce by job category, ethnicity, race, and gender

Employers have a legal obligation to collect this information and to comply with this requirement. However, to avoid potential liability for discriminatory conduct, employers should ensure that the information is collected outside the context of the recruiting process and that any information gathered is not considered when making decisions about other terms and conditions of employment.

KEY TERMS

- ✓ EEO-1 survey
- ✓ employment application
- ✓ employment eligibility verification (I-9) form
- ✓ Immigration and Nationality Act (INA)
- ✓ Immigration Reform and Control Act of 1986 (IRCA)
- ✓ implied contract
- ✓ interview
- ✓ offer letter

DISCUSSION QUESTIONS

Explain your response to each of the following questions with the understanding that in some cases there is no right or wrong answer. If you cannot make an informed decision with the facts provided, indicate the nature and significance of the additional information you would need. For the purposes of these questions, you can assume that the employers, employees and applicants mentioned below are covered by Title VII and other relevant federal workplace anti-discrimination laws.

1. Explain what is meant by *employment application* and *interview*, and the types of information each should be designed to elicit.
2. Provide some examples of discussion topics that should be avoided in interviews and explain the reason for your response.
3. Explain the type of information an employer would be permitted to request from a job applicant about her educational background, as well as the types of questions an employer would be prohibited from asking.
4. Explain why an employer might provide an individual with an offer letter and the type of information it might include.
5. Beth is the CEO of a music video company known for hiring "young and hip" employees. She wants to expand her workforce and decides she will accept only video cover letters and resumes that have been uploaded onto YouTube in the form of a 30-second video. She says she knows about Title VII and the prohibition against workplace discrimination, but she is not concerned because she requires all employees to have advanced technical skills. What do you think of Beth's recruitment plan?
6. A private university known for its eclectic student body decides that it will replace its recruitment process for tour guides with an application process requiring interested individuals to report to its office on a certain date, pick up one piece of blank paper, and return it within 24 hours illustrating why they are the ideal candidate for the position. The Dean applauds this recruitment technique. What do you think?
7. Your boss tells you that because you took a class about how to conduct employment interviews, he will let you handle the recruitment process. He also tells you that after you complete each interview, he will have lunch with each candidate to get to know them personally, and to determine whether they would fit into the work culture. What do you think about this idea?
8. Beau provides his manager Judy with a list of the following questions as a way to eliminate candidates for further consideration for cashier positions at his new sporting goods store. What do you think of the use of each of these questions?
   a. Have you ever worked as a cashier before?
   b. How many employers have you had since you graduated college?
   c. Can you work on holidays?
   d. Do you have any medical problems that would make it difficult to unload delivery trucks if the employee who is regularly scheduled to do that work calls in sick?
   e. Have you ever been arrested or convicted of a crime? If so, provide details.
   f. Are you willing to submit to a credit check?
   g. Is there anything else you would like us to know to better evaluate your qualifications?

9. Denise hires Glen, a pharmacist, and offers him a salary of $40,000 a year. She says she does not want to put anything in writing because she is afraid a written document will undermine the presumption that Glen is an at-will employee who can be fired for any reason at any time. Does Denise have a valid concern? Is there a way she can address it?

ENDNOTES

1. *See Gregory v. Litton Sys.*, 316 F. Supp. 401 (C.D. Cal. 1990).
2. 29 C.F.R. § 1625.5.
3. EEOC Compl. Man. § 13 (National Origin Discrimination) (Oct. 6, 2008) (available at *http://www.eeoc/gov/policy/docs/national-origin.html*).
4. 29 C.F.R. § 1625.5.
5. *See, e.g.*, N.Y. Exec. Law § 296(1)(d) ("It is unlawful for an employer or employment agency to print or circulate or cause to be printed or circulated any statement, advertisement or publication, or to use any form or application for employment, or to make any inquiry in connection with prospective employment, which expresses, directly or indirectly, any limitation, specification or discrimination as to age, race, creed, color, national origin, sexual orientation, military status, sex, disability, predisposing genetic characteristics, or marital status, or any intent to make any such limitation, specification, or discrimination. . . .").
6. EEOC Informal Discussion Letter from Peggy R. Mastroianni, Internet Hiring (Oct. 27, 2005) (available at *http://www.eeoc.gov/foia/letters/2005/internet_hiring.html*).
7. *See* Statement of Adam T. Klein, Esq. at U.S. Equal Employment Opportunity Commn. Meeting (May 16, 2007) (regarding Employment Testing and Screening) (available at *http://www.eeoc.gov/eeoc/meetings/archive/5-16-07/klein.html*).
8. EEOC Informal Discussion Letter from Peggy R. Mastroianni, Internet Hiring (Oct. 27, 2005) (available at *http://www.eeoc.gov/foia/letters/2005/internet_hiring.html*).
9. *See* U.S. Equal Employment Opportunity Commn., Transcr. Commission Meeting (May 16, 2007) (available at *http://www.eeoc.gov/abouteeoc/meetings/5-16-07/transcript.html*).
10. *See* Lisa Takeuchi Cullen, *It's a Wrap. You're Hired!*, Time (Feb. 22, 2007) (available at *http://www.time.com/time/magazine/article/0,9171,1592860,00.html*).
11. U.S. Equal Employment Opportunity Commn., Pre-Employment Inquiries and Citizenship (available at *http://www.eeoc.gov/laws/practices/inquiries_citizenship.cfm*).
12. EEOC Compl. Man. § 13-III (National Origin Discrimination) (available at *http://www.eeoc.gov/policy/docs/national-origin.html*).
13. *See generally* U.S. Equal Employment Opportunity Commn., National Origin Discrimination (available at *http://www.eeoc.gov/laws/types/nationalorigin.cfm*).
14. *EEOC v. Preferred Mgt. Corp.*, 216 F. Supp. 2d 763, 813 (S.D. Ind. 2002).
15. New York State Div. of Human Rights, Recommendations on Employment Inquiries (rev. Dec. 2004) (available at *http://www.dhr.state.ny.us/pdf/employment.pdf*).
16. *Id.*
17. Rania V. Sedhom, *The EEOC's eRace Initiative: Combating Systemic Racism*, Human Resources 2008 (Summer ed.) (available at *http://www.buckconsultants.com/buckconsultants/portals/0/documents/publications/published_articles/2008/Articles_Sedhom_Human_Resources_summer_08.pdf*).
18. *See* U.S. Equal Employment Opportunity Commn., Transcr. Commission Meeting (Feb. 28, 2007) (available at *http://www.eeoc.gov/abouteeoc/meetings/2-28-07/transcript.html*).
19. *See* Lisa Takeuchi Cullen, *It's a Wrap. You're Hired!*, Time (Feb. 22, 2007) (available at *http://www.time.com/time/magazine/article/0,9171,1592860,00.html*).

20. New York State Div. of Human Rights, Recommendations on Employment Inquiries (rev. Dec. 2004) (available at *http://www.dhr.state.ny.us/pdf/employment.pdf*).

21. *Id.*

22. *Id.*

23. *Id.*

24. Executive Order 13087, issued on May 28, 1998, prohibits discrimination based on sexual orientation within the Executive Branch for civilian employment. U.S. Office of Personnel Mgt., Addressing Sexual Orientation Discrimination in Federal Civilian Employment (available at *http://www.opm.gov/er/address2/guide01.asp*).

25. *See, e.g.,* Cal. Lab. Code § 1102.1. California, Connecticut, District of Columbia, Hawaii, Illinois, Maine, Maryland, Massachusetts, Minnesota, Nevada, New Hampshire, New Jersey, New Mexico, New York, Rhode Island, Vermont, Washington, and Wisconsin have laws that prohibit workplace discrimination on the basis of sexual orientation. California, Hawaii, Illinois, Maine, Minnesota, New Mexico, Rhode Island, and Washington also forbid gender identity discrimination. *See* AFL-CIO, Discrimination: Sexual Orientation and Gender Identity (available at *http://www.aflcio.org/issues/jobsecon omy/workersrights/rightsatwork_e/disc_sexorient.cfm*).

26. Colorado, Delaware, Indiana, Michigan, Montana, and Pennsylvania have laws that prohibit sexual orientation discrimination in public workplaces. Nolo, Sexual Orientation Discrimination in the Workplace (available at *http://www.nolo.com/article.cfm/ObjectID/ 0F606661-EF27-4560-9191693C7FFA61B3*). There are also more than 180 cities and counties that provide some other types of protection based on sexual orientation. *Id.*

27. *See* Steven Mitchell Sack, *The Working Woman's Legal Survival Guide* (1998) (available at *http://public.findlaw.com/bookshelf-working-woman/WMNCHP1_a.html*).

28. New York State Div. of Human Rights, Recommendations on Employment Inquiries (rev. Dec. 2004) (available at *http://www.dhr.state.ny.us/pdf/employment.pdf*).

29. 29 C.F.R. § 1625.4(b).

30. New York State Div. of Human Rights, Recommendations on Employment Inquiries (rev. Dec. 2004) (available at *http://www.dhr.state.ny.us/pdf/employment.pdf*).

31. *See id.*

32. *Espinoza v. Farah Mfg. Co.,* 414 U.S. 86, 92 (1973); 29 C.F.R. § 1060.5(a).

33. This component of the INA is enforced by the Department of Homeland Security. U.S. Dept. of Labor, Employment Law Guide, Authorized Workers (available at *http://www .dol.gov/compliance/guide/aw.htm*).

34. U.S. Equal Employment Opportunity Commn., Pre-Employment Inquiries and Citizenship (available at *http://www.eeoc.gov/laws/practices/inquiries_citizenship.cfm*).

35. New York State Div. of Human Rights, Recommendations on Employment Inquiries (rev. Dec. 2004) (available at *http://www.dhr.state.ny.us/pdf/employment.pdf*).

36. *Id.*

37. *See* U.S. Equal Employment Opportunity Commn., Enforcement Guidance: Pre-Employment Disability-Related Questions and Medical Examinations (available at *http://www.eeoc.gov/policy/docs/preemp.html*).

38. U.S. Equal Employment Opportunity Commn., Enforcement Guidance: Preemployment Disability-Related Questions and Medical Examinations (available at *http://www.eeoc.gov/ policy/docs/preemp.html*).

39. 42 U.S.C. § 12,112(d)(2).

40. 42 U.S.C. § 12,112(d)(3).

41. U.S. Equal Employment Opportunity Commn., Background Information for EEOC Notice of Proposed Rulemaking on Title II of the Genetic Information Nondiscrimination Act of 2008 (available at *http://www.eeoc.gov/policy/docs/qanda_geneticinfo.html*) ("This prohibition is absolute. Covered entities may not use genetic information in making employment decisions under any circumstances.").

42. New York State Div. of Human Rights, Recommendations on Employment Inquiries (rev. Dec. 2004) (available at *http://www.dhr.state.ny.us/pdf/employment.pdf*).

43. U.S. Equal Employment Opportunity Commn., Enforcement Guidance: Preemployment Disability-Related Questions and Medical Examinations (available at *http://www.eeoc.gov/policy/docs/preemp.html*).

44. *See id.*

45. New York State Div. of Human Rights, Recommendations on Employment Inquiries (rev. Dec. 2004) (available at *http://www.dhr.state.ny.us/pdf/employment.pdf*).

46. *Geller v. Markham*, 635 F.2d 1027 (2d Cir. 1980), *cert. denied*, 451 U.S. 945 (1981).

47. *Taggart v. Time, Inc.*, 924 F.2d 43 (2d Cir. 1991).

48. New York State Div. of Human Rights, Recommendations on Employment Inquiries (rev. Dec. 2004) (available at *http://www.dhr.state.ny.us/pdf/employment.pdf*).

49. *See, e.g.*, Kansas Human Rights Commn., Guidelines on Equal Employment Practices: Preventing Discrimination in Hiring (available at *http://www.khrc.net/hiring.htm*).

50. U.S. Equal Employment Opportunity Commn., ADA Enforcement Guidance: Preemployment Disability-Related Questions and Medical Examinations (available at *http://www.eeoc.gov/policy/docs/medfin5.pdf*).

51. *Id.*

52. *See, e.g.*, Wisconsin Dept. of Workforce Dev., *Fair Hiring & Avoiding Loaded Interview Questions*, Equal Rights Publication ERD-4825-PWEB (available at *http://dwd.wisconsin.gov/er/discrimination_civil_rights/publication_erd_4825_pweb.htm#15*).

53. *See generally* Statement of Adam T. Klein, Esq. at U.S. Equal Employment Opportunity Commn. Meeting (May 16, 2007) (regarding Employment Testing and Screening) (available at *http://www.eeoc.gov/eeoc/meetings/archive/5-16-07/klein.html*).

54. *See, e.g.* Wisconsin Dept. of Workforce Dev., *Fair Hiring & Avoiding Loaded Interview Questions*, Equal Rights Publication ERD-4825-PWEB (available at *http://dwd.wisconsin.gov/er/discrimination_civil_rights/publication_erd_4825_pweb.htm#15*).

55. *See, e.g.*, Susan K. Lessack, *Employers Trying to Curb Smoking Should Be Cautious Not to Get Legally Burned*, Lab. & Empl. L. Update (Pepper Hamilton LLP Feb. 27, 2007) (available at *http://www.pepperlaw.com/publications_update.aspx?ArticleKey=845*).

56. *See* Youth Action & Policy Assn., Smoking: Law and Policy for Youth Services (available at *http://www.yapa.org.au/youthwork/facts/smoking.php*).

57. David Pittman, *BSA Adopts No-Hire Policy for Smokers*, Amarillo Globe-News (Jan. 3, 2009) (available at *http://www.amarillo.com/stories/010309/new_12185039.shtml*).

58. *Id.*

59. U.S. Equal Employment Opportunity Commn., Enforcement Guidance: Preemployment Disability-Related Questions and Medical Examinations (available at *http://www.eeoc.gov/policy/docs/preemp.html*).

60. *Id.*

61. *Id.*

62. *Id.*

63. *See* New York State Div. of Human Rights, Recommendations on Employment Inquiries (rev. Dec. 2004) (available at *http://www.dhr.state.ny.us/pdf/employment.pdf*).

64. U.S. Dept. of Justice, Frequently Asked Questions (available at *http://www.usdoj.gov/crt/military/faq.htm*). This law provides individuals who believe they have been discriminated against based on military service with the right to file a claim with the Department of Labor or go directly to federal or state court.

65. *See, e.g.*, Nevada Equal Rights Commn., Pre-Employment Guide (available at *http://www.nvdetr.org/nerc/nerc_preemp.htm*).

66. *See* 10 Fair Empl. Prac. Cas. (BNA) 260, EEOC Dec. No. 74-25 ¶ 6400, 1973 WL 3919 (E.E.O.C.) (citing 1971 study showing that Black/African-American servicemembers received a lower proportion of honorable discharges and a higher proportion of general and undesirable discharges than Whites of similar aptitude and education, the consideration of which would have a foreseeable disproportionate impact on minorities); *Dozier v. Chupka*, 395 F. Supp. 836, 850–51 (S.D. Ohio 1975) (bonus points for honorable discharges invalidated in absence of evidence establishing that such criterion was related to job performance where Blacks/African-Americans received proportionately higher

dishonorable discharges from armed forces); *see, e.g.*, Idaho Commn. on Human Rights, Pre-Employment Inquiries—Discrimination Pitfalls (available at *http://humanrights. idaho.gov/discrimination/pre_employment.html*).

67. *See* New York State Div. of Human Rights, Recommendations on Employment Inquiries (rev. Dec. 2004) (available at *http://www.dhr.state.ny.us/pdf/employment.pdf*).

68. *See, e.g., Meade v. Cedarapids, Inc.*, 164 F.3d 1218 (9th Cir. 1999).

69. *See* Equal Employment Opportunity Commn., 2008 EEO-1 Survey: Frequently Asked Questions (available at *http://www.eeoc.gov/eeo1survey/faq.html*). All federal government contractors and first-tier subcontractors with 50 or more employees and a contract in the amount of $50,000 or more are also required to file the EEO-1 report.

Pre-Employment Testing

11

Chapter Objectives

This chapter explores the wide range of tests used by employers to assess whether an applicant is suitable for a position. The text explains what different types of pre-employment tests are designed to measure and emphasizes the importance of administering each test in a uniform and nondiscriminatory manner. Significant guidance is provided relating to the appropriate use of test results, and special attention is paid to background checks, credit checks, polygraph tests, and medical and drug testing.

After completing this chapter, students should have a fundamental understanding of the most commonly used pre-employment tests and the appropriate use of them in the hiring process.

Upon mastering the main objectives of this chapter students should be able to

- explain the reasons why an employer might use pre-employment tests;
- identify the most common pre-employment tests and what each is designed to measure;
- explain why the manner in which an employer administers a pre-employment test might result in employer liability for workplace discrimination;
- define *negligent hiring* and explain its relevance to the use of pre-employment tests;
- explain the significance of the Fair Credit Reporting Act (FCRA) to pre-employment testing;
- explain the appropriate use of arrest records and criminal convictions to disqualify applicants, and the reasons why the information is subject to different standards;
- explain when it might be appropriate for an employer to subject an applicant to a credit check;
- explain the significance of the Employee Polygraph Protection Act (EPPA) and the limitations it places on employees; and
- explain the rights of employers to request medical information and inquire about the drug use of their applicants.

INTRODUCTION

Pre-employment testing is administered immediately before an individual is hired (or post-hiring but prior to the start of employment), and other employment testing may occur immediately after an individual begins to work. Employers have historically used these tests to assess the ability of applicants to perform the tasks associated with a position as well as to avoid (or at least minimize) liability that may arise in the event an individual who is hired causes harm to others.

A pre-employment test might be characterized as an **eligibility test**, which means that an applicant would be required to achieve a minimum score to be eligible for the position. A typing test might be an eligibility test, for example, if an employer determined an applicant must be able to type 50 words per minute to be considered for a position. A test might also be characterized as an **ineligibility test**, which means that a certain result would disqualify an applicant from further consideration. A drug test would be an example of an ineligibility test if a positive result would render an applicant unsuitable for a particular position.

eligibility tests
pre-employment tests that require applicants to achieve a certain result to be considered qualified for a position

ineligibility tests
pre-employment tests that eliminate applicants from consideration based upon certain results

A. COMMON TESTS

Pre-employment testing can take a number of different forms, evaluate a number of different skills, and result in the production of a wide range of information. According to the EEOC, the most common categories of pre-employment tests are the following:

- ✓ **cognitive tests,** which measure skills such as memory, arithmetic, and reasoning, as well as knowledge of a specific job;
- ✓ **sample job tasks,** which require the performance of simulated projects comparable to anticipated job assignments;
- ✓ **personality tests,** which assess different components of an applicant's personality such as the likelihood to be a team player;
- ✓ **physical ability tests,** which measure strength and stamina;
- ✓ **medical inquiries and physical examinations,** which relate to an applicant's physical or mental health;
- ✓ **criminal background checks,** which provide information about an applicant's history of arrests and convictions;
- ✓ **credit checks,** which provide the credit and financial history of applicants; and
- ✓ **English proficiency tests,** which determine whether an individual has command of the English language.[1]

Because the results of pre-employment tests will be used as part of the recruitment process and can influence an individual's terms and conditions of employment, employers may be subject to liability if use of the tests does not comply with anti-discrimination laws.

B. LIABILITY FOR DISCRIMINATORY CONDUCT

The plain language of Title VII permits the use of pre-employment testing provided the selection tools are not "designed, intended or used to discriminate because of race, color, religion, sex or national origin."[2] Based on this, employers who use pre-employment tests must ensure that their use, like all other components of the recruitment process, complies with federal anti-discrimination laws. The EEOC reports that in one year, it received a record high of 304 charges filed relating to the alleged wrongful use of pre-employment testing to screen out applicants.[3] Consistent with how anti-discrimination laws are applied to other elements of the employment process, applicants can challenge the use of a pre-employment test by filing a disparate treatment or disparate impact claim. See Chapter 2, Title VII — The Foundation of Workplace Discrimination Law.

1. DISPARATE TREATMENT DISCRIMINATION

An individual may bring a claim for **disparate treatment discrimination** if an employer engages in intentional discrimination based on an individual's membership in a protected class. This type of claim would materialize if an employer decides that because women are more likely than men to have typing skills, male applicants will have to pass a typing test prior to being considered for an administrative assistant position, but female applicants will not be subject to the same requirement.

> **disparate treatment discrimination**
> basis for a claim under Title VII alleging an employer engaged in conduct intended to discriminate based on an individual's membership in a protected class

2. DISPARATE IMPACT DISCRIMINATION

An individual may bring a claim for **disparate impact discrimination** if an employer uses a test that has a disproportionate adverse impact on members of a protected class. For example, one court upheld a disparate impact claim against an employer because the strength test it used to eliminate applicants had a disproportionate impact on women. The court found that the test (which required the lifting of 35 pounds, 30 to 60 inches, at a rate of 1.25 lifts per minute) eliminated a disproportionate number of female candidates from the applicant pool and was not sufficiently job related to justify this result. The court based its finding, in part, on the fact that, because the test was more difficult than what the job required, it unlawfully eliminated female applicants who might have possessed the level of strength necessary to perform the job tasks.[4]

> **disparate impact discrimination**
> basis for a claim under Title VII alleging that the implementation of a facially neutral policy had a disproportionate adverse impact on members of a protected class

To provide assistance in determining whether a pre-employment test has a disparate impact on members of a protected class, the EEOC, through its Uniform Guidelines on Employee Selection Criteria, has established the **four-fifths (or 80%) rule,** which compares the selection rate of different groups of applicants. Under this rule, if the selection rate of the group with the lowest selection rate is less than 80% of the selection rate of the group with the highest selection rate, then the presumption is that a disparate impact exists.[5]

> **four-fifths (or 80%) rule**
> standard established by the EEOC that quantifies an adverse impact on a protected group as a selection rate that is less than 4/5 (or 80%) of the selection rate of the group with the highest selection rate

For example, suppose the following table represents the number of individuals who apply and are hired for a position to unload delivery trucks, which the employer has determined requires the applicant to lift 60 pounds.

Number of Applicants Based on Membership in a Particular Protected Class	Number of Individuals Hired Based on Membership in a Particular Protected Class	Selection Rate (Percentage Hired) Based on Membership in a Protected Class
10 women	1	10% (1/10)
20 men	4	20% (4/20)

Here, 10 women and 20 men applied for the position, and the employer hired one woman and four men for the positions. The employer hired 10% of the female candidates (one out of ten equals a 10% selection rate), and 20% of the male candidates (4 out of 20 equals a 20% selection rate). This information could be used as evidence to support a claim for disparate impact discrimination in violation of the four-fifths (or 80%) rule, because the 10% selection rate for women is 50% (or half) of the 20% selection rate for the men, which is less than the 80% (or four-fifths) threshold established by the EEOC.[6]

 ## ADMINISTRATION OF TESTS

The obligation of employers to comply with anti-discrimination laws applies to all components of the testing process, from the administration of the test, to the substance of the test, to how the results are used. Employers using pre-employment tests as part of their hiring process may be subject to liability for discriminatory behavior even before the actual substance of the test is considered. They may be subject to liability for failing to administer the test in a nondiscriminatory manner, which includes, among other things, the duty to provide a reasonable accommodation for disabled applicants and for those applicants who have sincerely held religious beliefs, which prevent them from being able to take the test under the conditions offered.

A. DISABILITY DISCRIMINATION

Because the Americans with Disabilities Act (ADA) protects disabled individuals from the beginning of the hiring process, an employer might be required to offer a disabled applicant a reasonable accommodation to enable the individual to take a pre-employment test.

1. PROVIDING A REASONABLE ACCOMMODATION

An employer has an obligation to accommodate disabled applicants to the same extent it must accommodate disabled employees. For example, if a pre-employment test is administered on the third floor of a building without an elevator, and an applicant confined to a wheelchair asks to complete the test in a conference room on the first floor, the employer might be required to offer this accommodation (or a different one that is deemed reasonable) provided that it does not result in an undue burden.[7] An employer might also be required to alter other conditions under which the pre-employment test is given, such as providing an applicant inflicted with cancer additional time to complete the test due to fatigue caused by a radiation treatment.[8] Similarly, an employer might have an obligation to provide an applicant with a reader if the individual has a vision disability that would prevent him from completing the test.[9]

2. ASSESSING THE NEED FOR AN ACCOMMODATION

Despite the general prohibition against asking disability-related questions until a conditional offer of employment is made, if an applicant requests an accommodation to take a pre-employment test, the employer is permitted to ask the applicant about the disability. All medical inquiries should be narrowly tailored to solicit enough information to determine whether the condition would fall within the coverage of the ADA and to better assess the type of accommodation that might be appropriate.[10] See Chapter 7, Disability Discrimination.

B. RELIGIOUS DISCRIMINATION

Consistent with Title VII's prohibition against religious discrimination, if an applicant indicates that a sincerely held religious belief or practice would conflict with the administration of a pre-employment test, the employer would be required to provide a reasonable accommodation provided it is not an undue burden. For example, if an applicant informs the employer that the proposed day for taking a pre-employment test falls on a religious holiday that would preclude the performance of work-related responsibilities, the employer might be obligated to offer the applicant an opportunity to take the test on an alternative date, provided it is not an undue burden. The applicant has the legal right to request this accommodation, and the request must not be considered when the employer makes a decision about whether the individual is qualified for the position.[11] See Chapter 4, Religious Discrimination.

 **JOB-RELATED SELECTION TESTS**

In addition to ensuring that pre-employment tests are administered in a nondiscriminatory manner, employers must also ensure that the skills the tests are designed to measure, and the information they are designed to gather, are necessary for the performance of the essential job tasks. **Selection tests** are the tests used to determine whether an applicant has the minimum qualifications necessary to perform the essential job functions.

selection tests
tests used to determine whether an applicant has the minimum qualifications necessary to perform essential job functions

Employers can utilize professionally developed selection tests to ensure hiring decisions are based on accurate information about an individual's qualifications, but the use of tests for this purpose has both benefits and drawbacks.

A. BENEFITS

The use of pre-employment selection tests can provide employers with a valuable source of information that can be used to determine whether an applicant is qualified for a position. Professionally developed tests can also be accurate predictors of an applicant's ability to succeed at a job, which will enhance the likelihood that the resources expended in the recruitment process will result in the selection of a well-suited candidate. In addition, in expanding an existing workforce by hiring a highly qualified candidate, an employer might achieve the added benefit of enhancing employee morale. Further, if a test disqualifies an applicant, particularly if the test is based on objective measurements, the results can be used as part of an employer's defense to a claim based on discriminatory hiring, in the event one materializes.

B. DRAWBACKS

Despite the benefits associated with the use of selection tests, there are also a number of potential drawbacks. The creation and validation of a test can be very expensive, take years to develop, and result in employer liability if the appropriate resources are not allocated to its creation and implementation. Also, the use of a test that includes objective measurements takes away some of the employer's flexibility in its hiring decisions. For example, a specific cut-off point may fail to account for the fact that an applicant's strength in one particular area might outweigh any shortcomings that are reflected in a sub-standard test score.

C. TYPES OF JOB-RELATED SELECTION TESTS

Assuming an employer determines that the benefits of selection tests outweigh their drawbacks, the next question to consider is what type of test will best address the needs of the employer.

1. COGNITIVE TESTS

cognitive tests
selection tests that measure basic skills as well as skills specific to a particular position

Cognitive tests focus on the responsibilities associated with the position and the skills necessary to complete the essential job functions. These types of tests can measure basic skills such as memory, arithmetic, and reasoning, or job-specific knowledge. A typing test for an administrative assistant position and a mathematics test administered for an accountant position are examples of cognitive tests. The types of cognitive tests least likely to produce discriminatory results are those that involve work samples, or that ask applicants to make decisions based on a specific set of facts. These tests are the least problematic because such exercises closely track the actual tasks that would be performed by the individual selected for the position.[12]

2. STRENGTH TESTS

Strength tests are used by employers for positions that require certain levels of physical strength. Although strength tests are not prohibited, courts closely scrutinize them based on particular concerns about their potential to have a disparate impact on women and older applicants.

3. PSYCHOLOGICAL AND PERSONALITY TESTS

Recent studies have shown that more than 30% of companies currently use some type of test to assess the personalities of their applicants to assist them in hiring decisions, and the number is expected to rise.[13] These psychological and **personality tests** are used by employers to determine whether an individual possesses certain characteristics, such as honesty, that the employer determines are necessary to perform the tasks associated with a position.

personality tests
tests that analyze different components of an individual's character to determine whether he or she possesses desirable traits for a position

D. GENERAL FRAMEWORK FOR TESTING

Because the results of selection tests are used to make employment decisions, anti-discrimination laws govern the gathering and use of information from those tests. Therefore, the tests should measure only job-related information about whether an applicant possesses the necessary skills to fill the position or to predict the future likelihood of acceptable performance.[14] The uniform administration of professionally developed tests that are narrowly tailored to assess a job skill and applied consistently within the parameters of anti-discrimination laws can be an effective part of a comprehensive recruitment plan.[15]

The EEOC recognizes the rights of employers to use pre-employment tests but also the potential for their use to produce discriminatory results. Based on this, the EEOC has provided some employer guidance to minimize potential liability, suggesting that employers (1) administer the tests uniformly, absent any consideration of whether applicants are members of a particular protected class; (2) ensure the tests are job related and narrowly tailored for the purpose for which they are used; (3) craft the tests to minimize the adverse impact their use might have on members of a protected class; and (4) continue to update the tests as the job requirements change.[16]

1. APPLY TEST UNIFORMLY

Employers should ensure that all pre-employment tests are administered in a uniform and nondiscriminatory manner.

a. Test All Applicants

The foundation for the nondiscriminatory use of the test is to require it for all applicants for a particular position, rather than limiting its use to applicants in a specific protected class. For example, an employer could be subject to liability for sex discrimination for requiring female applicants for a bus driver position to take a driving test but not subjecting male applicants to the same requirement.

An employer could also be subject to liability for limiting the use of a physical strength test to female applicants based on the preconceived notion they are less likely than men to be able to move heavy boxes. An employer could also be subject to liability under the Age Discrimination in Employment Act (ADEA) for requiring a physical strength test for applicants over 50 years of age based on a preconceived notion that strength decreases as a person ages.[17] To minimize the potential for a claim based on discriminatory conduct, employers seeking to fill positions that require lifting a certain amount of weight should require a physical strength test for all applicants so they can assess the physical strength of each person individually, rather than singling out members of certain protected classes based on stereotypes, prejudices, or preconceived notions about their abilities.[18]

b. Apply Uniform Standards

Once an employer implements a policy to test all applicants, it must also use uniform standards to analyze the test results. Title VII provides, "It shall be an unlawful employment practice for a respondent, in connection with the selection or referral of applicants or candidates for employment or promotion, to adjust the scores of, use different cutoff scores for, or otherwise alter the results of, employment related tests on the basis of race, color, religion, sex, or national origin."[19] For example, an employer would be prohibited from implementing a policy requiring female candidates to be able to lift 50 pounds to qualify for a position while requiring men to be able to lift 75 pounds.

2. LIMIT TESTS TO JOB-RELATED SKILLS

Even if an employer tests all applicants and applies the same standards, it should also be prepared to illustrate a clear connection between what the test measures and what is needed to complete the job responsibilities for the position. For example, although an employer might be able to illustrate why applicants for an accountant position would have to pass a test illustrating their ability to perform complex mathematical calculations, it would be more challenging to illustrate why applicants applying for an attorney position must have those skills.

a. Business Need

In determining whether a test is job related, employers should assess whether there is a business need for the test and whether the results are necessary to determine whether an applicant is qualified for the position. For example, if an employer is seeking to hire a candidate who has knowledge of a particular computer program, the employer can administer a test to determine whether an applicant possesses those skills. If, however, the employer would be willing to hire an applicant who is unfamiliar with a particular computer program and provide training with respect to it, then the employer should not utilize this test because the results would not necessarily qualify or disqualify an applicant from consideration.

If it can be shown that members of certain protected classes are less likely than nonmembers to pass such a test, and if it can also be shown that this knowledge is not necessary to perform the essential job tasks (because workplace training would be available), the employer could be subject to liability for discriminatory conduct. This is because the test would be eliminating candidates from consideration and therefore have a disparate impact on members of a protected class (because members are more likely than nonmembers to fail the test) without a business need for doing so (because knowledge of the program is unnecessary since it could be learned on the job).

b. Potential Liability Under the Americans with Disabilities Act (ADA)

Employers should pay particular attention to tests that eliminate applicants with disabilities.[20] The ADA specifically references the fact that employers will be subject to liability for "failing to select and administer tests . . . in the most effective manner to ensure that . . . such test results accurately reflect the skills [and] aptitude . . . that such test purports to measure, rather than reflecting the impaired sensory, manual, or speaking skills of . . . [a disabled applicant.]"[21]

Employers should also be careful that the use of psychological and personality tests does not identify medical conditions, because this could materialize into an ADA claim.[22] Although psychological and personality tests are permitted to assess such characteristics as honesty, tastes, and habits, an employer might be subject to liability if a test reveals that an individual suffers from anxiety, depression, or a compulsive disorder, and the test was determined to be a pre-employment medical test, which would be prohibited by the ADA.[23] For example, one employer had to pay a significant penalty for administering a pre-employment personality test that the court classified as a medical test because it had historically been used by psychologists "to diagnose and treat individuals with abnormal psychological symptoms and personality traits."[24]

3. NARROWLY TAILOR TESTS TO MINIMIZE ANY ADVERSE IMPACT

Even if an employer can show that a specific skill is necessary to perform the essential tasks associated with the job, the employer must also show that the required *level* of skill is necessary for an applicant to be qualified for the position.

a. Measure the Minimum Skills Necessary to Perform the Essential Job Tasks

Pre-employment tests should only require the level of skill critical for completing the essential tasks associated with the position. For example, if an employer wants to hire an administrative assistant who can type 90 words per minute and decides to administer a test to learn if a candidate possesses this skill, the employer should be prepared to explain why a candidate who types 70 words per minute would be unable to perform the essential functions of the job. If a candidate who possesses slower typing skills could perform the essential functions, then the employer should adjust its expectations to reflect this reality. This is particularly important if the higher standard results in the disqualification of a disproportionate number of candidates from a particular protected class.

b. Collect Information That Can Be Appropriately Considered

Because the presumption is that an employer will use all of the gathered information to make its hiring decisions, the employer should ensure that the results of any selection tests it uses do not provide information that, if considered by the employer in making an adverse decision, would constitute discriminatory behavior. For example, employers should try to avoid open-ended questions on selection tests, or those that would invite applicants to provide information that would reveal their protected class status. This is because if an individual responds to an open-ended question with information revealing his membership in a protected class and does not receive a job offer, the applicant can assert that the motivating factor behind the adverse employment decision was discriminatory.

4. MODIFY THE TEST AS CIRCUMSTANCES WARRANT

Employers who use pre-employment tests should also monitor their continued use to assess whether changes in the workplace suggest an adjustment is necessary. This is important because an employer who has a legitimate need for a test might lose this protection if a changed circumstance eliminates the original business need for the test, or if an alternative test that would minimize the resulting disparate impact on members of a protected class became available.[25]

For example, an employer might need applicants to be proficient in a particular computer program and therefore decide to assess this level of skill through a pre-employment test. If, however, the employer decides to automate some of that work, the particular skill that had been tested might become less relevant. This changed circumstance might eliminate the need for the use of that particular test, and the employer might be subject to liability for continuing to use it, particularly if use of the test disqualifies a disproportionate number of applicants who belong to a particular protected class.

IV BACKGROUND CHECKS GENERALLY

After an employer determines that a candidate has the minimum qualifications necessary to perform the essential job tasks, the employer often administers a number of other tests that extend beyond whether the applicant has the specific skills to fill the open position. The purpose of these types of tests is to verify information the applicant has provided and review other information that may have been requested to further assess the candidate's suitability for the position.

Because there are a number of laws that regulate an employer's right to collect information about its applicants, some employers are hesitant to aggressively gather it. However, this concern should be balanced against the potential liability that may materialize if an employer hires an individual that it knows, or should have known, would pose a danger in the workplace. This balance is particularly significant within the context of **background checks,** which can take a number of forms depending on the business needs of the employer. Components of a background check could include the following:

- ✓ **criminal background checks,** which provide information about an applicant's history of arrests and convictions;
- ✓ **credit checks,** which provide information about an applicant's credit and financial history; and
- ✓ **reference checks,** which confirm an applicant's prior work experience and may provide feedback from previous employers.[26]

background checks
information collected by an employer to verify information provided by an applicant and to further assess an applicant's suitability for a position

As workplace violence continues to rise and serious occurrences of misconduct are showcased on the local and national news, employers have become increasingly concerned about the potential for workplace violence. This reality, along with post-9/11 security concerns, has resulted in the increased use of background checks.[27] The enhanced scrutiny of applicants can serve the dual purpose of creating safer workplace environments and bolstering the defense of an employer in response to a negligent hiring claim if an individual is hired and causes harm to others.

A. NEGLIGENT HIRING

Employers have an obligation to investigate potential employees to ensure they do not pose a threat to others.

1. BASIS FOR A CLAIM

Most employers conduct some type of background check to determine whether an individual is fit for a position. In the event a background check is not conducted, an employer may be subject to liability based on the theory of **negligent hiring** if the individual causes harm to another person.

Under this doctrine, employers have an obligation to ensure that they do not hire individuals who pose a risk of injury or harm to others. Liability arises if an employer knows or should have known that a particular person was unfit for a position and that individual causes harm. This harm can take a number of forms, ranging from physical threats or assaults to the theft of personal property.

negligent hiring
claim that materializes when an individual, who an employer knows or should have known was unfit for a position, causes harm

2. FORESEEABILITY OF HARM

To avoid a negligent hiring claim, employers must assess whether an individual is fit to work alongside co-workers. This liability is not absolute, however, because the employer will be responsible only for injuries caused by the individual to the extent the behavior was foreseeable. The employer will not be subject to liability if the investigation it conducted did not reveal information that would suggest a potential danger, and if the employer had no other reason to believe that such a danger existed.[28]

B. TECHNOLOGICAL IMPACT

Background checks have often been used to eliminate unfit candidates from consideration, but the process was often time-consuming and cost-prohibitive because so many records had to be searched by hand. Today, many components of investigations can be done electronically, which greatly reduces their expense. These technological advances have also made the services more readily available because many companies now offer them.[29]

C. UNIFORM APPLICATION OF POLICIES

Employers have a vested interest in maintaining a safe workplace and avoiding a negligent hiring claim, but they must ensure policies relating to background checks are consistent with workplace anti-discrimination laws. Although Title VII does not prohibit employers from reviewing arrest and conviction records or credit histories, it does require the showing of a business necessity for the need for this review, and it requires the collection of such information to be done in a uniform and nondiscriminatory manner.[30]

For example, an employer who conducts background investigations of applicants from certain countries but not of applicants from other countries could be subject to liability under Title VII for national origin discrimination.[31] An employer might also be subject to liability for asking applicants born in the Middle East for information about their arrest or conviction records, but not asking for the same information from others, or for checking only the references of applicants belonging to certain minority groups.[32]

D. FAIR CREDIT REPORTING ACT (FCRA)

Fair Credit Reporting Act (FCRA)
federal law that requires the accurate and confidential reporting of consumer information

Employers using background checks as part of the hiring process should become familiar with the **Fair Credit Reporting Act (FCRA),** which is the federal law that focuses on the importance of accurately reporting consumer information and protecting the privacy of the collected information. The FCRA establishes a process for collecting information, using the information within the employment process, and providing notice to individuals about what will be collected and how it will be used. The information that falls within the scope of the FCRA is very broad, and despite the name of the law, the Act applies to far more information than what would be contained in an individual's credit report.[33]

1. INFORMATION COVERED

The FCRA applies to all of the information included in a **consumer report**, which is broadly defined to include written and oral information collected by a consumer reporting agency that relates to an individual's creditworthiness, credit standing, credit capacity, character, general reputation, and personal characteristics, and that will be used for employment purposes.[34]

Consumer reports also include information collected for a number of purposes outside the employment context, such as determining whether an individual is eligible for insurance or is a suitable candidate for the extension of certain levels of credit. The broad definition of the term makes the FCRA's regulations applicable to information obtained through background checks, reference checks, and any other information collected as part of the hiring process.[35] Thus, the Act would also apply to an employer request for a **credit report,** which is a specific type of consumer report that provides information about an applicant's residence as well as whether he pays his bills, and whether he has been sued, has been arrested, or has filed for bankruptcy.[36]

consumer report
broad term for consumer information provided by a reporting agency used to assess an individual's suitability for such things as employment, insurance, and credit

credit report
type of consumer report that provides information used to determine whether an applicant is a suitable candidate for the extension of credit

2. AUTHORIZATION FOR USE OF A CONSUMER REPORTING AGENCY

The FCRA also applies to any information collected by a **consumer reporting agency,** which is loosely defined as any party that regularly engages in assembling or evaluating consumer reports for a fee for the purpose of providing the information to a third party.[37] Employers who intend to retain the services of a consumer reporting agency must obtain written authorization from each applicant prior to requesting any information, and the authorization form should be a stand-alone document (as opposed to including the request in a more general authorization permitting the verification of any information provided on the application).[38] In addition, each applicant must be provided with a written "clear and conspicuous" disclosure indicating that a report will be requested from a third party.[39]

consumer reporting agency
entity that gathers and/or reviews information on a consumer report and provides it to a third party in exchange for compensation

3. USE OF INFORMATION AS THE BASIS FOR AN ADVERSE EMPLOYMENT DECISION

An employer's right to use the information contained in a consumer report as the basis for an adverse employment decision is also regulated. An employer who makes an adverse employment decision based on information obtained from a consumer report must provide the applicant with a summary of his rights under the FCRA along with a copy of the report and the name, address, and telephone number of the third party that provided it.[40] In addition, employers should implement any policies relating to the use of the information in a uniform and non-discriminatory manner. This includes ensuring that the consideration of certain information does not intentionally or unintentionally discriminate against members of a protected class.

The EEOC and the FCRA establish legal parameters for the reporting and use of the information, and some state laws place additional limitations on what may and may not be considered within the hiring process. Whether the employer's consideration of information contained in the report will materialize into a claim against the employer will vary depending on the process used to collect the information as well as the specific type of information from the report that is considered. There are some categories of information, however, that cannot not be used to disqualify applicants absent further employer inquiry, and the use of other types of information is closely scrutinized.

V CRIMINAL BACKGROUND CHECKS

Criminal background checks provide information about the conviction and arrest records of an applicant, and there are limitations on how this information can be appropriately used.

A. STATE LAWS IMPOSE RESTRICTIONS

A number of states have passed laws that place stringent limitations on the rights of employers to use arrest and conviction records in the hiring process. For example, California law prohibits employers from asking applicants to disclose information about an arrest that did not result in a conviction, seeking any other sources for this information, or utilizing it as a factor in hiring.[41] In Nevada, pre-employment questions regarding arrests are unacceptable, and questions regarding convictions must be accompanied by a statement that a convictions will not automatically eliminate a candidate from consideration.[42] Hawaii places similar restrictions on employers, making it an unlawful discriminatory practice for an employer to refuse to hire an applicant based on an arrest, and allowing consideration of a criminal conviction only where there is a rational relationship between it and the responsibilities of the position.[43]

B. BLANKET DISQUALIFICATIONS ARE GENERALLY PROHIBITED

Even absent this type of legislation, blanket policies that disqualify applicants because of an arrest record or conviction will likely violate Title VII based on the disparate impact such a policy would have on members of a protected class. Due to this potential for discriminatory results, the EEOC suggests that employers include language on their application that a past conviction or arrest will not necessarily disqualify a candidate from consideration.[44]

The fact that blanket prohibitions are closely scrutinized does not mean that employers are prohibited from independently evaluating this information based on the nature of the offenses and the position for which the individual is applying.[45] However, when reviewing an applicant's criminal history, an employer must also understand that information about arrests must be treated differently than information about convictions.

C. ARREST RECORDS AS THE BASIS FOR A DISQUALIFICATION

There are a number of reasons why the use of arrest records to disqualify applicants is subject to stringent review.

1. NOT CONCLUSIVE PROOF CRIME OCCURRED

An arrest record is not conclusive evidence that any illegal conduct occurred. As the Supreme Court stated, "The mere fact that a [person] has been arrested has very little, if any, probative value in showing that he has engaged in misconduct."[46]

2. DISPARATE IMPACT DISCRIMINATION

Because studies have shown that minorities are more likely than nonminorities to be arrested, using an arrest record to justify an adverse employment decision will likely have a disparate impact on minorities and could violate Title VII. Due to this reality and the potential for the misuse of information obtained from arrest records, a number of states and the District of Columbia have actually passed legislation that specifically prohibits or advises against the use of pre-employment questions about arrests.[47] In addition, some courts have advised against pre-employment inquiries about arrest records because the mere request might discourage qualified applicants from applying in the first place.[48]

3. APPROPRIATE USE OF INFORMATION

Because an arrest is not conclusive proof that illegal conduct occurred, and consideration of an arrest record would likely have a disparate impact on minority applicants, an employer should neither make broad pre-employment inquiries about an applicant's arrest nor automatically disqualify applicants upon learning of this information.[49] This is not to say, however, that an employer must ignore an arrest record, or that the consideration of it does not play an appropriate role in the hiring process. Instead, employers that learn information about an individual's arrest record are generally required to undergo a two-part analysis to determine whether it should disqualify the applicant.[50] Specifically, to support the use of an arrest record as the basis for making an adverse employment decision, the employer should be prepared to illustrate that (1) the applicant actually engaged in the conduct that was the basis for the arrest, and (2) the conduct would affect the individual's ability to perform the job responsibilities.[51]

It makes the most sense for the employer to initiate this analysis by focusing on the second component of the test first. This is because if the employer determines that the unlawful conduct in which the applicant might or might not have engaged would *not* impact whether the individual is qualified for the position, there will be no need to investigate whether the applicant actually engaged in it.

a. Connection Between the Charges and the Ability to Perform Essential Job Functions

To determine whether the arrest should disqualify an applicant, the employer should determine whether, if the applicant did engage in the behavior, it would hamper his ability to complete the essential tasks associated with the position. In making this determination, the employer should look at (1) the nature and gravity of the offense, (2) the time that has passed since the arrest, and (3) the nature of the position.[52]

Employers have been most successful at establishing a connection between an arrest and the applicant's qualifications within the context of security-sensitive positions such as those that involve law enforcement or crime prevention.[53] In addition, employers seeking candidates to fill positions that will require access to the possessions of others, as well as positions with responsibilities associated with the safety of others, are usually provided with significant discretion to determine whether the nature of the charges, if true, should disqualify an applicant from further consideration.[54]

b. Likelihood the Applicant Engaged in the Unlawful Conduct

Once an employer determines that if an applicant engaged in the conduct that was the basis for the arrest it would hamper his ability to perform the essential tasks associated with the position, the employer is required to engage in an investigatory step to determine whether the applicant actually engaged in misconduct. To minimize the potential liability for discriminatory conduct, the employer should ensure that any adverse employment decision is based on a finding that the applicant actually *engaged* in the behavior that was the subject of the arrest as opposed to basing the decision on the fact that the arrest took place.[55]

In conducting this modest investigation, the employer may ask the applicant about whether he engaged in the behavior, and if presented with a denial or a reasonable explanation for the arrest, the employer must take further steps to assess the applicant's credibility before imposing an adverse decision. One way for the employer to assess the applicant's credibility is to contact a previous employer or a police department for further information.[56] Note that because there is potential that an employer could violate a number of other laws by conducting this investigation, employers should be certain that those who are delegated with these investigatory responsibilities are appropriately trained.

D. CRIMINAL CONVICTIONS

Unlike an arrest, a criminal conviction establishes that the individual engaged in unlawful conduct beyond a reasonable doubt. Therefore, an employer does not need to investigate whether the individual convicted of the crime engaged in the behavior.[57] Instead, the employer can use the conviction as proof that the crime was committed. Depending on the nature of the conviction, an employer might actually be legally required to disqualify an applicant. In other instances, an employer might have the right to use the conviction as the basis for the imposition of an adverse employment decision.

1. STATUTORY OBLIGATIONS

Some federal laws require employers to conduct criminal background checks on applicants for certain positions, and to disqualify candidates based on certain findings. For example, the Federal Deposit Insurance Act provides that financial institutions cannot employ individuals who have been convicted of certain offenses involving dishonesty, a breach of trust, or money laundering, and employers may be subjected to a fine of up to $1 million per day for failing to comply with this provision.[58]

2. SECURITY RISK

Assuming there is no applicable law that would require an employer to disqualify an applicant based on a particular conviction, the question becomes whether the employer would have the right to do so. Employers have the greatest discretion to use a conviction to disqualify an applicant when the conviction suggests the individual may be a security risk. Thus, employers may decide to engage in more extensive background checks based on security concerns, but the checks should be administered in a uniform and nondiscriminatory manner. For example, an employer may not require applicants with certain ethnic backgrounds to undergo such checks if they do not impose the same requirements upon all other similarly situated applicants.[59]

3. CONNECTION BETWEEN THE CONVICTION AND THE ESSENTIAL JOB FUNCTIONS

Absent a showing that the applicant's conviction for a particular crime poses a security risk, employers will likely be prohibited from automatically disqualifying an applicant based on it. Instead, the conviction can be used as the basis for an adverse employment decision only if there is a sufficient link between the offensive conduct that resulted in the conviction and the candidate's fitness to perform the essential job tasks. Even for convictions for serious crimes, employers must show that the disqualification is job related and consistent with a business necessity.[60]

Before using a conviction as the basis for an adverse employment decision, an employer should consider (1) the severity of the offense, (2) whether the conviction was recent or occurred in the distant past, and (3) whether the conviction will have an impact on the applicant's ability to perform the essential job tasks.[61] For example, an employer might have difficulty showing that an applicant's conviction for driving under the influence of alcohol would impact her ability to perform the essential tasks associated with being an accountant. The employer would have significantly less difficulty, however, illustrating that a conviction for driving under the influence is sufficient to support the disqualification of an applicant for a position as a bus driver.

VI. REFERENCE CHECKS

In addition to reviewing the arrest and conviction records of applicants, employers usually verify other information provided by applicants to assess their suitability for a position. Employers usually perform **reference checks** on applicants that might include verifying applicants' past work history as well as other information provided on the employment application. Employers usually ask applicants to provide the name and contact information of prior employers on their employment application so their past work history can be verified.

reference checks
verification of an individual's past work history and other information submitted on an employment application to assess an applicant's suitability for a position

A. VERIFICATION OF INFORMATION

When verifying an applicant's references, employers may inquire about an applicant's dates of employment, job titles, responsibilities, job performance, and eligibility for rehire. Employers should be careful about asking questions that might give them information about an individual's membership in a protected class based on the presumption that an employer will use all information it possesses when making a hiring decision. For example, if a former employer indicates that the candidate made a valuable workplace contribution when he was feeling well enough to work a full shift, this could suggest the applicant had an illness that constituted a disability. The receipt of this information is significant, because if it influences a hiring manager's decision not to extend an offer of employment, the conduct could result in discriminatory conduct under the ADA. See Chapter 7, Disability Discrimination.

B. APPROPRIATE USE OF NEGATIVE INFORMATION

If an employer determines that an individual provided false information related to a material fact on an employment application, the employer generally has the right to refrain from extending an offer of employment to the candidate. In addition, an employer who learns negative information about an applicant through a reference check generally has the right to use the information as the basis for making an adverse decision.

C. DRAWING INFERENCES

Many companies have policies that specifically prohibit the providing of references due to concerns about the potential liability that may result if the information given in a reference leads to an adverse employment decision. Even in the absence of a specific prohibition, many employers remain reluctant to provide such information based on these same concerns. Therefore, those who are seeking references should be aware of the appropriate inferences to be drawn from a former employer's response to a reference request.

For example, because employers are not legally required to provide substantive references, a former employer's refusal to discuss an applicant may or may not be the result of a negative experience the employer had working with that individual.[62] Based on this reality, employers verifying the references of job applicants should understand the extent of a former employer's obligation to provide information and the potential sources of liability for doing so, both of which are discussed in further detail in Chapter 20, Severance and Post-Employment Obligations.

D. USE OF THIRD PARTIES TO CONDUCT REFERENCE CHECKS

An employer may check the references of an applicant internally, or it may hire an outside vendor to perform these services. In the event the employer does outsource this work, it should ensure the applicant is aware of and agrees to the disclosure of her information to a third party consistent with the terms of the FCRA, as discussed above. When implementing procedures to ensure its processes comply with the FCRA, an employer should understand that the Act also applies to the collection of other information, such as a credit history, that might be relevant to an applicant's suitability for a position.[63]

 VII **CREDIT CHECKS**

Employers should not ask applicants about their credit history during the interview process unless there is a specific business need to review the information.

A. USE OF CREDIT CHECKS CLOSELY SCRUTINIZED

The laws relating to credit checks are quite extensive, and such checks are usually closely scrutinized based, in part, on the findings that women and some minorities tend to have lower credit scores than men and nonminorities.[64] For example, one study showed that the credit scores of Blacks/African-Americans tend to be 10% to 35% lower than those of whites, and Hispanics had credit scores that were 5% to 25% lower than those of non-Hispanics.[65] Findings such as these raise concerns that the use of credit scores as the basis for adverse employment decisions might have a disparate impact on members of certain protected classes.

B. ASSESSING THE BUSINESS NEED FOR A CREDIT CHECK

Because the use of credit checks has the potential for discriminatory results, employers that use them as part of the hiring process should be prepared to illustrate the connection between an applicant's qualifications for the position and the information that the credit check would reveal. Employers have the most success in establishing this link if financial trustworthiness is connected to an essential job task. For example, while it might be appropriate to conduct a credit check of an individual applying for a position as a financial planner, it would be less relevant for an individual applying for a position as a mechanic. In addition, even if a credit score is relevant, employers should be prepared to show that the cut-off is a business necessity and explain why a certain cut-off is appropriate based on its job relatedness.[66]

POLYGRAPH TESTS

Although an employer will have some sense of whether an applicant is honest by determining whether the information obtained through a reference check or a credit check is consistent with information provided on an employment application, some employers may want to conduct other tests to assess this character trait.

A. DEFINITION

polygraph test
lie detector test, which employers are generally prohibited from using as part of their hiring process

A **polygraph test**, often referred to as a lie detector test, is used to determine whether an individual is responding honestly to the questions posed. Except in very limited instances, these tests cannot be used as part of an employer's hiring process.

Employee Polygraph Protection Act (EPPA)
federal law that prohibits most private-sector employers from using lie detector tests as part of the hiring process or during an individual's employment

B. EMPLOYEE POLYGRAPH PROTECTION ACT (EPPA)

The right of employers to use polygraph tests is governed by the **Employee Polygraph Protection Act (EPPA)**, which prohibits most private-sector employers from using polygraph tests as part of their pre-employment screening process as well as during the course of an individual's employment.[67] The EPPA is enforced by the Department of Labor, and employers may be subject to penalties up to $10,000 for each violation of the Act.[68] See Exhibit 11-1.

1. LIMITS ON USE

The EPPA prohibits employers from (1) requiring, requesting, or suggesting that an individual take a lie detector test; (2) using, accepting, or asking about the results of a previous test; and (3) disciplining, discriminating, or imposing any adverse employment decision on an employee based on the results of a test.[69] The Act covers polygraph tests, which record changes in cardiovascular and respiratory signals to assess the honesty of an individual, as well as other similar tests (such as those that analyze the stress in an individual's voice) used to assess these same characteristics.[70]

2. APPROPRIATE USE

Although the EPPA's prohibition against the use of polygraph tests is broad, there are a few exceptions to it. The employees who may be asked to take a polygraph test are the following: those who are suspected of being involved in a workplace incident that could result in an economic loss to an employer; prospective employees of certain businesses related to national security, health, and safety (such as security firms); and prospective employees whose job functions might give them access to controlled substances.[71] Even in these instances, the employer's rights to administer the tests are closely regulated.

a. Limited Scope of Permissible Use

Even if a polygraph is permissible, employers should exercise care to ensure that the questions posed are not otherwise prohibited. For example, an employer fitting within one of the limited exceptions permitting the use of a polygraph test might be subject to liability for asking an applicant about the use of any lawful medications, because this could compel an individual to reveal information about a disability and raise concerns under the ADA.[72] See Chapter 7, Disability Discrimination.

b. Rights of an Individual Subjected to a Polygraph Test

Employers permitted to administer a polygraph test will be subject to a number of legal obligations with respect to the administration of the test and the use of the results. The employer must provide the affected individual with written notification of the test requirements, which includes the scope of the questions that will be posed and how the results will be used. In addition, employees retain the right to refuse to take the test and to stop the questioning at any point during the process. After the test is administered, there are restrictions on how the employer can use the results. The results cannot be shared with anyone other than the individual tested and the employer who administered the test, unless providing the information is required by law.[73]

Exhibit 11-1

U.S. DEPARTMENT OF LABOR

EMPLOYMENT STANDARDS ADMINISTRATION

Wage and Hour Division
Washington, D.C. 20210

NOTICE

EMPLOYEE POLYGRAPH PROTECTION ACT

The Employee Polygraph Protection Act prohibits most private employers from using lie detector tests either for pre-employment screening or during the course of employment.

PROHIBITIONS

Employers are generally prohibited from requiring or requesting any employee or job applicant to take a lie detector test, and from discharging, disciplining, or discriminating against an employee or prospective employee for refusing to take a test or for exercising other rights under the Act.

EXEMPTIONS*

Federal, State and local governments are not affected by the law. Also, the law does not apply to tests given by the Federal Government to certain private individuals engaged in national security-related activities.

The Act permits *polygraph* (a kind of lie detector) tests to be administered in the private sector, subject to restrictions, to certain prospective employees of security service firms (armored car, alarm, and guard), and of pharmaceutical manufacturers, distributors and dispensers.

The Act also permits polygraph testing, subject to restrictions, of certain employees of private firms who are reasonably suspected of involvement in a workplace incident (theft, embezzlement, etc.) that resulted in economic loss to the employer.

EXAMINEE RIGHTS

Where polygraph tests are permitted, they are subject to numerous strict standards concerning the conduct and length of the test. Examinees have a number of specific rights, including the right to a written notice before testing, the right to refuse or discontinue a test, and the right not to have test results disclosed to unauthorized persons.

ENFORCEMENT

The Secretary of Labor may bring court actions to restrain violations and assess civil penalties up to $10,000 against violators. Employees or job applicants may also bring their own court actions.

ADDITIONAL INFORMATION

Additional information may be obtained, and complaints of violations may be filed, at local offices of the Wage and Hour Division. To locate your nearest Wage-Hour office, telephone our toll-free information and help line at 1 - 866 - 4USWAGE (1 - 866 - 487 - 9243). A customer service representative is available to assist you with referral information from 8am to 5 pm in your time zone; or if you have access to the internet, you may log onto our Home page at www.wagehour.dol.gov.

THE LAW REQUIRES EMPLOYERS TO DISPLAY THIS POSTER WHERE EMPLOYEES AND JOB APPLICANTS CAN READILY SEE IT.

*The law does not preempt any provision of any State or local law or any collective bargaining agreement which is more restrictive with respect to lie detector tests.

U.S. DEPARTMENT OF LABOR
EMPLOYMENT STANDARDS ADMINISTRATION
Wage and Hour Division
Washington, D.C. 20210

WH Publication 1462
June 2003

MEDICAL AND DRUG INQUIRIES AND TESTING

As employers assess the suitability of a candidate for a position, they might want to request information about an applicant's health to determine whether he will have the physical and mental stamina to report to work and complete the essential job functions. The collection of medical information and inquiries about drug use are closely regulated, and noncompliance with the governing laws has the potential to subject an employer to significant liability. The request for medical information, questions about past illegal drug use, and the administration of both medical and drug tests require employers to consider potential liability under the ADA which specifically states that the prohibition against discrimination based on disabilities extends to medical examinations and inquiries.[74] Employers are subject to different standards when requesting this type of information from applicants as opposed to those to whom offers of employment have been extended.

A. MEDICAL INQUIRIES

As a general rule, employers are not permitted to ask applicants information about their medical history, a specific medical condition, whether they are undergoing any medical treatments, whether they use or have ever used any assistive devices, whether they are currently taking any prescription drugs, or whether they have ever taken a medical leave.[75]

1. ABILITY TO PERFORM ESSENTIAL JOB TASKS

Although direct medical inquiries are not permitted, an employer may ask pre-employment questions about an applicant's ability to perform job-related functions with or without a reasonable accommodation.[76] For example, applicants could be asked whether they have the ability to lift crates weighing up to 75 pounds with or without a reasonable accommodation (presuming this is an essential job requirement), but it would be improper to ask an applicant whether he has a history of back problems that might prevent him from lifting heavy boxes.[77] Consistent with this, employers may ask applicants to describe or demonstrate how they will perform other essential job functions with or without a reasonable accommodation.[78]

2. NO OBLIGATION TO REVEAL MEDICAL CONDITIONS

The ADA does not impose any obligation on prospective employees to reveal a medical condition to a prospective employer unless an accommodation is necessary for the individual to move through the hiring process. Therefore, it is permissible for a qualified individual with a disability to wait until after an offer is extended and accepted before informing the employer of a need for an accommodation.[79]

In the event an applicant voluntarily reveals information about a medical condition, the employer is generally permitted to ask two questions related to the topic. The employer can ask whether the applicant would need an accommodation and, if so, what type of accommodation would be necessary. The employer may not ask applicants whether they were diagnosed with a particular medical condition, whether they take any medications, or whether the condition is under control.[80] For example, if an applicant for a receptionist position volunteers she will need regular breaks to administer her medication, the employer can ask questions relating to how often she will need these breaks and for what duration. The employer cannot, however, ask for further details about the nature of the medical condition that necessitates these breaks.[81]

B. MEDICAL EXAMINATIONS

1. CONDITIONAL OFFERS OF EMPLOYMENT ARE PERMISSIBLE

Once an offer of employment is made, an employer may require an individual to undergo a medical examination provided the medical test is administered uniformly to all of the individuals who will be employed in the same classification (regardless of an individual's disability or perceived disability), it is job related, and there is a business necessity for requiring the examination.[82]

A job offer may be conditioned on the results of a medical test, but if the results show that the applicant has a disability, the employer will not be permitted to automatically revoke the offer. Instead, the employer will have an obligation to comply with the ADA by providing the individual with a reasonable accommodation, provided it does not impose an undue burden on the employer.

2. OBLIGATION TO PROVIDE A REASONABLE ACCOMMODATION

An employer will be permitted to revoke the job offer of an individual who has a disability only if the disability renders the individual unable to perform the job-related task that is a business necessity and a reasonable accommodation would be an undue burden or would not remedy the situation. The precise nature of this obligation will vary based on the nature of the disability, but the employer might need to consider whether the job can be modified to accommodate the disabled individual.[83]

For example, an employer is not permitted to withdraw a job offer after learning an individual has cancer provided the individual can perform the essential job duties with or without a reasonable accommodation. To assess what type of accommodation might be appropriate, an employer is permitted to ask related follow-up questions about the condition, such as whether current treatments would require a scheduling accommodation, and whether there are any anticipated side effects that might interfere with the performance of job duties.[84] See Chapter 7, Disability Discrimination.

C. MAINTENANCE OF THE RESULTS OF MEDICAL INQUIRIES AND EXAMINATIONS

Medical information must also be kept confidential except when there is a recognized need for the employer (1) to release the information to a supervisor to provide information necessary to arrange for an accommodation, (2) to provide the information to safety personnel in the event the condition might necessitate emergency treatment, and (3) to release the information to officials investigating whether the employer complied with its obligations under the ADA.[85] An employer may also disclose information about an individual's medical condition if it is needed for the processing of a workers' compensation claim or for other insurance purposes.[86] Employers must also comply with the laws that regulate the collection of such information and require that it be maintained in separate medical files.[87]

D. DRUG INQUIRIES

Because the current use of illegal drugs is not protected under the ADA, an employer may ask applicants whether they currently use illegal drugs and may administer tests designed to identify illegal drug use.[88] Permissible inquiries would include questions about drugs that are inherently illegal, such as cocaine, as well as prescription drugs that have not been prescribed for the individual's use. Employers should not ask individuals whether they are former drug addicts, however, because such individuals who are no longer using illegal drugs could be found to have a disability as defined by the ADA if they (1) have successfully completed a supervised drug rehabilitation program or have otherwise been rehabilitated successfully, or (2) are participating in a supervised rehabilitation program such as Narcotics Anonymous, and therefore would be entitled to protections under the statute.[89] See Chapter 7, Disability Discrimination.

KEY TERMS

- ✓ background checks
- ✓ cognitive test
- ✓ consumer report
- ✓ consumer reporting agency
- ✓ credit report
- ✓ disparate impact
- ✓ disparate treatment
- ✓ eligibility tests
- ✓ Employee Polygraph Protection Act (EPPA)
- ✓ Fair Credit Reporting Act (FCRA)
- ✓ four-fifths (or 80%) rule
- ✓ ineligibility test
- ✓ negligent hiring
- ✓ personality test
- ✓ polygraph test
- ✓ reference check
- ✓ selection test

DISCUSSION QUESTIONS

Explain your response to each of the following questions with the understanding that in some cases there is no right or wrong answer. If you cannot make an informed decision with the facts provided, indicate the nature and significance of the additional information you would need. For the purposes of these questions, you can assume that the employers, employees and applicants mentioned below are covered by Title VII and other relevant federal workplace anti-discrimination laws.

1. Explain some types of pre-employment tests an employer might decide to use as part of its hiring process.
2. Explain the relevance of the ADA to the administration of pre-employment tests.
3. Discuss the reasons why the manner in which an employer administers a pre-employment test might result in liability for workplace discrimination.
4. What type of information might be collected pursuant to a background check?
5. Explain the appropriate use of an individual's arrest record and past convictions within the hiring process. Will the type of job for which an individual is applying affect your answer? Why or why not?
6. Can an employer ever require a job applicant to undergo a medical examination?
7. An employer hires an outside consultant to develop pre-employment tests for his use. The consultant provides a guarantee that "his tests will eliminate underachievers and identify top talent." Should this employer have any concerns about this guarantee?
8. Nathan is opening a new car dealership and decides to administer the same pre-employment credit check for all potential candidates to minimize his risk of workplace discrimination claims. Do you think this is a good idea?
9. Becky is an employer who wants to hire additional staff to handle basic administrative tasks and to catalogue the hundreds of dresses used in fashion shows around the world that are stored in her off-site warehouse. What pre-employment tests might Becky use?
10. Donna owns a cosmetic company and is hiring individuals to sell her products at parties in the homes of their friends, to business leads solicited by telephone inquiries, and at local schools. Donna decides she will not need to conduct any pre-employment tests because the job requires only basic skills. She will provide each employee with company invoices to be used to sell the products and to collect the money. Once Donna receives the order and payment, she will give the products to each employee, who will be responsible for delivering the items. Do you agree with Donna that there is no need for any pre-employment tests? Why or why not?

ENDNOTES

1. U.S. Equal Employment Opportunity Commn., Fact Sheet on Employment Tests and Selection Procedures (available at *http://www.eeoc.gov/policy/docs/factemployment_ procedures.html*).

2. 42 U.S.C. § 2000e-2(h).

3. U.S. Equal Employment Opportunity Commn., Fact Sheet on Employment Tests and Selection Procedures (available at *http://www.eeoc.gov/policy/docs/factemployment_ procedures.html*).

4. *EEOC v. Dial Corp.*, 469 F.3d 735 (8th Cir. 2006); *see* 42 U.S.C. § 2000e-2(k).

5. *See* 29 C.F.R. pt. 1607 (Uniform Guidelines on Employee Selection Procedures). Questions and answers to clarify and interpret the Uniform Guidelines were adopted by five federal agencies. *See* 44 Fed. Reg. No. 43 (Mar. 2, 1979) (available at *http://www.eeoc.gov/ policy/docs/qanda_clarify_procedures.html*).

6. *See* U.S. Equal Employment Opportunity Commn., 44 Fed. Reg. No. 43 (Mar. 2, 1979) (Adoption of Questions and Answers to Clarify and Provide a Common Interpretation of the Uniform Guidelines on Employee Selection Procedures, Purpose and Scope) (available at *http://www.eeoc.gov/policy/docs/qanda_clarify_procedures.html*).

7. U.S. Equal Employment Opportunity Commn., How to Comply with the Americans with Disabilities Act: A Guide for Restaurants and Other Food Service Employers (available at *http://www.eeoc.gov/facts/restaurant_guide.html*).

8. U.S. Equal Employment Opportunity Commn., Questions and Answers About Cancer in the Workplace and the Americans with Disabilities Act (ADA) (available at *http://www .eeoc.gov/facts.cancer.html*).

9. *See EEOC v. Daimler Chrysler Corp.*, No. 03-75137 (E.D. Mich. Jan. 12, 2004).

10. U.S. Equal Employment Opportunity Commn., Enforcement Guidance: Pre-Employment Disability-Related Questions and Medical Examinations (available at *http://www.eeoc.gov/ policy/docs/preemp.html*).

11. 42 U.S.C. § 12112(b)(7); *see Minkus v. Metropolitan Sanitary Dist.*, 600 F.2d 80 (7th Cir. 1979).

12. *See* Kathleen K. Lundquist, Ph.D., Co-Founder and President, APT, Inc., Statement at U.S. Equal Employment Opportunity Commn. Meeting (May 16, 2007) (regarding Employment Testing and Screening) (available at *http://www.eeoc.gov/eeoc/meetings/archive/5-16- 07/lundquist.html*).

13. *See* U.S. Equal Employment Opportunity Commn. and Department of Justice Civil Rights Div., Town Hall Listening Session on the ADAAA Proposed Regulations (Oct. 30, 2009) (available at *http://www.eeoc.gov/eeoc/events/transcript-phil.cfm*).

14. *See, e.g.*, Kathleen K. Lundquist, Ph.D., Co-Founder and President, APT, Inc., Statement at U.S. Equal Employment Opportunity Commn. Meeting (May 16, 2007) (regarding Employment Testing and Screening) (available at *http://www.eeoc.gov/eeoc/meetings/archive/ 5-16-07/lundquist.html*).

15. *See generally id.*

16. U.S. Equal Employment Opportunity Commn., Fact Sheet on Employment Tests and Selection Procedures (available at *http://www.eeoc.gov/policy/docs/factemployment_ procedures.html*).

17. *Id.*

18. *See* New York State Div. of Human Rights, Recommendations on Employment Inquiries (rev. Dec. 2004) (available at *http://www.dhr.state.ny.us/pdf/employment.pdf*).

19. 42 U.S.C. § 2000e-2(*l*).

20. 42 U.S.C. § 12112(b)(6).

21. 42 U.S.C. § 12112(b)(7).

22. *See* U.S. Equal Employment Opportunity Commn., Commission Meeting (May 16, 2007) (available at *http://www.eeoc.gov/eeoc/meetings/archive/5-16-07/*).

23. U.S. Equal Employment Opportunity Commn., Enforcement Guidance: Pre-Employment Disability-Related Questions and Medical Examinations (available at *http://www.eeoc.gov/ policy/docs/preemp.html*).

24. *Karraker v. Rent-A-Center, Inc.*, 431 F. Supp. 2d 883, 885 (C.D. Ill. 2006).

25. *Smith v. City of Jackson*, 544 U.S. 288 (2005).

26. U.S. Equal Employment Opportunity Commn., Fact Sheet on Employment Tests and Selection Procedures (available at *http://www.eeoc.gov/policy/docs/factemployment_ procedures.html*).

27. Rae T. Vann, General Counsel, Equal Employment Advisory Council, Statement at U.S. Equal Employment Opportunity Commn. Meeting (Nov. 20, 2008) (regarding Employment Discrimination Faced by Individuals with Arrest and Conviction Records) (available at *http://www.eeoc.gov/eeoc/meetings/11-20-08/vann.cfm*).

28. *See generally* Michael L. Foreman, Professor, Director of Civil Rights Appellate Clinic, Pennsylvania State University Dickinson School of Law, Statement at U.S. Equal Employment Opportunity Commn. Meeting (Nov. 2008) (regarding Employment Discrimination Faced by Individuals with Arrest and Conviction Records) (available at *http://www .eeoc.gov/eeoc/meetings/11-20-08/foreman.cfm*).

29. Rae T. Vann, General Counsel, Equal Employment Advisory Council, Statement at U.S. Equal Employment Opportunity Commn. Meeting (Nov. 20, 2008) (regarding Employment Discrimination Faced by Individuals with Arrest and Conviction Records) (available at *http://www.eeoc.gov/eeoc/meetings/11-20-08/vann.cfm*).

30. *See Gregory v. Litton Sys.*, 316 F. Supp. 401 (C.D. Cal. 1970); EEOC Informal Discussion Letter from Raymond Peeler, Title VII Arrest and Conviction Records (Dec. 1, 2005) (available at *http://www.eeoc.gov/eeoc/foia/letters/2005/titlevii_arrest_conviction_records.html*).

31. *See* U.S. Equal Employment Opportunity Commn., Questions and Answers About the Workplace Rights of Muslims, Arabs, South Asians, and Sikhs Under the Equal Employment Opportunity Laws (available at *http://www.eeoc.gov/facts/backlash-employee.html*).

32. *See, e.g., id.*

33. *See generally*, Federal Trade Commn., Facts for Consumers (available at *http://www.ftc .gov/bcp/edu/pubs/consumer/credit/cre01.shtm*).

34. Section 603(d) of the FCRA, 15 U.S.C. § 1681(a).

35. *See, e.g.*, FTC Staff Opinion Letter from William Haynes to John Beaudette (June 9, 1998) (available at *http://www.ftc.gov/os/statutes/fcra/beaudett.shtm*); *see generally* Federal Trade Commn. website, Summaries of Rights, Fair Credit Reporting Act (available at *http:// www.ftc.gov/bcp/edu/pubs/consumer/credit/cre35.pdf*).

36. Federal Trade Commn., Facts for Consumers (available at *http://www.ftc.gov/bcp/edu/ pubs/consumer/credit/cre01.shtm*).

37. Section 603(f) of the FCRA, 15 U.S.C. § 1681(a).

38. Section 604(b)(2)(A)(ii) of the FCRA, 15 U.S.C. § 1681(b); *see* Federal Trade Commn. website, Summaries of Rights, Fair Credit Reporting Act (available at *http://www.ftc.gov/ bcp/edu/pubs/consumer/credit/cre35.pdf*).

39. Section 604(b)(2)(A)(i) of the FCRA, 15 U.S.C. § 1681(b).

40. Section 604(b)(3) of the FCRA, 15 U.S.C. § 1681(b); *see also* FTC Staff Opinion Letter from William Haynes to John Beaudette (June 9, 1998) (available at *http://www.ftc.gov/os/ statutes/fcra/beaudett.shtm*); *see generally* Federal Trade Commn. website, Summaries of Rights, Fair Credit Reporting Act (available at *http://www.ftc.gov/bcp/edu/pubs/consumer/ credit/cre35.pdf*).

41. Cal. Lab. Code §§ 432.7, 432.8 (2002) (prohibiting discrimination based on convictions related to the possession of marijuana).

42. Nev. Rev. Stat. §§ 391.100, 449.179, 463A.030.

43. Haw. Rev. Stat. §§ 378.2-378.3; *see also* Colo. Rev. Stat. § 24-72-308 (prohibiting requiring the disclosure of information contained in sealed records); Mo. Rev. Stat. §§ 302.272, 630.317 (questioning an applicant about arrest and conviction records is inadvisable unless related to the applicant's ability to perform a specific job); Mich. Comp. Laws

§ 3.2205a (prohibiting the making of or maintaining of records of information regarding a misdemeanor, arrest, detention, or disposition where a conviction did not result).

44. *See* EEOC Informal Discussion Letter from Raymond Peeler, Title VII Arrest and Conviction Records (Dec. 1, 2005) (available at *http://www.eeoc.gov/eeoc/foia/letters/2005/titlevii_arrest_conviction_records.html*).

45. *See, e.g., McCraven v. City of Chicago*, 109 F. Supp. 2d 935 (N.D. Ill. 2000) (allowing the blanket disqualification of applicants with arrest records for police officers because of the "awesome responsibilities" of law enforcement).

46. *Schware v. Board of Bar Examiners*, 353 U.S. 232, 241 (1957).

47. Arizona, California, Colorado, District of Columbia, Hawaii, Idaho, Maryland, Massachusetts, Michigan, Minnesota, Mississippi, New Jersey, New York, Ohio, Oregon, Utah, Virginia, Washington, West Virginia, and Wisconsin have implemented this prohibition or advisement. U.S. Equal Employment Opportunity Commn., Policy Guidance on the Consideration of Arrest Records (available at *http://www.eeoc.gov/policy/docs/arrest_records.html*).

48. *Carter v. Gallagher*, 452 F.2d 315 (8th Cir. 1971).

49. U.S. Equal Employment Opportunity Commn., Policy Guidance on the Consideration of Arrest Records (available at *http://www.eeoc.gov/policy/docs/arrest_records.html*).

50. *Id.*

51. *Id.*

52. *Green v. Missouri Pac. R.R. Co.*, 549 F.2d 1158, 1160 (8th Cir. 1977); *Carter v. Maloney Trucking & Storage Inc.*, 631 F.2d 40 (5th Cir. 1980).

53. *United States v. City of Chicago*, 411 F. Supp. 218 (N.D. Ill. 1976).

54. *See, e.g., Osborne v. Cleland*, 620 F.2d 195 (8th Cir. 1980).

55. U.S. Equal Employment Opportunity Commn., Policy Guidance on the Consideration of Arrest Records (available at *http://www.eeoc.gov/policy/docs/arrest_records*); *see, e.g., Gregory v. Litton Sys.*, 316 F. Supp. 401 (C.D. Cal. 1970); *Carter v. Gallagher*, 452 F.2d 315 (8th Cir. 1971), *cert. denied*, 406 U.S. 950 (1972).

56. U.S. Equal Employment Opportunity Commn., Policy Guidance on the Consideration of Arrest Records (available at *http://www.eeoc.gov/policy/docs/arrest_records.html*). The number of times an applicant has been arrested may be considered when conducting a credibility assessment, but employers should not establish a threshold that would automatically disqualify an applicant. *See, e.g., Gregory v. Litton Sys.*, 316 F. Supp. 401 (C.D. Cal. 1990).

57. *See generally* Rania V. Sedhom, The EEOC's eRace Initiative: Combating Systemic Racism, Human Resources 2008 (Summer ed.) (available at *http://www.buckconsultants.com/buckconsultants/portals/0/documents/publications/published_articles/2008/Articles_Sedhom_Human_Resources_summer_08.pdf*).

58. Federal Deposit Insurance Act, 12 U.S.C. § 1833(a). In limited instances an employer can obtain permission from the Federal Deposit Insurance Corporation to retain such an employee. There are a number of other federal laws that have the same or similar requirements for background checks. *See, e.g.,* Violent Crime Control and Law Enforcement Act of 1994, 18 U.S.C. § 1033(e)(1); U.S. Patriot Act of 2001, 49 U.S.C. § 5103(a).

59. U.S. Equal Employment Opportunity Commn., EEOC Compl. Man. § 12 (Religious Discrimination) (July 22, 2008) (available at *http://www.eeoc.gov/policy/docs/religion.html*).

60. *See generally* Rania V. Sedhom, The EEOC's eRace Initiative: Combating Systemic Racism, Human Resources 2008 (Summer ed.) (available at *http://www.buckconsultants.com/buckconsultants/portals/0/documents/publications/published_articles/2008/Articles_Sedhom_Human_Resources_summer_08.pdf*). Not only are there discrimination concerns related to the use of convictions, but also studies have shown that those with convictions have a more difficult time finding employment, and this has the potential to result in higher crime rates. For example, one New York study shows that almost 60% of sex offenders remain unemployed one year after their release. The research also showed a link between reoccurring crime and unemployment, finding that 83% of ex-offenders who violated the

terms of their probation did not have a job at the time of the incident. Center for Employment Opportunities, Overview: Crime and Work (Jan. 24, 2007) (available at *http://www.ceoworks.org/roundcrime_work012802.pdf*).

61. Rania V. Sedhom, The EEOC's eRace Initiative: Combating Systemic Racism, Human Resources 2008 (Summer ed.) (available at *http://www.buckconsultants.com/buckconsultants/portals/0/documents/publications/published_articles/2008/Articles_Sedhom_Human_Resources_summer_08.pdf*).

62. *See, e.g., Davis v. Board of County Commrs. of Dona Ana County*, 987 P.2d 1172 (N.M. Ct. App. 1999).

63. *See generally*, Federal Trade Commn., Facts for Consumers (available at *http://www.ftc.gov/bcp/edu/pubs/consumer/credit/cre01.shtm*).

64. *See* Statement of Adam T. Klein, Esq., U.S. Equal Employment Opportunity Commn. Meeting (May 16, 2007) (regarding Employment Testing and Screening) (available at *http://www.eeoc.gov/eeoc/meetings/archive/5-16-07/klein.html*) (stating that there is a correlation between the quality of one's credit record and one's race); *see id.* (citing Theresa M. Beiner & Robert B. Chapman, Take What You Can, Give Nothing Back: Judicial Estoppel, Employment Discrimination, Bankruptcy, and Piracy in the Courts, 60 U. Miami L. Rev. 1, 3 (2005)) ("households with children are more likely to experience bankruptcy than childless households, and most individuals filing bankruptcy are women who depend on their jobs to climb their way out of financial distress").

65. Rania V. Sedhom, The EEOC's eRace Initiative: Combating Systemic Racism, Human Resources 2008 (Summer ed.) (available at *http://www.buckconsultants.com/buckconsultants/portals/0/documents/publications/published_articles/2008/Articles_Sedhom_Human_Resources_summer_08.pdf*).

66. *See generally* 29 C.F.R. pt. 1607.

67. 29 U.S.C. §§ 2001-2009.

68. Wage & Hour Div., Employment Standards Admin., U.S. Dept. of Labor, Fact Sheet #36: Employee Polygraph Protection Act of 1988 (available at *http://www.dol.gov/esa/whd/regs/compliance/whdfs36.pdf*); *see also* Office of Compliance Assistance Policy, U.S. Dept. of Labor, Employment Law Guide, Lie Detector Tests (available at *http://www.dol.gov/compliance/guide/eppa.htm*).

69. Wage & Hour Div., Employment Standards Admin., U.S. Dept. of Labor, Fact Sheet #36: Employee Polygraph Protection Act of 1988 (available at *http://www.dol.gov/esa/whd/regs/compliance/whdfs36.pdf*).

70. *Id.*

71. *Id.*

72. U.S. Equal Employment Opportunity Commn., Enforcement Guidance: Pre-Employment Disability-Related Questions and Medical Examinations (available at *http://www.eeoc.gov/policy/docs/preemp.html*).

73. Wage & Hour Div., Employment Standards Admin., U.S. Dept. of Labor, Fact Sheet #36: Employee Polygraph Protection Act of 1988 (available at *http://www.dol.gov/esa/whd/regs/compliance/whdfs36.pdf*); *see also* Office of Compliance Assistance Policy, U.S. Dept. of Labor, Employment Law Guide, Lie Detector Tests (available at *http://www.dol.gov/compliance/guide/eppa.htm*).

74. 42 U.S.C. § 12112(d)(1).

75. U.S. Equal Employment Opportunity Commn., Questions and Answers About Cancer in the Workplace and the Americans with Disabilities Act (ADA) (available at *http://www.eeoc.gov/facts.cancer.html*); U.S. Equal Employment Opportunity Commn., Questions and Answers About Deafness and Hearing Impairments in the Workplace and the Americans with Disabilities Act (July 26, 2006) (available at *http://www.eeoc.gov/facts/deafness.html*).

76. 42 U.S.C. § 12112(d)(4)(a).

77. U.S. Equal Employment Opportunity Commn., Questions and Answers About Cancer in the Workplace and the Americans with Disabilities Act (ADA) (available at *http://www.eeoc.gov/facts.cancer.html*).

78. 29 C.F.R. § 1630.14(a).

79. U.S. Equal Employment Opportunity Commn., Questions and Answers About Cancer in the Workplace and the Americans with Disabilities Act (ADA) (available at *http://www .eeoc.gov/facts.cancer.html*).

80. *Id.;* U.S. Equal Employment Opportunity Commn., Questions and Answers About Diabetes in the Workplace and the Americans with Disabilities Act (ADA) (available at *http:// www.eeoc.gov/facts/diabetes.html*).

81. U.S. Equal Employment Opportunity Commn., Enforcement Guidance: Pre-Employment Disability-Related Questions and Medical Examinations (available at *http://www.eeoc.gov/ policy/docs/preemp.html*).

82. 42 U.S.C. § 12112(d)(3); 29 C.F.R. § 1630.14(d).

83. U.S. Equal Employment Opportunity Commn., How to Comply with the Americans with Disabilities Act: A Guide for Restaurants and Other Food Service Employers (available at *http://www.eeoc.gov/facts/restaurant_guide.html*).

84. U.S. Equal Employment Opportunity Commn., Questions and Answers About Cancer in the Workplace and the Americans with Disabilities Act (ADA) (available at *http://www .eeoc.gov/facts/cancer.html*).

85. *Id.;* U.S. Equal Employment Opportunity Commn., How to Comply with the Americans with Disabilities Act: A Guide for Restaurants and Other Food Service Employers (available at *http://www.eeoc.gov/facts/restaurant_guide.html*).

86. 42 U.S.C. § 12112(d)(3).

87. U.S. Equal Employment Opportunity Commn., Questions and Answers About Deafness and Hearing Impairments in the Workplace and the Americans with Disabilities Act (July 26, 2006) (available at *http://www.eeoc.gov/facts/deafness.html*).

88. U.S. Equal Employment Opportunity Commn., Disability Discrimination (available at *http://www.eeoc.gov/types/ada.html*).

89. 29 C.F.R. § 1630.3(b).

Part III

Managing

© 1999 Randy Glasbergen.   www.glasbergen.com

"I'm sending you to a seminar to help you work harder and be more productive."

Compensation and Benefits

12

Chapter Objectives

This chapter provides an overview of the components of a compensation package an employer might offer its employees. The text includes a substantial discussion about the benefits and protections provided by the Fair Labor Standards Act (FLSA), which is the federal law that establishes a minimum hourly wage rate and the payment of overtime, regulates child labor, and imposes notice and recordkeeping obligations on the employer. In addition, the obligations of employers to compensate their employees in a uniform and nondiscriminatory manner and to provide equal pay for equal work pursuant to the Equal Pay Act (EPA) are examined.

This chapter also provides a basic introduction to medical plans, retirement benefits, and disability plans, which can be valuable components of a compensation package. After completing this chapter, students should have a fundamental understanding of each of these benefits. Upon mastering the main objectives of this chapter students should be able to

- explain the foundation for the payment of wages under the FLSA;
- explain what it means to be fully and partially exempt from the FLSA and explain the categories of employees who might be exempt;
- explain what is meant by compensation discrimination and the ways an employee might prove such a claim;
- identify the factors that are relevant in determining whether two positions are substantially equal for the purposes of the EPA; and
- identify the types of medical and retirement benefits an employee might receive as part of her compensation package.

Compensation is often discussed within the context of the amount of money an individual receives in a weekly paycheck, but most employees receive significant benefits from their employers well beyond this financial payment. There are a number of federal laws that regulate things of value that are provided to employees in exchange for the performance of services, and the nature of the benefit will determine which laws apply.

DEFINITION OF *COMPENSATION*

compensation
broad term that could include anything of current or future value an employer provides an individual in exchange for the performance of services

Compensation is a broadly defined term that could include anything of current or future value an employer provides an individual in exchange for the performance of services. Compensation encompasses both economic and noneconomic benefits offered to an individual at the time work is performed, or at an agreed-on future date.

A compensation package could include a number of components, such as the following:

✓ wages
✓ overtime pay
✓ bonuses
✓ vacation pay
✓ holiday pay
✓ gasoline allowances
✓ hotel accommodations
✓ use of a company car
✓ medical insurance
✓ retirement benefits
✓ stock options
✓ profit sharing
✓ bonuses
✓ expense accounts
✓ reimbursement for travel expenses.[1]

An employer's obligations with respect to an overall compensation package will vary depending on the specific element of the package that is at issue. For example, the Fair Labor Standards Act (FLSA) is the federal law that is the foundation for the payment of wages.

COMPENSATION PURSUANT TO THE FAIR LABOR STANDARDS ACT (FLSA)

Fair Labor Standards Act (FLSA)
federal law that regulates the minimum hourly wage rate, payment of overtime, recordkeeping, and the employment of children

U.S. Department of Labor (DOL)
federal agency charged with enforcing the Fair Labor Standards Act (FLSA)

The **Fair Labor Standards Act (FLSA)** is designed to ensure that employee compensation meets minimum standards.[2] While the Equal Employment Opportunity Commission (EEOC) enforces Title VII and other federal anti-discrimination laws, the **U.S. Department of Labor (DOL)** is the federal agency charged with the enforcement of the FLSA.

A. COVERAGE

The FLSA establishes a minimum hourly wage rate, the appropriate payment of overtime, the employer's recordkeeping obligations, and standards for the employment of minors.[3] As a general rule, businesses with employees who engage in or produce goods for interstate commerce and who have more than $500,000 in revenue, hospitals, schools for children, institutions of higher education, and federal, state, and local government agencies regardless of their annual income, are covered by the FLSA.[4] Employees who work for employers whose revenue is less than this $500,000 threshold may also be covered if they engage in *interstate commerce,* a term that is broadly defined.[5] Every private, federal, state, and local government entity employing any employee covered by the FLSA is required to compensate their employees pursuant to the statute and to post a notice outlining the protections offered by the statute.[6] See Exhibit 12-1.

B. MINIMUM HOURLY RATE OF PAY

The FLSA establishes a federal **minimum hourly rate of pay,** which is currently $7.25 per hour.[7] The FLSA also provides a different minimum hourly rate for "tipped" employees, who are generally defined as those employees who receive more than $30 per month in tips. This rate is currently set at $2.13 per hour provided that this amount, along with the amount received in tips, results in earnings that are equal to at least the standard hourly minimum wage.[8]

minimum hourly rate of pay
lowest hourly wage an employer can pay an employee covered by the FLSA

C. OVERTIME

In addition to establishing a minimum hourly rate of pay, the FLSA regulates the payment of **overtime,** which must be paid at a rate of one and one-half times the employee's regular rate of pay after 40 hours of work in a workweek.[9]

overtime
term for hours worked in excess of 40 hours in a workweek which must be paid at one and one-half times a covered employee's hourly rate of pay

**"It's a part-time position, 10 hours a week
with 30 hours of unpaid overtime."**

Exhibit 12-1

EMPLOYEE RIGHTS
UNDER THE FAIR LABOR STANDARDS ACT

THE UNITED STATES DEPARTMENT OF LABOR WAGE AND HOUR DIVISION

FEDERAL MINIMUM WAGE
$7.25 PER HOUR
BEGINNING JULY 24, 2009

OVERTIME PAY   At least 1½ times your regular rate of pay for all hours worked over 40 in a workweek.

CHILD LABOR   An employee must be at least **16** years old to work in most non-farm jobs and at least 18 to work in non-farm jobs declared hazardous by the Secretary of Labor.

Youths **14** and **15** years old may work outside school hours in various non-manufacturing, non-mining, non-hazardous jobs under the following conditions:

No more than
- **3** hours on a school day or **18** hours in a school week;
- **8** hours on a non-school day or **40** hours in a non-school week.

Also, work may not begin before **7 a.m.** or end after **7 p.m.**, except from June 1 through Labor Day, when evening hours are extended to **9 p.m.** Different rules apply in agricultural employment.

TIP CREDIT   Employers of "tipped employees" must pay a cash wage of at least $2.13 per hour if they claim a tip credit against their minimum wage obligation. If an employee's tips combined with the employer's cash wage of at least $2.13 per hour do not equal the minimum hourly wage, the employer must make up the difference. Certain other conditions must also be met.

ENFORCEMENT   The Department of Labor may recover back wages either administratively or through court action, for the employees that have been underpaid in violation of the law. Violations may result in civil or criminal action.

Employers may be assessed civil money penalties of up to $1,100 for each willful or repeated violation of the minimum wage or overtime pay provisions of the law and up to $11,000 for each employee who is the subject of a violation of the Act's child labor provisions. In addition, a civil money penalty of up to $50,000 may be assessed for each child labor violation that causes the death or serious injury of any minor employee, and such assessments may be doubled, up to $100,000, when the violations are determined to be willful or repeated. The law also prohibits discriminating against or discharging workers who file a complaint or participate in any proceeding under the Act.

ADDITIONAL   • Certain occupations and establishments are exempt from the minimum wage and/or overtime pay
INFORMATION   provisions.
- Special provisions apply to workers in American Samoa and the Commonwealth of the Northern Mariana Islands.
- Some state laws provide greater employee protections; employers must comply with both.
- The law requires employers to display this poster where employees can readily see it.
- Employees under 20 years of age may be paid $4.25 per hour during their first 90 consecutive calendar days of employment with an employer.
- Certain full-time students, student learners, apprentices, and workers with disabilities may be paid less than the minimum wage under special certificates issued by the Department of Labor.

For additional information:
1-866-4-USWAGE
(1-866-487-9243)   TTY: 1-877-889-5627

U.S. Wage and Hour Division

WWW.WAGEHOUR.DOL.GOV

U.S. Department of Labor | Wage and Hour Division

WHD Publication 1088 (Revised July 2009)

1. WORKWEEK

The FLSA defines **workweek** as any seven consecutive 24-hour periods. This definition permits the employer to calculate the payment of overtime based on whether an employee works more than 40 hours during a workweek that starts at 10:00 a.m. on Tuesday and ends at 10:00 a.m. the following Tuesday, or on any other seven consecutive 24-hour periods.[10]

workweek
the seven consecutive 24-hour periods that an employer uses to determine whether overtime is due

2. UNAUTHORIZED HOURS WORKED

The FLSA requires the payment of overtime regardless of the circumstances surrounding the working of those hours. For example, an employer who is aware that employees are working through their unpaid lunch, working at home, or staying after the end of their shift to complete their work must compensate those employees for each of those hours worked. If an employer is subject to the FLSA, then even if its employee stays late one evening to finish a project without getting permission from the employer, the employer will be required to compensate the employee for working those hours. Also, similar to other areas of the law, employers and employees do not have the right to jointly waive a provision of the FLSA by, for example, negotiating an agreement for working additional hours for a rate of pay less than the minimum wage or for no additional compensation.[11]

D. COMPENSATORY TIME

Compensatory time ("comp time") provides employees who work more than 40 hours in a workweek additional time off instead of additional compensation. The calculation is based on the overtime rate of one and one-half hours of time off for each hour worked in excess of 40 hours. Compensatory time is often granted when an employee wants to bank paid leave for a future occasion, or when an employer wants an employee to work extended hours in a particular week but does not want to provide, or does not have the financial resources to provide, additional compensation for the hours worked.

compensatory time
hours worked in excess of 40 hours in a workweek for which an employee receives time off rather than additional compensation (calculated one and one-half hours off for each hour worked in excess of 40 hours)

1. AVAILABILITY OF COMPENSATORY TIME FOR PRIVATE EMPLOYEES

Providing compensatory time in lieu of overtime compensation may be problematic for private employers covered by the FLSA because it is inconsistent with its terms. Since the Act requires employers to pay employees one and one-half times their regular rate of pay for all hours worked in excess of 40 hours in a workweek, a covered employer and employee are not permitted to enter into an agreement that would undermine this provision.[12]

2. AVAILABILITY OF COMPENSATORY TIME FOR PUBLIC EMPLOYEES

The FLSA includes a limited exception to the prohibition against compensatory time, which applies to a public agency that is a state, a political subdivision of a state, or an interstate government agency, to grant employees compensatory time in lieu of additional compensation pursuant to an agreement with employees, provided the time off is calculated at the overtime rate.[13] Thus, a public agency that wants to make this substitution must provide its employees one and one-half hours of compensatory time for each hour worked in excess of 40 hours in a workweek. In addition, prior to making this substitution, the public employer must reach an agreement with impacted employees about how the hours worked in excess of 40 hours in a workweek will be treated.[14]

3. AVAILABILITY OF COMPENSATORY TIME FOR EMPLOYEES NOT COVERED BY THE FAIR LABOR STANDARDS ACT (FLSA)

Although the FLSA does not allow private employers to provide compensatory time to their employees instead of overtime, this substitution might be permitted under state law, which could apply to private employers *not* covered by the FLSA. For example, pursuant to the California Labor Code, an employer can provide employees with compensatory time in lieu of overtime time if (1) the practice is implemented pursuant to a written agreement entered into before the employee performs the work; (2) the employee has not accrued more than 240 compensatory hours; (3) the employee made a written request that compensatory time be provided in lieu of overtime; and (4) the employee is regularly scheduled to work at least 40 hours per week.[15] Because this exchange is less than what is offered by the FLSA, it is an option available only for employers and employees who are not covered by the FLSA.

E. EXEMPTIONS FROM FAIR LABOR STANDARDS ACT (FLSA) COVERAGE

Some employers are outside of the scope of the FLSA's coverage and are not required to compensate employees pursuant to it. If a particular employer does not meet the minimum earnings threshold required by the FLSA or does not engage in interstate commerce, then it will not have an obligation to pay the minimum hourly rate of pay or overtime based on the terms of the federal law. It is also possible for an employer who is covered by the FLSA to be relieved from the obligation to pay the minimum hourly wage rate or overtime if an employee fits into one of the exceptions outlined in the statute.

1. PARTIAL OR FULL EXEMPTION

partial exemption
absence of the right to either the minimum hourly rate of pay *or* the payment of overtime under the FLSA, based on the nature of an employee's work

As discussed above, the FLSA provides covered employees with two significant benefits relating to their compensation: (1) payment of a minimum hourly rate of pay, and (2) payment of overtime at one and one-half of the employee's regular rate of pay for each hour worked in excess of 40 hours in a workweek. There are some categories of employees who are covered by the FLSA but are exempt from one or both of these provisions. Employees will be subject to a **partial exemption** if they are not entitled to either the minimum hourly wage rate for hours worked *or* the payment of overtime. Employees will be subject to a **full exemption** if they are not entitled to either benefit. For example, the FLSA requires employers to pay commissioned employees working in retail or service establishments and employees of motion picture theaters the minimum hourly rate of pay but not overtime, so they are examples of employees who are partially exempt from the Act.[16]

Because a determination that an employee is subject to or exempt from the FLSA has significant financial implications, the issue is often the subject of litigation. As one might expect, employees often assert they have a right to earn the minimum hourly rate of pay and overtime pursuant to the FLSA, and employers often assert certain employees are partially or fully exempt from these statutory provisions.

full exemption
the absence of a right to *both* the minimum hourly rate of pay and overtime that would be otherwise required by the FLSA, based on the nature of an employee's work

2. CATEGORIES OF EXEMPT EMPLOYEES

The most expansive exemptions under the FLSA relate to executive, administrative, or professional employees who are fully exempt from the Act, which means that an employer will not be required to pay such employees pursuant to the minimum wage or overtime provisions of the Act.[17] For this exemption to apply, the terms and conditions of an individual's employment must meet a number of conditions related to salary level, salary basis, and job responsibilities.[18]

a. Executive Employee Exemption

The first category of fully exempt employees are those who fit into the **executive employee exemption**. For this exemption to apply, each of the following conditions must be met:

executive employee exemption
category of employees who, based on salary paid and duties performed, including, but not limited to, supervisory responsibilities, are fully exempt from the FLSA and therefore not entitled to the minimum hourly wage rate or the payment of overtime

1. the employee must be compensated on a salary or fee basis of not less than $455 per week; and
2. the employee's primary duty must be to manage the business, or to manage a customarily recognized department or subdivision of the enterprise; and
3. the employee must customarily and regularly direct the work of at least two or more full-time employees; and
4. the employee must have the authority to hire or to fire other employees, or the employee's suggestions relating to the hiring, firing, promoting, and changing of status must be given particular weight.[19]

b. Administrative Employee Exemption

The second category of fully exempt employees are those who fit into the **administrative employee exemption**. For this exemption to apply, each of the following conditions must be met:

1. the employee must be compensated at a salary or fee basis of not less than $455 per week; and

administrative employee exemption
category of employees who, based on the high level of work performed and the independent judgment the job requires, are fully exempt from the FLSA and therefore not entitled to the minimum hourly wage rate or the payment of overtime

2. the employee's primary duty must be the performance of office or non-manual work directly related to the management or general business operations of the employer or the employer's customers; and

3. the employee's primary duty must include the exercise of discretion and independent judgment with respect to significant matters.[20]

c. Professional Employee Exemption

The third category of fully exempt employees are those who fit into the **professional employee exemption**. For this exemption to apply, each of the following conditions must be met:

professional employee exemption
category of employees who, based on the specialized nature of the work performed, are fully exempt from the FLSA and therefore not entitled to the minimum hourly wage rate or the payment of overtime provided under the statute

1. the employee must be compensated at a salary or fee basis of not less than $455 per week; and

2. the employee's primary duty must be the performance of work requiring *advanced knowledge,* defined as work that is predominantly intellectual and includes work that requires the consistent exercise of discretion and judgment; and

3. the advanced knowledge must be in a field of science or learning; and

4. the advanced knowledge must customarily be acquired by a prolonged course of specialized intellectual instruction.[21]

d. Outside Sales Capacity

Another category of fully exempt employees are those who work in an outside sales capacity. For this exemption to apply, both of the following conditions must be met:

1. the employee's primary duty must be making sales, or obtaining orders or contracts for services or for the use of facilities, for which consideration is paid by the client; and

2. the employee must be regularly engaged away from the employer's place of business.[22]

e. Other Exemptions

In addition to the fundamental categories of exempt employees, there are other employees who are fully exempt from coverage, such as some employees who work in the computer field. There is also a creative exemption that exempts employees whose work requires imagination or talent in a field of artistic or creative endeavor. *Highly compensated employees* (defined as employees who perform office or non-manual work and earn more than $100,000 per year, which must include at least $455 per week paid on a salary or fee basis) who regularly perform at least one of the duties of an exempt executive, administrative, or professional employee are also fully exempt from the Act.[23]

F. CATEGORIES OF COVERED EMPLOYEES

Just as the FLSA includes statutory language that exempts certain categories of employees from coverage, the Act also includes language that makes it clear that certain categories of employees are intended to be covered. Specifically, blue-collar workers, police officers, firefighters, paramedics, and other first responders are entitled to the benefits and protections under the Act, which includes both the payment of the minimum hourly wage rate and the payment of overtime.[24]

G. REGULATION OF CHILD LABOR

In addition to establishing a minimum hourly wage rate and the payment of overtime, the FLSA also regulates the employment of young employees. The Act provides that children under the age of 16 may not work more than (1) three hours on a school day; (2) 18 hours in a school week; (3) eight hours on a non-school day; or (4) 40 hours in a non-school week. In addition, all of these hours must be worked between 7:00 a.m. and 7:00 p.m. (except in the summer when the evening curfew is extended until 9:00 p.m.). In addition, the DOL prohibits children who are age 16 or 17 from accepting a number of jobs it characterizes as hazardous.[25]

H. OTHER WORKING CONDITIONS ARE NOT REGULATED

**"Instead of a raise, I'm adding you to the
Friends list on my MySpace page."**

Although the FLSA regulates employer conduct, its coverage is not all-inclusive. In fact, it does not regulate a number of terms and conditions of employment that have the potential to significantly impact an employee's compensation. For example, the Act does not regulate the length of a workday (other than the restrictions for the employment of children), changes in work schedules, or terminations. In addition, the FLSA does not require employers to offer annual salary increases, paid vacation days, sick days, holiday pay, or additional compensation for weekend or evening work.

1. ENHANCED COMPENSATION FOR HOURS WORKED UNDER DIFFERENT CONDITIONS

double time
payment of two times an employee's regular rate of pay for hours worked under certain conditions, which is a benefit not required by the FLSA

The FLSA does not require the payment of a certain wage for hours worked under strenuous conditions, provided covered employees earn at least the minimum hourly rate of pay and overtime when appropriate. For example, the Act does not require the payment of **double time**, which is the payment of two times an employee's regular rate of pay for hours worked during certain times of the day that might impose a burden on an employee or for hours worked in hazardous conditions that might place an employee in danger.

2. CLASSIFICATION OF PART-TIME AND FULL-TIME EMPLOYEES

The FLSA includes no restrictions on the classification of employees as part-time or full-time based on the number of hours worked, or the number of hours an employee can be required to work in a day or a week, provided that the employee is at least 16 years of age (or 18 years of age for certain jobs considered dangerous). For example, the FLSA would not prohibit an employer from requiring a 25-year-old employee who is paid the minimum hourly rate, and overtime after 40 hours in a workweek, from working 18 hours on a workday or 100 hours in a workweek.[26]

I. RELATIONSHIP BETWEEN STATE AND FEDERAL LAW

To determine whether the FLSA applies to a particular employee, the statutory language (and other sources of law that interpret or modify the statutory language) must be reviewed. Regardless of whether or not the FLSA applies, the applicable state laws that govern wages and working conditions must be researched to ensure that the appropriate compensation is paid. It is possible that the FLSA and a state law could both apply to an employee's work, that one law could apply, or that neither law would offer any protections. This analysis is critical because even if the FLSA did not require that an employer pay the minimum hourly rate of pay and overtime to a particular employee, and even though the FLSA did not require an employer to provide enhanced compensation for certain working conditions, it is possible that the employer would be subject to these types of regulations under state law.

1. STATE MINIMUM WAGE LAWS

Both employees who are covered by the FLSA and those who are exempt might be entitled to benefits and protections under state law that are comparable to or even exceed those provided by the FLSA. For example, Indiana has a state minimum wage law (currently set at $7.25), which applies to employers with two or more employees. Therefore, an employee working for a small employer in Indiana might be entitled to receive this minimum wage, even if the employer is not covered by the FLSA because it does meet the minimum revenue thresholds.

Similarly, although the FLSA might exempt an employer who has less than $500,000 in annual sales, Minnesota has a state minimum wage law that requires enterprises with annual receipts of less than $625,000 to pay a minimum hourly rate of $5.25. Therefore, an individual working in a small business in Minnesota would be covered by the state law (and therefore would be entitled to an hourly wage rate of at least $5.25 per hour) even if the FLSA does not apply to this employer.

There are also some states that link their minimum wage rate to the FLSA. For example, the minimum hourly wage rate in Washington, D.C. is $7.55 per hour, or $1 more than the hourly rate established by the FLSA, whichever is higher.[27] In addition, both New York and New Hampshire automatically replace their state minimum wage with the federal minimum wage if the federal minimum wage is higher.[28] See Exhibit 12-2.

2. CONFLICT BETWEEN STATE AND FEDERAL MINIMUM WAGE LAWS

If both the FLSA and a state law apply to an individual's employment and there is a conflict between the established minimum wage rates, the employee will be entitled to the higher rate of pay. This is an important concept because there are four states that have a state minimum wage that is less than the federal minimum wage; 13 states (and Washington, D.C.) have a state minimum wage that is higher than the federal minimum wage, and 28 states have a minimum wage rate that is the same as the federal minimum wage requirement. (There are also five states that have not passed a law establishing a minimum wage rate.[29])

For example, California law requires the payment of a minimum hourly wage of $8.00. If a California employee is subject to both the FLSA and state law, that individual will earn a minimum hourly wage of $8.00, because this is California's statutory minimum wage and it is higher than the $7.25 hourly rate required by the FLSA. Thus, those employees who are covered by the FLSA as well as those who are not covered should look to the applicable state law to determine their maximum entitlement under both federal and state law. This same type of research and review should be done for other terms and conditions of employment.

**Exhibit 12-2
Minimum Wage Standards Applicable for
Nonsupervisory Nonfarm Private Sector Employment
Under State Laws (As of July 24, 2009)[1]**

Federal Law Basic Minimum Hourly Rate Pursuant to the Fair Labor Standards Act (FLSA)	
$7.25	
State	**Basic Minimum Hourly Rate**
Alabama	No state minimum wage law.
Alaska	$7.25
Arizona	$7.25
Arkansas (applicable to employers with four or more employees).	$6.25
California	$8.00
Colorado	$7.28
Connecticut	$8.00 ($8.25 effective 1/1/10)
Delaware	$7.25
District of Columbia	$8.25
Florida	$7.25
Georgia (applicable to employers of six or more employees).	$7.25
Guam	$5.85
Hawaii	$7.25
Idaho	$7.25
Illinois (applicable to employers of four or more employees, excluding family members).	$8.00 $8.25 (effective 7/1/10)
Indiana (applicable to employers of two or more employees).	$7.25
Iowa	$7.25
Kansas	$2.65 $7.25 (effective 1/1/10)
Kentucky	$7.25
Louisiana	No state minimum wage law.
Maine	$7.25 $7.50 (effective 10/1/09)
Maryland	$7.25

Exhibit 12-2 *(continued)*

State	Basic Minimum Hourly Rate
Massachusetts	$8.00
Michigan (applicable to employers of two or more employees).	$7.40
Minnesota	$6.15 (enterprise with annual receipts of $625,000 or more) $5.25 (enterprise with annual receipts of less than $625,000)
Mississippi	No state minimum wage law.
Missouri	$7.25
Montana	$7.25 $4.00 (businesses with gross annual sales of $110,000 or less)
Nebraska (applicable to employers of four or more employees).	$7.25
Nevada	$7.55 (with no health benefits provided by the employer) $6.55 (with health insurance benefits provided by the employer and received by the employee)
New Hampshire	$7.25
New Jersey	$7.25
New Mexico	$7.50
New York	$7.25
North Carolina	$7.25
North Dakota	$7.25
Ohio	$7.30
Oklahoma	$7.25 (employers of ten or more full-time employees at any one location and employers with annual gross sales over $100,000 irrespective of number of full-time employees) $2.00 (all other employers)
Oregon	$8.40
Pennsylvania	$7.25
Puerto Rico	$4.10
Rhode Island	$7.40
South Carolina	No state minimum wage law.
South Dakota	$7.25
Tennessee	No state minimum wage law.

Exhibit 12-2 *(continued)*

State	Basic Minimum Hourly Rate
Texas	$7.25
Utah	$7.25
Vermont (applicable to employers of two or more employees).	$8.06
Virginia (applicable to employers of four or more employees)	$7.25
Virgin Islands (except businesses with gross annual receipts of less than $150,000).	$6.15
Washington	$8.55
West Virginia (applicable to employers of six or more employees at one location).	$7.25
Wisconsin	$7.25
Wyoming	$5.15

[1] U.S. Department of Labor, Wage and Hour Division, Minimum Wage Laws in the States-July 24, 2009 (available at *http://www.dol.gov/esa/minwage/america.htm*). Just like federal wage and hour laws, state law often exempts particular occupations or industries, as well as employers of a particular size, from the minimum labor standard generally applied to covered employment. Particular exemptions are not identified in this table. Students are encouraged to consult the laws of particular states in determining whether the State's minimum wage applies to a particular employment. This information can usually be found at the websites maintained by State labor departments, and the links to these websites are available at *http://www.dol.gov/esa/contacts/state_of.htm*.

3. TERMS AND CONDITIONS OF EMPLOYMENT MAY BE REGULATED BY STATE LAW

Some state laws regulate terms and conditions of employment that relate to compensation and are not regulated by the FLSA. For example, some state laws require employers to provide individuals working in certain industries (e.g., hotel or restaurant) at least 24 hours of rest in each calendar week. Other state laws require employers to provide employees who work a shift that exceeds a certain number of hours with an uninterrupted lunch period of at least a half hour.[30] Based on this, it is advisable for both employers and employees to research the applicable state laws to determine their respective rights and obligations under the law. In addition, in a number of circumstances employers offer their employees particular benefits, even in the absence of a legal obligation to do so.

4. TERMS AND CONDITIONS OF EMPLOYMENT THAT EXCEED STATE AND FEDERAL LAW

Neither the FLSA nor state law prevents two parties from negotiating terms and conditions of employment that exceed those an employer is legally obligated to provide. An employer might agree to provide enhanced compensation benefits for a number of reasons, such as to attract and to maintain a talented workforce. An employee might negotiate a higher hourly rate for hours worked after a certain number of hours in one day, or reach an agreement that would place an upper limit on the number of hours the employee could be required to work in one day or in one workweek. An employee might also negotiate a minimum rest period between the end of one shift and the start of the next, even though none of these benefits are required by the FLSA.

Similarly, the FLSA would not prevent employers from establishing their own minimum hourly wage that exceeds what is legally mandated, or paying employees overtime after 35 hours in a workweek (or any other number of hours less than the 40 hours required by the Act). In addition, employers may offer fully or partially exempt employees both the minimum hourly rate of pay and overtime, even if they have no legal obligation to do so.

J. RECORDKEEPING AND NOTICES

Based on the complexity of the FLSA, as well as its relationship to state law, the question of whether an employee is compensated properly pursuant to the terms of the statute is often in dispute. When an employee brings a claim under the FLSA, time-keeping records will be necessary to determine whether a violation occurred and both parties have an interest in ensuring accurate information is presented. Employers have an additional incentive to maintain accurate records because the FLSA explicitly imposes this obligation on them.

Although there is no specific requirement for employers to provide pay stubs, it is the most common method for employers to fulfill most of their time-keeping obligations under the Act based on the nature of the information that must be tracked. Specifically, employers are required to maintain the following information for each of their covered employees:

✓ personal information, including employee's name, home address, occupation, sex, and birth date if under 19 years of age;
✓ hour and day when the workweek begins;
✓ total hours worked each workday and each workweek;
✓ total daily or weekly straight-time earnings;
✓ regular hourly pay rate for any week when overtime is worked;
✓ total overtime pay for each workweek;
✓ deductions from or additions to wages;
✓ total wages paid each pay period; and
✓ date of payment and pay period covered.[31]

With respect to the child labor provisions, employers are required to maintain the dates of birth for all employees under the age of 19, the starting and ending time of their daily shifts, their weekly hours, and their work obligations.[32]

If the time-keeping records indicate that an employee was not paid according to the FLSA, then the employer can be subject to significant liability. The extent of the damages awarded will depend on the length of time for which the employee was underpaid, as well as whether the employer willfully violated the Act.

K. REMEDIES

Damages are imposed under the FLSA to compensate employees for an employer's failure to properly administer the provisions of the Act.

1. COMPENSATION VIOLATIONS

Employees who claim they were not compensated pursuant to the FLSA have the right to file a claim against an employer and request up to two years of back pay for a violation (with an additional year of back pay in the event of a willful violation), along with liquidated damages, attorney's fees, and court costs. The Act also specifically provides that an employee cannot be terminated or discriminated against for filing a complaint under this law.[33]

If the Department of Labor determines that a violation occurred, it can recommend that the employer immediately comply with the provisions and compensate its employees for any back pay due. Employers who willfully disregard the FLSA may be prosecuted criminally and fined up to $10,000 for a first offense, and a second conviction could result in the imprisonment of the offender. Repeat offenders who willfully violate the Act could also incur additional civil penalties of up to $1,100 for each violation.[34]

2. CHILD LABOR VIOLATIONS

In addition to the remedies available if an employer fails to comply with the minimum wage rate and overtime provisions, there are now increased penalties for violations of the child labor laws under the FLSA as amended by the Genetic Information Nondiscrimination Act of 2008 (GINA). Pursuant to the amendments, an employer who violates the child labor provisions may be subject to a civil penalty not to exceed $11,000 for each employee who was the subject of such a violation, or $50,000 for a violation that causes the death or serious injury of any employee under the age of 18 years, and a $100,000 penalty may be imposed if the violation is repeated or willful.[35]

serious injury
work-related injury resulting in harm to a child under the age of 18 years that could subject an employer to liability for violation of the child labor laws under the FLSA

The amendments also provide a definition of what constitutes a **serious injury** under the FLSA, which includes (1) permanent loss or substantial impairment of one of the senses (sight, hearing, taste, smell, tactile sensation); (2) permanent loss or substantial impairment of the function of a bodily member, organ, or mental faculty, including the loss of all or part of an arm, leg, foot, hand, or other body part; or (3) permanent paralysis or substantial impairment that causes loss of movement or mobility of an arm, leg, foot, hand, or other body part.[36]

 **EQUAL PAY ACT (EPA)**

In addition to facing liability under the FLSA for failing to properly compensate a covered employee or for violating the child labor provisions, an employer might be subject to an FLSA claim under the Equal Pay Act (EPA), which amended the FLSA and requires employers to pay equal pay for equal work.

A. COVERAGE

An employee can appropriately file a compensation discrimination claim under Title VII for sex discrimination by asserting an employer is unlawfully making compensation decisions based on sex. See Chapter 5, Sex, Pregnancy, and Genetic Discrimination. In addition, an employee who is compensated at a rate that is lower than what is paid to a counterpart of the opposite sex for the performance of equal work may bring an independent claim under the EPA.

The **Equal Pay Act (EPA)** is an amendment to the FLSA that prohibits an employer from discriminating "by paying wages to employees . . . at a rate less than the rate at which he pays wages to employees of the opposite sex . . . for equal work on jobs the performance of which requires equal skill, effort and responsibility, and which are performed under similar working conditions. . . ."[37] The EPA covers all employees who are covered by the FLSA, and covers virtually all employers.[38] Although EPA claims are usually filed by female employees claiming they are being compensated less for performing work that is equal to what is being performed by their male counterparts, a male employee also has the right to file a claim if he believes he is being paid less for performing work that is equal to what is being performed by his female counterpart.

> **Equal Pay Act (EPA)** amendment to the FLSA that requires employers to pay equal pay for equal work

B. POTENTIAL LIABILITY

The EPA, like other federal anti-discrimination laws, is administered by the EEOC, which reports that in 2009 it received 942 charges of compensation discrimination under the EPA, and in the same year it resolved 991 charges and recovered $4.8 million for aggrieved parties, not including monetary benefits obtained through litigation.[39] These figures represent the potential for significant liability for individual employers. For example, in one instance an employee who filed a claim under the EPA and Title VII received a $75,000 settlement and a salary increase based on a claim that a company failed to promote its Black/African-American female employees and paid them less than their White male counterparts.[40]

C. ASSERTING A CLAIM

To assert a claim under the EPA an employee must show that (1) a higher wage is paid to an employee of the opposite sex working in the same establishment; and (2) the two employees perform substantially equal work in terms of skill, effort, and responsibility, under similar working conditions. Once an employee satisfies this burden, the employer will have the opportunity to escape liability by showing that the pay disparity is based on seniority, a merit system, an incentive system, or any factor other than sex.[41]

1. HIGHER WAGE PAID TO AN EMPLOYEE OF THE OPPOSITE SEX

As a starting point, an employee must present evidence that an employee of the opposite sex earns a more generous salary. After this is established, the next question is whether the work performed by the two employees represents a meaningful comparison.

2. SUBSTANTIALLY EQUAL WORK

The foundation for an EPA claim is a comparison of substantially equal work, which is determined by examining whether the positions share a **common core of tasks**, which are job responsibilities that are central to a position and are used to assess whether two positions are substantially similar for the purposes of the EPA.

Once an employee illustrates that the positions share a common core of tasks and are therefore substantially similar and represent an appropriate comparison, courts will consider whether any additional tasks are significant enough to undermine this finding or whether the differences are peripheral job tasks that do not detract from the original determination.[42]

For example, one court found that the extra packing, lifting, and cleaning performed by night inspectors was inconsequential to the common core of tasks and therefore insufficient to support a showing that the job was not substantially equal to the day inspector.[43] Another court found that the job of a female employee was not substantially similar to that of her male counterpart because, even though the additional duties connected to the male's job did not require a significant amount of time, they were essential to the operation.[44] An employee asserting an EPA claim does not have to illustrate that the job responsibilities and/or titles are identical to those of another position. Instead, the issue is whether the positions are substantially equal and warrant equal compensation.[45]

In assessing whether the two positions require substantially equal work, the relevant consideration is whether the completion of the work of each job requires **equal skill, effort, and responsibility**. To establish an EPA claim, the employee must illustrate that *each* of these elements is comparable. If an employer can show that significant differences exist in one of these areas, then the EPA claim will likely not be sustained, regardless of the similarities that exist in the other areas.

a. Skill

The question of whether two positions require the same skills looks to whether successful job performance requires a similar level of experience, ability, education, and training. In making this determination, the focus is on the type of experience that is necessary to perform the job rather than the specific skills one employee may possess and the other may lack.[46]

common core of tasks
job responsibilities that are central to a position and are used to assess whether two positions are substantially similar for the purposes of an EPA claim

equal skill, effort, and responsibility
standard used to determine whether two positions are substantially similar and must be compensated equally pursuant to the terms of the EPA

i. Lower-Level Responsibilities Are Not Determinative

If the individual working in one of the positions performs functions that require lower-level skills, such as providing administrative support, this would not undermine a finding that the jobs require equal skills. For example, if two employees work as bookkeepers but only one is responsible for greeting clients who visit the office, this would not negate a finding that the work requires equal skills. This is because the court would likely view the greeting of clients as a lower-level job responsibility that could be performed by either employee.[47]

ii. Relevance of Skills to the Common Core of Tasks

If there are differences in the skills required for the two positions, the courts will examine the relevance of those particular skills to the common core of tasks for the job. Thus, if a skill required for the job performed by one employee, such as the creation of work policies for a national organization, was high-level work that was not required of, nor performed by, the individual working in the other position, this would likely result in a finding that the required skills are not equal.[48]

b. Effort

The physical or mental effort that is necessary to perform the tasks associated with a position is also a relevant inquiry. Positions that require the same amount of effort would support an employee's EPA claim, even if the exact nature of the effort is different.[49] For example, if male store clerks are required to stock the heavy items on the shelves, while females are required to stock the smaller items, these positions might still be considered to require the same effort under the EPA and not justify a pay disparity. This is because although the tasks performed by the men may require additional physical effort, the women's tasks are more repetitive, which could equalize the amount of effort required for the performance of the job tasks.[50]

c. Responsibility

Courts also look to the levels of responsibility associated with each position to determine whether they are substantially similar. The relevant factors include (1) the extent to which the employee works without supervision, (2) the extent to which the employee exercises supervisory functions, and (3) the impact the performance of the job functions has on the employer's business.[51]

i. Varying Levels of Responsibilities

If the employees working in the two positions have varying levels of responsibilities, this may justify different levels of compensation and undermine an individual's claim that the two positions are substantially similar. For example, if a male employee who is required to perform all of the tasks associated with closing a retail store on a regular basis is paid more than a female employee who is not expected to close, this may justify a difference in pay. However, if the responsibilities associated with closing the store are limited to turning off the office equipment, this would *be unlikely to undermine* an employee's position that the job required equal levels of job responsibilities.

The safeguarding of employer assets and supervisory functions are responsibilities that the courts have considered particularly significant.[52] For example, if a female is compensated less than her male counterpart and their job responsibilities are the same except that the male is solely responsible for determining whether to accept the personal checks of customers, this would *likely undermine* an employee's position that the jobs have similar levels of responsibilities. In this case, the male employee would be responsible for explaining the potential loss to the company if an error was made, and this represents a significant difference in the level of responsibility between the two positions.[53]

ii. Peripheral Duties May Become Significant

Even if the basic responsibilities associated with two positions are the same, the performance of a peripheral duty may be sufficient to distinguish the jobs and prevent a finding that the positions are substantially similar for the purposes of an EPA claim. However, such peripheral tasks will be closely scrutinized to determine their significance to the position. Some relevant factors include

1. whether the additional duties are actually performed;
2. whether the duties are required on a regular and recurring basis;
3. whether the duties are significant rather than mundane tasks that could be performed by any employee;
4. whether the additional duties are ever assigned to lower-paid employees; and
5. whether the extra duties justify the additional compensation.[54]

If the application of these factors suggests that a particular task is not critical or is insignificant, the performance of it will not prevent a finding that two positions are substantially similar.

For example, if a male employee is given an added responsibility of ensuring that the field offices open on time on the rare occasion when a supervisor is traveling for business, this probably would be insufficient to support the employer's position that the job responsibilities were substantially unequal and therefore did not represent a meaningful comparison for the assertion of an EPA claim. Under this set of facts, there is no indication that the peripheral responsibility was performed by the male employee on a regular basis or that it required the exertion of a heightened degree of effort or skill. Further, it is not clear that other employees, who were paid less but whom the supervisor trusted, could not have performed this peripheral task. Thus, the performance of this task by one of the employees from time to time would be unlikely to result in a finding that these two employees were assigned varying level of responsibilities that would be sufficient to support a finding that the positions were not substantially similar.[55]

3. WORKING CONDITIONS

The two positions used as the basis for an EPA claim must require the performance of work under similar working conditions. In assessing whether the working conditions are similar, the employee's physical surroundings and potential job hazards are relevant considerations. With respect to whether the physical surroundings are comparable, courts look at one physical space rather than a number of offices in different locations. An employee is generally prohibited from using different locations of a chain store to establish a pay disparity.[56]

An examination of **hazardous conditions** looks to whether the employees working in the two positions are subject to a comparable intensity and frequency of environmental factors such as bad weather, noise, odor, fumes, and ventilation, which could be relevant to the determination of whether the positions are comparable.[57]

hazardous conditions working conditions an employee might be expected to tolerate and that could be used by a court to determine whether two positions require equal levels of responsibilities for the purpose of an EPA claim

D. AFFIRMATIVE DEFENSES

The mere presence of a pay disparity between a man and a woman working in substantially similar jobs is not sufficient to show a violation of the EPA. In fact, the statute outlines four **affirmative defenses** that employers might assert to explain a pay differential between a man and a woman performing equal work, which would relieve an employer of liability under the Act.[58]

An employer providing evidence to support an affirmative defense will not be subject to liability under the EPA because the defense would justify the difference in pay between two substantially similar jobs. Specifically, an employer can defend a compensation disparity that appears discriminatory by showing that the disparity is based on a bona fide system that

affirmative defense justification that, if proven to be accurate, would absolve an employer from any liability under the EPA for a pay disparity between two employees performing substantially similar work

✓ was not imposed with a discriminatory intent;
✓ contains predetermined criteria for measuring the results;
✓ has been communicated to employees;
✓ has been consistently and evenhandedly applied to men and women; and
✓ is the basis for the pay disparity.[59]

Specifically, a male and female might be appropriately compensated differently if the salary levels are determined pursuant to the terms of (1) a seniority system, (2) a merit system, (3) a system that measures earnings by quantity or quality of production; or (4) any other factors other than sex.[60]

1. SENIORITY SYSTEMS

An employer might defend its decision to pay employees performing substantially similar work differently if the difference is the result of a **bona fide seniority system** that offers enhanced compensation based on an employee's length of service. Seniority systems should be applied to all employees based on their length of employment, and employees should be provided with advance notice about factors that could impact whether they will receive full credit for a particular year, such as whether a benefit will be reduced for the time during which an individual is out on a leave.

bona fide seniority system compensation structure that provides for enhanced compensation based on the length of an employee's service

2. MERIT SYSTEMS

merit system
compensation structure that offers enhanced compensation for superior job performance

A **merit system** offers enhanced compensation based on superior job performance and can be used by an employer to justify the compensation disparity between a male and a female employee who perform substantially similar work.

Merit systems should be based on criteria such as efficiency, accuracy, level of service, and other factors relevant to the work performed by the group of employees subject to it.[61] Both objective and subjective factors can be considered, but subjective tests are closely scrutinized to prevent abuse. For example, one employer successfully justified a pay differential by showing that all of the employees were aware of the details of the merit plan, and the administration of the benefits was based on the quality of their instruction, their research, and their service.[62] In contrast, another employer's attempt to justify a pay differential based on a merit plan was rejected because the benefits were administered in an informal and unsystematic manner, the employees were unaware of the existence of the plan, and the final decisions relating to what employees were to be compensated were based on inaccurate information.[63]

3. INCENTIVE SYSTEMS

incentive system
compensation structure that provides enhanced compensation based on the quality or quantity of work produced

An **incentive system** offers enhanced compensation based on the quality or quantity of work produced. An incentive system is generally tied to work production. For example, if an employer manages an insurance company, such a system might award bonuses to employees who resolve more than a certain number of claims in a particular week, month, or calendar quarter. Thus, if an employee filed an EPA claim against an employer, and the employer could present evidence that the pay disparity between a male and female employee who performed substantially similar work was a result of the payment of this bonus, this would constitute a valid employer defense and prevent the imposition of liability.

4. FACTORS OTHER THAN SEX

factors other than sex
affirmative defense under the EPA that provides employers with the opportunity to justify a pay disparity between a male and a female employee by showing it is based on a consideration other than sex

The fourth affirmative defense under the EPA is an expansive catch-all provision that provides employers with the flexibility to offer men and women different levels of compensation based on a consideration of any **factors other than sex.** Thus, employers can avoid liability under the EPA by asserting this defense and presenting evidence that the compensation differential between a man and a woman was based on anything other than their gender.[64]

a. Legitimate Considerations

As a starting point, an employer can consider an employee's education, experience, training, and other abilities when determining the appropriate compensation, provided these factors are related to job performance and will provide a benefit to the employer.[65] To rely on this defense, an employer must show that she was aware of these qualifications prior to offering the compensation at issue.[66]

The payment of higher hourly rates of pay to temporary or part-time employees who may not receive all of the benefits offered to full-time employees, the payment of additional compensation to employees being trained for higher positions, and the matching of the salaries of new hires for the purposes of recruitment and retention may all constitute legitimate considerations for variations in compensation based on this affirmative defense.

b. Red Circling

An employer may also present evidence to show it made the decision to **red circle** an employee's rate of pay as a defense to an EPA claim. An employer who decides to red circle a compensation rate basically agrees to retain the higher salary of the employee, even though the work responsibilities might not justify the enhanced compensation.

For example, if a long-term male employee is unable to continue to perform his job tasks, an employer might agree to place him in a lower-skilled and lower-paid position, red circle his salary, and continue to pay him at the higher rate for as long as he continued to work. Under these facts, if a female employee who worked in an identical lower-skilled and lower-paid position filed an EPA claim and proved the positions were substantially similar, the employer would assert a defense that a factor other than sex — the decision to red circle the male employee's salary in recognition of his lengthy service to the company — explained the pay disparity to avoid liability under the Act.[67]

red circling
defense under the EPA that justifies the pay differential between a male and a female performing equal work because the difference represents the maintenance of a prior salary associated with a higher position

E. LIABILITY

An employer who does not compensate men and women performing substantially the same work equally, and who does not successfully assert an affirmative defense, would be subject to liability under the EPA.

1. INTENT NOT REQUIRED

A showing of a pay disparity between a man and a woman who perform substantially equal work and the absence of a valid employer defense will result in the imposition of liability under the EPA. This liability will be imposed regardless of whether or not the employer intended to engage in this discriminatory behavior.

2. REMEDIES

An employer who violates the EPA must raise the compensation of the employee who is underpaid. The employer is not permitted to remedy the situation by lowering the compensation of the employee who received the more generous salary.[68] In addition, because the EPA is an amendment to the FLSA, the employer is also subject to the remedial provisions of the FLSA, which could include back pay equal to the difference between what the adversely impacted employee earned and the employer paid, plus any other statutory liquidated damages provided by the FLSA.

IV COMPENSATION DISCRIMINATION

Even if an employer is compensating its employees pursuant to the FLSA, which includes paying the minimum hourly wage rate, paying overtime, and offering equal pay for equal work as provided by the EPA, the employer might still be subject to other sources of liability. Specifically, an employer may be subject to claim for compensation discrimination for unlawfully considering an employee's member-ship in a protected class when making a decision related to payment of wages and other benefits. The right of employees to be free from discriminatory compensation decision is protected under several federal statutes, and the applicability of the statutes will vary depending upon the nature of the alleged discrimination.

A. MEMBERSHIP IN A PROTECTED CLASS

Employees who claim they were subjected to adverse compensation decisions based on their national origin, race, color, sex, or religion can file a claim under Title VII. If the discrimination is based on age, the behavior is prohibited by the Age Discrimination in Employment Act (ADEA), and if the discrimination is based on an individual's disability, the behavior is prohibited by the Americans with Disabilities Act (ADA).[69] These discrimination claims can usually be filed under a disparate treatment or disparate impact theory. See Chapter 2, Title VII — The Foundation of Workplace Discrimination Law; Chapter 6, Age Discrimina-tion; and Chapter 7, Disability Discrimination.

B. DISPARATE TREATMENT DISCRIMINATION

A disparate treatment claim will be based on employer conduct that intentionally compensates similarly situated employees differently based on their membership in a protected class. This situation would arise, for example, if an employer offers its Black/African-American employees a salary that is 10% less than what is offered to its similarly situated Caucasian employees.[70] This type of discrimination continues to be prevalent in the workplace for members of protected classes, as well as against members within protected classes. For example, one survey found that those with lighter skin earned 8% to 15% more than immigrants with the darkest skin color, even when the salaries were adjusted to reflect differences in education levels and language proficiency.[71]

C. DISPARATE IMPACT DISCRIMINATION

An employee may allege compensation discrimination by filing a disparate impact claim if the implementation of a compensation policy that is neutral on its face has an adverse impact on members of a protected class. A disparate impact claim can be asserted by presenting a facially neutral policy along with statistics that show the imposition of the policy had a disproportionate impact on members of a protected class.[72]

This situation would arise if, for example, an employer decides to compensate employees who graduated from a select group of colleges more than employees who graduated from other schools. If the policy resulted in certain minority groups' earning less compensation than nonminorities because the minorities were underrepresented in the schools with graduates receiving the higher compensation, these circumstances could support a disparate impact claim for compensation discrimination. Although the employer may not have intended to engage in discriminatory conduct, and although the policy did not appear to be discriminatory on its face, the employer could still be subject to liability for the discriminatory result. Similar issues could arise if an employer assigned different salaries to different job categories without a business justification, and it was determined that the positions assigned the lower salaries were predominantly filled by women or members of certain minority groups, while the positions assigned the higher salaries were filled by men or nonminorities.

V. BENEFITS

Employer obligations with respect to compensation also apply to other benefits that might be provided as part of an individual's overall compensation package. Although a discussion about compensation usually focuses on the amount of money an employee is paid, employers usually provide employees with a number of other valuable benefits, such as participation in medical and retirement plans, life insurance policies, and short-term and long-term disability plans. There are entire textbooks dedicated to the complex issues that surround the administration of benefits that are beyond the scope of this textbook. Nevertheless, a brief explanation of some of the most common offerings is worth mentioning here.

A. HEALTH INSURANCE

Health insurance is a significant component of an employee's compensation package. A medical plan covers all or part of the medical bills for employees and, in most cases, their spouses and dependent children. Most employers recognize that health insurance is a necessary component of a compensation package that is designed to recruit and maintain highly qualified employees. A recent study found that 85% of employees working in private industry have access to medical benefits.[73] In addition, on average, employers pay 83% of the cost of premiums for single coverage and 71% of the cost for family coverage for workers participating in employer-sponsored medical plans.[74]

Based on this prevalence, it is important to have a basic understanding of the different types of medical plans, the most common federal laws that regulate the plans, and the obligations of employers who provide employees with access to the plans.

health insurance
benefit that covers all or part of the medical expenses of employees and usually those of their spouses and dependent children

1. TYPES OF MEDICAL PLANS

indemnity plan
medical plan that provides plan participants with the option to select their providers

managed care plan
medical plan that requires participants to use the medical providers who are members of their network

Medical plans take a variety of forms, but most fit into one of two categories. An **indemnity plan** usually offers plan participants the flexibility to select their doctors, while a **managed care plan** usually limits the covered benefits to those offered by doctors, hospitals, and other professionals who are members of their network.

2. FEDERAL LEGISLATION THAT REGULATES MEDICAL PLANS

There are a number of significant pieces of legislation that regulate medical plans and the rights of plan participants.

a. Employee Retirement Income Security Act of 1974 (ERISA)

Employee Retirement Income Security Act (ERISA)
federal law that regulates the administration of most voluntary medical and retirement plans in the private industry

The **Employee Retirement Income Security Act (ERISA)** is a comprehensive federal law that regulates most voluntarily established medical and retirement plans in the private industry and provides extensive protections to plan participants. ERISA imposes significant obligations on employers to provide participants with information about the plan benefits, which includes such elements as what the plan provides and how it must be funded. It also establishes minimum standards relating to when benefits must be available, provides participants with access to an informal process to resolve disputes (rather than requiring participants to resort to expensive and time-consuming litigation), and guarantees some of the benefits provided by the plan.[75]

fiduciary duties
obligations imposed upon individuals who manage medical and retirement plans covered by ERISA to act for the exclusive benefit of plan participants and their beneficiaries

ERISA also imposes significant levels of responsibility upon those who manage and administer the plan benefits in the form of **fiduciary duties** and provides participants the right to sue for the breach of these duties.[76] These duties represent the obligations required of individuals who manage a medical or retirement plan subject to ERISA to make decisions for the exclusive benefit of the participants and their beneficiaries.[77]

b. Consolidated Omnibus Budget Reconciliation Act (COBRA)

Consolidated Omnibus Budget Reconciliation Act (COBRA)
amendment to ERISA that provides plan participants with a number of protections, such as the right to the continuation of medical coverage after certain qualifying life events

The **Consolidated Omnibus Budget Reconciliation Act (COBRA)** amended ERISA and requires most employers with 20 or more employees to notify employees of their eligibility to receive continuing medical coverage at a group rate on the occurrence of a **qualifying event** that results in the loss of medical coverage.[78]

qualifying event
life event that results in the loss of medical coverage and would provide an individual with a right, under COBRA, to continue to receive medical benefits at a group rate

The qualifying events for employees are voluntary or involuntary terminations for reasons other than gross misconduct, or a reduction in the number of hours of employment.[79] Individuals who elect COBRA coverage will likely pay higher premiums than what was paid while they were active employees because employers usually pay a portion of the cost of coverage for active employees. However, even with this added expense, the COBRA rates are generally less expensive than what an individual would have to pay for coverage on the open market.[80]

c. Health Insurance Portability and Accountability Act (HIPAA)

Another piece of significant federal healthcare legislation is the **Health Insurance Portability and Accountability Act (HIPAA)**, which offers plan participants privacy protections as well as rights with respect to medical coverage for preexisting medical conditions.[81] HIPPA (1) limits the ability of an employer's medical plan to exclude coverage for a condition that existed prior to a new employee's start of employment; (2) provides enrollment opportunities into a group health plan if coverage is lost based on certain qualifying events (which would likely be less expensive than the cost of individual coverage); and (3) prohibits discrimination against employees and their dependent family members based on any of their health factors, including prior medical conditions, previous claims experience, and genetic information.[82]

Health Insurance Portability and Accountability Act (HIPAA)
federal law that protects the privacy rights of plan participants and offers some protections against the denial of coverage based on preexisting medical conditions

3. OBLIGATION TO PROVIDE CONTINUING COVERAGE DURING JOB-PROTECTED LEAVE

Although employers do not have a legal obligation to provide employees with health benefits, once an employer makes the decision to offer them, the administration of the benefits and the employer's obligation to continue to provide them during certain types of approved leave are subject to regulation. For example, the Uniformed Services Employment and Reemployment Rights Act of 1994 (USERRA) requires employers to continue to provide medical and retirement coverage for certain servicemembers on military leaves for a duration of less than 31 days as if they were *not* on leave. Those employees who are on military leave for more than 30 days must be provided with the option to continue to receive employer-sponsored healthcare for up to 24 months, although they may be required to pay up to 102% of the full premium.[83] Employers also have an obligation to continue to provide medical benefits under certain terms for employees who are on disability leave or on leave for an FMLA-related condition. See Chapter 13, Paid and Unpaid Leave.

B. RETIREMENT BENEFITS

In addition to offering medical benefits to current employees, most employers also offer employees benefits they can access at the time of their retirement. Retirement benefits relate to the benefits employers provide their employees on their reaching retirement age and ceasing working. Although there is no federal law that requires employers to offer retirement benefits, one study found that 61% of private-industry employees do have access to them.[84] Employers who elect to provide these benefits can do so in a number of different forms.

1. DEFINED BENEFIT PLAN

Employers who provide retirement benefits pursuant to a **defined benefit plan** offer their employees a specific amount of compensation over a period of time,

defined benefit plan
retirement plan that offers participants a benefit based on a specific formula, that usually considers the age, salary, and years of service completed by the employee

usually for life, commencing at the time that an employee retires. The amount of compensation is based on a formula that usually considers as factors the age, salary, and years of service completed by the employee. When developing these plans, employers may (1) establish a retirement age for the receipt of benefits; (2) require employees to work for a certain number of years before becoming eligible to retire; (3) cap the amount of benefits an employee can receive, provided the limitation is not based on age; or (4) cap the number of years of service credit to which an employee would be entitled.[85]

early retirement incentives
enhanced retirement benefit offered to employees who agree to leave their employment prior to reaching retirement age

Although employers usually set the age an employee must reach before accessing the retirement plan benefit, some employers may offer **early retirement incentives**, which is an enhanced retirement benefit offered to those employees who voluntarily leave employment prior to reaching retirement age. These types of incentives might be offered in an effort to avoid layoffs that would otherwise be necessary to reduce payroll costs. See Chapter 6, Age Discrimination, for a detailed discussion about mandatory and voluntary retirement plans, as well as potential sources of liability associated with providing these benefits.

2. DEFINED CONTRIBUTION PLAN

defined contribution plan
retirement benefit that offers participants a benefit based on investment returns of deposited funds

Instead of offering employees a defined benefit retirement plan, some employers offer retirement benefits pursuant to a **defined contribution plan**. Under this type of plan, an employer agrees to deposit a specific amount of money into each employee's designated retirement account. Employees then have the right to invest the compensation in the funds available under the plan, and the retirement benefit will depend on the investment returns of the contributions.

In addition to providing employees with a monetary benefit at the time of their retirement, some employers offer employees the opportunity to participate in a tax-deferred savings plan during the term of their employment to supplement their retirement income. An employer might offer its employees a defined contribution **401(k) plan**, which is an employer-sponsored plan that allows employees to deposit pretax earnings into an account for use after they reach a certain age or during their retirement.

401(k) plan
employer-sponsored defined contribution retirement plan that allows employees to deposit pretax earnings into an account for use after they reach a certain age or during their retirement, the value of which will be based upon the investment returns of the funds deposited into the account

These plans are considered defined contribution plans because the amount of money employees will have in the account upon retirement will be based on the investment choices established by the plan and selected by the plan participant. In some cases, employers offer the employees who elect to participate in a 401(k) plan a **company match**, which represents an employer contribution to supplement the contributions made by the employees.

company match
employer contribution to the 401(k) account of a plan participant to supplement an employee's retirement benefit

C. MISCELLANEOUS BENEFITS

In addition to medical and retirement benefits, there are a number of other benefits that might be offered by employers.

1. LIFE INSURANCE

Life insurance policies provide a financial benefit to the designated **beneficiary** of an employee at the time of his death. A beneficiary may be a particular person, a group of people, or an entity, such as a charitable foundation or a university.

These policies can serve a number of purposes, such as replacing the income of the deceased, offsetting funeral expenses, establishing an inheritance for family members or friends by naming them as beneficiary, or paying taxes that might otherwise be paid by the beneficiaries of the deceased's estate.[86] Some employers pay the life insurance policy premiums for their employees, while some agree to share the cost of providing the insurance in the event an employee wishes to purchase the coverage. In other instances, employers offer a modest amount of coverage and provide employees with the option to increase the benefit at their own expense.

The most basic form of life insurance is a **whole life insurance** policy, which pays a benefit on an individual's death, regardless of when it occurs. **Term life insurance** policies are also common and provide a benefit during the term of the policy, which is usually selected based on the events occurring in an individual's life.

For example, an employee might purchase a 30-year term life insurance policy to cover the term of a mortgage to prevent it from becoming a financial burden on a surviving spouse or family members on the death of the insured. An employee might also purchase term life insurance at the time during which she is paying for the college tuition of her children to cover those expenses in the event of her death. If an individual is covered by a term life insurance policy, a death benefit will be paid only if the insured dies during the term. If the employee lives beyond the term of the policy, then a death benefit will not be paid.

2. DISABILITY BENEFITS

In addition to offering protections to employees in the event of an untimely death, some employers also provide protections to employees if they are injured or become ill, and are unable to continue their employment. Most employers offer paid sick leave, but many employers also provide disability benefits, which represent a more extensive benefit that covers all or part of an employee's salary should she become unable to work as a result of an injury or illness. The period of time for which an employee will receive the benefit will vary based upon the type of benefit offered.

A **short-term disability plan** will usually provide benefits for up to two years. More extensive illnesses or injuries might be covered under a **long-term disability plan**, which could provide the benefit for a few years and might even continue for the remainder of the employee's life.[87] It is common for a long-term disability plan to compensate a covered employee at a rate of 60% of her salary, and the benefits usually begin when any short-term disability benefits are exhausted.[88]

---

life insurance
benefit that may be offered to an employee to provide a financial benefit to a designated beneficiary at the time of the employee's death

beneficiary
person (or organization) designated to receive the life insurance benefit upon the death of the insured

whole life insurance
insurance policy that pays a death benefit to an individual's beneficiary upon the individual's death, regardless of when it occurs

term life insurance
insurance policy that pays a death benefit if the covered individual dies within the period of time for which coverage is purchased

short-term disability plan
benefit that provides an injured or ill employee with her full or partial salary in the event of an injury or illness that prevents her from working for a short period of time, usually not to exceed two years

long-term disability plan
benefit that provides an injured employee with full or partial salary in the event of an illness or injury that prevents her from working for an extended period of time

D. OBLIGATION TO PROVIDE COVERAGE ON A UNIFORM AND NONDISCRIMINATORY BASIS

Although employers have significant discretion to determine whether to provide medical, retirement, and other miscellaneous benefits, once the decision to offer them is made, the benefits represent a term and condition of employment and therefore must be offered in a uniform and nondiscriminatory manner to prevent the imposition of liability for discriminatory conduct. Discrimination claims based on the availability or administration of benefits can usually be filed under a disparate treatment or disparate impact theory, depending on whether the resulting discrimination was intentional or the result of the imposition of a facially neutral policy.

Although employers have the right to offer different levels of benefits to different employees, they should be prepared to explain the business justification for such decisions. A policy that intentionally discriminates against members of a protected class, such as a decision to provide medical benefits only to men but not to women, would likely subject an employer to liability, as would a decision to provide life insurance policies only to employees with more than three years remaining until reaching retirement age, which would likely have a disproportionate impact on older employees. The increased costs associated with providing benefits to older employees raise significant and unique concerns, however, and the obligations employers have to older employees (as well as some potential relief for these increased costs) are discussed in Chapter 6, Age Discrimination.

With respect to the actual medical benefits provided within a plan, employers should ensure that decisions relating to the amount of premiums to be paid, the deductibles required, the limits on coverage, and the waiting periods for new hires to receive benefits are not based on characteristics directly or indirectly related to an individual's membership in a protected class. For example, it could be problematic for an employer to impose different caps on coverage for the treatment of cancer than for the treatment of another disease that would constitute a disability if it can be showed that members of a certain protected class are more likely to become inflicted with a certain disease than nonmembers.[89]

KEY TERMS

- ✓ 401(k) plan
- ✓ administrative employee exemption
- ✓ affirmative defense
- ✓ beneficiary
- ✓ bona fide seniority system
- ✓ common core of tasks
- ✓ company match
- ✓ compensation
- ✓ compensatory time
- ✓ Consolidated Omnibus Budget Reconciliation Act (COBRA)
- ✓ defined benefit plan
- ✓ defined contribution plan
- ✓ double time
- ✓ early retirement incentives
- ✓ Employee Retirement Income Security Act (ERISA)
- ✓ Equal Pay Act (EPA)

✓ equal skill, effort, and responsibility
✓ executive employee exemption
✓ factors other than sex
✓ Fair Labor Standards Act (FLSA)
✓ fiduciary duties
✓ full exemption
✓ hazardous conditions
✓ health insurance

✓ Health Insurance Portability and Accountability Act (HIPAA)
✓ incentive system
✓ indemnity plan
✓ life insurance
✓ long-term disability
✓ managed care plan
✓ merit system
✓ minimum hourly rate of pay
✓ overtime
✓ partial exemption

✓ professional employee exemption
✓ qualifying event
✓ red circling
✓ retirement benefits
✓ serious injury
✓ short-term disability
✓ term life insurance
✓ U.S. Department of Labor (DOL)
✓ whole life insurance
✓ workweek

DISCUSSION QUESTIONS

Explain your response to each of the following questions with the understanding that in some cases there is no right or wrong answer. If you cannot make an informed decision with the facts provided, indicate the nature and significance of the additional information you would need. For the purposes of these questions, you can assume that the employers and employees mentioned below are covered by Title VII and other relevant federal workplace anti-discrimination laws.

1. Other than a financial payment, provide some examples of benefits that might constitute compensation.
2. What does the FLSA regulate?
3. Explain the difference between overtime and compensatory time, and provide an example of a category of employees who would not be entitled to receive these benefits under the FLSA.
4. Under what conditions might a child be permitted to work pursuant to the FLSA?
5. Explain what is meant by a statement that employees must receive "equal pay for equal work."
6. Provide an example of a "factor other than sex" that might justify paying a female employee more than a male employee who performs the same or similar work.
7. Provide an example of a type of medical plan and a type of retirement benefit that an employer might offer its employees.
8. Marge wants to file a claim against her employer for refusing to pay her the minimum hourly wage and overtime pursuant to the FLSA. Do you think she has a claim?
9. Stacey tells you she thinks her boss Jeff has no business sense because he pays her $2.00 more than the federal minimum wage. What do you think?

10. Claire tells her newly hired employee, Ian, to report to a meeting to discuss the two compensation packages available to him. Specifically, Claire tells Ian she will pay him an annual salary of $80,000 without any benefits (other than those required by law) or $40,000 with a number of benefits. What choice do you think Ian should make? What types of questions might he ask?

11. Dani, a 15-year-old high school student, wants to work in a toy store after school, but her parents tell her that it is illegal for her to work under the FLSA. What do you think?

12. Jamie pays her employees the minimum wage and overtime pursuant to the FLSA because she is under the impression that, with respect to employee coverage under the Act, "you are in or you are out." Is she correct?

13. Vivian, a news anchor, tells you she is going to sue her employer because she found out that her male friend who is also a news anchor for the company earns $5,000 per year more than what she earns. What do you think?

14. Alex is an employer who wants to compensate a female reporter more money than her male counterpart after she receives three awards for her investigative journalism. He is concerned about giving her this additional compensation, however, because of the potential for a claim under the EPA, because both employees have identical job responsibilities. What do you think?

15. Noreen finds out that her administrative assistant, Tom, who earns $450 per week, is looking for a new job. Because she does not want Tom to leave, she decides to offer him a promotion and a raise. Specifically, she tells Tom his new salary will be $550 per week and he will receive a new title. Noreen also informs Tom that his new salary will make him exempt from the FLSA as an administrative employee, and because of this, she will not be legally permitted to continue to pay him overtime. What do you think?

16. Roe hires three new receptionists for her new office building, and because she wants to establish long-term employment relationships with them, she tells them she will compensate them beyond what is required under the FLSA. Specifically, she offers them an hourly rate of $30 for the first 40 hours of work, and an overtime rate of $40 per hour. Do you think there are any potential problems with this compensation arrangement?

ENDNOTES

1. *See* EEOC Compl. Man. § 10 n.13 (Compensation Discrimination) (Dec. 5, 2000) (available at *http://www.eeoc.gov/policy/docs/compensation.html*).
2. 29 U.S.C. §§ 201-219.
3. Office of Compliance Assistance, U.S. Dept. of Labor, Employment Law Guide (available at *http://www.dol.gov/compliance/guide/minwage.htm*); Fair Labor Standards Act of 1938, 29 U.S.C §§ 201-219.
4. Office of Compliance Assistance, U.S. Dept. of Labor, Employment Law Guide (available at *http://www.dol.gov/compliance/guide/minwage.htm*).

5. U.S. Dept. of Labor, Handy Reference Guide to the Fair Labor Standards Act (available at *http://www.dol.gov/whd/regs/compliance/hrg.htm*).

6. U.S. Dept. of Labor, Poster Page: Workplace Poster Requirements for Small Businesses and Other Employers (available at *http://www.dol.gov/osbp/sbrefa/poster/matrix.htm*).

7. This rate is effective July 29, 2009. Wage & Hour Div., U.S. Dept. of Labor, Employee Rights Under the Fair Labor Standards Act (available at *http://www.dol.gov/whd/regs/compliance/posters/minwage.pdf*).

8. Office of Compliance Assistance, U.S. Dept. of Labor, Employment Law Guide, Minimum Wage and Overtime (available at *http://www.dol.gov/compliance/topics/wages-minimum-wage.htm*). The Department of Labor has also determined that some other categories of employees, such as student learners, or full-time students in retail or service establishments, may be paid below the statutory minimum hourly wage. Office of Compliance Assistance, U.S. Dept. of Labor, Wages and Hours Worked: Tips (available at *http://www.dol.gov/compliance/topics/wages-other-tips.htm*).

9. 29 U.S.C. § 207(a).

10. Wage & Hour Div., Employment Standards Admin., U.S. Dept. of Labor, Fact Sheet #23: Overtime Pay Requirements under the FLSA (available at *http://www.dol.gov/whd/regs/compliance/whdfs23.pdf*).

11. Note that employers do have the right to establish policies that prohibit working overtime without prior consent and generally have the right to discipline employees for failing to abide by those policies. However, the FLSA would still require the employers to compensate employees for any overtime hours worked, even if those hours were unauthorized. *Id.*

12. Wage & Hour Div., Employment Standards Admin., U.S. Dept. of Labor, Handy Reference Guide to the Fair Labor Standards Act (available at *http://www.dol.gov/whd/regs/compliance/wh1282.pdf*).

13. 29 U.S.C. § 207(o), U.S. Dept. of Labor, FLSA Overtime Calculator Advisor, Compensatory Time Off (available at *http://www.dol.gov./elaws/esa/flsa/otcalc/glossary.asp?p=compensatory%20time%20off*).

14. 29 C.F.R. § 553.23; 29 U.S.C. § 207(o)(5)(A), (B); U.S. Dept. of Labor, FLSA Overtime Calculator Advisor, Compensatory Time Off (available at *http://www.dol.gov./elaws/esa/flsa/otcalc/glossary.asp?p=compensatory%20time%20off*).

15. Cal. Lab. Code § 204.3.

16. Office of Compliance Assistance, U.S. Dept. of Labor, Employment Law Guide, Who Is Covered (available at *http://www.dol.gov/compliance/guide/minwage.htm#who*).

17. Fair Labor Standards Act § 13(a)(1); 29 C.F.R. § 516.3.

18. Wage & Hour Div., Employment Standards Admin., U.S. Dept. of Labor, Fact Sheet #17G: Salary Basis Requirement and Part 541 Exemptions Under the Fair Labor Standards Act (FLSA) (available at *http://www.dol.gov/whd/regs/compliance/fairpay/fs17g_salary.pdf*). The analysis of an employee's salary level includes commissions and nondiscretionary compensation and excludes credit for lodging, payments for medical insurance, and contributions for fringe benefits. Considerations relating to the salary basis generally require that employees regularly receive a predetermined salary that is not adjusted based on the amount of work performed. The inquiry about job responsibilities focuses on whether the individual performs managerial duties and work relating to the general business operations, and whether independent judgment is exercised.

19. Wage & Hour Div., Employment Standards Admin., U.S. Dept. of Labor, Fact Sheet #17A: Exemption for Executive, Administrative, Professional, Computer & Outside Sales Employees Under the Fair Labor Standards Act (FLSA) (available at *http://www.dol.gov/whd/regs/compliance/fairpay/fs17a_overview.htm*).

20. *Id.*

21. *Id.*

22. *Id.*

23. *Id.*

24. *Id.*

25. *See* 29 U.S.C. §§ 201 *et seq.; see also* U.S. Dept. of Labor, Employment Law Guide, Wages and Hours Worked: Child Labor Protections (Nonagricultural Work) (*available at http://www.dol.gov/compliance/guide/childlbr.htm*). Note that there is a broad exception that permits children of any age to deliver newspapers and perform in radio, television, movies, or theatrical productions, or work for their parents in non-farm businesses.

26. U.S. Dept. of Labor, Employment Law Guide, Wages and Hours Worked: Child Labor Protections (Nonagricultural Work) (*available at http://www.dol.gov/compliance/guide/childlbr.htm*). The classifications of employees are full-time and part-time, and the regulation of work schedules, just like a number of other issues not regulated by the FLSA, may be subject to regulations under state law.

27. Office of Compliance Assistance, U.S. Dept. of Labor, Employment Law Guide, Wages and Hours Worked: Minimum Wage and Overtime Pay (available at *http://www.dol.gov/compliance/guide/minwage.htm#_*); Fair Labor Standards Act of 1938, 29 U.S.C. §§ 201-219; *see generally* Wage & Hour Div., Employment Standards Admin., U.S. Dept. of Labor, Work Hours: Breaks & Meal Periods (available at *http://www.dol.gov/dol/topic/workhours/breaks.htm*).

28. Office of Compliance Assistance, U.S. Dept. of Labor, Employment Law Guide (available at *http://www.dol.gov/compliance/guide/minwage.htm#_*).

29. *See* Wage & Hour Div., U.S. Dept. of Labor, Minimum Wage Laws in the States (July 24, 2009) (available at *http://www.dol.gov/esa/minwage/america.htm#footnote*).

30. *See, e.g.,* New York State Dept. of Labor, Wages and Hours: Frequently Asked Questions (available at *http://www.labor.state.ny.us/workerprotection/laborstandards/faq.shtm#7*).

31. Wage & Hour Div., Employment Standards Admin., U.S. Dept. of Labor, Handy Reference Guide to the Fair Labor Standards Act (available at *http://www.dol.gov/whd/regs/compliance/hrg.htm*).

32. U.S. Dept. of Labor, Employment Law Guide, Wages and Hours Worked: Child Labor (Nonagricultural Work) (available at *http://www.dol.gov/compliance/guide/childlbr.htm*).

33. U.S. Dept. of Labor, Employment Law Guide, Wages and Hours Worked: Minimum Wage and Overtime (available at *http://www.dol.gov/compliance/guide/minwage.htm#Penalties*).

34. *Id.*

35. 29 U.S.C. § 216(e)(1)(A); U.S. Dept. of Labor, General Information on the Fair Labor Standards Act (FLSA) (available at *http://www.dol.gov/whd/regs/compliance/mwposter.htm*).

36. 29 U.S.C. § 216(e)(1)(B).

37. 29 U.S.C. § 206(d).

38. U.S. Equal Employment Opportunity Commn., Equal Pay and Compensation Discrimination (available at *http://www.eeoc.gov/laws/types/equalcompensation.cfm*).

39. U.S. Equal Employment Opportunity Commn., Equal Pay Act Charges (includes concurrent charges with Title VII, ADEA, and ADA) FY 1997–FY 2009 (available at *http://www.eeoc.gov/eeoc/statistics/enforcement/epa.cfm*).

40. *EEOC v. NASDAQ Stock Mkt., Inc.,* No. 06-1066 RWTV (D. Md. Aug. 30, 2006).

41. EEOC Compl. Man. § 10 (Compensation Discrimination) (Dec. 5, 2000) (available at *http://www.eeoc.gov/policy/docs/compensation.html*). Compensation under the EPA, just like other federal statutes, is broad and refers to all compensation, including deferred compensation such as a pension plan, fringe benefits such as a medical plan, vacation pay and other forms of paid leave, and premium pay for overtime and hazardous work.

42. *Stanley v. University of S. Cal.,* 178 F.3d 1069 (9th Cir.), *cert. denied,* 120 S. Ct. 533 (1999); *Stopka v. Alliance of Am. Insurers,* 141 F.3d 681, 685 (7th Cir. 1998).

43. *Corning Glass Works v. Brennan,* 417 U.S. 188, 203 n.24 (1974).

44. *Goodrich v. International Bhd. of Elec. Workers,* 815 F.2d 1519 (D.C. Cir. 1987).

45. U.S. Equal Employment Opportunity Commn., Equal Pay and Compensation Discrimination (available at *http://www.eeoc.gov/policy/docs/compensation.html*). An employee does not have to show a pay disparity between his position and that of a current employee, but rather an employee can prevail on an EPA claim if a higher wage was paid to someone of the opposite sex who worked in the position before the employee was hired.

46. *Id.*

47. EEOC Compl. Man. § 10 (Compensation Discrimination) (available at *http://www.eeoc.gov/policy/docs/compensation.html*).

48. *Stopka v. Alliance of Am. Insurers*, 141 F.3d 681, 686 (7th Cir. 1998).

49. U.S. Equal Employment Opportunity Commn., Equal Pay and Compensation Discrimination (available at *http://www.eeoc.gov/policy/docs/compensation.html*).

50. EEOC Compl. Man. § 10 (Compensation Discrimination) (Dec. 5, 2000) (available at *http://www.eeoc.gov/policy/docs/compensation.html*).

51. *Id.*

52. U.S. Equal Employment Opportunity Commn., Equal Pay and Compensation Discrimination (available at *http://www.eeoc.gov/policy/docs/compensation.html*).

53. EEOC Compl. Man. § 10 (Compensation Discrimination) (Dec. 5, 2000) (available at *http://www.eeoc.gov/policy/docs/compensation.html*).

54. 29 C.F.R. § 1620.20.

55. *Fallon v. Illinois*, 882 F.2d 1206 (7th Cir. 1989).

56. 29 C.F.R. § 1620.9.

57. EEOC Compl. Man. § 10 (Compensation Discrimination) (Dec. 5, 2000) (available at *http://www.eeoc.gov/policy/docs/compensation.html*).

58. *See generally* U.S. Equal Employment Opportunity Commn. (available at *http://www.eeoc.gov*).

59. EEOC Compl. Man. § 10 (Compensation Discrimination) (Dec. 5, 2000) (available at *http://www.eeoc.gov/policy/docs/compensation.html*).

60. *Id.*

61. *See, e.g., Willner v. University of Kan.*, 848 F.2d 1023, 1031 (10th Cir. 1988).

62. *Id.*

63. *Brock v. Georgia Sw. Coll.*, 765 F.2d 1026 (11th Cir. 1985).

64. There have been a number of legislative attempts to limit this exception that, to date, have not been signed into law. For example, the Paycheck Fairness Act, which was introduced in the House and Senate (and passed by the House on January 9, 2009), would, among other things, limit this defense to instances where an employer can show that the compensation difference is related to job performance and consistent with business necessity. *See generally* Paycheck Fairness Act Fact Sheet, National Women's Law Center (available at *http://www.nwlc.org/pdf/Broad_Paycheck_Fairness_Fact_Sheet_November_2008.pdf*).

65. *Tomka v. Seiler Corp.*, 66 F.3d 1295 (2d Cir. 1995*); see generally* EEOC Compl. Man. § 10 (Compensation Discrimination) (Dec. 5, 2000) (available at *http://www.eeoc.gov/policy/docs/compensation.html*).

66. *EEOC v. White & Son Enters.*, 881 F.2d 1006, 1010 (11th Cir. 1989).

67. EEOC Compl. Man. § 10 (Compensation Discrimination) (Dec. 5, 2000) (available at *http://www.eeoc.gov/policy/docs/compensation.html*).

68. 29 U.S.C.A. § 206(d)(3).

69. 42 U.S.C. § 2000e-2(a)(1) (Title VII); 29 U.S.C. § 623(a)(1) (ADEA); 42 U.S.C. § 12,112(a) (ADA); *see generally* EEOC Compl. Man. § 10 (Compensation Discrimination) (Dec. 5, 2000) (available at *http://www.eeoc.gov/policy/docs/compensation.html*).

70. EEOC Compl. Man. § 10 n.13 (Compensation Discrimination) (Dec. 5, 2000) (available at *http://www.eeoc.gov/policy/docs/compensation.html*).

71. Lizeth Cazares, *Study Reveals Skin Color Influences Wages: Discrimination Is a Major Problem for Both Immigrants, Non-immigrants*, America's Intelligence Wire (Feb. 2, 2007) (available at *http://www.accessmylibrary.com/coms2/summary_0286-29483123_ITM*).

72. EEOC Compl. Man. § 10 (Compensation Discrimination) (Dec. 5, 2000) (available at *http://www.eeoc.gov/policy/docs/compensation.html*).

73. Bureau of Labor Statistics, U.S. Dept. of Labor, Employee Benefits in the United States (Mar. 2008) (available at *http://www.bls.gov/news.release/ebs2.nr0.htm*).

74. *Id.*

75. U.S. Dept. of Labor, Retirement Plans, Benefits & Savings, Employee Retirement Income Security Act (ERISA) (available at *http://www.dol.gov/dol/topic/retirement/erisa.htm#doltopics*).

76. *Id.*

77. 19 U.S.C. § 1104(a)(1)(B).

78. U.S. Dept. of Labor, FAQs About COBRA Continuation Health Coverage (available at *http://www.dol.gov/ebsa/faqs/faq_compliance_cobra.html*). COBRA benefits are also available to retirees, spouses, former spouses, and dependent children.

79. *Id.*

80. *Id.*

81. *See generally* U.S. Dept. of Labor, Health Plans and Benefits (available at *http://www.dol.gov/dol/topic/health-plans/erisa.htm*).

82. U.S. Dept. of Labor, FAQs About Portability of Health Coverage and HIPAA (available at *http://www.dol.gov/ebsa/faqs/faq_consumer_hipaa.html*).

83. U.S. Dept. of Labor, Program Highlights, Veterans' Employment and Training Service (available at *http://www.dol.gov/vets/programs/userra/userra_fs.htm*).

84. Bureau of Labor Statistics, U.S. Dept. of Labor, Employee Benefits in the United States (Mar. 2008) (available at *http://www.bls.gov/news.release/ebs2.nr0.htm*).

85. 29 U.S.C. § 623(i)(1)(A).

86. *See* Insurance Info. Inst. of Am., Why Should I Buy Life Insurance? (available at *http://www.iii.org/individuals/life/basics/whybuy/*).

87. *See* Insurance Info. Inst. of Am., What Are the Types of Disability Insurance? (available at *http://www.iii.org/individuals/disability/types/*).

88. *See* Insurance Info. Inst. of Am., Will My Employer Provide Disability Insurance? (available at *http://www.iii.org/individuals/disability/employer/*).

89. EEOC Compl. Man. ch. 3 (Employee Benefits) (available at *http://www.eeoc.gov/policy/docs/benefits.html*).

Paid and Unpaid Leave

13

Chapter Objectives

This chapter examines the different types of paid and unpaid leave employers may offer their employees. The Family and Medical Leave Act (FMLA), which provides 12 weeks of job-protected unpaid leave for eligible employees to tend to family and medical issues, is discussed in detail, along with the National Defense Authorization Act (NDAA), which was the first set of amendments to the FMLA, and provides enhanced benefits and protections to covered servicemembers and their family caregivers. The text also provides information about the Uniformed Services Employment and Reemployment Rights Act (USERRA), which is the federal law that provides military leave benefits.

After completing this chapter, students should have a working knowledge of the wide range of leave entitlements an employer might provide. They should be aware of the most significant federal laws that require employers to provide certain types of leaves, as well as the benefits and protections that are attached to this time away from work.

Upon mastering the main objectives of this chapter students should be able to

- list the types of paid and unpaid leave an employer might offer to its employees;
- explain the significance of the FMLA and the NDAA and what each provides, including the qualifying reasons for a leave and how an employer can identify the time period for the entitlement;
- explain the benefits provided by USERRA;
- define *job-protected leave* and explain its significance to the FMLA and to USERRA; and
- explain why it might be problematic for an employer to subject its employees to a strict attendance policy.

Federal law does not require employers to provide paid time off in the form of sick days, vacation days, holiday pay, or personal leave, or paid time off to serve on a jury or provide military service. Some forms of leave are governed by state law, however, and most employees do receive a combination of paid and unpaid leave as a condition of their employment.

In the absence of a federal or state obligation, employers do retain some discretion to create and implement leave policies for their employees. Because such a policy is considered a term and condition of employment, employers must ensure that any such policies are administered in a uniform and nondiscriminatory manner. For example, an employer may decide to offer different categories of employees different leave entitlements. However, it could be problematic if certain minority groups or members of other protected classes are overrepresented in the categories of jobs that are offered the less generous benefits. An employer could also be subject to liability for discriminatory conduct for offering different military leave benefits to men and women based on assumptions about their responsibilities outside the home, or whether one is more likely to be the breadwinner in the family.[1]

Despite the potential for this liability, most employers offer their employees leave entitlements that can be used for a number of different reasons. The reason for such business decisions may vary, but these benefits may be offered because they are expected as part of a compensation package, or because an employer determines offering them is necessary to attract and retain qualified employees.

PAID LEAVE FOR ILLNESSES, HOLIDAYS, VACATIONS, FUNERALS, AND PERSONAL REASONS

The majority of private-industry employers provide paid leave in the form of sick days, vacation days, funeral leave, and other miscellaneous personal reasons. In addition, most employers offer paid time off for holidays; private employers offer an average of eight paid holidays per year.[2]

Percentage of U.S. Employers, Across All Industries, That Offer Paid Leave for Qualifying Reasons[3]

Sick Leave	Holidays	Vacation	Funeral Leave	Personal Leave
66%	76%	75%	71%	41%

paid holiday
day for which an employee is paid but not required to work, or is paid enhanced compensation for working

paid vacation
days for which an employee is paid but not required to work, usually selected by the employee and approved by the employer

personal leave
days for which an employee is paid but not required to work, which are used for miscellaneous purposes

A **paid holiday** has been defined as a "day for which employees who are not required to work receive pay for the time off, or for which employees who are required to work get premium pay or compensatory time off."[4] **Paid vacation** refers to "leave from work (or pay in lieu of time off) provided on an annual basis and normally taken in blocks of days or weeks."[5] Employees typically have the right to select which days will be taken as paid vacation, but the selection is usually subject to employer approval. The broader term for leave that can be used for any purpose the employee chooses is **personal leave,** and it is sometimes defined as the "catch-all" leave to "provide the employee with time off from work for miscellaneous purposes that may or may not be covered by other types of leave plans."[6]

These types of paid leave are not mandated by federal law. Therefore, employers retain some discretion to structure how these benefits are accrued and administered. An employer might implement a policy that starts the accrual of vacation time after the completion of a probationary period, rather than on the first day of employment. An employer might also have a policy to prorate or even deny paid vacation days to part-time employees.

Because paid leave is a term and condition of employment, the granting of the benefit must be implemented within the parameters of anti-discrimination laws, meaning employers should strive for the uniform application of objective policies. For example, an employer has the right to determine how many vacation days employees will be entitled to on an annual basis. However, an employer would violate Title VII by providing extra vacation days to female employees based on a belief that they have a greater need for paid leave to care for their children. See Chapter 5, Sex, Pregnancy, and Genetic Discrimination.

In addition, although employers do not have an obligation to provide employees with paid sick leave, they do have an obligation to provide reasonable accommodations to their disabled employees, provided it is not an undue burden, pursuant to the terms of the Americans with Disabilities Act (ADA). See Chapter 7, Disability Discrimination. Employers also have a legal obligation to provide employees with unpaid job-protected leave to tend to their serious medical conditions and to those of their family members within the parameters of the FMLA, which now also provides enhanced benefits and protections to covered servicemembers and their family caregivers.

 ## FAMILY AND MEDICAL LEAVE ACT (FMLA)

The **Family and Medical Leave Act (FMLA)** provides covered employees with job-protected leave to tend to family and medical issues, and the National Defense Authorization Act (NDAA) amended the FMLA to provide coverage for "qualifying exigency" leave to eligible employees with covered family members in the Regular Armed Forces and for "military caregiver leave" to eligible employees who are the spouse, son, daughter, parent, or next of kin of certain veterans with a "serious injury or illness."[7]

Family and Medical Leave Act (FMLA)
federal law that provides job-protected leave to employees to tend to family, medical, and in some cases military, issues

The FMLA is considered one of the most significant advancements for American workers who are also caregivers, and millions of eligible employees take advantage of its leave provisions each year.[8]

A. CAREGIVERS RECEIVE NO SPECIFIC PROTECTIONS UNDER TITLE VII

Although Title VII prohibits workplace discrimination, it does not specifically prohibit the implementation of policies that have a discriminatory impact on caregivers. In fact, when policies have been challenged on the basis that they have an disparate impact on caregivers, courts have suggested that employees who care for their children are not entitled to special protections, even though women are more likely than men to assume this role.[9] Despite this absence of protections from discriminatory conduct under Title VII, caregivers may be entitled to job-protected leave to tend to family and medical issues pursuant to the terms of the FMLA.

B. LEAVE ENTITLEMENT

To be eligible for FMLA benefits an employee must (1) work for a covered employer, (2) have worked for the employer for a total of 12 months, (3) have worked at least 1,250 hours over the previous 12 months, and (4) have worked at a location where at least 50 employees are employed by the employer within 75 miles.[10]

The FMLA provides eligible employees with 12 weeks of job-protected unpaid leave to tend to family and medical issues, which means that employees must be granted the leave, may not be penalized for taking the time off, and must be returned to the same or an equivalent position on their return to work, provided the appropriate notice and certification requirements are met.[11] The NDAA amended the FMLA and provides up to 26 weeks of unpaid job-protected leave in a 12-month period (inclusive of the original 12 weeks' entitlement) for eligible employees to care for a servicemember (spouse, son, daughter, parent, or next of kin) who was injured in the line of duty, and also allows 12 weeks of this leave entitlement to be used for "qualifying exigencies" arising out of an active duty or call-to-duty status of a spouse, son, daughter, or parent.[12]

C. SCOPE OF COVERAGE

U.S. Department of Labor (DOL)
federal agency charged with enforcing a number of federal employment laws, including the FMLA

The **U.S. Department of Labor (DOL),** which is the federal agency charged with enforcing the FMLA, requires employers with 50 or more employees who have worked 20 or more weeks in the current or previous calendar year to provide FMLA leave to employees consistent with the terms of the Act.[13] To be entitled to this benefit, an employee must have worked for a covered employer within the parameters outlined above, including having worked at least 1,250 hours in the previous 12 months.[14]

D. CALCULATION OF LEAVE

The FMLA provides for 12 weeks of unpaid leave for traditional family care (and 26 weeks for military caregivers) during a 12-month period. There are a number of rules relating to the calculation of this annual allotment and how the time may be used.

1. TWELVE-MONTH PERIOD

Employers have four options to frame the 12-month period used for the purpose of calculating the time period during which the 12- or 26-week leave allotment must be provided to employees. Specifically, an employer may calculate this benefit based on:

- ✓ a calendar year;
- ✓ any fixed 12-month period (such as the employer's fiscal year or the employee's anniversary date);

✓ the 12-month period that begins on the date an employee first uses FMLA leave; or

✓ the rolling 12-month period measured backward from the date an employee uses this leave.[15]

2. TWELVE WEEKS OF LEAVE

The FMLA does not require eligible employees to take all of their FMLA leave at a single time. Instead, the leave may be taken "intermittently or on a reduced leave schedule."[16]

a. Intermittent Leave

Intermittent leave refers to time off at a number of different times for the same underlying reason. This type of leave might be used by a person with a chronic health condition who requests a few hours of weekly work relief to receive a treatment, or who has sudden flare-ups that prevent the individual from reporting to work. If the intermittent leave is taken for planned medical treatments, then the employee has an obligation to make a "reasonable effort to schedule the treatment so as not to disrupt unduly the employer's operations."[17] In the event an employee requests an intermittent leave for the birth of a new child, then the employer must consent to the arrangement.[18]

intermittent leave
FMLA-related leave taken sporadically to allow an employee to tend to a family or medical issue

b. Reduced Leave Schedule

Employees can also use FMLA to work a **reduced leave schedule**, which refers to the shortening of a workday or workweek (such as a reduction from full-time to part-time status) to enable an employee to address the problem for which the leave is requested.[19] Just as with intermittent leave, in the event an employee wants to work a reduced leave schedule for the birth of a new child, the employer must consent to this arrangement.[20]

reduced leave schedule
adjustment of work hours or workdays to allow an employee to take FMLA-related leave

E. TRADITIONAL REASONS FOR LEAVE

Employees are entitled to job-protected leave under the FMLA only if the request is based on a qualifying reason under the Act.

1. FAMILY CARE

Until recently, the only qualifying reasons for FMLA-related leave were (1) the birth and care of an eligible employee's child (or placement of an adopted or foster child with the employee); (2) the care of an employee's immediate family member (spouse, child, or parent) who has a serious health condition; and (3) the care of a covered employee's own serious health condition.[21] As noted above, the recent amendments to the FMLA by the NDAA expanded the leave entitlements to include "qualifying exigencies," which relate to exigencies arising out of the fact that an employee's spouse, son, daughter, or parent is on active duty, or has been notified of an impending call or order to active duty, in support of a contingency operation.[22]

2. SERIOUS MEDICAL CONDITION

serious health condition
severe illness that may require more extensive sick leave than what standard policies provide and for which the use of FMLA-related leave may be appropriate

Although most people are familiar with the FMLA within the context of the care of a newborn child, it is also commonly used to tend to serious medical conditions. Employees are not entitled to use FMLA leave for any minor ailment. Instead, the leave is available only for **serious medical conditions**, which are severe illnesses that require more extensive sick leave than what is generally offered by an employer's sick leave policy.

a. Definition

Generally speaking, a serious medical condition includes the following:

✓ any treatment connected with inpatient care;
✓ a period of incapacity that requires continuing treatment from a healthcare provider, or that requires an absence of more than three calendar days off from work;
✓ a period of incapacity due to pregnancy;
✓ a period of incapacity due to a chronic serious health condition (such as diabetes);
✓ a period of incapacity that is permanent for which there is no treatment (such as Alzheimer's disease); or
✓ any absence to receive treatments from a healthcare provider for a condition that would likely result in an absence from work for more than three days if left untreated.[23]

b. Legislative History

The legislative history of the FMLA provides guidance about what constitutes a serious health condition and states the term is "intended to cover conditions or illnesses that affect an employee's health to the extent that he or she must be absent from work on a recurring basis or for more than a few days for treatment or recovery."[24] The language is not intended to cover all illnesses and is "not intended to cover short-term conditions for which treatment and recovery are very brief. It is expected that such conditions will fall within even the most modest sick leave policies."[25] By way of example, heart conditions, back conditions that require extensive therapy or surgical procedures, severe arthritis, and complications or illnesses related to pregnancy and recovery from childbirth, would be considered serious health conditions for the purpose of the FMLA.[26]

c. Relationship Between Serious Medical Conditions and Disabilities

Some serious health conditions that fall within the scope of the FMLA's coverage would also be considered disabilities for the purpose of the ADA, while others may not. For example, an aggressive form of cancer may be both a serious health condition and a disability, while a broken leg might be considered an FMLA-related condition, but it might not rise to the level of a disability if the condition does not substantially limit an individual's ability to engage in a major life activity such as walking.[27] See Chapter 7, Disability Discrimination.

d. Healthcare Provider

Because one of the definitions of a serious health condition refers to the necessity of treatment by a healthcare provider, there is extensive guidance about what this would include. For the purposes of the FMLA, the term includes doctors of medicine or osteopathy authorized to practice medicine or surgery (as appropriate) by the state in which the doctor practices, podiatrists, dentists, optometrists, and any other healthcare provider who offers services through the health plan offered by the employer.[28]

F. MILITARY FAMILY LEAVE ENTITLEMENTS

The **National Defense Authorization Act (NDAA)** was the first set of FMLA amendments, and provides more extensive leave entitlements to allow eligible employees to care for a covered servicemember with a serious injury or illness and allows for the use of a portion of this leave to tend to issues related to a call, or impending call, to duty.[29]

National Defense Authorization Act (NDAA) the first set of amendments to the FMLA, which provides extended job-protected leave to allow eligible employees to care for a covered servicemember who has a serious injury or illness and allows for the use of 12 weeks of the leave for "qualifying exigencies" arising out of an active duty or call-to-duty status of a spouse, son, daughter, or parent

1. COVERED EMPLOYEES AND LENGTH OF LEAVE

The NDAA provides family member caregivers the right to take up to 26 weeks of unpaid leave in any 12-month period to provide care to a covered servicemember with a serious injury incurred in the line of duty.[30] Twelve weeks of this entitlement can be used to tend to family military leave issues that fit within the statutory definition of a "qualifying exigency," which did not previously fall within the scope of the FMLA's coverage. This NDAA leave entitlement is significant because it extends the leave time (from 12 weeks to 26 weeks), the categories of people for whom the benefit is available (i.e., next of kin), and the reasons for which a portion of the leave can be taken (qualifying exigency leave).[31]

2. MILITARY CAREGIVER LEAVE

The NDAA allows an employee who is the spouse, son, daughter, parent, or next of kin of a covered servicemember who has a serious injury or illness, to take up to 26 weeks of unpaid leave to care for that servicemember. This would include time off needed to care for a servicemember who is undergoing medical treatment, recuperation, or therapy, is in an outpatient status, or is otherwise on the temporary disability retired list as a result of a serious illness or injury. Further, a serious injury could be one incurred by a servicemember in the line of active duty, which rendered the individual unfit to perform the duties of his or her office, grade, rank, or rating.[32] This entitlement is significant because it provides individuals more than two times the original entitlement of 12 weeks of unpaid leave available under the FMLA. In addition, it is also significant that under these amendments, 12 weeks of this leave can be used for expanded purposes related to the call to duty.

3. QUALIFYING EXIGENCY LEAVE

qualifying exigency leave
expanded reasons for which caregivers of servicemembers may use 12 weeks of their leave entitlement under the FMLA

Under the NDAA, employees who have a family member on active duty in the National Guard or Reserves (which includes a spouse, son, daughter, or parent) are entitled to use the 12 weeks of job-protected leave under the FMLA for **qualifying exigency leave**.

This represents an expansion of FMLA rights because before the passage of the NDAA, an employee was not permitted to use FMLA leave for these purposes. The FMLA, as amended, provides a benefit for a family member of a covered servicemember who is on active duty or who is called to support a contingency operation. The leave can be used for (1) short-notice deployment, (2) military events and related activities, (3) childcare and school activities, (4) financial and legal arrangements, (5) counseling, (6) rest and recuperation, (7) post-deployment activities, and (8) additional reasons mutually agreed to by the employer and employee.[33]

G. EMPLOYER CANNOT DENY THE LEAVE REQUEST

Once it is determined that an employee is entitled to a leave under the FMLA (which includes its amendments), provided the employee complies with the appropriate notice provisions of the Act, a covered employee is entitled to take this unpaid job-protected time away from work. An employer cannot deny a leave request even if it may have a significant impact on the employer, or if the employee might be able to continue to work under different conditions.[34]

This right to a leave is in contrast to an employee's rights (and an employer's obligations) under the ADA. Under the ADA, disabled employees are entitled to a reasonable accommodation, which might include an unpaid leave. However, such disabled employees would not have the right to be completely relieved of their workplace responsibilities if it would impose an undue burden on the employer's business. Under the FMLA, employers are required to grant the leave that falls within the parameters of the Act, notwithstanding the impact it might have on the employer's business. See Chapter 7, Disability Discrimination.

Employers are also prohibited from retaliating against an employee for requesting a leave by imposing an adverse employment decision in response to an employee's assertion of a legal right, or by considering it when making any decision relating to an employee's terms and conditions of employment.[35]

While this right to be fully relieved from work responsibilities without the imposition of any negative consequences is a significant benefit for employees, a number of other protections also coincide with this time away from work.

H. PARAMETERS OF LEAVE

In addition to actually providing employees with the right to take a leave from work, the FMLA provides employees with additional benefits and protections related to that leave. For example, because the FMLA provides only for unpaid leave, many employees are not in a financial position to take advantage of the full entitlement. In recognition of this reality, the FMLA offers some ways for employees to minimize the financial impact that might result from their assertion of their right to take this unpaid leave from work.

1. SUBSTITUTION OF PAID LEAVE

Although the FMLA only provides for unpaid leave, employees may choose to use their paid leave (such as vacation days or sick days) to cover all or part of the time away from work. In addition, employers have the right to establish policies that require the use of accrued paid time and FMLA leave to run concurrently.[36] An employer may also run the FMLA leave at the same time as workers' compensation benefits (which is a leave provided for job-related injuries) provided that the same qualifying illness is the reason for the use of both benefits and that employees are made aware of this policy.[37]

2. JOB-PROTECTED LEAVE

Regardless of whether or not an employee is paid for all or a portion of the time away from work, the entire leave period is **job-protected leave**, which means that employees returning from it must be placed in the same position they held before the start of their leave.

    This means that an employee returning from leave must be reinstated to his original job or an equivalent job. The post-leave position must offer the same pay, benefits, and other terms and conditions of employment as the previous position, as long as the employee can perform the essential functions of the position on his return to work. In short, returning employees must be placed in their original or in a comparable position and receive all of the benefits and protections they would have earned had they continued to work through the period of the leave.[38] In the event an employee is unable to perform the essential job functions of the position on returning to work at the conclusion of the leave period, the FMLA does not require the employer to offer the employee an accommodation or a different position.[39] The employer may, however, have an obligation to provide a reasonable obligation under state law, the ADA, or both. See Chapter 7, Disability Discrimination.

job-protected leave
absence from work after which an employee must be returned to the same or equivalent position held before the absence, as if the leave did not occur

3. FRINGE BENEFITS

Another component of this job-protected leave is the obligation imposed on employers to extend certain benefits to employees who exercise their right to use the benefit.

a. Medical Benefits

While an employee is away from work on FMLA-related leave, an employer has an obligation to continue to provide medical coverage on the same terms and conditions that were provided before the leave. This obligation continues until the employer receives notice that the employee has no intention of returning to work at the conclusion of the leave period.[40] If an employee is not required to pay medical premiums while working, the employee cannot be required to pay medical premiums while on leave. By the same token, if an employee is required to pay medical premiums while working, the employer can require the employee to continue to make these contributions while on FMLA leave, provided this requirement is also imposed on employees who are on other types of leave.[41]

b. Life Insurance and Disability Insurance

Because the right to take an FMLA leave is a term and condition of employment, employers cannot discriminate against individuals who take advantage of it. Thus, employers must continue to provide other benefits such as life insurance or disability insurance to employees on FMLA-related leave on the same basis as those who are on leave for other reasons, because refusing to extend this benefit under the circumstances would be discriminatory conduct.[42]

4. OTHER TERMS AND CONDITIONS OF EMPLOYMENT

The FMLA does not require employers to allow for the accrual of vacation days, sick days, or seniority for employees on FMLA-related leave. However, if an employer allows these accruals for employees on other types of leave, employees on FMLA-related leave are entitled to this same treatment.[43]

I. NOTICE

The granting of job-protected leave to an employee has the potential to have a detrimental impact on the operations of an employer's business. Because of this, the FMLA contains notice provisions that relate both to the notice employees must provide to their employers when they want to utilize their FMLA-related leave, as well as to the notice that employers must provide their employees when they intend to deduct an absence from their employees' leave entitlement for the applicable 12-month period. An employee who is faced with a family or medical issue that falls within the scope of the FMLA is required to comply with these notification requirements, just as the employer is required to comply with the notification requirements related to deducting the leave from the employee's leave entitlement.

1. EMPLOYEE NOTICE OF INTENT TO TAKE FMLA-RELATED LEAVE

Historically, employees who wanted to take FMLA-related leave had to provide 30 days' advance notice of this intention to their employer. If an employee was not aware of the need for a leave 30 days in advance, the employee had to inform the employer of the situation "as soon as practicable," which was interpreted to mean one to two business days after the need for the leave materialized.[44]

The recent FMLA amendments, however, have tightened this notification requirement based on concerns raised by employers relating to the detrimental impact the lack of notice had on their operations. Currently, under the FMLA as amended, employees requesting FMLA-related leave are required to follow the "usual and customary call-in procedures for the reporting of an absence, absent unusual circumstances."[45]

2. EMPLOYER NOTICE OF FMLA-RELATED LEAVE DESIGNATION

Just as employees have an obligation to provide their employers with notice of their intention to take FMLA-related leave, employers have a reciprocal obligation to provide their employees with notice of their intention to deduct a leave from the employees' benefit entitlement.[46]

Once an employer learns that a leave is being taken for a qualifying reason, it must promptly notify the employee that the time will be deducted from the employee's FMLA allotment (usually within two days).[47] Employers are generally not permitted to retroactively label an employee's leave as FMLA-related leave and deduct it from the 12- or 26-week benefit. However, if an employer learns that an employee is on leave for a qualifying reason while the leave is in progress, it may be able to deduct the days from the allotment if the employee is notified about this intention while the leave is in progress, or within two business days after the employee returns to work.[48] If the employee takes leave and the employer does not provide the employee with notice within these parameters, then the employer will be prohibited from deducting these days from the employee's entitlement under the Act.[49]

J. RIGHTS OF EMPLOYERS TO REQUEST INFORMATION ABOUT THE NATURE OF THE LEAVE

Although an employer is obligated to grant an employee's leave request for an FMLA-related purpose if the notification is given, employers do have some rights to ask for information about the nature of the employee's request. Generally speaking, an employer is permitted to ask for medical documentation to substantiate an employee's claim that leave is being requested for an FMLA-related condition. The inquiry should, however, be strictly limited to the health condition for which the leave is being requested, to ensure the request for documentation does not violate the stringent requirements for requesting medical documentation under the ADA.[50] The employer may also offer to pay for a second or third opinion to substantiate the need for a leave, and request an update about an employee's condition as well as whether the individual intends to return to work.[51] See Chapter 7, Disability Discrimination.

K. EMPLOYER'S OBLIGATION TO NOTIFY EMPLOYEES OF THEIR FMLA RIGHTS

Employers are required to provide their employees with specific information about their FMLA leave policies, such as when other paid leave (such as vacation time or sick days) must be used concurrently with FMLA-related leave. In addition, employers are required to post a general notice to educate employees about their rights under the FMLA, and employers who willfully refuse to post a notice outlining the rights of employees may be subject to a fine not to exceed $100 for each offense.[52] See Exhibit 13-1.

 PAID JURY LEAVE AND MILITARY LEAVE

An employee who does not have the need to take a leave for a qualifying reason under the FMLA might be entitled to paid leave from work for a number of other reasons. The majority of employers offer paid jury leave and military leave, even though in many instances they have no legal obligation to do so.

Percentage of U.S. Employers, Across All Industries, That Offer Paid Leave for Qualifying Reasons[53]

Type of Leave	Jury Leave	Military Leave
Percentage of Employers Offering the Benefit	74%	52%

A. JURY LEAVE

Leave time for employees required to report for jury duty is generally governed by state law. Some states require employers to pay employees for work time spent on jury duty, some states require employers to offer unpaid leave, and some states are more specific, such as, for example, requiring employers to permit their employees to use vacation days to cover this time away from work.[54] Even if an employer is not required to provide this benefit, many do so because declining to offer it might deter qualified candidates from applying for certain positions or make it difficult to retain top candidates.[55]

B. MILITARY LEAVE PURSUANT TO THE UNIFORMED SERVICES EMPLOYMENT AND REEMPLOYMENT RIGHTS ACT (USERRA)

Surveys have found that the majority of employers provide their employees with some amount of paid leave during their military service.[56] In addition, federal law provides employees serving in the Armed Forces Reserve, in the National Guard, or

Exhibit 13-1

EMPLOYEE RIGHTS AND RESPONSIBILITIES
UNDER THE FAMILY AND MEDICAL LEAVE ACT

Basic Leave Entitlement

FMLA requires covered employers to provide up to 12 weeks of unpaid, job-protected leave to eligible employees for the following reasons:

- For incapacity due to pregnancy, prenatal medical care or child birth;
- To care for the employee's child after birth, or placement for adoption or foster care;
- To care for the employee's spouse, son or daughter, or parent, who has a serious health condition; or
- For a serious health condition that makes the employee unable to perform the employee's job.

Military Family Leave Entitlements

Eligible employees with a spouse, son, daughter, or parent on active duty or call to active duty status in the National Guard or Reserves in support of a contingency operation may use their 12-week leave entitlement to address certain qualifying exigencies. Qualifying exigencies may include attending certain military events, arranging for alternative childcare, addressing certain financial and legal arrangements, attending certain counseling sessions, and attending post-deployment reintegration briefings.

FMLA also includes a special leave entitlement that permits eligible employees to take up to 26 weeks of leave to care for a covered servicemember during a single 12-month period. A covered servicemember is a current member of the Armed Forces, including a member of the National Guard or Reserves, who has a serious injury or illness incurred in the line of duty on active duty that may render the servicemember medically unfit to perform his or her duties for which the servicemember is undergoing medical treatment, recuperation, or therapy; or is in outpatient status; or is on the temporary disability retired list.

Benefits and Protections

During FMLA leave, the employer must maintain the employee's health coverage under any "group health plan" on the same terms as if the employee had continued to work. Upon return from FMLA leave, most employees must be restored to their original or equivalent positions with equivalent pay, benefits, and other employment terms.

Use of FMLA leave cannot result in the loss of any employment benefit that accrued prior to the start of an employee's leave.

Eligibility Requirements

Employees are eligible if they have worked for a covered employer for at least one year, for 1,250 hours over the previous 12 months, and if at least 50 employees are employed by the employer within 75 miles.

Definition of Serious Health Condition

A serious health condition is an illness, injury, impairment, or physical or mental condition that involves either an overnight stay in a medical care facility, or continuing treatment by a health care provider for a condition that either prevents the employee from performing the functions of the employee's job, or prevents the qualified family member from participating in school or other daily activities.

Subject to certain conditions, the continuing treatment requirement may be met by a period of incapacity of more than 3 consecutive calendar days combined with at least two visits to a health care provider or one visit and a regimen of continuing treatment, or incapacity due to pregnancy, or incapacity due to a chronic condition. Other conditions may meet the definition of continuing treatment.

Use of Leave

An employee does not need to use this leave entitlement in one block. Leave can be taken intermittently or on a reduced leave schedule when medically necessary. Employees must make reasonable efforts to schedule leave for planned medical treatment so as not to unduly disrupt the employer's operations. Leave due to qualifying exigencies may also be taken on an intermittent basis.

Substitution of Paid Leave for Unpaid Leave

Employees may choose or employers may require use of accrued paid leave while taking FMLA leave. In order to use paid leave for FMLA leave, employees must comply with the employer's normal paid leave policies.

Employee Responsibilities

Employees must provide 30 days advance notice of the need to take FMLA leave when the need is foreseeable. When 30 days notice is not possible, the employee must provide notice as soon as practicable and generally must comply with an employer's normal call-in procedures.

Employees must provide sufficient information for the employer to determine if the leave may qualify for FMLA protection and the anticipated timing and duration of the leave. Sufficient information may include that the employee is unable to perform job functions, the family member is unable to perform daily activities, the need for hospitalization or continuing treatment by a health care provider, or circumstances supporting the need for military family leave. Employees also must inform the employer if the requested leave is for a reason for which FMLA leave was previously taken or certified. Employees also may be required to provide a certification and periodic recertification supporting the need for leave.

Employer Responsibilities

Covered employers must inform employees requesting leave whether they are eligible under FMLA. If they are, the notice must specify any additional information required as well as the employees' rights and responsibilities. If they are not eligible, the employer must provide a reason for the ineligibility.

Covered employers must inform employees if leave will be designated as FMLA-protected and the amount of leave counted against the employee's leave entitlement. If the employer determines that the leave is not FMLA-protected, the employer must notify the employee.

Unlawful Acts by Employers

FMLA makes it unlawful for any employer to:

- Interfere with, restrain, or deny the exercise of any right provided under FMLA;
- Discharge or discriminate against any person for opposing any practice made unlawful by FMLA or for involvement in any proceeding under or relating to FMLA.

Enforcement

An employee may file a complaint with the U.S. Department of Labor or may bring a private lawsuit against an employer.

FMLA does not affect any Federal or State law prohibiting discrimination, or supersede any State or local law or collective bargaining agreement which provides greater family or medical leave rights.

FMLA section 109 (29 U.S.C. § 2619) requires FMLA covered employers to post the text of this notice. Regulations 29 C.F.R. § 825.300(a) may require additional disclosures.

For additional information:
1-866-4US-WAGE (1-866-487-9243) TTY: 1-877-889-5627
WWW.WAGEHOUR.DOL.GOV

U.S. Wage and Hour Division

U.S. Department of Labor | Employment Standards Administration | Wage and Hour Division

WHD Publication 1420 Revised January 2009

Uniformed Services Employment and Reemployment Rights Act (USERRA)
federal law that provides covered employees serving in the military with certain rights to take leave and to return to their position upon completion of their service

in other uniformed service with significant leave entitlements. The **Uniformed Services Employment and Reemployment Rights Act (USERRA),** which is enforced by the DOL, provides employees with, among other things, job-protected leave, and prohibits employers from denying an individual's application for reemployment based on an obligation to serve, the filing of an application to serve, or an intent to serve in the Armed Forces.[57] USERRA also provides veterans, reservists, and National Guard members with reemployment rights after a military leave.[58]

1. EMPLOYEE NOTICE OF INTENT TO TAKE MILITARY LEAVE

Employees who wish to exercise their right to take military leave must provide their employers with as much advance written or verbal notice as possible.[59]

2. LENGTH OF LEAVE

Employees on military leave must report back to work (or apply for reemployment) within the time frames specified in USERRA to be entitled to its benefits and protections. Employees who are on leave for a period of less than 31 days must return to work on the first full workday after their release from military service. Employees who are on leave for more than 30 days but less than 181 days must submit their application for reemployment within 14 days of their release. Those employees who are on leave for more than 180 days have 90 days from their release to file their application for reemployment.[60]

3. REEMPLOYMENT RIGHTS

As long as an employee is covered by USERRA, reemployment rights will not vary based on the timing, frequency, length, or nature of the military service.[61] Employers have an obligation to place employees returning from military leave in the same position they would have been in had they continued their employment during the length of the leave. Thus, a returning employee must be offered the position she had before her leave, enhanced by the application of the appropriate level of seniority, status, promotions, additional job responsibilities, salary, and other benefits she would have been entitled to had her employment not been interrupted.[62] If the employee's position significantly changed during the term of the leave, and the returning employee is no longer qualified for the original position, then the employer will have an obligation to provide training to assist the employee to qualify for reemployment.[63]

4. VETERANS

USERRA provides disabled veterans with additional protections. Employers have an obligation to accommodate the disability of a veteran, which might require offering the returning veteran employee the opportunity to either return to the preexisting position or to apply for reemployment, for a period of up to two years from the date of completion of military service.[64]

5. EMPLOYER'S OBLIGATION TO POST NOTIFICATION OF RIGHTS

Employers are required to place their employees on notice of their rights under USERRA, and the full text of a notice must be provided to each employee who is entitled to rights and benefits under USERRA. Although there are no penalties for a failure to provide this information, an individual does have the right to request that the DOL file an action to require employers to provide employees with notice of their rights.[65] See Exhibit 13-2.

 **ATTENDANCE**

It is not surprising that the providing of different types of leave entitlements for such a wide range of issues, along with the extensive laws that regulate the rights of employers to require employees to report to work, has led to litigation relating to the appropriate treatment of certain types of leave for the purpose of administering attendance policies. Employers may believe that because they are compensating employees for performing their work, they can implement strict policies to mandate work attendance. However, an employer's right to implement these policies is not absolute and has the potential to result in liability if attendance policies are not enforced in a uniform and nondiscriminatory manner.

A. STRICT ATTENDANCE POLICIES

Strict attendance policies may result in discrimination issues because of the potential for such policies to have a disparate impact on members of certain protected classes. For example, a strict attendance policy could have a significant impact on women because they are more likely than men to assume primary responsibility for caring for children and aging parents, which might result in a higher rate of absenteeism. Primary caretakers may also need to report to their shifts later or leave their shifts earlier than co-workers who are not tied to the schedules of daycare or medical providers. This disparity is even greater for women of color, who are less likely to have alternative backup care plans in the event an emergency arises.[66] Employers could also face problems if they consider the likelihood that an employee will be able to meet their high expectations relating to attendance, based on stereotypes and personal opinions, when making decisions about work assignments and promotional opportunities.[67]

B. PERFECT ATTENDANCE AWARDS

Some employers give employees an added incentive to report to work instead of imposing penalties for excessive absences. However, an employer could actually face

Exhibit 13-2

YOUR RIGHTS UNDER USERRA
THE UNIFORMED SERVICES EMPLOYMENT
AND REEMPLOYMENT RIGHTS ACT

USERRA protects the job rights of individuals who voluntarily or involuntarily leave employment positions to undertake military service or certain types of service in the National Disaster Medical System. USERRA also prohibits employers from discriminating against past and present members of the uniformed services, and applicants to the uniformed services.

REEMPLOYMENT RIGHTS

You have the right to be reemployed in your civilian job if you leave that job to perform service in the uniformed service and:

☆ you ensure that your employer receives advance written or verbal notice of your service;

☆ you have five years or less of cumulative service in the uniformed services while with that particular employer;

☆ you return to work or apply for reemployment in a timely manner after conclusion of service; and

☆ you have not been separated from service with a disqualifying discharge or under other than honorable conditions.

If you are eligible to be reemployed, you must be restored to the job and benefits you would have attained if you had not been absent due to military service or, in some cases, a comparable job.

RIGHT TO BE FREE FROM DISCRIMINATION AND RETALIATION

If you:

☆ are a past or present member of the uniformed service;
☆ have applied for membership in the uniformed service; or
☆ are obligated to serve in the uniformed service;

then an employer may not deny you:

☆ initial employment;
☆ reemployment;
☆ retention in employment;
☆ promotion; or
☆ any benefit of employment

because of this status.

In addition, an employer may not retaliate against anyone assisting in the enforcement of USERRA rights, including testifying or making a statement in connection with a proceeding under USERRA, even if that person has no service connection.

HEALTH INSURANCE PROTECTION

☆ If you leave your job to perform military service, you have the right to elect to continue your existing employer-based health plan coverage for you and your dependents for up to 24 months while in the military.

☆ Even if you don't elect to continue coverage during your military service, you have the right to be reinstated in your employer's health plan when you are reemployed, generally without any waiting periods or exclusions (e.g., pre-existing condition exclusions) except for service-connected illnesses or injuries.

ENFORCEMENT

☆ The U.S. Department of Labor, Veterans Employment and Training Service (VETS) is authorized to investigate and resolve complaints of USERRA violations.

☆ For assistance in filing a complaint, or for any other information on USERRA, contact VETS at **1-866-4-USA-DOL** or visit its **website at http://www.dol.gov/vets**. An interactive online USERRA Advisor can be viewed at **http://www.dol.gov/elaws/userra.htm**.

☆ If you file a complaint with VETS and VETS is unable to resolve it, you may request that your case be referred to the Department of Justice or the Office of Special Counsel, as applicable, for representation.

☆ You may also bypass the VETS process and bring a civil action against an employer for violations of USERRA.

The rights listed here may vary depending on the circumstances. The text of this notice was prepared by VETS, and may be viewed on the internet at this address: http://www.dol.gov/vets/programs/userra/poster.htm. Federal law requires employers to notify employees of their rights under USERRA, and employers may meet this requirement by displaying the text of this notice where they customarily place notices for employees.

U.S. Department of Labor
1-866-487-2365

U.S. Department of Justice

Office of Special Counsel

1-800-336-4590

Publication Date—July 2008

liability for implementing a "perfect attendance" award if an employee is denied the award based on an absence that an employee has a legal right to take and that cannot be used as the basis for the imposition of an adverse decision. This is because under some statutes, employees returning from preapproved leaves must be placed in the same position they would have been in had the leave not occurred, and therefore cannot be subjected to any penalty based upon those absences.[68]

There does seem to be an indication, however, that there is now a shift away from the idea that employees on leave cannot be subject to any adverse consequences.[69] Historically, employees could not be penalized for taking FMLA-related leave, which was interpreted to mean that employees could not be denied a perfect attendance award if their only absences were FMLA related. However, the recent FMLA amendments reversed this position, and, under the current law, employers are permitted to disqualify employees from receiving a "perfect attendance award" based on FMLA-related absences provided that employees returning from other types of leaves are treated in the same manner. Before these amendments, an employee who had perfect attendance except for the leave covered by the FMLA could not be denied a perfect attendance award.[70]

C. ATTENDANCE AS AN ESSENTIAL JOB FUNCTION

Employers will be in the best position to defend a strict attendance policy if they can illustrate that the nature of their business operation justifies the strict policy. For example, an employer might assert that the policy is necessary because its operation is minimally staffed, runs 24 hours a day, or employs highly skilled technical employees who perform time-sensitive work that cannot be completed by other colleagues. An employer could also support the need for a strict policy by showing that an individual's physical presence at work is actually an essential job function. In a number of instances, courts have recognized this argument under the ADA by refusing to require employers to accommodate the needs of disabled employees who could not report to work for their regularly scheduled shifts if attendance was an essential job task and providing such an accommodation would be an undue burden.[71] See Chapter 7, Disability Discrimination.

D. ALTERNATIVES TO STRICT POLICY

If the nature of an employer's business does not justify a strict attendance policy, or if an employer wants to adopt a less restrictive policy, there are some options to reduce the impact workplace absences will have on its operation. For example, an employer could implement a flexible scheduling policy to enable employees to plan for anticipated absences relating to religious practices and personal appointments. Some employers have policies that permit alternative work schedules, give a certain number of "floating" holidays, or provide employees with permission to mutually agree to exchange shifts, so employees have some leeway to adjust their schedules.

Depending on the extent of the leave needed, an employer may still need to make arrangements for other accommodations on a case-by-case basis to avoid liability for religious discrimination under Title VII or disability discrimination under the ADA. Nevertheless, using alternatives to a strict policy could reduce the adverse impact of absences on the employer's business as well as ease the administrative burden of having to consider each employee's request for some type of work relief.[72] See Chapter 4, Religious Discrimination, and Chapter 7, Disability Discrimination.

E. TELECOMMUTING

telecommuting
working from home or a location other than the employer's worksite

Telecommuting refers to an arrangement for an employee to work from home or from a location other than the employer's worksite. Technological advancements have enabled employers to serve clients in geographically diverse locations, and these same advancements have made it much easier for employees to work from remote locations. Despite the benefits that may be derived from such working arrangements, employers may prohibit telecommuting based on fundamental managerial issues such as wanting to be able to closely supervise their employees. Such a prohibition would likely not be inconsistent with the law if it is applied in a uniform and nondiscriminatory manner to all employees, or if there is a business justification for permitting the arrangement for some positions and prohibiting it for others.[73]

KEY TERMS

- ✓ Family and Medical Leave Act (FMLA)
- ✓ intermittent leave
- ✓ job-protected leave
- ✓ National Defense Authorization Act (NDAA)
- ✓ paid holiday
- ✓ paid vacation
- ✓ personal leave
- ✓ qualifying exigency leave
- ✓ reduced leave schedule
- ✓ serious health condition
- ✓ telecommuting
- ✓ U.S. Department of Labor (DOL)
- ✓ Uniformed Services Employment and Reemployment Rights Act (USERRA)

DISCUSSION QUESTIONS

Explain your response to each of the following questions with the understanding that in some cases there is no right or wrong answer. If you cannot make an informed decision with the facts provided, indicate the nature and significance of the additional information you would need. For the purposes of these questions, you can assume that the employers and employees mentioned below are covered by Title VII and other relevant federal workplace anti-discrimination laws.

1. Explain some of the types of leave employers may offer their employees as part of a compensation package.
2. Does the FMLA require employers to allow their employees to take time off whenever they have to care for a sick child? Explain your answer.
3. Provide some example of how an employee may request an FMLA-related leave to be scheduled.
4. Explain the benefits military members and their caregivers are entitled to under the NDAA and USERRA.
5. Jared is an employer who is trying to save money and decides that he will only pay employees their salary on the days they report to work. What do you think about this idea?
6. Charlie is an employer who is trying to predict the future costs of providing medical leave to his employees. He sends out a memo asking each of them to document any existing health problems as well as any other medical conditions that are prevalent in their families. What do you think about this idea?
7. Caroline is an employer who is having trouble running her business. Her employees are out of the office for 18 weeks each year because they regularly use their four weeks of vacation, two weeks of sick leave, and 12 weeks of FMLA-related leave. Do you have any suggestions about how she can manage this situation?
8. On January 15 while Dorian is on the telephone, her employee Victoria waves good-bye, says she is leaving to take care of a sick friend, and instructs her to deduct the time off from her FMLA leave bank. Victoria tells Dorian she is not sure when she will return, but she has 12 weeks left in her bank because she has not taken any FMLA leave since January 1. What do you think about Victoria's assertion of her rights? Is she accurate?
9. Urmi is a social worker whose lifelong dream is to play professional soccer with her three sisters. While on vacation at a tournament that recruits professional players, she collides with another player. The other player suffers a serious brain injury, and although Urmi recovers, she is told she will never be able to play the sport professionally. Immediately after the accident she contacts Jessica, her boss, to request additional time off. Jessica tells Urmi that because she has recovered from her head injury and has used all of her vacation and sick days for the year, she must report back to work as scheduled. Do you think Jessica has the right to require Urmi to return to work? What other information might you want to know?
10. Janet is an employee who tells her employer she is leaving for military service and then plans to take off some additional time to finish writing a book she has been working on for a number of years. Her employer, Syd, makes a note in his file indicating that the company must protect Janet's job until she completes her book and decides to return to work. Do you think Syd is legally required to offer this protection?

ENDNOTES

1. *See generally* U.S. Equal Employment Opportunity Commn., Perspectives on Work/ Family Balance and the Federal Equal Employment Opportunity Laws, Commission Meeting (Apr. 17, 2007) (available at *http://www.eeoc.gov/eeoc/meetings/archive/4-17-07/*).

2. Bureau of Labor Statistics, U.S. Dept. of Labor, Employee Benefits Survey, Leave Benefits (Mar. 2008) (available at *http://www.bls.gov/ncs/ebs/benefits/2008/ownership/civilian/ table21a.htm*).

3. Bureau of Labor Statistics, U.S. Department of Labor, Employee Benefits in the United States tbl. 6 (Selected paid leave benefits: Access, National Compensation Survey) (Mar. 2009) (available at *http://www.bls.gov/ncs/ebs/sp/ebnr0015.pdf*) (sick leave); Bureau of Labor Statistics, U.S. Dept. of Labor, Employee Benefits Survey, Leave Benefits (Mar. 2008) (available at *http://www.bls.gov/ncs/ebs/benefits/2008/ownership/civilian/table21a.htm*) (holiday, vacation, funeral, and personal leave).

4. Bureau of Labor Statistics, U.S. Dept. of Labor, Program Perspective on Paid-Leave Benefits, Issue 2 (Feb. 2009) (available at *http://www.bls.gov/opub/perspectives/issue2for11by17 .pdf*).

5. *Id.*

6. *Id.*

7. Wage & Hour Div., Employment Standards Admin., U.S. Dept. of Labor, Fact Sheet #28A: The Family and Medical Leave Act Military Family Leave Entitlements (available at *http:// www.dol.gov/whd/regs/compliance/whdfs28a.pdf*).

8. In 2005, between 6.1 and 13 million workers took FMLA-related leave. *See* Family and Medical Leave Act Regulations: A Report on the Department of Labor's Request for Information, 72 Fed. Reg. No. 124, at 35,551 (June 28, 2007). The FMLA regulations can be found at 29 C.F.R. pt. 825.

9. *See, e.g., Guglietta v. Meredith Corp.*, 301 F. Supp. 2d 209 (D. Conn. 2004) (refusing to require an employer to limit an employee's shift assignments to those that coincide with the available hours of her daycare provider); *Fejes v. Gilpin Ventures, Inc.*, 960 F. Supp. 1487 (D. Colo.1997) (refusing to require an employer to offer an employee a part-time schedule to accommodate her request to breastfeed or care for her children). Even under the ADA, employers are not required to provide reasonable accommodations to employees who are responsible for providing care to disabled family members. *See* EEOC Interpretive Guidance, 29 C.F.R. § 1630.8 app. at 348 (1996) (stating "an employer need not provide the applicant or employee without a disability with a reasonable accommodation because that duty only applies to qualified applicants or employees with disabilities. Thus, for example, an employee would not be entitled to a modified work schedule as an accommodation to enable the employee to care for a spouse with a disability."); *see also Den Hartog v. Wasatch Acad.*, 129 F.3d 1076 (10th Cir. 1997) (refusing to require an employer to offer a reasonable accommodation to the associate of a disabled employee since "the lack of any reference to the associates or relatives of the employee or applicant in Section 12112(b)(5)'s articulation of the ADA's 'reasonable accommodation' requirement is not due to any inadvertent omission").

10. Wage & Hour Div., Employment Standards Admin., U.S. Dept. of Labor, Fact Sheet #28A: The Family and Medical Leave Act Military Family Leave Entitlements (available at *http:// www.dol.gov/whd/regs/compliance/whdfs28a.pdf*).

11. Family and Medical Leave Act of 1993, Pub. L. No. 103-3, 107 Stat. 6 (codified at 29 U.S.C. §§ 2601 *et seq.*).

12. Wage & Hour Div., Employment Standards Admin., U.S. Dept. of Labor, Fact Sheet #28A: The Family and Medical Leave Act Military Family Leave Entitlements (available at *http:// www.dol.gov/whd/regs/compliance/whdfs28a.pdf*).

13. FMLA § 101(2).

14. FMLA § 101(4).

15. *See* Wage & Hour Div., Employment Standards Admin., U.S. Dept. of Labor, Family and Medical Leave Act (available at *http://www.dol.gov/whd/regs/compliance/1421.htm*).

16. 29 C.F.R. § 825.203.

17. *Id.* (scheduling of intermittent or reduced schedule leave).

18. FMLA § 102; 29 C.F.R. § 825.203(b).

19. 29 C.F.R. § 825.203(a).

20. FMLA § 102; 29 C.F.R. § 825.203(b).

21. FMLA § 102; 29 U.S.C. § 2612.

22. Wage & Hour Div., Employment Standards Admin., U.S. Dept. of Labor, Fact Sheet #28A: The Family and Medical Leave Act Military Family Leave Entitlements (available at *http://www.dol.gov/whd/regs/compliance/whdfs28a.pdf*).

23. *See* Wage & Hour Div., Employment Standards Admin., U.S. Dept. of Labor, Family and Medical Leave Act (available at *http://www.dol.gov/whd/regs/compliance/1421.htm*).

24. H. Rep. No. 103-8, at 40 (1991); S. Rep. No. 103-3, at 28 (1993).

25. *Id.*

26. *Id.*

27. *See generally* U.S. Equal Employment Opportunity Commn., Fact Sheet: The Family and Medical Leave Act, The Americans with Disabilities Act, and Title VII of the Civil Rights Act of 1964 (available at *http://www.eeoc.gov/policy/docs/fmlaada.html*).

28. *See* Wage & Hour Div., Employment Standards Admin., U.S. Dept. of Labor, Family and Medical Leave Act (available at *http://www.dol.gov/whd/regs/compliance/1421.htm*).

29. Wage & Hour Div., Employment Standards Admin., U.S. Dept. of Labor, Fact Sheet #28A: The Family and Medical Leave Act Military Family Leave Entitlements (available at *http://www.dol.gov/whd/regs/compliance/whdfs28a.pdf*).

30. Wage & Hour Div., Employment Standards Admin., U.S. Dept. of Labor, Fact Sheet #28A: The Family and Medical Leave Act Military Family Leave Entitlements (available at *http://www.dol.gov/whd/regs/compliance/whdfs28a.pdf*); DOL's Final Rule on Family and Medical Leave Providing Military Family Leave and Updates to the Regulations (available at *http://www.dol.gov/whd/fmla/finalrule/factsheet.pdf*).

31. DOL's Final Rule on Family and Medical Leave Providing Military Family Leave and Updates to the Regulations (available at *http://www.dol.gov/whd/fmla/finalrule/factsheet.pdf*).

32. Wage & Hour Div., Employment Standards Admin., U.S. Dept. of Labor, Fact Sheet #28A: The Family and Medical Leave Act Military Family Leave Entitlements (available at *http://www.dol.gov/whd/regs/compliance/whdfs28a.pdf*). Covered employees are entitled to a combined total of 26 weeks of leave under the NDAA, which would be inclusive of the 12-week entitlement that could be used for qualifying exigency leave or for another qualifying FMLA-related reason for leave.

33. *Id.*

34. 29 C.F.R. § 825.702(d)(1).

35. *See* Wage & Hour Div., Employment Standards Admin., U.S. Dept. of Labor, Family and Medical Leave Act (available at *http://www.dol.gov/whd/regs/compliance/1421.htm*).

36. Wage & Hour Div., Employment Standards Admin., U.S. Dept. of Labor, Fact Sheet #28: The Family and Medical Leave Act of 1993 (available at *http://www.dol.gov/WHD/regs/compliance/whdfs28.pdf*).

37. *See* Wage & Hour Div., Employment Standards Admin., U.S. Dept. of Labor, Family and Medical Leave Act (available at *http://www.dol.gov/whd/regs/compliance/1421.htm*).

38. *See* 29 U.S.C. § 2614. The FMLA does have a limited exception for key employees, who do not have to be reinstated after a leave because it would cause "substantial and grievous economic injury" to its operations. The definition of a key employee and the procedure for invoking this exception are detailed in the language of the statute. *See* Wage & Hour Div., Employment Standards Admin., U.S. Dept. of Labor, Family and Medical Leave Act (available at *http://www.dol.gov/whd/regs/compliance/1421.htm*).

39. 29 C.F.R. § 825.214(b).

40. *See* Wage & Hour Div., Employment Standards Admin., U.S. Dept. of Labor, Family and Medical Leave Act (available at *http://www.dol.gov/whd/regs/compliance/1421.htm*).

41. 29 C.F.R. §§ 825.209-825.210.

42. 29 C.F.R. § 825.220(c).

43. *See* Wage & Hour Div., Employment Standards Admin., U.S. Dept. of Labor, Family and Medical Leave Act (available at *http://www.dol.gov/whd/regs/compliance/1421.htm*).

44. *Id.*

45. DOL's Final Rule on Family and Medical Leave Providing Military Family Leave and Updates to the Regulations (available at *http://www.dol.gov/esa/whd/fmla/finalrule/factsheet.pdf*).

46. 29 C.F.R. § 825.208(a).

47. 29 C.F.R. § 825.208(b)(1).

48. *See* Wage & Hour Div., Employment Standards Admin., U.S. Dept. of Labor, Family and Medical Leave Act (available at *http://www.dol.gov/esa/whd/regs/compliance/1421.htm*).

49. 29 C.F.R. § 825.700(a).

50. U.S. Equal Employment Opportunity Commn., Fact Sheet: The Family and Medical Leave Act, The Americans with Disabilities Act, and Title VII of the Civil Rights Act of 1964 (available at *http://www.eeoc.gov/policy/docs/fmlaada.html*).

51. Wage & Hour Div., Employment Standards Admin., U.S. Dept. of Labor, Fact Sheet #28: The Family and Medical Leave Act of 1993 (available at *http://www.dol.gov/whd/regs/compliance/whdfs28.htm*).

52. Wage & Hour Div., Employment Standards Admin., U.S. Dept. of Labor, Fact Sheet #28: The Family and Medical Leave Act of 1993 (available at *http://www.dol.gov/WHD/regs/compliance/whdfs28.pdf*); U.S. Dept. of Labor, Poster Page: Workplace Poster Requirements for Small Businesses and Other Employers (available at *http://www.dol.gov/osbp/sbrefa/poster/matrix.htm*).

53. Bureau of Labor Statistics, U.S. Dept. of Labor, Employee Benefits Survey, Leave Benefits (Mar. 2008) (available at *http://www.bls.gov/ncs/ebs/benefits/2008/ownership/civilian/table21a.htm*).

54. *See* Steven Mitchell Sack, The Working Woman's Legal Survival Guide (1998) (available at *http://public.findlaw.com/bookshelf-working-woman/*).

55. Some surveys indicate that up to 87% of employers provide paid time off for jury duty. *See, e.g.*, U.S. Dept. of Labor, Leave Benefits, Jury Duty (available at *http://www.dol.gov/dol/topic/benefits-leave/juryduty.htm*).

56. Bureau of Labor Statistics, U.S. Dept. of Labor, Employee Benefits Survey, Leave Benefits (Mar. 2008) (available at *http://www.bls.gov/ncs/ebs/benefits/2008/ownership/civilian/table21a.htm*).

57. U.S. Dept. of Labor, Program Highlights, Veterans' Employment and Training Service (available at *http://www.dol.gov/vets/programs/userra/userra_fs.htm*). USERRA also prohibits employers from denying an individual's application for employment based on these same considerations. See Chapter 10, Collection of Information: The Application and Interview.

58. 38 U.S.C. §§ 4301 *et seq.*; U.S. Office of the Special Counsel, Uniformed Services Employment and Reemployment Rights Act (available at *http://www.osc.gov/userra.htm*). Military members on active duty are also provided with other protections not related to employment. For example, the Service Members Civil Relief Act of 2003 provides protection for such things as rental agreements, credit card interest rates, and automobile leases. *See* 50 U.S.C.S. app. §§ 501-596. In addition, a full-time federal civilian employee whose appointment is not limited to one year is entitled to paid military leave under certain circumstances. 5 U.S.C. § 6323(a).

59. U.S. Dept. of Labor, Program Highlights, Veterans' Employment and Training Service (available at *http://www.dol.gov/vets/programs/userra/userra_fs.htm*).

60. *Id.*

61. *Id.*

62. U.S. Dept. of Labor, Program Highlights, Veterans' Employment and Training Service (available at *http://www.dol.gov/vets/programs/userra/userra_fs.htm*); *see also* U.S. Dept. of Justice, Frequently Asked Questions (available at *http://www.usdoj.gov/crt/military/faq .htm*).

63. U.S. Dept. of Labor, Program Highlights, Veterans' Employment and Training Service (available at *http://www.dol.gov/vets/programs/userra/userra_fs.htm*).

64. *Id.*

65. U.S. Dept. of Labor, Poster Page: Workplace Poster Requirements for Small Businesses and Other Employers (available at *http://www.dol.gov/osbp/sbrefa/poster/matrix.htm*).

66. *See* Lynette Clemetson, *Work vs. Family, Complicated by Race*, N.Y. Times, Feb. 9, 2006, at G1; *see generally* U.S. Equal Employment Opportunity Commn., Enforcement Guidance: Unlawful Disparate Treatment of Workers with Caregiving Responsibilities (available at *http://www.eeoc .gov/policy/docs/caregiving.html*).

67. *See generally* Anne-Marie Mizel, Family Responsibility and Discrimination: The Hidden Violations (available at *http://www.sheastokes.com/resources/legal_amizel01.shtml*).

68. *See, e.g.,* Wage & Hour Div., Employment Standards Admin., U.S. Dept. of Labor, Fact Sheet #28: The Family and Medical Leave Act of 1993 (available at *http://www.dol.gov/ WHD/regs/compliance/whdfs28.pdf*).

69. *See* DOL's Final Rule on Family and Medical Leave Providing Military Family Leave and Updates to the Regulations (available at *http://www.dol.gov/esa/whd/fmla/finalrule/ factsheet.pdf*).

70. *Id.*

71. *See, e.g., Maziarka v. Mills Fleet Farm, Inc.,* 245 F.3d 675 (8th Cir. 2001) (refusing to require an employer to accommodate a clerk in a retail store under the ADA because he was unable to report to work on a regular basis and this was an essential job task); *Nowak v. St. Rita High Sch.,* 142 F.3d 999 (7th Cir. 1998) (refusing to consider a disabled teacher "qualified" for a position under the ADA because regular attendance was an essential job task).

72. *See* U.S. Equal Employment Opportunity Commn., Best Practices for Eradicating Religious Discrimination in the Workplace (available at *http://www.dol.gov/WHD/regs/ compliance/whdfs28.pdf*); *see generally* Zachary D. Fasman, Remarks at U.S. Equal Employment Opportunity Commn. Meeting (Apr. 1, 2007) (regarding Perspective on Work/ Family Balance and the Federal Equal Employment Opportunity Laws) (available at *http://www.eeoc.gov/eeoc/meetings/archive/4-17-07/*).

73. *See generally* Zachary D. Fasman, Perspective on Work/Family Balance and the Federal Equal Employment Opportunity Laws, Remarks at U.S. Equal Employment Opportunity Commn. Meeting (Apr. 1, 2007) (available at *http://www.eeoc.gov/eeoc/meetings/archive/ 4-17-07/*).

14

Performance Management

Chapter Objectives

This chapter explores the tools used by employers to manage the work performance of their employees, with a focus on the use of probationary periods, progressive discipline policies, and performance evaluations. The text explains the purpose of each tool and provides employers with guidance about how to minimize issues that may arise as a result of the improper use of these tools. The obligations of employers to assign work and to provide access to training and promotional opportunities in a uniform and nondiscriminatory manner are also discussed.

After completing this chapter, students should have a fundamental understanding about the rights of employers to manage their workforce and how the use of performance management tools may impact the expansive rights employers have to terminate their at-will employees. Students should also be able to explain how employers can use performance management tools in a manner that minimizes their potential liability for discriminatory conduct.

Upon mastering the main objectives of this chapter students should be able to

- define *probationary period* and explain why it might be used;
- explain the purpose of a progressive discipline policy and identify the most common steps used in the process;
- explain the benefits of strictly adhering to the steps in a progressive discipline process and when a deviation might be appropriate;
- explain the relationship between at-will employment and the use of probationary periods and progressive discipline policies; and
- explain the framework for the appropriate use of performance evaluations and how to avoid liability for their improper use.

Employers have the right to use performance management tools to monitor employee work performance. While performance management is usually discussed within the context of identifying and remedying problematic behavior, it can also be used to reward employees for work performance that exceeds the expectations of an employer. Regardless of whether performance management tools are used for one or both of these purposes, because they have the potential to impact an employee's terms and conditions of employment, the tools must be used in a uniform and nondiscriminatory manner to minimize potential employer liability under Title VII and other anti-discrimination laws.

∏ PROBATIONARY PERIOD

probationary period
initial period of employment during which employers retain the right to terminate a newly hired employee for any legal reason

Employers can initiate performance management on the first day of employment by subjecting new hires to a **probationary period**, which is a length of time at the beginning of employment during which employees can be terminated for any legal reason. This broad termination right assumes that the motivation for the termination is not inconsistent with Title VII or any other law that regulates employer conduct.

employees at will
employees who can be terminated with or without cause, and with or without any notice

The majority of working individuals are **employees at will**, who can be terminated with or without cause and with or without notice. However, even with respect to their at-will employees, employers retain more extensive termination rights during a probationary period than they do after its completion due to the creation of a large number of legislative and judicial limitations on the at-will doctrine. Based on this, employers should pay careful attention to the work performance of new employees during the probationary period. In the event an employer determines an employee is not suitable for a position, it should terminate the employee and end the employment relationship before the expiration of this time period. See Chapter 18, Employment at Will.

A. LENGTH OF THE PROBATIONARY PERIOD

The length of a probationary period is established by the employer, and the most common durations are for 30, 60, or 90 days. Most employers establish a uniform probationary period for all employees, but there are some circumstances that may justify different lengths of time.

1. LINKING THE LENGTH OF THE PROBATIONARY PERIOD TO A JOB TITLE

An employer is permitted to vary the length of the probationary period for different positions, but any unequal treatment could give rise to a discrimination claim. For example, an employer might be subject to a disparate impact discrimination claim for imposing longer probationary periods on employees hired for lower-skilled positions if those positions tend to be filled by members of a particular protected class. Based on this potential, employers should be prepared to explain the business justification for any variations that exist to refute an allegation of discriminatory conduct in the event a claim materializes.

2. EXTENDING THE PROBATIONARY PERIOD

Employers often retain the right to extend the length of an employee's probationary period if they determine more time is needed to assess an employee's suitability for a position, which can be memorialized in a company handbook. Employers exercising their right to extend, however, should remember that such an extension, just like the probationary period itself, is a term and condition of employment. Therefore, any extension must be implemented in a uniform and nondiscriminatory manner to avoid a discrimination claim.

Assuming the reason for the extension is not discriminatory, even if the right to such an extension is not pursuant to an established policy, in practical terms, the employer retains significant control over the decision of whether one will be imposed. This is because if an employer decides there is a need to extend the probationary period and the employee objects, the employer can merely exercise its right to terminate the employment relationship before the end of the initial time period and the relationship will end.

B. RIGHT TO TERMINATE AT THE CONCLUSION OF THE PROBATIONARY PERIOD

Employees who pass their probationary periods will continue to work in the positions for which they were hired. However, even at the conclusion of a probationary period, it is unlikely that an employee will have guaranteed employment for any specific period of time. Instead, employers retain varying degrees of termination rights, depending on the nature of their employment relationships, the company policies that govern the continued employment of their employees, and state laws.

Even those employers who retain significant rights to terminate their employees after the conclusion of the probationary period are often reluctant to exercise those rights. Instead employers often utilize a number of methods to manage employee performance, particularly in response to minor infractions. This is especially true for employers who invest a significant amount of time and money in their recruitment processes. In addition, employers recognize that qualified candidates will likely be deterred from applying for positions with employers who have a reputation for making rash termination decisions or set unreasonable expectations for work performance. For this reason, many employers implement progressive disciplinary processes to manage the work performance of their employees.

 **PROGRESSIVE DISCIPLINE**

Although employers have the right to discipline employees, they should pay close attention to the impact the discipline may have on other employees. Employers who earn a reputation for imposing discipline in a discriminatory manner, or for imposing penalties that bear no relationship to the nature of the misconduct, may have a difficult time recruiting and retaining talented employees. In addition, the imposition of harsh discipline may have a detrimental effect on other employees, resulting in poor employee morale or decreased productivity. The resulting situation could become more problematic for the employer than the initial misconduct that the discipline was intended to address.

progressive discipline
imposition of escalating levels of discipline designed to identify and to remedy problematic behavior

Based on these concerns, many employers implement **progressive discipline** policies to manage their employees, which involves the imposition of escalating levels of discipline designed to identify problematic behavior and provide opportunities for it to be modified. Progressive discipline policies are often favored methods of discipline because they are not designed to punish employees for unsatisfactory behavior. Instead, the goal is to educate employees about employer expectations and provide employees with the opportunity to alter their conduct and continue the employment relationship.

Employers that decide to use a progressive discipline process as a performance management tool should consider following the well-established steps.

A. STEPS

Progressive discipline policies include a number of steps linked to increased penalties for repeat offenses of the same or similar behavior the employer determines is unsatisfactory. The most common steps of a progressive discipline process include (1) a counseling session, (2) a verbal warning, (3) a written warning, (4) a suspension, and (5) a termination.[1]

1. COUNSELING

counseling
initial step in the progressive discipline process that places an employee on notice about unacceptable behavior

The first step of the progressive discipline process, a **counseling** session, is actually a bit of a misnomer because, even though it is considered part of the disciplinary process, it is not technically disciplinary in nature. Instead, a counseling session is a conversation between an employee and a supervisor that places the employee on notice of a potential problem and provides possible corrective options. A supervisor might counsel an employee about what would constitute appropriate workplace behavior. For example, if an employee reports to work five minutes late every morning, the supervisor may want to have a counseling session to let the employee know she is expected to report to work at the start of her shift, and any lateness will not be tolerated. The employer may not want to discipline an employee for this behavior but instead want merely to clarify the employee's work hours and the employer's expectation that the employee will report to work at the designated time. In most cases, employees who are counseled about a workplace issue will modify their behavior, which eliminates the need for any further action.

2. VERBAL WARNING

verbal warning
step in the progressive discipline process that involves a conversation with an employee, identifying problematic behavior and placing the employee on notice that if the behavior is not corrected, further discipline will be imposed

If an employee does not modify the problematic behavior after counseling, a **verbal warning** is the next step in the progressive discipline process. This includes a conversation between the employer and employee in which the employer identifies the employee's problematic behavior and makes it clear the behavior must be corrected or further discipline, up to and including termination, might occur.

In contrast to a counseling session, during this meeting the individual issuing the verbal warning should make it clear to the employee that he is being subjected to formal discipline, which will escalate unless the problem is remedied. Since, by definition, a verbal warning is not formally memorialized in writing, it is advisable for the individual issuing the warning to have another supervisor or member of the Human Resources Department present at these discussions so they can, in the event of a dispute, be called to corroborate that a verbal warning was issued. By way of example, an employee who continues to report to work after the designated start time of her regularly scheduled shift could be verbally warned by her supervisor, in the presence of at least one witness, that lateness will not be tolerated and that, if it continues, more serious discipline, up to and including termination, will be imposed.

In some cases employers place a notation of a verbal warning in an employee's personnel file to maintain a record of past discipline. However, employers should ensure that any written document maintained in the file reflects that the warning was verbal, because any memorialized representation of the discipline might be incorrectly construed as a written warning, which would be inconsistent with the level of discipline imposed.

3. WRITTEN WARNING

If an employee is verbally warned about inappropriate behavior and the behavior continues, the employer can move to the next step in the progressive discipline process and issue a **written warning**. At this step in the process, the employer provides the employee with a written document describing the inappropriate conduct, explaining how the situation must be addressed, and making it clear that if the behavior continues, more serious discipline will be imposed.

written warning
step in the progressive discipline process that includes documenting the details of the inappropriate behavior and placing a record of it in an employee's personnel file

The written warning should detail the unacceptable behavior and reference the prior levels of discipline. For example, a written warning might state that the employee was counseled on a particular date about the importance of reporting to work on time, then received a verbal warning, and continued to report to work late. The written warning should be placed in the employee's personnel file as a record of the problematic behavior.

4. SUSPENSION

If a written warning is issued and the behavior continues, a **suspension** is the next step in the progressive discipline process. A suspension involves unpaid time away from work, and the length of the leave will vary depending on, among other things, the severity of the inappropriate conduct.

suspension
step in the progressive discipline process that includes forced unpaid leave from work in response to an employee's problematic conduct

Employers who impose a suspension should provide the affected employee with a written document outlining the reason for the suspension and its terms. It should include the length of the suspension (i.e., one, three, or five days, or perhaps longer depending on the gravity of the offense), and a confirmation that the time away from work will be unpaid. In addition, the letter should reference the prior levels of discipline imposed for the same behavior, and make it clear that if the problem is not remedied, the employee will be subject to further discipline, up to and including termination. A copy of this letter should be maintained in the employee's personnel file as a record of the unacceptable behavior.

5. TERMINATION

The final step in the progressive discipline process is **termination**, which ends the employment relationship. The use or absence of progressive discipline is often a significant consideration in assessing the appropriateness of a termination, in the event the termination is challenged by the employee. If progressive discipline was followed, the employer can use this to defend its position that the termination was appropriate, because it can be used to illustrate that the employee was placed on notice about the problematic behavior and was given the opportunity to remedy it. Similarly, a terminated employee may use the absence of a progressive discipline process to support her position that the termination was inappropriate, because she had no knowledge that the behavior was problematic and was not given the opportunity to remedy it.

B. IMPORTANCE OF FOLLOWING STEPS

Generally speaking, employers should move through each step of the progressive discipline process, provide employees with a clear explanation of the reason for the discipline at each level, and maintain detailed records of each step. Implementing this framework will provide employees with the opportunity to correct unacceptable behavior, which is the ultimate goal because presumably the employer will want to continue to employ the individual as long as the work performance issue is addressed. In addition, if an employee alleges that the discipline was imposed in a discriminatory manner, an employer can defend itself by presenting evidence to illustrate that all employees were subjected to the same process.[2]

C. STEPS SHOULD BE LINKED TO PROBLEMATIC BEHAVIOR

Employers should follow the disciplinary steps for each *type* of offense and avoid moving to the next level of discipline based on prior discipline issued for a different type of unacceptable behavior. For example, if an employee is counseled, verbally warned, and issued a written warning for being late to work, it would likely be inappropriate for an employer to then suspend the employee for poor work performance. Instead, if a new problem arises, the employer should start with the first step in the process, a counseling session, to provide the employee with the opportunity to remedy that particular behavior. In some cases, however, employers may be able to group different types of inappropriate behavior together if a commonality exists between them.

1. BENEFITS OF NARROWLY TAILORED DISCIPLINE

Employers should narrowly tailor the imposed discipline to address the specific problematic conduct. For example, if a data entry clerk makes a number of typographical errors on loan applications, which is a key job responsibility, any resulting discipline should specifically reference this behavior. Under these circumstances, if the employee continues to submit loan applications with errors, the employer could escalate the discipline to the next step. If the discipline is challenged and the employee claims that he was not on notice about the problematic behavior, the employer could support this escalation by referencing the prior discipline, which was imposed to address that specific behavior.

2. BENEFITS OF BROADLY DEFINED DISCIPLINE

Sometimes an employer may elect to impose discipline in a broader fashion by referencing overall job performance and providing specific examples. This could provide an employer with the right to impose a higher level of discipline for more general performance issues, rather than having to start at the first step for an unrelated problem. For example, if an employee inputs incorrect information on loan applications and also has a tendency to miss important deadlines and act inappropriately toward customers, the employer might decide to impose discipline based on poor work performance. Based on this, the employer would have the right to escalate the discipline if any of the behavior referenced in the earlier steps was repeated.

Keep in mind that an employee might have more success challenging broadly defined discipline based on a lack of notice (stating he was unaware that the particular conduct would not be tolerated) than he would have challenging discipline that pinpointed the exact behavior the employee was expected to modify. Thus, the potential benefit of issuing discipline that references broad categories of behavior should be balanced against the benefits of implementing narrowly tailored discipline designed to eliminate any question about the specific behavior an employee must alter to avoid more serious consequences.

D. JUSTIFICATION FOR DEVIATION FROM STEPS IN THE PROCESS

If an employer decides to impose discipline to address specific misconduct, it should adhere to the steps of the progressive discipline process as closely as possible to minimize the potential liability for a discrimination or wrongful termination claim. An employer's adherence to the steps suggests that the employer applied the discipline in a uniform and nondiscriminatory manner.

Despite the benefits of closely adhering to the steps, however, there may be some circumstances that warrant a deviation from this framework. Based on this, employers should determine whether escalation is appropriate on a case-by-case basis, because a blanket rule requiring strict adherence to the steps without consideration of extenuating circumstances might actually be deemed unreasonable and present a problem for an employer if the discipline is challenged. In some instances, extenuating circumstances do warrant a deviation from the usual progression through the steps of an employer's progressive discipline policy.

Put simply, depending on the relevant facts, employers should try to adhere to the steps as closely as possible but also be willing to consider extenuating circumstances suggesting that a deviation would be appropriate, either in the form of skipping a step or repeating a step, and then be prepared to present a justification for any such deviation.

1. SKIPPING OF STEPS

Some inappropriate conduct might warrant imposing a high level of discipline at its first occurrence. For example, if an employee decides to voice his opposition to a new work assignment by assaulting a supervisor, the employer would likely have the right to terminate the employee. The employer would not have an obligation to counsel, warn (in a verbal or written form), or even suspend an employee engaging in such behavior, because it is well established that a physical attack is not an appropriate response to the receipt of an undesirable work assignment. In contrast, a data entry clerk who is terminated for filling out an invoice incorrectly would likely have a strong argument that the presence of a progressive discipline policy would make the termination decision inappropriate. This would be a particularly strong argument if the clerk was not subjected to any prior discipline and was not provided with the opportunity to remedy the behavior.

2. REPETITION OF STEPS

Just as some circumstances justify the skipping of a step in the progressive discipline process, some circumstances warrant the repetition of a step. For example, there may be times when the behavior is not egregious enough to move to the next step but is serious enough that the employer does not want to let it continue unaddressed. There also may be other mitigating circumstances that would warrant the repetition of a step as opposed to the escalation to the next.

a. Nature of Behavior

As a starting point, there might be circumstances in which the next level of discipline seems too harsh. For example, suppose an employee is counseled about the importance of reporting to work on time and issued a verbal and written warning for the behavior. The next step in the process would be a suspension. If the next time the employee reports to work late he presents evidence of extenuating circumstances that caused his lateness, such as involvement in a serious car accident, the employer might decide to issue another written warning to address the behavior (or a lesser form of discipline depending on the specific facts). An employer might make this decision based on a determination that this conduct did not warrant the withholding of the employee's salary in the form of a suspension.

b. Passage of Time Since Prior Misconduct and Imposition of Discipline

Employers should also consider the length of time that passes between the imposition of one level of discipline and the next infraction. For example, suppose an employee was counseled and received a verbal and written warning for lateness, and there was no repeat of the inappropriate behavior for a period of 12 months. Because of the length of time between the incidents, it would be challenging to support a suspension after the next occurrence, even though it is the next step in the progression. Instead, the employer may want to have another counseling session (or issue another verbal or written warning) to reiterate its expectations.

On the other hand, if an employee is issued a written warning for acting in a hostile manner toward an employee and engages in the same behavior a year later, the nature of the behavior might warrant the continued escalation of discipline despite the passage of an extended period of time between the incidents.

E. COMMON CHALLENGES

Employers should also be aware of a number of situations that often form the basis for challenges to discipline imposed pursuant to a progressive discipline policy.

1. LACK OF DOCUMENTATION

Employers will have a difficult time escalating discipline for unacceptable behavior through the progressive discipline process absent any documentation indicating that prior discipline was imposed. Specifically, an employer who indicates that a written warning is appropriate because an employee has been counseled and given a verbal warning about unacceptable behavior should have some proof that the counseling and verbal warning did, in fact, occur. As previously discussed, an employer might ask another supervisor or member of the Human Resources Department to be present at these discussions so they can be called to corroborate that an employee was counseled about a particular behavior or that a verbal warning was issued. In addition, an employer should maintain a record of any counseling sessions or verbal warnings. While formal documentation is preferred, personal notes as to what was said and who was present during the discussions can be sufficient.

2. PASSAGE OF TOO MUCH TIME BETWEEN MISCONDUCT AND IMPOSITION OF DISCIPLINE

Employees often challenge discipline that is imposed a significant amount of time after the occurrence of the problematic behavior by stating that if the behavior was truly intolerable, the employer would have acted quickly to address it. This problem will also surface if an employer imposes one level of discipline, such as a verbal warning, and then allows the behavior to continue for months before moving to the next step in the process.

For example, it will be difficult for an employer to justify a high level of discipline for an employee who regularly arrives ten minutes late for work if the employer knew about the problem and let it continue unaddressed for years. Similarly, if an employee receives a verbal warning for this behavior but then is not subjected to any further discipline over the next six months even though the behavior continued, this would be problematic. In short, the longer an employer waits to impose the initial discipline, or the longer an employer waits to move to the next step in the process, the more challenging it will be to illustrate that the behavior cannot be tolerated and that discipline is warranted. To avoid this potential problem, employers should monitor employee conduct so that unacceptable behavior does not continue unaddressed and should move through the progressive discipline process at a pace that tracks that of the problematic behavior. Keep in mind, however, an employer's failure to enforce a policy does not always mean it has given up its right to do so; it just represents an additional hurdle to overcome to sustain the discipline in the event it is challenged.

3. PASSAGE OF TOO LITTLE TIME BEFORE ESCALATION TO THE NEXT STEP

Just as employers should not move through the steps of the progressive discipline process too slowly, they should not move through the steps too rapidly to avoid a challenge on the basis that the escalation occurred too soon. The rapid escalation of discipline could be problematic because the failure of an employer to provide an employee with adequate time to correct the unacceptable behavior could undermine the remedial value of the steps. Further, if an employer seems to be moving through the process at an accelerated pace, this could be used to suggest that the employer was trying to use the process to cover up the true discriminatory motivation for a termination.

F. POTENTIAL FOR DISCRIMINATION CLAIMS

Because discipline is a term and condition of employment, its imposition constitutes an adverse employment action. Therefore, to minimize the potential for the filing of a discrimination claim, employers should ensure that discipline is imposed in a uniform and nondiscriminatory manner and that employees are on notice that they will be subject to progressive discipline for unacceptable workplace behavior.

1. IMPOSE DISCIPLINE IN A UNIFORM MANNER

On the most basic level, employers will be subject to liability for imposing discipline on only a select group of employees, or for imposing discipline that has a disparate impact on members of a protected class. For example, if an employer counsels one employee for reporting to work 15 minutes late, but issues a verbal warning to another employee who happens to be of a different national origin, it could give rise to a discrimination claim.[3] See Chapter 3, Race, Color, and National Origin Discrimination.

An employer could also face liability for allowing certain employees to engage in specific types of behavior while prohibiting others from engaging in the same conduct. For example, an employer would be prohibited from permitting one employee to report to work 30 minutes late each morning to attend Catholic services, while disciplining another employee who reports late each morning to attend services of a different denomination. This does not mean that an employer must grant all employees who wish to attend religious services the right to report to work late. However, an employer who provides an accommodation for one employee must be prepared to offer a legitimate nondiscriminatory reason for declining to provide the same accommodation to a similarly situated employee. Additionally, because in the example both employees would be requesting an accommodation to attend religious services, the employer would likely have an obligation to accommodate both employees, provided it is not an undue burden.[4] See Chapter 4, Religious Discrimination.

2. PLACE EMPLOYEES ON NOTICE OF PROCESS

Employers that use progressive discipline can minimize potential liability for discriminatory conduct not only by imposing discipline in a uniform manner but also by ensuring that all employees are fully aware they will be subject to progressive discipline for inappropriate or unsatisfactory workplace behavior. One common method employers use to disseminate this information is to include a description of the policy in a company handbook. Employers should outline the parameters of the disciplinary process and be certain to retain the right to deviate from the steps if the circumstances warrant it. Employers should review these policies with all new employees and should reinforce the existence of the policies by reminding employees of them on a regular basis (i.e., annually).

 # PERFORMANCE MANAGEMENT TOOLS AND EMPLOYMENT AT WILL

Most employers find that the use of probationary periods and progressive discipline policies are effective performance management tools that produce desirable results. A probationary period allows an employer to assess an individual's initial suitability for a position, and progressive discipline allows for the isolating and remedying of unacceptable behavior so that performance can be improved and continuous employment can be maintained. Employers who use these tools, however, should be aware of potentially unintended consequences.

As previously discussed, most working individuals are considered employees at will, meaning they can be terminated for any reason at any time, subject to certain limitations. The relevance of the at-will doctrine to the performance management tools discussed here is, that by subjecting an employee to a probationary period or a system of progressive discipline, an employer may be undermining its position that it intended to retain the right to terminate the employee for any reason at any time. See Chapter 18, Employment at Will, for a detailed discussion of this doctrine and the rights of employers to terminate employees working pursuant to it.

A. PROBATIONARY PERIOD

The use of a probationary period for at-will employees raises this concern. By informing new hires they will be subjected to a probationary period, the employer is suggesting that at the end of the time period employees will be entitled to some degree of job security. This perception is what might conflict with the employer's right to terminate an at-will employee with or without cause at any time during the employment relationship.

B. PROGRESSIVE DISCIPLINE

The use of progressive discipline to manage at-will employees raises a similar concern because its fundamental purpose is to assure employees they will have the opportunity to correct problematic behavior and continue their employment. A progressive discipline process represents an employer's commitment to work with employees to address their unacceptable behavior, rather than ending the employment relationship. In contrast, under the at-will doctrine, an employer can terminate an employee with or without cause, and this would include the right to terminate an employee the first time a workplace issue surfaces.

For example, under the at-will doctrine, an employer might have the right to terminate an employee who is ten minutes late for the start of his shift. However, an employer who follows a progressive discipline policy would likely be required to counsel the late employee about his unacceptable lateness, and then proceed through the other steps (verbal warning, written warning, and suspension) before ending the employment relationship.

C. MINIMIZING THE IMPACT

In recognition of the potential inconsistency between an employer's desire to maintain the at-will status of its employees and the use of performance management tools, employers should clearly state the terms of the probationary period and the progressive discipline policy in their company handbooks. Additionally, the handbook should include a disclaimer stating that neither the probationary period nor the progressive discipline policy is intended to alter the at-will relationship between the employer and employee or to undermine any other termination rights that may have been negotiated between the parties.

The disclaimer should be located in a clear and conspicuous place in the handbook. Some employers include the disclaimer in a number of places throughout the handbook to ensure it is not overlooked. Other employers require employees to sign a separate document that includes the disclaimer to be certain that each employee is aware of it and understands that neither the probationary period, the progressive discipline policy, nor any other provision in the handbook is intended to alter the at-will status of the employee.

While neither a separate document nor a disclaimer guarantees that the termination rights of the employer will not be affected by the use of a probationary period or progressive discipline policy, each is a piece of evidence that can be used to illustrate that the employer intended to retain the broad termination rights that were mutually agreed to by the parties. A more detailed discussion about at-will disclaimers and the importance of ensuring they are clear and conspicuous, as well as other methods employers use to emphasize their intention to maintain the at-will status of their employees, appears in Chapter 18, Employment at Will.

PERFORMANCE EVALUATIONS

In addition to using probationary periods and progressive discipline policies as tools to address problematic behavior, some employers use other tools, such as performance evaluations, for this same purpose.

Copyright 2001 by Randy Glasbergen. www.glasbergen.com

"I always give 110% to my job.
40% on Monday, 30% on Tuesday, 20% on
Wednesday, 15% on Thursday, and 5% on Friday."

A. REASONS FOR THE USE OF EVALUATIONS

Performance evaluations are often used by employers to assess the work performance of those they supervise to identify problematic behavior. They can also be used to reward positive workplace contributions by determining whether enhanced terms and conditions of employment should be offered.

performance evaluations
managerial tool used to assess employee work performance by identifying problematic behavior and rewarding positive workplace contributions

1. IDENTIFYING AND REMEDYING PROBLEMATIC BEHAVIOR

The use of a performance evaluation to place an employee on notice about problematic behavior is closely tied to the progressive discipline process. The notice element is important because by identifying problematic behavior, a performance evaluation will give the employee the opportunity to remedy it and avoid formal discipline. Courts place significant value on the remedial component of a performance evaluation. For example, in one instance a court found that an employer's inaccurate characterization of a minority employee's performance as satisfactory (to avoid conflict) was discriminatory because it deprived her of the opportunity to remedy her behavior and continue her employment.[5]

Further, if an employee challenges the imposition of disciplinary action based on a lack of notice, an employer can use a performance evaluation that referenced similar unacceptable behavior to support its position that the employee was aware of the problem and the discipline was warranted.

2. DETERMINING THE APPROPRIATE TERMS AND CONDITIONS OF EMPLOYMENT

In addition to assessing whether an employee is satisfactorily performing his work responsibilities, a performance evaluation can also be used to determine the appropriate compensation for an employee as well as eligibility for desirable work assignments, training programs, and promotional opportunities. When using the evaluation for any of these purposes, however, employers should ensure they do so in a nondiscriminatory manner.

B. WORKPLACE DISCRIMINATION

Although employers view the providing of feedback to employees as a favorable exercise, they should be aware of the potential liability that might materialize if the performance evaluations are used in a discriminatory manner. Federal law makes it unlawful "to discriminate . . . with respect to . . . compensation, terms, conditions, or privileges of employment." Because a performance evaluation can be used as the basis for determining whether an employee will receive enhanced or reduced terms and conditions of employment, the evaluation must be conducted in a uniform and nondiscriminatory manner to avoid potential liability.[6] As one court stated, "We hold that an evaluation that directly disentitles an employee to a raise of any significance is an adverse employment action under Title VII."[7] Based on this, there is a potential for any member of a protected class who is denied a raise (or any other enhancement) based on the contents of a performance evaluation to file a discrimination claim.

1. DISPARATE TREATMENT DISCRIMINATION

The use of performance evaluations can subject employers to disparate treatment claims (for intentional discrimination) if the evaluations are used to intentionally discriminate against members of a protected class. This could result if, for example, only men are provided with evaluations, and those evaluations are used to support the employer's decisions relating to promotional opportunities. It would also be discriminatory to evaluate only minority employees, and then to use the results of the evaluation to justify the imposition of adverse employment decisions or discipline on those employees.

Intentional discrimination may also arise in a less obvious manner, such as when older employees receive more unfavorable reviews than their younger counterparts who appear to perform at the same level. In addition, dramatic changes in the substance of an evaluation, absent a mitigating factor, could suggest a discriminatory motive. For example, if after a new supervisor is hired, the performance evaluations of a minority employee start to identify significant work performance issues and are more critical than the evaluations prepared for nonminority counterparts who acted in a similar manner, it could suggest racially discriminatory behavior, in violation of Title VII.[8]

2. DISPARATE IMPACT DISCRIMINATION

Even if all employees are evaluated, an employer might still be subject to a disparate impact claim (for unintentional discrimination) if the use of the evaluations results in the denial of enhanced terms and conditions of employment for a disproportionate number of employees in a protected class. In these cases the employer should be prepared to defend the use of the evaluations by showing they are administered in a uniform and nondiscriminatory manner and by explaining the business need for them. See Chapter 2, Title VII — the Foundation of Workplace Discrimination Law.

3. RETALIATION

An employer might also be subject to liability for issuing a negative performance appraisal to retaliate against an employee for bringing an issue to the attention of the employer, or for filing, considering filing, or assisting another employee in filing a discrimination claim (or any other type of action) against the employer. For example, in one instance an employer was required to pay an employee $3,000 for issuing what was determined to be a retaliatory performance appraisal.[9]

C. DEFAMATION

Because an employer might communicate unfavorable statements about an employee's work performance within the context of a performance evaluation, some employees have tried to use a negative evaluation as the basis for asserting a defamation claim, which is a cause of action based on the communication of information that harms an individual's reputation.[10] Employees have had minimal success with these types of claims unless the negative information is conveyed with malicious intent. This is because by agreeing to be evaluated (which is often a term and condition of employment), employees are presumed to have consented to allow the communication of any information the evaluation elicits. Some courts have made it clear that employers have a qualified privilege to discuss employee work performance as part of this evaluative process, which means they generally cannot be subject to liability for comments made in that context, provided the comments were not made with a malicious intent.[11]

In the event a claim is filed, employers should recognize that truth is an absolute defense to a defamation claim, so evidence that the negative information conveyed accurately described the work performance of the evaluated employee will prevent the imposition of liability, regardless of whether the employer is also entitled to a qualified privilege. Because defamation claims may also arise within the context of providing employment references for former employees, this cause of action is discussed in greater detail in Chapter 20, Severance and Post-Employment Obligations.

D. LITIGATION VALUE OF EVALUATIONS

Some employers use performance evaluations to establish a written record of the objective, uniform, and nondiscriminatory treatment of their employees. Specifically, some employers conduct performance evaluations to document the specific justifications for enhanced or reduced terms and conditions of employment so they can be prepared to defend their decisions in the event a discrimination claim is filed.

Although using evaluations to ensure benefits are administered in a nondiscriminatory manner is a legitimate business justification for their use, this value may never materialize if the evaluations are conducted in a haphazard manner. In addition, the presentation of a history of positive performance evaluations followed by a negative evaluation and adverse employment decision could support an employee's position that the negative evaluation was merely a pretext (cover-up) for an illegal or improper discriminatory motive.[12] See Chapter 2, Title VII — The Foundation of Workplace Discrimination Law.

Based on this, employers who conduct performance evaluations should ensure the evaluations accurately reflect employee work performance. Evaluations that are inflated could suggest that an employer is attempting to justify the inappropriate promotion of an individual who is not a member of a protected class, to the exclusion of an individual who might be protected.[13] Evaluations that are artificially low could be used to suggest that the employer is using the evaluation as a pretext for a discriminatory decision.

Employers retain broad discretion to determine the content of evaluations. However, to maximize the potential value of an evaluation as part of a defense to a discrimination claim, and to minimize a discrimination claim for the use of the evaluation itself, employers who use them should take steps to ensure the legitimacy of the process. Those evaluations that have the greatest potential to be legally sound are those that are fair measuring tools, which means they are uniformly administered and consistent with a business necessity.[14]

E. FRAMEWORK FOR THE EVALUATION PROCESS

Although there is no generic evaluation process that will prevent an employer from being subject to liability, there are some well-established trends related to their use.

1. TRAIN EVALUATORS

Due to the potential risks associated with the inappropriate use of performance evaluations, the individuals who will be expected to complete them should be trained about the potential claims that could arise from their use. An evaluation usually covers a specific period of time (generally one year), so this training should be conducted well in advance of the time the evaluations will be administered. This will provide managers with the opportunity to track the performance of the employees they will be expected to evaluate, rather than merely focusing on the recent past, which could be problematic if an employee's work performance is not consistent over an extended period of time.

2. ENSURE EVALUATORS HAVE DIRECT KNOWLEDGE OF EMPLOYEE WORK PERFORMANCE

In selecting who will conduct the evaluations, employers should make sure that those individuals who will perform them have direct knowledge of the work of the employees they are expected to evaluate. The evaluators should be familiar with the job descriptions and duties required for each position, as well as the actual work performance of the employees. Because the evaluation can be used to determine whether an employee will receive enhanced terms and conditions of employment (in the form of, for example, a promotion or salary increase), it should reflect the evaluator's direct knowledge of the employee's work. In one case a court determined that the evaluation process was a "sham" intended to cover up illegal motives, because the evaluators did not have significant direct knowledge about the employee's work and did not seem to have even reviewed the personnel file.[15]

3. EVALUATIONS AS EMPLOYMENT TESTS AND SELECTION PROCEDURES

Although employers are not legally required to conduct performance evaluations, those who do so must understand that the EEOC considers performance appraisals a type of employment test and selection procedure. Therefore, the laws that govern the use of pre-employment tests apply to performance evaluations, which means, among other things, that the evaluations must be administered in a uniform and nondiscriminatory manner.[16] See Chapter 11, Pre-Employment Testing.

a. Employees Evaluated

Uniformity does not require employers to evaluate all employees, but employers should have a business justification for deciding which job classifications will be evaluated. It would be problematic to evaluate female employees, but not male employees, or to evaluate some minority groups, and not others. In addition, because the evaluations may be used to determine whether salary increases are warranted, it could be problematic to evaluate some higher-level employees and not lower-level employees if the employees working in those positions are not diverse, meaning the absence of the evaluation process in one group could have a disparate impact on members of a protected class.

b. Substance of Evaluations

Once it is decided who will be evaluated, employers must decide what types of factors will be used to assess whether work performance is satisfactory. Although there is no universal form used to evaluate employee job performance, most evaluations consider a combination of objective and subjective factors. Objective considerations are favored, but there is a recognition that subjective considerations are also likely to be part of the evaluation process.

i. Objective Considerations

objective considerations
factors reviewed in performance evaluations that are based on measurable data

Due to the potential for an evaluation to be introduced as evidence in a judicial proceeding, to the extent possible, evaluations should be based on **objective considerations**, which are criteria that are based on measurable data. The nature of what is measured will be based upon the requirements of the individual's job and may include measurable components such as the number of units produced or number of products sold. While it is usually easier to objectively evaluate the job performance of employees working in lower-skilled jobs, there is a recognition that this measure of objectivity becomes more challenging as employees move into higher-skilled positions.[17]

ii. Subjective Considerations

subjective considerations
factors reviewed in performance evaluations that are based on the opinion or personal perspective of the evaluator

Not every job task or position is conducive to an objective measurement, and most performance evaluations include some **subjective considerations** that are based on the opinion or personal perspectives of the evaluators.

The use of subjective considerations in a performance evaluation is less desirable than objective measurements because it is more difficult to show that such factors are true measures of work performance and not the result of improper motivations. Although courts recognize the necessity for the use of subjective considerations, evaluations that include specific illustrative examples to support negative comments are considered more credible than those that rely on generalizations. Based on this, all comments should be as fact specific as possible. Additionally, to the extent possible, evaluators should attempt to secure independent verification of any subjective conclusions. For example, to the extent time sheets, invoices, customer evaluations, or other documents support the subjective comments of the evaluator, they should be included in the evaluative process.

c. Application of Standards

Once an employer decides which factors will be considered when conducting the evaluations, the next step is to ensure that the standards are uniformly applied. This uniformity requirement goes beyond who receives an evaluation — it also requires the application of the same standards to all employees. For example, an employer is prohibited from determining that a certain level of performance is satisfactory for its male employees, but the same level of performance is less than satisfactory for its female employees because they have the potential to perform better.[18]

4. LOGISTICS

Employers should inform their employees of their intent to conduct performance evaluations, the general time frame when the evaluations will occur, and how the results will be used. After evaluations are completed, employers should discuss and explain the results with each employee and request each individual to sign a copy of the evaluation to acknowledge its receipt and that the discussion occurred. Employees should also be given a copy of the evaluation along with the opportunity to submit a written response to any of the information it contains.

This response, along with the evaluation, should be kept in the employee's personnel file.

In some instances an employer might decide to alter the working conditions of an employee as a result of a performance evaluation. Although this is permissible, employers must remember that because such decisions affect terms and conditions of employment, they, too, must be made in a nondiscriminatory and uniform manner.

 **WORK SCHEDULES AND ASSIGNMENTS**

The assignment of work schedules and responsibilities is a term and condition of employment and therefore could be the basis for the filing of a workplace discrimination claim. Based on this, employers must pay attention to both the intentional and unintentional consequences of work schedules and assignments, particularly if such decisions are not made pursuant to the terms of a structured process.

A. WORK HOURS

Because the start and end time of an employee's shift is a condition of employment, the hours cannot be assigned based on an individual's membership in a protected class. For example, an employer could be subject to liability for regularly assigning minorities to the less desirable overnight shift while assigning nonminorities to the more desirable day shifts. This is not to say, however, that an employer may not have a business need for shifts to start and end at a specific time. If it does have a business need for specific starting and ending times, the employer has the right to assign employees to undesirable shifts as long as the scheduling decisions are based on uniform and nondiscriminatory factors.

B. WORK ASSIGNMENTS

The same rationale applies to the type of work that is assigned to employees, because it, too, must be assigned in a nondiscriminatory manner. For example, an employer could be held liable for discrimination for assigning minorities to "back of the house" jobs such as dishwashers and busboys, and for refusing to consider minorities for promotions to the more desirable "front of the house" positions, such as maître d's, in favor of nonminorities who are less qualified and have less seniority.[19] Other work assignments could subject an employer to liability for these same reasons. For example, employees who work on commission could file a claim for discrimination if potential client lists are distributed in a discriminatory manner and because of that members of protected classes earn less than nonmembers.

C. OVERTIME

Although employers have the right to determine the work schedules of their employees, issues may also arise if the shifts most likely to include opportunities for earning additional compensation through overtime work are assigned in a nonuniform or discriminatory manner. This does not mean that an employer has an obligation to offer the same amount of overtime to all employees, because there may be business justifications that support differential treatment. For example, if the work performed during overtime hours is tied to the employer's most well-established clients, the employer might assign the work to its most talented employees. Such decisions may be problematic, however, if the members of a protected class can illustrate that the reason they are not the top performers is a result of the employer's failure to provide training and promotional opportunities on a uniform and nondiscriminatory basis.

VI TRAINING

Many employers provide training to their employees, and this can benefit both parties. Employers have an incentive to invest in training because it may enhance employee work performance, which, in turn, could enhance the employer's business. In addition, offering training might be an effective tool to recruit and retain qualified employees.

Employees will also benefit from training because it will provide them with opportunities to update and enhance their own skill sets, and increase the likelihood they will be qualified for career advancement opportunities. Training constitutes a term and condition of employment, and it, just like all other terms and conditions of employment, must be offered in a uniform and nondiscriminatory manner.

A. ACCESS

The federal prohibition against workplace discrimination applies to access and enrollment in training programs. In addition, some state laws actually specify that employers must provide employees with equal rights to apply for, be admitted to, and participate in training programs, apprenticeship programs, on-the-job training programs, or any other retraining programs, without consideration of whether an individual is a member of a protected class.[20] The purpose of these laws is to ensure that all employees are given equal access to opportunities to enhance their skills and qualify for promotional opportunities.

B. QUALIFICATIONS

Employers should also ensure that any tests used to determine whether an employee is granted the opportunity to participate in a training program are not discriminatory.

Employers must not discriminate intentionally (i.e., through disparate treatment), such as by requiring female applicants to take a strength test prior to being admitted to a training program but not subjecting male applicants to the same requirement.

Employers must also pay close attention to any admissions tests that have the potential to result in a disparate impact on a member of a protected class. Under these circumstances, an employer would have an obligation to ensure that there is not a less discriminatory alternative that could serve the same purpose. In one case a large employer and the labor union that represented its employees paid more than $8 million to settle a suit filed by a group of Black/African-American employees, who claimed that a test required to gain access to an apprenticeship program had a disparate impact on minorities. The court determined that the test was discriminatory because the company continued to use the test that resulted in the disproportionate impact on minorities even after the development of a less discriminatory test that would satisfy the employer's needs.[21]

PROMOTIONS

As employees successfully complete training, their employers may want to reward them by providing them with opportunities for career advancement. This might include offering promotions, which could include new job responsibilities, better working conditions, and enhanced compensation. Title VII prohibits employers from considering membership in a protected class when making decisions about such promotional opportunities.[22] Some states explicitly prohibit discrimination as it relates to promotions, and some provide even greater details such as prohibiting the denial of a promotion based on a sincerely held religious belief that might prevent an individual from working on certain days considered holy.[23]

The same practices employers use to minimize the potential for discrimination claims relating to the initial hiring process should be implemented to minimize the potential for discrimination claims relating to promotions.

A. APPLICATION FOR PROMOTION

Employers who require employees to submit written materials or participate in an interview to be considered for a promotion should recognize that the same rules that apply to the hiring process apply to the process used to determine who will be provided with promotional opportunities. For example, just as employers should not request an applicant's age, date of birth, or national origin when filling a position unless the information is necessary to evaluate his candidacy, employers should not request this type of information as part of any other evaluative process that occurs during an individual's employment—which includes a process to determine an employee's eligibility for a promotion.[24] Employers are presumed to use all of the gathered information to reach decisions about granting enhanced terms and conditions of employment, and by requesting information about an employee's membership in a protected class, it will be presumed that the information is being considered in the decision-making process in violation of Title VII and other anti-discrimination laws.[25] See Chapter 10, Collection of Information: The Application and Interview.

B. CUSTOMER PREFERENCE

Just as an employer is prohibited from refusing to hire an applicant of a certain race (or a member of any other protected class) based on its own prejudices or the prejudices of its customers, employers are prohibited from making decisions about promotions based on these considerations. An employer would be prohibited from denying a promotion to a practicing Buddhist, who was the most qualified applicant for a position, in favor of a practicing Christian based on a belief that the Christian applicant would be able to secure stronger working relationships with the majority of the firm's clients, who also happened to be Christians.[26] Such discriminatory decisions based on customer preference can result in significant financial penalties. For example, in one case an employer settled a discrimination claim by agreeing to pay $45,000 for refusing to promote minority employees based on the CEO's position that the company was situated in "redneck country" and its clients would not work with a Black/African-American account manager.[27]

KEY TERMS

- ✓ counseling
- ✓ objective considerations
- ✓ performance evaluations
- ✓ probationary period
- ✓ progressive discipline
- ✓ subjective considerations
- ✓ suspension
- ✓ termination
- ✓ verbal warning
- ✓ written warning

DISCUSSION QUESTIONS

Explain your response to each of the following questions with the understanding that in some cases there is no right or wrong answer. If you cannot make an informed decision with the facts provided, indicate the nature and significance of the additional information you would need. For the purposes of these questions, you can assume that the employers and employees mentioned below are covered by Title VII and other relevant federal workplace anti-discrimination laws.

1. What is a probationary period and why might it be used by an employer?
2. Explain the most common steps used in a progressive discipline process, and explain why the steps might not be strictly followed.

3. Explain the benefits of the use of performance evaluations. Provide an example of a set of facts that might subject an employer to liability for the misuse of evaluations. Are there ways employers can minimize their potential liability?

4. Jen is an employer who decides it is too much trouble to subject employees to a probationary period or progressive discipline. Since she only hires at-will employees, she believes she can just terminate any of her employees, for any reason, at any time. What do you think?

5. Steve is an employer who decides he does not want to implement a progressive discipline policy because it is a rigid system, and he wants to retain flexibility to discipline his employees. What do you think?

6. Duffy is an employee who is terminated for serious misconduct. As he is escorted from the building, he waves a page from the company handbook that indicates the employer is committed to using progressive discipline, says he will consider himself counseled about the inappropriateness of his behavior, and says he will report to work tomorrow at the start of his shift. What do you think about Duffy's statement?

7. Heidi receives counseling, a verbal warning, a written warning, and suspension for her poor work performance, and is then terminated. The day after her termination she files a discrimination claim against her employer, Bill, alleging she was terminated because she was a woman. Bill says he is not concerned about the claim because the manager's use of progressive discipline will provide a "rock solid" defense to such a claim. What do you think?

8. Nancy, Heidi's direct supervisor, overhears Bill's comments in the question immediately above, and reminds him that last week she actually gave Heidi a performance evaluation that identified her problematic behavior. Nancy said the evaluation would be further evidence that the termination was not discriminatory. What do you think?

9. David is a restaurant owner who settled a discrimination lawsuit by agreeing to actively recruit minority employees. Soon after the agreement, he learns about a valuable three-week training opportunity for a new cooking technique that is expected to "revolutionize" the restaurant business. David wants to minimize the potential liability for any further workplace discrimination claims, so he implements a uniform policy allowing anyone to use vacation time to cover the three-week period to attend the training sessions. He also decides that those employees who complete the training will be eligible for promotional opportunities. What do you think about this idea?

ENDNOTES

1. Some disciplinary policies are more creative and deviate from these traditional steps. Such policies may impose fines, recapture commissions, or limit participation in certain incentive programs as part of the escalation of discipline.

2. *See generally* U.S. Equal Employment Opportunity Commn., EEOC Compl. Man. § 13-III (National Origin Discrimination) (available at *http://www.eeoc.gov/policy/docs/ national-origin.html*).

3. *See id.*

4. EEOC Compl. Man. § 12 (Religious Discrimination) (July 22, 2008) (available at *http:// www.eeoc.gov/policy/docs/religion.html*).

5. *Vaughn v. Edel*, 918 F.2d 517 (5th Cir. 1990).

6. *See* 42 U.S.C. § 2000e-2(a)(1); *see* U.S Equal Employment Opportunity Commn., Questions and Answers: Compliance Manual Section on Compensation Discrimination (available at *http://www.eeoc.gov/policy/docs/qanda-compensation.html*).

7. *Gillis v. Georgia Dept. of Corr.*, 400 F.3d 883, 888 (11th Cir. 2005).

8. *See Thomas v. Eastman Kodak Co.*, 183 F.3d 38 (1st Cir. 1999).

9. *Alvarado v. Department of the Navy*, EEOC Appeal No. 0120081910 (July 17, 2008); *see* Office of Federal Operations, 19 Digest Equal Empl. Opportunity L. No. 3 (Summer 2008) (available at *http://www.eeoc.gov/federal/digest/xix-3.cfm*).

10. *See, e.g., Bratt v. International Bus. Machs. Corp.*, 467 N.E.2d 126 (Mass. 1984) (holding communication of an unfavorable review does not support a defamation claim); *Shamley v. ITT Corp.*, 869 F.2d 167, 173 (2d Cir. 1989) (holding "[e]valuations of employees made by their supervisors enjoy a qualified privilege in defamation actions").

11. *Shamley v. ITT Corp.*, 869 F.2d 167, 173 (2d Cir. 1989).

12. *See Green v. National Sci. Found.*, EEOC Appeal No. 01A33221 (Feb. 16, 2006).

13. U.S. Equal Employment Opportunity Commn., Best Practices for Employers and Human Resources/EEO Professionals, How to Prevent Race and Color Discrimination (available at *http://www.eeoc.gov/eeoc/initiatives/e-race/upload/bestpractices-employers.pdf*).

14. *See* Kathleen K. Lundquist, Ph.D., Co-Founder and President of APT, Inc., Statement at U.S. Equal Employment Opportunity Commn. Meeting (May 16, 2007) (regarding Employment Testing and Screening) (available at *http://www.eeoc.gov/eeoc/meetings/ archive/5-16-07/lundquist.html*).

15. *Woodson v. Scott Paper Co.*, 109 F.3d 913 (3d Cir.), *cert. denied*, 522 U.S. 914 (1997).

16. U.S. Equal Employment Opportunity Commn., Employment Tests and Selection Procedures (available at *http://www.eeoc.gov/policy/docs/factemployment_procedures.html*).

17. *See generally* U.S. Equal Employment Opportunity Commn., Transcr. Commission Meeting (May 16, 2007) (available at *http://www.eeoc.gov/eeoc/meetings/archive/5-16-07/ transcript.html*).

18. U.S. Equal Employment Opportunity Commn., Questions and Answers About Race and Color Discrimination in Employment (available at *http://www.eeoc.gov/policy/docs/ qanda_race_color.html*).

19. *EEOC v. Restaurant Daniel*, No. 07-6845 (S.D.N.Y. Aug. 2, 2007); *see also* EEOC Compl. Man. § 13-III (National Origin Discrimination) (available at *http://www.eeoc.gov/policy/ docs/national-origin.html*).

20. *See, e.g.*, N.Y. Exec. Law § 296(1-a)(b) (It is unlawful for an employer to "deny or withhold from any person because of race, creed, color, national origin, sexual orientation, military status, sex, age, disability, or marital status, the right to be admitted to participate in a guidance program, an apprenticeship training program, on-the-job training program, executive training program, or other occupational training or re-training program. . . .").

21. *EEOC v. Ford Motor Co.*, No. 1:04-CV-00845 (S.D. Ohio June 16, 2005); *see also* Press Release, U.S. Equal Employment Opportunity Commn., EEOC, Ford, UAW, Class Members Voice Approval of Landmark Race Discrimination Settlement (June 1, 2005) (available at *http://www.eeoc.gov/press/6-1-05.html*).

22. EEOC Compl. Man. § 13-III (National Origin Discrimination) (available at *http://www .eeoc.gov/policy/docs/national-origin.html*).

23. *See, e.g.*, N.Y. Exec. Law § 296(10)(a) ("It shall be an unlawful discriminatory practice for any employer . . . to impose upon a person as a condition of obtaining or retaining employment, including opportunities for promotion, advancements or transfers, any terms or conditions that would require such person to violate or forgo a sincerely held

practice of his or her religion, including but not limited to the observance of any particular day or days or any portion thereof as a Sabbath or other holy day in accordance with the requirements of his or her religion. . . .").

24. 29 C.F.R. § 1625.5.

25. *See generally* EEOC Compl. Man. § 13-III (National Origin Discrimination) (available at *http://www.eeoc.gov/policy/docs/national-origin.html*).

26. *See, e.g., Noyes v. Kelly Servs., Inc.*, 488 F.3d 1163 (9th Cir. 2007); EEOC Compl. Man. § 12 (Religious Discrimination) (July 22, 2008) (available at *http://www.eeoc.gov/policy/docs/religion.html*).

27. *EEOC v. Frontier Materials Corp.*, No. H-03-856 (S.D. Tex. Mar. 2, 2004).

Workplace Harassment

15

Chapter Objectives

This chapter explores workplace harassment that is linked to an individual's membership in a protected class, with a particular emphasis on sexual harassment and claims based on religion, national origin, and disabilities. Claims for *quid pro quo* harassment, and those based on a hostile work environment, are discussed. In addition, the text explains the type of conduct that might subject an employer to liability and discusses how employers can minimize these potential risks.

After completing this chapter, students should have a fundamental understanding of workplace harassment and the types of conduct that could support such a claim. Upon mastering the main objectives of this chapter students should be able to

- identify the types of conduct that would rise to the level of workplace harassment;
- distinguish between *quid pro quo* and hostile work environment harassment claims;
- identify sources of risk for the employer by listing the categories of people for whom an employer might be subject to liability for harassment; and
- explain how an employer can minimize the risk of a harassment claim and bolster its defense in the event one does materialize.

INTRODUCTION

Workplace harassment might constitute employment discrimination in violation of Title VII, the Americans with Disabilities Act (ADA), or the Age Discrimination in Employment Act (ADEA), depending on the nature of the harassing behavior. Most people are aware of claims relating to sexual harassment, but under federal anti-discrimination laws, harassment can also be alleged based on race, color, sex, religion, national origin, age, and disability. The EEOC reports that in 2009 it received 30,641 charges of harassment under Title VII, which could be based on an individual's membership in any protected class under the statute. In the same year it resolved 28,100 charges and recovered $80.5 million for aggrieved parties, which does not include monetary benefits obtained through litigation.[1]

SEXUAL HARASSMENT

A. SEX DISCRIMINATION UNDER TITLE VII

sexual harassment
form of sex discrimination under Title VII that occurs when individuals are subjected to unwelcome sexual advances that impact their working conditions

Title VII prohibits discrimination based on sex, which includes **sexual harassment** that occurs when individuals are subject to unwelcome sexual advances that impact their working conditions.[2] The Supreme Court has specifically held that "[u]nwelcome sexual advances, requests for sexual favors, and other verbal or physical conduct of a sexual nature constitute sexual harassment when this conduct explicitly or implicitly affects an individual's employment, unreasonably interferes with an individual's work performance, or creates an intimidating, hostile, or offensive work environment."[3] In 2009 the EEOC received 12,696 charges of sexual harassment under Title VII. In the same year the Agency resolved 11,948 charges and recovered $51.5 million for aggrieved parties, which does not include monetary benefits obtained through litigation.[4]

B. IDENTITY OF HARASSER AND VICTIM

Sexual harassment occurs in a number of forms. The harasser may be a supervisor, a co-worker, an agent of the employer, or a nonemployee such as a customer, an employee of another business with whom the employee must work, or a vendor entering the workplace to provide a service to an employer.[5] The harasser may be a man or a woman, and the victim does not have to be a member of the opposite sex. Instead, the relevant issue is whether the harassment is "because of . . . sex."[6] In addition, the victim may be anyone impacted by the offensive conduct and does not necessarily have to be the person against whom the conduct is directed.[7]

C. EXTENT OF WRONGFUL CONDUCT

To determine whether conduct rises to the level of sexual harassment, courts impose a "reasonable person" standard, which usually requires more than one isolated incident for the conduct to be actionable.[8] A particularly egregious incident, such as an intentional touching of the alleged victim's intimate body area, however, might be sufficiently offensive to constitute sexual harassment.[9]

Two distinct types of sexual harassment are actionable under Title VII. The first is *quid pro quo* harassment, which is the conditioning of a favorable employment

decision upon the granting of sexual favors or the imposition of adverse consequences for the refusal to grant sexual favors. The second type of harassment is
a hostile work environment, which is the creation of an atmosphere so intolerable a
reasonable person is not expected to endure it.

D. *QUID PRO QUO* HARASSMENT

Quid pro quo is the Latin term for "this for that," and this type of harassment
occurs when a person with power imposes a **tangible employment action** on a
subordinate because of the latter's compliance with or refusal to comply with a
request for a sexual favor.[10] A tangible employment action refers to conduct that
represents a significant change in an individual's employment status.

A decision relating to a hiring, firing, promotion, or demotion would constitute a tangible employment action, as would an undesirable work reassignment, or
a decision that causes a significant change in benefits or compensation.[11] Each
exemplifies the results of a decision that, when made in exchange for the granting
of sexual favors (or the refusal to grant such favors) would constitute *quid pro quo*
sexual harassment. For example, both an individual who is demoted in response
to her refusal to grant her supervisor a sexual favor, and an individual who is
informed she will not receive a promotion unless she responds favorably to her
supervisor's sexual advances, could file a *quid pro quo* sexual harassment claim.[12]

quid pro quo harassment
Latin term meaning "this
for that," which, within the
context of sex discrimination,
refers to harassment that
occurs when an individual is
subjected to a tangible
employment action in response
to either granting or refusing to
grant a favor of a sexual nature

tangible employment action
change in employment status
such as a promotion,
termination, or an undesirable
reassignment, which could be
the basis for a harassment
claim

E. HOSTILE WORK ENVIRONMENT

The second type of sexual harassment claim is related to the creation of a **hostile
work environment**, which encompasses an atmosphere consisting of "unwelcome
sexual advances, requests for sexual favors, and other verbal or physical conduct of
a sexual nature" that creates an atmosphere so intolerable a reasonable person is
not expected to endure it.[13] Sexual comments, sexual electronic communications,
comments about physical attributes, offensive touching and gesturing, and posting
of pornographic pictures in the workplace are examples of behavior that could
create a hostile work environment.

hostile work environment
within the context of sex
discrimination, refers to
harassment that occurs when
an individual is subjected to
pervasive unwelcome sexual
advances, requests for sexual
favors, and other verbal or
physical conduct of a sexual
nature that creates an
atmosphere so intolerable a
reasonable person is not
expected to endure it

1. ISOLATED OR ANNOYING COMMENTS
ARE INSUFFICIENT TO SUPPORT A CLAIM

A hostile work environment exists if the negative atmosphere is "so pervasive that it
materially alters the terms and conditions of employment."[14] To sustain a sexual
harassment claim based on a hostile work environment, an individual must be subjected to an intimidating and offensive sexual atmosphere, and this is distinguishable
from rude or annoying conversations or isolated jokes (unless egregious), which,
although not desirable, would not be sufficient to support the existence of such a
claim.[15] The Supreme Court has also warned that "mere utterances of an . . . epithet
which engenders offensive feelings in an employee" would not rise to the level of the
establishment of a hostile work environment.[16] Instead, the determination requires a

case-by-case analysis to determine whether the workplace behavior could "reasonably be perceived, and is perceived, as hostile or abusive."[17]

Courts examine such factors as the frequency and severity of the discriminatory conduct, whether it is physically threatening or humiliating, and whether it unreasonably interferes with an employee's work performance to determine whether the environment is hostile or whether it is merely an annoying situation that must be tolerated.[18]

2. BEHAVIOR MUST BE UNWELCOME

Once an offensive environment is found to exist, the second key component of a hostile work environment claim is a showing that the behavior was unwelcome.[19] The establishment of the unwelcome nature of conduct is often a challenge, as courts have recognized that there is a distinction between sexual advances that are "invited, uninvited-but-welcome, offensive-but-tolerated, and flatly rejected."[20] One court tried to clarify the issue by stating that unwelcome behavior is that which the individual "did not solicit or incite . . . [and] the employee regarded . . . as undesirable or offensive."[21]

a. Participation in Behavior Is Not Determinative

An individual's participation in the behavior is not sufficient to establish that the conduct was welcome. This is because there may be a number of explanations for the participation, such as the fear of negative repercussions for noncompliance.[22] Therefore, when confronted with conflicting evidence as to whether particular conduct was unwelcome, courts consider the *totality* of the circumstances and evaluate each situation on a case-by-case basis.[23]

b. Contemporaneous Complaint Is Not Determinative

Another relevant inquiry relating to whether conduct was unwelcome is whether the individual reported it soon after it occurred. Although an individual who raises the issue will have a stronger case if he can show he reported the behavior soon after it occurred, this is not a necessary element of a claim because there could be a number of explanations for a decision not to do so, such as the fear of retaliation from the alleged aggressor. Based on this, the relevance of whether the victim has complained will vary, depending upon "the nature of the sexual advances and the context in which the alleged incidents occurred."[24]

 OTHER FORMS OF DISCRIMINATORY HARASSMENT

Although most individuals associate harassment claims with incidents of a sexual nature, both *quid pro quo* and hostile work environment claims can be filed under Title VII (for discrimination based on sex, religion, race, national origin, and color) and other federal anti-discrimination laws.

This extension of actionable forms of harassment under Title VII was confirmed by a Supreme Court decision stating that "[w]hen the workplace is permeated with discriminatory intimidation, ridicule, and insult that is sufficiently severe or pervasive to alter the conditions of the victim's employment and create an abusive working environment, Title VII is violated."[25] Other forms of actionable harassment can be filed under the particular federal law that protects the individual who is subjected to the inappropriate conduct. Claims based on disability harassment can be filed under the ADA, and claims based on age harassment would be filed under the ADEA.[26]

The analysis for all types of harassment is essentially the same. For *quid pro quo* harassment, the threshold question is whether a decision to impose a desirable or adverse working condition is based on an individual's agreement to engage in or refrain from a particular behavior that is linked to her membership in any protected class. For a hostile work environment claim, the threshold question is whether an individual's status as a member (or perceived member) of a protected class results in the creation of a work environment that would be intolerable and offensive to a reasonable person.[27] Because a harassment claim can be filed based on an individual's membership in *any* protected class, a discussion of a few examples is warranted here. See Chapter 2, Title VII — The Foundation of Employment Discrimination Law; Chapter 7, Disability Discrimination; and Chapter 6, Age Discrimination, respectively.

A. HARASSMENT BASED ON NATIONAL ORIGIN

Harassment based on national origin is common and represents the primary reason for the filing of claims for national origin discrimination under Title VII. Between 1993 and 2003 the number of claims filed rose from 1,383 to 2,719, and in 2002, 30% of the claims based on national origin discrimination included a component of harassment.[28] As with all other forms of harassment, the conduct used to support a claim based on a hostile work environment based on an individual's national origin must be so pervasive and severe that a reasonable person would not be expected to tolerate it.

For claims based on national origin discrimination, the inappropriate conduct might be ethnic slurs, jokes, graffiti, or other behavior related to an individual's place of birth, cultural customs or dress, or foreign accent. The relevant considerations include whether the conduct was threatening or intimidating, the number of times the conduct occurred, and whether the employer responded in a timely and appropriate manner when the harassment was discovered. Consistent with other forms of harassment, the individual responsible for creating the intolerable work environment could be a co-worker, supervisor, or nonemployee such as a customer or vendor conducting business in the workplace.[29]

B. HARASSMENT BASED ON RELIGION

A claim for religious harassment could be filed under Title VII if an employee (1) is compelled to abandon, alter, or adopt a particular religious practice as a condition of employment; or (2) is subjected to unwelcome statements of a religious nature that rise to the level of the creation of a hostile work environment.[30]

1. *QUID PRO QUO* HARASSMENT

Religious discrimination in the form of *quid pro quo* harassment might arise from conduct such as requiring participation in a religious activity (for example, saying a particular prayer at the beginning of each workday with co-workers) in exchange for continued employment. It could also include an individual's agreement not to leave work during the busy time of the day to attend a church service, in exchange for continued employment.

Note that employers do retain some rights to impose reasonable job-related restrictions on an individual's right to engage in religious practices, depending on the burden it places on the operation of the employer's business. The employer's obligation with respect to an employee's request for work relief to engage in a religious belief or practice is limited to providing a reasonable accommodation provided it does not impose an undue burden on the employer.[31] See Chapter 4, Religious Discrimination.

2. HOSTILE WORK ENVIRONMENT

To sustain a religious discrimination claim in the form of a hostile work environment, an individual must show that the harassment was (1) based on the individual's religion or participation in a religious practice; (2) unwelcome; and (3) sufficiently severe or pervasive to alter the conditions of employment by creating an intimidating, hostile, or offensive work environment.[32] Hostile work environment harassment might arise from repeated, pervasive, and egregious jokes of a religious nature directed toward an employee of a particular faith by a group of employees. In addition, religious expression that is directed toward other employees (such as passing out religious pamphlets) might constitute religious harassment, particularly if co-workers indicate that being offered such information is unwelcome.[33] See Chapter 4, Religious Discrimination.

C. HARASSMENT BASED ON A DISABILITY

An employer might be liable for workplace harassment under the ADA if the offensive conduct relates to an individual's disability and rises to the level of severe or pervasive conduct that creates a hostile or abusive work environment. As with all forms of harassment, rude or offensive comments will not be sufficient to establish liability. Instead, the alleged victim must be subjected to conduct that would be perceived as hostile and abusive to a reasonable person.[34] See Chapter 7, Disability Discrimination.

 IV **EMPLOYER LIABILITY**

The presence of workplace harassment can result in significant liability for an employer who knows or should have known about the problematic behavior and does not prevent its continuance. In addition, an employer may be directly or indirectly responsible for the harassing conduct of its employees.

A. EXTENT OF POTENTIAL LIABILITY

Employers must recognize the potential for significant liability for participating in conduct that constitutes harassment or for failing to address the problematic behavior engaged in by individuals under their direction and control. For example, one nationally known restaurant agreed to settle a harassment claim by paying $2.2 million to its female, Black/African-American, and Hispanic employees. In that instance, the EEOC charged the restaurant with racial and national origin harassment (including directing epithets toward Black/African-American and Hispanic employees and ridiculing Hispanics for their accents) as well as sexual harassment (including graphic comments, demands for sexual favors, and unwelcome groping).[35]

In another case, a company was charged with racial harassment for subjecting a Black/African-American employee to a hostile work environment by calling him "Cornelius," an ape character in the movie "Planet of the Apes," as well as retaliating against other employees who objected to the behavior.[36] Another employer settled a hostile work environment claim for $600,000 after being charged with displaying Nazi symbols such as swastikas, racially charged graffiti such as nooses, and KKK videos at its worksite.[37]

B. LIABILITY FOR SUPERVISOR CONDUCT

If a supervisor engages in harassing behavior that materializes into an adverse employment decision (such as reassigning an employee to a less desirable shift based on her refusal to have a drink with her supervisor), the employer could be subject to liability for the unlawful behavior.[38] Under some circumstances an employer might be able to avoid liability, however, by proving that (1) it exercised reasonable care to prevent and to correct the harassing behavior, and (2) the employee failed to take advantage of the processes the employer made available to address these situations.[39]

C. NEGLIGENCE CLAIM FOR THE FAILURE TO ACT

If an employee brings a claim of harassment to the attention of a supervisor and the employer fails to respond, the employer may be held responsible under a negligence theory for failing to exercise an appropriate level of care to address the situation. Further, if the employer knew or should have known about the harassment engaged in by a co-worker, an agent of the employer, a vendor entering the workplace to provide a service to the employer, or another nonemployee (which would include a customer, or an employee of another business with whom the employee must work), and failed to act to remedy the behavior, the employer also could be held responsible for the unlawful harassing conduct.[40]

D. MINIMIZATION OF RISK

There are a number of things an employer can do to minimize both the potential for the filing of a harassment claim and the size of a potential damage award in the event one is imposed.

1. ESTABLISH AN ANTI-HARASSMENT POLICY

Because employers can face significant liability for the harassing acts of their supervisors and employees, they should establish and communicate a specific anti-harassment policy to all employees to make it clear that such conduct will not be tolerated. The most effective policies clearly define the types of conduct that constitute harassment, provide specific examples of the unlawful conduct, and advise all employees the behavior will not be tolerated.

The policy should also clearly state that an employee will not be subject to any adverse consequences for alerting the employer to the unlawful behavior.[41] This is significant because Title VII's prohibition against workplace harassment based on membership in a protected class, as well as the prohibition in other federal anti-discrimination laws, includes a prohibition against **retaliation**, which is the imposition of an adverse employment decision on an individual for, among other things, opposing an unlawful employment practice.

retaliation
an employer's imposition of an adverse employment decision in response to an employee's assertion of rights, which includes opposing an unlawful employment practice under Title VII or another anti-discrimination law

2. ESTABLISH A PROCESS TO ADDRESS COMPLAINTS

Once an employer establishes and implements a policy that prohibits workplace harassment, it should establish a process that employees can access if the policy is violated. This is critical because an employer's demonstration that it established a process for the investigation of harassment complaints and that the alleged victim failed to utilize the process could be a significant component in an employer's defense. The EEOC has said that if an employee fails to use the established complaint procedure, the employer will not be responsible for the supervisor's harassing behavior provided (1) the harassment did not result in a tangible employment action, and (2) fear of retaliation was not the reason the employee did not utilize the procedure.[42] By the same token, the absence of an anti-harassment policy or the absence of a process to obtain relief can be used by an individual to bolster his harassment claim.

3. TRAIN SUPERVISORS

Employers should educate their supervisors about the types of behavior that constitute harassment, that it will not be tolerated, and the appropriate way to respond to a complaint. The Supreme Court has made it clear that employers have an obligation to take reasonable steps to prevent workplace harassment. When discussing the elements that comprise a reasonable plan to accomplish this result, the Court specifically mentioned that training is a critical component of any plan.[43] Some states specifically incorporate this judicial guidance into their own laws. For example, with respect to sexual harassment training, California law requires employers to train new hires within the first six months of their employment and to retrain their supervisors at least once every two years.[44] Based on this, an investment in training has the potential to assist an employer to accomplish the dual goals of eliminating (or at least minimizing) workplace harassment and the need for the filing of such claims, while also minimizing employer liability in the event a claim does materialize.

KEY TERMS

- ✓ hostile work environment
- ✓ *quid pro quo* harassment
- ✓ retaliation
- ✓ sexual harassment
- ✓ tangible employment action

DISCUSSION QUESTIONS

Explain your response to each of the following questions with the understanding that in some cases there is no right or wrong answer. If you cannot make an informed decision with the facts provided, indicate the nature and significance of the additional information you would need. For the purposes of these questions, you can assume that the employers and employees mentioned below are covered by Title VII and other relevant federal workplace anti-discrimination laws.

1. Explain the two types of harassment claims that may be filed and provide an example of a set of facts that might support each.
2. Provide a set of facts that might support a claim for a hostile work environment based on an individual's religion.
3. How can an employer minimize potential liability that might arise from a claim of harassment based on national origin? Provide examples of employer conduct that a court might consider when deciding the appropriate damage award.
4. Jen tells you she is miserable at work because her co-workers continue to make jokes about her hair, which is always tied back tightly and covered. She said she told her supervisor she was being harassed under Title VII, but he said that she has no claim for sexual harassment because her co-workers never expressed a romantic interest in her. What do you think?
5. Leilani is uncomfortable working late hours alongside Caroline, who works as part of the evening cleaning staff, because she constantly tells sexually offensive jokes. Leilani believes it is useless complaining to her boss because she knows Caroline is only kidding around to pass the time, and even if she felt uncomfortable there is nothing anyone can do, because the cleaning staff is made up of employees from an outside cleaning company. What do you think?
6. Kat's co-worker told her a joke she found to be sexually inappropriate, violent, and offensive. She went to her supervisor, who said to let her know if it happens again,

because although one comment does not create a hostile work environment, if it happens again, she might be able to file a complaint. What do you think?

7. Will is an employee who says he finds the erotic pictures posted behind the desk of his co-worker Erin offensive. Will's employer asks him a few questions and determines that Erin has never made any sexual advances toward Will, nor discussed the pictures with him. Instead, Will just sees the pictures posted behind her desk when he passes by each morning. Do you think this employer could be subject to liability for a claim for sexual harassment?

8. Brandon is an employee who continues to have problems with co-workers who taunt him based on a speech impediment that constitutes a disability. His supervisor, Kathleen, has spoken with the co-workers on a number of occasions, but their behavior has continued. After a work conference that is the scene of another taunting session, Kathleen takes Brandon aside and tells him if he can tolerate the behavior for a few months until the close of the fiscal year, she will process the promotion she had been promising him, which would include a transfer to a different office. What do you think of this resolution?

ENDNOTES

1. U.S. Equal Employment Opportunity Commn., Harassment Charges, EEOC & FEPAs Combined: FY 1997–FY 2009 (available at *http://www.eeoc.gov/eeoc/statistics/enforcement/harassment.cfm*).

2. *Meritor Sav. Bank, FSB v. Vinson*, 477 U.S. 57, 65 (1986); U.S. Equal Employment Opportunity Commn., Sexual Harassment (available at *http://www.eeoc.gov/types/sexual_harassment.html*).

3. U.S. Equal Employment Opportunity Commn., Sexual Harassment (available at *http://www.eeoc.gov/laws/types/sexual_harassment.cfm*).

4. U.S. Equal Employment Opportunity Commn., Sexual Harassment Charges, EEOC & FEPAs Combined: FY 1997–FY 2009 (available at *http://www.eeoc.gov/eeoc/statistics/enforcement/sexual_harassment.cfm*).

5. U.S. Equal Employment Opportunity Commn., Sexual Harassment (available at *http://www.eeoc.gov/laws/types/sexual_harassment.cfm*). The EEOC also reports that 15.9% of the claims for sexual harassment were filed by men.

6. *Oncale v. Sundowner Offshore Servs.*, 523 U.S. 75, 79 (1998).

7. U.S. Equal Employment Opportunity Commn., Sexual Harassment (available at *http://www.eeoc.gov/laws/types/sexual_harassment.cfm*); 29 C.F.R. § 1604.11(a)(3).

8. *Rogers v. EEOC*, 454 F.2d 234 (5th Cir. 1971).

9. U.S. Equal Employment Opportunity Commn., Policy Guidance on Current Issues of Sexual Harassment (available at *http://www.eeoc.gov/policy/docs/currentissues.html*).

10. U.S. Equal Employment Opportunity Commn., Questions & Answers for Small Employers on Employer Liability for Harassment by Supervisors (available at *http://www.eeoc.gov/policy/docs/harassment-facts.html*).

11. *Id.*

12. *See id.*

13. 29 C.F.R. § 1604.11(a)(3).

14. 29 C.F.R. § 1604.11(a).

15. *See generally* U.S. Equal Employment Opportunity Commn., Policy Guidance on Current Issues of Sexual Harassment, Determining Whether Conduct Is Unwelcome (available at *http://www.eeoc.gov/policy/docs/currentissues.html*).

16. *Meritor Sav. Bank, FSB v. Vinson*, 477 U.S. 57, 65 (1986).

17. *Harris v. Forklift Sys., Inc.*, 510 U.S. 17 (1993).

18. *Id.* at 23.

19. 29 C.F.R. § 1604.11(a).

20. *Barnes v. Costle*, 561 F.2d 983, 999 (D.C. Cir. 1977) (MacKinnon, J., concurring).

21. *Henson v. City of Dundee*, 682 F.2d 897, 903 (11th Cir. 1982).

22. *McMillan v. Pennsylvania*, 477 U.S. 79 (1986).

23. 29 C.F.R. § 1604.11(b).

24. *Id.*

25. *Oncale v. Sundowner Offshore Servs.*, 523 U.S. 75, 79 (1998).

26. U.S. Equal Employment Opportunity Commn., Disability Discrimination (available at *http://www.eeoc.gov/laws/types/disability.cfm*); U.S. Equal Employment Opportunity Commn., Age Discrimination (available at *http://www.eeoc.gov/laws/types/age.cfm*).

27. *See* U.S. Equal Employment Opportunity Commn., Disability Discrimination (available at *http://www.eeoc.gov/laws/types/disability.cfm*); U.S. Equal Employment Opportunity Commn., Age Discrimination (available at *http://www.eeoc.gov/laws/types/age.cfm*).

28. EEOC Compl. Man. § 13 (National Origin Discrimination) (available at *http://www.eeoc.gov/policy/docs/national-origin.html*).

29. *Id.*

30. EEOC Compl. Man. § 12 (Religious Discrimination) (available at *http://www.eeoc.gov/policy/docs/religion.html*).

31. *Id.*

32. *Meritor Sav. Bank, FSB v. Vinson*, 477 U.S. 57, 67 (1986); *see also* EEOC Compl. Man. § 12 (Religious Discrimination) (available at *http://www.eeoc.gov/policy/docs/religion.html*).

33. *See* EEOC Compl. Man. § 12 (Religious Discrimination) (available at *http://www.eeoc.gov/policy/docs/religion.html*).

34. U.S. Equal Employment Opportunity Commn., Questions and Answers About Deafness and Hearing Impairments in the Workplace and the Americans with Disabilities Act (July 26, 2006) (available at *http://www.eeoc.gov/facts/deafness.html*).

35. Press Release, U.S. Equal Employment Opportunity Commn., Tavern on the Green to Pay $2.2 Million for Harassment of Females, Blacks, Hispanics (June 2, 2008) (available at *http://www.eeoc.gov/press/6-2-08*). According to the EEOC, the restaurant also retaliated against employees for objecting to the harassment.

36. *EEOC v. Dairy Fresh Foods, Inc.*, No. 2:0 CV 14085 (E.D. Mich. Sept. 27, 2000).

37. *EEOC v. AK Steel Corp.* (W.D. Pa. Jan. 30, 2007).

38. *See Burlington Indus., Inc. v. Ellerth*, 524 U.S. 42 (1998).

39. *Faragher v. City of Boca Raton*, 524 U.S. 75 (1998); *see also* U.S. Equal Employment Opportunity Commn., Questions & Answers for Small Employers on Employer Liability for Harassment by Supervisors (available at *http://www.eeoc.gov/policy/docs/harassment-facts.html*).

40. U.S. Equal Employment Opportunity Commn., Sexual Harassment (available at *http://www.eeoc.gov/types/sexual_harassment.html*).

41. U.S. Equal Employment Opportunity Commn., Questions & Answers for Small Employers on Employer Liability for Harassment by Supervisors (available at *http://www.eeoc.gov/policy/docs/harassment-facts.html*).

42. *Id.*

43. *Faragher v. City of Boca Raton*, 524 U.S. 775 (1998); *see Burlington Indus., Inc. v. Ellerth*, 524 U.S. 742 (1998).

44. *See* Fair Employment and Housing Commn., Sexual Harassment Training and Education Regulations Approved by the Office of Administrative Law on July 18, 2007 (available at *http://www.fehc.ca.gov/pdf/SexualHarassmentTrainingRegulations_Approved_by_OAL_July_18_2007.pdf*)

Workplace Privacy and Personal Expression

16

Chapter Objectives

This chapter explores the tension between the rights of employers to manage their workforce and protect their business interests and the privacy rights of employees. A number of sources for privacy rights are discussed, including rights that emanate from statutory law and common law. Significant attention is paid to areas that are most conducive to workplace privacy issues, including searches and inspections, monitoring of employee communications, and video and audio surveillance. Students will also learn about the rights of employees to express themselves through their attire and grooming choices, as well as the rights of employers to enforce dress codes.

After completing this chapter, students should have a fundamental understanding about the rights of employees to be free from workplace intrusions and the rights of employers to monitor employee conduct. Students should be familiar with the concept of a reasonable expectation of privacy and be able to identify the types of employer and employee conduct that would be used to determine whether a reasonable expectation of privacy exists.

Upon mastering the main objectives of this chapter students should be able to

- identify a number of sources of workplace privacy rights;
- list some federal laws that regulate workplace privacy and explain the significance of each;
- explain the four common law causes of action related to an invasion of privacy;
- define *reasonable expectation of privacy* and explain the factors a court might use to determine whether it exists;
- explain the factors used to determine whether an employer has the right to search employee property such as briefcases and purses, and employer property such as company lockers and work computers;
- provide examples of employer conduct that might minimize the privacy rights of employees at work, and employee conduct that might enhance these rights;
- explain the significance of the Electronic Communications Privacy Act of 1986 (ECPA), the extent to which it prevents the monitoring of work e-mail accounts, and the exceptions to its coverage;

- ■ define *video surveillance* and *audio surveillance* and explain the rights of employers to use them to monitor their employees; and
- ■ explain the extent to which an employer can implement a dress code or grooming requirement, and the extent to which an employer might be required to provide a reasonable accommodation to an employee whose dress or grooming is tied to that individual's protected class membership.

Employers have the right to manage their employees, and in some cases they can be subject to liability for failing to do so. However, these rights must be balanced against their employees' rights to privacy and personal expression.

SOURCES OF PRIVACY PROTECTIONS

Privacy rights emanate from a number of different sources, and each can be the source of a claim for an intrusion.

A. CONSTITUTIONAL PROTECTIONS

Fourth Amendment of the U.S. Constitution
establishes a right to privacy by prohibiting unreasonable searches and seizures

The **Fourth Amendment of the U.S. Constitution** protects the rights of individuals to be free from unreasonable searches and seizures.[1] Because the Constitution applies only to government employers (which includes public employers), this amendment cannot be used as the basis for the filing of a privacy claim against a private employer. Some states do, however, include privacy protections in their state constitutions, and this has been used to support a showing that, as a matter of public policy, invasive employer conduct within the private sector should be prohibited.[2]

B. STATUTORY PROTECTIONS

Fair Credit Reporting Act (FCRA)
federal law that regulates, among other things, the administration of background checks

Employee Polygraph Protection Act (EPPA)
federal law that regulates the administration of lie detector tests

Health Insurance Portability and Accountability Act (HIPAA)
federal law that regulates, among other things, the disclosure of an individual's medical information

A number of federal statutes regulate privacy in the workplace. For example, the **Fair Credit Reporting Act (FCRA)** is the federal law that regulates the administration of background checks as well as how information obtained through a check may be used,[3] and the **Employee Polygraph Protection Act (EPPA)** is the federal law that regulates the administration of lie detector tests and the use of the results.[4] See Chapter 11, Pre-Employment Testing.

In addition, the **Health Insurance Portability and Accountability Act (HIPAA)** is the federal law that is a significant source of privacy protections for employees by, for example, regulating the purposes for which health information obtained by health plans and providers can be disclosed, and how the information must be maintained.[5]

C. COMMON LAW

Under common law, an employee might file an **invasion of privacy** claim based on (1) appropriation of name or likeness; (2) public disclosure of truthful but private facts; (3) defamation; or (4) an intrusion upon seclusion. Although an intrusion upon seclusion claim is the cause of action that arises most often within the context of an employer–employee relationship, a basic understanding of each cause of action is important.

invasion of privacy
violation of duty to refrain from intruding into an individual's private life

1. APPROPRIATION OF NAME OR LIKENESS

The **appropriation of name or likeness** refers to the unauthorized use of an individual's likeness for a commercial purpose.[6] Under this cause of action, liability arises from the utilization of the name or likeness of a public figure absent consent. For example, under this theory Johnny Carson was successful in preventing a small manufacturer from marketing a line of "here's Johnny" portable toilets,[7] and the estate of Martin Luther King, Jr., was able to block the manufacturing and marketing of a plastic bust resembling him.[8]

appropriation of name or likeness
right to privacy cause of action relating to the unauthorized use of an individual's image for a commercial benefit

2. PUBLIC DISCLOSURE OF TRUTHFUL BUT PRIVATE FACTS

Another type of invasion of privacy claim is the **public disclosure of truthful but private facts**, which materializes if an employer makes information about an employee public, and the disclosure, even though true, would be considered highly offensive to a reasonable person.

public disclosure of truthful but private facts
cause of action based on public attention given to an individual's private life that a reasonable person would consider offensive

For example, an employer who reveals to its employees that another employee had undergone reconstructive surgery could be subject to liability under this theory. As one court reasoned, liability is appropriate when an individual "exposes private facts to a public whose knowledge of those factors would be embarrassing," and the public could include "a particular public such as fellow employees, club members, church members, family or neighbors."[9] In contrast, a court rejected an employee's privacy claim against an employer for disclosing her attendance record to her husband (which enabled him to determine she was having an affair), because it was not reasonable for an employee to believe that such information would remain private.[10]

3. DEFAMATION

Another cause of action that might arise within the context of a privacy claim is **defamation,** which is defined as a "communication that tends to harm the reputation of another so as to lower him in the estimation of the community to deter third persons from associating or dealing with him."[11] Although an employee could file a defamation claim against a current employer, these issues often arise within the context of an employer's providing an employment reference for a former employee, which is discussed in detail in Chapter 20, Severance and Post-Employment Obligations.

defamation
cause of action relating to the communication of false information about an individual that causes harm to his reputation or deters third persons from dealing with the individual

4. INTRUSION UPON SECLUSION

Although an employee can file any of the privacy claims described above against an employer within the context of an employment relationship, workplace privacy claims usually materialize within the context of an **intrusion upon seclusion**.

intrusion upon seclusion
violation of the duty to refrain from interfering in an individual's private matters

This type of invasion could arise if an employer intentionally intrudes (physically or otherwise) upon the solitude or seclusion of another, or into a private affair or concern. Such conduct would result in liability for an employer if the intrusion would "be highly offensive to a reasonable person."[12] The intrusion might be related to a physical invasion of an individual's personal space intended to be kept private, or it can refer to the use of one's senses, with or without mechanical assistance, to overhear a conversation.[13] For example, an employer who places a video camera in an employee locker room provided for the changing into work uniforms might be subject to an intrusion upon seclusion claim. Under this cause of action, potential liability attaches once the intrusion occurs rather than resulting from what is done with the information after it is uncovered.[14]

a. Establishing a Reasonable Expectation of Privacy

reasonable expectation of privacy
threshold question in an invasion of privacy claim used to assess whether an individual had the right to expect an area or concern would be free from an outside intrusion

The basis for an intrusion upon seclusion claim is whether the alleged misconduct violated an individual's **reasonable expectation of privacy**, which means that the individual had the right to assume an area or matter of concern would be private.[15] For example, an employee whose personal briefcase is searched by an employer might claim that this conduct violated her reasonable expectation of privacy, as would an employee who learns that his employer eavesdrops on his personal telephone calls. Under each of these circumstances, if the employee can show that it was reasonable to expect that those matters would remain private and therefore the employer's conduct was intrusive, the employer could be subject to liability under an intrusion upon seclusion cause of action.

Although these examples might seem straightforward, most situations are not as definitive. For example, although an employer's questioning of an employee about "her personal sexual proclivities" would likely violate an individual's right to privacy,[16] an invitation for intercourse, though offensive, would be less likely to rise to the level of an intrusive invasion.[17] Because this reasonable expectation of privacy has been loosely defined as the "objective entitlement founded on broadly based and widely accepted community norms," the analysis used to determine whether it exists requires the consideration of a number of factors.[18]

i. Physical Space

As a starting point, a court might look at the physical environment where the conduct occurred to assess whether it should be considered a place of solitude, which would support an individual's claim that a right to privacy exists there. There would be a significant difference between the monitoring of an employee's conduct at a public event such as a company picnic (not a place of solitude) and the monitoring of an employee in an employer workspace (possibly a place of solitude, depending on, among other things, how it is set up).

ii. Ownership

Courts also consider who owns the property that is subject to the intrusion to determine whether a right to privacy exists there. Individuals have more privacy rights in their own homes as compared to their rights while on their employer's property. Similarly, individuals have greater privacy rights for items they personally own, such as purses or briefcases, than for items that are owned by their employers, such as company lockers and computers.

b. Establishing the Offensive Nature of Intrusion

If a determination is made that an employee has a reasonable expectation of privacy in a matter that has been intruded upon, the next inquiry is whether the intrusion was offensive. In determining offensiveness, courts look at the "context, conduct and circumstances surrounding the intrusion as well as the intruder's motives and objectives."[19] For example, the installation of a hidden video camera by an employer who is investigating the assault of a number of employees after work hours would likely be less offensive than the installation of a hidden video camera by an employer who is attempting to track which employees report late to their shifts. In addition, while a court would be unlikely to consider an employer's administration of a test for illegal drug use as offensive behavior, it could be considered offensive if the employer insists on directly observing the providing of the specimen.[20]

 ## SIGNIFICANCE OF NOTICE AND CONSENT

A determination of whether a reasonable expectation of privacy exists is closely tied to the issue of whether the employee had notice of and consented to the employer intrusion. If an employer can show an employee was on notice of and consented to its monitoring policy, this will undermine the employee's claim that it was reasonable to assume privacy rights existed in the area or matters of concern the policy covered.[21]

A. NOTICE

Notice relates to whether an employee is aware of the potential for an intrusion, which has an impact on the reasonableness of a privacy expectation. For example, courts have held that an employee's awareness about the potential for the monitoring of work e-mail accounts "undermines the reasonableness of an employee's claim that he or she believes such information was private and not subject to search."[22] If, however, an employee is not aware that an employer reserves the right to monitor work e-mail communications, and there is no indication that the employer intended to engage in this type of monitoring, then a court might find that it was reasonable for an employee to assume those communications would be private.[23]

> **notice**
> within the context of workplace privacy, the awareness of the potential for an intrusion

The question about whether an employee was on notice of the potential for an intrusion is a key element in a privacy claim. Because of this, employers should place their employees on notice of any policies that might be considered intrusive, which can be done in a number of ways.

1. VERBAL NOTICE

An employer can provide verbal notice to its employees during a new hire orientation or at a staff meeting that certain work areas or property will *not* be private. In addition, employers should consider providing notice to employees about potential intrusions more than once. Some employers send employees annual reminders about the most significant workplace policies, or direct employees to company websites for updates. Employers who use audio surveillance to record telephone calls might program their system to play a statement at the beginning of each call to alert call participants that the calls may be monitored.

Employers using a verbal notification method should devise a method to confirm that notice was provided. For example, if a recording is played at the beginning of each monitored call, employers should determine whether the system can generate a report to corroborate that the recording is regularly played. For other types of verbal notifications, employers should document what was communicated. For example, if an employer explains a policy to an employee or group of employees in an informal meeting, sending a follow-up e-mail after the discussion that confirms what was communicated would be evidence to support an employer's claim that notice was provided, in the event of a challenge. If the issue is discussed at a staff meeting, the employer might also create and maintain a meeting agenda along with an attendance sheet signed by each of the employees in attendance, which can be used by the employer to support a position that notice of a particular policy was provided to all employees in attendance.

2. WRITTEN NOTICE

Because the issue of whether an employee had notice of a monitoring policy is often in dispute, employers should not rely exclusively on the verbal communication of such policies. Although there is nothing inherently wrong with verbally notifying employees about the terms of a monitoring policy, employers should also present a written policy confirming the details of the verbal notification. Effective methods of providing written notice are the inclusion of the monitoring policy in the company handbook and the posting of the notice in work areas where monitoring will take place.

a. Memorialize Policy in a Company Handbook

Employers can include policies relating to the privacy rights employees can expect while at work in their company handbooks. In the handbook, employers can explain the specific parameters of a monitoring policy and what employees can expect will and will not remain private.

For example, as electronic communication has become an ordinary and customary method of workplace communication, it is becoming increasingly more common for employers to include monitoring policies relating to workplace computers and electronic communications in their company handbooks. In addition, because the use of the Internet is subject to the same privacy parameters as e-mail accounts, many policies reference the rights of employers to monitor both e-mail communications and Internet use.

With respect to policy content, employers may want to create a broad policy allowing the interception, monitoring, and accessing of all e-mails and files contained in a workplace computer. Employers who want to monitor the Internet browsing of employees might also decide to make it clear that the monitoring would include an employee's history of website viewing, as well as any postings made to other websites. Employers may also want to remind employees that using workplace computers for illegal and improper activities such as gambling and the viewing of pornographic materials is inappropriate and will not be tolerated.

By outlining such a policy in a handbook, an employer is placing its employees on notice of what matters might be subject to an intrusion. The document can be a significant piece of employer evidence to refute an employee's claim that certain workplace electronic communications or a history of website browsing would be private. Further, the policy could be used to show that because the employee was aware of the potential for an intrusion, the employee had no reasonable expectation of privacy in her electronic communications or record of browsing activities.

b. Post a Notification

In addition to incorporating a monitoring policy in the company handbook, some employers post signs in the areas they intend to monitor, to place employees on notice that it would be unreasonable to expect a right to privacy there. This might be done by employers who decide to use video surveillance to track employee behavior to alert individuals as to the location of the cameras. With respect to electronic communications, some employers program their workplace computers to display the policy on the screen as it starts up, so that employees are notified of the potential for monitoring of their computer use each time the intrusion might occur.[24]

B. CONSENT

After an employer places its employees on notice of a monitoring policy, it should ensure that the employees consent to the terms of the policy. **Consent** to a monitoring policy relates to whether an employee agrees to be bound by its terms.

> **consent**
> within the context of a privacy claim, the granting of permission for certain workplace monitoring

Courts have specifically noted that the "presence or absence of opportunities to consent voluntarily to activities impacting privacy interests obviously affects the expectations of the participants."[25] If an employee consents to a monitoring policy that would subject an area or property to an intrusion, a court is unlikely to determine that the employee had a reasonable expectation of privacy regarding those interests. Employers can minimize their liability for an invasion of privacy claim by obtaining express or implied consent from employees before engaging in the monitoring.

1. EXPRESS CONSENT

Express consent to a monitoring policy refers to providing affirmative verbal or written confirmation to be subject to the policy's terms. For example, employees who sign a document saying they understand the employer monitoring policy

> **express consent**
> an affirmative agreement to be bound

found in a company handbook and agree to be subject to it would be providing express consent. Employers who decide to implement surveillance techniques or intrusive conduct that extends beyond standard business practice might ask their employees to sign a separate document indicating awareness of the specific policy related to the monitoring, rather than relying on the more general consent to work under the terms of the entire handbook.

2. IMPLIED CONSENT

implied consent
conduct suggesting an
agreement to be bound

Implied consent to a monitoring policy refers to conduct that suggests an employee agrees to be subject to its terms. If an employee knows that the employer intends to monitor her computer use and she continues to work under those conditions, this constitutes implied consent. Under these circumstances, if an employee asserts that the monitoring was intrusive or violated a reasonable expectation of privacy, the employer would respond that the employee's conduct constituted her implied consent to work subject to the terms of the employer's monitoring policy.

For example, an employee who sees the computer monitoring policy on the screen of a work computer when it is turned on and continues to use the equipment will have a difficult time asserting that the monitoring constitutes wrongful conduct. Her continued use of the computer after reading the policy would constitute implied consent to the terms of the policy and would undermine a claim that it was reasonable for the employee to assume her communications would be private. Similarly, if an employee hears a recorded message stating that a call will be monitored when using a work telephone and continues to participate in the conversation, this also constitutes implied consent to the monitoring.

Although some employers require employees to provide express consent to comply with the provisions of a company handbook, others rely on implied consent. Some employers e-mail the company handbook and subsequent updates to employees and maintain an electronic receipt to prove the document was sent, received, and opened. Under these circumstances, if the handbook included a monitoring policy, the employer would use these confirmation records to support its position that by continuing to work for the employer after reviewing the handbook, the employee provided implied consent to be monitored consistent with the policy.

Whether an employer decides to obtain express or implied consent for a particular monitoring policy will vary depending on the nature of the intrusion, and privacy claims related to these intrusions usually materialize within the context of three broad categories: searches and inspections, employee communications, and video and audio surveillance.

SEARCHES AND INSPECTIONS

Employers do not retain the full discretion to search and inspect their employees' workspaces and persons because, as discussed above, employees have varying degrees of privacy rights while at work. Two significant issues to address in determining the appropriate degree of privacy are who owns the property and what was the purpose for which the property was purchased.

A. EMPLOYEE PROPERTY

Employees have significant expectations of privacy in their personal belongings such as their briefcases, purses, and cars. However, these privacy rights may be diminished somewhat if they bring the items onto the premises of an employer. For example, one court rejected an invasion of privacy claim filed against an employer for searching an employee's car based on the written policy allowing for the random search of any cars leaving the property. The court reasoned that because the employee was aware of this policy, by continuing to drive a personal car to work, the employee consented to a diminished expectation of privacy for his personal belongings.[26]

B. EMPLOYER PROPERTY

Employers do not have exclusive access and control over the property and work-spaces they provide for their employees to perform their jobs. Thus, even if an employer provided the property for an employee to use at work (such as a company car), the employee might still maintain some privacy rights with respect to it. This is because, although ownership is significant, it must be evaluated along with a number of other factors.

1. OFFICE SPACE, DESKS, AND LOCKERS

Employers that provide office space, furniture, and lockers to their employees retain some degree of control over the property, but issues often materialize relating to whether employers have the right to search the contents of that property. One court found that an employer did not invade the privacy of an employee when it entered his office and searched the desk for evidence it needed to conduct an investigation. Although the employee claimed that the employer's search was an invasion of privacy, the court found this right to be diminished because the employee knew the employer retained copies of the office and desk keys.[27] In contrast, when an employee used her personal lock to secure a work locker and was never informed it might be subjected to a search, a court found that a subsequent search violated her privacy rights.[28] Consistent with this line of reasoning, one court noted that if "the employer equips the employee's office with a safe or file cabinet or other receptacle in which to keep his private papers, [the employee] can assume that the contents of the safe are private."[29]

2. COMPUTERS AND LAPTOPS

Issues often arise with respect to company computers, and courts have provided employers with some latitude to monitor computer use because of the potential for abuse. One court even determined that an employer could attach whatever conditions it wanted to the use of a work computer because "the abuse of access to workplace computers is so common (workers being prone to use them as media of gossip, titillation, and other entertainment and distraction) that reserving a right of inspection is so far from being reasonable that the failure to do so might well be thought irresponsible."[30]

Despite this monitoring right, and in some cases obligation, employers should be certain to provide employees with notice of their intention to exercise it, because a failure to provide notice could be used to support the employee's position that an expectation of privacy was reasonable. For example, one court determined a reasonable expectation of privacy attached to an employee's work computer because he had no reason to believe it would be subject to search, he did not share his office or computer with his co-workers, and his employer did not access or monitor work computers on a regular basis.[31]

3. MANAGING PRIVACY EXPECTATIONS

Employees can engage in behavior that will maximize their privacy expectations, which in turn would minimize the rights of employers to engage in such monitoring. However, employers can also engage in conduct to counter this employee behavior and minimize the privacy expectations of employees, which would then maximize the employers' monitoring rights.

Generally speaking, employees will find it challenging to establish a reasonable expectation of privacy in places where others (including the employer, co-workers, customers, or members of the public) have access. However, employees that take affirmative steps to create privacy expectations through the use of personal locks or other safeguards (such as locking computer files with passwords) can use this conduct to support a position that a reasonable expectation of privacy exists.[32]

Employers can take steps to block this type of behavior and prevent employees from creating these types of privacy expectations. For example, employers can adopt work rules that prohibit the use of personal locks, maintain keys for all company locks, and ensure that employees are aware of the fact that company property is subject to search and inspection. Employers can also prohibit the use of password-protected files, or make it clear that the employer retains the right to access those passwords for monitoring purposes.

C. EMPLOYEE COMMUNICATIONS

Although privacy issues often arise within the context of physical property, privacy rights also extend to employee communications, with particular issues linked to those communications that are created, sent, and stored in an electronic format. There has been a significant amount of litigation surrounding the rights of employers to monitor the workplace communications of their employees. The nature of the employer–employee relationship necessitates some type of employer monitoring — because the employer is responsible for the acts of its employees while they are acting within the scope of their employment. This monitoring, however, has to be balanced against the privacy rights of employees.

1. TELEPHONE AND MAIL COMMUNICATIONS

As a starting point, employees have privacy protections related to personal telephone conversations and to mail delivered through the postal service. However, telephone conversations can be monitored if monitoring is done in the ordinary course of business, such as by an alarm company that illustrates the need to engage in this monitoring to provide emergency services to its customers, or by an employer who has a reasonable belief an employee is sharing confidential information with its competitors.[33] Calls of a personal nature, however, cannot be monitored, and if an employer intercepts a call that is unrelated to its business, the monitoring must stop.[34] Mail delivered through the postal service is afforded similar protection. For example, one court recognized the potential for an invasion of privacy claim when an employer opened and read employee mail marked "personal."[35]

More technologically advanced forms of communication like voicemail and e-mail messages raise additional concerns because they are commonly stored long after the communication takes place. The extended life span of the information, along with employer control over its access, has led to questions about the appropriate level of privacy each should be afforded.

2. ELECTRONIC COMMUNICATIONS

© 2001 by Randy Glasbergen.

"Be careful what you write. My wonderful, charming, brilliant boss reads everyone's e-mail."

Because employees are provided work e-mail accounts to perform work responsibilities, not personal matters, courts have been willing to provide employers with significant leeway to monitor workplace e-mail communications. However, there has been litigation relating to whether e-mail communications should be treated like mail received through the postal service, or whether the appropriate treatment should be comparable to the rights afforded to lockers and desks.[36]

For example, some courts have held that employees should understand the ease with which e-mail messages can be passed along to others, which would make it unreasonable to attach meaningful privacy rights to these communications.[37] Most significant, however, is some of the judicial reluctance to impose liability on employers who monitor e-mail accounts, because this would be inconsistent with their obligation to monitor employee behavior. Specifically, under the legal theory of *respondeat superior,* an employer is responsible for the actions of its employees that occur within the scope of their employment. Thus, because employers might be held liable for misconduct engaged in by an employee through work e-mail communications, they must have the right to monitor these accounts to protect their interests, as it has the potential to subject them to liability.[38] See Chapter 8, Employees versus Independent Contractors, for a more detailed discussion about *respondeat superior.*

Even though employers have the right to monitor work e-mail accounts, these rights are not absolute and must be exercised within the context of privacy law. There are a number of federal and state laws that might subject an employer to liability for monitoring those electronic communications of employees presumed to be private, and one of the most significant is the Electronic Communications Privacy Act of 1986 (ECPA).[39]

3. ELECTRONIC COMMUNICATIONS PRIVACY ACT (ECPA)

Electronic Communications Privacy Act (ECPA)
federal law that, among other things, prohibits the interception of electronic communications

The **Electronic Communications Privacy Act (ECPA)** amended the Wiretap Act and regulates the use of electronic communications by prohibiting (1) the intentional interception (or attempted interception) of any wire, oral, or electronic communication; (2) the intentional use of (or the directing of another individual to use) any electronic, mechanical, or other device to intercept any oral communication; and (3) the intentional use of information in violation of the ECPA.[40]

Because e-mail communications fall within the scope of the definition of *electronic communications* under this statute, an employer may be subject to liability for intercepting or for monitoring the e-mail accounts of its employees.

a. Scope of Coverage

The ECPA does not completely bar employers from monitoring electronic communications because of its limitations. First, the law prohibits only *the interception* of e-mail communications, and most invasion of privacy claims relate to intrusions that occur post-transmission.[41] As one court explained, an interception "require[s] participation by the one charged with an 'interception' in the contemporaneous acquisition of the communication through the use of the device."[42] Thus, an employer would likely be permitted to review electronic communications housed in network storage after their transmission, without being subject to liability under the statute.[43]

b. Statutory Exceptions

In addition to the statutory language that narrows the application of the ECPA, there are also three specific exceptions that would prevent the imposition of liability on an employer: (1) the business use exception, (2) the system provider exception, and (3) consent.

i. Business Use Exception

The first exception to the ECPA allows an employer to intercept the wire communications of its employees if the interception is accomplished (1) through the use of equipment supplied by a provider of wire or electronic communication service; (2) or "in the ordinary course of the subscriber's, user's or provider's business."[44] The expansive interpretation of the term *ordinary course of business* provides employers with wide latitude to monitor business communications but provides employers with very little, if any, latitude to monitor personal communications.[45] Even if monitoring is permissible under that statute, courts have held that the moment an employer determines that an intercepted e-mail communication is personal, it must refrain from reading it any further.[46]

ii. System Provider Exception

The second exception under the ECPA allows the provider of the technology used to transmit the communication to intercept it in the normal course of business if the interception is required to (1) provide the service or (2) protect the rights or property of the employer.[47] This exception might be invoked if, for example, there is a reasonable belief that trade secrets (which refers to formulas, devices, or other information an employer might have the right to prevent an employee from disclosing to others) are being transmitted via e-mail. See Chapter 20, Severance and Post-Employment Obligations, for a more detailed discussion about trade secrets.

iii. Consent Exception

The final exception under the EPCA permits employers to intercept the e-mail communications of employees if prior consent is obtained.[48] Under this exception employers will not be held liable for any monitoring about which their employees knew or should have known.[49]

The general trend is to broadly interpret the consent exception to include both express and implied consent. As discussed above, express consent could be obtained by having employees sign a document acknowledging their awareness that e-mail communications will be monitored and possibly intercepted. Implied consent would be obtained through employee conduct such as, for example, an employee's decision to continue to use a work computer after being told that e-mail communication sent through it might be monitored or intercepted. Some state laws legislate the type of conduct that would constitute consent. For example, a Delaware state law requires employers to provide employees with daily notice that their electronic communications may be monitored.[50]

D. MONITORING OF INTERNET USE

Some employers monitor the Internet use of their employees. Issues regarding this type of workplace monitoring often materialize within the context of the viewing and downloading of pornographic materials, as opposed to other non-work-related viewing of news, sports, or celebrity gossip websites. When such issues do arise, courts look to the same types of factors that apply to e-mail communications, including whether (1) the employer regularly monitors website access, (2) there is a monitoring policy in place, and (3) employees are on notice of and consent to this monitoring.[51] In addition, some courts attach significance to the location of the computer screen. For example, one court determined it was unreasonable for an employee to believe his website browsing was private because the employee worked in an office that did not have a door, and his screen was visible from the hallway unless he specifically obstructed the view from those who walked by.[52]

IV EMPLOYEE SURVEILLANCE

In addition to arising under the types of monitoring discussed above, privacy issues may materialize in response to the monitoring of the physical movements and behavior of employees. Employers have the most latitude to monitor unhidden employee conduct. For example, in one case a court determined an employee's right to privacy was not invaded when an employer watched his house and ran a license check on a number of vehicles parked there. The Court found it particularly significant that there was no physical intrusion and all of the monitored activity occurred in public view and could have been seen by anyone who passed by.[53]

Technological advances have resulted in a number of sophisticated forms of surveillance techniques to track employee movement and behavior.[54] Two common forms of monitoring include video or audio surveillance, both of which are subject to significant regulation.[55]

A. VIDEO SURVEILLANCE

video surveillance
the use of visible or hidden cameras to track employee movement and behavior

Video surveillance relates to using visible or hidden cameras to monitor employee conduct, and an employer may want to engage in this type of monitoring for security purposes or to monitor employee work performance. A fundamental issue in determining whether such monitoring is appropriate is the location of the surveillance device, and a consideration of both state law and what expectations of privacy, if any, the employees have in the monitored areas are the relevant inquiries.

1. REGULATION UNDER STATE LAW

State laws vary on the rights of employers to use video surveillance, and whether the camera will be hidden or in plain view is particularly significant under these laws. A number of states (approximately 24) prohibit the use of hidden cameras in areas that are deemed private. Although many of these laws limit this prohibition to the recording of nudity, state law should still be reviewed to determine the extent of any such limitations and an employer's potential liability.[56]

2. ASSESSING WHETHER A REASONABLE EXPECTATION OF PRIVACY EXISTS

Assuming the use of hidden cameras is permissible (or the camera is not hidden), whether the camera intrudes on the privacy rights of employees will depend on a number of factors used to establish whether a reasonable expectation of privacy exists. In addition to whether the camera is hidden or in plain view, relevant issues relate to the physical location of the cameras and whether an employee might expect to be videotaped in the surveillance area.

For example, this issue might materialize within the context of a work locker room. Because people enter a locker room freely, it might be unreasonable to assume their conduct there would be private. However, courts have found that an individual's right to privacy in a locker room might not be diminished to the point where one could expect to be videotaped.[57] This is in contrast to taping that occurs in open spaces used by a number of employees and located in heavy traffic areas, such as building entrances or exits, or in hallways that connect a number of offices. Under these circumstances, courts have allowed the use of video surveillance based on the unreasonableness of assuming anything that occurred in these areas would be private.[58]

Other significant factors relate to who is being videotaped, the reasons for the recording, and whether the monitored individuals consented to the monitoring. An employer can minimize privacy expectations by placing the cameras in plain view, posting signs about their use, or asking employees to sign a consent form agreeing to the monitoring. Even employers who are confident that their employees do not have a reasonable expectation of privacy in a particular area should expend efforts to minimize the expectations of their employees. This is important because courts have recognized that the invasive nature of the actual creation of a permanent record of an employee's workplace conduct might warrant some protections. Specifically, one court acknowledged the potential for a privacy claim when a reporter secretly videotaped employees in their cubicles because even though it might be unreasonable to think that their conversations and actions were private, the actual taping of the behavior implicated heightened concerns.[59]

B. AUDIO SURVEILLANCE

audio surveillance
the use of technology to record the conversations of others, which is regulated by state and federal law

Audio surveillance refers to the use of technology to record the conversations of others and is regulated by state and federal law. Generally speaking, federal law permits the recording of telephone and other electronic communications if the person engaging in the recording is a call participant, or if one of the participants has given consent to the recording, and the purpose of the recording is not to commit a criminal or tortuous act.[60]

one-party consent states
states that either permit individuals to record telephone and other electronic conversations if they are call participants or, in some cases, by non-participants if one participant provides prior consent

The majority of states (e.g., Alabama, New Jersey, New York, Texas) are considered **one-party consent states** and permit the recording of conversation to which an individual is a participant without informing the other parties he is doing so and, in some cases, permit the recording of conversations by non-participants if one participant provides prior consent.[61] In contrast, a few states (e.g., California, Connecticut, Florida, Massachusetts, Pennsylvania) are generally considered **two-party consent states** and require *all* parties to a conversation to consent to the recording for it to be lawful.[62]

two-party consent states
states that permit the recording of telephone and other electronic communications only if consent is obtained from all call participants

Even if the audio recording of an employee's conversation is permissible under federal and state law, it can still materialize into a claim for the invasion of privacy. Within this context, the recording is generally prohibited if it would be reasonable for the individual speaking to believe that her conversation would not be overheard or recorded.[63] Thus, just as with other monitoring issues, the relevant consideration is whether the person who was subjected to the audio surveillance had a reasonable expectation that a certain conversation would be private.

The intrusiveness of this kind of monitoring in the workplace continues to be closely scrutinized, and it is allowed only for verbal communications relating to business matters. Thus, even an employer who is appropriately monitoring calls must cease and desist the monitoring once it is determined that the call relates to a personal, not business, matter.[64]

V ABSENCE OF MONITORING

Although the restrictions placed on the rights of employers to monitor employee conduct may seem onerous and deter employers from engaging in any type of monitoring, this is not necessarily a desirable result. Employers should understand the limitations on their rights to engage in employee monitoring to avoid liability, but they should also understand the risks of not doing any monitoring. This is because just as an employer might be subject to liability for engaging in prohibited employee monitoring, an employer might also be subject to liability for failing to properly monitor and address inappropriate workplace behavior.

Courts have required employers to monitor the conduct that occurs on their equipment and have imposed liability on those employers who do not exercise due care to do so. For example, one court found that an employer could be subject to liability for failing to take action against an employee for viewing child pornography at work, after his sexual abuse of his stepdaughter surfaced. The court determined that an employer who is on notice that an employee is viewing pornography at work has a duty to investigate the conduct and take prompt action to address it.[65] Another court subjected an employer to liability for allowing a hostile work environment to continue over e-mail because of the employer's failure to make reasonable efforts to address the conduct. This was based on the theory that an employer's e-mail system is an extension of its workplace, which an employer has an obligation to ensure is in compliance with federal anti-discrimination laws.[66] See Chapter 15, Workplace Harassment, for a detailed discussion about hostile work environment claims.

Because employers may be subject to liability for failing to adequately monitor their employees, they will need to balance their right to monitor with the potential risks associated with infringing on the rights of their employees and minimize those risks where possible. Ideally, employers should create policies that outline their monitoring practices, place employees on notice of the terms of the policy, and obtain their employees' consent.

 **GROOMING AND DRESS CODES**

Even if employers minimize the potential for privacy claims related to workplace monitoring, they may be subject to privacy claims in other contexts. In addition to the privacy rights employees have in their work areas and with respect to their property, they also have privacy rights related to their personal expression. Because individuals might express themselves through their personal appearance, workplace privacy issues could materialize as a result of the implementation of dress codes and grooming requirements.

Employers have the right to establish dress codes and grooming requirements, but these policies, like all other terms and conditions of employment, must be consistent with anti-discrimination laws. For example, an employer who decides to regulate the wearing of head coverings and jewelry must ensure the policy is implemented in a uniform and nondiscriminatory manner, meaning the policy does not intentionally discriminate against or have a disparate impact on members of a protected class.

A. CHARACTERISTIC MUST BE RELATED TO MEMBERSHIP IN A PROTECTED CLASS

In assessing whether a grooming or dress code policy is discriminatory, courts have made it clear that the basis for the allegation that a policy is discriminatory must be linked to an individual's membership in a protected class. For example, a court would allow a grooming policy that prohibits mustaches and requires short sideburns, despite a claim that it constituted discriminatory behavior because Black/African-American men would likely have to exert more effort than white men to comply with it. Because neither mustaches nor sideburns are characteristics unique to Black/African-American men, having a policy that regulates their growth cannot be the basis for the filing of a discrimination claim based on racial discrimination.[67]

The court used this same rationale when a Black/African-American woman challenged her employer's prohibition against "corn row" style hair, asserting that the hair style "has been historically, a fashion and style adopted by Black American women reflective of cultural, historical essence of the Black women in American society."[68] In determining that the prohibition against corn rows was permissible, the court cited other decisions that clarified "[n]ational origin must not be confused with ethnic or socio-cultural traits," and discrimination (other than religion) is usually based on characteristics that are "beyond the victim's power to alter."[69] This court found it particularly significant that the employer told the employee she could style her hair as desired while off-duty, and while working she could tie it back and use a hairpiece to alleviate the potential unsanitary condition that was the basis for the implementation of the policy.[70]

Although grooming and dress codes could be challenged based on membership in any protected class, they often arise with respect to religion and race.

B. RELIGIOUS DISCRIMINATION

A potential challenge to a dress code could materialize if an employer implements a policy to require all employees to wear identical uniforms. Under these circumstances, the issue would be the extent to which an employer would have an obligation to provide a reasonable accommodation to an employee who asserts that an established dress code policy conflicts with one of her sincerely held religious beliefs or practices. The obligation of an employer is to provide a reasonable accommodation if it does not impose an **undue burden** on the employer. Thus, if an employee requests a reasonable accommodation to allow the wearing of religious garb, the relevant inquiries would relate to the reason for the policy and the impact of allowing an exception to it.

undue burden
a hardship that exceeds what an employer would be required to withstand in order to accommodate an employee's religious beliefs or practices

For example, it would be unlikely that a court would require an employer who imposes a dress code based on safety concerns to provide an accommodation, particularly if the accommodation would not alleviate the potential danger to its employees or customers. In addition, a police department could likely deny an employee's request to wear a cross on his uniform because it would be an undue burden for an employer to risk that the conduct would suggest the department endorsed a specific religion, in violation of the constitutional requirement to separate church and state.[71]

In contrast, an employer would likely be prohibited from requiring an employee to cover a visible religious tattoo based on the employer's view that the message was incompatible with its family-oriented and kid-friendly image since "[h]ypothetical hardships based on unproven assumptions typically fail to constitute undue hardship."[72] An employer might also be required to permit an employee to wear religious clothing if the sole purpose of uniforms is to present a consistent appearance to potential customers. See Chapter 4, Religious Discrimination.

C. RACIAL DISCRIMINATION

A number of grooming policies also raise issues relating to racial discrimination, and employers who implement grooming policies that discriminate against members of a particular race must illustrate a business necessity for such policies. For example, Title VII would prohibit an employer from preventing its Black/African-American female employees from wearing their hair in its natural state unless the employer could present evidence of a business necessity for this policy and the absence of an accommodation that, if permitted, would address its concern. Thus, if the employer asserts that the reason for the policy relates to food safety concerns, the employer might be asked to explain why, for example, requiring all employees to tie their hair back or to wear a hair net would not adequately resolve this issue. Further, even if an accommodation such as this would not be sufficient, the employer might still face liability if the imposed policy applies only to women of a particular race, as opposed to being a uniform and nondiscriminatory policy that applies to all employees.[73]

A facially neutral policy that has a disparate impact on members of a protected class is also problematic. For example, although an employer might want to implement a no-beard policy for its employees to promote a clean image, to avoid a discrimination claim an employer would likely have to make an exception to accommodate an individual who has *pseudofolliculitis barbae*, a medical condition that prevents those afflicted with it from shaving and that most commonly affects Black/African-American men.[74] The employer would likely be required to make this modification because of the disproportionate impact the no-beard policy would have on African-American men, because they would be less likely than nonmembers of the protected class to be able to comply with this policy. See Chapter 3, Race, Color, and National Origin Discrimination.

KEY TERMS

- ✓ appropriation of name or likeness
- ✓ audio surveillance
- ✓ consent
- ✓ defamation
- ✓ Electronic Communications Privacy Act (ECPA)
- ✓ Employee Polygraph Protection Act (EPPA)
- ✓ express consent
- ✓ Fair Credit Reporting Act (FCRA)
- ✓ Fourth Amendment to the U.S. Constitution
- ✓ Health Insurance Portability and Accountability Act (HIPAA)
- ✓ implied consent
- ✓ intrusion upon seclusion
- ✓ invasion of privacy
- ✓ notice
- ✓ one-party consent state
- ✓ public disclosure of truthful but private facts
- ✓ reasonable expectation of privacy
- ✓ two-party consent state
- ✓ undue burden
- ✓ video surveillance

DISCUSSION QUESTIONS

Explain your response to each of the following questions with the understanding that in some cases there is no right or wrong answer. If you cannot make an informed decision with the facts provided, indicate the nature and significance of the additional information you would need. For the purposes of these questions, you can assume that the employers and employees mentioned below are covered by Title VII and other relevant federal workplace anti-discrimination laws.

1. What are some sources of privacy rights?
2. Explain the different types of claims that an individual might file that stem from an invasion of privacy under common law.
3. Define the terms *notice* and *consent*, and explain their relevance to a discussion relating to whether an individual has a reasonable expectation of privacy at work.
4. Explain why an individual might have more privacy rights in her home than while at work.
5. Can an employer read through the messages in the work e-mail accounts of his employees on a weekly basis to confirm the accounts are being used only for work purposes?
6. Do employees have privacy rights in their offices? Is there a way an employer can enhance or minimize these rights?
7. Do you think a terminated employee would have a valid invasion of privacy claim against an employer who reads the e-mails sent to his personal Yahoo! account accessed through his work computer? What factors would you consider when making a decision?
8. Pam owns a summer camp and is inspecting the cabins where the counselors and campers sleep, in preparation for parent visitation day. During the inspection, Pam sees a picture of a nude model taped inside the door of a locker that belongs to Chris, a counselor, and she immediately terminates his employment. Do you think Pam's decision could subject her to liability for an invasion of privacy? Why or why not?
9. Janet decides to install video surveillance in every area of her restaurant so she can see how her wait staff interacts with the customers and with one another. Do you think Janet's employees will have a viable invasion of privacy claim against her for engaging in this type of surveillance? How should she proceed to minimize their privacy expectations?
10. Logan owns a bubble gum factory in the center of a big metropolitan city, and she knows that everyone is fascinated by how the product is produced. She does not have the staff to offer guided tours, so she sets up video cameras in the factory and streams the images onto the Internet for potential customers to view. Do the employees who are opposed to use of the video cameras have a valid invasion of privacy claim? Present the arguments Logan could make to support the use of video cameras in this manner, as well as the arguments the employees could make against it. Even if all of the employees indicate they

approve of the videotaping, are there any safeguards Logan might put into place to fend off a potential claim for an invasion of privacy?

11. Could an employer require its bus driver employees to wear a uniform that includes pants even if an employee claims wearing the uniform is inconsistent with her religious beliefs? Why or why not?

ENDNOTES

1. U.S. Const. amend. IV.
2. *See, e.g., Hennessey v. Coastal Eagle Point Oil Co.*, 129 N.J. 91 (1992) (holding the privacy rights granted in the state's constitution could support the argument that drug testing is impermissible based on public policy).
3. 15 U.S.C. §§ 1681 *et seq.*
4. 29 U.S.C. §§ 2001 *et seq.*
5. *See generally* 18 U.S.C. §§ 1 *et seq.*
6. Restatement (Second) of Torts § 652C (1977).
7. *Carson v. Here's Johnny Portable Toilets*, 698 F.2d 831 (6th Cir. 1983).
8. *Martin Luther King, Jr. Ctr. for Soc. Change v. American Heritage Prods.*, 296 S.E.2d 69 (Ga. 1982).
9. *Beaumont v. Brown*, 257 N.W.2d 522, 531 (Mich. 1977).
10. *Kobeck v. Nabisco*, 305 S.E.2d 183 (Ga. Ct. App. 1983).
11. *See, e.g., Feldman v. Lafayette Green Condo Assn.*, 806 A.2d 497, 500 (Pa. Commw. Ct. 2002) (citations omitted).
12. Restatement (Second) of Torts § 652B (1977).
13. Restatement (Second) of Torts § 652B cmt. A.
14. Restatement (Second) of Torts § 652B cmt. B.
15. *See O'Connor v. Ortega*, 480 U.S. 709 (1987).
16. *Phillips v. Smaller Maint. Servs., Inc.*, 435 So. 2d 649 (Ala. 1983).
17. *McIsaac v. WZEM-FM*, 495 So. 2d 649 (Ala. 1986).
18. *Hill v. National Collegiate Athletic Assn.*, 7 Cal. App. 4th 1, 36 (1994).
19. *See, e.g., Sorrentino v. Textron Lycoming*, No. 3:93CV02262, 1995 U.S. Dist. LEXIS 21754, at *8 (D. Conn. Mar. 24, 1995).
20. *See Kelly v. Schlumberger Tech. Corp.*, 849 F.2d 41 (1st Cir. 1988).
21. *See, e.g., George v. Carusone*, 849 F. Supp. 159 (D. Conn. 1994).
22. *United States v. Bailey*, 272 F. Supp. 2d 822, 835 (D. Neb. 2003); *see Thygeson v. U.S. Bancorp*, No. CV-03-467-ST, 2004 WL 2066746, at *20 (D. Or. Sept. 15, 2004).
23. *See United States v. Bailey*, 272 F. Supp. 2d 822 (D. Neb. 2003).
24. *See, e.g., United States v. Greinder*, 235 Fed. Appx. 541 (9th Cir. 2007).
25. *Hill v. National Collegiate Athletic Assn.*, 7 Cal. App. 4th 1, 36 (1994).
26. *Gretencord v. Ford Motor Co.*, 538 F. Supp. 331 (D. Kan. 1982).
27. *Sorrentino v. Textron Lycoming*, No. 3:93CV02262, 1995 U.S. Dist. LEXIS 21754 (D. Conn. Mar. 24, 1995).
28. *K-Mart Corp. Store No. 7441 v. Trotti*, 677 S.W.2d 632 (Tex. Ct. App. 1984).
29. *Muick v. Glenayre Elecs.*, 280 F.3d 741, 743 (7th Cir. 2002).
30. *Id.*
31. *Leventhal v. Knapek*, 266 F.3d 64 (2d Cir. 2001).
32. *See O'Connor v. Ortega*, 480 U.S. 709 (1987); *see also United States v. Barrows*, 481 F.3d 1246 (10th Cir. 2007) (holding a reasonable expectation of privacy might have been established had an individual installed a password system for his personal computer files).

33. *See Arias v. Mutual Cent. Alarm Servs., Inc.*, 182 F.R.D. 407 (S.D.N.Y. 1998), *aff'd*, 202 F.3d 553 (2d Cir. 2000) (upholding monitoring by alarm company); *Briggs v. American Air Filter Co.*, 630 F.2d 414 (5th Cir. 1980) (upholding monitoring to investigate misconduct).

34. *Watkins v. L.M. Berry & Co.*, 704 F.2d 577, 581 (11th Cir. 1983).

35. *Doe v. Kohn Nast & Graf, P.C.*, 866 F. Supp. 190 (E.D. Pa. 1994).

36. *See, e.g., Thygeson v. U.S. Bancorp*, No. CV-03-467-ST, 2004 WL 2066746, at *18 (D. Or. Sept. 15, 2004); *Fraser v. Nationwide Mut. Ins. Co.*, 135 F. Supp. 2d 623 (E.D. Pa. 2001).

37. *Commonwealth v. Proetto*, 771 A.2d 823, 831 (Pa. Super. Ct. 2001).

38. *See, e.g., Booker v. GTE.net, LLC*, 350 F.3d 515 (6th Cir. 2003).

39. *See, e.g.,* Electronic Communications Privacy Act, 18 U.S.C. §§ 2510 *et seq.*; New Jersey Wiretapping Act and Electronic Surveillance Control Act, N.J. Stat. Ann. §§ 2A:156A-1 *et seq.*

40. Electronic Communications Privacy Act of 1986, 18 U.S.C. §§ 2510 *et seq.*

41. *Id.*

42. *United States v. Turk*, 526 F.2d 654, 658 (5th Cir. 1976); *see, e.g., Steve Jackson Games, Inc. v. United States Secret Serv.*, 36 F.3d 457 (5th Cir. 1994).

43. *See United States v. Turk*, 526 F.2d 654, 658 (5th Cir. 1976).

44. 18 U.S.C. § 2510(5)(a).

45. *See, e.g., James v. Newspaper Agency Corp.*, 591 F.2d 579, 581-582 (10th Cir. 1979) (holding that providing quality service and employee training as well as protecting the interests of the company are each legitimate business reasons to engage in employee monitoring).

46. *See, e.g., Briggs v. American Air Filter Co.*, 630 F.2d 414 (5th Cir. 1980).

47. 18 U.S.C. § 2511(2)(a)(i).

48. 18 U.S.C. § 2511(2)(d).

49. *See, e.g., Watkins v. L.M. Berry & Co.*, 704 F.2d 577 (11th Cir. 1983).

50. Del. Code Ann. tit. 19, § 705.

51. *See United States v. Ziegler*, 474 F.3d 1184 (9th Cir. 2007).

52. *Doe v. XYC Corp.*, 887 A.2d 1156 (N.J. Super. Ct. App. Div. 2005).

53. *Fayard v. Guardsmark, Inc.*, 1989 U.S. Dist. LEXIS 14211 (E.D. La. 1989).

54. *See* Kristina Dell & Lisa Takeuchi Cullen, *Snooping Bosses*, Time, Sept. 11, 2006, at 62-64 (explaining technological advancements in workplace surveillance) (available at *http://www.csea9200.com/pdfs/Community/TIMEMagazineSnoopingBosses.pdf*).

55. Employers who retain the services of an outside vendor to conduct surveillance should pay close attention to the FCRA, since the reports from those investigators would be considered "investigative consumer reports" under the FCRA and therefore its requirements relating to consent, notice, and other issues will apply. See Chapter 11, Pre-Employment Testing, for a more detailed description of the FCRA and an employer's obligations under it.

56. Reporters Comm. for Freedom of the Press, A Practical Guide to Taping Phone Calls and In-Person Conversations in the 50 States and D.C. (2008) (available at *http://www.rcfp.org/taping/index.html*).

57. *See, e.g., Trujillo v. City of Ontario*, 428 F. Supp. 2d 1094 (C.D. Cal. 2006).

58. *See Acosta v. Scott Labor, LLC*, 377 F. Supp. 2d 647 (N.D. Ill. 2005) (open spaces); *Marrs v. Marriott Corp.*, 830 F. Supp. 274 (D. Md. 1992) (security desk).

59. *Sanders v. American Broad. Co.*, 20 Cal. 4th 907 (1999). There has been significant litigation relating to whether the introduction of video surveillance cameras into a unionized workplace is a term and condition of employment for which an employer must bargain with the union. This issue was specifically addressed in *Anheuser-Busch, Inc., No. 14-CA-25299, 342 NLRB No. 49* (St. Louis, Mo. July 22, 2004), where the court determined that an employer had to provide unions with notice about the installation of hidden cameras in work areas and provide them with the opportunity to bargain over its impact.

60. 18 U.S.C. § 2511(d) (It is not unlawful "for a person not acting under the color of state law to intercept a wire, oral, or electronic communication where such person is a party to the communication or where one of the parties to the communication has given prior consent to such interception unless such communication is intercepted for the purpose of

committing any criminal or tortuous act in violation of the Constitution or laws of the United States or of any state").

61. *Compare, e.g.*, Alaska Stat. §§ 42.40.300(a) & 42.20.310(a)(1), *and Palmer v. State*, 604 P.2d 1106, 1108 n. 5 (Alas. 1979) (stating that the statute is intended to prohibit third-party eavesdropping and does not apply if a participant is the party engaging in the recording), *and* Ind. Code Ann. § 35-33.5-1 -5(2) (allowing the recording of a telephone conversation by either the sender or receiver of the communication, *with, e.g.*, Miss. Code Ann. § 41-29-531(e) (no civil liability if the person recording the conversation is a party to the communication *or* has received the prior consent of a party to the communication). *See generally* Reporters Comm. for Freedom of the Press, A Practical Guide to Taping Phone Calls and In-Person Conversations in the 50 States and D.C. (2008) (available at *http://www.rcfp.org/taping/index.html*); *see also* Association of Am. Physicians & Surgeons, Inc., Summary of Consent Requirements for Taping Telephone Conversations (available at *http://www.aapsonline/org/judicial/telephone.htm*).

62. *See, e.g.*, Del. Code. Ann. tit. 11, § 1335(a)(4) (statutory violation to intercept a telephone conversation without the consent of *all* parties); *see generally* Reporters Comm. for Freedom of the Press, A Practical Guide to Taping Phone Calls and In-Person Conversations in the 50 States and D.C. (2008) (available at *http://www.rcfp.org/taping/index.html*); *see also* Association of Am. Physicians & Surgeons, Inc., Summary of Consent Requirements for Taping Telephone Conversations (available at *http://www.aapsonline/org/judicial/telephone.htm*). In some cases, there is a disagreement as to whether a state is considered a one- or two-party consent state. For example, according to Montana law, it is violation of privacy to record a conversation "without the knowledge of all parties to the conversation." Mont. Code Ann. § 45-8-213. However, at least one Montana case held that, in the criminal setting, recording a conversation is permissible if one call participant consents. *State v. Coleman*, 616 P.2d 1096 (Mont. 1980); *see also State v. Brown*, 755 P.2d 1364, 1368 (Mont. 1988); *State v. Cannon*, 68 P.2d 705, 708 (Mont. 1984). Vermont law is also unclear. One Vermont court suggested that the federal statute on interception and disclosure of wire communications was applicable in a state setting. *State v. Fuller*, 503 A.2d 550, 551 (Vt. 1985). Another case indicated that in a criminal setting, a challenge to the recording of a conversation could be made on constitutional grounds, pursuant to the Fourth, Fifth, and Sixth amendments. *State v. Kasper*, 404 A.2d 85, 92-93 (Vt. 1979). Various interpretations might also arise in Illinois because a state statute prohibits recording a telephone conversation without the consent of "all parties to [the] conversation." 720 ILCS 5/14-2(a). However, an Illinois court found that the recording of a conversation by a party to the conversation is not a violation of the statute even if another party to the conversation is unaware of the recording. *People v. Jansen*, 561 N.E.2d 312, 314 (Ill. App. Ct. 1990).

63. 18 U.S.C. § 2510(2).

64. *See, e.g., Watkins v. L.M. Berry & Co.*, 704 F.2d 577 (11th Cir. 1983).

65. *Doe v. XYC Corp.*, 887 A.2d 1156 (N.J. Super. Ct. App. Div. 2005).

66. *Blakely v. Continental Airlines*, 751 A.2d 538 (N.J. 2000).

67. *Smith v. Delta Air Lines*, 486 F.2d 512 (5th Cir. 1973).

68. *Rogers v. American Airlines*, 527 F. Supp. 229, 231 (S.D.N.Y. 1981).

69. *Gloor v. Garcia*, 618 F.2d 264, 269 (5th Cir. 1980).

70. *Rogers v. American Airlines*, 527 F. Supp. 229, 233 (S.D.N.Y. 1981).

71. *Daniels v. City of Arlington*, 246 F.3d 500 (5th Cir. 2001), *cert. denied*, 122 S. Ct. 347 (2001).

72. *EEOC v. Red Robin Gourmet Burgers, Inc.*, 2005 WL 2090677 (W.D. Wash. Aug. 29, 2005).

73. Rania V. Sedhom, The EEOC's eRace Initiative: Combating Systemic Racism, Human Resources 2008 (Summer ed.) (available at *http://www.buckconsultants.com/buckconsultants/portals/0/documents/publications/published_articles/2008/Articles_Sedhom_Human_Resources_summer_08.pdf*).

74. *Id.*

17

Regulation of Off-Duty Conduct

Chapter Objectives

This chapter explores the rights of employers to regulate the off-duty conduct of their employees, which refers to employee behavior that occurs outside their regularly scheduled workday. The methods an employer might use to regulate off-duty conduct as well as the factors an employer should consider before using that conduct as the basis for the imposition of discipline are explained in detail. The chapter also contains an extensive discussion about legitimate business interests and public policy considerations that might be used to justify an off-duty intrusion, as well as potential liability under state laws for attempting to regulate off-duty legal conduct (such as smoking and eating unhealthy foods) and under Title VII and other federal anti-discrimination laws for failing to impose the regulations in a uniform and nondiscriminatory manner.

After completing this chapter, students should have a fundamental under-standing of the potential sources of liability for an employer who regulates the off-duty conduct of its employees. Students should be able to explain the factors that are considered when determining whether an employer has the right to use off-duty conduct as the basis for discipline, which includes analyzing the nature of the conduct, the employee's position, the likelihood the conduct will reoccur, and whether the behavior will affect an employer's reputation.

Upon mastering the main objectives of this chapter students should be able to

- define *off-duty conduct* and provide examples;
- explain the methods employers might use to regulate the off-duty conduct of their employees;
- define *legitimate business interest* and *public policy consideration*, and explain the relevance of each to the regulation of off-duty conduct;
- explain the factors that are considered to determine whether particular off-duty conduct might be an appropriate basis for the imposition of discipline;
- explain the significance of Title VII and other federal anti-discrimination laws as they relate to the regulation of off-duty conduct; and
- define *lifestyle choices* and their significance to a discussion about the regulation of off-duty conduct.

INTRODUCTION

The publisher of Archie Comics once wrote a scathing letter to the chairman of Viacom expressing his outrage at the behavior of Melissa Joan Hart, the actress who played "Sabrina" on the popular children's television show of the same name. In an attempt to change her wholesome image, the underage actress posed for semi-nude pictures in *Maxim* and *Bikini* magazines, and provided each with an extensive interview in which she discussed sex and drinking games. The publisher stated that the actress's behavior violated the wholesome image of the Sabrina character. He demanded that the company immediately terminate the actress unless she publicly apologized, admitted the interviews and pictures were a poor exercise in judgment, agreed not to repeat the behavior, and voluntarily participated in an anti-drinking campaign.[1]

off-duty conduct
behavior that occurs outside an employee's regularly scheduled workday, which an employer might try to use as the basis for the imposition of discipline

Today, employers remain concerned about the **off-duty conduct** of their employees and often use that conduct as the basis for discipline when it has an impact (or the potential to impact) their operational needs. For example, employees have been fired for off-duty conduct that includes posting certain materials on a MySpace page,[2] blogging,[3] dating married men,[4] refusing to obtain a divorce,[5] smoking,[6] drinking,[7] asking a controversial question at an anti-war political rally,[8] and participating in hate groups such as the Ku Klux Klan.[9] Other employees have been terminated for placing a bumper sticker on a car supporting a candidate their employer did not support[10] and for cross-dressing while away from the office.[11]

Although employees may believe they are subject to the control of their employer only during the workday, there has been litigation that has provided employers with limited rights to subject their employees to discipline, up to and including termination, for conduct occurring outside the employees' scheduled shifts. These rights are not absolute, however, so an employer seeking to use off-duty conduct as the basis for imposing discipline must determine whether a specific federal or state law, or the nature of the employment relationship it has with the employee, would prevent it from engaging in this type of regulation.

METHODS USED TO REGULATE OFF-DUTY CONDUCT

A. EARLY REGULATION

Employer control over the off-duty conduct of employees is not a new phenomenon. For example, nineteenth-century coal mines and steel mills provided housing for employees so employers could confirm their employees' church attendance.[12] One of the earliest publicized cases of this monitoring involved the Ford Motor Company's early twentieth century employment of more than

100 employees for its sociology department. The department's primary responsibility was to monitor the behavior of its employees (often in their homes) to make sure they did not drink too much, lead blemished sex lives, keep unclean homes, or spend their leisure time improperly.[13] Today, the rights of employers to regulate the off-duty conduct of employees are derived from a number of sources.

B. STATE REGULATION

Some states have legislated the extent to which an employer can regulate the off-duty conduct of its employees. For example, New York labor laws protect specific forms of private behavior, the scope of which was intended to cover legal, off-duty conduct that is not work related.[14] States such as Illinois, Nevada, North Carolina, and Wisconsin have legislated a response to their concerns about intrusive employer regulations and now protect the off-duty lawful use of any legal product.[15] So, for example, in these states employers would not be permitted to discipline employees for smoking cigarettes or drinking alcohol outside their regularly scheduled workday (if the individual is of legal age), because both cigarettes and alcohol are legal products. A number of other states have passed laws that protect other specific types of off-duty conduct. For example, some states protect the rights of individuals to be involved in politics and retain their employment.[16]

If there is no state law that prohibits the regulation of a particular type of off-duty conduct, an employer may look for ways to retain the right to use such conduct as the basis for the imposition of discipline. An employer seeking to regulate its employees' off-duty conduct might try to achieve this result by negotiating a morals clause, including a policy about the off-duty conduct in its company handbook, or taking the position that such regulation is permissible pursuant to the at-will doctrine since, under it, employees can be terminated for any legal reason.

C. MORALS CLAUSES

An employer seeking to regulate employee off-duty conduct could negotiate a **morals clause** for employees working pursuant to the terms of an individual employment contract. These provisions could provide an employer with a right to discipline, and in many cases terminate, an employee for engaging in off-duty conduct found to be morally offensive to the employer, its consumers, or to the community.

morals clause
contractual provision that provides the employer with the right to terminate an employee for conduct considered morally offensive

1. EARLIEST USES

Morals clauses received their most prominent attention in 1947 when the U.S. House of Representatives' Un-American Activities Committee (HUAC) held a hearing in which 11 prominent screenwriters were asked whether they were members, or had ever been members, of the Communist Party. The group of 11 writers collectively agreed that they would not answer the question, and as a result, were charged with contempt of Congress.[17]

Soon after this incident, MGM Studios conditioned the future employment of one of its employees on his testifying under oath that he was not associated with the Communist Party. When the employee refused to comply, MGM terminated his employment based on the morals clause in his employment contract, which stated he would "not do or commit any act or thing that [would] tend to degrade him in society or bring him into public hatred, contempt, scorn or ridicule, or that [would] tend to shock, insult or offend the community or ridicule the public morals or decency, or prejudice the producer or the motion picture, theatrical, or radio industry in general."[18] When the employee filed a lawsuit for wrongful termination, the court determined that the employee acted within his rights in refusing to testify because he was led to believe his association with the Communist Party would not impact his employment. The Ninth Circuit Court of Appeals, however, reversed the decision and upheld the termination.[19]

2. MODERN USE

Today, some employers use morals clauses or comparable provisions to control off-duty employee behavior with which they would not want to be associated. The employment contracts of sports, entertainment, and news figures may include morals clauses, such as one basketball player's contract that required him to "always be fully and neatly attired in public and at all times (on and off the basketball court), conduct himself in accordance with the highest standards of morality, honesty, fair play and sportsmanship, and not do anything which shall be detrimental or prejudicial to the Club, Association, or professional sports or which shall subject any thereof to ridicule or contempt."[20] In one case, a university employer terminated its new football coach, who was married with children, after he spent time in a topless bar and then in his hotel room with a number of strippers while attending a golf tournament.[21] An NFL coach was also recently fined $50,000 for making an obscene gesture at a public event.[22]

Other employers have disciplined, terminated, or compelled employees to resign for conduct that is viewed as immoral, or at least not consistent with the image an employer wishes to portray. For example, one school district required its new superintendent to sign a morals clause as part of his employment contract. The language in his contract stated that he would voluntarily leave his position, without pay, if any alcohol-related problems arose during the term of his contract.[23] In another case, when photographs of a dean from a Catholic high school were discovered on a sexually explicit website, he was forced to resign.[24]

The issue of whether the parties to an employment contract will negotiate a morals clause depends on a number of factors, such as what rights both parties have under state law, as well as whether the individual's off-duty conduct could be traced back to the employer. This is particularly relevant when an employee is a public figure whose off-duty conduct would likely be publicized and associated with the employer. However, because the majority of employees do not work under employment contracts, an employer might look for alternative ways to control the off-duty conduct of its workforce.

D. COMPANY HANDBOOKS

An employer might be permitted to regulate the off-duty conduct of its employees if such a policy is contained in its company handbook. Such a policy might allow the regulation of, for example, off-duty conduct that the company determines is immoral, or it might extend beyond the regulation of immoral behavior. For example, some employers have policies that restrict an individual's right to work at a second job or that require employees to obtain their supervisor's approval before making such an arrangement. This is usually justified based on a conflict of interest that might materialize if the two employers compete with one other, or if the sharing of information from one company to another might be detrimental. When implementing such policies, employers should ensure that the policy clearly states the type of conduct it will cover, and that it is applied in a uniform and nondiscriminatory manner.

E. EMPLOYEES AT WILL

Most working individuals are employees at will, which means they can be terminated with or without cause at any time. For at-will employees, then, in the absence of some type of prohibition such as a state law, employers will likely have the right to use off-duty conduct as a basis for discipline (up to and including termination) even in the absence of a written policy. The relevant question in these circumstances is whether the off-duty behavior engaged in by the employee fits into one of the exceptions to the at-will doctrine that would prevent the termination, such as, for example, the limitation on an employer's termination rights linked to certain public policies. For example, an employer is more likely to have the right to regulate an employee's decision to work as an exotic dancer after the conclusion of his workday than an employee's decision to participate in an evening labor demonstration. This is because as a public policy matter, courts will be more likely to support an employee's right to participate in a labor demonstration than a person's right to work as an exotic dancer. See Chapter 18, Employment at Will.

Employers should be aware that, even if they retain the right to regulate off-duty employee conduct using any of these methods, this will not guarantee that an adverse employment decision based on that conduct will not be challenged.

 **JUSTIFYING THE INTRUSIVE NATURE OF THE REGULATION**

Because, by definition, off-duty conduct occurs while an employee is not working, an inherent tension exists between the rights of employees to be free from employer intrusions while away from work and the rights of employers to control employee conduct that has the potential to impact their business operations. Based on this, all employees, even those who may be subject to a specific contractual provision or policy that would enable an employer to regulate their off-duty conduct, might challenge this employer behavior by asserting that the regulation was beyond the scope of rights retained by the employer, or the regulation should not be permissible because of its intrusiveness. Thus, employers should be prepared to justify any regulation that intrudes upon the rights of employees outside their regularly scheduled workday.

In some instances employers have provided an appropriate justification by showing that the regulation of off-duty conduct furthers a legitimate business interest or advances a particular public policy consideration. In determining whether either supports the intrusion, or in instances where an employer is asserting another justification for the intrusion, decision makers often apply a balancing test that considers a number of factors relating to the nature of the job and the nature of the behavior at issue to determine whether the off-duty can be used to support the imposition of the discipline.

A. ESTABLISHING A LEGITIMATE BUSINESS INTEREST FOR THE REGULATION

legitimate business interest
a justification for imposing discipline on an employee based on behavior that occurs outside the employee's regularly scheduled workday that usually relates to the potential for the behavior to adversely affect the employer's operations

Employers may be able to support their decision to regulate off-duty conduct by illustrating a **legitimate business interest** for the intrusion, which is an explanation as to why the intrusion is necessary. The most compelling business interests are those that are reasonable and supported by a showing that absence of regulation could harm the business interests of the employer or would be an impediment to the efficient operation of its business.[25]

In some cases, employers have been able to successfully establish a legitimate business interest that enabled them to impose discipline on employees as a result of the employees' marriage, dating, or cohabitation with a member of the opposite sex.[26] For example, when a deputy sheriff was terminated for refusing to end his relationship with the wife of a well-known organized crime figure, the court allowed the regulation of the off-duty conduct and the infringement on his right to privacy, and upheld the termination. The court reasoned that because the department that terminated the individual was investigating organized crime, the deputy had access to confidential materials, and the reputation of the entire department might be adversely affected by the relationship between the sheriff and the crime figure's wife, the discharge was appropriate.[27] Another employer was able to illustrate that it had a legitimate business interest in disciplining an employee who was a teacher for having an affair with a student.[28]

Employers have been able to establish legitimate business interests to regulate off-duty conduct in other contexts. For example, one court determined an employer could prohibit the use of off-duty drugs by its employees, based on the possibility that such employees might be required to report to work outside their regularly scheduled workdays in the event of an emergency.[29] The Supreme Court also supported an employer's right to terminate a police officer for off-duty conduct relating to the sale of videos depicting himself engaging in sexual acts due to the department's interest in ensuring its employees adhered to certain standards of behavior, rejecting the individual's claim that this action violated his First Amendment right to freedom of speech or that the off-duty regulation was intrusive.[30]

B. LINKING THE REGULATION TO A PUBLIC POLICY CONSIDERATION

Even in the absence of a showing that the regulation is necessary to further a legitimate business interest, employers seeking to regulate off-duty conduct may assert the regulation is appropriate because it advances a **public policy consideration**, which is a justification for the imposition of discipline in response to behavior that our society wants to discourage. For example, some courts have upheld the imposition of discipline on employees for off-duty drunk driving because our society has an interest in discouraging this behavior.[31] In another case, the termination of an employee who attended a company party accompanied by a mistress was upheld, because the court determined that the public policy frowning on extramarital affairs outweighed the value placed on an individual's right to privacy and free association while off-duty.[32]

public policy consideration
justification for the imposition of discipline in response to behavior our society wants to discourage

There are some other courts, however, that have protected the privacy rights employees have with respect to their personal lives more aggressively and have issued contrary decisions. For example, in one instance an employer's decision to terminate a married police officer because he was living with a married woman other than his wife was overturned. The court determined that because there was no indication that the living arrangement had an impact on the officer's ability to perform his job responsibilities, even though the behavior might not reflect a desirable societal result, the invasion of privacy that resulted from the rgulation of the off-duty conduct was not justified.[33]

When intending to rely on a public policy consideration, employers should be certain to research the applicable laws to determine the types of public policy considerations that have been accepted by the governing courts as well as those that have been rejected and found to be insufficient to warrant the imposition of discipline.

C. BALANCING TEST

In assessing whether a legitimate business interest or public policy consideration justifies the intrusion, and in instances in which an employee challenges the regulation of off-duty conduct on the basis of its overall intrusiveness, decision makers usually evaluate a number of different factors, weighing the rights of employees to engage in particular conduct outside work hours against the rights of employers to manage their operations, control their workforce, and protect their business interests. When applying this balancing test the nature of the conduct, the nature of the employer's business, and the harm to an employer's reputation that would result in the absence of regulation are each considered.

1. NATURE OF CONDUCT

The nature of the off-duty conduct that is the reason for the discipline is a significant component of the balancing test. For example, a court would be more likely to allow for the imposition of discipline in response to the conviction of an employee for a violent crime that occurred outside of work hours than for a conviction for tax evasion. (This would assume, however, that the conviction for tax evasion would not disqualify the individual from performing his job tasks as discussed below.) Similarly, an employer would have less difficulty defending the imposition of discipline in response to an employee's off-duty felony conviction for the sale of marijuana than for the employee's off-duty misdemeanor conviction for the possession of marijuana.[34]

2. NATURE OF EMPLOYMENT

The weight given to the nature of the off-duty conduct is also directly linked to the nature of the employer's business and the employee's position. Certain off-duty conduct may have to be tolerated by one employer but constitute an appropriate basis for termination of an employee for another. For example, it is not difficult to demonstrate the significance of the off-duty conduct of a police officer who commits a felony, a teacher who molests a child, a sales clerk who is convicted of shoplifting, or a bank teller who embezzles money from a local church fund.[35] (An employer, in fact, might actually be subject to liability for continuing to employ an individual who engages in these types of behaviors.) Similarly, it is unlikely that an individual who commits a sex crime or property theft will have the right to continued employment in a position that requires entering the homes of his employer's customers.[36] An employer would also likely have greater rights to discipline a news reporter for attending a high-profile protest against a politician she was expecting to interview in the upcoming week than another employee who also attended the protest, but whose job responsibilities were limited to playing the appropriate commercials during the interview breaks.

Along these same lines, when the off-duty conduct of an employee of the Department of Housing and Urban Development suggested he was a slumlord, the court upheld his termination because his off-duty behavior was clearly inconsistent with the goals of the employer.[37] Similarly, the termination of a police officer for engaging in an off-duty relationship with a 17-year-old female cadet attending a program to introduce high school students to the field of law enforcement was upheld, based on a finding that the officer's behavior would undermine public confidence in the police department as well as in law enforcement officers in general.[38]

3. LIKELIHOOD THE CONDUCT WILL REOCCUR

Another consideration is whether the off-duty conduct is likely to be repeated within the workplace. For example, one court upheld the discipline of an employee who engaged in disrespectful behavior toward his supervisor while off-duty because this incident occurred while both parties were on the employer's worksite, and the employee had previously been disciplined for similar behavior during work hours.[39]

In contrast, the termination of an employee of a shipowner for his off-duty drug use was overturned because the employee was closely supervised at work and the behavior was unlikely to occur again. In addition, because the employee's primary responsibilities included cooking, cleaning, and shopping, his off-duty conduct did not invoke safety concerns. The lack of a connection between the drug use and his job requirements, coupled with the unlikelihood of its reoccurrence, was used to overturn the termination.[40]

Similarly, the termination of a supermarket employee for moonlighting at a mini-market outside of his work hours was overturned, because the decision maker determined that the mini-market was not a true competitor, and the nature of the conduct (obtaining a second job to supplement the employee's income) was not deemed sufficient to support the employer's decision to end the employment relationship.[41]

4. OFF-DUTY CONDUCT THAT HARMS THE EMPLOYER'S REPUTATION

An employer would also be likely to have the right to regulate off-duty conduct if the conduct would harm the employer's reputation. This would include behavior that would jeopardize the employer's business operations by creating negative publicity that would have a detrimental impact on the organization's public image. If the conduct is unlikely to have an adverse effect on the business, the discipline is unlikely to withstand judicial scrutiny.[42]

For example, the termination of an employee by a world-class hotel was upheld after he was convicted of petty theft. The owner and manager of the hotel asserted that in addition to the strong likelihood that the employee would have an opportunity to engage in the same misconduct on a future occasion and the fact that honesty was a fundamental job requirement, its business would be unable to survive if they were forced to continue to employ dishonest employees. The employer argued that the nature of the conduct was particularly significant, because the employee's position required him to have regular unsupervised access to the rooms of the hotel guests.[43]

a. Determining the Impact of Off-Duty Conduct

A number of factors may be considered when determining whether off-duty conduct would have a detrimental impact on the employer's reputation.

i. Services Offered

The type of services that a business offers is relevant in determining whether the damage to the company's reputation is significant enough to justify the imposition of discipline. Damage to an employer's reputation may present a more significant concern for businesses that operate in consumer-oriented markets (e.g., airlines, retail stores, private schools, health clubs, daycare centers) than for companies operating in a product-oriented market (e.g., factory).[44] For example, in one case the termination of a hospital employee convicted of shoplifting was upheld because the employee's primary job responsibility was to tend to sick people in a small community. The rationale for upholding the termination was that because the employee was often alone in the rooms of the hospital's patients, the business would suffer irreparable harm if it became known that it continued to employ dishonest employees who would not be able to satisfactory complete their job responsibilities.[45]

ii. Potential for Publicity

The potential for an employee's off-duty conduct to be publicized is also a relevant consideration. The physical location of an employee's business is part of this analysis because it is linked to the amount of publicity an incident will receive and the impact the awareness of an incident will have on an employer's reputation. When public attention is focused on off-duty conduct and the employee has been clearly identified as employed by the employer, the damage to the employer may become evident. One decision maker recognized this by acknowledging that a prominent employer in a small, isolated town may suffer more harm as a result of a scandal stemming from the off-duty conduct of an employee than would an unknown employer in a large metropolitan area.[46] In upholding the termination of an employee charged with murder, an acknowledgment was made that in the small town where the crime was committed, "the crime was headlined in the local press [and] [l]iterally, every citizen was aware of the incident and it would be naïve to assume that the public would fail to associate [the employee] with the Company should she return to her job."[47] In another instance, the "sensational negative publicity" that surrounded an altercation involving an off-duty intoxicated officer was used to justify his termination.[48]

If the publicity specifically names the employer, this is particularly significant because absent any mention of the employer, it might be challenging to establish a connection between the off-duty conduct and the employer, which would be necessary to illustrate that its reputation would be harmed by the continued employment of the employee. In one case a police officer stopped a woman for a traffic violation and proceeded to kiss and fondle her without consent. The incident received a great deal of media attention and was covered on the front pages of the local newspapers. The decision overturning the termination of this employee from his second position as a hospital security guard, however, reasoned that because the newspaper coverage failed to mention or even suggest the guard's affiliation with the hospital, it was unlikely anyone would connect the off-duty conduct to the employer and impact its reputation.[49]

b. Establishing Proof of Damages

In assessing damages to an employer's reputation, the majority view is that an employer must show actual damage to its reputation to justify the imposition of discipline, but there is a minority view that permits the imposition of discipline based on the potential for this result. To support the termination of an employee based on her off-duty conduct, the employer is usually required to provide proof that continuing the individual's employment will harm the company's reputation. Because it is always possible to suggest that the conduct engaged in by an employee would result in the loss of a customer, or have a detrimental impact on an employer's reputation, most decision makers require employers to present specific evidence illustrating the harm that will occur if the individual remains employed, as opposed to just predicting that this will be the result. As one decision maker reasoned, "[M]ere surmise, conjecture, or speculation" that harm will occur will be insufficient to establish that the employer should have the right to terminate an employee for conduct that occurred while he was not at work. Instead, the employer will be required to provide proof that damages have occurred.[50]

D. OFF-DUTY CONDUCT THAT LEADS TO THE RELUCTANCE OR INABILITY OF OTHER EMPLOYEES TO PERFORM THEIR WORK

An employer might also have the right to impose discipline if the employee's off-duty conduct has a direct impact on other employees. If, for example, an individual who is convicted of a violent crime works late at night alongside other employees, and they refuse to continue to work under these conditions, this could provide the employer with the right to terminate the convicted employee.

E. OFF-DUTY CONDUCT THAT RENDERS AN EMPLOYEE UNABLE TO PERFORM JOB DUTIES

An employer will usually have the right to terminate an employee for engaging in off-duty conduct that renders him unable to complete his work responsibilities. For example, suppose an employee's license was suspended after he was convicted of drunk driving after a weekend wedding. If this individual worked as a bus driver, then he could likely be terminated for this off-duty conduct, even if the behavior could not be connected to the employer. This is because the nature of the off-duty conduct — the suspension of the employee's license — would prevent the employee from being able to continue to perform his work. The same result would be likely if an employee who worked as a professional (such as a doctor or a lawyer) had her license revoked due to off-duty conduct since, under these circumstances, the off-duty conduct would impact the ability of the employee to complete the work that she was hired to perform.

One caveat in these cases is that even if off-duty conduct prevents an employee from being able to perform the tasks associated with the position, the employer may still not have an absolute right to end the employment relationship. Instead, this right might be limited by an individual employment contract, a collective bargaining agreement, or a company policy established by the employer. For example, if the affected employee is a union member whose terms and conditions of employment are governed by a collective bargaining agreement, the agreement might include job security language that would require an employer to modify the employee's job responsibilities if an employee is unable to complete them, particularly if the employee can continue to perform the majority of the tasks associated with his position.

So, in the example above, if the bus driver whose license was revoked was working pursuant to a collective bargaining agreement, was only responsible for picking up students at the start of the day, and supervised the children in their gym class during the remainder of his scheduled shift, the employer might have an obligation to continue to employ the individual. The extent to which this obligation exists, if at all, would depend on whether the governing collective bargaining agreement included contract language that obligated the employer to reassign the employee's driving duties to another employee, and to provide the employee who lost his license with alternative tasks during the time he would have otherwise been driving.

F. MITIGATING FACTORS

Although all of the above factors are relevant in determining whether an employee's off-duty conduct can be the basis for the imposition of discipline, they cannot be looked at in isolation. Instead, there may be other factors related to an individual's employment that might impact the appropriateness of a particular level of discipline, or the decision regarding whether discipline should be imposed at all. As with many disputes relating to whether a particular level of discipline is appropriate, **mitigating factors**, which are extenuating circumstances that might affect the level of discipline imposed, are often relevant.

mitigating factors
extenuating circumstances or other factors that an employer might consider when determining the appropriate level of discipline

Generally speaking, mitigating factors do not excuse the improper conduct but instead are used to suggest that a lesser degree of discipline should be imposed. For example, an employee subjected to discipline based on a weekend drunk driving arrest might present evidence that earlier in that day he learned about a family tragedy, which he responded to by having a number of drinks. While this situation would not excuse the behavior, an employer might determine that the circumstance warrants a lesser degree of discipline, such as a suspension, as opposed to a termination.

Quite often employees point to their satisfactory or exceptional work performance, lack of disciplinary record, or long-term employment with a company as relevant mitigating factors to support the reduction or even revocation of any discipline imposed. For example, one employee was reinstated after being found guilty of shoplifting, based on her unblemished four-year record with the same employer and a showing that she never engaged in any other conduct that called her honesty into question.[51] Along these same lines, the termination of a teacher involved in a vehicular homicide was overturned, based on a showing of her 17 years of solid service, and a 14-month record of satisfactory service since the accident. In deciding that the isolated incident did not render the teacher unfit to counsel school children, the decision maker reasoned, "There is no evidence that the accident was anything other than an isolated occurrence in an otherwise unblemished past and, by itself, the accident would not justify the dismissal."[52]

G. REGULATIONS LINKED TO MEMBERSHIP IN A PROTECTED CLASS

The regulation of off-duty conduct that is closely linked to an individual's membership in a protected class is also closely scrutinized. Employers should pay careful attention to them because such regulations could be used as the basis for an independent discrimination claim which would represent an additional source of potential liability.

1. PREGNANCY

Because pregnancy is a protected condition under Title VII, employers who want to use it as the basis for imposing discipline must pay close attention to the potential for a discrimination claim. The regulation may be permitted if the employer can establish that the pregnancy conflicts with the employer's legitimate business interest. For example, one court upheld the termination of a pregnant employee based on an employer policy that allowed for the discharge of unmarried employees who became pregnant or caused a pregnancy, because the employer illustrated that, under these circumstances, the presence of an unmarried pregnant woman directly contradicted the mission of the employer to provide young girls with role models.[53]

In instances in which the connection between the pregnancy and the employer's mission was more tenuous, however, courts have disallowed the imposition of discipline. For example, when a public school required a pregnant, unmarried teacher to take a leave of absence, the court determined that the action violated Title VII because there was no established connection between the pregnancy and the woman's ability to teach her classes.[54] See Chapter 5, Sex, Pregnancy, and Genetic Discrimination.

2. RELIGION

Religious activities have also been subject to employer regulations despite the religious protections offered under Title VII that require employers to provide reasonable accommodations to enable employees to engage in religious practices. Employers have been most successful in regulating off-duty religious conduct when there is a potential for violence to result. For example, in one case in which the media publicized a bus driver's position as a leading member of a local Ku Klux Klan group, the termination of the employee was upheld. In supporting the employer's right to restrict the off-duty conduct of this employee in this manner, the factors the decision maker determined to be significant were the potential for (1) violence, (2) the striking by other drivers, and (3) a passenger boycott.[55] See Chapter 4, Religious Discrimination.

 **LIFESTYLE CHOICES**

Even as employers seek to avoid discrimination claims by ensuring they have a legitimate business interest that justifies the regulation of off-duty conduct linked to protected class membership, they should be aware that even more neutral regulations have the potential to result in discriminatory conduct. For example, as the cost of healthcare continues to rise, more companies are attempting to regulate the **lifestyle choices** of their employees with regard to their decisions about healthy eating, refraining from smoking, and exercising.[56]

lifestyle choices
day-to-day decisions that may impact an individual's health and well-being

A. APPLYING THE REGULATION IN A NONDISCRIMINATORY MANNER

As a starting point, employers should ensure that any attempts to regulate the lifestyle choices of employees are not discriminatory. For example, they should refrain from requiring members of a protected class to participate in certain wellness programs, designed to assist them in making better choices, based on stereotypes or preconceived notions about whether they would be more likely than others to make unhealthy lifestyle choices. Employers should also ensure that any regulations imposed do not have a disparate impact on members of certain protected classes. This might occur if, for example, the problem the regulation is seeking to address (such as the high costs of medical care for cancer or arthritis) is more prevalent in older employees, and that results in more stringent behavioral control over those employees. See Chapter 6, Age Discrimination.

B. ESTABLISHING A LEGITIMATE BUSINESS INTEREST

Employers can place themselves in the best position to defend the regulation of lifestyle choices by illustrating the legitimate business interest that supports their decision to regulate such choices. This business interest is the justification that would permit an employer to exert control over an employee's conduct outside the employee's regularly scheduled workday. As discussed above, the most compelling business interests are those that are reasonable and supported by a showing that an absence of regulation could harm the employer's business or be an impediment to the efficient operation of the business.[57]

Employers often establish their legitimate business interest in regulating lifestyle choices by pointing out that certain lifestyle choices lead to fewer incidents of chronic illnesses such as diabetes, heart disease, and arthritis, which could dramatically decrease insurance costs, as well as the productivity losses associated with extensive use of medical leave.[58] These concerns are supported by the fact that the Centers for Disease Control has found that heart disease, which killed more than 800,000 people in 2006, affects about 80 million Americans and is primarily caused by poor diet and lack of exercise over a lifetime.[59] This situation has compelled some employers to formalize their efforts to regulate the off-duty conduct of their employees through the offering of wellness programs.

C. FORMALIZED REGULATIONS THROUGH A WELLNESS PROGRAM

wellness programs
employer-sponsored benefit programs that provide employees with resources to make better lifestyle choices

Some statistics indicate that more than 81% of employers with 50 or more employees offer some type of **wellness program**, which are employer-sponsored plans designed to assist employees in making informed and healthy choices.[60] Employers justify the use of these programs by focusing on their potential benefits. For example, one study suggested that wellness plans that shift the focus of our health care system to prevention through positive choices rather than treatment could prevent 40 million cases of cancer, heart disease, and other chronic illness in the next 15 years and could translate into savings of more than $1.1 trillion in medical care costs and loss in workplace productivity.[61] Consistent with this justification for their use, some programs focus on healthy eating in an attempt to battle obesity and prevent the onset of certain related diseases, some focus on the cessation of smoking, and others provide information and incentives linked to overall health and workplace productivity.[62]

Even if an employer has a legitimate business interest to justify a wellness program, it must also keep in mind a number of potential legal issues associated with the administration of these programs.

1. RELEVANCE OF THE GENETIC INFORMATION NONDISCRIMINATION ACT (GINA)

Genetic information, in the form of genetic testing and family medical histories, that is used to determine susceptibility to certain diseases might be collected in conjunction with a wellness plan. Therefore, employers must understand the limitations that the Genetic Information Nondiscrimination Act (GINA) places on the collection and maintenances of such information. GINA is the federal law that prohibits workplace discrimination based on genetics and genetic information and places stringent controls on the circumstances under which information can be gathered and how it must be maintained.[63] Although GINA does not prohibit all requests for genetic information pursuant to a wellness program, rights to do so are limited. Specifically, GINA permits employers to ask for genetic information as part of a wellness program provided participation in the program is voluntary.[64]

a. Voluntariness of Wellness Program

If an employer does not require employees to participate in a wellness program and does not penalize those employees who decline to participate, then the wellness program will be considered voluntary.[65] Issues of voluntariness continue to evolve, such as whether a wellness plan that offers compensation for participation should be considered voluntary since those who decline to participate are arguably penalized because they are denied the opportunity to receive the compensation associated with the program.[66] Even if voluntariness is achieved, the collection of this genetic information is still subject to other requirements.

b. Gathering and Maintaining Information

GINA places stringent control on gathering genetic information pursuant to a wellness program. Specifically, the collection of information must be authorized in writing and can only be shared with the employee and a licensed healthcare professional or licensed genetic counselor.[67] Further, the information is subject to stringent confidentiality requirements and generally must be treated in the same manner as medical information, meaning it must be kept confidential and maintained in a file other than the employee's primary personnel file.[68] Based on these obligations, employers who ask employees to provide information about their medical histories to perform an overall assessment of their health as part of the overall wellness program must be careful not to solicit information that would violate GINA. See Chapter 5, Sex, Pregnancy, and Genetic Discrimination, for a more detailed discussion of GINA.

2. RELEVANCE OF THE AMERICANS WITH DISABILITIES ACT (ADA)

Employers who offer wellness programs must also understand the potential liability that might materialize under the Americans with Disabilities Act (ADA) because it permits only medical examinations and the collection of medical information that is job related and consistent with a business necessity.[69] As discussed above, GINA eases some of these restrictions on employers by allowing genetic information that may be medical in nature to be collected if the wellness program is voluntary and GINA's other requirements are met. Nevertheless, any medical information the employer collects still must be kept confidential and separate from personnel records.[70] Thus, employers who decide to gather this information must abide by this structure to avoid liability under the statute. See Chapter 7, Disability Discrimination.

3. RELEVANCE OF STATE LAWS AND OTHER POTENTIAL RESTRAINTS

Even employers who are confident that they have a legitimate business interest that will warrant the regulation of lifestyle choices and who collect and maintain medical and genetic information within the parameters established by GINA and the ADA must also determine whether there is an independent prohibition against the regulation of legal behavior. Although this is important to consider before attempting to regulate any off-duty behavior, it is particularly true for wellness programs because a number of states have laws that could impact an employer's right to regulate smoking and obesity, which are usually key components of such programs.

a. Smoking

The link between smoking and health, and the fact that one of the largest elements of the healthcare costs of a smoker relates to cancer treatment, has led to a significant increase in the number of employers attempting to encourage their employees to alter this behavior.[71] Most employers have the right to regulate smoking on their premises, and in some states employers actually have an obligation to do so. For example, the Tennessee Non-Smokers Protection Act makes it illegal to smoke in almost all enclosed public spaces, including restaurants, public and private educational facilities, hotels, shopping malls, sports arenas, restrooms, and lobbies.[72]

Despite these restrictions, there are a number of states that continue to protect the rights of individuals to engage in legal conduct outside work hours (which would include smoking), and other states protect the lawful use of lawful products (which would include tobacco).[73] Some states such as California go even further by prohibiting employers from demoting, suspending, or discharging an employee for engaging in lawful conduct that takes place away from an employer's business during nonwork hours.[74]

Even if an employer is permitted to regulate the off-duty smoking of its employees, it could be subject to a discrimination claim for failing to apply the rule in a uniform and nondiscriminatory manner. For example, if an employer attempted to regulate only the smoking habits of older employees, it could give rise to a claim of intentional discrimination under the Age Discrimination Employment Act (ADEA). Furthermore, employers should not limit the lifestyle regulations to certain job classifications without a legitimate business justification for doing so, because this decision could have a disparate impact on members of a certain protected class if they tend to be overrepresented in those job classifications, which could result in liability for unintentional discriminatory conduct pursuant to a disparate impact claim.

b. Obesity

Obesity has also become the subject of increased employer regulation due to concerns about higher insurance premiums for greater incidences of related medical conditions, as well as the potential productivity loss if related health problems necessitate the use of extended sick leave. However, the regulation of obesity has the potential to result in liability from a number of different sources.

Just as with all other types of regulations, employers that regulate obesity must do so in a uniform and nondiscriminatory manner. For example, an employer who attempts to regulate the level of obesity for its female employees, while not subjecting male employees to the same restrictions, could be subject to a claim for sex discrimination. In addition, in some situations obesity might constitute a disability under the ADA, in which case an employer would be prohibited from discriminating against an employee because of his obesity. Such regulations might also be prohibited under a state law.[75] Furthermore, some states have laws that prohibit workplace discrimination on the basis of physical appearance, which could include using an individual's weight as the basis for an adverse employment decision.[76]

KEY TERMS

- ✓ legitimate business interest
- ✓ lifestyle choices
- ✓ mitigating factors
- ✓ morals clause
- ✓ off-duty conduct
- ✓ public policy consideration
- ✓ wellness program

DISCUSSION QUESTIONS

Explain your response to each of the following questions with the understanding that in some cases there is no right or wrong answer. If you cannot make an informed decision with the facts provided, indicate the nature and significance of the additional information you would need. For the purposes of these questions, you can assume that the employers and employees mentioned below are covered by Title VII and other relevant federal workplace anti-discrimination laws.

1. What is off-duty conduct, and what factors are considered when determining whether an employer has the right to regulate it?

2. What is a mitigating factor that might support an employee's claim that discipline imposed for off-duty conduct should not be allowed or should be reduced?

3. Can an employer ever regulate off-duty conduct that is linked, either directly or indirectly, to an individual's membership in a protected class?

4. Jenn is a corporate executive negotiating her employment agreement. She tells her employer that what she does after her regularly scheduled workday is private, unless he wants to pay her a salary equal to her hourly rate based on a 24-hour workday, seven days a week. Do you agree with her?

5. If an employer wants to regulate the off-duty conduct of her employees but does not want to negotiate individual employment contracts, how else can the employer accomplish this result?

6. Liz is an employer who understands she has some rights to regulate the off-duty conduct of her employees, but does not believe these rights would allow her to regulate conduct linked to membership in a protected class. Provide examples of the conduct she might be permitted to regulate.

7. Do you think an employer would have the right to terminate its company president for marrying a woman who is a well-known adult film star? What additional facts would help you make a decision?

8. What would you need to know to assess whether an employer has the right to regulate the off-duty conduct of an employee related to his posting of messages on publicly displayed Internet message boards?

9. Do you think the owner of a world-class gym could require its employees to eat healthily and exercise five times a week as a condition of continued employment? Why or why not? What are the relevant considerations?

ENDNOTES

1. Adam Buckman, *Sabrina Told: Say Sorry, or So Long*, N.Y. Post, Sept. 30, 1999, at 5. Because Archie Comics owns the trademark for the Sabrina character, many of the issues surrounding this particular situation relate to the use of the trademark. However, the parallel between this situation and the one in which an employer attempts to control the off-duty behavior of its employees is what makes the situation relevant here.

2. *Fla. Teacher Fired over MySpace Page*, Local6.com (Jan. 25, 2007) (available at *http://www .clickorlando.com/education/10838194/detail.html*).

3. *See* Stephanie Armour, *Warning: Your Clever Little Blog Could Get You Fired*, USA Today, June 15, 2005, at 1B (available at *http://www.usatoday.com/money/workplace/2005-06-14-worker-blogs-usat_x.htm*).

4. *New York v. Wal-Mart Stores*, 9 Lab. Arb. Rep. (BNA) 143 (N.Y. Sup. Ct. 1993), *rev'd*, 621 N.Y.S.2d 158 (App. Div.1995).

5. *Frankel v. Warwick Hotel*, 881 F. Supp. 183 (E.D. Pa. 1995).

6. *See, e.g., Grusendorf v. City of Oklahoma City*, 816 F.2d 539, 543 (10th Cir. 1987) (finding an employee could be discharged for violating the company ban on on- and off-duty smoking during a training period).

7. *Best Lock Co. v. Review Bd.*, 572 N.E.2d 520 (Ind. 1991).

8. Chris Erikson, *Firing Lines*, N.Y. Post, Oct. 8, 2007, at 39 (describing other examples of terminations for off-duty conduct) (available at *http://www.nypost.com/p/item_UAKi6IyQ2WFiCANY27NxSI/1*).

9. *Slater v. King Soopers*, 809 F. Supp. 809 (D. Colo. 1992).

10. Timothy Noah, *Bumper Sticker Insubordination*, Slate (Sept. 14, 2004) (available at *http://www.slate.com/id/2106714/*).

11. *Olier v. Winn-Dixie*, 2002 WL 31098541 (E.D. La. 2002); *see generally* Jeremy W. Peters, *Company's Smoking Ban Means Off-Hours, Too*, N.Y. Times (Feb. 8, 2005) (available at *http://www.nytimes.com/2005/02/08/business/08smoking.html*).

12. *See* Peter T. Kliborn, *Privacy vs. Profit: Workers Are Being Watched and Tested: How Far Is Too Far?*, Des Moines Register, June 19, 1994, at 1.

13. David F. Linowes & Ray C. Spencer, *Privacy: The Workplace Issue of the '90s*, 23 J. Marshall L. Rev. 591, 597-598 (1990).

14. N.Y. Lab. Law § 20-d(5) to (7).

15. *See, e.g.*, Ill. Ann. Stat. § 80(1); Nev. Rev. Stat. Ann. § 608.017; N.C. Gen. Stat. § 95-130; Wis. Stat. § 111.31.

16. *See, e.g.*, Conn. Gen. Stat. Ann. § 203a (prohibiting discrimination based on an individual's candidacy or election to office); Wis. Stat. Ann. § 12.07 (prohibiting employers from enjoining employees from working as elected officials).

17. Paul C. Weiler, Entertainment, Media, and the Law 58 (1997). Prior to this hearing it was generally accepted that performers would not be penalized for their beliefs as long as those beliefs did not interfere with the performers' work. However, as a consequence of HUAC's highly publicized meeting, the major studios agreed to the Waldorf-Astoria Declaration, which said, among other things: "We will not knowingly employ a communist or a member of any party or group which advocates the overthrow of the government of the United States by force, or by an illegal unconstitutional method."

18. *Loew's Inc. v. Cole*, 185 F.2d 641 (9th Cir. 1950).

19. *Id.; see* Paul C. Weiler, Entertainment, Media, and the Law 58 (1997).

20. *Vaughn v. American Basketball Assn.*, 419 F. Supp. 1275 (S.D.N.Y. 1976).

21. Rick Bragg, *In Alabama, Where Coaches Are Revered, Sinning Not Tolerated*, N.Y. Times, May 9, 2009, at C13(available at *http://www.nytimes.com/2003/05/09/sports/ncaafootball/09alabama.html?ex=1053488451&ei=1&en=26fb6aebab619eda&pagewanted=all*).

22. Erik Matuszewski, *Jets Coach Rex Ryan Won't Face NFL Fine for Obscene Gesture*, Bloomberg.com (Feb. 3, 2010) (reporting the Jets fined the coach $50,000 for making an obscene gesture at a public event, but the National Football League declined to impose additional discipline) (available at *http://www.bloomberg.com/apps/news?pid=20601079&sid=atPHvlstEePM*).

23. Linda K. Wertheimer, *Board Hires Rojas as Superintendent*, Dallas Morning News, May 26, 1999, at A1.

24. S. Mitra Kalita, *Paul VI School Dean Resigns over Photo on Lurid Web Sites*, Wash. Post(Feb. 26, 2003) (available at *http://www.encyclopedia.com/doc/1P2-236979.html*).

25. *Best Lock v. Review Bd. of the Ind. Dept. of Employment & Training Servs.*, 572 N.E.2d 520 (Ind. Ct. App. 1991) (citing 76 Am. Jur. 2d § 57 (1975)).

26. *See, e.g.*, *Beechman v. Henderson County*, 422 F.3d 372 (6th Cir. 2005) (upholding termination based on an employee's dating of married individuals); *McCavitt v. Swiss Reinsurance Am. Corp.*, 237 F.3d 166 (2d Cir. 2001) (upholding termination based on off-duty romantic relationship); *State v. Wal-Mart Stores*, 1995 N.Y. App. Div. LEXIS 17 (upholding termination for violating company policy prohibiting married employees from dating unmarried employees).

27. *Baron v. Meloni*, 602 F. Supp. 614 (W.D.N.Y.), *aff'd*, 779 F.2d 36 (2d Cir. 1985).

28. *Naragon v. Wharton*, 572 F. Supp. 1117 (M.D. La. 1983).

29. *City of Palm Bay v. Bauman*, 475 So. 2d 1322 (Fla. 1985).

30. *City of San Diego v. Roe*, 543 U.S. 77 (2004); *see Ruiz v. Brown*, 579 N.Y.S.2d 47 (App. Div. 1992) (upholding termination of police officer who consorted with prostitutes, even though no money was exchanged).

31. *Maddox v. University of Tenn.*, 62 F.3d 843 (6th Cir. 1996); *Despears v. Milwaukee County*, 63 F.3d 635 (7th Cir. 1995). *But see Whitaker v. New Orleans Police Dept.*, 863 So. 2d 572, 574 (La. Ct. App. 2003) (overturning termination of police officer for driving while intoxicated outside his regularly scheduled work hours because employee might not have understood that the policy providing for such terminations applied to off-duty conduct).

32. *States v. Ohio*, 620 F. Supp. 118 (W.D. Pa. 1985).

33. *Briggs v. North Muskegon Police Dept.*, 563 F. Supp. 585 (W.D. Mich. 1983), *aff'd*, 46 F.2d 1475 (6th Cir. 1984).

34. *West Monona Cmty. Sch. Dist.*, 93 Lab. Arb. Rep. (BNA) 414 (1989) (Hill, Arb.) (citing Hill & Kahn, *Discipline and Discharge for Off-Duty Misconduct: What Are the Arbitral Standards?*, Arbitration 1986: Current and Expanding Roles, Proceedings of the 39th Annual Meeting, National Academy of Arbitrators 121-154); *see also Beck v. Florida Unemployment Appeals Commn.*, 768 So. 2d 522 (Fla. 2000) (illustrating that, on balance, a terminated employee's isolated failure to report an off-duty traffic violation was not sufficient to give rise to the denial of unemployment benefits).

35. *See, e.g., Shaddox v. Bertani*, 2 Cal. Rptr. 3d 808 (1st Dist. 2003) ("That a person's unfitness for law enforcement can clearly be found in off-duty behavior has become an established incident of public employment").

36. *West Monona Cmty. Sch. Dist.*, 93 Lab. Arb. Rep. (BNA) 414 (1989) (Hill, Arb.).

37. *Wild v. U.S. Dept. of Hous. & Urban Dev.*, 692 F.2d 1129 (7th Cir. 1982).

38. *City of Warwick v. Kelly*, 2005 WL 1006045 (R.I. Super. Ct. 2005).

39. *King v. Department of Veterans Affairs*, 248 Fed. Appx. 192 (Fed. Cir. 2007), *cert. denied*, 128 S. Ct. 1468 (2008).

40. *State of Alaska & Alaska State Employees Assn.*, 93-2 Lab. Arb. Awards (CCH) ¶ 3494 (1993) (Wilkinson, Arb.).

41. *Kroger Co. & United Food & Commercial Workers Union Local No 536*, 91-1 Lab. Arb. Awards (CCH) ¶ 8263 (1991) (Goldstein, Arb.).

42. *Whirlpool Corp.*, 90 Lab. Arb. Rep. (BNA) 41 (1987) (citing Staff of BNA, Grievance Guide 95 (6th ed. 1982).

43. *CSX Hotels*, 93 Lab. Arb. Rep. (BNA) 1037 (1989) (Zobrak, Arb.).

44. *West Monona Cmty. Sch. Dist.*, 93 Lab. Arb. Rep. (BNA) 414 (1989) (Hill, Arb.) (citing Hill & Kahn, *Discipline and Discharge for Off-Duty Misconduct: What Are the Arbitral Standards?*, Arbitration 1986: Current and Expanding Roles, Proceedings of the 39th Annual Meeting, National Academy of Arbitrators 121-154).

45. *Fairmont Gen. Hosp.*, 58 Lab. Arb. Rep. (BNA) 1293 (1971) (Dybeck, Arb.).

46. *West Monona Cmty. Sch. Dist.*, 93 Lab. Arb. Rep. (BNA) 414 (1989) (Hill, Arb.) (citing Hill & Kahn, *Discipline and Discharge for Off-Duty Misconduct: What Are the Arbitral Standards?*, Arbitration 1986: Current and Expanding Roles, Proceedings of the 39th Annual Meeting, National Academy of Arbitrators 121-154).

47. *Motor Cargo*, 96 Lab. Arb. Rep. (BNA) 181 (1990) (Jones, Arb.).

48. *Police Officers — Discharge*, Conn. L. Trib., Feb. 22, 1993, at L9.

49. *Government of the V.I.*, 91-2 Lab. Arb. Awards (CCH) 8543 (1991).

50. *Raytheon Co.*, 66 Lab. Arb. Rep. (BNA) 67 (1976) (Tarkus, Arb.).

51. *American Airlines*, 68 Lab. Arb. Rep. (BNA) 1245 (1977) (System Bd. of Adjustments: Harkless, Neutral Referee).

52. *West Monona Cmty. Sch. Dist.*, 93 Lab. Arb. Rep. (BNA) 414 (1989) (Hill, Arb.). Note that the arbitrator eventually upheld the discharge because it was determined the employee was under the influence of drugs and alcohol at the time of the accident and her job required her to counsel students on drug- and alcohol-related issues.

53. *Chambers v. Omaha Girls Club*, 834 F.2d 697 (8th Cir. 1987).

54. *Ponton v. Newport News Sch. Bd.*, 632 F. Supp. 1056 (E.D. Va. 1986).

55. *Baltimore Transit Co. v. Amalgamated Transit Union*, 47 Lab. Arb. Rep. (BNA) 62 (1966); *see also Matus v. GRMI, Inc.*, 885 So. 2d 48 (Fla. 2004) (finding an employee's off-duty aggressive behavior directed to a supervisor was sufficient to support a termination and disqualification for unemployment benefits).

56. In some cases, employers are permitted to charge individuals who smoke higher premiums for healthcare coverage. This issue is generally governed by state law and is beyond the scope of this discussion.

57. *Best Lock v. Review Bd. of the Ind. Dept. of Employment & Training Servs.*, 52 N.E.2d 520 (4th Cir. 1991) (citing 76 Am. Jur. 2d § 57 (1975)).

58. *See generally* Susan Combs, Fighting Obesity — The Business Response (available at *http://www.window.state.tx.us/specialrpt/obesitycost/06fightingobesity.html*); Counting Costs and Calories, Measuring the Cost of Obesity to Texas Employers (Mar. 2007) (available at *http://www.window.state.tx.us/specialrpt/obesitycost/*).

59. Matt Cover, *Insurance-Premium Regulation in Health Care Bill Rewards Bad Behavior, Penalizes Good*, Cnsnews.com (Aug. 21, 2009) (available at *http://www.cnsnews.com/news/article/52847*). In 2007, the average annual cost to employers and employees was reported to be respectively $3,785 and $694 for individual coverage, and $8,824 and $3,281 per year for family coverage. American Cancer Society Cancer Facts & Figures 2008 (available at *http://www.cancer.org/downloads/STT/2008CAFFfinalsecured.pdf*).

60. Wellness Council of Am., Building a Well Workplace (available at *http://www.welcoa.org/wellworkplace/index.php?cat=1&page=1*).

61. Michelle Andrews, *Desperate to Control Healthcare Costs, Employers Are Rolling Out Wellness Programs with Teeth*, U.S. News & World Rep. (Oct. 25, 2007) (available at *http://health.usnews.com/articles/health/health-plans/2007/10/25/americas-best-health-plans.html?PageNr=1*).

62. *See* Alison Harding, *Company Wellness Programs Improve Health, Cut Costs*, CNN Health (Sept. 1, 2009) (available at *http://www.cnn.com/2009/HEALTH/09/01/hcif.healthy.living/*).

63. U.S. Equal Employment Opportunity Commn., Background Information for EEOC Notice of Proposed Rulemaking on Title II of the Genetic Information Nondiscrimination Act of 2008 (available at *http://www.eeoc.gov/policy/docs/qanda_geneticinfo.html*).

64. 29 C.F.R. § 1635.8(b)(2) (allowing collection of genetic information, under specified conditions, when an employer offers health or genetic services as part of a voluntary wellness program); *see* Jeremy Gruber, J.D., President and Executive Director, Counsel for Responsible Genetics, Statement at U.S. Equal Employment Opportunity Commn. Meeting (Feb. 25, 2009) (regarding Notice of Proposed Rulemaking on Implementation of Title II of the Genetic Information Nondiscrimination Act of 2008) (available at *http://www.eeoc.gov/eeoc/meetings/2-25-09/gruber.cfm*).

65. U.S. Equal Employment Opportunity Commn., Enforcement Guidance: Disability-Related Inquiries and Medical Examinations of Employees Under the Americans with Disabilities Act (ADA) (available at *http://www.eeoc.gov/policy/docs/guidance-inquiries.html*).

66. *See* Jeremy Gruber, J.D., President and Executive Director, Counsel for Responsible Genetics, Statement at U.S. Equal Employment Opportunity Commn. Meeting (Feb. 25, 2009) (regarding Notice of Proposed Rulemaking on Implementation of Title II of the Genetic Information Nondiscrimination Act of 2008) (available at *http://www.eeoc.gov/eeoc/meetings/2-25-09/gruber.cfm*).

67. Genetic Information Nondiscrimination Act of 2008 § 202(b)(2).

68. Genetic Information Nondiscrimination Act of 2008 § 202(a); *see* 42 U.S.C. § 12,112(d)(3)(B); *see also* U.S. Equal Employment Opportunity Commn., Background Information for EEOC Notice of Proposed Rulemaking on Title II of the Genetic Information Nondiscrimination Act of 2008 (available at *http://www.eeoc.gov/policy/docs/qanda_geneticinfo.html*).

69. 42 U.S.C. § 12,112(d)(4)(A) (2000) ("A covered entitled shall not require a medical examination and shall not make inquiries of an employee as to whether such employee is an individual with a disability or as to the nature of severity of the disability, unless such examination or inquiry is shown to be job-related and consistent with business necessity").

70. *See* H.R. Rep. No. 101-485, pt. 2, at 75 (1990) ("As long as the programs are voluntary and the medical records are maintained in a confidential manner and not used for the purpose of limiting health insurance eligibility or preventing occupational advancement, these activities would fall within the purview of accepted activities"); U.S. Equal Employment Opportunity Commn., Enforcement Guidance: Disability-Related Inquiries and Medical Examinations of Employees Under the Americans with Disabilities Act (ADA) (available at *http://www.eeoc.gov/policy/docs/guidance-inquiries.html*).

71. *See generally* Jeremy W. Peters, *Company's Smoking Ban Means Off-Hours, Too*, N.Y. Times (Feb. 8, 2005) (available at *http://www.nytimes.com/2005/02/08/business/08smoking.html*); American Cancer Society Cancer Facts & Figures 2008 (available at *http://www.cancer.org/ downloads/STT/2008CAFFfinalsecured.pdf*).

72. *See* Tennessee Dept. of Health, Smokefree Tennessee: Tennessee Non-Smokers Protection Act (available at *http://health.state.tn.us/smokefreetennessee/*).

73. *See, e.g.,* Wyo. Stat. Ann. § 27-9-105; W. Va. Code § 21-3-19; N.C. Gen. Stat. § 95-28.2. Illinois, Maine, and Wisconsin have similar protections.

74. Cal. Lab. Code § 96(k); *see also* Colo. Rev. Stat. § 24-34-402.5(1) (2001) (protecting lawful activities); N.D. Cent. Code § 14-02.4-01 (2005) (protecting lawful participation in lawful activities).

75. *See, e.g., Viscik v. Fowler Equip. Co.*, 13 N.J. 1 (2002) (finding obesity is a handicap under the New Jersey Law Against Discrimination); *State Div. of Human Rights v. Xerox Corp.*, 480 N.E.2d 695 (N.Y. 1985) (finding obesity may be a disability under state law). *But see Philadelphia Elec. Co. v. Pennsylvania Human Relations Commn.*, 448 A.2d 701, 707 (Pa. Commw. Ct. 1982).

76. *See, e.g.,* Wis. Stat. Ann. §§ 111.31 *et seq.;* Mich. Comp. Laws Ann. §§ 37.1202, 37.2201 *et seq.*

Part IV

Firing

"When I have to fire someone, it's less traumatic if I use my helium voice."

Employment at Will

Chapter Objectives

This chapter explores employment at will, which is the doctrine that permits employers to terminate employees working pursuant to it with or without cause, and with or without notice. The most significant limitations on the rights of employers to terminate at-will employees are explained in detail, including those imposed by federal and state law, the public policy exception, promissory estoppel, and the duty of good faith and fair dealing. A number of sources of implied contracts that might limit the rights of employers to terminate their at-will employees are also discussed.

After completing this chapter, students should have a fundamental understanding about what it means to be an at-will employee and the reasons such employees might be terminated. Upon mastering the main objectives of this chapter students should be able to

- define *employment at will* and explain the termination rights employers retain under the doctrine;
- explain the relationship between employment at will and state and federal laws;
- explain the public policy exception and provide examples of behaviors that might fall under it;
- explain each element of a promissory estoppel claim and the potential relevance of such a claim to an employee at will;
- define *implied contract* and provide some examples of such contracts that might limit an employer's termination rights; and
- explain the significance of including an at-will disclaimer in an employee handbook.

INTRODUCTION

Most working individuals do not work pursuant to the terms of an employment contract. Instead, they are **employees at will**, meaning they can be terminated for any reason at any time.[1] Sometimes the at-will doctrine is defined as allowing a termination for good cause, bad cause, or no cause, and with or without notice.[2] Put another way, at-will employees can be terminated with or without cause, and with or without notice.[3]

employment at will
doctrine that allows for the termination of an employee with or without cause, and with or without any notice

A. TERMINATION FOR CAUSE

Under the employment at will doctrine, an employee's failure to report to work on time, to respect a supervisor, or to satisfactorily perform a job duty could constitute a valid reason for termination. An employer might also have the right to terminate an at-will employee because he did not fit in with the culture of the workforce — for example, if he appeared rigid with respect to work rules, while the workplace prided itself on its relaxed atmosphere.

B. TERMINATION FOR NO CAUSE

The employment at will doctrine permits an employer to terminate an at-will employee without cause, meaning there need be no particular reason for the employer's decision to end the employment relationship.[4] Therefore, an employer could simply tell an at-will employee that, effective immediately, her services are no longer needed and she is terminated.

Even though employers technically have this right, for a number of reasons, they rarely take advantage of this option. As a starting point, because it is expensive and time-consuming to recruit, hire, and train new employees, employers are unlikely to terminate employees for minor infractions that can be remedied or that have little impact on their business operations. In addition, terminations for minor infractions may have a negative impact on employee morale, which has the potential to affect the overall work performance and the productivity level of an entire workforce. An employer might also decline to terminate an at-will employee for no cause because earning a reputation for aggressively ending employment relationships, particularly for minor incidents of misconduct, could hinder its ability to attract and retain a talented workforce.

C. PRACTICAL APPLICATION OF THE DOCTRINE

Despite what seems to be the clear language of the at-will doctrine, there is a significant and persistent tension between those who favor a strict application of it, enabling employers to retain full discretion to terminate employees for any legal reason, at any time, and those who believe employees should have the right to continued employment provided they continue to satisfactorily perform their job responsibilities.

1. LITERAL APPLICATION PROVIDES EXPANSIVE TERMINATION RIGHTS

Proponents of an expansive application of the at-will doctrine argue that because at-will employees have the right to leave their employment at any time, employers should retain the reciprocal right to terminate these employees without any restrictions. A number of judicial decisions support this broad application.[5] For example, in one case a court held that an at-will employee who was terminated as a result of a company merger that was not discussed during the recruitment and interview process did not have a valid claim against the employer because, pursuant to the at-will doctrine, the employee could be terminated for any reason at any time.[6] Other courts haves supported this expansive application of the doctrine, holding an at-will employee might have to accept a termination decision even if malice or bad faith was the basis for it.[7]

Those who support the maintenance of broad termination rights for employers of at-will employees also point out that, although it is customary for an employee to provide a minimum of two weeks' notice of an intent to resign from a position, it is generally not required. Some suggest that employees who want to restrict an employer's termination rights should bargain for enhanced job security at the *beginning* of their employment, which would provide employers with an opportunity to decide whether this is agreeable and, if so, to bargain for a benefit in exchange for providing this additional protection.

2. RESTRICTIVE APPLICATION LIMITS TERMINATION RIGHTS

Not everyone, however, agrees that it is appropriate to provide employers with significant latitude to terminate their employees. Some people view employment as the right of an individual to earn a living, and some courts provide at-will employees with some protections by restricting the rights of employers to interfere with an employee's right to be gainfully employed.[8] Those who support this more restrictive application suggest there is an inherent imbalance of power between employers and employees that makes it unlikely an at-will employee will have sufficient bargaining power to demand any limitations on an employer's termination rights.[9] Thus, they argue that placing the burden on individuals to bargain for job security is not a practical solution, making some type of intervention necessary.

3. MIDDLE GROUND

The current landscape relating to the application of the at-will doctrine rests somewhere in between the above two positions. Employers continue to have wide latitude to terminate at-will employees, but this right is far from absolute. Instead, there are a number of well-established limitations on these rights, which provide at-will employees with some job security, depending on the reason their employer makes a decision to terminate their employment.

 **LIMITATIONS ON TERMINATION RIGHTS**

A. APPLICATION OF FEDERAL AND STATE LAW

For the most part, even those who support the most expansive application of the employment-at-will doctrine acknowledge that the right of employers to terminate at-will employees for no cause does not extend to allowing terminations that are motivated by discriminatory or illegal considerations. This means, on the most fundamental level, that the expansive termination rights provided for under the at-will employment doctrine do not include the right to terminate individuals for reasons that are otherwise prohibited by law.

1. PROHIBITION AGAINST WORKPLACE DISCRIMINATION

The prohibition against workplace discrimination is an expansive limitation on the rights of employers to terminate their at-will employees.[10] For example, because Title VII is a federal law that prohibits discrimination based on race, an employer could not terminate an employee because she was a member of a particular race and defend the discriminatory conduct by stating that, because the employee was working pursuant to the at-will doctrine, she could be terminated for any reason at any time. See Chapter 3, Race, Color, and National Origin Discrimination.

Similarly, an at-will employee could not be terminated based on her membership in any other protected class under federal or state law. For example, because marital status is a protected class under Wisconsin state law (meaning an employer is prohibited from using it as the basis for an adverse employment decision), an employer cannot defend its decision to terminate an at-will employee based on her marital status, even if there was an understanding that her employment was at-will and she could be terminated for any reason at any time.[11]

2. OTHER STATUTORY RESTRICTIONS ON TERMINATION RIGHTS

In addition to laws that prohibit workplace discrimination, there are other federal and state laws that place restrictions on the rights of employers to terminate at-will employees. For example, New Jersey's Conscientious Employee Protection Act (CEPA) prohibits employers from retaliating against employees for reporting actual or suspected unlawful conduct by their employers. Therefore, CEPA would prohibit a New Jersey employer covered by the law from terminating an employee for reporting unlawful conduct, which is a limitation on the rights of employers to terminate their at-will employees for any reason at any time.[12]

Some federal laws place additional restrictions on the rights of employers to terminate their at-will employees. For example, the National Labor Relations Act (NLRA) is the federal law that governs the relationship between employers and labor unions, and it prohibits employers from terminating an at-will employee for attempting to organize a workplace. Therefore, the NLRA places another limitation on an employer's right to terminate an at-will employee because an employer cannot use the employee's at-will status to defend conduct that would violate the NLRA by, for example, terminating an employee for exercising his legal right to participate in protected union activity such as participating in a peaceful labor demonstration.[13]

B. JUDICIAL MODIFICATIONS

In addition to these statutory limitations, courts have also placed further restrictions on the rights of employers to terminate at-will employees. Some of these limitations have developed over a number of years as courts have worked to balance the rights of employers to select their workforce and the rights of employees to sustain their employment. Because these exceptions are judicially created, whether or not they will apply to a particular termination will depend on which state laws govern a particular employment relationship.

1. PUBLIC POLICY EXCEPTION

In most states at-will employees cannot be terminated for reasons that conflict with a "clear mandate of public policy."[14] This is because the **public policy exception** is accepted by the majority of states, and it gives employees some degree of job security if the conduct that causes their employment to be placed at risk furthers a public policy or represents a type of behavior our society wants to encourage.[15]

public policy exception
limitation on employer termination rights under state law that could prohibit the termination of an at-will employee for conduct society wants to encourage

For example, an at-will employee who is terminated for refusing to follow her employer's instructions to complete an accident report in a manner she believed violated the law could assert the public policy exception to attempt to block this termination because our society wants to encourage employees to refuse to engage in behavior they believe is illegal.[16] Along these same lines, an at-will employee who is terminated for filing a workers' compensation claim, which is a statutory right employees have to receive a benefit for injuries sustained at work, could assert that the public policy exception to the at-will doctrine should be used to block this termination because our society wants to encourage people to assert their rights under state and federal laws absent the fear of losing their employment.[17]

a. No Precise Definition

The public policy exception is recognized by about 40 states and generally provides at-will employees with latitude to illustrate that a termination implicates a public policy.[18] Most courts agree that "'public policy' as a concept is notoriously resistant to precise definition."[19] However, there is a significant disagreement relating to what sources of law can be the appropriate basis for determining that a particular termination implicates a public policy.

Some courts provide individuals with significant leeway to assert what constitutes public policy for the purpose of this exception. For example, one court stated the policy could be established by "the state constitution; in the letter and purpose of a constitutional, statutory or regulatory provision or scheme; in the judicial decisions of the state and national courts; in the constant practice of government officials; and, in certain instances, in professional codes of ethics."[20] Other courts limit the circumstances under which the exception will apply, such as one court that held, "Unless an employee identifies a 'specific' expression of public policy violated by his discharge, it will not be labeled as wrongful and within the sphere of public policy."[21] Still other courts are reluctant to decide that a certain behavior furthers a public policy, holding that "courts should venture into this area, if at all, with great care and due deference to the judgment of the legislative branch to avoid judicial policymaking."[22]

b. Broad Categories

Despite the absence of a precise definition of what constitutes a clear mandate of public policy that would enable an at-will employee to successfully assert this exception, there are a few broad categories of conduct that are generally accepted as examples of the behavior that would fit within its scope. Specifically, employers are generally prohibited from terminating at-will employees for (1) refusing to engage in illegal behavior, (2) attempting to perform a duty required by law, or (3) reporting the illegal or inappropriate conduct of an employer.[23]

By way of example, an at-will employee terminated for refusing to falsify the payroll records of an employer could assert that the termination should be prohibited because society wants to encourage employees to challenge this type of behavior; supporting this termination would encourage employees to follow the instructions of their supervisors, even if they are directed to engage in questionable behavior, in order to protect their employment. Because this is not a desired societal result, the termination would likely not be upheld by a state that recognizes the public policy exception.[24] Similarly, the termination of an at-will employee for providing testimony in response to a subpoena probably would likely not be upheld, because our society wants to encourage employees to comply with the law.[25]

c. Exception Not Universally Accepted

It is important to research whether this exception is recognized under the state law in which an at-will employee intends to invoke it, because some states have rejected the application of this exception to at-will employment, and other states have restricted its application.[26] In outwardly refusing to apply this exception, for example, one court reasoned that the intent of at-will employment is to permit employers to retain extensive termination rights, which might include the ending of employment relationships for reasons that do not necessarily have a universal appeal.[27] Consistent with this line of reasoning, another court refused to impose a blanket rule that an employee terminated for exercising a statutory right or refusing to violate the law has a viable claim for wrongful discharge.[28]

2. PROMISSORY ESTOPPEL/DETRIMENTAL RELIANCE

Some states provide employees with the right to challenge an employer's termination decision, even in the presence of broad termination rights, based on a theory of promissory estoppel.[29] This theory, commonly referred to as "detrimental reliance," is an exception to the at-will doctrine that is rooted in contract law and provides for the imposition of a contract when technically one does not exist.[30]

promissory estoppel
legal theory that a promise should be enforced if an individual reasonably relied on the promise and injustice can be avoided only by such enforcement

a. Framework

Promissory estoppel is based on the idea that if an employer makes an individual a promise with respect to a job opportunity or continued employment (or any other promise), and the individual relies on that promise, then the promise should be enforced if injustice can be avoided only by the enforcement of it.[31] The concept of promissory estoppel was first introduced in 1898 when a woman left her job in reliance on her grandfather's promise to pay her $2,000. When the grandfather passed away before paying the money to his granddaughter, she sued his estate, which refused to make the payment, stating it had no obligation to do so. In requiring the estate to pay the money, the court determined that individuals have the right to enforce a promise if it was reasonable for them to act in reliance on it and it would be unjust not to enforce it.[32]

An at-will employee (or any other employee who is terminated but expected some degree of job security based on an employer's promise) can use this theory to challenge an employer's right to terminate his employment, provided the applicable state law recognizes this cause of action. The assertion of a promissory estoppel claim requires showing that

1. the employer made a promise;
2. it was reasonable for the employee to rely on the promise;
3. the employer would expect the employee to rely on the promise;
4. the employee acted in reliance on the promise; and
5. the employee would suffer significant harm if the promise was not enforced.[33]

b. Reasonable to Rely on an Employer's Statement

An individual asserting a promissory estoppel claim must show that reliance on an employer's promise was reasonable. By way of example, suppose an East Coast employer offers an individual living and working in California an executive position in its headquarters. In response, the individual informs the employer she has no interest in moving across the country, particularly because the real estate market is at its lowest point in years. From there, suppose the employer provides assurances that the individual's rapid salary escalation in the new job would compensate her for any loss she might suffer as a result of the sale of her home during this economic climate. In addition, suppose the employer provides the applicant with the names of a number of real estate agents to assist her in selling her home on the West Coast and purchasing one on the East Coast.

Under these circumstances, if the employee accepts the job offer, moves across the country, and is terminated within two weeks for no cause pursuant to the at-will doctrine, the employee might rely on the theory of promissory estoppel (assuming the applicable state law recognizes this cause of action) to attempt to block the termination or recover damages or both. In this instance, it would likely be deemed reasonable for the applicant to reply on the employer's statement and promise of job security since he exerted significant efforts (such as providing assistance in the selling of her home) in an effort to entice her to accept the employment opportunity.[34]

In contrast, in one case a court held that it was unreasonable for an individual to rely on an employer's statement that a position would provide any type of job security since the job posting clearly indicated that the position was a temporary opportunity.[35] In another instance, a court found that it was unreasonable for an individual to rely on a statement by a human resources employee about whether

her employment was guaranteed since it was established that only senior executives had the authority to alter the at-will status of an individual's employment.[36]

c. Failure to Enforce the Promise Would Produce an Unjust Result

An individual asserting a promissory estoppel claim would also have to show that a failure to require enforcement of the promise would produce an unjust result. Based on the above example, the newly hired at-will employee would allege that the employer should be prohibited from terminating her employment because of the representation it made that her future salary would offset the real estate loss incurred by selling her home at a loss. In addition, the employee would point out that it was reasonable to assume the employer knew she was acting in reliance on this promise, because the employer provided the assistance of a real estate broker. The employee would also have to show that by not enforcing this promise, she would suffer significant harm because she would not receive additional compensation to offset the loss she incurred based on her reliance on the employer's representation. The employee might illustrate additional harm she incurred by leaving her prior employment for what she was led to believe would be a long-term employment opportunity. See Chapter 19, Ending the Employment Relationship, for further discussion about promissory estoppel.

3. DUTY OF GOOD FAITH AND FAIR DEALING

Even if an employee did not expect some type of security as a result of a promise made by an employer, the individual might still have claim for wrongful discharge if the employer acted in bad faith when making the decision to end the employment relationship. A few states (approximately 11) apply the contractual theory relating to the **duty of good faith and fair dealing** to employment relationships, which is another limitation on the rights of employers to terminate their at-will employees.[37]

duty of good faith and fair dealing
contractual theory that may impose an obligation on both parties in an employment relationship to act in good faith

This obligation requires the parties who enter into an employment relationship to act appropriately toward one another because neither has the right to take advantage of the other, regardless of whether or not the at-will doctrine applies.[38] Some courts have interpreted this standard as a general obligation to act in good faith, while others have suggested it prohibits employers only from engaging in intentional deception and fraud or from denying an individual a benefit to which he was previously entitled.[39] One court held that an arbitrary termination decision would constitute a breach of this covenant,[40] and another court narrowed its applicability, finding that it applies only if an employer would receive an unjust financial benefit by depriving a former employee of compensation for past services performed.[41]

Although some states impose this obligation on the parties to an employment relationship, the majority continue to reject the idea that this standard applies to at-will employees, based on the view that the right to terminate such employees for no cause is intended to alleviate any restrictions, and, as one court stated, the imposition of covenant of good faith and fair dealing on an employer "irreconcilably conflicts with the employment-at-will doctrine."[42] Consistent with this line of reasoning, some courts have readily acknowledged that the at-will doctrine might require an employee to accept a termination for a reason that might be generally undesirable.[43]

C. IMPLIED CONTRACTS

An employer who wants to terminate an at-will employee for a reason that does not conflict with another law or does not fit into one of the above exceptions may still be subject to other restrictions. If an employer engages in conduct that suggests its intention was to provide the individual with some degree of job security, the at-will employee may attempt to compel the employer to act in accordance with that conduct. The at-will employee will assert that the employer, through its conduct, entered into an **implied contract** with the employee, and therefore will seek to enforce its contemplated terms.[44]

implied contract
contractual obligation that may arise based on employer conduct or statements

In evaluating whether an implied contract exists, the totality of circumstances is reviewed to determine whether the employer conduct was sufficient to override the presumption that the employer retained broad termination rights. The employee will argue that the employer acted in a manner that suggested employment was not governed by the at-will doctrine, while the employer will argue that nothing that was said or done was intended to limit its right to terminate the employee with or without cause. Sources of implied contracts include statements made during the recruitment process or interviews, language used in job advertisements, and company documents that establish terms and conditions of employment. See Chapter 10, Collection of Information: The Application and Interview.

1. STATEMENTS ABOUT SATISFACTORY JOB PERFORMANCE MAY SUGGEST CONTINUED EMPLOYMENT IS GUARANTEED

A claim that an implied contract exists might be based on an employer's statement relating to job expectations. For example, suppose an employer tells an employee he is only required to report to work at the start of a regularly scheduled shift and perform his job responsibilities. If this employee was terminated but could show that he reported to work on time and had satisfactorily completed his work, he could assert that the employer's statement limited his termination rights because it implied this was all that was necessary to guarantee his continued employment.

2. VERBAL AND WRITTEN STATEMENTS MAY SUGGEST EMPLOYMENT IS GUARANTEED FOR A SPECIFIC LENGTH OF TIME

Employers also have to be cautious about suggesting that an at-will employee is entitled to continued employment for any length of time. For an at-will employee to establish that some type of job security was contemplated, some courts require that an employer have made a clear and definitive promise to an individual that employment for a particular period of time is guaranteed.[45] However, some courts recognize that an employer's verbal or written statement might have also created an implied contract that guaranteed employment for a certain period of time.[46]

For example, suppose an employer tells an applicant that one benefit of working for the company will be the exponential salary increases he could expect to receive over the next three years due to the anticipated public offering of the company stock. If the employer terminates this employee before the stock's going public, the employee could assert that the termination was improper because it violated the terms of the implied contract. The at-will employee will argue that the comments made by the employer during the recruitment process implied that he would have a position for three years, or at least until the stock went public. Along these same lines, if an at-will employee is told that he should not be concerned about his job while he was out sick, this statement could be used by the employee to try to block the future termination of that employee due to absences related to an illness.[47]

The determination of whether an implied contract exists will be based on a fact-specific analysis that considers the totality of the circumstances. For example, one court held that by asking an applicant about his availability to work for one year, and basing a salary offer on a annual salary, the employer did not alter the at-will status of the employee. Thus, under this set of facts, the employer was not required to continue to employ the individual for a full year and could terminate him pursuant to the at-will doctrine.[48] Contrast this situation with another, in which an employer told an employee who was reluctant to leave her job to work for a start-up company that the position he was offering represented a better opportunity with respect to long-term career opportunities. Under that set of facts, when the individual accepted the new position and was terminated after two months, she used the statements made by her employer to assert that a certain degree of job security was contemplated by the parties, and the court agreed with her position, holding that the employer's statement promised a "reasonable" term of employment, which it defined as at least one year.[49]

Along these same lines, one court determined that a guarantee of a $1,000 weekly salary for 12 months could be interpreted as a one-year employment contract.[50] Another court held that when an employee received a letter confirming that 50% of his moving expenses would be payable immediately and the balance would be paid after one year, this was also a guarantee of one year of employment.[51]

Based on the uncertainty surrounding how a particular court might view such statements, employers should pay careful attention to the statements made and documents given to at-will employees relating to the employees' job security. In addition, employers must carefully draft any company handbook provisions that are designed to highlight workplace policies or to offer benefits to employees because these, too, might be used as the basis for an implied-contract claim, which could obligate the employer to provide the promised benefits and protections.

3. COMPANY HANDBOOKS

At-will employees often look to company handbooks to support their claim that their employment was not at will or at least that the employer did not intend to retain broad rights to terminate them for any reason at any time.

a. Content

There is no magic formula for the creation of a company handbook. The length and format will vary based on a number of factors, such as the nature of the employer's business and the size of its workforce. The most common provisions are those relating to expectations for employee behavior, paid time off (such as sick days, vacation days, and holiday pay), maternity leave and other leaves of absence, the process for the imposition of discipline, termination and layoff provisions, and anti-discrimination policies.

Other provisions that might be included relate to confidentiality and conflicts of interest, attendance policies, rules on moonlighting (working a second job), access to personnel files, acceptance of gifts, access to company premises, hiring of relatives, travel expenses, dress codes, and Internet and e-mail use. Depending on the industry for which the handbook is used, it might also include information about the employee's work product and who will retain the rights to any product created. The handbook might also include a noncompetition or non-solicitation clause designed to restrict the conduct of individuals during the term of their employment, but which most often refer to an individual's post-employment obligations to their former employer. See Chapter 20, Severance and Post-Employment Obligations, for a detailed discussion about restrictive covenants.

b. Binding Nature

Generally speaking, employees do not negotiate for the right to receive the benefits contained in the company handbook, and employers reserve the right to modify the terms in their sole discretion. Based on this, many courts have concluded that handbooks are not binding on an employer.[52] Consistent with this line of reasoning, one court held that at-will employees continue to be employed at will, even if a handbook exists, unless there is an agreement specifying a duration of employment or limiting the termination rights of the employer.[53]

In contrast, some courts have held that handbook language created an implied contract between an employer and at-will employee that provided for a degree of job security beyond that which would ordinarily be associated with at-will employment. For example, one court found that because the employer distributed a manual establishing a progressive discipline policy and just-cause standard for termination, employees could "justifiably rely" on the terms of the manual and expect those provisions to govern the employees' terms and conditions of employment.[54]

c. Poential for Certain Provisions to Limit Termination Rights

A company handbook is a useful tool to spell out the policies and expectations of an employer, and it can also be a valuable component of an employer's defense to a discrimination claim when used to support an employer's position that it has policies in place that are uniformly enforced. However, because of the uncertainty regarding whether a particular court will determine that company handbook language will create an implied contract and impose certain obligations on an employer, employers should pay close attention to the particular types of provisions that have the potential to undermine an employer's position that it intended to retain wide latitude to terminate its at-will employees.

i. Progressive Discipline

Many handbooks describe the employer's progressive discipline policy, which uses the gradual escalation of discipline to give employees the opportunity to remedy problematic behavior. The presence of a progressive discipline process suggests that employees cannot be terminated for a first offense (particularly for a minor infraction), but instead must be given guidance about how to resolve the problematic conduct and continue their employment. An employee at will might use the handbook language that sets forth the employer's progressive discipline process as evidence that a termination would not be appropriate unless progressive discipline was used. This was the result in one case, where a court held that an at-will employee could not be terminated after a first offense for misconduct because there was no evidence that progressive discipline was imposed, and the steps of the progressive discipline process were clearly outlined in the handbook that was disseminated to all employees.[55] See Chapter 14, Performance Management, for a detailed discussion about progressive discipline policies and their relevance to at-will employment.

ii. Termination Rights

Company handbook language that references termination rights may impact the rights of employers to terminate their at-will employees, unless the language mirrors the doctrine by stating that at-will employees may be terminated with or without cause and with or without notice. For example, if a handbook indicates employees will be terminated only for just cause — a standard for termination that is more restrictive than what is provided under the at-will doctrine — an employee would likely argue that this standard should apply to her employment even if she understood her employment was at will.[56] See Chapter 19, Ending the Employment Relationship, for a detailed discussion of the just cause standard for terminations.

iii. Severance Policy

If a handbook contains a severance policy that provides terminated employees with a monetary benefit or a provision that offers employees advance notice of the ending of their employment (usually a minimum of two weeks), this would also suggest the employer did not intend to retain expansive rights to terminate its employees with or without cause, or with or without notice. In addition, a layoff provision stating that employees will be laid off on the basis of seniority (number of years of service with the employer) suggests that even an employee at will cannot be laid off unless she is the least senior employee. See Chapter 20, Severance and Post-Employment Obligations.

d. At-Will Disclaimer

Despite the concerns associated with including provisions in a company handbook that might restrict the rights of employers to terminate their at-will employees with or without cause and with or without notice, some employers still desire to document their policies in this manner. There are some ways, however, that these employers can balance that desire with the desire to retain broad termination rights for at-will employees.

Many of the judicial decisions holding that a provision in a company handbook was intended to alter the status of an at-will employee have also recognized that the handbook might also include language that could refute this presumption. Specifically, in anticipation of a claim by an at-will employee asserting job security was contemplated by the parties based on certain handbook provisions, an employer could include a clear and conspicuous **at-will disclaimer** in its company handbook making it clear that the benefits contained in the handbook are not intended to override the at-will status of their employees.

i. Content

An at-will disclaimer might be as simple as a statement indicating that, notwithstanding any of the handbook language, at-will employees can still be terminated with or without cause and with or without notice. Some disclaimers are more extensive and include statements indicating that the handbook is provided for informational purposes only and does not constitute a contract or promise of a benefit of any kind. The language may go even further and say that neither the handbook, nor any other company documents, nor any verbal or written documentation from a supervisor constitutes an express or implied contract that can alter the at-will status of an employee.

ii. Format

An employer that incorporates an at-will disclaimer into a handbook must ensure that it is **clear and conspicuous**, which means that it is prominently displayed and distinguishable from the remainder of the handbook text. For example, in declining to attach any significance to a disclaimer that was not clear and conspicuous, one court noted it was not printed in a font distinguishable from the other text of the handbook, not capitalized, and not set off with a border.[57]

iii. Judicial Response

Most courts recognize that the inclusion of an at-will disclaimer in a company handbook weakens the claims of employees asserting the handbook imposes some type of contractual obligation on their employer and that their employment is not governed by the at-will doctrine.[58] For example, one court upheld the termination of a 30-year employee with no prior discipline pursuant to the at-will doctrine based on the employer's assertion that the individual simply did not have the same level of English-speaking skills as other employees. In its decision, the court noted that the at-will disclaimer clearly stated that the employer intended to retain the right to terminate its at-will employees in its sole discretion, and long-term seniority with an employer, even with a stellar record of work performance, did not impact the employer's established termination rights.[59]

Employers intending to rely on the use of a clear and conspicuous at-will disclaimer to maintain its broad termination rights must understand that decisions

at-will disclaimer
language included in a company handbook that makes it clear that the benefits described in the handbook are not intended to alter the at-will status of the company's employees

clear and conspicuous
standard used to determine whether an at-will disclaimer is displayed in a manner that makes it enforceable

about their legal significance are made on a case-by-case basis, and there is still no judicial consensus as to their precise impact.[60] Some courts give a disclaimer a significant amount of weight, ruling that its presence will defeat any suggestion that at-will employees are entitled to anything other than what is provided under the doctrine.[61] Other courts attach only minimal significance to an at-will disclaimer, ruling that there is an element of fundamental unfairness in allowing employers to provide benefits and protections to employees through a handbook but also providing employers with the sole discretion to decide that certain benefits and protections do not apply. As one court stated, "The mere inclusion of boilerplate language [i.e., at-will disclaimer] providing that the employee relationship is at-will cannot negate any implied contract and procedural protections created by an employee handbook."[62]

In most cases, the use of an at-will disclaimer, standing alone, is not sufficient to prove that an employer intended for its employees to remain subject to the at-will doctrine. Instead, courts look to the totality of the evidence and weigh the presence of a disclaimer (and whether it is clear and conspicuous) against the other evidence (including the types of provisions the handbook contains and any other circumstance that might affect the employees' employment status) to determine the ultimate impact of a disclaimer.[63]

KEY TERMS

- ✓ at-will disclaimer
- ✓ clear and conspicuous
- ✓ duty of good faith and fair dealing
- ✓ employment at will
- ✓ implied contract
- ✓ promissory estoppel
- ✓ public policy exception

DISCUSSION QUESTIONS

Explain your response to each of the following questions with the understanding that in some cases there is no right or wrong answer. If you cannot make an informed decision with the facts provided, indicate the nature and significance of the additional information you would need.

1. Define *employment at will*. Provide two reasons an employer would likely be permitted to terminate an at-will employee, and two reasons an employer would likely not be permitted to end an at-will employment relationship.

2. Provide a set of facts that would support an at-will employee's claim that her employer should not be permitted to terminate her employment, provided the

law of the state in which the claim is filed recognizes all potential causes of action and exceptions.

3. What is an *implied contract,* and what is the relevance of the term to at-will employment?

4. What is a disclaimer, and what is its relevance to employment at will?

5. Do you think the law should allow employers to retain expansive rights to terminate their at-will employees, or do you think that employers should be required to continue to employ individuals as long as the employees satisfactorily complete their job tasks?

6. Two friends are arguing about whether an employer can terminate an employee at will for forgetting to punch in using a time clock twice in the same week. What do you think?

7. Marci opens an art consulting company, and because she expects to be very busy during the grand opening, she hires 25 new employees. She knows she will need only four employees on a long-term basis, but she is not concerned, because she tells them they are at-will employees who can be fired for any reason at any time. Do you think this is a good idea? Why or why not? Do you have any other ideas about how she should proceed?

8. Jason just relocated to a new city to accept a new position and comes to your dinner party looking depressed. You ask him why he is upset, and he tells you he lost his job and there is nothing he can do because before he was hired he signed a document confirming he was an employee at will, who could be terminated for any reason. Are there any circumstances under which Jason might be able to challenge the termination?

9. Harper found out her boss was not paying any taxes and reported him to the Internal Revenue Service. Two weeks later, you see her in a bar, and she says the good news is that her boss is now paying his taxes but the bad news is she is unemployed. She tells you that her boss found out she reported him to the IRS, terminated her employment, and posted a statement on the Internet saying that she had a poor work ethic and should not be trusted. She says she feels helpless because she was an employee at will and knows there is nothing she can do about the situation. Do you agree?

10. Sloane left her job as the CEO of a Fortune 500 company to accept a new position based on the representations of her new employer, Fred. Specifically, Fred told her she would make a lot of money in her new position and receive season tickets for the upcoming football season. One month after she started her new job (and three months before the start of the football season), Fred told her that the company was going in a different direction and her services were no longer needed. Sloane went directly to Adam, who was head of the Human Resources Department, and he laughed and said there was a reason Fred never puts any promises in writing. (For purposes of this question, you can assume that Sloane was told she would be an employee at will.) Do you think Sloane might have a basis to challenge the termination?

11. Ryan is an employer who wants to draft a company handbook. He intends to use progressive discipline to manage his employees and to protect himself from workplace discrimination claims. However, he does not want to include the progressive discipline policy in the handbook, because he wants to be sure

to maintain the at-will status of his employees. Do you think this is a sound business practice?

ENDNOTES

1. *See Port Auth. of Allegheny County v. Unemployment Comp. Bd. of Review*, 955 A.2d 1070 (Pa. Commw. Ct. 2008) (employment is usually considered to be at will); *Foote v. Simmonds Precision Prods. Co.*, 613 A.2d 1277, 1279 (Vt. 1992) (holding an at-will employee can be terminated at any time, for any reason).

2. *See, e.g., Baker v. Tremco, Inc.*, 917 N.E.2d 650, 654-655 (Ind. 2009) (holding under the employee at will doctrine, an employee may be terminated with or without reason); *Montgomery County Hosp. Dist. v. Brown*, 965 S.W.2d 501, 502 (Tex. 1998).

3. *See, e.g., Tony v. Elkhart County*, 851 N.E.2d 1032, 1034 (Ind. Ct. App. 2006) (holding under the employment-at-will doctrine, employees can be terminated with or without cause); *Cress v. Recreation Servs., Inc.*, 795 N.E.2d 817 (Ill. 2003) (stating Illinois is an employment-at-will state).

4. *See Guarascio v. New Hanover Health Network, Inc.*, 592 S.E.2d 612, 614 (N.C. 2004) (at-will employment is terminable by either party at any time, regardless of the quality of the performance by the other party).

5. *See, e.g., Brown v. Hammond*, 810 F. Supp. 644, 645 (E.D. Pa. 1993) (holding an employer's right to terminate an at-will employee is "virtually absolute").

6. *Smalley v. Dreyfus Corp.*, 10 N.Y.3d 55 (2008).

7. *See, e.g., Jones v. Keogh*, 409 A.2d 581, 582 (Vt. 1979).

8. *See, e.g., Pearson v. Simmonds Precision Prods., Inc.*, 624 A.2d 1134 (Vt. 1993) (holding that neither an at-will provision in an employment contract, nor a contractual disclaimer indicating an employer had broad termination rights, would prevent the assertion of a negligence claim (arising from a termination) based on an employer's failure to disclose or misrepresentation of certain facts that had an influence on an individual's decision to accept an employment offer based on an expectation of job security).

9. *See Murphy v. American Home Prods.*, 448 N.E.2d 86, 89-90 (N.Y. 1983).

10. *See Kurtzman v. Applied Analytical Indus., Inc.*, 493 S.E.2d 420, 422 (N.C. 1997) (holding "federal and state statutes have created exceptions [to at-will employment] prohibiting employers from discharging employees based on impermissible considerations such as the employee's age, race, sex, religion, national origin, or disability, or in retaliation for filing certain claims against the employer").

11. *See* Wis. Stat. §§ 111.31-111.395 (prohibiting workplace discrimination based on, among other things, arrest records, sexual orientation, and the use of lawful products off the employer's premises during nonworking hours).

12. New Jersey's Conscientious Employee Protection Act (CEPA), N.J. Stat. Ann. §§ 34:19-1 et *seq.*

13. National Labor Relations Act § 7, 29 U.S.C. § 158(a)(1), (3).

14. *See, e.g., Borse v. Piece Goods Shop, Inc.*, 963 F.2d 611, 614 (3d Cir. 1992); *Clay v. Advanced Computer Applications*, 522 Pa. 86, 88, 559 A.2d 917, 918 (1989) (holding that if the discharge of an at-will employee threatens a clear mandate of public policy, there is a cause of action against the employer).

15. *See* Charles Muhl, *The Employment-at-Will Doctrine: Three Major Exceptions*, Mthly. Lab. Rev. (Jan. 2001) (available at *http://www.bls.gov/opub/mlr/2001/01/art1full.pdf*); *Considine v. Compass Group USA, Inc.* 551 S.E.2d 179, 181 (N.C. 2001) (recognizing the public policy exception to the at-will doctrine).

16. *See McClanahan v. Remington Freight Lines*, 517 N.E.2d 390, 393 (Ind. 1988) (allowing a cause of action for wrongful discharge by an at-will employee discharged for refusing to engage in behavior, at the direction of his employer, that would violate state law).

17. *See, e.g., Tony v. Elkhart County*, 851 N.E.2d 1032 (Ind. Ct. App. 2006) (blocking the termination of an employee for filing a workers' compensation claim).

18. *See, e.g., Palmateer v. International Harvester Co.*, 421 N.E.2d 876, 878 (Ill. 1981) (holding public policies can be found "in the state's constitution and statutes and, when they are silent, in its judicial decisions"); *Parnar v. Americana Hotels*, 652 P.2d 625, 631 (Haw. 1982) (allowing judicial decisions to "establish the relevant public policy"); *see generally* American Bar Assn., *Leaving a Job: Being Fired*, Family Legal Guide: Law and the Workplace (available at *http://public.findlaw.com/abaflg/flg-12-5a.html*).

19. *Gantt v. Sentry Ins.*, 824 P.2d 680, 687-688 (Cal. 1992).

20. *Boyle v. Vista Eyewear, Inc.*, 700 S.W.2d 859, 871 (Mo. Ct. App. 1985); *see Mat v. Advanced Clinical Commcns., Inc.*, 846 A.2d 604, 607 (N.J. 2004) (holding a clear mandate of public policy required under a statute can be established by something "other than a public policy statement in a statute, rule, or regulation"); *Green v. Ralee Engg. Co.*, 960 P.2d 1046 (Cal. 1999) (expanding sources of public policy to include federal regulations intended to protect public safety); *Parnar v. Americana Hotels*, 652 P.2d 625, 631 (Haw. 1982) (stating that prior judicial decisions may establish the relevant public policy).

21. *McGonagle v. Union Fid. Corp.*, 556 A.2d 878, 885 (Pa. Super. Ct. 1989); *see also Smith v. Calgon Carbon Corp.*, 917 F.2d 1338, 1344 (3d Cir. 1990), *cert. denied*, 499 U.S. 966 (1991) ("[A] 'clear mandate of public policy' [is] embodied in a constitutionally or legislatively established prohibition, requirement, or privilege").

22. *Gantt v. Sentry Ins.*, 824 P.2d 680, 687-688 (Cal. 1992).

23. *See, e.g., Ivy v. Army Times Publg. Co.*, 428 A.2d 831 (D.C. 1981) (refusing to commit perjury as requested by an employer); *Tacket v. Delco Remy Div. of Gen. Motors Corp.*, 937 F.2d 1201 (7th Cir. 1991) (filing a claim against an employer); *Hausman v. St. Croix Care Ctr.*, 571 N.W.2d 393 (Wis. 1997) (reporting abuse of nursing home residents); *Flenker v. Willamette Indus., Inc.*, 967 P.2d 295 (Kan. 1998) (reporting a safety violation).

24. *See Haas Carriage, Inc. v. Berna*, 651 N.E.2d 284, 288 (Ind. Ct. App. 1995) (upholding a claim by an employee who alleged he was wrongfully discharged for refusing to drive with a certain amount of weight in his truck, as directed by his employer, because it would violate the law to do so).

25. *Daniel v. Carolina Sunrock Corp.*, 436 S.E.2d 835, 836 (N.C. 1993).

26. *See e.g., Ed Rachal Found. v. D'Unger*, 207 S.W.3d 330, 332 (Tex. 2006) (holding that the limited public policy exception protected employees who were required to commit a crime, not those who were asked not to report a crime).

27. *See Winters v. Houston Chronical Publg. Co.*, 795 S.W.2d 723 (Tex. 1990) (refusing to extend the public policy exception to at-will employment).

28. *See Cantrell v. Morris*, 849 N.E.2d 488, 494 (Ind. 2006).

29. *Cohen v. Cowles Media Co.*, 479 N.W.2d 387, 391 (Minn. 1992); *Madden v. Omega Optical Inc.*, 683 A.2d 386, 392 (Vt. 1996) (holding promissory estoppel may modify an employment relationship that is otherwise terminable at will). *But see Van Brant v. Rauschenberg*, 799 F. Supp. 1467, 1474 (S.D.N.Y. 1992).

30. *See* Restatement (Second) of Contracts § 90 (1981).

31. Restatement (Second) of Contracts § 90 (1981); *see Orr v. Westminster Vill. N., Inc.* 689 N.E.2d 712, 718 (Ind. 1997).

32. *Ricketts v. Scothorn*, 77 N.W. 365 (Neb. 1898). This theory is memorialized in the Restatement (Second) of Contracts, which provides that an individual will be able to enforce a promise that "a promisor should reasonably expect to induce action or forbearance on the part of the promisee or a third person and which does induce such action or forbearance . . . if injustice can be avoided only by enforcement of the promise." Restatement (Second) of Contracts § 90 (1981).

33. *See* Restatement (Second) of Contracts § 90 (1981).

34. *See Ricketts v. Scothorn*, 77 N.W. 365 (Neb. 1898).

35. *See Watson v. Public Serv. Co. of Colo.*, 207 P.3d 860 (Colo. Ct. App 2008), *cert. denied*, 2009 WL 1280496 (Colo. 2009).

36. *See Jordan v. Radiology Imaging Assocs.*, 577 F. Supp. 2d 771 (D. Md. 2008).

37. *See* Charles Muhl, *The Employment-at-Will Doctrine: Three Major Exceptions*, Mthly. Lab. Rev. (Jan. 2001) (available at *http://www.bls.gov/opub/mlr/2001/01/art1full.pdf*).

38. Restatement (Second) of Contracts § 205 (Duty of Good Faith and Fair Dealing) ("[e]very contract imposes upon each party a duty of good faith and fair dealing in its performance and its enforcement"); *see 511 W. 232nd Owners Corp. v. Jennifer Realty Co.*, 98 N.Y.2d 144, 153 (2002) (holding that "neither party shall do anything which will have the effect of destroying or injuring the right of the other party to receive the fruits of the contract"); *Shelton v. Oscar Mayer Foods Corp.*, 325 S.C. 248, 481 S.E.2d 706 (1997) (holding "there exists in *every* contract an implied covenant of good faith and fair dealing"); *McHugh v. University of Vt.*, 758 F. Supp. 945, 953 (Vt. 1991) (holding there is an implied covenant of good faith and fair dealing in all contracts).

39. *E.I. DuPont de Nemours & Co. v. Pressman*, 679 A.2d 436, 442-444 (Del. 1996) (intentional deception and fraud); *Fortune v. National Cash Register Co.*, 364 N.E.2d 1251 (Mass. 1971) (earned benefit).

40. *Berube v. Fashion Cent.*, 771 P.2d 1033, 1049 (Utah 1989).

41. *Fortune v. National Cash Register Co.*, 364 N.E.2d 1251, 1257 (Mass. 1977).

42. *Madden v. Omega Optical, Inc.*, 683 A.2d 386 (Vt. 1996). Some courts have held that there is no duty of good faith and fair dealing in any employment context. *See, e.g., City of Midland v. O'Bryant*, 18 S.W.3d 209 (Tex. 2000); *see also Northern Heel Corp. v. Compo Indus. Inc.*, 851 F.2d 456, 466 (1st Cir. 1988) ("[not our role to] accomplish by judicial fiat what a party has neglected to achieve contractually"); *Federal Express Corp. v. Dutschmann*, 846 S.W.2d 282, 289 (Tex. 1993) (refusing to recognize the implied covenant of good faith and fair dealing within the employment context).

43. *See, e.g., Payne v. Western & A.R.R.*, 81 Tenn. 507, 519-520 (1884), *overruled on other grounds by Hutton v. Watters*, 132 Tenn. 527, 179 S.W. 134 (1915) (allowing discharge under the at-will doctrine for good cause, for no cause, or even for cause morally wrong).

44. *See* Charles Muhl, *The Employment-at-Will Doctrine: Three Major Exceptions*, Mthly. Lab. Rev. (Jan. 2001) (available at *http://www.bls.gov/opub/mlr/2001/01/art1full.pdf*) (indicating that 38 states recognize the implied-contract exception to employment-at-will doctrine).

45. *Giusti v. Sterling Wentworth Corp.*, 2009 UT 2, 201 P.3d 966 (Utah 2009).

46. *See Pickell v. Arizona Components Co.*, 931 P.2d 1184 (Colo. 1997).

47. *See Lopez v. Kline*, 953 P.2d 304, 306 (N.M. 1997). Depending on the nature of the illness, such an employee might also have a viable claim for the violation of his rights under the ADA, FMLA, or some other source of law.

48. *McIntyre v. Guild, Inc.*, 659 A.2d 398 (Md. 1995); *Cassel v. Ancilla Dev. Group, Ltd.*, 704 F. Supp. 865, 868 (N.D. Ill. 1989) (holding an agreement to compensate an employee on a monthly or annual basis did not create a guarantee of employment for a year).

49. *See Pickell v. Arizona Components Co.*, 931 P.2d 1184 (Colo. 1997).

50. *Berutti v. Dierks Foods., Inc.*, 496 N.E.2d 350, 354 (Ill. 1986).

51. *Miller v. Community Disc. Ctrs., Inc.*, 228 N.E.2d 113, 115 (Ill. 1967).

52. *See, e.g., Johnson v. National Beef Packing Co.*, 551 P.2d 779, 782 (Kan. 1976) (holding a handbook is a unilateral declaration of company policy that is not bargained for by employees).

53. *See Grose v. Procter & Gamble Paper Prods.*, 866 A.2d 437, 441 (Pa. Super. Ct. 2005) ("employee handbook does not overcome the 'at-will' presumption unless the handbook's language clearly expresses the employer's intent to do so"); *Fralin v. C & D Sec., Inc.*, 2008 WL 2345957, at *5 (E.D. Pa. 2008) (holding that for a handbook to become an express contract, it "must contain unequivocal provisions that the employer intends to be bound by it and renounces the long-held principle of at-will employment").

54. *Toussaint v. Blue Cross & Blue Shield*, 292 N.W.2d 880, 893 (Mich. 1980); *see Taylor v. National Life Ins. Co.*, 652 A.2d 466 (Vt. 1993) (company handbook can be used as

evidence that an at-will employee can only be terminated for good cause even though the employee did not bargain for its terms).

55. *See Ross v. Times Mirror, Inc.*, 665 A.2d 580 (Vt. 1995) (holding an employer must follow progressive discipline policies established in an employee handbook even if the employee is otherwise an at-will employee); *Farnham v. Brattleboro Retreat, Inc.*, 671 A.2d 1249 (Vt. 1995) (holding whether a handbook creates an implied contract with respect to the use of a progressive discipline policy is a question to be decided by a jury).

56. *See Tritle v. Crown Airways, Inc.*, 928 F.2d 81, 85 (4th Cir. 1990) (finding a handbook can create a unilateral contract if it states a definite promise that an employee will only be terminated for just cause).

57. *McDonald v. Mobil Coal Producing, Inc.*, 820 P.2d 986 (Wyo. 1991).

58. *See Grose v. Procter & Gamble Paper Prods.*, 866 A.2d 437, 441 (Pa. 2005) (holding an at-will disclaimer in a company handbook would undermine a claim that the handbook imposed a contractual obligation on the employer).

59. *Kang v. PB Fasteners*, No. 06-55913 (9th Cir. Feb. 27, 2008).

60. *Compare, e.g., Farnum v. Brattleboro Retreat, Inc.*, 671 A.2d 1249, 1254 (Vt. 1995) (finding that a boilerplate disclaimer cannot negate "any implied contract and procedural protections created by an employee handbook"), *with, e.g., Davis v. Wyoming Med. Ctr., Inc.*, 934 P.2d 1246, 1250-1252 (Wyo. 1997) (finding that a disclaimer is enforceable against a promissory estoppel claim).

61. *See, e.g., Peters v. USA Today*, 893 F.2d 1335 (6th Cir. 1990) (finding an employer retained the right to terminate an at-will employee with or without cause and with or without notice based upon the explicit disclaimer in the company handbook).

62. *Farnum v. Brattleboro Retreat, Inc.*, 671 A.2d 1249 (Vt. 1995).

63. *See id.* (holding disclaimers "must be evaluated in the context of all the other provisions" in a handbook, along with "any other circumstances bearing on the status of the employment agreement").

19

Ending the Employment Relationship

Chapter Objectives

This chapter explores the ways in which employment relationships end, by natural conclusions, layoffs, just-cause terminations, and resignations. The discussion includes information about the rights of employers to lay off employees to reduce costs as well as the obligations such decisions may trigger under the federal Worker Adjustment and Retraining Notification (WARN) Act. The just-cause standard for termination is discussed in detail, including an explanation of each of its elements and the circumstances under which it might apply to an employment relationship.

After completing this chapter, students should have a fundamental understanding of a number of ways an employment relationship might end. Upon mastering the main objectives of this chapter students should be able to

- provide some examples of how an employment relationship might end;
- define *layoff* and explain an employer's obligation to affected employees under the federal WARN Act;
- define *duty of good faith and fair dealing* and *promissory estoppel* and explain the significance of each;
- define *just cause* and explain its elements;
- explain why an employer might terminate an employee only for just cause, and provide some examples of implied contracts that might require the application of this standard; and
- define *constructive discharge* and explain its significance.

NATURAL CONCLUSION TO THE EMPLOYMENT RELATIONSHIP

Despite the extensive litigation surrounding employment terminations, many employment relationships end absent any dispute or ill will.

A. LENGTH OF TIME

One common situation that results in the conclusion of an employment relationship is the expiration of the period of time for which employment was contemplated. For example, two parties may agree to a specific term of employment, such as three years. In this case, the employee will perform services for the employer for this period of time in exchange for the agreed-on compensation. After the passage of this length of time, the relationship will come to its natural and mutually agreed-on end.

In some cases the parties will document their agreement in a written employment contract. It is important to understand that, even if the parties agree to enter into an employment relationship for a fixed period of time, they can mutually decide to alter its terms based on a change in circumstances. Therefore, even if the parties agree to a particular term and memorialize this understanding, there is nothing that would prohibit the parties from mutually agreeing that the relationship will end before that original agreed-on date.

For example, if an employee signs a three-year employment contract and his spouse is relocated to a different city at the end of the first contract year, the employee could ask his employer for a release from the existing agreement, meaning he would be relieved of his obligations to continue to work until the end of the negotiated term. The employer would have the right to refuse the employee's request, and might choose to do so, particularly if the services the employee offers are unique. If the employer declines to release the employee from the contract, the employee would have an obligation to continue to perform his work responsibilities for the duration of the three-year period. However, even though the employer may not have an obligation to consider such a release, it may be amenable to doing so, particularly if the employee is willing to provide assistance in finding a replacement and ensuring a smooth transition. Under this scenario, assuming both parties agree to this modification, the relationship will come to an end before the negotiated end date, and no liability would attach.

An employer that is itself faced with changed circumstances and wanting to make a staff change could also discuss the possibility of releasing an employee from a contract before the anticipated end date. However, just as the employer would have the right to decline to modify the contract term on the request of the employee, the employee would have a similar right if approached by the employer. Thus, if the employee declined to shorten the contract term and wanted to continue to work for the duration of the contract pursuant to its terms, the employer would have to continue to fulfill its obligation under the agreement. In some cases employers anticipate a potential change in circumstance and actually negotiate contract language that would provide them with the right to end the contract before the end date, usually in exchange for paying the employee all or part of whatever remaining compensation would otherwise be due under the agreement.

B. PROJECT-BASED EMPLOYMENT RELATIONSHIP

In addition to agreeing to a term of employment based on a specific period of time, two parties might also agree that the length of the employment relationship will be based on how long it will take for a project to be completed. For example, a law firm might hire an attorney to handle a lawsuit expected to last for a number of months. The parties may come to a mutual understanding that the employment relationship will continue until the case is resolved, at which point the relationship will come to its agreed-on end.[1]

C. CONTEMPLATED TERMS

Although two parties may agree that the employment relationship will end after the passage of a specific period of time or the completion of a project, there may be a disagreement as to what terms were contemplated. One such disagreement might relate to whether a fixed period of time was intended by the parties. This is significant because if the parties contemplate that the employment will continue for an indefinite duration, absent an agreement relating to a fixed term, most states will consider the employment to be at will, which means that the employer retains the right to terminate the employee with or without cause and with or without notice.[2] See Chapter 18, Employment at Will.

When disputes arise relating to whether the parties intended their employment relationship to end at the end of a specific time period, a court may be asked to determine if the parties' actions or discussions suggested a definitive end date. For example, one court found that a professional boxer had entered into a contract for a definitive period with his trainer, even in the absence of a written contract, after verbally agreeing to work with him for "as long as the boxer fights professionally." Based on this finding the court reasoned that because a definitive period was contemplated, the employee (the trainer) was not an employee at will, and his employer (the boxer) could not terminate the trainer's employment without cause. This is a right that the boxer would have retained had the court determined the parties did not contemplate a definitive term of employment and therefore the at-will doctrine governed the employment relationship.[3]

 ## LAYOFFS

There may be times when the parties to an employment relationship are satisfied with their working arrangement, but an employer makes the decision to end the employment relationship earlier than either party anticipates or even desires.

layoff
ending of an employment relationship, usually due to budget restraints, initiated by an employer due to a business need to reduce the size of its staff

For example, an employer might be faced with a business need that warrants a reduction in its staff due to budget restraints, perhaps in response to a decline in sales or the automation of certain functions previously performed by an employee.[4] Under these circumstances, an employer could implement the **layoff** process, which would end its employment relationships with the affected employees. (Note that an employer's right to lay off an employee within the parameters below assumes the parties have not entered an agreement — such as an employment contract or collective bargaining agreement — that restricts the employer's right to lay off the employee.)

A. DETERMINING WHICH EMPLOYEES TO LAY OFF

Although an employer generally has the right to determine the size of its workforce, it does not have the right to reduce the numbers of workers in a discriminatory manner. Instead, the employer must make decisions about who will be laid off using objective and nondiscriminatory considerations, avoiding the intentional or unintentional consideration of an employee's race, color, religion, sex, national origin, age, disability, or membership in any other protected class.[5] For example, employers are usually prohibited from basing layoffs on the salary earned by an employee because this policy would have a disproportionate impact on older employees.[6] In addition, some courts have held that basing a layoff decision on an employee's "years of service" or "pension eligibility" would constitute prohibited age discrimination under the Age Discrimination in Employment Act (ADEA), based on the disproportionate impact the consideration of these factors would have on older employees.[7] See Chapter 6, Age Discrimination.

B. PROVIDING NOTICE AND NOTICE PAY

notice
amount of advance warning an employee receives that employment will end

In many cases, employers provide laid off employees with some type of notice of the anticipated date of the end of their employment as well as a financial payment. **Notice** refers to how far in advance employees are told that their employment will end. An employer might provide two weeks' notice of a layoff, but some employers make the business decision to offer a significantly longer notice period, perhaps up to three months, during which time an affected employee will continue to work but will be actively seeking alternative employment.

notice pay
payment of an employee's salary for the period of time he would ordinarily continue to work after being informed his employment would end (but relieving him from his employment responsibilities)

Alternatively, some employers offer **notice pay** in lieu of notice. An employee entitled to notice pay would receive the amount of money equivalent to his salary for the period of time he would ordinarily continue to work after being informed his employment would end but would be relieved of his work obligations during that period of time. Some employers offer notice pay instead of notice to provide employees some financial support during the time they dedicate to their job search. An employer might also offer an employee notice pay in lieu of notice if the employer is concerned that the employee's continued presence at a worksite, while knowing his employment will end, would be disruptive to its business operations.

C. OFFERING SEVERANCE

In addition to providing a laid-off employee with notice, or notice pay, some employers offer additional compensation at the time the relationship is severed in the form of severance. **Severance** is a monetary benefit provided to a laid-off or terminated employee, usually in exchange for an agreement that the employer's decision to terminate the relationship under the particular circumstances will not be challenged, and will generally include additional language indicating that the individual will not assert any other claims arising out of their employment.

severance
monetary benefit provided to a terminated employee, usually in exchange for an agreement that the decision to end the employment relationship will not be challenged

1. CALCULATING THE BENEFIT

The calculation of a severance payment is usually based on a formula that provides a certain number of weeks' salary for each year of service completed by the impacted employee. For example, an employer may have a policy that provides employees two weeks' notice of a layoff (or two weeks' notice pay) along with a severance payment in the amount of two weeks of pay for each year of *completed* service. Under these circumstances, an employer who decides to lay off an employee who was employed for five years and six months would give the employee two weeks' notice that her employment will end, during which the employee will either work, or be relieved of her job responsibilities, but still be paid. In addition, this employee would receive an additional ten weeks of pay (calculated at the rate of two weeks' salary for each year of completed service) at the time of the layoff.

Some employers would also provide the full two weeks of pay for a partial year of service, meaning that this employee would receive another two weeks' pay for the last six months of service. Other employers might provide a prorated benefit for a partial year of severance, meaning this employee would receive one additional week of pay for the last six months of her employment prior to the layoff.

Employers generally have wide discretion to calculate this benefit, although, just like all other terms and conditions of employment, any severance policy must be applied in a uniform and nondiscriminatory manner. Employers can minimize the potential for a discrimination claim based on the payment of severance by establishing a clear policy outlining who is eligible for the benefit and how it will be calculated, and documenting the terms in a company handbook.

2. USING RELEASE AGREEMENTS

Employers can minimize the potential for the filing of discrimination claims in response to layoff decisions, as well as the filing of claims to address other potential issues related to the employment of the laid-off employees, by conditioning the payment of this severance benefit on the signing of a release agreement. Pursuant to the terms of the release, laid-off employees would waive their legal rights to file certain claims against their employer in exchange for the economic and noneconomic elements of an exit package. A more detailed discussion about severance, the use of release agreements, and the enhanced obligations required for those agreements intended to apply to claims arising under the ADEA can be found in Chapter 20, Severance and Post-Employment Obligations.[8] That chapter also includes a discussion about the rights of laid-off employees to receive unemployment benefits, a benefit provided under state law to qualifying individuals who lose their employment through no fault of their own (which would include laid-off employees).

D. NOTIFYING EMPLOYEES OF LAYOFF

Although employers will have significant latitude to determine whether to provide laid-off employees with financial assistance to supplement benefits that may be provided under state law, it is possible that employers will have less latitude with respect to the amount of notice they must provide to affected employees. Whether or not an employer has a legal obligation to provide notice in excess of what the employer would be obligated to provide pursuant to its company policy will depend on the number of employees affected as well as the state in which the individuals are employed. Generally speaking, small employers that have a business need to reduce staff have more flexibility with respect to notifying their employees they will lay them off than do larger employers that have the need to lay off large groups of employees or close their entire operation. The extent of this flexibility with respect to the notification requirements is governed by federal, and in some cases state, law.

E. COMPLYING WITH THE FEDERAL WORKER ADJUSTMENT AND RETRAINING NOTIFICATION (WARN) ACT

Worker Adjustment and Retraining Notification (WARN) Act
federal law that requires large employers (generally those with 100 or more employees) to provide 60 days' written notice to those employees who will lose their jobs due to a plant closing or mass layoff

The **Worker Adjustment and Retraining Notification (WARN) Act** is a federal law that requires employers of large businesses (generally those with 100 or more employees) to provide a minimum of 60 days' advance written notice to employees who will lose their positions as a result of a plant closing or mass layoff.[9] The intent of the WARN Act is to balance the needs of employers to streamline their operations by closing worksites and laying off employees with the needs of employees to have time to seek alternative employment.

The laws of many states, such as New York, New Jersey, California, and Illinois, provide greater protections for laid-off employees than the federal WARN Act by imposing obligations on smaller employers and providing more extensive notice requirements.[10] For example, private-sector New York employers employing 50 individuals (as opposed to employing 100 individuals, which is the threshold for coverage under the federal WARN Act) are required to provide 90 days' written notice of mass layoffs that will result in both plant closings and relocations (as opposed to the 60-day notice period required by the federal WARN Act).[11]

1. PLANT CLOSING AND MASS LAYOFF

The federal WARN Act provides extensive details about what constitutes a plant closing and a mass layoff. A **plant closing** refers to the shutting down of a single site of employment that results in the loss of a job for 50 or more employees (excluding part-time employees) for any period lasting 30 days or longer.[12] This notification is required even if the employer closes the site for a limited period, such as during a time period when the company is renovating its facilities. A **mass layoff** relates to a loss of employment for at least 30 days at a single site for (1) 500 or more employees (excluding part-time employees) or (2) 50 to 499 employees (excluding part-time employees) if the latter make up at least 33% of the employer's active workforce.[13]

An employer's business decision that would result in job losses or a break in employment that falls within these parameters will trigger notice obligations for the employer, and a failure to comply with these obligations could result in significant financial liability.

2. OBLIGATION TO PROVIDE NOTICE

The cornerstone of the federal WARN Act relates to the obligations of an employer to notify its employees that they will be laid off, which means that their employment will come to an end.

a. Length of Notice Period

The intent of the WARN Act is not to alter any existing notification period, so the 60-day notification period required under the Act may run concurrently with any other notification period that might apply to an individual's employment. For example, suppose an employer outlines its layoff policy in a company handbook, which provides that employees will receive two weeks' written notice of a layoff. If the circumstances of an employee's layoff fall within the coverage of the WARN Act, the employee would be entitled to a total of 60 days' written notice of the layoff rather than 60 days' notice plus an additional two weeks based on the benefit provided in the company policy.[14]

b. Exemptions

In some circumstances, an employer might be fully relieved from its obligation to provide the 60-day notice period to its affected employees, and in other circumstances less than the full 60 days' notice might be sufficient.

i. No Notice Required

The WARN Act provides two significant exemptions that completely relieve employers from the obligation to provide 60 days' written notice of a layoff. Specifically, employers do not have to provide this notice if the closing of a worksite is due to the closing of a temporary facility or the completion of a particular project. However, this exception applies only if the employees were *aware* of the temporary nature of their work at the time of their hiring. This provision of the WARN

plant closing
the shutting down of a single worksite that results in a job loss for 50 or more employees (excluding part-time employees) for any 30-day period (or longer) that triggers notification obligations for employers under the federal WARN Act

mass layoff
business decision that results in the loss of employment for at least 30 days at a single site for (1) 500 or more employees (excluding part-time employees) or (2) 50 to 499 employees (excluding any part-time employees) if the latter make up at least 33% percent of the employer's active workforce, and that triggers notification obligations for employers under the federal WARN Act.

Act represents another reason why it is critical for employers to clarify the terms and conditions of employment for employees at the time they are hired. See Chapter 10, Collection of Information: The Application and Interview, which discusses the ways employers can document an employee's key terms and conditions of employment.

The second category of employees who are not entitled to 60 days' written notice of a layoff consists of those employees who do not expect continued employment. Employees who voluntarily quit, resign, retire, are terminated for cause, are on strike, or have been locked out as a result of a labor dispute are not entitled to any notification under the WARN Act. In addition, all federal, state, and local government employees fall outside the scope of the statute's coverage and therefore are not entitled to 60 days' written notice of a layoff.[15]

ii. Partial Notice May Be Sufficient

Even if an employer is not fully exempt from its obligation to provide 60 days' written notice of a layoff, there are three other situations that might provide an employer with the right to provide its employees with a shorter notice period. In these instances, an employer may be able to avoid liability under the Act that would ordinarily be imposed if 60 days' notice is not given. However, for these exceptions to apply, the notice that is given must be provided as soon as it is practicable to do so and it must include the relevant information. Further, to assert a right to be relieved of some or all of the notice obligations, the employer is required to submit a statement supporting its position that one of these exceptions applies.[16]

(a) Faltering Company

faltering company
employer that is actively seeking financial assistance during what comprises the 60-day required notice period under the WARN Act, which prevents the employer from being in a position to provide notice to its affected employees

Partial notice may be permissible for a **faltering company**, which is a company that is actively seeking additional financial resources during the time that comprises the 60-day notification period. If this exception applies, a shorter notification period will be justified based on an employer's showing that alerting employees to the situation (and therefore presumably alerting potential investors) would have negatively affected the employer's ability to secure the funding that might have enabled the employer to avoid some (or all) of the layoffs.

(b) Unforeseen Consequences

An employer that makes the decision to lay off its employees for a reason it could not have reasonably foreseen might also be relieved of its obligation to provide the full 60 days' notice required by the WARN Act. For example, one court found that an employer's decision to lay off 200 employees three days after one of its largest customers decided to stop doing business with the company did not trigger WARN obligations because the employer did not anticipate this loss of revenue and had a business need to immediately respond to it.[17]

(c) Natural Disasters

The final type of situation that could relieve an employer of the obligation to provide 60 days' written notice of a lay-off relates to natural disasters. For example, a business that is forced to close as a result of a disaster such as a tornado or flood would likely be relieved of the obligation to provide the full 60 days' notice that would have been otherwise required by the Act if the unforeseen circumstance required the employer to reduce its payroll costs in fewer than 60 days after the occurrence of the event that warranted the layoffs.[18]

3. CONTENT OF NOTIFICATION

The WARN Act provides very little guidance as to what information needs to be included in the required written notice. Rather, it defers to the regulations promulgated by the **U.S. Department of Labor** (DOL), which is the federal agency that is charged with enforcing the WARN Act.

U.S. Department of Labor (DOL)
federal agency that enforces several federal statutes, including the WARN Act

a. U.S. Department of Labor (DOL) Guidance

The DOL has promulgated regulations that require WARN notifications to include the date of the layoff or plant closing as well as the name and contact information of the company representative to be contacted for additional information. Because written notification is required, a verbal announcement at a staff meeting will not constitute sufficient notification. In addition, due to the job-specific information that must be provided, it is unlikely that a press release to the media or a generic memo attached to the paychecks of affected employees will constitute sufficient notice.[19]

b. Unionized Employees

Because the terms and conditions of employment for unionized employees are governed by a collective bargaining agreement, employers of represented employees have additional reporting obligations under the WARN Act, and might also have additional notice and financial obligations pursuant to the terms of the existing collective bargaining agreement.

In addition, if the collective bargaining agreement provides covered employees with bumping rights, the notice provided to unionized employees must include technical information about those rights, so affected employees can assess whether they are entitled to other positions in the company, or whether they might lose their position to someone else who has more seniority (years of service).[20] **Bumping rights** are derived from some collective bargaining agreements and may provide employees with greater seniority (years of service) the right to displace other employees with less seniority in the event a position is eliminated. Information about bumping rights must be included in the notification sent to the union because there is a presumption that because the union is responsible for administering the collective bargaining agreement that governs their represented employees, they must be aware of the rights of their members working pursuant to the terms of the agreement.[21]

bumping rights
rights derived from a collective bargaining agreement that provide employees with more seniority the right to displace other employees, usually in the same job classification, if a position is eliminated

F. LIABILITY

Employer adherence to the WARN Act is important because a violation of the Act can result in significant financial penalties, which includes back pay and benefits for each affected employee for each day of the 60-day notice period during which the employee was not informed of the layoff. For example, an employee who was given ten days' written notice of a layoff instead of the 60 days required by the WARN Act could be awarded 50 days of back pay and benefits as a result of this violation.[22]

Even if an employer does not have a specific business need to reduce its staff, it may have other reasons for wanting to end an employment relationship. However, the rights of an employer to terminate its employees will vary depending on what the employer intentionally or unintentionally promised an employee, as well as other obligations that might be legally imposed.

TERMINATION RIGHTS PURSUANT TO A CONTRACTUAL OBLIGATION

As discussed in Chapter 18, Employment at Will, the majority of working individuals do not work pursuant to the terms of a written employment contract but instead are at-will employees who can be terminated with or without cause and with or without notice. However, in some cases an employment contract governs the employment relationship.

A. FACT-SPECIFIC TERMINATION RIGHTS

Some parties enter into a written employment agreement that will establish an individual's terms and conditions of employment. Under these circumstances, the parties usually intend to create a mutual obligation for employment. An employee will likely be willing to commit to work for an employer for a specific period of time in exchange for an employer's commitment to continue to employ the individual for a fixed term. When the parties enter into a written agreement, a significant issue relates to the circumstances under which an employer retains the right to terminate the relationship prior to the end of the agreed-on term.

The parties entering into an employment agreement for a specific duration (i.e., three years) may decide to negotiate the specific reasons an employer may terminate an employee prior to the end of this established term. For example, an individual may enter into a three-year employment contract to serve as the CEO of a company, and the employer may retain the right to end the individual's employment if stock prices fall below a certain price. Thus, the CEO's employment would continue for the three-year period, the end of the mutually agreed-on term, unless the stock price falls below the agreed-on price, at which point the employer could terminate the employment relationship.

An employee might also negotiate for the right to end the employment relationship before the expiration of the term. For example, a news anchor working in a small city might negotiate a contractual provision that would allow her to end the employment relationship before the end of the contract term in the event she is offered a position with a network news program. Under these circumstances, both parties would be bound by the terms of the employment contract for the full term, unless these circumstances materialized.

B. DUTY OF GOOD FAITH AND FAIR DEALING

The parties to an employment agreement might also negotiate termination language that clearly outlines the obligations each party will have to the other. This language can become significant because both parties to the agreement may be subject to a **duty of good faith and fair dealing**, which is the obligation imposed on employers to refrain from engaging in any conduct that will "have the effect of destroying or injuring the right of the other party to receive the fruits of the contract. . . ."[23]

duty of good faith and fair dealing
obligation imposed on the parties entering into an agreement not to engage in any conduct that will destroy or injure the rights of one another

In support of the imposition of this mutual obligation, one court made it clear that when two parties enter into a contract, it would be incorrect to "suppose that one party was to be placed at the mercy of the other."[24] Based on this, an employer who exercises a termination right under a negotiated contract might still be required to show that there was a legitimate business need for this decision to prevent a finding that the decision violated its duty of good faith and fair dealing.[25]

C. PROMISSORY ESTOPPEL/DETRIMENTAL RELIANCE

Even if the parties do not enter into an employment contract that establishes the termination rights of the employer, an employee might assert that a contract should be judicially imposed through the assertion of a promissory estoppel claim.

Under the theory of **promissory estoppel**, a terminated employee asserts her right to some type of enhanced job security (or other term and condition of employment), because an employer made a promise suggesting this result. This theory, commonly referred to as detrimental reliance, is rooted in contract law and provides for the imposition of a contract when technically one does not exist. A promissory estoppel claim is based on the idea that if an employer makes an individual a promise with respect to a job opportunity or continued employment, and the employee relies on that promise, then the promise should be enforced if injustice can be avoided only by the enforcement of it."[26]

promissory estoppel
limitation on an employer's right to terminate an employee if it was reasonable for the employee to act in reliance on the employer's statement that suggested some degree of job security or other term or condition of employment would be provided

Promissory estoppel is a cause of action that might be available under state law if the employee seeking to enforce a promise can show

1. the employer made a promise;
2. it was reasonable for the employee to rely on the promise;
3. the employer would expect the employee to reliance on the promise;
4. the employee acted in reliance on the promise; and
5. the employee would suffer significant harm if the promise was not enforced.[27]

When faced with termination, the terminated employee would assert a claim for promissory estoppel by arguing that even though a contract for employment did not exist, a court should impose one to prevent an unjust result. Promissory estoppel can be asserted by any individual who relies on a promise within the parameters outlined above.

At-will employees often assert a promissory estoppel claim suggesting they were promised some degree of job security. Thus, this cause of action might be relevant to parties who enter into an employment contract without a fixed term because such contracts are generally interpreted as an indication the parties intended for the employment to be at will.[28] Further, in the absence of contract language that establishes an employer's termination rights, the relationship will likely be presumed to be at will. Because of the potential relevance of a promissory estoppel claim, all employers (and employees) should be aware of its existence. Because it usually arises within the context of at-will employment, however, the cause of action is discussed in further detail in Chapter 18, Employment at Will.

APPLICABILITY OF THE JUST-CAUSE STANDARD

Although the parties to an employment relationship have significant latitude to negotiate the particular rights an employer will have to terminate the relationship, employers often terminate employees only for **just cause**, which is a broad standard that might be used to determine the appropriateness of an employer's decision to end an employment relationship in a number of different contexts.

The obligation to adhere to the just-cause standard may arise because the employer intentionally agrees to adhere to it, the standard is judicially or legislatively imposed, or the employer's conduct suggests this was the intended result. A just-cause standard provides employees with more job security than what is provided for under the at-will doctrine, which allows for the termination of employment with or without cause and with or without notice, but the just-cause standard also makes it clear that employment is not guaranteed.

just cause
broad standard that might be used to determine the appropriateness of an employer's decision to end an employment relationship in a number of different contexts

A. INDIVIDUAL EMPLOYMENT CONTRACTS

Employees working under a fixed-term employment contract might have negotiated contract language that establishes the just-cause standard will govern the employment relationship. For example, if an employee and employer negotiate a three-year contract with a just-cause provision, this means that the intent is for the employment relationship to continue for the three-year period, provided that the employee does not engage in conduct that would support a just-cause termination.[29]

The contractual language itself may refer to just cause, or the language might include more specific contractual guidance as to what types of behavior would constitute just cause and therefore provide the employer with the right to terminate the employment relationship. For example, if an employee is hired to increase the price of the company stock, the parties may agree to language stating that if the stock does not rise to a certain price by a certain date, this will constitute the just cause necessary for the employer to terminate the employment relationship.

The contractual language might also specify employee conduct that would not be acceptable to the employer and would, therefore, constitute just cause for termination if the employee engages in it. For example, the employer of a news anchor might negotiate a contract provision that says the employee will be terminated only for just cause, defined as accepting something of value from a interviewee in exchange for favorable news coverage, or failing to remain objective while conducting a news interview.

B. COLLECTIVE BARGAINING AGREEMENTS

Unionized employees are not employees at will. Instead, the rights of an employer to terminate unionized employees will be established by a **collective bargaining agreement**, which is a negotiated contract that establishes the terms and conditions of employment for the employees working under it

The parties have flexibility to negotiate termination rights that address their mutual needs, but the termination rights negotiated in a collective bargaining agreement will likely be much more restrictive than the termination rights provided for under the at-will doctrine. Many collective bargaining agreements provide for a just-cause standard for termination. A collective bargaining agreement might include basic language indicating that employees working under it are subject to a just-cause standard, it might provide a list of specific behaviors that would constitute just cause for termination, or it might include a lengthy explanation of what would and would not support a termination under this standard.

In addition to establishing a standard for terminations, most collective bargaining agreements also establish a **grievance and arbitration process**, which details the process the union can use to challenge the employer's administration of the agreement, which would include the exercising of any termination rights established by the agreement. This process is particularly relevant to a discussion about terminations, because it would be used by a union to challenge an employer's decision to terminate a unionized employee for a reason that did not rise to the level of just cause (or whatever standard was agreed to by the parties).[30]

collective bargaining agreement
contract negotiated between an employer and the labor union representing the employees of that employer that governs their terms and conditions of employment

grievance and arbitration process
method for unionized employees to challenge an employer's administration of a provision in a collective bargaining agreement, which would include the exercising of termination rights

C. STATE LAWS

Some states have laws that mandate the imposition of a just-cause standard for all terminations, regardless of whether the employment is at will or whether some other termination standard was negotiated by the parties.[31] In addition, employers who employ individuals governed by civil service laws are generally required to ensure their terminations are supported by just cause.[32]

D. JUDICIAL IMPOSITION BASED ON PRINCIPLE

Some courts have imposed the just-cause standard to terminations based on a general reluctance to provide employers with wide discretion to terminate their employees. As one court stated, an employer's right to terminate an employee must rise to the level of just cause "even where the employment contract, by its terms, purports to reserve to the employer the right to terminate the contract at-will."[33]

E. JUDICIAL IMPOSITION BASED ON EMPLOYER STATEMENTS OR CONDUCT

Other courts have imposed the just-cause standard based on employer statements and conduct that suggest the parties did not intend for the employer to retain broad termination rights.

1. VERBAL STATEMENTS

Courts usually will consider an employer's verbal statements when deciding whether the parties intended a just-cause standard (or some other standard that restricts the termination rights of an employer) to apply to their employment relationships. For example, an employee might present an employer's statement that the employee would be guaranteed employment for "as long as her job performance met the minimum standards" as evidence that she was promised she would be terminated only for just cause and could not be fired for any reason at any time pursuant to the at-will doctrine.[34] Other courts, however, suggest that a more definitive statement would be needed to provide the employee with any job security. For example, one court reasoned, "An employer must do something more than promise continuous employment to take an employee out of an at-will status."[35]

2. COMPANY HANDBOOKS

Courts have also held that a company handbook could contractually obligate an employer to apply a just-cause standard to all employees, including those who are at will. This result may be intentional, such as if an employer makes it clear in its handbook that all employees will be subject to a just-cause standard for termination, or it may be unintentional, such as if an employer includes other company policies in its handbook, like those discussed below, that would ordinarily be applicable only to employees whom the employer intended to be subject to a just-cause standard for termination.

a. Termination Language

The presence of language in a company handbook establishing a just-cause standard for termination could obligate the employer to subject all employees to that standard, regardless of whether an employee is at will or is working pursuant to an employment contract that provides the employer with expansive termination rights.[36] A handbook that intends to subject employees to a just-cause standard could do so by simply stating that all employees will be terminated only for just cause. Another alternative is for a handbook to provide a definition of just cause, to identify the types of behavior that would constitute just cause for termination (such as workplace violence or theft), or to reserve the right for the employer to determine whether misconduct rises to the level of just cause necessary for a termination based on the specific facts surrounding each particular incident. See Chapter 18, Employment at Will, for a detailed discussion relating to the impact a company handbook might have on an individual's status as an at-will employee.

b. Probationary Periods and Progressive Discipline

Even in the absence of clear language adopting a just-cause standard for terminations, an employer might adopt other policies in its handbook suggesting that the employer did not intend to retain the discretion to terminate its employees unless an employee's misconduct rises to the level that constitutes just cause for termination. For example, requiring new hires to serve a probationary period (a period of time at the start of an individual's employment during which the employer retains the right to terminate the employee in its sole discretion) and subjecting all employees to a process of progressive discipline (the imposition of escalating levels of discipline designed to identify and remedy problematic behavior) are policies suggesting that an employer intends to forgo some of the broad termination rights to which it might otherwise be entitled.

By subjecting newly hired employees to a probationary period during which they can be terminated for any reason, employers are suggesting that after the end of that period, a just-cause standard (or some other standard for workplace performance that offers some degree of job security) will be required to support a termination. By subjecting employees to a progressive discipline process, employers are suggesting that they intend to use a just-cause standard (or some other variation) as the basis for a termination. This is because pursuant to a progressive discipline policy, employees are not terminated the first time they engage in problematic behavior but instead are provided with the opportunity to address the problem in order to remain employed. This is in contrast to the at-will doctrine, for example, which provides the employer with the right to terminate an at-will employee the first time problematic behavior is exhibited.[37] See Chapter 14, Performance Management, for a detailed discussion about probationary periods and progressive discipline policies, and their relevance to at-will employment.

In many cases employers recognize the potential inconsistency between wanting to maintain broad termination rights with respect to their employees and including these types of policies in their handbooks. This perceived inconsistency can be addressed for at-will employees, however, through the use of a clear and conspicuous at-will disclaimer in a company handbook which makes it clear that the use of these policies is not intended to alter the at-will status of the company's employees. See Chapter 18, Employment at Will, for a detailed discussion about at-will disclaimers and their legal significance.

3. VOLUNTARY USE

Even in the absence of a contractual or statutory obligation to use a just-cause standard for termination, or a judicial decision imposing it, an employer may voluntarily apply the standard for a number of reasons. First, the consistent use of the just-cause standard is an effective way for employers to minimize the potential for a discrimination claim and maximize their ability to defend a claim in the event one materializes. This is because evidence of the presence of the just-cause standard could be used to refute a claim that a termination was arbitrary or the result of a discriminatory motive. In addition, some employers have determined that it is a sound business practice to apply this uniform standard for terminations so employees are confident they will be treated fairly as long as they continue to make a productive workplace contribution. Employers may also apply the just-cause standard to avoid earning a reputation for making rash and/or biased termination decisions, which could hamper their ability to recruit and retain talented employees.

ESTABLISHING JUST CAUSE

Once it is determined that, for whatever reason, an employer will apply the just-cause standard to a termination, the next question is how the standard is applied. Whether or not misconduct would constitute just cause for a termination will depend on a fact-specific examination of the circumstances that led up to the making of the termination decision.

"Since you love office gossip, here's a hot rumor
for you. Someone in this room is going to be
fired if they don't stop gossiping!"

A. DEFINITION

There is no precise definition of the term *just cause*, and this is likely because of the well-established understanding that whether an employee's conduct warrants the termination of employment will depend on the nature of the job and the offending behavior.[38] For example, an employer might be able to support the just-cause termination of a sales clerk who regularly arrives to work ten minutes late if that employee is responsible for opening the store each morning. This same behavior, however, might not rise to the level of warranting a just-cause termination for a sales clerk whose sole responsibility is to unpack boxes in a warehouse.

This does not mean that an employer cannot demand that all of its employees report to work at the start of their regularly scheduled shifts. However, the question as to whether an employee's lateness would permit an employer to terminate an employee whose employment is governed by the just-cause standard will depend on, among other things, the nature of the individual's employment, which is relevant to a number of the components of the just-cause standard.

B. FRAMEWORK

Regardless of the type of position to which the just-cause standard is applied, an examination of whether an employee's misconduct rises to this level usually examines (1) whether the employee had notice of the rule that prohibited the conduct, (2) whether the rule was reasonable, (3) whether the employer conducted an investigation before the termination, (4) whether the rule was uniformly enforced, and (5) whether the penalty was appropriate based on the nature of the misconduct.[39] An employer will be in the best position to defend a just-cause termination if each of the listed elements is present, and the absence of any one component will likely be problematic. However, an employer could minimize the impact of a weakness in one element by illustrating that the presence of one or more of the other elements is particularly compelling.

1. NOTICE

The first element in the just-cause framework relates to whether the terminated employee was on notice that the behavior at issue was impermissible and could result in termination. The relevant inquiries for this element relate to whether the employer had an obligation to communicate a rule to place an employee on notice of it, and if so, what type of notice would be sufficient.

a. Value of Communicating Work Rules and Expectations

Employers should communicate workplace rules and expectations to their employees and make it clear that the violation of the rules or the failure to meet the expectations of the employer will place their employment at risk. This is important, because if an employer cannot show that an employee was aware of a workplace rule, then the employer will have a difficult time justifying a termination based upon a violation of it under the just-cause standard.

i. Refrain from Making Assumptions About Acceptable Standards of Behavior

Employers should not assume that employees will share their views about what constitutes acceptable workplace behavior. Instead they should clearly communicate their workplace expectations along with the consequences of failing to meet them. For example, suppose an employee is entitled to a one-hour lunch break, regularly takes a one-hour and ten-minute lunch break, and is subsequently terminated for not adhering to work rules, which the employer determines supports a just-cause termination. Although an employer might assume its employees know they are required to return from their lunch breaks on time, this may not be accurate. Some employers might be more flexible in enforcing the start and end time of breaks, and others may not be concerned about minor infractions as long as their employees satisfactorily complete their job tasks. Thus, employers who expect their employees to strictly comply with the start and end times of their shifts and want to minimize challenges to discipline imposed for not adhering to those time frames should make sure this expectation is clearly communicated to those it affects.

ii. Communication of Rule May Not Be Necessary

Despite the importance of educating employees about workplace rules, in some instances employers can establish an employee had notice of a rule absent proof that it was actually communicated. In making this determination, some courts impose a *reasonable person standard*, meaning they look to whether the conduct is something that a reasonable person should know would not be tolerated.[40] For example, if a supervisor asks an employee to complete a work assignment and the employee responds by assaulting the supervisor, the employee would have a difficult time asserting that he was unaware of the prohibition against physical violence because the rule was not communicated to him. If a bus driver is caught drinking a beer immediately before reporting for his shift, it would likely be considered unreasonable for him to assert he was unaware this behavior would not be tolerated, even if the employer did not clearly communicate that this was the expectation.

Although employers may be able to overcome the notice component of the just-cause framework depending on the nature of the misconduct, most err on the side of caution when establishing standards for their workforce and expend efforts to ensure employees are on notice of the rules and consequences of noncompliance. It is simply easier to present evidence that an employer placed an employee on notice of a rule than to litigate whether the conduct warrants an exception to the notice requirement because employees should have known that certain conduct would not be tolerated.

b. Methods of Providing Notice

Once the employer determines what rules will be communicated to employees, there are a number of ways this can be accomplished. If possible, employers should utilize a number of methods to communicate those workplace rules to decrease the likelihood a decision maker will determine that an employee was unaware of the rule and therefore could not be disciplined or terminated for a failure to adhere to it. When deciding which methods to use, employers should consider how they would provide evidence that the information was communicated to the employees in the event of a legal challenge.

i. Verbal Notice

Some employers, particularly those with a limited number of employees, put employees on notice of a workplace rule by verbally explaining the rule and the consequences of failing to adhere to it.

(a) Face-to-Face Conversation
Some employers believe that the best way to place employees on notice of a workplace rule is to verbally communicate it in a face-to-face conversation. To the extent possible, employers should not rely exclusively on verbal notification since it is difficult to prove that such a conversation took place. This is particularly true because a significant amount of time might pass between the time a rule is communicated and the time a violation occurs, and if there is disagreement as to what was said, the burden will be on the employer to show notice was provided. There are, however, a number of ways to address a potential challenge to an assertion that an employee was on notice of a rule based on a verbal notification.

(b) Verbal Notice in Group Setting
One way for an employer to counter an anticipated employee claim that the verbal notification of a rule never occurred is to have the conversation in a group setting and engage in conduct that will corroborate the fact that notice was provided. For example, suppose an employer is particularly worried about the theft of office supplies. The employer could place the issue on the written agenda of a mandatory staff

meeting, request all attendees to sign in, and explain to employees that office supplies should not be removed from the premises. The employer might also want to make it clear that there is a zero-tolerance policy for theft and that anyone caught stealing office supplies will be subjected to discipline up to and including termination.

Suppose a few weeks after this meeting, an employee is caught leaving the employer's premises with a box of ballpoint pens, is terminated, and claims the employer permitted employees to take home a few pens from time to time for personal use. In defending the decision to terminate this employee for misconduct that rose to the level of just cause, the employer might be asked to illustrate that the employee was on notice about its no-tolerance policy for the stealing of office supplies.

As a starting point, the employer could point out that theft is a crime, which suggests that notice of the inappropriateness of the conduct is not necessary. In addition, the employer could illustrate that, despite the fact affirmative notice might not have been necessary, it exerted significant efforts to ensure employees had a clear understanding of its expectations. The employer might say that it verbally communicated its policy at a staff meeting. The employer could then submit both the meeting agenda outlining its zero-tolerance policy for the theft of office supplies and the attendance sheet with the employee's signature. The employer might also be prepared to call another witness to testify about what was communicated at the meeting and to confirm the attendance of the terminated employee. Under these circumstances, even though technically the employee was placed on notice of the rule verbally, the employer would have other forms of evidence to corroborate its position that the employee was placed on notice of the rule and was aware of the consequences of violating it.

ii. Written Notice

An employer might also want to create a written record of a workplace rule to further ensure employees are on notice of it.

(a) Company Handbook

An employer can illustrate that an employee was aware of a workplace rule by providing a copy of a written policy that establishes its terms, which might be included in a company handbook. This is particularly strong evidence if the employer can also produce an acknowledgment signed by the employee indicating that she received, read, understood, and agreed to be bound by its terms.

(b) Written Correspondence

Employers that are unsure whether employees have a firm understanding of existing policies (or who want to implement a new rule) may also want to send out a correspondence stating the rule and making it clear there will be consequences for not adhering to it. An employer that is particularly cautious might decide to attach the document outlining the rule to the paychecks or paystubs of each employee to ensure it is received.

iii. Posting of the Rule

Even if a rule is verbally communicated to employees and presented in a written document, an employer may want to communicate the rule in another way, such as by posting it in a conspicuous place, to bolster its claim that employees were placed on notice of it. Some employers have bulletin boards in their workplace and tell their employees (verbally or in a company handbook) that they are responsible for information posted on it. In addition, if employees use a particular lunchroom for their meals and scheduled breaks, the document can be posted in those locations. Some employers also post important notices at eye level near a time clock, where employees are required to punch in and out at the end of each day, to further support the position that these employers satisfied their notification obligations.

iv. Providing Assistance to Comply with the Rules

Employers can also show that their employees were on notice of workplace rules and expectations if they provided them with assistance in complying with the rules.

(a) Training

An employer might illustrate that an employee was on notice of the inappropriateness of a particular behavior by presenting evidence that training was provided related to that behavior. For example, suppose an employee is terminated for sexual harassment for repeatedly telling offensive jokes to a co-worker, and he claims he was not aware that this behavior was unacceptable. An employer can support its position that employees were placed on notice that sexual harassment is a terminable offense by showing that the employee attended a mandatory sexual harassment training program which addressed the specific issue relating to the telling of offensive jokes at work.

(b) Financial Assistance

In some cases, an employer can illustrate that an employee had notice of a rule by showing it provided the employee with financial assistance (or some other type of assistance) to comply with it. For example, suppose an employer requires its employees to wear business suits to work, an employee claims he had no knowledge of the policy, and the employer states it was discussed during the interview process. The employer could bolster its position that the employee was on notice about the dress code in the interview if, in response to the employee's statement he did not own any business suits, the employer agreed to provide him with a $500 signing bonus to defray the cost of purchasing new clothing.

Similarly, if an employee claims that she was never placed on notice of a rule that required her to receive a certain license as a condition of continued employment, an employer might present evidence that the employee was provided with a financial payment to offset some of the costs associated with enrolling in a course to prepare for the examination necessary to obtain a license. An employer might also show that the employee was provided with materials about how to apply for funding for a preparatory course, which indicated that obtaining the appropriate license was a condition of continued employment.

(c) Alteration of Working Conditions

An arrangement between an employer and employee about a particular working condition can also be used to establish that the employee was on notice of a rule. Suppose an employee regularly reports to work ten minutes after the start of her shift and, when asked about her untimeliness, she states that the operating hours of her daycare provider prevent her timely arrival. Suppose also that, when the employee was first hired, the employer agreed to change the employee's 8:30 a.m. to 4:30 p.m. shift to 9:00 a.m. to 5:00 p.m. to accommodate her scheduling needs. In the event the employee is subsequently disciplined or terminated for regularly reporting to work at 9:10 a.m. instead of 9:00 a.m. and claims that she was not aware of the employer's expectation with respect to timeliness, the employer can use their prior conversations and the adjustment of her schedule to counter her assertion.

v. Progressive Discipline

Even in the absence of a widely disseminated verbal or written notification about the existence of a particular rule, an employer might illustrate an employee was on notice of a rule by showing that the employee was subjected to progressive discipline for violating it. The purpose of progressive discipline is to impose escalating levels of discipline on an employee in an attempt to provide him with notice of any inappropriate behavior and to give him an opportunity to correct it. Depending on which steps of the progressive discipline process were imposed, its use could illustrate that notice was provided in a number of different forms. If an employer can show that the employee was counseled about the importance of a particular workplace rule, or issued a verbal warning for failing to comply with it, this employer conduct could constitute a verbal notification of a rule. Consistent with this, both a written warning and a suspension would constitute written notice of the rule and the employer's expectation that the employee adhere to it.

For example, suppose a supervisor tells an employee she is not permitted to park her car in the reserved parking spots because they are reserved for important clients. If the employee claims she mistakenly believed the spots were reserved for employees, the supervisor could correct her misconception and direct her not to park in any of the reserved spots. Suppose two weeks after this conversation, the employee repeats the conduct, and the supervisor reiterates that the reserved spots are for important clients, and informs the employee she is being verbally warned that the conduct must stop immediately. Suppose also that the employee parks in a reserved spot a third time, receives a written warning for the misconduct, and after the fourth occurrence is suspended for inappropriate conduct.

In this case, if a subsequent offense results in the employee's termination, it would be difficult for her to successfully argue that there was no just cause for her termination based on absence of notice since there was no written policy memorializing it. Here, the employer could overcome the absence of a written policy reserving certain parking spots for clients by asserting that the use of the progressive discipline policy to identify and attempt to correct the inappropriate conduct constituted sufficient notice of its expectations. See Chapter 14, Performance Management, for a detailed discussion about progressive discipline.

c. Employer Conduct That May Undermine Notice

Even if an employer provides its employees with notice of its workplace rules, it must also ensure that its supervisors and managers do not engage in behavior that undermines the effectiveness of it. This is important because even if a rule is in place and employees are aware of it, an employer's historical failure to enforce the rule may undermine any notice that has been provided.

i. Establishing a Past Practice

By ignoring an existing rule or making the decision not to enforce it, an employer may have developed a **past practice**, which can be used by employees to argue that even though they were on notice of the content of the rule, they were not on notice that it would be enforced or that they could be subject to discipline for failing to adhere to it.

past practice
employer conduct that deviates from company policy and establishes a revised standard to which employees may expect adherence

For example, suppose an employer has a company policy that specifically states that employees are required to provide medical documentation to explain the use of a sick day on the day the employee returns to work. Suppose also that the employer does not have the staffing resources to keep track of this information on a daily basis, so he verifies receipt of it on the last business day of each month. As a result of this practice, most employees know that they have until the last day of the month to provide this documentation because the employer just ensures that the medical information was provided and does not maintain any record of *when* it was received.

If this practice goes on for a number of months, and employees continue to provide documentation by the end of the month without any adverse consequences, it would be difficult for an employer to terminate an employee for failing to comply with this policy, since employees were not aware of its strict enforcement. This is not to say, however, that employers who have failed to enforce a rule for a significant period of time do not have the right to start to enforce it. However, there is a process that should be used before taking such action.

ii. Reverting to Prior Policy

Employers that intentionally or unintentionally establish a past practice generally have the right to revert back to the enforcement of the original policy. However, employers will generally be required to place their employees on notice of the change as it if was a *new* policy. For example, under the facts stated above, suppose the employer receives funding to hire additional staff who will be responsible for tracking the attendance of its employees. At this point, the employer may want to start to enforce the sick leave policy as written and require employees to provide medical documentation at the time they return to work after the use of a sick day.

In this case, the employer can likely require employees to adhere to the rule consistent with how it was written but only *after* it is clearly communicated to the affected employees. Without this communication, employees disciplined for violating the rule will likely challenge its enforcement, stating that the employer established a past practice to verify medical documentation at the end of the month and they were not provided with any notice that failing to provide medical documentation on returning to work would not be tolerated. To avoid such a challenge, employers that want to alter a past practice relating to the enforcement of a rule should place employees on notice about this change *before* beginning to discipline employees for failing to comply with it.

2. REASONABLENESS OF THE RULE

If an employer can establish that an employee was placed on notice of a rule, and the employer did not act in a manner suggesting it did not intend to enforce the rule, the next component in establishing just cause is to show that the rule was reasonable; an employer will be able to support a termination for the violation of a rule only if the rule is a reasonable one. There is no precise definition for the term *reasonableness*, because it requires a fact-specific analysis of the nature of the misconduct and the business of the employer. However, an employer will be in the best position to establish reasonableness by showing that the rule serves a legitimate business purpose, is common among other employers in the industry, or is necessary to address a specific safety concern.

For example, a court is unlikely to permit the just-cause termination of an employee who arrives to work 15 seconds late (in violation of the rule that requires employees to report at the start of their regularly scheduled shift), even if the employee acknowledges he was on notice of the rule, because the rule will likely be deemed unreasonable. Similarly, even if an employer places its employees on notice of a rule that personal calls are prohibited during work hours, a court would likely prohibit the just-cause termination of an employee who accepts a telephone call from a school principal informing her about an emergency situation with her child. Because these rules would likely be considered unreasonable, even if the employees were aware of the rules and admitted they violated them, it is unlikely that an employer would be able to support a just-cause termination based on these violations.

3. INVESTIGATION

Although in the examples above there might not be a dispute regarding the identity of the employee who engaged in the conduct that is the basis for the termination or whether that conduct occurred, in many cases the facts are not so clear. Because of this, employers have an obligation to conduct a complete and impartial investigation to determine whether an employee actually engaged in the misconduct prior to using it as the basis for the imposition of discipline or a termination.

The employer should exert efforts to ensure that the investigation is an unbiased and thorough process and that the employer makes a final decision as to whether the termination is appropriate only after completion of the investigation. The presentation of evidence illustrating that the employer conducted an appropriate investigation prior to terminating an employee is another factor used to support a showing that a termination decision was supported by just cause.

The investigations that are most likely to survive a legal challenge are completed within the following framework.

a. Timeliness

For a number of reasons, an employer should conduct an investigation as soon as possible after an incident occurs.

i. Supports Severity of Misconduct

The termination of an employee is a serious form of discipline, and the immediate allocation of resources to an investigation supports an employer's position that the misconduct warrants this aggressive response. If an employer is troubled by the employee's behavior, and particularly if the conduct implicates safety concerns, the employer should impose a **suspension pending the investigation**, which means that the employer will instruct the employee that he is not permitted to report to work until the investigation has been completed and the employer has determined whether the employee engaged in any misconduct and, if so, what level of discipline is appropriate.

    If an employee is not paid while suspended pending the investigation, and the investigation determines the misconduct did not occur, the employee should be returned to work and paid for the lost time.

suspension pending the investigation
imposition of a paid or unpaid leave on an employee accused of misconduct until a determination is made as to whether the individual engaged in the misconduct and, if so, what level of discipline is appropriate

ii. Increases Accuracy of Information

It is important for the investigation to be conducted as soon as practicable, because the investigator will receive the most accurate information from witnesses immediately after the incident takes place. As time passes individuals are likely to have more difficulty recalling the details of the incident. Some investigators obtain or prepare written statements from each witness and have each signed by the appropriate witness to confirm the accuracy of its contents. Other investigators prepare an investigation report summarizing the witness statements and findings, and sign it themselves, attesting to its accuracy.

    It is important to have a written document to support the findings of an investigation since any litigation relating to the termination might occur a significant amount of time after the interviews take place. The absence of written documentation outlining key pieces of evidence could be problematic because a witness's recollection of the events may fade, a witness may no longer be working for the company, or for some other reason, a witness may be unavailable at a future point in time when a decision maker is retained to make a decision and requests that the employer present evidence to support its position that the termination was supported by just cause.

iii. Minimizes Undue Influence

An expedited investigation will also minimize the likelihood that the witnesses will be improperly influenced. In the event an incident implicates a number of individuals, it will also minimize the amount of time employees will have to speak with one another about how they intend to respond to the investigator's inquiries.

b. Proof

Another component of a thorough investigation is the collection and review of sufficient evidence before concluding that the terminated employee engaged in the misconduct. An investigation may include direct and circumstantial evidence, and the evidence should come from a number of different sources that might suggest that the conduct did, or did not, occur.

c. Due Process

Employers should ensure that employees accused of misconduct are provided with **due process** throughout the investigatory process. Due process requires that the investigation be thorough and unbiased, and that it provide the employee with the opportunity to present his recollection of the events. Due process also prohibits threats against or harassment of the terminated employee or any of the witnesses, or the making of any assumptions about whether or not the conduct occurred.

d. Interviews of Witnesses

Anyone who might have witnessed the incident should be interviewed as part of the investigative process. The initial witness list should be flexible, because one witness might reveal information that could lead to other witnesses who might provide key information. For example, if a female is interviewed about whether she was sexually harassed by an employee, she might reveal the names of other employees who were subjected to similar behavior. In addition, a witness whose credibility is in question might provide the names of other witnesses who can corroborate her statements.

e. Physical Evidence

In the event the investigation relies on any physical evidence, the employer should use its best efforts to preserve it. For example, if company property is damaged, it should be saved, or if there is vandalism that needs to be removed, photographs should be taken. If there is a surveillance tape that is relevant to the investigation it should be maintained, because the original piece of evidence is more desirable than a report about its contents.

4. UNIFORM APPLICATION OF THE RULE

Even if, as a result of an investigation, an employer determines the employee engaged in the misconduct, the just-cause termination might still be challenged if other employees engaged in similar behavior and were not subject to the same level of discipline. The issue will focus on whether there was **selective enforcement** of the rule, which is the employer's failure to subject all employees to the same standards when deciding whether the violation of a rule warrants the imposition of adverse consequences.

Selective enforcement could result in a discrimination claim if the decision regarding whether a particular rule will be enforced or about the appropriate penalty for violating the rule is based upon whether an individual is a member of a protected class. Selective enforcement is also problematic because it is closely tied to the issue of whether the employee was on notice that the rule would be enforced and, even if it was enforced, whether it could result in a termination.

For example, suppose an employer terminates an employee it determines stole employer property and cites its zero-tolerance policy for theft as the basis for the termination. The terminated employee could present a compelling defense by

---

due process
the conducting of a disciplinary investigation in accordance with rules and principles for protecting and enforcing the rights of individuals, which would include conducting a thorough and unbiased investigation of the employee's alleged misconduct and giving the individual accused of wrongdoing the opportunity to present his recollection of the events

selective enforcement
inconsistent enforcement of a workplace rule, which could undermine an employer's position that the behavior supports a just-cause termination

presenting evidence that three co-workers who stole from the employer were not terminated but instead were given the opportunity to pay back the money for the stolen goods, and continued to work for the employer with enhanced supervision. This selective enforcement (inconsistent application) of the rule could be used by the terminated employee to support her claim that she was not on notice that violation of the rule could tesult in her termination (or that she was on notice of the rule but not that it would be strictly enforced). This selective enforcement of the rule could also be used by the terminated employee to claim that the true motive for the decision to end the employment relationship was discriminatory or based on some other inappropriate consideration, particularly if the terminated employee is a member of a protected class, and the employee subjected to a lesser form of discipline was not.

Although employers should strive to uniformly apply workplace rules to avoid a selective enforcement issue, this does not mean employers are required to respond to the same misconduct in the same way each time it occurs. In fact, it is generally not advisable for employers to be so rigid that they refuse to consider any **mitigating factors** when deciding whether termination is appropriate. Mitigating factors are extenuating circumstances that suggest a more lenient form of discipline might be appropriate to address misconduct that might ordinarily support a just-cause termination.

> **mitigating factors**
> circumstances that may warrant more lenient forms of discipline for similar misconduct

An employer might consider the nature of an employee's position when determining whether certain conduct warrants a termination, such as deciding that an employee who is rude to a customer should not be terminated because, even though the behavior was unacceptable and other employees were terminated for similar behavior, this employee's job did not require her to come in contact with customers and the only reason she was dealing directly with customers on the day of the misconduct was because she was asked to cover the shift of a co-worker who called out sick at the last minute. Other mitigating factors that might affect an employer's decision as to whether a termination is appropriate include an employee's long-term service and dedication to the employer, a lack of prior discipline, or an employee's personal circumstances at the time of the incident.

Suppose an employer determines that an employee's hostile and verbally abusive reaction to constructive criticism offered by a supervisor is a terminable offense and suspends the employee pending the investigation of the incident. Also suppose that during the course of the investigation the individual, a long-term employee with no prior discipline, expresses sincere regret for the outburst and informs the employer that he was under a significant amount of stress due to a recent family tragedy. Under these circumstances the employer might determine the conduct warrants a written warning or suspension, rather than a termination. If after this incident a different employee engages in similar misconduct, is terminated for just cause, and challenges that decision based on the employer's selective enforcement of the rule, the employer could defend the termination (and its earlier decision not to terminate the other employee who engaged in similar behavior) by noting the presence of a mitigating factor that supported this differential treatment.

5. APPROPRIATENESS OF THE PENALTY

The final issue relevant to whether a termination is supported by just cause relates to whether the ending of the employment relationship in response to the violation of a rule is a reasonable response based on the nature of the misconduct. Even if an employer can establish that an employee violated a reasonable rule that was uniformly enforced, the employer must still be prepared to illustrate that termination is the appropriate level of punishment for the misconduct. Although employers have wide latitude to establish their workplace rules, a just-cause termination is likely to be challenged in the event the termination is viewed as an overly harsh response to the misconduct. A harsh penalty might also suggest that the reference to the violation of a workplace rule was actually a pretext (cover-up) for the true discriminatory motive for the decision.

For example, it might be reasonable for an employer to impose a workplace rule that prohibits employees from eating at their desks based on customer comments indicating it was unprofessional. However, the termination of an employee who, hidden from the view of any customers, reaches into her bag to take a bite of a sandwich because an early-morning delay prevented her from having time to eat breakfast might be considered an overly aggressive reaction, based on the nature of the misconduct. The perception that this response was too harsh might also be bolstered if the terminated employee presented evidence of mitigating factors such as a ten-year work history with the employer and the absence of any prior discipline history. Although an employer may have the right to hold its employees to high standards, the determination as to whether the termination was a measured response to the misconduct is a component of the just cause standard, and the appropriateness of the decision will be based on an analysis of the specific facts relating to the nature of the misconduct and its impact on the operations of the employer's business.

C. CATEGORIES OF BEHAVIOR THAT MAY CONSTITUTE JUST CAUSE

Because the details of an incident are so critical to a determination as to whether the just-cause standard is met, there is no precise list of misconduct that will provide a legally sound basis for termination under the standard. However, just-cause terminations often relate to unsatisfactory job performance or serious misconduct.

1. UNSATISFACTORY JOB PERFORMANCE

An employee's failure to satisfactorily perform the duties associated with a position is often the basis for a just-cause termination. For example, suppose an employer wants to terminate an employee for his failure to accurately process 100 invoices on a daily basis, as required by his position. If an employee consistently enters 73 invoices a day with a number of errors, the employer can assert that his failure to meet the minimum threshold supports a just-cause termination. To establish notice, the employer can present a copy of an employee's job description, along with an acknowledgment of receipt of the qualifications signed by the employee, explaining this requirement. The employer might also show that this standard is reasonable because the entry of 110 invoices per day is the industry standard. The employer could also provide evidence of its profit margin indicating that it must meet these minimum standards to remain profitable and sustain its operations.

With respect to an investigation, the employer would need to show reliable evidence, such as logs or an internal tracking mechanism, to prove that the terminated employee regularly completed fewer than the 100 invoices required. The employer could then present the records of its other employees from the past three years, illustrating that only those who met these minimum requirements continued to be employed, while those who fell below the threshold on a regular basis no longer worked for the company. Finally, to illustrate that the termination was the appropriate level of discipline, the employer could show a history of progressive discipline, including a number of counseling sessions, a verbal warning, a written warning, and a suspension, all based on the employee's failure to meet the minimum productivity levels required for the position.

2. SERIOUS MISCONDUCT

In addition to unsatisfactory work performance, workplace behavior that constitutes serious misconduct commonly serves as the basis for just-cause terminations. There are some categories of serious misconduct, such as the physical assault of a co-worker, that will, standing alone, be sufficient to establish the just cause necessary to support a termination. As stated above, if the conduct is inherently offensive (such as workplace violence), the employer will point out that it is reasonable to assume that employees should have been aware that violence will not be tolerated, even in the absence of a clearly stated rule to that effect.

For misconduct that is not inherently offensive, an employer can support a just-cause termination by showing the terminated employee was aware of the rule because it was detailed in a memo distributed with employee paychecks, and the employee had been disciplined for violating it on prior occasions. Further, the employer can explain the business need for the rule, that all other employees are held to the same standard with respect to its enforcement, and that the termination is appropriate based on the resulting harm that would be caused to the employer's company and reputation in the event the rule was not enforced.

 ## IMPORTANCE OF WRITTEN DOCUMENTATION

Regardless of the source of the employer's right to end an employment relationship and the standard that applies, the importance of written documentation relating to the basis for making the decision cannot be overstated. As soon as a workplace issue arises, employers should begin to document the circumstances surrounding the misconduct, as well as the steps taken to address the inappropriate behavior.

A. ESTABLISH A RECORD OF PAST PROBLEMATIC BEHAVIOR

The purpose of written documentation is to establish a record of the misconduct and the steps taken to address the problematic behavior in an attempt to avoid a termination, as well as to prepare to defend a just-cause termination in the event the situation escalates. Courts have found the documentation of past problematic behavior, through the use of a progressive discipline process or for any other reason, to be particularly significant. For example, one court sustained a termination based on an employer's presentation of a "detailed counseling memoranda [that] document[ed] job performance deficiencies and attendance problems" that continued until the termination."[41] Another court found that an employer met its burden that the termination was not discriminatory based on its providing of "specific, substantial, and undisputed performance deficiencies contemporaneously documented."[42]

B. REFUTE ALLEGATIONS OF DISCRIMINATORY CONDUCT

Courts have also considered the *absence* of written documentation establishing a record of an employee's past poor work performance significant when finding that the termination was a pretext for illegal discriminatory motivations. This consideration suggests that an employer will have difficulty supporting a just-cause termination by showing only written documentation that is created near or at the time a termination occurs as opposed to presenting documentation illustrating a gradual escalation of discipline leading up to the termination.[43]

 RESIGNATION AND CONSTRUCTIVE DISCHARGE

Despite all of the attention paid to the rights of employers to end an employment relationship, it is also possible for an employee to initiate the end of an employment relationship or for there to be a dispute as to which party initiated its conclusion.

A. RESIGNATION

resignation
the ending of an employment relationship initiated by an employee

Most working individuals are at-will employees, who can be terminated with or without cause and with or without notice and who retain the reciprocal right to end their employment relationship for any reason at any time. A **resignation** is an employee's decision to terminate an employment relationship.

While there is no federal law that requires employees to provide notice of their intent to resign, the standard business practice is to provide an employer with at least two weeks' notice before leaving a position. Employees should put their resignation in writing to establish that notice was given, and the document can be useful evidence if future questions arise relating to whether the employee voluntarily ended the employment relationship, or whether the employer initiated the termination for just cause, or for some other reason that was related to the employee's work performance. During the notice period employees usually complete open tasks and train those who will perform their work after the departure. In addition, the notice period provides the employer with time to look for a replacement for the departing employee.

B. CONSTRUCTIVE DISCHARGE

Because an employer will have limited obligations to employees who resign from its employment, issues have arisen relating to whether an employee's decision to leave was truly voluntary, or whether employer conduct compelled the employee to leave her position against her will. Under a theory of **constructive discharge**, an employer would be subject to liability for wrongful termination based upon making an employee's working conditions so intolerable that it would compel a reasonable employee to resign.[44]

constructive discharge
legal theory (often referred to as a forced resignation) whereby an employment relationship ends based on the presence of working conditions that are so intolerable a reasonable person would not be expected to continue to work subject to them

Under the theory of constructive discharge, which is sometimes referred to as a forced resignation, a resignation that is tendered to escape intolerable employment requirements is considered a wrongful termination.[45] Most courts will not require an employee to show that the employer's intent was to force an employee to resign, but rather a showing that a reasonable person would not have agreed to continue to work under the working conditions is sufficient.[46] An employee could assert a constructive discharge claim if an employer significantly alters the working conditions of that employee, or if an employer is aware of intolerable working conditions and allows them to continue.

1. ALTERING OF WORKING CONDITIONS

Although employers have the right to alter the working conditions of their employees, it is important for employers to have a valid business justification for making significant changes and to be aware of the potential for a constructive discharge claim, which could materialize if those changes are so intolerable a reasonable person would not be expected to continue to work pursuant to them. This is important because in the event a claim for wrongful termination is upheld, the employee could be awarded significant damages in the form of reinstatement, back pay (with interest), and other damages, including attorney fees.[47]

For example, suppose a 65-year-old employee has been working in the same position with a company for 30 years without any prior discipline, and the employer decides to change the employee's shift from the day shift (which he has worked during his tenure with the company) to the night shift. In addition, suppose the employer tells the employee his office will be moved to its satellite location

25 miles from the company headquarters where he has worked since he started with the company. Also, assume that the company has a severance policy that requires the payment of two weeks' salary for each year of completed service (which would translate to 60 weeks of pay for this employee) in the event of a layoff or separation from employment for a reason other than just cause.

On the implementation of these changes, the affected employee could file a claim for constructive discharge against the employer. The employee would argue that the reason for the changes to his working conditions was to compel him to resign to avoid the expense of the 60 weeks' pay he would otherwise be owed pursuant to the severance policy in the company handbook if he was laid off or terminated without cause. The employee's position would be that because a reasonable person would not be expected to tolerate such drastic changes to his working conditions, the employer should be obligated to pay him the 60 weeks' of pay he would be entitled to pursuant to the handbook along with any other appropriate damages. In addition, the employee might also have a claim under ADEA (or a state law that prohibits age discrimination) if he can prove that his age (or an age-related characteristic) was the motivating factor behind the employer's decision to make such significant and adverse changes to his working conditions.

In response, the employer would have the opportunity to defend its conduct by illustrating the legitimate business need for these changes. For example, the employer might refute the employee's claim that it was trying to compel him to resign by presenting objective evidence of the decline of work that can be performed during the day, that it has future plans to close its headquarters and employ staff only at its satellite offices, and that it subjected other similarly situated employees, who were younger than 40 years of age and non-members of other protected classes, to these same changes. See Chapter 6, Age Discrimination.

Although these changes to an employee's working conditions may seem extreme, the changes do not necessarily have to rise to this level to support a claim for constructive discharge. However, an individual asserting a constructive discharge claim will have a high burden to show that the conditions are intolerable, and changes to the employee's working conditions must go beyond the basic rights employers have to manage their workforce, and must result in distress to the employee that goes beyond ordinary challenges that may be associated with job responsibilities.[48] Most successful constructive discharge cases involve significant changes to job responsibilities, or those that dramatically alter the working conditions under which the tasks are performed. Further, a change to an individual's working conditions that place her in physical harm could rise to the level of intolerable working conditions sufficient to support a constructive discharge claim.[49]

2. ALLOWING INTOLERABLE WORKING CONDITIONS TO CONTINUE

A constructive discharge claim could also materialize if an employee's job responsibilities remain the same, but he is expected to perform the work in a hostile work environment. In resigning from his employment and asserting a constructive discharge claim based on a hostile work environment, the employee could assert that a resignation was not voluntary because the environment in which he was expected to work was intolerable and beyond what a reasonable person would be expected to endure. This is significant because employers have an obligation to address situations in which employees are subject to conduct that exceeds the level of what must be tolerated.

An employee asserting a constructive discharge claim based on a hostile work environment will have a very high burden to show the conditions are intolerable, based on the established understanding that employees might be expected to accept some "boorish colleagues."[50] If, however, the employee can show that the conditions were truly intolerable, he brought the issue to the attention of his supervisor, and it went unaddressed, then he might have a valid claim for a constructive discharge, which could result in employer liability in the form of the payment of severance and/or any other damages appropriate for a wrongful termination.

KEY TERMS

- ✓ bumping rights
- ✓ collective bargaining agreement
- ✓ constructive discharge
- ✓ due process
- ✓ duty of good faith and fair dealing
- ✓ faltering company
- ✓ grievance and arbitration process
- ✓ just cause

- ✓ layoff
- ✓ mass layoff
- ✓ mitigating factors
- ✓ notice
- ✓ notice pay
- ✓ past practice
- ✓ plant closing
- ✓ promissory estoppel
- ✓ resignation
- ✓ selective enforcement
- ✓ severance

- ✓ suspension pending the investigation
- ✓ U.S. Department of Labor (DOL)
- ✓ Worker Adjustment and Retraining Notification (WARN) Act

DISCUSSION QUESTIONS

Explain your response to each of the following questions with the understanding that in some cases there is no right or wrong answer. If you cannot make an informed decision with the facts provided, indicate the nature and significance of the additional information you would need.

1. Explain a number of ways an employment relationship might end.
2. What is the federal WARN Act and what obligations does it impose on an employer?
3. Explain the number of circumstances under which an employee might become subject to a just-cause standard for termination.
4. Assuming an employer agrees that all terminations will be supported by just cause, what factors are reviewed to determine whether this standard has been met?

5. Jayne accepts a new position at a recruitment agency and tells you her plan is to decline to consider any applicants who are not currently employed, because people who are not working must have been fired from a previous job based on poor performance or some type of misconduct. Do you agree? Why or why not?

6. Parisa owns a large factory that manufactures clothing and accessories for dogs. One morning she wakes up, decides she wants a new career, and announces to her staff she is moving to Canada and the factory is closed. Do you see any problems with her behavior? Is there any other information you would like to know?

7. Sharon is a real estate broker who has just accepted a new job and received her first employment contract. The contract says it is for a three-year term and she can only be terminated for just cause. Since she knows you just completed an employment law course, she asks you to explain what the term *just cause* means. What do you tell her?

8. Sharon in the example above ends up signing the employment contract and calls you again six months later. This time, she tells you she was terminated because she sold only one apartment since the start of her employment. She tells you she plans to consult an attorney but wants to know your opinion. What do you think? Is there any other information you would like to know?

9. After you provide Sharon with your opinion about her termination, she tells you another story about her co-worker Fred, who was terminated for taking home all of the extra food from an open house he had held, which violated company policy. Sharon said the situation was very tense because as Fred was being escorted out of the building, he was yelling that his termination was unjust because he was never told about the rule, and he thought the food was going to be thrown away. Do you think Fred was terminated for just cause? Why or why not? What other information might you want to know?

10. Marge, the owner of a large company, tells you that she wants to impose new rules about how the store should be closed at the end of the day, and she intends to discipline employees who do not comply with this new procedure. How do you think she should communicate the new process to her employees?

11. Shelly is an employer who has a company handbook that includes a provision requiring employees to provide a note from a doctor if they want to use a sick day on a summer Friday or a day preceding or immediately following a holiday weekend. She has never enforced the policy in the past, but now she suspects that employees are abusing their sick day benefits, and she wants to start to enforce it. Can Shelly start to enforce the policy immediately?

ENDNOTES

1. An employer might hire an independent contractor, rather than an employee, to work on a particular project, or even an individual to work under a different work arrangement.

Variations on the traditional employer–employee relationship are discussed in greater detail in Chapter 8, Employees versus Independent Contractors.

2. *Janis v. AMP, Inc.*, 856 A.2d 140 (Pa. Super. Ct. 2004) (holding an employment contract for an unspecified duration does not overcome the presumption that an employee is an at-will employee); *see, e.g., Valentine v. General Am. Credit, Inc.*, 362 N.W.2d 628 (Mich. 1984).

3. *Rooney v. Tyson*, 91 N.Y.2d 685, 694 (1998).

4. *See Winarto v. Toshiba Am. Elecs. Components, Inc.*, 274 F.3d 1276, 1295 (9th Cir. 2001) (holding an employer's decision to lay off an employee can be a legitimate nondiscriminatory reason for ending an employment relationship).

5. EEOC Compl. Man. § 13-III (National Origin Discrimination) (available at *http://www.eeoc.gov/policy/docs/national-origin.html*); *see Coburn v. Pan Am. World Airways, Inc.*, 711 F.2d 339 (D.C. Cir.), *cert. denied*, 464 U.S. 994 (1983) (explaining an employer can use an objective measure of performance to determine which employees will be laid off).

6. *Metz v. Transit Mix, Inc.*, 828 F.2d 1202 (7th Cir. 1987).

7. *See EEOC v. City of Altoona*, 723 F.2d 4 (3d Cir.), *cert. denied*, 467 U.S. 1204 (1983).

8. Although the focus of the discussion about release agreements in this textbook relates to their use within the context of employment terminations, their use is not limited to these circumstances. For example, the parties in an employment relationship might negotiate a release agreement during the course of an individual's employment to resolve a wide number of employment issues, such as a claim for a discriminatory decision related to a promotional opportunity. Under this circumstance, the same framework for the release agreement will apply, and the employee must receive a benefit in exchange for an agreement not to pursue a legal claim on the specific issue the agreement is intended to resolve for the agreement to constitute a legally enforceable contract.

9. 29 U.S.C.§§ 2101-2109.

10. *See, e.g.*, Illinois Worker Adjustment and Retraining Notification Act (Illinois WARN) (available at *http://www.commerce.state.il.us/NR/rdonlyres/39715255-2DCF-42F8-845C-ED9B6D90C004/0/IllinoisWARNSB2665.pdf*); *see* Illinois Department of Commerce and Economic Opportunity, New Illinois WARN Act Signed into Law (available at *http://www.commerce.state.il.us/dceo/Bureaus/Workforce_Development/WARN/warn_default.htm*) (definition of *mass layoff* gives employees greater protections by applying to employers with 25 or more full-time employees and by providing that employees are laid off if they constitute one-third or more of the full-time employees at the site or 250 or more full-time employees).

11. N.Y. Lab. Law art. 25-A (N.Y. WARN Act); *see* Press Release, Labor Department Announces Legislation Requiring Region Companies to Provide a 90-Day Layoff Notice or Face Strict Penalties (Sept. 2, 2008) (available at *http://www.labor.state.ny.us/pressreleases/2008/September2_2008.htm*).

12. 29 U.S.C. § 2101(a)(2). When determining whether a layoff triggers federal WARN obligations, the issue relating to what constitutes a single facility is often in dispute. An employer who decides to lay off a number of employees from a number of different worksites might argue that the impacted worksites are not a single facility and therefore the statute does not apply. In contrast, the employees may argue that the employer's multiple worksites are not distinct and should be treated as a single facility, meaning that the cumulative number of employees laid off is the appropriate figure to assess whether the employer is required to provide the employees with notice pursuant to the WARN Act. *See, e.g., Bader v. Northern Line Layers, Inc.*, 503 F.3d 813, 818-819 (9th Cir. 2007)(finding geographically dispersed worksites do not constitute a single facility).

13. 29 U.S.C. § 2101(a)(3).

14. *See* U.S. Dept. of Labor, Employer's Guide to Advance Notice of Closing and Layoffs, Frequently Asked Questions (FAQS) About WARN, Other Laws and Contracts (available at *http://www.doleta.gov/layoff/pdf/EmployerWARN09_2003.pdf*).

15. *See id; see also Deveraturda v. Globe Aviation Sec. Servs.*, 454 F.3d 1043, 1049-1050 (9th Cir. 2006) (determining that layoffs required by the government do not trigger WARN obligations).

16. *See* Employment & Training Admin., U.S. Dept. of Labor, Fact Sheet: The Worker Adjustment and Retraining Notification Act (available at *http://www.doleta.gov/programs/factsht/warn.htm*).

17. *Gross v. Hale-Halsell Co.*, 554 F.3d 870 (10th Cir. 2009).

18. *See* Employment & Training Admin., U.S. Dept. of Labor, Fact Sheet: The Worker Adjustment and Retraining Notification Act (available at *http://www.doleta.gov/programs/factsht/warn.htm*).

19. *See* U.S. Dept. of Labor, Worker's Guide to Advance Notice of Plant Closings and Layoffs, Notice That Does Not Satisfy WARN Requirements (available at *http://www.doleta.gov/layoff/pdf/WorkerWARN2003.pdf*).

20. *See id.*

21. *See* U.S. Dept. of Labor, Worker's Guide to Advance Notice of Plant Closings and Layoffs (available at *http://www.doleta.gov/layoff/pdf/WorkerWARN2003.pdf*).

22. *See* U.S. Dept. of Labor, Worker's Guide to Advance Notice of Plant Closings and Layoffs, Frequently Asked Questions (FAQs) About WARN: Penalties for Failure to Give Notice (available at *http://www.doleta.gov/layoff/pdf/WorkerWARN2003.pdf*).

23. *Kirk La Shelle Co. v. Paul Armstrong Co.*, 188 N.E. 163 (N.Y. 1933); *see Carter v. Bradlee*, 245 A.D. 49, 50 (N.Y. 1964).

24. *Wood v. Lucy, Lady Duff-Gordon*, 118 N.E. 214 (N.Y. 1917).

25. *See id.*

26. Restatement (Second) of Contracts § 90 (1981).

27. *See id.*

28. Cal. Lab. Code § 2922 (2005); *Murphy v. American Home Prods.*, 448 N.E.2d 86, 89-90 (N.Y. 1983) (agreeing to work for an indefinite term is presumed to be at-will employment).

29. In some cases the parties may negotiate language that provides for termination for cause, or good cause, but for purposes of this textbook, these terms are interchangeable.

30. Some employers also offer an internal process for the resolution of workplace disputes for nonunionized employees that is similar to the grievance and arbitration processes established for unionized employees pursuant to the terms of a collective bargaining agreement.

31. *See* Mont. Code Ann. §§ 39-2-901 to -914; 29 P.R. Laws Ann. § 185a-I; *Rodriguez v. Eastern Air Lines, Inc.*, 816 F.2d 24, 29 (1st Cir. 1987); *Vargas v. Royal Bank of Can.*, 604 F. Supp. 1036, 1039 (D.P.R. 1985) (statute provides exclusive remedy).

32. *See, e.g., County of Dallas v. Wiland*, 124 S.W.3d 390 (Tex. 2003); 5 U.S.C. § 7513(a), enacted in 1978 (indicating federal government employees can be demoted or fired "only for such cause as will promote the efficiency of the service"); 42 U.S.C. § 1983 (establishing remedies for terminating government employees without due process, which has been used to suggest a just-cause standard must be applied).

33. *Gallagher v. Savarese*, No. 99 CV 4181, 2001 U.S. Dist. LEXIS 18112 (S.D.N.Y. Nov. 6, 2001).

34. *See, e.g., Tennessee Walking Horse Breeders Assn. of Am.*, 476 S.W.2d 644 (Tenn. Ct. App. 1971).

35. *Ross v. Times Mirror, Inc.*, 665 A.2d 580 (Vt. 1995).

36. *See Burton v. Atomic Workers Fed. Credit Union*, 803 P.2d 518, 520 n.1 (Idaho 1990) (employment manual may modify terms of employment); *Sadler v. Basin Elec. Power Co-op.*, 431 N.W.2d 296, 300 (N.D. 1988) (an original employment contract may be modified or replaced by a subsequent unilateral contract in employee handbook).

37. *See, e.g., Ferguson v. Host Intl., Inc.*, 757 N.E.2d 267, 272-273 (Mass. App. Ct. 2001) (holding handbook provisions such as progressive discipline policies are enforceable if they instill a reasonable belief in employees that management will adhere to them).

38. *See Crider v. Spectrulite Consortium, Inc.*, 130 F.3d 1238 (7th Cir. 1997) (stating just cause is a flexible concept that considers equity and fairness).

39. *See Grief Bros. Cooperage Corp.*, 42 Lab. Arb. Rep. (BNA) 555 (1964) (Daugherty, Arb.); *Whirlpool Corp.*, 58 Lab. Arb. Rep. (BNA) 421 (1972).

40. *See Luteran v. Loral Fairchild Corp.*, 688 A.2d. 211, 214 (Pa. Super. Ct. 1997).

41. *Arroyo v. New York State Ins. Dept.*, No. 91 Civ. 4200, 1995 U.S. Dist. LEXIS 15376, at *9 (S.D.N.Y. Oct. 18, 1995).

42. *Turner v. Schering-Plough Corp.*, 901 F.2d 335, 344 (3d Cir. 1990).

43. *See, e.g., Montana v. First Fed. Sav. & Loan Assn.*, 869 F.2d 100 (2d Cir. 1989).

44. *See Derr v. Gulf Oil Corp.*, 796 F.2d 340 (10th Cir. 1986); *Goss v. Exxon Office Sys. Co.*, 747 F.2d 885, 888 (3d Cir. 1984); *Nolan v. Cleland*, 686 F.2d 806, 812-815 (9th Cir. 1982); *Held v. Gulf Oil Co.*, 684 F.2d 427 (6th Cir. 1982); *Clark v. Marsh*, 655 F.2d 1168, 1175 (D.C. Cir. 1981); *Bourque v. Powell Elec. Mfg. Co.*, 617 F.2d 61, 65 (5th Cir. 1980); *Turner v. Anheuser-Busch, Inc.*, 7 Cal. 4th 1238 (1994) (establishing standards for constructive wrongful discharge claims under California law).

45. *See, e.g., Henson v. Dundee*, 682 F.2d 897 (11th Cir. 1982).

46. *See, e.g., Calhoun v. Acme Cleveland Corp.*, 798 F.2d 559 (1st Cir. 1986). *But see EEOC v. Federal Reserve Bank of Richmond*, 698 F.2d 633, 672 (4th Cir. 1983) (accepting the minority view that the employer will be subject to liability for constructive discharge only if there is adequate proof that the employer imposed the intolerable conditions with the intent of forcing the victim to leave).

47. *See, e.g., Henson v. Dundee*, 682 F.2d 897 (11th Cir. 1982).

48. *See Ongsiako v. City of New York*, 199 F. Supp. 2d 180, 187 (S.D.N.Y. 2002) (finding that to support a constructive discharge claim, the working conditions must be even more egregious than the high standard for a hostile work environment because an employee ordinarily is expected to remain employed while seeking redress for the alleged discrimination or unfair treatment); *Travis v. Alcorn Labs., Inc.*, 504 S.E.2d 419 (W. Va. 1998) (explaining the infliction of emotional distress as the basis for a constructive discharge claim).

49. *Ongsiako v. City of New York*, 199 F. Supp. 2d 180, 187 (S.D.N.Y. 2002) (holding an "unreasonable risk of physical harm . . ." might support a constructive discharge claim); *see Simpson v. Borg-Warner Auto., Inc.*, 196 F.3d 873, 878 (7th Cir. 1999).

50. *Lindale v. Tokheim Corp.*, 145 F.3d 953, 956 (7th Cir. 1998).

20

Severance and Post-Employment Obligations

Chapter Objectives

This chapter explores the concept of severance and what an employee might be asked to agree to in exchange for this benefit. The text explains a common method for the calculation of the financial element of a severance package, some of the noneconomic benefits that might be offered, as well as the availability of unemployment benefits. There is also an extensive discussion about the types of release agreements that may be signed by the parties at the end of an employment relationship, which explains the limitations on the types of claims that an employee can waive as well as what is required under the Older Workers Benefit Protection Act (OWBPA) to ensure that the release constitutes a knowing and voluntary waiver of rights. Restrictive covenants that impose post-employment obligations on the parties are also discussed, along with types of employer liability that might arise from the providing of references, and from defamation and retaliation claims.

After completing this chapter, students should have an understanding of the economic and noneconomic benefits that an employer might offer a terminated employee, as well as the rights an employee might be asked to waive as a condition of the receipt of those benefits. In addition, students should understand the elements that comprise a knowing and voluntary waiver, and the types of restrictive covenants that might restrict the post-employment behavior of both employers and their former employees.

Upon mastering the main objectives of this chapter students should be able to

- explain the different benefits an employee might receive as part of a severance package and how the financial component might be calculated;
- explain why an employer might place a significant value on a release agreement and provide examples of the types of claims an individual might be asked to waive;
- explain the significance of the OWBPA and what it requires to ensure a waiver is a knowing and voluntary waiver of an individual's rights;
- provide examples of some restrictive covenants and explain the business interests each is designed to protect;

■ explain the obligation of an employer to provide references and its relevance to a claim for negligent referral; and

■ explain the elements of a defamation claim and some of the affirmative defenses that an employer might assert to avoid liability.

An employer's decision to terminate an employee will not immediately sever all ties between the two parties. First, depending on the reason the employment relationship ends, an employee might challenge the termination, which could result in a lengthy dispute resolution process and could ultimately require reinstatement of the terminated employee. In addition, the parties may be subject to a number of post-employment obligations that could be the subject of litigation.

To limit the exposure to these potential risks, and, for a number of other reasons, on the employees' departure some employers provide terminated employees with either a financial benefit, a noneconomic benefit, or both, often conditioned on their signing a release that would limit their rights to assert certain claims.

SEVERANCE

severance
a benefit offered to a terminated employee, usually in exchange for an agreement that the termination will not be challenged and that the departing employee will not file any other claims against his employer arising out of his employment

Severance refers to the benefit an employer might offer a terminated employee, usually in exchange for the signing of an agreement that the departing employee will not challenge the termination or file any claims arising from his employment. Severance usually refers to a financial payment, but it could be part of a more extensive exit package that includes valuable *noneconomic* benefits.

Although employers generally do not have a legal obligation to provide terminated employees with any economic or noneconomic benefits on their departure, offering them does have the potential to benefit both employers and departing employees, including enhancing the likelihood that the separation from employment will be a smooth transition.

A. BENEFITS TO EMPLOYEES

1. FINANCIAL BENEFIT

The payment of severance provides a financial benefit to terminated employees. Terminated employees can use the compensation as a bridge, supporting them for a period of time until they can secure alternative employment. Additionally, even if an employee believes the termination is unjustified, the severance payment offers an immediate and guaranteed financial benefit, while a legal challenge to a termination could require the expenditure of a significant amount of time and money, without a guarantee of a successful outcome.

2. JOB SECURITY

The availability of severance also provides employees with a degree of job security. An employer would be less likely to terminate an employee for an illegitimate reason (or an insignificant reason) if there is a financial cost tied to making such a decision. This benefit is most significant for employees who have worked for an employer for an extended period of time, and whose years of service may entitle them to a significant financial payment in the event of termination.

B. BENEFITS TO EMPLOYERS

Even if an employer has the right to end the employment relationship, there are still a number of significant business justifications for providing severance to terminated employees.

1. RECRUIT AND RETAIN QUALIFIED EMPLOYEES

Offering a severance package may assist an employer in recruiting employees. New employees want some level of job security as well as an indication that their employer is committed to their position, and a severance policy is one way an employer can respond to those concerns. First, as stated above, depending upon the amount of severance that would be payable in the event of termination, an employee may perceive the benefit as a source of protection against an arbitrary or unjustified termination, because it would impose a financial cost on the employer for engaging in this conduct. Further, offering a severance package would guarantee a new employee some financial stability should the employment relationship end.

2. GOOD WILL

An employer might also decide to offer its employees severance as a showing of good will since providing this benefit could enhance the employer's reputation among its workforce as well as within the broader community, which could include potential clients and business partners. In addition, treating departing employees fairly is considered a sound business practice, because an employer might need to contact former employees for information about work projects they were involved in before their departure or to provide assistance in litigation that occurs after the end of their employment.

3. AVOID LITIGATION

Perhaps one of the most significant reasons an employer may offer its employees a severance benefit is to avoid litigation. This is because an employer's providing severance is usually conditioned on the employee's signing of a release, which is an agreement that prevents an employee from challenging a termination or filing a legal claim relating to an issue that arose from her employment. The value of a release to the employer will vary based on the circumstances surrounding the ending of the employment relationship.

If an employee is terminated for serious misconduct, an employer may be confident it has the right (and perhaps obligation) to terminate the employee. Assuming neither the employer's company policy nor any other promises made to the employee require the payment of severance under these circumstances, the employer may determine there is no business need to attempt to secure a release to prevent the employee from filing a claim for wrongful termination. However, if the employer suspects the terminated employee might allege that the termination was based on a discriminatory motive, the employer might be concerned about the filing of a discrimination claim and determine that obtaining a release has significant value that would justify the financial expenditure that might be necessary to secure the release.

Even if an employer is confident that it has the right to terminate an employee, the employer might still determine that the release has a value. This is because if an employee challenges a termination, the employer will still have to invest time and money into gathering relevant information to defend its conduct and perhaps hire an attorney to prepare documents and appear in a judicial proceeding. In addition, because employment issues are fact-specific terminations, there is always the risk that a fact finder will determine that a termination was not warranted, and impose some type of liability.

C. FINANCIAL COMPONENT OF SEVERANCE BENEFIT

Employers who decide to offer a severance benefit to their employees have wide discretion to implement a policy of their own choosing. Because it is considered a term and condition of employment, however, the benefit must be offered and calculated in a uniform and nondiscriminatory manner. In creating a severance policy, two key components relate to who will be entitled to the benefit, and how the amount of the payment will be calculated.

1. ELIGIBLE EMPLOYEES

An employer may decide to limit the offering of severance to employees who have been working for a specific length of time, such as those who have completed at least one year of service. Severance is not offered to employees who are terminated during their probationary period. In addition, an employer may limit the availability of the benefit to employees who are terminated for specific reasons. For example, an employer may implement a policy that severance will be offered to employees who are terminated for work performance issues, but will not be offered to employees terminated for serious misconduct, such as theft or the threat of workplace violence. Some employers offer severance to all employees except those who are terminated for cause, or for just cause, which is a common standard that may apply to terminations. See Chapter 19, Ending the Employment Relationship.

2. CALCULATION OF BENEFIT

Once an employer establishes under what circumstances it intends to offer a severance benefit, the next question is how to calculate its precise value. There is no set formula for the calculation of a financial component of the severance benefit, although it is usually tied to an individual's salary and length of service with the company. For example, an employer might offer a benefit in the amount of one week of pay for each full year of employment, and some employers also provide a prorated benefit for any partial year of employment. Under this formula, an employee who earns $500 per week and is terminated after five and one-half years of employment would receive a severance payment in the amount of $2,750, which represents $500 for each year of the five years of completed service ($2,500), and half of the weekly salary ($250) for the final six months of employment. Employers generally use the same formula for the calculation of a severance payment for a termination for cause as they do for layoffs, which is discussed in Chapter 19, Ending the Employment Relationship.

a. Calculation Must Be Nondiscriminatory

While employers have discretion to establish the formula for calculation of this benefit, they do not have the right to link the formula to characteristics associated with membership in a protected class. For example, an employer would not be permitted to reduce the amount of severance paid to older employees based on the assumption they might be more eager to retire and leave their employment. Employers are also prohibited from applying more generous calculation formulas to men than to women, because of an assumption that men are more likely to be the sole breadwinners in their families. See Chapter 6, Age Discrimination, and Chapter 5, Sex, Pregnancy, and Genetic Discrimination, respectively.

b. Minimum and Maximum Payments

Some employers establish a minimum severance payment, such as a policy that guarantees a payment of at least two weeks' pay regardless of whether, at the time of the termination, the employee has completed the length of service that would obligate the employer to make this payment under its policy. Some employers impose a cap on severance, which limits the value of the benefit an employee would be eligible to receive. For example, an employer might implement a policy stating that a terminated employee will never be entitled to more than 26 weeks of severance, regardless of the length of his employment. Pursuant to a policy such as this, an employer who provides a severance benefit calculated at the rate of two weeks' salary for each year of service would offer an employee who completed 13 years of service with the employer at the time of termination 26 weeks of severance (two weeks' salary for each year of completed service), just as an employee who completed 20 years of service would receive (calculated at the rate of two weeks' salary for each year of completed service, with a maximum allowable benefit of 26 weeks of pay).

c. Reimbursement of Partial Payment on Obtaining Employment

Some employers require their former employees to reimburse them for the amount of severance that exceeds the actual time the individual is out of work. For example, if an employee is terminated after eight years of employment, receives 16 weeks of severance pay (calculated at the rate of two weeks' salary for each year of completed service), and finds a new position after six weeks, then, if the employer includes this limitation in its severance policy, the former employee would be required to reimburse the employer for 10 of the 16 weeks of the severance pay received.[1]

d. Timing of Benefit

Although employees may expect their severance to be paid in one lump sum at the time of their termination, employers have some latitude to determine how the payments will be made (subject to any restrictions that may be imposed under state law). An employer may have a policy that provides for the payment of severance in one payment at the end of the employment relationship. However, an employer may also have a policy that establishes a different schedule, such as continuing to pay the employee on a weekly basis for the duration of the severance period, or making the payment at the close of its fiscal year.

Although employers do have some discretion to determine who will be eligible for a severance benefit, how it will be calculated, and when it will be paid (subject to other restrictions that might be imposed under state law), to minimize the potential for a claim for discriminatory conduct, employers should establish a clear policy that outlines the details about the benefit, place employees on notice of the rules, and ensure the rules are implemented in a uniform and nondiscriminatory manner.

3. UNEMPLOYMENT BENEFITS

unemployment benefits
payments made to eligible individuals who lose their employment through no fault of their own, as determined by state law

In addition to the financial component of a severance package that may be provided by an employer, terminated employees may also be entitled to **unemployment benefits**, which refers to money paid to eligible individuals who lose their employment through no fault of their own (as defined by state law).

a. Purpose of Unemployment Benefits

The purpose of unemployment benefits is to provide qualifying individuals with temporary financial assistance. With the exception of three states that require minimal employee contributions, the funding for unemployment benefits is provided solely through a tax on employers. Each state administers its own unemployment insurance program, which must be established within guidelines established by federal law.[2]

b. Eligibility for Unemployment Benefits

Eligibility for unemployment benefits, the amount of the payments, and the period of time for which the benefits are paid are issues governed by state law.

In most states the benefit amount is a percentage of the individual's earnings in a recent 52-week period, up to a state maximum, and is paid for a maximum of 26 weeks. During periods of high unemployment, individuals may be eligible for extended benefits, which can provide up to an additional 13 weeks of payments.[3]

The ultimate decision as to whether an individual receives unemployment benefits is determined by the state that administers the program, but the employer has the right to contest the individual's application for benefits if it does not believe the individual should be entitled to them. Under these circumstances, the parties will appear before an administrative law judge, who will make the ultimate decision as to whether the reason for the termination should disqualify the individual from receiving benefits or whether benefits should be awarded.[4]

D. NONECONOMIC BENEFITS

Although terminated employees are usually most concerned about their eligibility for the financial component of severance and unemployment benefits, some employers also offer terminated employees a number of valuable noneconomic benefits as part of their exit package. When making decisions about offering severance, neither employers nor employees should underestimate the value of the resources an employer can provide terminated employees to assist them in securing new employment. Some employers, for example, offer departing employees access to outplacement services, which might include job search assistance such as training opportunities, a resume critique, access to interviewing skills workshops, and the identification of sources of vacant positions.

USE OF RELEASE AGREEMENTS TO COMPEL INDIVIDUALS TO WAIVE CERTAIN RIGHTS

The availability of a severance package that includes economic and noneconomic benefits will likely be viewed as very important to individuals who have been informed that their employment is ending. Because employers are not required to offer severance, however, they have the right to condition its payment on the signing of a **release agreement**. Among other things, a release can prevent terminated employees from filing a legal claim challenging the termination as well as for any other issues arising out of their employment.[5]

Employers who decide to condition the receipt of severance on the execution of a release should make this stipulation clear in the company handbook or in the document that establishes rules for eligibility and for calculation of the benefit. The terms of the release agreement, including the nature of the rights an employee will be asked to and will agree to waive, will vary depending upon the specific facts surrounding each termination.

release agreement
agreement negotiated by an employer and terminated employee, usually in exchange for severance, in which an employee waives her rights to challenge the termination or file a claim against an employer for issues arising from her employment

A. DETERMINING RIGHTS TO BE WAIVED

The primary purpose of a release agreement is to prevent terminated employees from challenging their termination and from filing a claim against an employer arising out of their employment relationship. Employers have some discretion to structure releases to protect themselves from potential liability arising from a number of difference sources. For example, an employer could include release language that would prevent employees from filing claims under Title VII, state anti-discrimination laws, or the employment contract that governed the terms and conditions of the terminated employee's employment.[6] However, even if an employer and a departing employee agree to specific release language, the enforceability of the agreement may be challenged for a number of reasons, one of which is the legal limitations on the types of claims an individual has the right to waive.

1. LIMITATIONS UNDER FEDERAL LAW

Individuals are granted some rights under federal law that cannot be waived, regardless of whether two parties entered into an agreement to this effect. For example, individuals cannot waive their rights under the National Labor Relations Act (NLRA), which is the federal law that governs the relationship between employers and labor unions.[7] Therefore, an agreement signed by an individual that purports to waive his rights to file a claim under the NLRA will not impact those rights because such rights cannot be waived.

   In some instances there is a disagreement as to whether certain claims can be waived. One example concerns claims under the Uniformed Services Employment and Reemployment Rights Act (USERRA), the federal law that provides employees serving in the military with certain rights to take leave and to return to employment upon completion of their service. According to a decision issued by a California court, a claim arising under USERRA cannot be waived in a release agreement.[8] However, a federal court suggested that a claim to reemployment under USERRA could be waived if the name of the statute was specifically referenced in the release agreement.[9] See Chapter 13, Paid and Unpaid Leave, for a detailed discussion about USERRA and the benefits and protections it provides.

2. LIMITATIONS UNDER STATE LAW

Just as federal laws limit the types of claims that can be waived in a release agreement, some state laws prohibit employees from waiving their rights to file certain claims that arise under state law. Therefore, even if two parties enter into an agreement designed to waive the employee's rights to file certain claims under a state law, the agreement will not have an impact on those rights of the employee if the state law prevents such a waiver. For example, under New York law, individuals are barred from waiving their rights to New York State unemployment insurance.[10] Thus, even if an employee signs a release agreement in which she waives her right to New York State unemployment insurance, she is still entitled to assert her rights to

New York State unemployment insurance because, pursuant to state law, those rights cannot be waived.

Other state laws will allow the parties to enter into an agreement intended to waive an individual's right to file certain claims but will only permit those waivers to be enforced if certain safeguards are imposed. For example, New York law prohibits the waiver of an employee's workers' compensation claim, unless the waiver is preapproved by the Workers' Compensation Board. Therefore, even if an employee (who is subject to New York law) signs an otherwise valid waiver giving up the right to file a workers' compensation claim, if it was not preapproved as required by the state law, the document would not prevent the employee from filing such a claim.[11]

3. LIMITATIONS ON THE TIMING OF THE CONDUCT THAT GIVES RISE TO A CLAIM

In addition to substantive limitations on release agreements such as those discussed above, there are also legal limitations relating to the period of time that a waiver can cover. A release agreement can only impact the rights of an employee to file a claim based on past conduct; it cannot waive an individual's right to file a claim that may arise in the future. Thus, an individual could be asked to sign a release to waive any discrimination claims that occurred *up to* the date of the signing of the agreement, but the release would not apply to claims that arise *after* the agreement is signed. For example, the release agreement would not prevent an individual from filing a retaliation claim against an employer who provides an untruthful and negative reference about the former employee after her departure (and therefore, presumably, after her signing of a release agreement), in response to the individual's prior threat to file a claim against them.[12]

This current landscape of federal and state limitations on the types of claims individuals have the right to waive makes it important to thoroughly research the federal and state laws that govern the release agreement to ensure that only claims that can be appropriately waived are included in the agreement. If an employer enters into a release agreement absent an understanding of the claims that can be waived, it may end up offering a terminated individual a significant amount of money in exchange for the individual's agreement not to file a particular claim, only to later learn that such rights cannot be waived and that, notwithstanding the waiver, the employer might still be required to defend a claim arising under a particular statute and potentially be subject to liability under it. Similarly, it is important for a departing employee to have this same knowledge so that she can make an informed decision relating to what rights she can and cannot waive, and which rights her employer is most interested in having her waive (for which, presumably, she can attempt to negotiate the most significant severance benefit).

Assuming that the scope of the release is limited to the types of claims that can be waived, the employer must still ensure that the formation and execution of the agreement complies with other relevant laws to ensure it has the desired effect of preventing a terminated employee from challenging the termination decision and from filing certain claims arising out of his employment.

B. APPLICABILITY OF CONTRACT LAW

A release agreement is a contract between two parties; therefore, contract law applies to it.[13] For an agreement to be a legally enforceable contract, both parties must receive **consideration**, which is a benefit that is derived from the agreement which the parties would not otherwise receive. In a properly executed release agreement, the terminated employee will receive a benefit in the form of a severance package, and the employer will receive a benefit in the form of the elimination of the costs associated with defending a claim arising out of the employment of the terminated employee, as well as the potential risk that liability will be imposed. Under this set of facts, both parties signing the agreement will receive a benefit from it that they would not otherwise receive absent the execution of the agreement, and this would constitute the consideration that is required for a contract to be legally enforceable.

Based on the legal requirement for both parties to receive consideration for a release agreement to create a legally binding contract, it would be problematic for an employer to guarantee the payment of severance in a company policy without making it clear that the receipt of this benefit will be conditioned on the signing of a release. Absent this clarification, the departing employee could assert that the employer would have received a benefit from the release agreement (the avoidance of liability for a claim arising out of the individual's employment), but the departing employee would not have received a benefit because, per the company handbook, even before he signed the agreement, he would have had a pre-existing right to the severance payment. Thus, the position of the terminated employee would be that he would retain the right to file a claim against the employer, notwithstanding the fact he received the severance benefit and signed the release agreement, because the release agreement lacked consideration and therefore was not a legally enforceable contract.

C. KNOWING AND VOLUNTARY

Even if both parties receive consideration from the release agreement, it will be still be enforced only if it represents a **knowing and voluntary** waiver of an individual's rights.[14]

1. REQUIREMENTS

The requirements to establish that a release agreement constituted a knowing and voluntary waiver of an individual's rights will vary depending on which statute is at issue, but common law, which is the collection of judicial decisions rendered on a particular issue, provides significant guidance on how to evaluate whether the standard is met. Because the judicial decisions evaluate the circumstances surrounding the negotiation and execution of a release agreement to determine whether it was a "knowing and voluntary" waiver of rights, and because courts in different jurisdictions have found different factors to be significant, the governing laws should be researched to determine how to structure a release that will be the most likely to withstand judicial scrutiny and prevent a terminated employee from asserting a claim for wrongful termination or a claim arising out of another term or condition of employment.[15]

Most courts look to the totality of the circumstances surrounding the negotiation of the release agreement to determine whether it was a "knowing and voluntary" waiver of the individual's rights. The factors that are routinely determined to be significant include (1) whether the release was written in a manner that was clear and specific enough for the departing employee to understand, (2) whether the release was induced by fraud or other improper conduct by the employer, (3) whether the departing employee had enough time to review the agreement and consult with an attorney, and (4) whether the departing employee received consideration for signing the release or whether the departing employee had a preexisting right to the severance benefit.[16]

For example, in one case a court determined that an educated individual who was represented by an attorney and received consideration (in the form of a financial payment) and 60 days to consider the terms entered into a knowing and voluntary waiver of his rights under Title VII.[17] In contrast, another court determined that a release would not be considered knowing and voluntary because the individual was not provided with sufficient time to review the terms, consult with an attorney, or negotiate enhanced terms.[18]

2. NO SPECIFIC STATUTORY REFERENCES REQUIRED OTHER THAN FOR THE WAIVER OF A CLAIM FOR AGE DISCRIMINATION

Release agreements generally list the statutes under which the employee waives her right to file a claim. However, with the exception of a waiver of the right to file an age discrimination claim under the Age Discrimination in Employment Act (ADEA) as discussed below, there is no blanket requirement that the agreement refer to a specific statute, such as Title VII, for a waiver to be deemed knowing and voluntary and constitute a valid waiver of a particular claim.[19] Nevertheless, if a release agreement is challenged based on the absence of a reference to a specific statute, the determination as to whether this omission will be sufficient to prevent the release from being deemed a knowing and voluntary waiver of rights will be based upon a review of the circumstances surrounding the execution of the agreement such as those factors listed above. For example, in one case a court held that a release agreement that was intended to apply to "all claims relating to an individual's employment or layoff" constituted a knowing and voluntary waiver of claims that arose under the WARN Act, even though the statute was not mentioned, because the individual had an extensive period of time to consider the release agreement and consult with an attorney.[20]

Age discrimination claims that arise under the ADEA, however, are subject to the established statutory exception to the rule that a statute does not have to be specifically named in a release agreement in order for the waiver of rights to apply to it. This is because Congress has imposed additional obligations upon employers attempting to secure a waiver intended to prevent employees who are 40 years of age or older from filing an age discrimination claim under the ADEA, one of which is the requirement that the release language specifically reference the statute.

D. RELEASE OF CLAIMS PURSUANT TO THE OLDER WORKERS BENEFIT PROTECTION ACT (OWBPA)

Older Workers Benefit Protection Act (OWBPA) amendment to the ADEA that details the elements that must be included in a release agreement for it to constitute a knowing and voluntary waiver and to effectively prohibit an employee from filing an age discrimination claim under the statute

Employers seeking to prevent a terminated employee from filing an age discrimination claim under the ADEA must ensure that the release complies with the **Older Workers Benefit Protection Act (OWBPA).** The OWBPA amended the ADEA to ensure older employees had accurate information about their rights to be free from age discrimination, and to prevent employers from denying older employees benefits and protections without their full knowledge and consent.[21] The purpose of the OWBPA is to require employers to take extra measures to ensure that a release signed by an older employee that is intended to prevent the filing of a claim for age discrimination is knowing and voluntary.

1. RELEASE REQUIREMENTS FOR INDIVIDUAL EMPLOYEES

There is significant overlap between the most common requirements for a general release and for those that are intended to waive an individual's right to file a claim under the ADEA. Specifically, pursuant to the statutory language of the ADEA, as amended by the OWBPA, for a waiver to apply to age discrimination claims it must

1. be in writing and be understandable;
2. specifically reference the Age Discrimination in Employment Act (ADEA);
3. waive only past claims and have no impact on claims that might arise in the future;
4. be in exchange for valuable consideration;
5. include a written provision suggesting that the affected employee consult an attorney prior to signing the waiver;[22]
6. provide the employee with at least 21 days to review and consider the agreement; and
7. provide the employee with a seven-day period after execution of the agreement during which the individual retains the right to revoke it.[23]

The Supreme Court has reinforced these requirements, noting that they are clear and absolute, and if a release agreement is missing one of these elements, it will not constitute a voluntary and knowing waiver of an individual's rights and will therefore not block the terminated individual's right to file an age discrimination claim under the ADEA.[24] For example, if the employer drafted a complex release agreement that was difficult to understand, but strongly encouraged the departing employee in both the written agreement and in the verbal conversations surrounding the negotiation of the release terms to consult an attorney, the release agreement could be challenged on the basis that it did not represent a knowing and voluntary waiver of the individual's rights. The failure of the employer to adhere to one of the elements established by the OWBPA (the obligation to write in clear and understandable language) would prevent the waiver from being considered knowingly and voluntary and would not prevent the individual from filing a claim under the ADEA—notwithstanding the fact the employer may have complied with its other obligations under the statute, including providing the employee the opportunity to consult with an attorney.[25]

2. RELEASE REQUIREMENTS FOR A GROUP OF EMPLOYEES

In some cases, an employer may offer severance to a group of laid off employees, or provide a group of employees with the opportunity to participate in an **exit incentive program**, which usually includes offering two or more employees (such as those in certain job functions) enhanced compensation in exchange for a voluntary resignation and the signing of a release.[26]

exit incentive program
employer plan that would provide certain employees the opportunity to receive enhanced compensation in exchange for a voluntary resignation and the signing of a release

Employers who intend to obtain release agreements from a group of laid off employees, or from a group of employees resigning from their employment pursuant to the terms of an exit incentive program, who may also potentially have a claim under the ADEA, are subject to additional requirements under the OWBPA to ensure that the employees are knowingly and voluntarily waiving their rights. In addition to the requirements outlined above, the employer must provide all affected employees with written notice of the date of their separation from employment and 45 days to consider the agreement, rather than the 21 days required for the review of an agreement presented to a single individual. The employer must also provide the affected employees with additional information, including the entire group of employees from which the employer chose those who would be affected (which might include, for example, all employees who held the same positions as the impacted employees, or all employees who worked for a particular department or at a particular worksite), and the ages of the employees who were in the same job classifications and offered continued employment.[27]

Courts have determined that the information that an employer is required to provide pursuant to the OWPBA is necessary for an individual to make an informed decision as to whether he wishes to waive his rights to assert an age discrimination claim. Therefore, an employer's failure to produce this information, or decision to only partially comply with its obligations, would likely result in a finding that the waiver was not knowing and voluntary and therefore would not prohibit the affected individuals from asserting a claim under the ADEA.[28] See Chapter 6, Age Discrimination, for further discussion about age discrimination and the significance of the OWBPA.

USE OF RELEASE AGREEMENTS TO PROTECT OTHER INTERESTS

A. CONFIDENTIALITY OF THE RELEASE AND ITS TERMS

As the parties agree to the terms of the release agreement, for a number of reasons, the parties may decide there is a value in keeping the terms confidential. A confidentiality clause could be included in the agreement to prohibit either party from disclosing details about the reasons for the ending of the employment relationship, the terms of the severance package, or other information relating to the individual's separation from employment. For example, an employer might offer an enhanced severance package to an employee based on the significant value placed on securing a release from that particular employee but not want this information revealed to other employees who might be terminated under different circumstances and for whom the employer might not want to offer comparable terms.

The confidentiality agreement could also prohibit the departing employee from discussing any potential claims she might have had against the company with other employees who might consider filing a similar claim, and who would *not* be prohibited from pursuing it because they were not a party to the release agreement. Further, if the release agreement refers to the reason for the ending of the employment relationship, such as the terminated employee's inability to meet the employer's work performance expectations, the departing employee might want to ensure that this information is not disclosed.

B. CONFIDENTIALITY OF INFORMATION OBTAINED DURING EMPLOYMENT

In addition to the interests that the parties might have to ensure the terms of the release agreement remain confidential, an employer might have an interest in ensuring that other information obtained during the term of the individual's employment is not disclosed by a departing employee. Whether or not a former employee has an obligation to keep information obtained during employment confidential absent an independent agreement to that effect is based on a fact-specific analysis of the nature of the information. For example, a departing employee would likely have an obligation to maintain the confidentiality of information that constitutes a trade secret. The definition of what constitutes a **trade secret** is very broad and refers to "any formula, pattern, device, or information compilation that is used in an employer's business and that gives the employer an opportunity to gain an advantage over competitors who do not know or use it."[29]

trade secret
broadly defined term for a formula, pattern, device, or other information an employer might seek to prevent former employees from disclosing to its competitors

Terminated employees are generally prohibited from sharing the trade secrets of their former employer because doing so breaches the post-termination fiduciary duty owed to their former employer.[30] For example, an employer who invested millions of dollars to research a new medication would likely be able to show that it has an interest in keeping the ingredient list confidential. Such an employer would be able to prevent a former employee from sharing the ingredient list with others after the employment relationship ends because it would likely constitute a trade secret, even in the absence of a confidentiality agreement.[31] In contrast, departing employees do not have an obligation to maintain the confidentiality of information that is known by the public or that an employer shares liberally with third parties, meaning this type of information can be shared with others.[32]

Although the trade secrets of an employer are protected, an employer might still want additional protections because whether certain information fits within the definition of trade secret is often in dispute. Further, the employer might want to maintain the confidentiality of information that falls outside of the definition of a trade secret, and this desired result can be achieved by incorporating a confidentiality clause into a release agreement and listing the specific information that the clause is intended to cover.

 ## RESTRICTIVE COVENANTS

Some employers have legitimate business interests (other than, or in addition to, a desire to keep certain information confidential) that will surface after an employment relationship ends. Depending on the nature of those interests, the parties may agree to certain **restrictive covenants** which limit the rights of former employees to engage in certain conduct that could result in competition for the employer or the sharing of confidential business information after the employment relationship ends.[33] The parties are not obligated to include any of these types of provisions in a release agreement, although an employer right require a departing employee to agree to its terms in exchange for the severance payment, provided the payment is not otherwise guaranteed. The types of restrictive covenants that are relevant will vary depending upon the nature of the employer's business, the reason for termination, and the future plans of each party to the employment relationship.

Because, by definition, restrictive covenants limit the rights of individuals, they are generally disfavored. In particular, courts and legislatures seek to achieve a delicate balance between the business interests the restrictive covenants are designed to protect and the societal interest in encouraging a competitive marketplace. The precise nature of the types of covenants that will be enforced is governed by state law and subject to stringent judicial review.

A. TYPES OF RESTRICTIVE COVENANTS

There are a number of restrictive covenants that might be relevant to an employment relationship, depending upon the concerns the parties are seeking to address. As stated, most restrictive covenants are subjected to significant judicial scrutiny based on the societal interest in fostering free and vigorous economic competition.[34]

1. NON-SOLICITATION AGREEMENT

A **non-solicitation agreement** is designed to prevent a former employee from recruiting the employees of a former employer or approaching clients of a former employer for business.[35]

There is often an overlap between an employer's interest in maintaining the confidentiality of its trade secrets and its interest in subjecting a former employee to a non-solicitation agreement. This overlap stems from a common disagreement between the parties as to whether or not particular information related to clients and client lists constitutes a trade secret. If the information does constitute a trade

restrictive covenants
contractual provisions that limit the rights of former employees to engage in certain conduct that could result in competition for the employer or the sharing of confidential business information after the employment relationship ends

non-solicitation agreement
agreement that a former employee will not recruit the employees of a former employer or approach clients of a former employer for business

secret, a former employee would have a post-employment obligation not to disclose the information by virtue of its being a trade secret. However, if the information is not determined to be a trade secret, the former employee would have the right to reveal and use that information absent an independent restriction such as a confidentiality clause or non-solicitation agreement. One court even stated that because, as a matter of law, it is challenging to determine what constitutes a trade secret, a restrictive covenant is the "pragmatic solution" to problems relating to the protection of confidential information.[36]

Courts have determined that customized customer lists and highly specialized marketing strategies that were discussed internally would be considered trade secrets deserving of protection. This means that an employer would not necessarily need a non-solicitation agreement to prevent a former employee from disclosing the information or using it for his personal gain.[37] However, if an employer is unable to show that the client lists were created through specialized techniques, the information might not be protected. The judicial reluctance to classify all client lists as trade secrets is best illustrated by one court's rejection of an employer's argument that a client list was a trade secret, despite the fact the employer established that it compiled the list from information on file with the secretary of state, which it paid $60,000 to access.[38]

2. NONCOMPETE CLAUSE

noncompete clause
restrictive covenant that prohibits an individual from working for the competitor of a former employer for a period of time after the end of that former employment relationship

Another type of restrictive covenant is a **noncompete clause**, sometimes referred to as a noncompetition clause, which seeks to limit the employers for whom an individual can work after an employment relationship ends. For example, a news anchor might be subject to a noncompete clause that would prevent her from accepting a position as a news anchor in the same city as the former employer, at a station that directly competes with that particular television station, for a period of six months after the conclusion of her employment.[39] Noncompete clauses are generally disfavored and subject to significant judicial scrutiny because they restrict the rights of employees to work in the field in which they are trained.[40]

3. NON-DISPARAGEMENT CLAUSE

non-disparagement clause
restrictive covenant that prohibits former employees from publicly ridiculing or vilifying a former employer, the other individuals who work at the company, or the company's products; a non-disparagement clause might also place the same restrictions on the employer, namely, prohibiting the employer from publicly ridiculing or vilifying a former employee

A **non-disparagement clause** is a restrictive covenant that prohibits former employees from publicly ridiculing or vilifying a former employer, the other individuals who work at the company, or the company's products.

This type of provision would prohibit a terminated employee from disparaging a former employer, or someone or something associated with it, because such remarks could have a negative impact on the employer's reputation. Although a non-disparagement clause could be limited to prohibiting a former employee from making any negative remarks, in some instances this restrictive covenant imposes mutual obligations on the parties, meaning that both parties agree not to make such comments about each other.

Even without this contractual language, both parties would have some recourse to address the making of *untruthful* disparaging remarks about one another through the filing of a defamation claim. However, as discussed later in this chapter, because truth is an affirmative defense to a defamation claim, an individual would not be entitled to any recovery within the context of a defamation claim for harm caused as a result of a *truthful* statement. Therefore, the parties may have a mutual interest in agreeing to a non-disparagement clause that could provide broader protections than a defamation claim because the non-solicitation clause would likely prohibit the communication of *both* truthful and untruthful derogatory statements.

B. LIMITATIONS ON RESTRICTIVE COVENANTS

Restrictive covenants are regulated by state law. Some states completely prohibit the use of certain types of covenants, and some states prohibit covenants in certain industries or for certain occupations. Most states that will enforce restrictive covenants place limitations on their use.[41] Although different restrictive covenants protect different interests, most courts require the restrictive covenants to fit within the same general parameters, enforcing them only if (1) their purpose is to protect a legitimate business interest of the employer, (2) they are supported by consideration, and (3) they are reasonable in scope.[42] For example, one court determined that a non-solicitation agreement was reasonable because its application was limited to a two-year period, covered six states, and applied only to specific contracts.[43]

1. MUST PROTECT A LEGITIMATE BUSINESS INTEREST

An employer seeking to restrict an individual's right to obtain future employment or to restrict the free flow of information in the marketplace must be prepared to illustrate that the restrictive covenant is narrowly tailored to address the legitimate business interest the covenant is designed to protect.[44] For example, an employer may assert a legitimate business interest in subjecting an individual to a non-solicitation clause based on the amount of time and resources that were expended to establish the working relationships with its clients, and this might be a particularly compelling interest if the customer leads were developed through an intricate research process.[45]

Although an employer might have a legitimate business interest in protecting its business relationships and client lists, non-solicitation agreements that are used to achieve this result must be narrowly tailored to protect the specific interest the covenant is designed to protect — namely, to "protect [the employer] from losing customers [to someone] who, by virtue of his employment, gained special knowledge and familiarity with the customers' requirements."[46] A court would likely refuse to apply a non-solicitation agreement to clients the former employee knew personally before he started his employment, because his continued contact with such individuals would likely have occurred even absent the employment relationship.[47] Under these circumstances, the employer would have difficulty showing its legitimate business interest should override the right of the former employee to continue to maintain a relationship with such individuals.[48]

An employer who wants to subject an employee to a noncompetition clause might assert that it has a legitimate business interest in protecting the financial investment it made to train the employee, and a competitor should not be permitted to achieve an immediate benefit from this financial expenditure.[49] Employers must recognize, however, that some courts are reluctant to recognize a business interest such as this since it restricts the rights of individuals to obtain employment in their fields. Some courts have determined that the knowledge and skills an employee acquires during her employment become part of the employee's person.[50] Other courts have suggested that an interest in restricting an individual's right to obtain alternative employment based on a prior financial expenditure to train the individual would not be a legitimate interest because the employer will have received a return on its investment during the time the individual was in its employ.[51]

Within the context of non-disparagement clauses, employers may assert they have a legitimate interest in protecting their company and its reputation from the harm that might be caused by a former employee who might speak unfavorably about the company after his separation from employment. An employer might have a particularly compelling business interest to enforce a non-disparagement clause in small industries, or for employers located in isolated areas where the terminated employee would be likely to continue to work.[52]

2. MUST BE SUPPORTED BY CONSIDERATION

Because a restrictive covenant is a contract between an employer and a former employee, it must be supported by consideration. Consideration is the benefit an individual receives in exchange for being subjected to the terms of the provision. Thus, an employer who asks an individual to sign a restrictive covenant on his last day of work as a matter of company policy would likely be unable to enforce its terms unless the individual received some type of independent benefit (such as additional compensation) for signing the agreement. Based on this, an employer who wants to incorporate a restrictive covenant into a release agreement must make it clear that the payment of severance is conditioned upon signing the release (or that something else of value is being provided in exchange for the agreement to be subject to the restrictive covenant). Assuming the employer intends for the severance to be the consideration, the employer will assert that the severance is the benefit received by the departing employee in exchange for the departing employee's agreement to be subject to the terms of the restrictive covenant which, therefore, creates a legally enforceable contract.[53]

3. MUST BE REASONABLE IN SCOPE

Because restrictive covenants are generally disfavored, most courts require that any covenant be supported by a general showing of reasonableness, which examines whether the restriction is narrowly defined to address the business interests the employer seeks to protect. In assessing reasonableness, most courts evaluate the type of conduct that is prohibited, the geographic scope of the restriction, and the amount of time for which it lasts.[54]

a. Conduct

Restrictive covenants should prohibit conduct only to the extent necessary to protect the interest the covenant is designed to protect. For example, one court held that a restrictive covenant that prohibited an artist employee from painting *any* birds — anywhere and forever — was void and unenforceable because the employer was unable to show it had an interest in restricting a former employee's behavior to this extent.[55] Similarly, a court refused to enforce a restrictive covenant that prohibited a janitor from working as a janitor for a period of ten years after the end of his employment.[56] A restrictive covenant that prohibited a former employee from performing any services for former clients was also found to be unenforceable because it was overbroad and did not specify the specific business activities that were prohibited.[57]

With respect to a noncompete clause, an employer headquartered in New York who does a majority of its business there would likely have difficulty enforcing a restrictive covenant that limits a former employee from engaging in any related work across the country. This restriction would likely be deemed unreasonable because the scope of the restriction would effectively prevent the employee from obtaining employment in the entire field in which he has expertise.[58] In contrast, a New York–based employer in a specialized industry would likely be more successful in placing limitations on its former employees who continue to work in the same industry in New York.[59]

b. Geography

Restrictive covenants should only prohibit conduct in the specific geographic location that is necessary to protect the employer's interests, and an absence of a limitation will likely mean the covenant is unreasonable.[60] For example, a restrictive covenant imposed by a medical clinic employer that was limited to the area that was serviced by the clinic was found to be reasonable.[61] In contrast, a restrictive covenant that covered a 100-mile radius around a large city was not.[62] Some courts suggest that if an employer has an interest in protecting its relationships with certain customers, it should limit the covenant to those specific customers rather than attempting to restrict an individual's conduct in a particular geographic location, since that might result in a finding that the covenant is overbroad, unreasonable, and therefore unenforceable.[63]

c. Duration

Employers should also ensure that their restrictive covenants are limited to a specific duration, because a lifelong prohibition would likely be deemed unreasonable, even if there are other limitations on the scope of a covenant's application.[64] The amount of time that a court will determine is reasonable will vary depending on the nature of the employer's business and the interests the covenant is designed to address.[65] For example, one court determined that because cardiology is a competitive business and it takes a significant amount of time to build a practice, a restrictive covenant that prohibited a departing doctor from practicing within a two-mile radius of the former employer's office for a period of three to five years was reasonable.[66]

V EMPLOYMENT REFERENCES

Copyright 2001 by Randy Glasbergen.
www.glasbergen.com

"I don't have any references, but 4 out of 5
phone psychics say I'm destined for greatness."

Regardless of how an employment relationship ends, there is always the possibility that a prospective employer will contact a former employer seeking an employment **reference.** A reference request might ask for the verification of an individual's dates of employment, salary, or title. The prospective employer conducting the reference check might also ask a former employer about an applicant's job performance, skills, attendance record, or personality to assess whether the person would be a match for the position the company is seeking to fill.

reference
information provided by a former employer to a prospective employer related to details about an individual's past employment

A. NO OBLIGATION TO PROVIDE REFERENCES

Generally speaking, an employer does not have an affirmative legal obligation to provide employment references.[67] Even though a former employer's decision to decline to provide a reference might suggest that any information provided would be negative, courts have generally upheld an employer's right to remain silent. This is because, in response to a former employer's decision to decline to provide any information, the prospective employer can make its own determination as to whether the situation warrants further investigation.[68]

One of the reasons some employers decline to provide references about their former employees is the potential liability that an employer might be subject to for supplying such information. Based on this risk, many employers incorporate reference policies into their company handbooks, making it clear they will provide only basic information about former employees, such as their dates of employment and job titles. Employers who provide references that include additional details about the work records of their employees should pay careful attention to the potential risks associated with sharing this type of information.

B. NEGLIGENT REFERRAL

Once an employer makes the decision to provide a reference, it must ensure that the reference is complete, because a failure to do so could subject it to liability for **negligent referral.** This cause of action imposes liability on an employer who misrepresents information about the qualifications and character of a former employee that could result in foreseeable harm. Once an employer provides *any* information about an individual's work performance, it is not permitted to withhold negative information that could present a risk to others.[69]

> **negligent referral**
> legal theory that holds a former employer responsible for harm caused by its former employee based on the employer's misrepresentation about a foreseeable risk

For example, in one case a court held an employer liable for negligent referral after the employer praised a former employee to a prospective employer even though he had knowledge of his previous sexual misconduct. The court determined that the former employer had an obligation to "complete the picture by disclosing material facts regarding charges and complaints of [the employee's] sexual improprieties."[70] In another case, an employer settled a claim after a former employee killed three co-workers, wounded two others, and killed himself at the workplace of his new employer. The settlement was based on the fact that the former employer provided a referral letter that did not indicate that the individual was terminated for bringing a weapon to work.[71]

C. LIABILITY FOR PROVIDING REFERENCES UNDER TITLE VII

Because providing references is part of the employment process, their use is subject to the provisions of Title VII and other anti-discrimination laws. Based on this, employers should establish a uniform and nondiscriminatory policy for providing references and avoid intentionally or unintentionally providing them based on whether or not individuals are members of a protected class. With the understanding that once an employer provides information it is generally not permitted to withhold negative information, employers should attempt to give information that is based on measurable factors, because an employer could be subject to liability if it appears that members of certain protected classes (or nonmembers) receive positive references while members of other protected classes receive less favorable reviews. Measurements about work performance could include such information as the number of claims an insurance adjuster successfully resolved, how much money a financial analyst saved the company, or the number of cars a salesperson sold. Employers who provide such information, whether it is positive or negative, should ensure that it is based on documented facts that can be verified, as opposed to being based on office gossip or rumors.

D. INFORMAL REFERENCE CHECKS

The potential risks employers face when providing references for former employees often makes it challenging for prospective employers to obtain extensive information about its job applicants. This situation often compels prospective employers to engage in other informal reference checks. Technological advances have created opportunities for employers to initiate these informal reference checks through the Internet with a basic Google search on an applicant's name, or through social networking sites where individuals post an abundance of personal and professional information.

Although such checks may provide an employer with extensive information, their use may also result in the imposition of liability. Further, as these techniques become more widespread, they will likely be the subject of significant litigation relating to whether an employer has the right to use the information it gathers through these informal reference checks, and what obligations, if any, it has to verify the type of information found. There is also a question as to whether an employer would have an obligation to notify applicants if information gathered through an informal reference check is used as the basis for the imposition of an adverse employment decision, such as a decision not to invite the applicant to move forward in the hiring process.

Employers should be careful about using these informal investigatory processes because the parameters surrounding the collection and use of information in this manner have not been fully tested. Additionally, such techniques have the potential to reveal a significant amount of information about an individual's membership in a protected class. For example, an employer might locate a newspaper article referencing an individual's attendance at a religious conference or association with a professional group linked to a particular national origin. The consideration of this information in making an adverse employment decision could constitute discriminatory conduct. Further, because an employer is presumed to use any information it has in its possession, even the fact that the employer initiated an Internet search and had such information could be used to suggest the employer unlawfully considered it as a basis for making an adverse employment decision. See Chapter 10, Collection of Information: The Application and Interview.

 VI OTHER POTENTIAL SOURCES OF POST-EMPLOYMENT LIABILITY

Although the extent to which an employer might be subject to liability for the use of informal reference checks is still developing, there are some other sources of post-employment liability that are fairly well established. In addition to liability that may arise within the context of references, both parties to an employment relationship may be subject to liability for a number of other types of post-employment conduct.

A. DEFAMATION

Defamation relates to the communication of false information about an individual that results in harm to his reputation or deters third persons from dealing with the individual.[72] An individual might file a defamation claim against a former employer who makes untruthful disparaging remarks about his past work performance that harms his reputation. A current employee might file a defamation claim about her employer, and an employer might file a defamation claim against an employee or a former employee for making statements that harm its reputation.

defamation
cause of action relating to the communication of false information about an individual (in a verbal or written form) that causes harm to his reputation or deters third persons from dealing with the individual

1. ELEMENTS OF DEFAMATION CLAIM

A defamation claim is filed to recover damages in response to a verbal or written communication that (1) harms an individual's reputation, (2) is communicated to a third party, and (3) is false.[73]

a. Communication Harms an Individual's Reputation

In determining whether a communication is defamatory, the first issue is whether "it tends to hurt the reputation of another so as to lower him in the estimation of the community or to deter third persons from associating or dealing with him."[74] Defamatory communications have also been defined as those that tend to expose another to "public hatred, contempt, ridicule or degradation."[75] In assessing whether a communication has a detrimental impact on one's reputation, the current reputation of the individual is relevant. As one court stated, "If an individual's reputation cannot be further damaged, a defamation suit serves no purpose, wastes judicial resources, and hinders First Amendment interests."[76]

There is no precise definition of what statement would fit within this description, and it is interpreted broadly. Within the context of providing references, it is significant that the law does not require proof of actual harm to an individual's reputation, but rather the communication must "prejudice a person in the eyes of a substantial and respectable minority of persons in the community or association."[77] For example, a former employee might file a defamation claim against an employer who makes untruthful remarks about his work performance at industry events and on the Internet, if he can show those remarks prevent him from being able to obtain employment in the industry.[78] An employer might also assert a defamation claim by, for example, demonstrating that a false statement harmed its reputation and led to lost business, or that a communication resulted in some other type of harm, such as causing the employer's landlord to decline to renew its long-standing lease.

b. Publication

The next element of a defamation claim is **publication**, which is the communication of the information to a third party. Publication requires the actual

publication
communication of information to a third party, which is a critical element of a defamation claim

communication of the harmful statement, and the term is interpreted liberally.[79] If an individual can show that a third party was able to understand the statement and knew to whom it was attributed, the publication element of defamation will be established.[80]

The manner in which the information is communicated will determine the type of defamation claim filed. **Slander** refers to a defamation claim based on communication that is spoken, while **libel** refers to a claim based on a written communication.[81] For example, a supervisor would likely be subject to liability for slander for lying to a group of employees by telling them a particular employee gave him a sexually transmitted disease.[82] If this same comment was made in writing, such as in a letter or on the Internet, the supervisor could be subject to liability for libel.[83]

slander
defamation claim based on a spoken communication

libel
defamation claim based on a written communication

c. False

The final component of a defamation claim is showing that the communication was false.[84] It is critical to understand that a truthful statement will not subject an individual to liability for defamation — even if the statement causes harm to an individual's reputation. For example, suppose an employer announces at a business dinner party that a former employee was a thief and posts a statement on the Internet saying that the individual was a thief, and then the individual loses three job opportunities because of these statements. If this individual files a defamation claim against the employer and the employer can present evidence that the individual was a thief (such as, for example, proof of a conviction for shoplifting), then the employer will not be subject to liability. An individual would not be subject to liability arising out of a defamation claim for making any truthful statements, regardless of their impact.[85]

2. AFFIRMATIVE DEFENSES

There are a number of affirmative defenses that can be asserted in response to the filing of a defamation claim. **Affirmative defenses** are conditions that, if true, would act as a complete bar to recovery for the claim.

affirmative defense
condition that, if true, will act as a complete bar to recovery for a particular claim

a. Truth

Truth is an affirmative defense to a defamation claim.[86] Thus, if an individual can show that a communication is true, it would prevent the imposition of liability for a defamation claim even if the statement was disparaging, offensive, or harmed another person's reputation.[87] Consistent with the example presented above, suppose an individual says that his former employer is a liar, this statement harms the reputation of the former employer, and the employer files a defamation claim. In defending the claim, if the individual presents evidence that his former employer is, in fact, a liar, then it would be an affirmative defense to the defamation claim and bar any recovery.

The fact that truth is an affirmative defense for a defamation claim also prevents the imposition of liability for the expression of an opinion. Suppose an individual leaves a movie theatre and yells that a certain film was the worst movie he had seen in years, and this statement causes a number of people to decline to purchase tickets for the film. Then suppose the director of the film files a defamation claim against the individual who made the statement, stating it harmed his reputation. The director would not be able to recover any damages from the individual, because the movie viewer would likely testify that, in his opinion, the movie was the worst he had seen in years, and because that statement was true (in his opinion), it cannot be used as the basis for the imposition of liability for a defamation claim.

b. Absolute Privilege

An **absolute privilege** protects an individual from liability for a defamation claim based on the role the person is acting in when the statement is made. Individuals who are entitled to an absolute privilege will not be subject to liability for defamation, even if their comments harm someone's reputation. For example, witnesses who testify to facts they believe to be true or legislators who make comments while on the legislative floor enjoy an absolute privilege, meaning they will not be subject to liability for defamatory statements made while they are acting in those capacities.[88]

absolute privilege
bar to recovery for a defamation claim based upon the role the person is acting in when the statement is made

c. Qualified Privilege

A **qualified privilege** offers a narrower source of protection and will prevent the imposition of liability on an individual acting in a certain role, provided that there is no malicious intent associated with the communication.[89] For example, an individual would also be unlikely to successfully assert a defamation claim against an employer for a written statement made pursuant to an investigation of a workplace incident, because the supervisor would likely have a qualified privilege for engaging in this conduct, provided he had a good faith belief that his statements were an accurate description of the events that took place.[90]

qualified privilege
defense to a defamation claim that may bar recovery for a statement that might otherwise be defamatory based on the role the person is acting in when the statement is made and on the circumstances surrounding the communication

Further, in most states supervisors who conduct performance evaluations are afforded a qualified privilege and therefore cannot be subject to liability for a defamation claim based on the statements made within the context of providing those evaluations, provided the statements are not made maliciously.[91] What distinguishes a qualified privilege from an absolute privilege, is that the qualified privilege will be lost if it is abused. Therefore, within the context of a performance evaluation, an employer could lose the privilege for making an unwarranted negative comment with a "conscious indifference or reckless disregard as to its results or effects."[92]

d. Consent

The final affirmative defense to a defamation claim is consent. If an employee agrees to the communication of a defamatory statement, this consent would prevent the imposition of liability.[93] For example, most employers seek consent from prospective employees for the right to check their employment references, and this consent would extend to whatever information is obtained through a reference check. This consent would therefore be sufficient to prevent the success of a defamation claim asserted by the applicant against a former employer if, for example, the potential employer obtains information through an authorized reference check and the applicant is subsequently not offered the position and claims the discussion harmed his reputation. Even though the statement by the former employer to the potential employer may have harmed the applicant and resulted in his not receiving an offer of employment (or in the withdrawal of a conditional offer of employment), by consenting to the reference check, the individual would have agreed to permit the communication of the information within this context.[94]

B. TORTIOUS INTERFERENCE WITH CONTRACTUAL RELATIONSHIPS

tortious interference with contractual relationships
cause of action relating to conduct intended to unlawfully block an individual from forming a contract with a third party or inducing a third party not to abide by its terms

In addition to the liability that may be imposed on an employer for making defamatory comments about a former employee, there is another potential source of liability that may materialize if an employer engages in conduct that interferes with the rights of its former employees to enter into other contractual relationships. The **tortious interference with contractual relationships** imposes liability on an employer who "intentionally and improperly interferes with the performance of a contract between another and a third person by inducing or otherwise causing the third person not to perform the contract."[95]

While the elements necessary to support a claim for this cause of action vary under state law, to sustain a claim a former employee must generally show that (1) the former employer knew about an existing or contemplated contract between the former employee and a third party, (2) the former employer engaged in conduct with the intention of blocking the creation or implementation of the contract, and (3) the intended result materialized.[96]

In assessing whether the employer is subject to liability for this interference, courts consider a number of factors, such as

1. the nature of the conduct;
2. the motive for the behavior;
3. the interests of the other person with whom the conduct interferes;
4. the interests of the person who attempts to interfere; and
5. the relationship between the parties.[97]

For example, this type of claim could arise if an employer terminates an employee and, on learning that two other employers extended employment offers to her, contacts those employers and advises against their hiring the individual. If the new potential employers revoke their offers to the individual based on this suggestion, the former employer could be subject to a claim for tortious interference with contractual relationships. An employer who engages in this type of conduct might also be subject to a retaliation claim depending on the reason he reached out to the potential employers.

C. POST-EMPLOYMENT RETALIATION

A claim for **retaliation** can arise under a number of circumstances, as discussed in Chapter 2, Title VII — The Foundation of Employment Discrimination Law. Such claims can materialize in response to an individual's assertion of any legal right, but within the context of workplace discrimination, retaliation claims relate to the imposition of an adverse employment action on an individual in response to his assertion of his rights (or intention to assert his rights) by filing a discrimination claim or by participating in the process to assert the rights of someone else.[98]

An **adverse action** is employer conduct that has a negative impact on an individual and that would discourage a reasonable person from filing or supporting the filing of a discrimination claim.[99] The Supreme Court has made it clear that the rights of employees to file retaliation claims continue even *after* the employment relationship ends. In making this determination, the Court reasoned that ruling that individuals could not file a retaliation claim post-termination would actually encourage employers to terminate employees they suspected were planning to file a claim, to prevent the filing of it.[100] For example, an employer who gives a negative reference about a former employee because the former employee previously filed a Title VII claim against its company could be subject to a post-employment retaliation claim.[101]

Even if the prior protected activity related to a different employer, retaliatory adverse actions are unlawful. Thus, a current employer who assigns a new employee to an undesirable work schedule in response to her pursuing a discrimination claim against a former employer could be subject to liability for engaging in retaliatory conduct.[102] Further, the Supreme Court indicated that an employer could be held liable for retaliation for engaging in retaliatory conduct outside the workplace by, for example, filing false criminal charges against a former employee in response to the former employee's filing of a prior discrimination claim.[103]

retaliation
employer imposition of an adverse action in response to a former employee's assertion of a legal right

adverse action
employer conduct that has a negative impact on an individual and that would discourage a reasonable person from filing or supporting the filing of a discrimination claim, or a claim that stems from the assertion of a number of other legal rights

KEY TERMS

- ✓ absolute privilege
- ✓ adverse action
- ✓ affirmative defense
- ✓ consideration
- ✓ defamation
- ✓ exit incentive program
- ✓ knowing and voluntary
- ✓ libel
- ✓ negligent referral
- ✓ noncompete clause
- ✓ non-disparagement clause
- ✓ non-solicitation agreement
- ✓ Older Workers Benefit Protection Act (OWBPA)
- ✓ publication
- ✓ qualified privilege
- ✓ reference
- ✓ release agreement
- ✓ restrictive covenants
- ✓ retaliation
- ✓ severance
- ✓ slander
- ✓ tortious interference with contractual relationships
- ✓ trade secret
- ✓ unemployment benefits

DISCUSSION QUESTIONS

Explain your response to each of the following questions with the understanding that in some cases there is no right or wrong answer. If you cannot make an informed decision with the facts provided, indicate the nature and significance of the additional information you would need. For the purposes of these questions, you can assume that the employers and employees mentioned below are covered by Title VII and other relevant federal workplace anti-discrimination laws.

1. Explain why an employer might want to provide a terminated employee a financial benefit in the form of severance. Why might an employer provide a noneconomic severance benefit?
2. Explain a common method for the calculation of severance.
3. Explain some factors that would be considered to determine whether a release agreement constituted a knowing and voluntary waiver of an individual's rights.
4. What is the OWBPA and what does it require?
5. Explain the types of restrictive covenants an employer might want to use to impose some post-employment obligations on a departing employee. What business interests do each of these convenants seek to protect?
6. Marsha is an employer who wants to terminate four employees. She is very concerned about the potential liability that might arise from two of the terminations, but because she is a small employer, she does not have any money to offer as a financial incentive to compel all of the employees to sign a release. Based on this, she says she has no options other than to just cross her fingers and hope the employees are too busy looking for new jobs to pursue any legal claims against her. Do you agree?
7. Morey is married to Marsha in the example above, and he tells her that he cannot believe she is concerned about the situation. He says he never worries about his employees suing because he makes all terminated employees sign a release in order to get their coats and personal belongings from their offices. Do you think this is a wise business decision? Why or why not?
8. Eric is the son of Marsha and Morey, and he thinks that both of his parents are overly cautious employers and that his current business practice would address all of their concerns. He says he processes a check for the severance that would be owed pursuant to company policy and hands it to any termi-nated employee along with the following release:

    "I, _____ (name of employee), acknowledge that I was an employee at will who could be fired for any reason at any time. Based on this, I agree not to file a claim against my employer for any reason. In addition, I understand that if I do not return this release by the close of business, my employer retains the right to stop payment on this severance check."

    Do you think the use of this release is a sound business practice? Should Marsha and Morey follow Eric's advice?

9. Maxine is an employer who is thrilled she finished negotiating a release agreement for an individual who had been a problem employee for almost three years. As soon as his severance is paid, Maxine goes out with her husband, Alan, for a celebratory drink. She says she is thrilled to have severed all ties with the individual and will never have to hear his name again. Her husband, a lawyer, smiles but knows this may not be true. What do you think?

10. When Maxine and Alan leave the restaurant, they notice that the tires on her car have been slashed. Maxine is furious because she is certain that her former employee was responsible for the damage and immediately e-mails all of her business contacts that he is a violent criminal who should be avoided. Also, because she heard he had two pending job offers, she posts a notice on her Internet blog (which is linked to a number of professional networks to which they both belong) to tell anyone who might be considering offering him an employment contract to immediately revoke it. Do you think Maxine could be subject to any liability for her conduct?

11. Terrence is a nervous employer who despises lawyers and is always looking for ways to avoid lawsuits and the exorbitant legal bills that always come along with them. Based on this, he implements a company policy that requires the Human Resources Department to use the following script to provide references for all former employees: "_____ (employee's full name) worked here from _____ (start date) to _____ (end date). We take great pride in our employees and the important contributions they make to our workplace. We were very disappointed when _____ (employee name) decided to leave his/her position with our company, but we know s/he will be a valuable asset to a new employer." Do you think this policy will be a useful tool for Terrence to reach his desired result? Why or why not?

ENDNOTES

1. Note that if an employer conditions the receipt of the severance benefit on the signing of a release agreement, a recoupment policy such as this could be problematic if the employer intended the severance payment to be the consideration necessary for the agreement to be a legally enforceable contract.

2. Employment & Training Admin., U.S. Dept. of Labor, State Unemployment and Insurance Benefits (available at *http://workforcesecurity.doleta.gov/unemploy/uifactsheet.asp*).

3. *Id.*

4. *See generally id.*

5. Although the focus of the discussion about release agreements in this textbook relates to their use within the context of employment terminations, their use is not limited to these circumstances. For example, the parties in an employment relationship might negotiate a release agreement during the course of an individual's employment to resolve a wide number of employment issues, such as a claim for a discriminatory decision related to a promotional opportunity. Under this circumstance, the same framework for the release agreement will apply, and the employee must receive a benefit in exchange for an agreement not to pursue a legal claim on the specific issue the agreement is intended to resolve for the agreement to constitute a legally enforceable contract.

6. *See, e.g., Hampton v. Ford Motor Co.*, 561 F.3d 709, 716 (7th Cir. 2009) (holding an employee may waive past claims that would arise under Title VII); *EEOC v. SunDance Rehab. Corp.*, 466 F.3d 490, 499 (6th Cir. 2006) (holding an employee may waive past claims that would arise under the Equal Pay Act).

7. *See U-Haul Co.*, 347 No. 34, at *13, 347 NLRB 375 (2006) (holding employees cannot waive their right to file a claim under the National Labor Relations Act).

8. *See Perez v. Unline, Inc.*, 157 Cal. App. 4th 953, 955 (2007).

9. *See Wrigglesworth v. Brumbaugh*, 121 F. Supp. 2d 1126, 1132 (W.D. Mich. 2000).

10. N.Y. Lab. Law § 595 (2008).

11. *See, e.g.*, N.Y. Workers' Comp. Law § 32(a) (2005).

12. *See* U.S. Equal Employment Opportunity Commn., Understanding Waivers of Discrimination Claims in Employee Severance Agreements (available at *http://www.eeoc.gov/policy/docs/qanda_severance-agreements.html*). In some cases courts disagree as to whether a particular prohibition relates to all claims that arise under a statute, or whether the prohibition only relates to future claims. This is the situation relating to claims that arise under the Family and Medical Leave Act (FMLA). Specifically, the Department of Labor regulations state that "employees cannot waive, nor may employers induce employees to waive, their rights under FMLA." 29 C.F.R. § 825.220(d). Despite what seems to be clear language, courts disagree as to whether this provision applies to both past and future claims. *See Dougherty v. TEVA Pharms. USA*, No. 05-CV-2336, 2008 U.S. Dist. LEXIS 13255, at *12-13 (E.D. Pa. Feb. 20, 2008) (holding the statutory language does not prohibit an employee from waiving past FMLA claim). *But see Taylor v. Progress Energy, Inc.*, 493 F.3d 454, 456-457 (4th Cir. 2007) (holding the statutory language prohibits an employee from waiving past and future claims). The recent FMLA regulations attempt to provide some clarity on the issue by stating that the language should be interpreted to mean that employees have the right to settle their existing FMLA claims but do not have the right to waive their rights with respect to future claims. *See* 29 C.F.R. §§ 825.100 *et seq.*

13. *See Bachiller v. Turn On Prods., Inc.*, 2003 WL 1878416 (S.D.N.Y. Apr. 14, 2003) (applying contract principles to determine the enforceability of a release agreement).

14. U.S. Equal Employment Opportunity Commn., Understanding Waivers of Discrimination Claims in Employee Severance Agreements (available at *http://www.eeoc.gov/policy/docs/qanda_severance-agreements.html*).

15. *See, e.g., Syverson v. International Bus. Machs. Corp.*, 2007 WL 8119 (9th Cir. 2007) (considering the education level of the individual to whom release is presented when determining whether it represents a knowing and voluntary waiver of rights).

16. *See Hampton v. Ford Motor Co.*, 561 F.3d 709 (7th Cir. 2009); *Wagner v. NutraSweet Co.*, 95 F.3d 527 (7th Cir. 1996); *Blum v. Lucent Techs., Inc.*, 2005 WL 4044579, at *6 (N.J. Super. Ct. App. Div. May 30, 2006) (considering the totality of circumstances, including such things as whether the agreement was written in clear language, whether consideration was provided, whether the individual had the appropriate time to review the agreement, and whether the individual was represented by an attorney); *Pilon v. University of Minn.*, 710 F.2d 466 (8th Cir. 1983) (upholding a release where the employee was represented by counsel, the release language was clear, and there was no claim of fraud or duress).

17. *Myricks v. Federal Reserve Bank of Atlanta*, 480 F.3d 1036 (11th Cir. 2007).

18. *Cole v. Gaming Entmt., L.L.C.*, 199 F. Supp. 2d 208, 213 (D. Del. 2002).

19. *See Hampton v. Ford Motor Co.*, 561 F.3d 709, 716 (7th Cir. 2009); *Smith v. Amedisys Inc.*, 298 F.3d 434, 443 (5th Cir. 2002) (holding a release does not have to specifically reference Title VII or other federal causes of action to constitute a valid waiver).

20. *Williams v. Phillips Petroleum Co.*, 23 F.3d 930, 936 (5th Cir. 1994).

21. *See* 29 U.S.C. § 626(f); 29 C.F.R. pt. 1625 (Waiver of Rights and Claims Under the Age Discrimination in Employment Act (ADEA)).

22. *See American Airlines, Inc. v. Cardoza-Rodriguez*, 133 F.3d 111, 118 (1st Cir. 1998) (by failing "to directly advise their employees to consult a lawyer before making the election,

we rule, as a matter of law, that [the employer] failed to meet its burden under the OWBPA").

23. 29 U.S.C. § 626(f); *see* 29 C.F.R. pt. 1625 (Waiver of Rights and Claims Under the Age Discrimination in Employment Act (ADEA)).

24. *Oubre v. Energy Operations, Inc.*, 522 U.S. 422 (1998); *see also Kruchowski v. Weyerhaeuser Co.*, 446 F.3d 1090, 1095 (10th Cir. 2006) (finding that if one of the statutory elements is missing from the release agreement, the waiver will not be valid as it relates to ADEA claims).

25. *See Syverson v. International Bus. Machs. Corp.*, 461 F.3d 1147 (9th Cir. 2006); *Thomforde v. International Bus. Machs. Corp.*, 406 F.3d 500 (8th Cir. 2005) (holding that the lack of clarity in the release language made it an ineffective waiver of an employee's right to a claim under the ADEA).

26. U.S. Equal Employment Opportunity Commn., Understanding Waivers of Discrimination Claims in Employee Severance Agreements (available at *http://www.eeoc.gov/policy/docs/qanda_severance-agreements.html*).

27. *Id; see* 29 C.F.R. pt. 1625 (Waiver of Rights and Claims Under the Age Discrimination in Employment Act (ADEA)).

28. *See Ruehl v. Viacom, Inc.*, 2007 WL 2555244 (3d Cir. 2007) (finding that the failure to provide the required demographic information relating to who is and who is not covered by a layoff would invalidate a waiver); *Currier v. United Techs. Corp.*, 393 F.3d 246, 251 n.4 (1st Cir. 2004) (listing the types of information an employee must receive to waive a claim under the ADEA, including the ages of other individuals who were selected for the program or were ineligible); *Adams v. Ameritech Servs., Inc.*, 231 F.3d 414, 431 (7th Cir. 2000) (waiver invalid if it does not include the job titles of other individuals affected by the group layoff); *Pagliolo v. Guidant Corp.*, 483 F. Supp. 2d 847, 864 (D. Minn. 2007) (refusing to bar employees from filing claims under the ADEA because the release contained misrepresentations that made it challenging for the affected individuals to make an informed decision as to whether they had a valid age discrimination claim, which was inconsistent with the requirements under the OWBPA).

29. Restatement of Torts § 757 cmt. (b) (1939).

30. *See, e.g., McKay v. Communispond, Inc.*, 581 F. Supp. 801 (S.D.N.Y. 1983).

31. *See id.* Employers should ask new employees if they are subject to any restrictive covenants because, depending upon the circumstances, the employers can be subject to liability for engaging in conduct that violates the terms of a restrictive covenant. For example, a new employer who benefits from the disclosure of a protected trade secret could be subject to liability for the use of the information along with the individual who discloses it. *See, e.g., A.H. Emery Co. v. Marcan Prods. Corp.*, 268 F. Supp. 289, 300 (S.D.N.Y. 1967), *aff'd*, 389 F.2d 11 (2d Cir.), *cert. denied*, 393 U.S. 835 (1968).

32. *See, e.g., GTI Corp. v. Calhoon*, 309 F. Supp. 762 (S.D. Ohio 1969).

33. It is important to recognize that although restrictive covenants may be negotiated as part of a release agreement, they may also be negotiated at the start of an individual's employment as part of an employment contract, or in some instances they may be incorporated into a company handbook and even restrict the behavior of at-will employees. *See, e.g., Camco, Inc. v. Baker*, 936 P.2d 829 (Nev. 1997) (enforcing post-hire restrictive covenant on at-will employee based on continued employment); *Ackerman v. Kimball Intl., Inc.*, 634 N.E.2d 778 (Ind. Ct. App. 1994); *Robert Half Intl., Inc. v. Van Steenis*, 784 F. Supp. 1263 (E.D. Mich. 1991) (enforcing a noncompete restrictive covenant against an at-will employee based on the consideration received in the form of continued employment).

34. *See Maryland Metals, Inc. v. Metzner*, 382 A.2d 564 (Md. 1978) (emphasizing the societal interest in fostering free and vigorous competition in the economic sphere).

35. Although these agreements limit the rights of individuals, many courts view non-solicitation agreements more favorably than noncompete agreements because they would not necessarily prevent individuals from earning a living in the field in which they have been trained. *See, e.g., Freiburger v. J-U-B Engrs.*, 111 P.3d 100 (Idaho 2005).

36. *Waters Servs., Inc. v. Tesco Chems., Inc.*, 410 F.2d 163, 170-171 (5th Cir. 1969) (referencing a covenant not to compete).

37. *See U.S. Reinsurance Corp. v. Humphreys*, 205 A.D.2d 187, 618 N.Y.S.2d 270 (1st Dept. 1994) (sales techniques); *Arnold's Ice Cream Co. v. Carlson*, 330 F. Supp. 1185 (E.D.N.Y. 1971) (customer lists).

38. *Hamer Holding Group, Inc. v. Elmore*, 560 N.E.2d 907 (Ill. App. Ct. 1990).

39. *See, e.g., Wessel Co. v. Busa*, 329 N.E.2d 414 (Ill. App. Ct. 1975) (upholding reasonableness of a three-year non-solicitation agreement that covered a 250-mile radius).

40. *See Hill v. Hill Mobile Auto Trim*, 725 S.W.2d 168 (Tex. 1987) (rejecting reasonableness of noncompetition agreement because it prevented the employee from earning a living where he lived); *State v. New Jersey Trade Waste Assn.*, 465 A.2d 596 (N.J. 1983).

41. *See, e.g.*, Cal. Bus. & Prof. Code § 16,601; Nev. Rev. Stat. § 613.200; Wis. Stat. Ann. § 103.465; Ala. Code § 8-1-1 (Contract Restraining Business Void (professionals)); Colo. Rev. Stat. § 8-2-113(3) (physicians).

42. Wis. Stat. Ann. § 103.465 (West 2001) (a covenant is enforceable within a specified territory and during a specified time if the restrictions imposed are reasonably necessary for the protection of the employer or principal); *see Gillespie v. Carbondale Marion Eye Ctrs.*, 622 N.E.2d 1267 (Ill. App. Ct. 1993) (enforceability depends on reasonable duration and scope designed to protect a legitimate business interest).

43. *Morrison Metalweld Process Corp. v. Valent*, 422 N.E.2d 103 (Ill. App. Ct. 1981).

44. *See* Restatement (Second) of Contracts § 188(1)(a) (1981); *Bishop v. Lakeland Animal Hosp.*, 644 N.E.2d 33 (Ill. App. Ct. 1994) (enforceability depends upon reasonableness and the protection of a legitimate business interest that is more than an attempt to stifle competition).

45. *See U.S. Reinsurance Corp. v. Humphreys*, 205 A.D.2d 187, 618 N.Y.S.2d 270 (1st Dept. 1994) (sales techniques); *Arnold's Ice Cream Co. v. Carlson*, 330 F. Supp. 1185 (E.D.N.Y. 1971) (customer lists).

46. *Instrumentalist Co. v. Band, Inc.*, 480 N.E.2d 1273, 1281 (Ill. App. Ct. 1985).

47. *Servomation Mathias v. Englert*, 333 F. Supp. 9 (M.D. Pa. 1971) (disallowing prohibition against solicitation of customers with whom former employee had no contact during his employment).

48. *Com-Co Ins. Agency, Inc. v. Service Ins. Agency, Inc.*, 321 Ill. App. 3d 816 (2001).

49. *Freund v. E.D. & F. Man Internation, Inc.*, 199 F.3d 382, 385 (7th Cir. 1999) (suggesting an investment in an employee's training might be sufficient grounds to enforce a non-compete agreement).

50. *Ingersoll-Rand Co. v. Ciavatta*, 542 A.2d 879 (N.J. 1988); *see Masterclean of N.C., Inc. v. Guy*, 345 S.E.2d 692 (N.C. Ct. App. 1986) (finding that employee's skills at removing asbestos belonged to him).

51. *Taylor v. Cordis Corp.*, 634 F. Supp. 1242 (S.D. Miss. 1986).

52. *See Wolff v. Protégé Sys. Inc.*, 506 S.E.2d 429 (Ga. Ct. App. 1998).

53. *See Sherman v. Pfefferkorn*, 135 N.E. 568 (Mass. 1922) (consideration required).

54. *American Broad. Cos. v. Wolf*, 52 N.Y.2d 394, 403 (1981) (stating "an otherwise valid covenant will not be enforced if it is unreasonable in time, space or scope or would operate in a harsh or oppressive manner").

55. *Nature House, Inc. v. Sloan*, 515 F. Supp. 398 (N.D. Ill. 1981).

56. *Frederick v. Professional Bldg. Maint. Indus., Inc.*, 344 N.E.2d 299 (Ind. Ct. App. 1976).

57. *Avion Sys., Inc. v. Thompson*, 650 S.E.2d 349 (Ga. Ct. App. 2007); *Stulz v. Safety & Compliance Mgmt., Inc.*, 648 S.E.2d 129 (Ga. Ct. App. 2007) (absence of a limitation on the type of conduct the former employee was prohibited from engaging in was unreasonable because it was overbroad).

58. *See Roanoke Engg. Sales Co. v. Rosenbaum*, 290 S.E.2d 882, 884 (Va. 1982).

59. *See Omniplex World Servs. Corp. v. US Investigations Servs., Inc.*, 618 S.E.2d 340, 342 (Va. 2005).

60. *See Trujillo v. Great S. Equip. Sales, LLC*, 2008 WL 269606 (Ga. Ct. App. Feb. 1, 2008) (unenforceable due to lack of geographic limitations); *American Family Life Assurance*

Co. v. Tazelaar, 482 N.E.2d 1072 (Ill. App. Ct. 1985) (unreasonableness of restrictive covenant that does not include a geographic limitation). *But see Intelus Corp. v. Barton*, 7 F. Supp. 2d 635 (D. Md. 1998) (upholding restrictive covenant that did not include a geographic limitation because the employee worked for clients around the world); *Superior Consulting Inc. v. Walling*, 851 F. Supp. 839, 851 (E.D. Mich. 1994) (holding geography may not have to be limited if the "business is sufficiently national and international in scope").

61. *Ellis v. McDaniel*, 596 P.2d 222, 224 (Nev. 1979).

62. *Hansen v. Edwards*, 426 P.2d 792 (Nev. 1967).

63. *See Frontier Corp. v. Telco Commcns. Group*, 965 F. Supp. 1200 (S.D. Ind. 1997).

64. *See, e.g., House of Vision, Inc. v. Hiyane*, 225 N.E.2d 21 (Ill. 1967) (refusing to enforce covenant that applied to a 30-mile radius in the absence of time limitation).

65. *Compare Shipley Co. v. Clark*, 728 F. Supp. 818, 828 (D. Mass. 1990) (upholding one-year covenant), *with EarthWeb v. Schlack*, 71 F. Supp. 2d 299, 313 (S.D.N.Y. 1999) (finding a one-year noncompete clause to be unreasonable because the individual's knowledge would quickly lose value based on the fast-paced nature of the industry), *and Blalock v. Perfect Subscription Co.*, 458 F. Supp. 123, 127-128 (S.D. Ala. 1978) (finding a 120-day restrictive covenant unreasonable).

66. *Mohanty, M.D. v. St. John Heart Clinic*, 2006 WL 3741970 (Ill. Dec. 21, 2006).

67. *See Davis v. Board of County Commrs. of Dona Ana County*, 987 P.2d 1172 (N.M. Ct. App. 1999).

68. *See, e.g., Saucedo v. Rheem Mfg. Co.*, 974 S.W.2d 117, 122 (Tex. App. 1998).

69. *See Randi W. v. Muroc Joint Unified Sch. Dist.*, 14 Cal. 4th 1066 (1997).

70. *Randi W. v. Muroc Joint Unified Sch. Dist.*, 14 Cal. 4th 1066, 1082 (1997).

71. *Jerner v. Allstate Ins. Co.*, No. 93-09472 (Fla. Cir. Ct. 1995).

72. *See* Restatement (Second) of Torts § 559 (1977).

73. Restatement (Second) of Torts § 558 (1977).

74. Restatement (Second) of Torts § 559 (1977).

75. *Phipps v. Clark Oil & Ref. Corp.*, 408 N.W.2d 569, 573 (Minn. 1987).

76. *Davis v. Hamilton*, 92 N.W. 512, 515 (Minn. 1902); *Finklea v. Jacksonville Daily Progress*, 742 S.W.2d 512, 517 (Tex. App. 1987).

77. Restatement (Second) of Torts § 559 (1977).

78. *See id.*

79. *See Houston Belt & Terminal Ry. Co. v. Wherry*, 548 S.W.2d 743, 751 (Tex. 1977); *Applewhite v. Memphis State Univ.*, 495 S.W.2d 190, 192 (Tenn. 1973).

80. Restatement (Second) of Torts, § 559 cmt. a (1977) ("the word 'communication' is used to denote the fact that one has brought an idea to the perception of another").

81. Restatement (Second) of Torts, § 568(1), (2); *see Draghetti v. Chmielewski*, 416 Mass. 808, 812 n.4 (1994).

82. *See Lewis v. Oregon Beauty Supply Co.*, 733 P.2d 430 (Or. 1987).

83. *See* Restatement (Second) of Torts § 568(1), (2).

84. *Janklow v. Newsweek, Inc.*, 759 F.2d 644, 648 (8th Cir. 1985), *cert. denied*, 479 U.S. 883 (1987) ("[i]n order for a statement to be defamatory . . . it must be false").

85. *See* Restatement (Second) of Torts § 581A (1977)("One who publishes a defamatory statement of fact is not subject to liability for defamation if the statement is true").

86. Restatement (Second) of Torts § 558; *see Fowle v. Donnelly*, 358 P.2d 485 (Or. 1960).

87. *Moore v. St Joseph Nursing Home, Inc.*, 459 N.W.2d 100, 103 (1990).

88. Restatement (Second) of Torts § 585 cmt. c (1977); *see Twelker v. Shannon & Wilson, Inc.*, 564 P.2d 1131 (Wash. 1977).

89. *See Wallace v. Skadden, Arps, Slate, Meagher & Flom*, 715 A.2d 873, 879 (D.C. 1998).

90. *Knox v. Neaton Auto Prods. Mfg., Inc.*, 375 F.3d 451 (6th Cir. 2004).

91. *See, e.g., Shamley v. ITT Corp.*, 869 F.2d 167, 173 (2d Cir. 1989).

92. *Moss v. Stockard*, 580 A.2d 1011, 1025 (D.C. 1990).

93. Restatement (Second) of Torts § 583 ("[C]onsent of another to the publication of defamatory matter concerning him is a complete defense," even as to defamatory statements); *see also LaBaron v. Board of Pub. Def.*, 499 N.W.2d 39, 42 (Minn. Ct. App. 1993).

94. *Miron v. University of New Haven Police Dept.*, 284 Conn. 35 (2007).

95. Restatement (Second) of Torts § 766 (1979).

96. Restatement (Second) of Torts § 766 (1979); *see Prudential Ins. Co. of Am. v. Stella*, 994 F. Supp. 318 (E.D. Pa. 1998); *see also Hibbs v. K-Mart Corp.*, 870 F.2d 435 (8th Cir. 1989); *Pacific Gas & Elec. Co. v. Bear Stearns & Co.*, 50 Cal. 3d 1118, 1126, 791 P.2d 587 (1990); *Hughes v. City of Chicago*, 2003 WL 21518592 (N.D. Ill. 1999); *Sklar v. Beth Israel Deaconess Med. Ctr.*, 59 Mass. App. Ct. 550 (2003).

97. Restatement (Second) of Torts § 767 (1979).

98. U.S. Equal Employment Opportunity Commn., Retaliation (available at *http://www.eeoc.gov/laws/types/retaliation.cfm*).

99. *Burlington N. & Santa Fe Ry. Co. v. White*, 548 U.S. 53 (2006).

100. *Robinson v. Shell Oil Co.*, 519 U.S. 337 (1996).

101. U.S. Equal Employment Opportunity Commn., Retaliation (available at *http://www.eeoc.gov/laws/types/retaliation.cfm*).

102. *Id.*

103. *Burlington N. & Santa Fe Ry. Co. v. White*, 548 U.S. 53 (2006). *Accord Berry v. Stevinson Chevrolet*, 74 F.3d 980, 984 (10th Cir. 1996).

Glossary of Key Terms

401(k) plan employer-sponsored defined contribution plan that allows employees to deposit pretax earnings into an account for use after they reach a certain age or during their retirement. The value of the account will be based on the investment returns of the funds deposited into the account. Some employers also contribute funds to the 401(k) accounts of their employees. See company match.

absolute privilege defense asserted to a defamation claim to bar recovery based on the role the person was acting in when he made the statement. A witness in a judicial proceeding who testifies to facts he believes to be true would assert an absolute privilege as a defense to a defamation claim.

ADA see Americans with Disabilities Act of 1990.

ADA Amendments Act of 2008 (ADAAA) amendments to the Americans with Disabilities Act (ADA) that reinforce the broad scope of the term *disability* and provide guidance relating to the benefits and protections available under the ADA.

ADAAA see ADA Amendments Act of 2008.

ADEA see Age Discrimination in Employment Act of 1967.

administrative employee exemption category of employees who, based on the high level of work performed and independent judgment required to perform the job, are fully exempt from the Fair Labor Standards Act (FLSA) and therefore not entitled to the minimum hourly wage rate or the payment of overtime under the Act.

administrative regulations rules promulgated by federal and state agencies that have the power delegated to them by Congress or a state legislature. The rules issued by the Department of Labor (DOL) relating to how the Fair Labor Standards Act (FLSA) is applied are examples of administrative regulations.

adverse action see adverse employment decision.

adverse employment action see adverse employment decision.

adverse employment decision decision that has a negative impact on the working conditions of an individual. Within the context of a retaliation claim, it refers to an action that an employer cannot impose (such as assigning an employee to an undesirable shift) if it is in response to the employee's assertion of a legal right, such as filing a workplace discrimination claim under Title VII. An adverse action is a similar decision but does not relate to a term and condition of employment. For example, an employer's decision to file false criminal charges against a former employee because the former employee previously filed a Title VII claim against a company supervisor is an example of an adverse action.

affirmative defense set of facts that, if true, will act as a complete bar to recovery for a particular claim. For example, under the Equal Pay Act (EPA), a showing that the reason for a pay disparity between a man and a woman performing substantially similar work was based on any factor other than sex (such as the possession of an advanced academic degree) would constitute an affirmative defense. If it is true, it would prevent an award of damages to the individual asserting the EPA claim. Within the context of a defamation claim, truth is an affirmative defense, meaning that if an individual can prove that the statement alleged to be defamatory is true, it will bar any recovery.

after-acquired evidence rule rule that allows the consideration of a legitimate reason for an adverse employment decision that is discovered *after* the adverse decision was imposed for a discriminatory reason. Although after-acquired evidence will generally not bar recovery, it is often considered by a court when determining the appropriate damage award for discriminatory conduct.

Age Discrimination in Employment Act of 1967 (ADEA) federal law that prohibits workplace discrimination based on age and age-related factors against individuals forty (40) years of age and older.

Americans with Disabilities Act of 1990 (ADA) federal law that prohibits discrimination against qualified individuals with physical and mental disabilities.

applicant pool group of candidates who will be considered for an open position.

appropriation of name or likeness right of privacy cause of action relating to the unauthorized use of an individual's image for a commercial benefit.

at-will disclaimer see disclaimer.

atheism absence of religious beliefs, which falls within the scope of beliefs protected under Title VII's prohibition against religious discrimination.

audio surveillance use of technology to record the conversations of others that is regulated by state and federal law; see one-party consent states and two-party consent states.

back pay damage award that represents wages lost as a result of unlawful conduct.

background checks information collected by an employer to verify information provided by an applicant to assess an applicant's suitability for a position. A background check might include a review of an applicant's criminal history, credit history, or record of past employment.

beneficiary person (or organization) designated to receive the life insurance benefit on the death of the insured. In some cases beneficiaries are designated for other benefits.

BFOQ see bona fide occupational qualification.

bona fide occupational qualification (BFOQ) employer's defense to an employment discrimination claim that illustrates the business necessity of considering an individual's protected class status, a consideration that otherwise would be prohibited. Race and color are never considered BFOQs.

bona fide seniority system plan that provides enhanced benefits to employees based on their length of employment and is permissible, despite the disparate impact it might have on members of a protected class, provided the purpose of setting up or administering the plan is not to produce a discriminatory result.

bumping rights rights derived from a collective bargaining agreement that provide employees with more seniority the right to displace other employees, usually in the same job classification, if a position is eliminated.

business necessity showing by an employer that a practice or policy is essential to its operations despite its disparate impact on members of a protected class.

circumstantial evidence information that suggests particular conduct occurred but does not prove it definitively.

Civil Rights Act of 1991 federal law that, among other things, subjects employers to liability for adverse employment decisions that are motivated by both legitimate and discriminatory considerations (see mixed motive). The Act also expands the types of damages that may be awarded for intentional discrimination claims to include compensatory and punitive damages.

clear and conspicuous standard used to determine whether a disclaimer (i.e., at-will disclaimer) is displayed in a manner that makes it enforceable. Relevant considerations include the placement of the disclaimer language (i.e., whether it is printed at the front of a company handbook or in a footnote) and whether the font is distinguishable from the remainder of the text.

COBRA see Consolidated Omnibus Budget Reconciliation Act.

cognitive tests pre-employment selection tests that measure basic skills as well as skills specific to a particular position.

collective bargaining agreement contract negotiated by an employer and the labor union that represents its employees which establishes the employees' terms and conditions of employment.

common core of tasks job responsibilities that are central to a position and are used to assess whether two positions are substantially similar for purposes of the Equal Pay Act (EPA).

common law also referred to as case law, the principles established by the courts through the issuance of judicial decisions.

company match employer contribution to the 401(k) account of a plan participant to supplement the employee's retirement benefit. These employer contributions are made within the context of a defined contribution plan, a plan in which the retirement benefit is not guaranteed but instead depends on the investment returns of the funds in the account.

compensation broad term that includes anything of current or future value an employer provides an individual in exchange for the performance of services. Base salary, vacation pay, stock bonuses, and car allowances are all examples of types of compensation.

compensatory damages damages awarded to an individual for actual losses suffered.

compensatory time hours worked in excess of forty (40) hours in a workweek for which an employee who is not covered by the Fair Labor Standards Act

(FLSA) (and, in some instances, public-sector employees who are covered by the FLSA) may receive time off rather than additional compensation. See Fair Labor Standards Act (FLSA).

consent an agreement to be bound. Within the context of a claim for an invasion of privacy, the term means the granting of permission for certain workplace monitoring, which could arguably be considered intrusive. See express consent and implied consent.

consideration the benefit each party must receive to create a legally enforceable contract. For example, because a release agreement is a contract, both the departing employee and the employer must receive consideration to create a legally binding contract. In such an agreement, consideration may come in the form of the employee's waiver of the right to file certain claims upon termination of employment in exchange for a severance benefit paid by the employer.

Consolidated Omnibus Budget Reconciliation Act (COBRA) amendment to the Employee Retirement Income Security Act (ERISA) that provides plan participants with a number of protections, such as the right to the continuation of medical coverage after certain qualifying life events.

constitution group of principles that govern the relationship between a government and the people it represents.

constructive discharge legal theory whereby an employment relationship ends based on the presence of working conditions that are so intolerable, a reasonable person would not be expected to continue to work subject to them. A constructive discharge is sometimes referred to as a compelled or forced resignation.

consumer report broad term for consumer information provided by a reporting agency used to assess an individual's suitability for such things as employment, insurance, and credit.

consumer reporting agency entity that gathers and/or reviews information on a consumer report and provides it to a third party (i.e., an employer) in exchange for compensation. Agencies are subject to certain federal regulations relating to the consent necessary to collect the information, how it may be used, and how it must be maintained. See the Fair Credit Reporting Act (FCRA).

counseling a conversation that represents an initial step in the progressive discipline process that places an employee on notice about problematic behavior.

The most common steps in a progressive discipline process are a counseling session, verbal warning, written warning, suspension, and termination.

credit report type of consumer report that provides information used to determine, among other things, whether an applicant is a suitable candidate for the extension of credit.

de minimis Latin term for minimal importance, referring to a burden an employer would likely be obligated to undertake in an effort to reasonably accommodate an individual's religious belief or practice or disability.

defamation cause of action relating to the communication of false information about an individual (in a verbal or written form) that causes harm to the individual's reputation or deters third persons from dealing with him. See libel and slander.

defined benefit plan retirement plan that offers participants a benefit based on a specific formula that usually considers the age, salary, and years of service completed by the employee.

defined contribution plan retirement plan that offers participants a benefit based on the investment returns of deposited funds. See 401(k) plan.

Department of Labor (DOL) see United States Department of Labor.

direct evidence information that is clear proof that particular conduct occurred.

disclaimer within the context of at-will employment, language included in a company handbook that makes it clear that the benefits described in the handbook are not intended to alter the at-will status of the company's employees.

disparate impact claim employment discrimination claim under Title VII (or another workplace anti-discrimination law) alleging that an employer engaged in unintentional discrimination based on the implementation of a policy or practice that is neutral on its face but results in an adverse impact on members of a protected class.

disparate treatment claim employment discrimination claim under Title VII (or another workplace anti-discrimination law) alleging that an employer engaged in intentional discrimination based on an individual's membership in a protected class.

double time the payment of two times an employee's regular rate of pay for hours worked under certain conditions such as those that are hazardous. This benefit is not required by the Fair Labor Standards Act (FLSA), but it may be regulated by state law.

due process clause   constitutional provision that, among other things, provides individuals with the right to a fair legal proceeding, including the opportunity to be heard. Within the context of the imposition of discipline, due process requires that a disciplinary investigation be conducted in accordance with rules and principles for protecting and enforcing the rights of individuals, which would include conducting a thorough and unbiased investigation of the employee's alleged misconduct and giving the individual accused of wrongdoing the opportunity to present her recollection of the events.

duty of good faith and fair dealing   contractual theory that may impose an obligation on both parties in an employment relationship to act in good faith. Also, it may refer to the obligations imposed on the two parties who enter into a contract not to engage in any conduct that will destroy or injure the rights of the other party.

early retirement incentives   enhanced retirement benefit offered to employees who agree to leave their employment before reaching retirement age. Employers often condition the receipt of these benefits on the employees' signing of a release agreement.

economic realities test   test that focuses on the extent to which individuals are economically dependent on their employers to determine whether they should be treated as employees or as independent contractors. Working individuals who are economically dependent on a particular employer are generally classified as employees, as compared to working individuals who are not economically dependent on a particular employer, who are generally classified as independent contractors.

ECPA   see Electronic Communications Privacy Act of 1986.

eligibility test   pre-employment test (such as a typing test) that requires applicants to achieve a certain result to be considered qualified for a position.

EEO-1 survey   government form employers that employ 100 or more individuals must submit on an annual basis that counts their workforce by job category, ethnicity, race, and gender.

EEOC   see Equal Employment Opportunity Commission.

Electronic Communications Privacy Act of 1986 (ECPA)   federal law that regulates the use of electronic communications by prohibiting (1) the intentional interception (or attempted interception) of any wire, oral, or electronic communication; (2) the intentional use of (or the directing of another individual to use) any electronic, mechanical, or other device to intercept any oral communication; and (3) the intentional use of information in violation of the Act.

employee   broad term for an individual who is subject to the control of an employer and provides services on the employer's behalf in exchange for compensation.

employee at will   see employment at will.

Employee Polygraph Protection Act (EPPA)   federal law that prohibits most private-sector employers from using lie detector tests as part of their hiring process or during an individual's employment. In the limited circumstances where use of the tests is permissible, the EPPA also regulates the administration of the test and the maintenance of the test results.

Employee Retirement Income Security Act of 1974 (ERISA)   federal law that regulates the administration of most voluntary medical and retirement plans in private industry and provides extensive protections to plan participants.

employment application   broad term for any written information provided by an applicant during the hiring process.

employment at will   doctrine that provides that employees working are under it can be terminated with or without cause, and with or without notice. An at-will employee will generally retain their reciprocal right to leave their employment for any reason at any time.

employment eligibility verification (I-9) form   federal document used by employers to verify an individual's eligibility to work in the United States. The Immigration and Nationality Act (INA) is the federal law that imposes an obligation on employers to verify an individual's eligibility to work, which requires the completion of this form.

English-only rules   workplace rules that prohibit employees from speaking any language other than English while at work.

EPA   see Equal Pay Act.

EPPA   see Employee Polygraph Protection Act.

equal-cost defense   employer's justification for providing older employees with lesser benefits based on a showing that it spent an equal amount of money to provide the lower level of benefits as it spent to provide the higher level of benefits to other younger employees.

Equal Employment Opportunity Commission (EEOC)   federal agency charged with enforcing a number of federal anti-discrimination employment laws, including Title VII, the Age Discrimination in Employment Act (ADEA), and the Americans with Disabilities Act (ADA).

Equal Pay Act (EPA)   an amendment to the Fair Labor Standards Act (FLSA) that requires employers to provide equal pay for substantially equal work.

equal skill, effort, and responsibility   standard used to determine whether two positions are substantially similar and must be compensated equally pursuant to the terms of the Equal Pay Act (EPA).

ERISA   see Employee Retirement Income Security Act.

essential job functions   see essential job tasks.

essential job tasks   in contrast to tangential job tasks, responsibilities that represent a necessary component of a position and will be performed by the individual filling the position. An employer is generally not obligated to significantly alter or reassign an essential job task to accommodate a disabled employee or an individual who expresses a desire to engage in a religious belief or practice; comparable to essential job functions.

ethnic group   group of people who share one or more social characteristics. An ethnic group may be the basis for the filing of a claim for workplace discrimination under Title VII based on national origin discrimination.

executive employee exemption   a category of employees who, based on the salary paid and duties performed, including, but not limited to, supervisory responsibilities, are fully exempt from the Fair Labor Standards Act (FLSA) and not entitled to the minimum hourly wage rate or the payment of overtime provided under the statute.

exit incentive program   an employer plan that provides certain employees the opportunity to receive enhanced compensation in exchange for a voluntary resignation, which is usually conditioned on the signing of a release agreement.

express consent   affirmative agreement to be bound, such as an employee's signing of a document agreeing that she will be subject to a company policy relating to the monitoring of work e-mail accounts. Contrast implied consent.

factors other than sex   affirmative defense under the Equal Pay Act (EPA) that provides employers with the opportunity to justify a pay disparity between a male and a female employee performing substantially similar work by showing the disparity is based on a consideration other than sex.

Fair Credit Reporting Act (FCRA)   federal law that regulates the administration of background checks. The FCRA also requires the accurate and confidential reporting of consumer information.

Fair Labor Standards Act (FLSA)   federal law that regulates the minimum hourly wage rate, payment of overtime, employer recordkeeping, and the employment of children.

faltering company   employer that was seeking financial assistance during what would have comprised the 60-day required notice period under the Worker Adjustment and Retraining Notification (WARN) Act, which prevented the employer from being in a position to provide notice to its affected employees.

Family and Medical Leave Act (FMLA)   federal law that provides 12 weeks of unpaid job-protected leave to employees to tend to family and medical issues. See National Defense Authorization Act (NDAA), which was the first set of amendments to the FMLA and provides enhanced benefits (up to 26 weeks of unpaid job-protected leave) to covered military members and their family caregivers.

FCRA   see Fair Credit Reporting Act.

fiduciary duties   obligations imposed on individuals who manage medical and retirement plans covered by the Employee Retirement Income Security Act (ERISA) to act for the exclusive benefit of plan participants and their beneficiaries. Fiduciary duties might be imposed on individuals in other contexts where they have the duty to act for the exclusive benefit of a particular party.

FLSA   see Fair Labor Standards Act.

FMLA   see Family and Medical Leave Act.

Form SS-8   federal tax form that can be filed by an employer or individual to seek Internal Revenue Service (IRS) assistance in determining the appropriate classification of certain work as being performed by an independent contractor or an employee.

four-fifths (or 80%) rule   standard established by the Equal Employment Opportunity Commission (EEOC) that quantifies an adverse impact on a protected class as a selection rate that is less than 4/5 (or 80%) of the selection rate of the group with the highest selection rate.

Fourth Amendment to the U.S. Constitution   constitutional amendment that establishes a right to privacy by prohibiting unreasonable searches and seizures.

front pay   damage award that represents future wages from the time a judgment is made until reinstatement or until a date certain if reinstatement is not possible.

full exemption   absence of a right to both the minimum hourly rate and overtime that would be otherwise required by the Fair Labor Standards Act (FLSA), based on the nature of an employee's work.

genetic information   broad term for information revealed through genetic testing of an individual or a family member as well as a family medical history.

Genetic Information Nondiscrimination Act of 2008 (GINA)   federal law that prohibits workplace discrimination based on genetics and genetic information. GINA also prohibits the collection of genetic information except under very limited circumstances.

genetic testing   tests used to assess the potential for an individual to develop certain diseases that are hereditary in nature.

GINA   see Genetic Information Nondiscrimination Act of 2008.

grievance and arbitration process   method for unionized employees to challenge their employer's administration of a provision in a collective bargaining agreement, which would include the right to challenge a termination decision. Some employers have a similar process for nonunionized employees to challenge adverse employment decisions.

hazardous conditions   working conditions an employee might be expected to tolerate (such as cold weather or dangerous conditions) and that could be used by a court to determine whether two positions require equal levels of responsibilities. This is relevant to whether the two positions are substantially similar for the purpose of an Equal Pay Act (EPA) claim.

health insurance   company benefit that covers all or part of the medical expenses of employees and usually those of their spouses and dependent children.

Health Insurance Portability and Accountability Act (HIPAA)   federal law that regulates, among other things, the disclosure of an individual's medical information. HIPAA also protects other privacy rights of health plan participants and offers some protections against the denial of coverage based on preexisting medical conditions.

HIPAA   see Health Insurance Portability and Accountability Act.

hostile work environment   work conditions for which a discrimination claim can be filed when an individual is subject to unwelcome, offensive, and pervasive objectionable comments or ridicule at the workplace based on her membership in a protected class, creating an atmosphere so intolerable a reasonable person is not expected to endure it. Within the context of sex discrimination, sexual harassment occurs when an individual is subjected to pervasive unwelcome sexual advances, requests for sexual favors, and other verbal or physical conduct of a sexual nature that creates such an atmosphere.

I-9 form   see employment eligibility verification (I-9) form.

Immigration and Nationality Act (INA)   amendment to the Immigration Reform and Control Act (IRCA) that prohibits employers from hiring individuals who are not legally authorized to work in the United States

and requires employers to verify this eligibility through the completion of an employment eligibility verification (I-9) form. See employment eligibility verification (I-9) form.

Immigration Reform and Control Act of 1986 (IRCA)   federal law that prohibits employment discrimination based on an individual's citizenship status and prohibits employers from hiring individuals not authorized to work in the United States. The IRCA was amended by the Immigration and Nationality Act (INA).

implied consent   conduct that suggests an agreement to be bound. Contrast express consent.

implied contract   contractual obligation that may arise based on employer statements or conduct.

INA   see Immigration and Nationality Act.

incentive system   a compensation structure that provides for enhanced compensation based on the quality or quantity of work produced.

indemnity plan   medical plan that generally provides plan participants with the option to select their providers.

independent contractor   broad term for an individual who is generally not subject to the control of an employer and provides services on the employer's behalf in exchange for compensation.

ineligibility test   pre-employment test that would disqualify an applicant from further consideration based on a certain result. A test for illegal drugs test would be an example of an ineligibility test because a positive result would likely disqualify an applicant.

intermittent leave   FMLA-related leave taken sporadically to allow an employee to tend to a family or medical issue.

interview   broad term for the exchanges between a potential employer and job applicant that occur during the recruitment and hiring process.

intrusion upon seclusion   cause of action stemming from the privacy right that relates to another person's duty to refrain from interfering in an individual's private matters.

invasion of privacy   violation of a duty to refrain from intruding into an individual's private life.

IRCA   see Immigration Reform and Control Act of 1986.

job-protected leave   absence from work after which an employee must be returned to the same or equivalent position held before the absence, as if the leave did not occur. The Family and Medical Leave Act (FMLA) and the Uniformed Services Employment and Reemployment Rights Act (USERRA) are examples of federal statutes that offer job-protected leave.

just cause broad standard that might be used to determine the appropriateness of an employer's decision to end an employment relationship in a number of different contexts. Just cause is a common standard used in collective bargaining agreements. An examination of whether an employee's misconduct rises to this level usually examines (1) whether the employee had notice of the rule that prohibited the conduct, (2) whether the rule was reasonable, (3) whether the employer conducted an investigation before the termination, (4) whether the rule was uniformly enforced, and (5) whether the penalty was appropriate based on the nature of the misconduct.

knowing and voluntary standard used to determine whether the individual who signed a release agreement understood its terms such that the agreement should be enforced.

layoff ending of an employment relationship, usually due to budget restraints, initiated by an employer due to a business need to reduce the size of its staff.

Ledbetter Fair Pay Act of 2009 federal law stating that the statute of limitations for filing a compensation discrimination claim starts to run each time the substandard wages are paid as opposed to running from only the initial discriminatory decision to pay those wages.

legitimate business interest within the context of the regulation of off-duty conduct, the justification for an intrusion that results in the imposition of discipline based on behavior that occurs outside an individual's regularly scheduled workday that has the potential to adversely affect the employer's operations.

legitimate, nondiscriminatory reason employer's burden of proof to present evidence illustrating a valid business justification for the imposition of an adverse employment decision that an individual alleges was based on the improper consideration of her membership in a protected class.

libel defamation claim based on a written communication. Contrast slander.

life insurance benefit that may be offered to an employee that provides a financial benefit to a designated beneficiary at the time of the employee's death.

lifestyle choices day-to-day decisions that may impact an individual's health and well being. Examples of lifestyle choices are eating a balanced diet, exercising, and refraining from smoking.

long-term disability plan benefit that provides injured or ill employees with their full or partial salary in the event of an injury or illness that prevents them from working for an extended period of time.

major life activity function that is significant to an individual's daily life (such as walking and speaking) that must be substantially limited for a condition to constitute a disability for the purposes of the Americans with Disabilities Act (ADA).

managed care plan medical plan that generally requires participants to use the medical providers who are members of a particular network.

mass layoff a loss of employment for at least 30 days at a single site for (1) 500 or more employees (excluding part-time employees) or (2) 50 to 499 employees (excluding part-time employees) if the latter make up at least 33% of the employer's active workforce that triggers notification obligations for employers under the federal Worker Adjustment and Retraining Notification (WARN) Act.

McDonnell Douglas Corporation. v. Green Supreme Court case establishing the framework for the presentation of proof for a claim of intentional discrimination.

mental impairment mental or psychological disorder that may constitute a disability under the Americans with Disabilities Act (ADA).

merit system compensation structure that offers enhanced compensation for superior job performance.

minimum hourly rate of pay the lowest hourly wage rate an employer can pay an employee covered by the Fair Labor Standards Act (FLSA).

mitigating factors circumstances that may warrant more lenient forms of discipline for similar misconduct. An employee's lack of prior discipline and long-term service to an employer are examples of mitigating factors.

mitigating measures assistance that may eliminate or reduce the extent to which an impairment limits a major life activity, which is a relevant consideration within the context of an ADA claim. Eyeglasses and a pair of crutches are examples of mitigating measures.

mitigation of damages affirmative obligation imposed on an individual to make a reasonable effort to limit any damages incurred. A terminated employee would likely be obligated to mitigate her damages in a wrongful termination claim by seeking alternative employment during the time during which his case is being litigated to reduce the amount of back pay that might be awarded.

mixed motive motive for an employment decision that is based on both legitimate and discriminatory considerations and may impact the amount of damages awarded. See Civil Rights Act of 1991.

morals clause contractual provision that provides the employer with the right to terminate an employee for conduct considered morally offensive.

National Defense Authorization Act (NDAA) the first set of amendments to the Family and Medical Leave Act (FMLA), which provides twenty-six (26) weeks of unpaid job-protected leave to allow eligible employees to care for a covered servicemember who has a serious injury or illness and allows for the use of 12 weeks of the leave for "qualifying exigencies" arising out of the active duty or call-to-duty status of a spouse, son, daughter, or parent.

national origin group group of people who share one or more social characteristics; may be the basis for a claim of national origin discrimination under Title VII.

NDAA see National Defense Authorization Act.

negligent hiring claim that materializes when an individual, whom an employer knows or should have known was unfit for a position, causes harm.

negligent referral legal theory that holds an employer responsible for harm caused by its former employee based on the employer's misrepresentation about a foreseeable risk.

nepotism providing favorable treatment to the family members of current employees when making employment decisions.

noncompete clause restrictive covenant that prohibits an individual from working for the competitor of a former employer for a period of time after the end of their employment relationship; also called a noncompetition clause.

non-disparagement clause restrictive covenant that prohibits former employees from making negative comments about a former employer, the individuals who work at the company, or the company's products. A non-disparagement clause might also prohibit an employer from publicly ridiculing or vilifying a former employee.

non-solicitation agreement a restrictive covenant that prohibits an individual from recruiting the employees of a former employer or approaching clients of a former employer for business.

notice amount of advance warning an employee receives that her employment will end. Within the context of workplace privacy, notice refers to the awareness of the potential for an intrusion. Within the context of the imposition of discipline, notice relates to whether an individual was aware of a particular workplace rule as well as the employer's expectation that she adhere to it.

notice pay payment of an individual's salary for the period of time an employee would ordinarily continue to work after being informed his employment would end (but relieving him from his job responsibilities).

objective considerations factors reviewed in performance evaluations that are based on measurable data.

off-duty conduct behavior that occurs outside an employee's regularly scheduled workday and that an employer might use as the basis for the imposition of discipline.

offer letter written document provided to a new employee to confirm the key terms and conditions of employment.

Older Workers Benefit Protection Act (OWBPA) amendment to the Age Discrimination in Employment Act (ADEA) that details elements that must be included in a release agreement for it to constitute a knowing and voluntary waiver and to effectively prohibit an employee from filing an age discrimination claim under the statute. For a waiver to be a knowing and voluntary under the OWBPA it must (1) be in writing and be understandable; (2) specifically reference the Age Discrimination in Employment Act (ADEA); (3) waive only past claims and have no impact on claims that might arise in the future; (4) be in exchange for valuable consideration; (5) include a written provision suggesting that the affected employee consult an attorney before signing the waiver; (6) provide the employee with at least 21 days to review and consider the agreement; and (7) provide the employee with a seven-day period after execution of the agreement, during which the individual retains the right to revoke it.

one-party consent states states that permit the recording of telephone and other electronic conversations by individuals if they are call participants or, in some cases, by non-participants if one participant provides prior consent.

opposition claim retaliation claim based on an employer's imposition of an adverse action on an individual in response to the individual's conduct that challenges employer behavior believed to be discriminatory.

overtime term for hours worked in excess of 40 hours in a workweek, which must be paid at one and one-half times a covered employee's hourly rate of pay if the employee is covered by the Fair Labor Standards Act (FLSA).

OWBPA see Older Workers Benefit Protection Act.

paid holiday day for which an employee is paid but not required to work or is paid enhanced compensation for working.

paid vacation   days for which an employee is paid but not required to work. The exact days classified as vacation days are usually selected by the employee and subject to employer approval.

partial exemption   absence of the right to either the minimum hourly rate *or* the payment of overtime under the Fair Labor Standards Act (FLSA) based on the nature of an employee's work.

participation claim   retaliation claim based on an employer's imposition of an adverse action on an individual in response to the individual's decision to participate in a proceeding relating to a claim or to assist another individual in filing such a claim.

past practice   employer conduct that deviates from a company policy and establishes a revised standard to which employees expect adherence.

PDA   see Pregnancy Discrimination Act.

performance evaluation   managerial tool used to assess employee work performance. These evaluations may be used to identify problematic behavior or to reward positive workplace contributions.

personal leave   days for which an employee is paid but not required to work which are used for miscellaneous purposes.

personality tests   pre-employment tests that analyze different components of an individual's character to determine whether the individual possesses desirable traits for a position.

physical impairment   physiological disorder or condition, cosmetic disfigurement, or anatomical loss that may constitute a disability under the Americans with Disabilities Act (ADA).

plant closing   the shutting down of a single worksite that results in a job loss for 50 or more employees (excluding part-time employees) for any 30-day period (or longer) that triggers notification obligations for employers under the federal Worker Adjustment and Retraining Notification (WARN) Act.

polygraph test   lie detector test that employers are generally prohibited from using as part of their hiring process or during an individual's employment. In the limited instances in which the tests are permissible, their use is strictly regulated. See Employee Polygraph Protection Act (EPPA).

precedent   first time the court hears and makes a decision on an issue which establishes how that issue should be interpreted or applied in future cases.

Pregnancy Discrimination Act (PDA)   federal law that prohibits discrimination in employment based on pregnancy, childbirth, and related medical conditions.

pretext   employer's justification for the making of an adverse employment decision that is actually a cover-up for the true discriminatory motivating factor.

pretext-plus   requirement for an applicant or employee to show both that the employer's explanation for making an adverse employment decision was untrue *and* that the true motivating factor was discriminatory.

***prima facie* case**   individual's initial burden of proof when asserting an employment discrimination claim.

probationary period   initial period of employment during which an employer retains the right to terminate a newly hired employee for any legal reason.

professional employee exemption   a category of employees who, based on the specialized nature of the work performed, are fully exempt from the Fair Labor Standards Act (FLSA) and not entitled to the minimum hourly wage rate or the payment of overtime provided under the statute.

progressive discipline   imposition of escalating levels of discipline designed to identify and remedy problematic behavior.

promissory estoppel   limitation on an employer's right to terminate an employee if it was reasonable for the employee to act in reliance on the employer's promise that suggested some degree of job security. Under this theory, the promise will be enforced if injustice can be avoided only by enforcement of that promise.

protected activity   employee conduct that generally cannot be the basis for the imposition of an adverse employment action because the behavior stems from a legal right.

protected class   group of people who share a common characteristic that entitles them to protection from discriminatory and harassing conduct under Title VII or another anti-discrimination law.

public disclosure of truthful but private facts   right to privacy cause of action based on the public attention given to an individual's private life that a reasonable person would consider offensive.

public policy consideration   justification for the imposition of discipline in response to behavior our society wants to discourage.

public policy exception   limitation on an employer's right to terminate an at-will employee for engaging in conduct our society wants to encourage. This exception is governed by state law and might, for example, prohibit an employer from terminating an employee for refusing to follow the directions of a supervisor which the terminated employee believed would violate the law.

publication communication of information to a third party, which is a critical element of a defamation claim.

punitive damages damages awarded to punish an employer for engaging in inappropriate conduct.

qualified individual with a disability individual possessing the skills and experience to perform the essential functions of a job with or without a reasonable accommodation.

qualified privilege defense asserted to a defamation claim that may bar recovery based on the role the person was acting in when he made the statement and the circumstances surrounding the communication. A supervisor who makes statements to an employee within the context of a performance evaluation would be entitled to a qualified privileged, meaning if the evaluated employee filed a defamation claim against the supervisor he would not be subject to liability provided the statements were not made maliciously.

qualifying event life event that results in the loss of medical coverage and would provide an individual with a right to continued medical benefits at a group rate pursuant to the terms of the Consolidated Omnibus Budget Reconciliation Act (COBRA). Voluntary or involuntary terminations for reasons other than gross misconduct, or a reduction in the number of hours of employment are examples of qualifying events.

qualifying exigency leave expanded reasons for which caregivers of servicemembers may use a portion of their leave entitlement under the Family and Medical Leave Act (FMLA). Leaves of absence arising from a covered military member's short-notice deployment, military events and related activities, and certain childcare and related activities are examples of qualifying exigency leaves.

quid pro quo harassment Latin for "this for that," harassment that occurs when, for example, an individual is subjected to a tangible employment action in response to either granting or refusing to grant a favor of a sexual nature (for sexual harassment) or harassment that occurs when an individual is required to forgo his right to engage in a religious practice in exchange for continued employment (for religious harassment).

reasonable accommodation alteration made to the working conditions of a qualified individual with a disability or for an individual to engage in religious conduct or practice that must be provided unless it will impose an undue burden on the employer.

reasonable expectation of privacy threshold question in an invasion of privacy claim used to assess whether an individual had the right to expect an area or concern would be free from an outside intrusion.

reasonable factor other than age an employer's basis for the imposition of an adverse employment decision on an individual forty (40) years of age or older that is unrelated to age and therefore not a violation of the Age Discrimination in Employment Act (ADEA). An individual's education or prior work experience, as well as other measures of the quality or quantity of an individual's work performance are examples of reasonable factors other than age that would likely be appropriate factors to consider when making employment decisions.

record of an impairment history of a past medical condition that might entitle an individual to protections under the Americans with Disabilities Act (ADA).

red circling defense under the Equal Pay Act (EPA) that justifies the pay differential between a male and a female performing substantially equal work because the difference represents the maintenance of a prior salary associated with a higher-level position.

reduced leave schedule adjustment of work hours or workdays to allow an employee to take FMLA-related leave.

reference information provided by a former employer to a prospective employer relating to details about an individual's past employment.

reference checks verification of an individual's past work history and other information submitted on an employment application to assess an applicant's suitability for a position.

regarded as having an impairment basis for adverse employer action rooted in the employer's belief that an individual has a disability, which could entitle an individual to protection under the Americans with Disabilities Act (ADA).

release agreement document negotiated by an employer and terminated employee, usually in exchange for severance, in which the employee waives her rights to challenge the termination and to file a claim against her employer for issues arising from her employment. Both parties may agree to certain post-employment obligations within the context of this type of agreement. Release agreements may also be negotiated with current employees to resolve disputes that arise during the term of an individual's employment (such as whether a certain monetary benefit is due).

religion broad term that covers all aspects of religious observances, practices, and beliefs. Religion is a protected class under Title VII.

religious conduct behavior for which an employer covered by Title VII would be required to provide a reasonable accommodation to avoid liability for discriminatory behavior under Title VII, provided the accommodation does not impose an undue burden on the employer. Wearing a particular head covering (such as a Muslim headscarf) is an example of religious conduct.

religious corporation employer for which there is a limited exception to the prohibition against religious discrimination under Title VII that permits it to consider an individual's religion when making employment decisions.

religious expression term used for the displaying of or speaking about religious content, which is protected under Title VII's prohibition against religious discrimination.

religious practice protected behavior under Title VII for which an employer might be required to provide a reasonable accommodation, provided the accomodation does not impose an undue burden on the employer. Praying is an example of a religious practice.

resignation the ending of an employment relationship initiated by an employee.

respondeat superior Latin for "let the master answer," the legal theory that imposes liability on an employer for harm caused by its employees that occur during the scope of their employment.

restrictive covenants contractual provisions that limit the rights of former employees to engage in certain conduct. Employers might use a restrictive covenant to limit an individual's post-employment conduct that could result in competition for the employer or the sharing of confidential business information. See noncompete clause, non-disparagement clause, and non-solicitation agreement.

retaliation employer's imposition of an adverse employment decision in response to an employee's assertion of a right under Title VII or another anti-discrimination law, or an employee's decision to oppose an unlawful employment practice. A retaliation claim may also be filed if an adverse action is imposed in response to an individual's attempt to assist another person in asserting that person's legal rights. Retaliation claims may be filed in other contexts beyond the scope of Title VII and other federal anti-discrimination laws.

retirement benefits compensation employees may receive after they cease working. See defined benefit plan and defined contribution plan.

right to control test compilation of factors used to determine whether the extent of control an employer exerts over an individual supports the classification of that individual as an employee or an independent contractor. Employers generally have the right to control their employees and do not have the right to control their independent contractors.

right to sue letter document from the Equal Employment Opportunity Commission (EEOC) that provides an individual with the right to file a workplace discrimination claim in a federal court.

selection tests pre-employment tests used to determine whether an applicant has the minimum qualifications necessary to perform the essential functions of a job.

selective enforcement inconsistent application of a workplace rule, which could undermine an employer's position that a violation of the rule rises to the level of just cause, which might be the standard required to support an employee's termination.

seniority measure of an employee's length of service with an employer that might be used to determine her eligibility for certain benefits.

seniority system see bona fide seniority system.

serious health condition severe illness that may require more extensive sick leave than what standard policies provide and for which the use of FMLA-related leave may be appropriate.

serious injury within the context of a claim under the Fair Labor Standards Act (FLSA), a work-related injury suffered by a child under the age of 18 years that could subject an employer to liability for violation of the Act's child labor laws.

severance benefit provided to a terminated employee, usually in exchange for an agreement that the decision to end the employment relationship will not be challenged and that the departing employee will not file any other claims arising out of his employment.

sex discrimination discrimination based on sex or gender stereotypes that is prohibited by Title VII.

sex-plus discrimination discrimination based on an individual's gender as well as on an additional characteristic not unique to the gender.

sexual harassment form of sex discrimination under Title VII that occurs when tangible employment actions are imposed in response to either granting or refusing to grant a favor of a sexual nature or when individuals are subject to unwelcome sexual advances that affect their working conditions. See *quid pro quo* harassment and hostile work environment.

short-term disability plan benefit that provides an injured or ill employee with her full or partial salary in the event of an injury or illness that prevents her from working for a short period of time, usually not to exceed two years.

slander   defamation claim based on a spoken communication. Contrast libel.

statute of limitations   time period within which an individual can file a claim asserting a legal violation occurred under a particular statute.

statutory law   laws passed by Congress and state legislatures.

subjective considerations   factors reviewed in performance evaluations that are based on the opinions or personal perspectives of the evaluators.

substantial limitation   extent to which a major life activity must be restricted by an impairment for it to be considered a disability for the purpose of coverage under the Americans with Disabilities Act (ADA).

suspension   step in the progressive discipline process that includes forced unpaid leave from work in response to an employee's problematic conduct. The most common steps in a progressive discipline process are a counseling session, verbal warning, written warning, suspension, and termination.

suspension pending the investigation   imposition of a paid or unpaid leave on an employee accused of misconduct until a determination is made as to whether the individual engaged in the misconduct and, if so, what level of discipline would be appropriate.

tangential job functions   see tangential job tasks.

tangential job tasks   in contrast to essential job tasks, non-critical responsibilities associated with a position that an employer might be required to alter or reassign to accommodate a disabled employee or an individual's religious beliefs or practices. Within the context of recruiting candidates to fill a position, tangential job tasks are responsibilities that may be assigned to an individual working in a position but that are not a necessary component of the position, comparable to tangential job functions.

tangible employment action   within the context of a *quid pro quo* sexual harassment claim, a change in employment status such as a promotion, termination, or undesirable reassignment, which could be the basis for a harassment claim if it is imposed in response to an employee's refusal to grant a sexual favor or conditioned on the employee's granting of the sexual favor.

telecommuting   working from home or a location other than the employer's worksite.

term life insurance   insurance policy that will pay a death benefit to the designated beneficiary if the covered individual dies within the period of time for which coverage is purchased. Contrast with whole life insurance.

termination   ending of an employment relationship which is also the final step in a progressive discipline process. The most common steps in a progressive discipline process that precede a termination are a counseling session, verbal warning, written warning, and suspension.

Title VII of the Civil Rights Act of 1964   federal law that prohibits workplace discrimination based on race, color, religion, sex, and national origin.

tortious interference with contractual relationship   cause of action relating to conduct intended to unlawfully block an individual from forming a contract with a third party or inducing a third party not to abide by its terms.

trade secret   broadly defined term for formula, pattern, device, or other information an employer might seek to prevent former employees from disclosing to its competitors.

two-party consent states   states that only permit the recording of telephone and other electronic communications if consent is obtained from all call participants.

undue burden   hardship that exceeds what an employer would be required to withstand to accommodate a qualified individual with a disability or an employee's religious beliefs or practices; also referred to as an undue hardship.

undue hardship   see undue burden.

unemployment benefits   payments made to eligible individuals who lose their jobs through no fault of their own, as determined by state law.

Uniformed Services Employment and Reemployment Rights Act (USERRA)   federal law that provides employees serving in the military with certain rights to take job-protected leave and to return to employment on completion of their service under certain conditions.

United States Department of Labor (DOL)   federal agency charged with enforcing a number of federal employment laws, such as the Family and Medical Leave Act (FMLA), the Fair Labor Standards Act (FLSA), and the Worker Adjustment and Retraining Notification (WARN) Act.

USERRA   see Uniformed Services Employment and Reemployment Rights Act.

verbal warning   step in the progressive discipline process that involves a conversation with an employee, identifying problematic behavior, and placing the employee on notice that if the behavior is not corrected, further discipline will be imposed. The most common steps in a progressive discipline process are a counseling session, verbal warning, written warning, suspension, and termination.

video surveillance   use of visible or hidden cameras to track employee movement and behavior.

WARN   see Worker Adjustment and Retraining Notification Act.

wellness programs   employer-sponsored benefit programs that provide employees with resources to make better lifestyle choices.

whole life insurance   insurance policy that pays a death benefit to an individual's designated beneficiary on the individual's death. Contrast with term life insurance.

Worker Adjustment and Retraining Notification (WARN) Act   federal law that requires large employers (generally those with 100 or more employees) to provide 60 days' written notice to those employees who will lose their jobs due to a plant closing or mass layoff, provided they do not fit within one of the exceptions provided for under the statute. See, e.g., faltering company.

workers' compensation   compensation provided to employees for injuries sustained during the course of their employment.

workweek   within the context of the Fair Labor Standards Act (FLSA), the seven (7) consecutive twenty-four (24) hour periods that an employer uses to determine whether overtime is due.

written warning   step in the progressive discipline process that includes documenting the details of the inappropriate behavior and placing a record of it in an employee's personnel file. The most common steps in a progressive discipline process are a counseling session, verbal warning, written warning, suspension, and termination.

Index